Taste of Home

most requested

RECIPES

TASTE OF HOME BOOKS • RDA ENTHUSIAST BRANDS, LLC • MILWAUKEE, WI

Taste of Home

EDITORIAL
Editor-in-Chief: Catherine Cassidy
Vice President, Content Operations: Kerri Balliet
Creative Director: Howard Greenberg

Managing Editor, Print & Digital Books: Mark Hagen
Associate Creative Director: Edwin Robles Jr.

Editors: Amy Glander, Hazel Wheaton
Associate Editors: Molly Jasinski, Julie Kuczynski
Art Director: Raeann Thompson
Graphic Designer: Courtney Lovetere
Layout Designers: Catherine Fletcher, Sophie Beck, Dalma Vogt
Editorial Services Manager: Dena Ahlers
Editorial Production Coordinator: Jill Banks
Copy Chief: Deb Warlaumont Mulvey
Copy Editors: Dulcie Shoener (senior), Ronald Kovach,
Chris McLaughlin, Ellie Piper
Editorial Services Administrator: Marie Brannon

Content Director: Julie Blume Benedict
Food Editors: Gina Nistico; James Schend; Peggy Woodward, RDN
Recipe Editors: Sue Ryon (lead), Irene Yeh

Culinary Director: Sarah Thompson
Test Cooks: Nicholas Iverson (lead), Matthew Hass
Food Stylists: Kathryn Conrad (lead), Lauren Knoelke, Shannon Roum
Prep Cooks: Bethany Van Jacobson (lead), Melissa Hansen, Aria C. Thornton
Culinary Team Assistant: Maria Petrella

Photography Director: Stephanie Marchese
Photographers: Dan Roberts, Jim Wieland
Photographer/Set Stylist: Grace Natoli Sheldon
Set Stylists: Melissa Franco (lead), Stacey Genaw, Dee Dee Schaefer
Set Stylist Assistant: Stephanie Chojnacki

Business Architect, Publishing Technologies: Amanda Harmatys
Business Analyst, Publishing Technologies: Kate Unger
Junior Business Analyst, Publishing Technologies: Shannon Stroud

Editorial Business Manager: Kristy Martin
Editorial Business Associate: Andrea Meiers

BUSINESS
Publisher: Donna Lindskog
Business Development Director, Taste of Home Live: Laurel Osman
Strategic Partnerships Manager, Taste of Home Live:
Jamie Piette Andrzejewski

TRUSTED MEDIA BRANDS, INC.
President & Chief Executive Officer: Bonnie Kintzer
Chief Financial Officer: Dean Durbin
Chief Marketing Officer: C. Alec Casey
Chief Revenue Officer: Richard Sutton
Chief Digital Officer: Vince Errico
Senior Vice President, Global HR & Communications:
Phyllis E. Gebhardt, SPHR; SHRM-SCP
General Counsel: Mark Sirota
Vice President, Product Marketing: Brian Kennedy
Vice President, Operations: Michael Garzone
Vice President, Consumer Marketing Planning: Jim Woods
Vice President, Digital Product & Technology: Nick Contardo
Vice President, Digital Content & Audience Development: Kari Hodes
Vice President, Financial Planning & Analysis: William Houston

For other Taste of Home books and products,
visit us **at tasteofhome.com.**

International Standard Book Number: 978-1-61765-654-5
Library of Congress Control Number: 2017935150

Cover Photographer: Grace Natoli Sheldon
Set Stylist: Melissa Franco
Food Stylist: Kathryn Conrad

Pictured on front cover (clockwise from left): Priscilla's Vegetable Chowder, page 113; No-Knead Knot Rolls, page 289; Chocolate Strawberry Punch Bowl Trifle, page 311; Best Lasagna, page 213
Pictured on back cover (clockwise from left): Crustless Spinach Quiche, page 76; Citrus & Herb Roasted Turkey Breast, page 411; Apricot Lemonade Iced Tea, page 41; Slow-Cooked Swiss Steak, page 264
Pictured on page 1: Southwestern Casserole, page 218

Printed in China.
1 3 5 7 9 10 8 6 4 2

PAGE 388

GET SOCIAL WITH US!

 LIKE US
facebook.com/
tasteofhome

 FOLLOW US
@tasteofhome

 PIN US
pinterest.com/
taste_of_home

TWEET US
twitter.com/
tasteofhome

To find a recipe
tasteofhome.com

To submit a recipe
tasteofhome.com/submit

To find out about other
Taste of Home products
shoptasteofhome.com

PAGE 70

PAGE 43

PAGE 185

PAGE 358

Serve Up the Very Best Dishes

Your family deserves nothing but the best—and that's what you'll find with *Most Requested Recipes!* Inside, you'll discover 633 of the most-popular, highest-rated, all-time favorite recipes from **Taste of Home.** These are the dishes that take center stage on kitchen tables from coast to coast. Now it's your turn to enjoy them in your own home.

With *Most Requested Recipes,* you can plan a stunning, yet easy, meal in no time at all. Check out each chapter and you will find **appetizing snacks, sweet sips, sunny brunch offerings, comforting casseroles** and **main dishes, soothing soups, hearty sandwiches, light salads, savory side dishes** and, last but not least, **dazzling desserts!** And the **bonus chapter** of **Seasonal Specialties** offers a year's worth of deliciously impressive ideas for holiday get-togethers.

Also, don't forget to check out all of the **helpful reviews** and suggestions from *tasteofhome.com* throughout the book.

Give them a read to find out why other family cooks loved these special recipes so much, then try them out for yourself!

We've included **four At-a-Glance icons** to make it easy for you to find just the sort of recipe you're looking for, whether it's a make-ahead dish or a meal you can have on the table without much effort.

Check out:

> FAST FIX ▸ Finished in 30 minutes or less

> SLOW COOKER 🍲 Made in a slow cooker

> (5)INGREDIENTS Made with 5 or fewer ingredients (excluding water, salt, pepper and canola/olive oil)

> FREEZE IT Freezing and reheating instructions are included

Since every recipe inside has been **tested and approved** by the *Taste of Home Test Kitchen* and recommended by our readers, you can cook and bake your way through the book with confidence. With *Most Requested Recipes,* you've got **633 new ways** to say, "Yum!"

table of contents

★★★★★ READER REVIEWS

Check out what today's family cooks are saying about the top-rated recipes found inside. As you flip through the book, you'll find even more raves!

WHITE CHOCOLATE FRUIT TART, PAGE 345

★★★★★ **READER REVIEW**

"Absolutely delicious! Nice alternative to the usual custard tart fillings. The cream cheese and white chocolate paired so nicely with the fruit I added—strawberries, kiwi, blueberries and raspberries."

SUZYSEWS TASTEOFHOME.COM

★★★★★ **READER REVIEW**

"Made this for the family Christmas gathering and now I'm designated to make it every year. It really is amazing and hearty and just as good heated up the next day."

RACHELRENO TASTEOFHOME.COM

ROASTED RED PEPPER TRIANGLES, PAGE 18

FONTINA ROLLED CHICKEN, PAGE 194

★★★★★ **READER REVIEW**

"Loved this! Easy to make and tastes great. I used half panko and half Italian bread crumbs. Either way, this recipe is definitely a keeper."

CLERSKINE TASTEOFHOME.COM

CHUNKY TACO SOUP, PAGE 117

FRESH HEIRLOOM TOMATO SALAD, PAGE 128

THREE-CHEESE MEATBALL MOSTACCIOLI, PAGE 216

BUTTER PECAN LAYER CAKE, PAGE 346

APPETIZERS, SNACKS, BEVERAGES

It's time to get the party started! Mix and match to your heart's content with these tantalizingly tasty bites. Pick from cheesy dips, hot-from-the-oven sliders, fresh salsa and so much more. And don't forget about beverages—find both kid-friendly and adult-only options inside.

MARINATED OLIVE & CHEESE RING

We love to make Italian meals into celebrations, and a colorful antipasto always kicks off the party. This one is almost too pretty to eat, especially when sprinkled with pimientos, fresh basil and parsley.
—**PATRICIA HARMON** BADEN, PA

PREP: 25 MIN. + CHILLING
MAKES: 16 SERVINGS

- 1 **package (8 ounces) cream cheese, cold**
- 1 **package (10 ounces) sharp white cheddar cheese, cut into ¼-inch slices**
- ⅓ **cup pimiento-stuffed olives**
- ⅓ **cup pitted Greek olives**
- ¼ **cup balsamic vinegar**
- ¼ **cup olive oil**
- 1 **tablespoon minced fresh parsley**
- 1 **tablespoon minced fresh basil or 1 teaspoon dried basil**
- 2 **garlic cloves, minced**
- 1 **jar (2 ounces) pimiento strips, drained and chopped**
  Toasted French bread baguette slices

1. Cut cream cheese lengthwise in half; cut each half into ¼-in. slices. On a serving plate, arrange cheeses upright in a ring, alternating cheddar and cream cheese slices. Place olives in center.

2. In a small bowl, whisk vinegar, oil, parsley, basil and garlic until blended; drizzle over the cheeses and olives. Sprinkle with pimientos. Refrigerate, covered, at least 8 hours or overnight. Serve with baguette slices.

☆ ☆ ☆ ☆ ☆ **READER REVIEW**

"I made this for a New Year's party, and it was a hit! The olives are perfectly flavored to accompany the cheese."

MAYZR97 TASTEOFHOME.COM

HONEY-GARLIC GLAZED MEATBALLS

My husband and I raise cattle on our farm in southwestern Ontario, so it's no surprise that we're fond of these saucy meatballs. They're perfect for parties and potlucks. I know your family will like them, too.

—MARION FOSTER KIRKTON, ON

PREP: 25 MIN. • **BAKE:** 15 MIN.
MAKES: 5½ DOZEN

- 2 **large eggs**
- ¾ **cup milk**
- 1 **cup dry bread crumbs**
- ½ **cup finely chopped onion**
- 2 **teaspoons salt**
- 2 **pounds ground beef**
- 4 **garlic cloves, minced**
- 1 **tablespoon butter**
- ¾ **cup ketchup**
- ½ **cup honey**
- 3 **tablespoons soy sauce**

1. In a large bowl, combine eggs and milk. Add the bread crumbs, onion and salt. Crumble beef over mixture and mix well. Shape into 1-in. balls. Place on greased racks in shallow baking pans. Bake, uncovered, at 400° for 12-15 minutes or until meat is no longer pink.

2. Meanwhile, in a large saucepan, saute the garlic in butter until tender. Stir in the ketchup, honey and soy sauce. Bring to a boil. Reduce heat; cover and simmer for 5 minutes. Drain the meatballs; add to sauce. Carefully stir to evenly coat. Cook for 5-10 minutes.

FAST FIX
MAPLE CRUNCH POPCORN

For a snack that's sure to bring smiles, try this medley of popcorn and pecans covered in a sweet and buttery coating. You won't be able to stop nibbling!

—ELMIRA TROMBETTI PADUCAH, KY

START TO FINISH: 25 MIN.
MAKES: 3½ QUARTS

- 10 **cups popped popcorn**
- 1½ **cups pecan halves, toasted**
- 1⅓ **cups sugar**
- 1 **cup butter, cubed**
- ¼ **cup maple syrup**
- ¼ **cup corn syrup**
- ½ **teaspoon salt**
- 1 **teaspoon maple flavoring**

1. Place popcorn and pecans in a large bowl; set aside. Using a large heavy saucepan, combine the sugar, butter, maple syrup, corn syrup and salt. Cook and stir over medium heat until a candy thermometer reads 300° (hard-crack stage). Remove from the heat and stir in the maple flavoring. Quickly pour over the popcorn blend and mix well.

2. Transfer to baking sheets lined with waxed paper to cool. Break into clusters. Store in airtight containers.

NOTE *We recommend that you test your candy thermometer before each use by bringing water to a boil; the thermometer should read 212°. Adjust your recipe temperature up or down based on your test.*

HONEY-GARLIC GLAZED MEATBALLS

LEMONADE ICED TEA

I have always loved iced tea with lemon, and this great thirst-quencher takes it one step further. The lemonade gives the drink a nice color, too. I dress up each glass with a piece of lemon on the rim.

—**GAIL BUSS** BEVERLY HILLS, FL

PREP: 15 MIN. + CHILLING
MAKES: 12 SERVINGS (ABOUT 3 QUARTS)

- 3 **quarts water**
- 9 **individual tea bags**
- ¾ **to 1¼ cups sugar**
- 1 **can (12 ounces) frozen lemonade concentrate, thawed**
  Lemon slices, optional

In a Dutch oven, bring water to a boil. Remove from the heat; add the tea bags. Cover and steep for 5 minutes. Discard tea bags. Stir in the sugar and lemonade concentrate. Cover and refrigerate until chilled. Serve over ice. If desired, garnish with lemon slices.

★ ★ ★ ★ ★ **5 STAR TIP**

Make this iced tea or other lemony chilled beverages extra special by dipping the rims of the glasses in fresh lemon juice, then twisting the glasses in a little bit of sugar. Set trays of glasses in the refrigerator until ready to serve.

LEMONADE ICED TEA

APPETIZER
PIZZAS

APPETIZER PIZZAS

To keep a summer kitchen cool, prepare pizzas on the grill. Quick-prep ingredients let you create three different flavor sensations, or let party guests build their own.

—TASTE OF HOME TEST KITCHEN

PREP: 30 MIN. • **GRILL:** 10 MIN.
MAKES: 9 APPETIZER PIZZAS

- 9 **flour tortillas (6 inches)**
- 3 **tablespoons olive oil**

TRADITIONAL PIZZAS
- ⅓ **cup chopped pepperoni**
- ¾ **cup shredded Colby-Monterey Jack cheese**
- 1 **jar (14 ounces) pizza sauce**

MEDITERRANEAN PIZZAS
- ½ **cup chopped seeded tomato**
- ⅓ **cup sliced ripe olives**
- ¾ **cup crumbled feta cheese**
- ¼ **cup thinly sliced green onions**
- 1 **carton (7 ounces) hummus**

MARGHERITA PIZZAS
- 9 **thin slices tomato**
- 1 **package (8 ounces) small fresh mozzarella cheese balls, sliced**
- 1 **tablespoon minced fresh basil**
- 1 **cup prepared pesto**

Brush one side of each tortilla with oil. Place oiled side down on grill rack. Grill, uncovered, over medium heat for 2-3 minutes or until puffed. Brush tortillas with oil; turn and top with pizza toppings.

FOR TRADITIONAL PIZZAS *Top three grilled tortillas with pepperoni and cheese. Cover and grill for 2-3 minutes or until cheese is melted. Cut into wedges; serve with pizza sauce.*

FOR MEDITERRANEAN PIZZAS *Top three grilled tortillas with tomato, olives, feta cheese and onions. Cover and grill for 2-3 minutes or until cheese is heated through. Cut into wedges; serve with hummus.*

FOR MARGHERITA PIZZAS *Top three grilled tortillas with tomato slices, mozzarella cheese and basil. Cover and grill for 2-3 minutes or until cheese is melted. Cut into wedges; serve with pesto.*

---

⑤ INGREDIENTS FAST FIX ▶
WHITE CHOCOLATE BRIE CUPS

Try these unique little tarts as an appetizer before a special meal, or save them for a surprisingly different dinner finale. They're sweet, creamy and crunchy—and addictive!

—ANGELA VITALE DELAWARE, OH

START TO FINISH: 25 MIN.
MAKES: 15 APPETIZERS

- 1 **package (1.9 ounces) frozen miniature phyllo tart shells**
- 1½ **ounces white baking chocolate, chopped**
- 2 **ounces Brie cheese, chopped**
- ⅓ **cup orange marmalade**
    Kumquat slices, optional

1. Preheat oven to 350°. Fill each tart shell with chocolate, then cheese. Place on an ungreased baking sheet. Top with marmalade.
2. Bake 6-8 minutes or until golden brown. Serve warm. If desired, top with kumquat.

MAPLE JALAPENOS

Craving something sweet and salty with a little bit of heat? Try my maple-flavored baked jalapeno snacks.

—NICOLE LARSON AMERICAN FORK, UT

PREP: 45 MIN. • **BAKE:** 20 MIN.
MAKES: 50 APPETIZERS

- 25 **jalapeno peppers**
- 1 **package (8 ounces) cream cheese, softened**
- 1 **cup (4 ounces) crumbled feta cheese**
- ½ **cup maple syrup**
- ½ **pound bacon strips, cooked and crumbled**
- ¼ **cup packed brown sugar**

1. Cut jalapenos in half lengthwise and remove seeds. Set aside. In a small bowl, beat the cream cheese, feta cheese and syrup until smooth. Spoon into pepper halves.
2. Place in two greased 15x10x 1-in. baking pans. Top with bacon and sprinkle with brown sugar. Bake at 350° for 20 minutes for spicy flavor, 30 minutes for medium, and 40 minutes for mild.
NOTE *Wear disposable gloves when cutting hot peppers; the oils can burn skin. Avoid touching your face.*

FAST FIX ▶
SALSA ROJA

With the help of my food processor, I can have fresh, homemade salsa ready in 15 minutes. The lime juice works wonders bringing out all the flavors, and you can really taste the cilantro.

—AMBER MASSEY ARGYLE, TX

START TO FINISH: 15 MIN.
MAKES: 7 CUPS

- 1 **can (28 ounces) whole tomatoes, drained**
- 1 **can (14½ ounces) diced tomatoes with garlic and onion, drained**
- 1 **can (14½ ounces) Mexican stewed tomatoes, drained**
- 1 **can (10 ounces) diced tomatoes and green chilies, drained**
- 1 **medium onion, quartered**
- 2 **banana peppers, seeded and coarsely chopped**
- 2 **jalapeno peppers, seeded and coarsely chopped**
- 3 **garlic cloves, minced**
- 2 **teaspoons salt**
- ¼ **teaspoon ground cumin**
- ½ **cup minced fresh cilantro**
- ¼ **cup lime juice**
- 2 **medium ripe avocados, peeled and cubed**
    Tortilla chips

1. Place the first 10 ingredients in a food processor; cover and process until chopped. Add cilantro and lime juice; cover and pulse until combined.
2. Transfer to a bowl; stir in avocados. Serve with tortilla chips.
NOTE *Wear disposable gloves when cutting hot peppers; the oils can burn skin. Avoid touching your face.*

SWISS MUSHROOM LOAF

I get lots of recipe requests when I serve this outstanding loaf stuffed with Swiss cheese and mushrooms. It's excellent as an appetizer or served with pasta.

—HEIDI MELLON WAUKESHA, WI

PREP: 15 MIN. • **BAKE:** 40 MIN.
MAKES: 10-12 SERVINGS

- 1 **unsliced loaf (1 pound) Italian bread**
- 1 **block (8 ounces) Swiss cheese, cut into cubes**
- 1 **cup sliced fresh mushrooms**
- ¼ **cup butter, cubed**
- 1 **small onion, finely chopped**
- 1½ **teaspoons poppy seeds**
- 2 **garlic cloves, minced**
- ½ **teaspoon seasoned salt**
- ½ **teaspoon ground mustard**
- ½ **teaspoon lemon juice**

1. Cut the bread diagonally into 1-in. slices to within 1 in. of bottom. Repeat the cuts in opposite direction. Place the cheese cubes and mushrooms in each slit.

2. In a microwave-safe bowl, combine the remaining ingredients; cover and microwave on high for 30-60 seconds or until butter is melted; stir until blended. Spoon over bread.

3. Wrap loaf in foil. Bake at 350° for 40 minutes or until cheese is melted.

NOTE *This recipe was tested in a 1,100-watt microwave.*

★ ★ ★ ★ ★ **READER REVIEW**

"I took this loaf to a party when asked to bring garlic bread. One of the guests remarked that it was the best item at the party. Delicious! I have made it several times."

BROWNSUGAR TASTEOFHOME.COM

SWISS
MUSHROOM
LOAF

FREEZE IT
CRISPY BAKED WONTONS

These quick, versatile wontons are great for a savory snack or paired with a bowl of warm soup on a chilly day.

—**BRIANNA SHADE** BEAVERTON, OR

PREP: 30 MIN. • **BAKE:** 10 MIN.
MAKES: ABOUT 4 DOZEN

- ½ **pound ground pork**
- ½ **pound extra-lean ground turkey**
- 1 **small onion, chopped**
- 1 **can (8 ounces) sliced water chestnuts, drained and chopped**
- ⅓ **cup reduced-sodium soy sauce**
- ¼ **cup egg substitute**
- 1½ **teaspoons ground ginger**
- 1 **package (12 ounces) wonton wrappers**
  Cooking spray
  Sweet-and-sour sauce, optional

1. In a large skillet, cook the pork, turkey and onion over medium heat until meat is no longer pink; drain. Transfer to a large bowl. Stir in the water chestnuts, soy sauce, egg substitute and ginger.
2. Position a wonton wrapper with one point toward you. (Keep the remaining wrappers covered with a damp paper towel until ready to use.) Place 2 heaping teaspoons of filling in the center of wrapper. Fold bottom corner over filling; fold sides toward center over filling. Roll toward the remaining point. Moisten top corner with water; press to seal. Repeat with remaining wrappers and filling.
3. Place on baking sheets coated with cooking spray; lightly coat wontons with additional cooking spray.
4. Bake at 400° for 10-12 minutes or until golden brown, turning once. Serve warm, with sweet-and-sour sauce if desired.

FREEZE OPTION *Freeze the cooled baked wontons in a freezer container, separating layers with waxed paper. To use, reheat on a baking sheet in a preheated 400° oven until crisp and heated through.*

⑤INGREDIENTS FAST FIX
MINI REUBEN CUPS

Treat your company to this hot and delicious nibble. The prebaked wonton wrappers hold all the savory flavors of a reuben sandwich.

—**GRACE NELTNER** LAKESIDE PARK, KY

START TO FINISH: 30 MIN.
MAKES: 2 DOZEN

- 24 **wonton wrappers**
- 3 **packages (2 ounces each) thinly sliced deli corned beef, chopped**
- ⅓ **cup sauerkraut, rinsed and well drained**
- ⅓ **cup Thousand Island salad dressing**
- ⅔ **cup shredded Swiss cheese**

1. Press wonton wrappers into miniature muffin cups coated with cooking spray. Bake at 350° for 6-7 minutes or until lightly browned.
2. Meanwhile, in a small bowl, combine the corned beef, sauerkraut and dressing. Spoon into wonton cups. Sprinkle with cheese.
3. Bake for 8-10 minutes or until filling is heated through. Serve warm.

⑤INGREDIENTS FAST FIX
QUICK WATERMELON COOLER

Summer means cooling off with a slice of watermelon and a glass of cold lemonade. This recipe combines two favorites in one.

—**DARLENE BRENDEN** SALEM, OR

START TO FINISH: 10 MIN.
MAKES: 4 SERVINGS

- 2 **cups lemonade**
- 3 **cups seedless watermelon, coarsely chopped**
- 1 **cup crushed ice**

In a blender, combine all ingredients; cover and process until smooth. Pour the mixture into chilled glasses; serve immediately.

VIETNAMESE PORK LETTUCE WRAPS

Casual, flavorful and low in carbs, these wraps are a perfect low-fuss way to feed a group. Place the ingredients in separate dishes, and let your guests assemble their own wrap, which allows them to personalize each one to suit their tastes.

—GRETCHEN BARNES FAIRFAX, VA

PREP: 25 MIN. + STANDING • **COOK:** 10 MIN.
MAKES: 8 SERVINGS

- ½ cup white vinegar
- ¼ cup sugar
- ⅛ teaspoon salt
- 2 medium carrots, julienned
- ½ medium onion, cut into thin slices

FILLING
- 1 pound ground pork
- 1 tablespoon minced fresh gingerroot
- 1 garlic clove, minced
- 2 tablespoons reduced-sodium soy sauce
- 1 tablespoon mirin (sweet rice wine)
- ¼ teaspoon salt
- ¼ teaspoon pepper
- 1 teaspoon fish sauce, optional

ASSEMBLY
- 8 Bibb lettuce leaves
- ½ English cucumber, finely chopped
- 1 small sweet red pepper, finely chopped
- 3 green onions, chopped
- ½ cup each coarsely chopped fresh basil, cilantro and mint
- 1 jalapeno pepper, seeded and finely chopped
- ¼ cup salted peanuts, chopped
  Hoisin sauce
  Lime wedges

1. In a small bowl, mix the vinegar, sugar and salt until blended. Stir in carrots and onion; let stand at room temperature 30 minutes.

2. In a large skillet, cook pork, ginger and garlic over medium heat 6-8 minutes or until pork is no longer pink, breaking up pork into crumbles; drain. Stir in soy sauce, mirin, salt, pepper and, if desired, fish sauce.

3. To serve, drain carrot mixture. Place pork mixture in lettuce leaves; top with cucumber, red pepper, green onions, carrot mixture and herbs. Sprinkle with jalapeno and peanuts; drizzle with hoisin sauce. Squeeze lime juice over the tops. Fold the lettuce over the filling.

FAST FIX
GARLIC-CHEESE FLAT BREAD

As an appetizer or side, this cheesy flat bread will be devoured in less time than it takes to bake. And that's not long!

—SUZANNE ZICK MAIDEN, NC

START TO FINISH: 25 MIN.
MAKES: 12 SERVINGS

- 1 tube (11 ounces) refrigerated thin pizza crust
- 2 tablespoons butter, melted
- 1 tablespoon minced fresh basil
- 4 garlic cloves, minced
- ¾ cup shredded cheddar cheese
- ½ cup grated Romano cheese
- ¼ cup grated Parmesan cheese

1. Unroll the dough into a greased 15x10x1-in. baking pan; flatten dough to 13x9-in. rectangle and build up the edges slightly.

2. Drizzle with butter. Sprinkle with basil, garlic and cheeses.

3. Bake at 425° for 11-14 minutes or until bread is crisp. Cut into squares; serve warm.

VIETNAMESE PORK LETTUCE WRAPS

SLOW COOKER
CHEESY MEATBALLS

Can meatballs be lucky? My guys think so, and they want them for game time. My beef, sausage and cheese recipe has a big fan following.

—JILL HILL DIXON, IL

PREP: 1 HOUR • **COOK:** 4 HOURS
MAKES: ABOUT 9 DOZEN

- 1 large egg
- ½ cup 2% milk
- 2 tablespoons dried minced onion
- 4 tablespoons chili powder, divided
- 1 teaspoon salt
- 1 teaspoon pepper
- 1½ cups crushed Ritz crackers (about 1 sleeve)
- 2 pounds ground beef
- 1 pound bulk pork sausage
- 2 cups shredded process cheese (Velveeta)
- 1 can (26 ounces) condensed tomato soup, undiluted
- 2½ cups water
- 1 cup packed brown sugar

1. Preheat the oven to 400°. In a large bowl, whisk egg, milk, minced onion, 2 tablespoons chili powder, salt and pepper; stir in crushed crackers. Add beef, sausage and cheese; mix lightly but thoroughly.
2. Shape the mixture into 1-in. balls. Place the meatballs on greased racks in 15x10x1-in. baking pans. Bake for 15-18 minutes or until browned.
3. Meanwhile, in a 5- or 6-qt. slow cooker, combine soup, water, brown sugar and remaining chili powder. Gently stir in the meatballs. Cook, covered, on low 4-5 hours or until meatballs are cooked through.

APPLE SALSA WITH CINNAMON CHIPS

FAST FIX
APPLE SALSA WITH CINNAMON CHIPS

Both my husband and I were raised on farms, and we prefer home cooking to anything processed that comes out of a bag or box. I've served this fresh, colorful salsa as an appetizer and as a snack. It's even sweet enough to be a dessert. It's easy to transport, too, if you're going to a potluck or party.

—CAROLYN BRINKMEYER GOLDEN, CO

START TO FINISH: 25 MIN.
MAKES: 4 CUPS SALSA

SALSA
- 2 medium tart apples, chopped
- 1 cup chopped strawberries
- 2 medium kiwifruit, peeled and chopped
- 1 small orange
- 2 tablespoons brown sugar
- 2 tablespoons apple jelly, melted

CHIPS
- 8 flour tortillas (7 or 8 inches)
- 1 tablespoon water
- ¼ cup sugar
- 2 teaspoons ground cinnamon

1. In a bowl, combine the apples, strawberries and kiwi. Grate orange peel to measure 1½ teaspoons; squeeze juice from orange. Add the peel and juice to apple mixture. Stir in brown sugar and jelly.
2. For chips, brush tortillas lightly with water. Combine sugar and cinnamon; sprinkle over tortillas. Cut each tortilla into eight wedges. Place in a single layer on ungreased baking sheets.
3. Bake at 400° for 6-8 minutes or until lightly browned. Cool. Serve with salsa.

CAPPUCCINO PUNCH

CAPPUCCINO PUNCH

When I tried this beverage at a friend's wedding shower, I had to have the recipe. Guests will eagerly gather around the punch bowl when you ladle out this frothy mocha ice cream drink.

—**ROSE REICH** NAMPA, ID

PREP: 10 MIN. + CHILLING
MAKES: ABOUT 1 GALLON

- ½ cup sugar
- ¼ cup instant coffee granules
- 1 cup boiling water
- 2 quarts whole milk
- 1 quart vanilla ice cream, softened
- 1 quart chocolate ice cream, softened
  Grated chocolate, optional

1. Combine sugar and coffee; stir in boiling water until dissolved. Cover and refrigerate until chilled.
2. Just before serving, pour coffee mixture into a 1-gal. punch bowl. Stir in milk. Add scoops of ice cream; stir until melted. If desired, sprinkle with grated chocolate.

FAST FIX

BLUEBERRY FRUIT DIP

After a long day at school, my kids like to snack on this fruit-filled dip.

—**RENEE SEVIGNY** WAYLAND, MI

START TO FINISH: 10 MIN.
MAKES: 1 CUP

- 4 ounces cream cheese, softened
- ½ cup confectioners' sugar
- ½ teaspoon ground cinnamon
- ½ teaspoon lemon juice
- ½ cup fresh blueberries
  Assorted fresh fruit, graham crackers and/or cookies

In a small bowl, beat the cream cheese, confectioners' sugar, cinnamon and lemon juice until smooth. Fold in blueberries. Serve with fruit, crackers and/or cookies.

GRILLED SHRIMP WITH SPICY-SWEET SAUCE

These finger-lickin' shrimp practically fly off the platter at my get-togethers. Play with the amount of Sriracha sauce to get the spice level just the way you like it.

—**SUSAN HARRISON** LAUREL, MD

START TO FINISH: 30 MIN.
MAKES: 15 SERVINGS (⅓ CUP SAUCE)

- 3 tablespoons reduced-fat mayonnaise
- 2 tablespoons sweet chili sauce
- 1 green onion, thinly sliced
- ¾ teaspoon Sriracha Asian hot chili sauce or ½ teaspoon hot pepper sauce
- 45 uncooked large shrimp (about 1½ pounds), peeled and deveined
- ¼ teaspoon salt
- ¼ teaspoon pepper

1. In a small bowl, mix mayonnaise, chili sauce, green onion and Sriracha. Sprinkle shrimp with salt and pepper. Thread three shrimp onto each of 15 metal or soaked wooden skewers.
2. Moisten some paper towel with cooking oil; using long-handled tongs, rub on grill rack to coat lightly. Grill shrimp, covered, over medium heat or broil 4 in. from heat 3-4 minutes on each side or until shrimp turn pink. Serve with sauce.

★ ★ ★ ★ ★ **5 STAR TIP**
Before you head to your backyard for some fun outdoor cooking on the grill, keep these tips in mind. Bring foods to a cool room temperature before grilling. Cold foods may burn on the outside before the interior is cooked. Use tongs to turn meat, fish or poultry instead of a meat fork to avoid piercing and losing juices. Use an instant-read thermometer to check the internal temperature of foods before the recommended cooking time is up.

SAUSAGE BISCUIT BITES

SAUSAGE BISCUIT BITES

I sometimes bake these pop-in-your-mouth noshes in the evening and refrigerate them overnight. Then in the morning, I put them in the slow cooker so my husband can take them to work to share with his co-workers. They're always gone in a hurry.

—**AUDREY MARLER** KOKOMO, IN

START TO FINISH: 30 MIN.
MAKES: 40 APPETIZERS

- 1 tube (7½ ounces) refrigerated buttermilk biscuits
- 1 tablespoon butter, melted
- 4½ teaspoons grated Parmesan cheese
- 1 teaspoon dried oregano
- 1 package (8 ounces) frozen fully cooked breakfast sausage links, thawed

1. On a lightly floured surface, roll out each biscuit into a 4-in. circle; brush with butter. Combine Parmesan cheese and oregano; sprinkle over biscuits. Place a sausage link in the center of each roll; roll up.
2. Cut each widthwise into four pieces; insert a toothpick into each. Place on an ungreased baking sheet. Bake at 375° for 8-10 minutes or until golden brown.

★ ★ ★ ★ ★ **READER REVIEW**
"Made these for a holiday get-together and they went fast. I was asked for the recipe, which I happily shared, several times."
CINDIAK TASTEOFHOME.COM

MUSHROOM BACON BITES

ROASTED RED PEPPER TRIANGLES

Robust meats, cheeses and veggies fill a flaky, golden crust in this snack. I recommend using marinara sauce for dipping.

—**AMY BELL** ARLINGTON, TN

PREP: 35 MIN. • **BAKE:** 50 MIN.
MAKES: 2 DOZEN

- 2 tubes (8 ounces each) refrigerated crescent rolls
- 1½ cups finely diced fully cooked ham
- 1 cup shredded Swiss cheese
- 1 package (3 ounces) sliced pepperoni, chopped
- 8 slices provolone cheese
- 1 jar (12 ounces) roasted sweet red peppers, well drained and cut into strips
- 4 large eggs
- ¼ cup grated Parmesan cheese
- 3 teaspoons Italian salad dressing mix

1. Unroll one tube of crescent dough into a long rectangle; press onto the bottom and ¾ in. up the sides of a greased 13x9-in. baking dish. Seal seams and perforations. Top with half of the ham; layer with Swiss cheese, pepperoni, provolone cheese and remaining ham. Top with red peppers.
2. In a small bowl, whisk the eggs, Parmesan cheese and salad dressing mix; set aside ¼ cup. Pour remaining egg mixture over peppers.
3. On a lightly floured surface, roll out the remaining crescent dough into a 13x9-in. rectangle; seal seams and perforations. Place over filling; pinch edges to seal.
4. Cover and bake at 350° for 30 minutes. Uncover; brush with the reserved egg mixture. Bake 20-25 minutes longer or until the crust is golden brown. Cool on a wire rack for 5 minutes. Cut the dish into triangles. Serve warm.

(5)INGREDIENTS **FAST FIX**
MUSHROOM BACON BITES

When we have a big cookout, these tasty bites always make an appearance. They're easy to assemble and then brush with prepared barbecue sauce.

—**GINA ROESNER** ASHLAND, MO

START TO FINISH: 20 MIN.
MAKES: 2 DOZEN

- 24 medium fresh mushrooms
- 12 bacon strips, halved
- 1 cup barbecue sauce

1. Wrap each mushroom with a piece of bacon; secure with a toothpick. Thread onto metal or soaked wooden skewers; brush with barbecue sauce.
2. Grill, uncovered, over indirect medium heat for 10-15 minutes or until the bacon is crisp and the mushrooms are tender, turning and basting occasionally with remaining barbecue sauce.

ROASTED RED
PEPPER TRIANGLES

VIDALIA ONION SWISS DIP

Here's a recipe for one of those sweet, creamy dips you can't resist. Bake it in the oven, or use the slow cooker to make it ooey-gooey marvelous.

—JUDY BATSON TAMPA, FL

PREP: 10 MIN. • **COOK:** 25 MIN.
MAKES: 20 SERVINGS (¼ CUP EACH)

- 3 **cups chopped Vidalia or other sweet onion (about 1 large)**
- 2 **cups shredded Swiss cheese**
- 2 **cups mayonnaise**
- ¼ **cup prepared horseradish**
- 1 **teaspoon hot pepper sauce**
  Fresh coarsely ground pepper, optional
  Assorted crackers or fresh vegetables

1. Preheat oven to 375°. In a large bowl, mix the first five ingredients. Transfer to a deep-dish pie plate.
2. Bake, uncovered, 25-30 minutes or until the edges are golden brown and onion is tender. If desired, sprinkle with pepper. Serve warm with crackers.

★ ★ ★ ★ ★ **READER REVIEW**

"Ooey-gooey marvelous is the best way to describe this delicious dip. We tried it with scoop-style corn chips. It's definitely a keeper."

ANNRMS TASTEOFHOME.COM

VIDALIA ONION
SWISS DIP

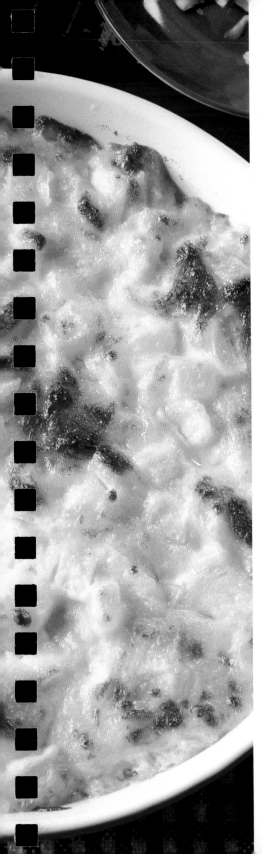

SHRIMP CORN CAKES WITH SOY MAYO

Feel free to add hot sauce to the dip that accompanies these savory corn cakes.

—**KATTY CHIONG** HOFFMAN ESTATES, IL

PREP: 30 MIN. • **COOK:** 5 MIN./BATCH
MAKES: 2 DOZEN (⅔ CUP SAUCE)

- ½ **cup mayonnaise**
- 1 **tablespoon reduced-sodium soy sauce**
- 1 **tablespoon ketchup**
- 2 **teaspoons Dijon mustard**
- ½ **teaspoon garlic powder**
- ½ **teaspoon hot pepper sauce, optional**
- ⅛ **teaspoon pepper**

SHRIMP CORN CAKES

- ½ **cup chopped onion (about 1 small)**
- 1 **tablespoon oil plus additional for frying, divided**
- 2 **garlic cloves, minced**
- ½ **pound uncooked peeled and deveined shrimp, finely chopped**
- ¾ **cup all-purpose flour**
- ¼ **cup cornmeal**
- 1 **tablespoon cornstarch**
- 1 **teaspoon baking powder**
- ¼ **teaspoon salt**
- ¼ **teaspoon pepper**
- 1 **cup cream-style corn**
- 1 **cup whole kernel corn**
- 1 **large egg, lightly beaten**

1. In a small bowl, combine the first seven ingredients. Cover and chill until serving.
2. In a large skillet, cook and stir the onion in 1 tablespoon oil over medium-high heat until tender. Add garlic; cook 1 minute longer. Add shrimp; cook and stir until shrimp turn pink. Remove from the heat.
3. In a large bowl, mix the flour, cornmeal, cornstarch, baking powder, salt and pepper. In a small bowl, mix the corn, egg and shrimp mixture; stir into the dry ingredients just until moistened.
4. In an electric skillet, heat ¼ in. of oil to 375°. In batches, drop the corn mixture by rounded tablespoonfuls into oil; fry 1½ minutes on each side or until golden brown. Drain on paper towels. Serve with sauce.

FAST FIX ▶
DILL BLOODY MARYS

With a nice level of pepper and just enough dill from the pickle, these Bloody Marys are sure to please. Fun garnishes make them like a meal unto themselves!

—**JAY FERKOVICH** GREEN BAY, WI

START TO FINISH: 10 MIN.
MAKES: 2 SERVINGS

- 1½ **cups Clamato juice, chilled**
- 2 **tablespoons dill pickle juice**
- 1 **tablespoon Worcestershire sauce**
- ¼ **teaspoon celery salt**
- ⅛ to ¼ **teaspoon pepper**
- ⅛ **teaspoon hot pepper sauce**
- ¼ **cup vodka, optional**
  Ice cubes
- 2 **celery ribs**
- 2 **pepperoni-flavored meat snack sticks**
- 2 **dill pickle spears**
- 2 **pitted ripe olives**

In a small pitcher, combine the first six ingredients. Stir in the vodka if desired. Pour into two glasses filled with ice; garnish with celery, snack sticks, pickles and olives.

MARYLAND CORN POPS

Fresh-picked sweet corn is a big thing in Maryland in the summer. Here is my homespun version of Mexican street corn that brings in local Bay flavors.
—**KRISTIE SCHLEY** SEVERNA PARK, MD

PREP: 25 MIN. • **GRILL:** 10 MIN.
MAKES: 2 DOZEN

- 8 **medium ears sweet corn, husks removed**
- 2 **tablespoons canola oil**
- 1½ **cups mayonnaise**
- 1½ **teaspoons garlic powder**
- ¼ **teaspoon freshly ground pepper**
- 24 **corncob holders**
- 2 **cups crumbled feta cheese**
- 2 **tablespoons seafood seasoning**
- ¼ **cup minced fresh cilantro**
  Lime wedges, optional

1. Brush all sides of corn with oil. Grill, covered, over medium heat 10-12 minutes or until tender and lightly browned, turning occasionally. Remove from grill; cool slightly.
2. Meanwhile, in a small bowl, mix the mayonnaise, garlic powder and pepper. Cut each ear of corn into thirds. Insert one corncob holder into each piece. Spread the corn with the mayonnaise mixture; sprinkle with the cheese, seafood seasoning and cilantro. If desired, serve with lime wedges.

MARYLAND CORN POPS

JALAPENO POPPER POCKET

For a fresh take on fried jalapeno poppers, we stuff chicken, cheeses and jalapenos into puff pastry and bake.
—**SALLY SIBTHORPE** SHELBY TOWNSHIP, MI

PREP: 15 MIN. • **BAKE:** 20 MIN. + STANDING
MAKES: 12 SERVINGS

- 2 **cups chopped rotisserie chicken (about 10 ounces)**
- 1 **carton (8 ounces) spreadable chive and onion cream cheese**
- 1 **cup shredded pepper jack or Monterey Jack cheese**
- 1 **can (4 ounces) diced jalapeno peppers**
- 1 **sheet frozen puff pastry, thawed**
- 1 **large egg, lightly beaten**

1. Preheat oven to 425°. In a bowl, mix chicken, cream cheese, pepper jack cheese and peppers.
2. On a lightly floured surface, unfold puff pastry; roll into a 13-in. square. Place on a parchment paper-lined baking sheet. Spread one half with chicken mixture to within ½ in. of edges. Fold remaining half over filling; press edges with a fork to seal.
3. Brush lightly with beaten egg. Cut slits in pastry. Bake 20-25 minutes or until golden brown. Let stand 10 minutes before cutting.

★ ★ ★ ★ ★ **5 STAR TIP**
Frozen puff pastry dough is available in sheets or individual shells. It has paper-thin layers of dough separated by butter. As the pastry bakes, steam created from water in the dough makes the layers rise up and pull apart, resulting in a crisp, flaky pastry. Before handling, thaw pastry at room temperature for about 20 minutes. Puff pastry is delicate, so handle it as little as possible to avoid stretching and tearing.

(5)INGREDIENTS | SLOW COOKER 🍲
HOT SPICED CHERRY CIDER

There's nothing better than coming in from the cold and smelling the aroma of this heartwarming cider that's been simmering in the slow cooker.
—MARLENE WICZEK LITTLE FALLS, MN

PREP: 5 MIN. • **COOK:** 4 HOURS
MAKES: 4 QUARTS

- 1 gallon apple cider or juice
- 2 cinnamon sticks (3 inches)
- 2 packages (3 ounces each) cherry gelatin

Place cider in a 6-qt. slow cooker; add cinnamon sticks. Cover and cook on high for 3 hours. Stir in gelatin; cook 1 hour longer. Discard the cinnamon sticks before serving.

(5)INGREDIENTS
SUGARED PEANUTS

I tend to prepare this treat only for special occasions because I cannot keep my husband and son (and myself!) away from them. The food never lasts long, so you might want to make a double batch.
—POLLY HALL ROCKFORD, MI

PREP: 20 MIN. • **BAKE:** 30 MIN. + COOLING
MAKES: 5 CUPS

- 5 cups unsalted peanuts
- 1 cup sugar
- 1 cup water
- ¼ teaspoon salt

1. In a large heavy saucepan, combine peanuts, sugar and water. Bring to a boil; cook until syrup has evaporated, about 10 minutes.
2. Spread peanuts in a single layer in a greased 15x10x1-in. baking pan; sprinkle with salt.
3. Bake at 300° for 30-35 minutes or until dry and lightly browned. Cool completely. Store in an airtight container.

PIZZA ROLLS

PIZZA ROLLS

This is my husband's version of store-bought pizza rolls, and our family loves them. They take some time to make, but they freeze well. So when all the prep work is done, we get to enjoy the fruits of our labor for a long time!
—JULIE GAINES NORMAL, IL

PREP: 50 MIN. • **COOK:** 5 MIN./BATCH
MAKES: 32 ROLLS

- 4 cups shredded pizza cheese blend or part-skim mozzarella cheese
- 1 pound bulk Italian sausage, cooked and drained
- 2 packages (3 ounces each) sliced pepperoni, chopped
- 1 medium green pepper, finely chopped
- 1 medium sweet red pepper, finely chopped
- 1 medium onion, finely chopped
- 2 jars (14 ounces each) pizza sauce
- 32 egg roll wrappers
  Oil for frying
  Additional pizza sauce for dipping, warmed, optional

1. Using a large bowl, combine the cheese, sausage, pepperoni, peppers and onion. Stir in pizza sauce until combined. Place about ¼ cup filling in the center of each egg roll wrapper. Fold bottom corner over filling; fold the sides toward center over filling. Moisten remaining corner with water and roll up tightly to seal.
2. In an electric skillet, heat 1 in. of oil to 375°. Fry pizza rolls for 1-2 minutes on each side or until golden brown. Drain on paper towels. Serve with additional pizza sauce if desired.

BACON CHEESEBURGER SLIDER BAKE

I created this meaty dish to fill two pans because these sliders disappear in a flash. Just cut the recipe in half if you only need one pan's worth.

—NICK IVERSON MILWAUKEE, WI

PREP: 20 MIN. • **BAKE:** 25 MIN.
MAKES: 2 DOZEN

- 2 packages (18 ounces each) Hawaiian sweet rolls
- 4 cups shredded cheddar cheese, divided
- 2 pounds ground beef
- 1 cup chopped onion
- 1 can (14½ ounces) diced tomatoes with garlic and onion, drained
- 1 tablespoon Dijon mustard
- 1 tablespoon Worcestershire sauce
- ¾ teaspoon salt
- ¾ teaspoon pepper
- 24 bacon strips, cooked and crumbled

GLAZE
- 1 cup butter, cubed
- ¼ cup packed brown sugar
- 4 teaspoons Worcestershire sauce
- 2 tablespoons Dijon mustard
- 2 tablespoons sesame seeds

BACON CHEESEBURGER SLIDER BAKE

1. Preheat oven to 350°. Without separating rolls, cut each package of rolls horizontally in half; arrange bottom halves in two greased 13x9-in. baking pans. Sprinkle each pan of rolls with 1 cup cheese. Bake 3-5 minutes or until cheese is melted.

2. In a large skillet, cook beef and onion over medium heat 6-8 minutes or until beef is no longer pink and onion is tender, breaking up beef into crumbles; drain. Stir in tomatoes, mustard, Worcestershire sauce, salt and pepper. Cook and stir 1-2 minutes or until combined.

3. Spoon beef mixture evenly over rolls; sprinkle with remaining cheese. Top with bacon. Replace tops. For the glaze, in a microwave-safe bowl combine the butter, brown sugar, Worcestershire sauce and mustard. Microwave, covered, on high until butter is melted, stirring occasionally. Pour over rolls; sprinkle with sesame seeds. Bake, uncovered, for 20-25 minutes or until golden brown and heated through.

FREEZE OPTION *Cover and freeze unbaked sandwiches; prepare and freeze glaze. To use, partially thaw in refrigerator overnight. Remove from refrigerator 30 minutes before baking. Preheat oven to 350°. Pour glaze over buns and sprinkle with sesame seeds. Bake the sandwiches as directed, increasing time by 10-15 minutes or until the cheese is melted and a thermometer inserted in the center reads 165°.*

★ ★ ★ ★ ★ **READER REVIEW**

"These are awesome! I made them exactly as written and wouldn't change a thing. The only problem is now I have to make them for every Sunday football game for my grown children and their friends!"

KDURK522 TASTEOFHOME.COM

TOPSY-TURVY
SANGRIA

TOPSY-TURVY SANGRIA

I got this recipe from a friend a few years ago. It's perfect for relaxed get-togethers. It tastes best when you make it the night before and let the flavors steep. But be careful—it goes down easy!

—**TRACY FIELD** BREMERTON, WA

START TO FINISH: 10 MIN.
MAKES: 10 SERVINGS (¾ CUP EACH)

- 1 **bottle (750 milliliters) merlot**
- 1 **cup sugar**
- 1 **cup orange liqueur**
- ½ **to 1 cup brandy**
- 3 **cups cold lemon-lime soda**
- 1 **cup sliced fresh strawberries**
- 1 **medium orange, sliced**
- 1 **medium lemon, sliced**
- 1 **medium peach, sliced**
  Ice cubes

In a pitcher, stir first four ingredients until sugar is dissolved. Stir in soda and fruit. Serve over ice.

FAST FIX ▶

NUTS & SEEDS TRAIL MIX

Need an excuse to show off a favorite serving bowl? My party mix combines seeds, nuts, fruit and chocolate. It's one I feel good about sharing with my family.

—**KRISTIN RIMKUS** SNOHOMISH, WA

START TO FINISH: 5 MIN.
MAKES: 5 CUPS

- 1 **cup salted pumpkin seeds or pepitas**
- 1 **cup unblanched almonds**
- 1 **cup unsalted sunflower kernels**
- 1 **cup walnut halves**
- 1 **cup dried apricots**
- 1 **cup dark chocolate chips**

Place all ingredients in a large bowl; toss to combine. Store in an airtight container.

HOW TO CUT A PINEAPPLE

With a chef's knife, remove the crown and the base. Stand the pineapple upright and cut down the length to remove the eyes and rind in strips.

Cut pineapple into quarters; remove the core. Cut the remainder into wedges or cubes, or use as recipe directs.

GRILLED PINEAPPLE WITH LIME DIP

GRILLED PINEAPPLE WITH LIME DIP

Serve this dish as an appetizer or dessert—the choice is yours! If you like, roll the pineapple wedges in flaked coconut before throwing them on the grill.

—TASTE OF HOME TEST KITCHEN

PREP: 20 MIN. + MARINATING
GRILL: 10 MIN.
MAKES: 8 SERVINGS

- 1 fresh pineapple
- ¼ cup packed brown sugar
- 3 tablespoons honey
- 2 tablespoons lime juice

LIME DIP
- 1 package (3 ounces) cream cheese, softened
- ¼ cup plain yogurt
- 2 tablespoons honey
- 1 tablespoon brown sugar
- 1 tablespoon lime juice
- 1 teaspoon grated lime peel

1. Peel and core the pineapple; cut into eight wedges. Cut each wedge into two spears. In a large resealable plastic bag, combine the brown sugar, honey and lime juice; add pineapple. Seal the bag and turn the fruit to coat; refrigerate for 1 hour.

2. In a small bowl, beat cream cheese until it is smooth. Beat in the yogurt, honey, brown sugar, lime juice and peel. Cover and refrigerate the blend until serving.

3. Coat grill rack with cooking spray before starting the grill. Drain and discard marinade. Grill pineapple, covered, over medium heat for 3-4 minutes on each side or until golden brown. Serve with lime dip.

CHICKEN SKEWERS WITH MARMALADE

CHICKEN SKEWERS WITH MARMALADE

My father-in-law loved this chicken dish and said that it reminded him of growing up in southern California. What a great way to bring a dose of summer sunshine to cold winter days.

—LAUREL DALZELL MANTECA, CA

PREP: 25 MIN. + MARINATING • **BROIL:** 5 MIN.
MAKES: 8 SERVINGS (1 CUP SAUCE)

- 1 pound boneless skinless chicken breasts
- ¼ cup olive oil
- ¼ cup reduced-sodium soy sauce
- 2 garlic cloves, minced
- ⅛ teaspoon pepper

SAUCE
- 2 teaspoons butter
- 2 tablespoons chopped seeded jalapeno pepper
- 1 teaspoon minced fresh gingerroot
- ¾ cup orange marmalade
- 1 tablespoon lime juice
- 1 tablespoon thawed orange juice concentrate
- ¼ teaspoon salt

1. Preheat broiler. Pound chicken breasts with a meat mallet to ¼-in. thickness; cut lengthwise into 1-in.-wide strips. In a large resealable plastic bag, combine oil, soy sauce, garlic and pepper. Add chicken; seal bag and turn to coat. Refrigerate for 4 hours or overnight.

2. In a small saucepan, heat butter over medium-high heat. Add jalapeno; cook and stir until tender. Add ginger; cook 1 minute longer. Reduce heat; stir in marmalade, lime juice, orange juice concentrate and salt.

3. Drain the chicken, discarding marinade. Thread chicken strips, weaving back and forth, onto eight metal or soaked wooden skewers. Place in a greased 15x10x1-in. baking pan. Broil 6 in. from heat 2-4 minutes on each side or until chicken is no longer pink. Serve with sauce.

NOTE *Wear disposable gloves when cutting hot peppers; the oils can burn skin. Avoid touching your face.*

APPETIZER
BLUE CHEESE LOGS

Three kinds of cheese and some curry powder make this cheese log a little more lively than most. Guests are sure to like the tasty surprise

—ETHEL JOHNSON NORTH SAANICH, BC

PREP: 20 MIN. + CHILLING
MAKES: 2 CHEESE LOGS

- 1 **package (8 ounces) cream cheese, softened**
- 1 **cup shredded sharp cheddar cheese**
- ½ **cup crumbled blue cheese**
- 1½ **teaspoons curry powder**
- 1 **tablespoon butter**
- ½ **cup finely chopped pecans**
- 2 **tablespoons minced fresh parsley**
  Assorted crackers

1. In a bowl, beat the cream cheese. Fold in cheddar cheese and blue cheese. Cover and refrigerate for at least 2 hours.
2. In a small skillet, saute the curry powder in butter for 1-2 minutes. Stir in pecans; cook and stir for 1 minute. Stir in the parsley. Cool slightly. Roll cheese mixture into two logs, about 5 in. long. Roll in pecan mixture. Cover and refrigerate until serving. Serve with crackers.

APPETIZER BLUE CHEESE LOGS

STROMBOLI RING

A friend of mine gave me this party-perfect recipe years ago, and it's so incredibly good. I serve it warm with marinara sauce.
—**BARRIE PEAGLER** SCOTTSDALE, AZ

PREP: 20 MIN. + RISING • **BAKE:** 30 MIN.
MAKES: 12 SERVINGS

- 1 **pound bulk Italian sausage**
- 1½ **cups shredded Monterey Jack or part-skim mozzarella cheese**
- 2 **large eggs, divided use**
- ½ **teaspoon Italian seasoning**
- 1 **loaf (1 pound) frozen bread dough, thawed**
- 1 **tablespoon grated Parmesan cheese**
  Marinara sauce, warmed, optional

1. In a large skillet, cook sausage over medium heat until no longer pink; drain. Stir in the Monterey Jack cheese, one egg and Italian seasoning.
2. On a lightly floured surface, roll dough into an 18x6-in. rectangle. Spoon sausage mixture over dough to within ½ in. of edges. Roll up jelly-roll style, starting with a long side; pinch seam to seal.
3. Place seam side down on a greased baking sheet; pinch ends together to form a ring. With scissors, cut from outside edge to two-thirds of the way toward center of ring at 1-in. intervals.
4. Beat remaining egg; brush over dough. Sprinkle with Parmesan cheese. Cover and let rise in a warm place until doubled, about 30 minutes.
5. Bake at 350° for 28-32 minutes or until golden brown. Serve with marinara sauce if desired.

⑤ INGREDIENTS | FAST FIX ▶
GARBANZO-STUFFED MINI PEPPERS

Mini peppers are so colorful and they're the perfect size for a two-bite appetizer. They have all the crunch of a pita chip, without the extra calories.
—**CHRISTINE HANOVER** LEWISTON, CA

START TO FINISH: 20 MIN.
MAKES: 32 APPETIZERS

- 1 **teaspoon cumin seeds**
- 1 **can (15 ounces) chickpeas, rinsed and drained**
- ¼ **cup fresh cilantro leaves**
- 3 **tablespoons water**
- 3 **tablespoons cider vinegar**
- ¼ **teaspoon salt**
- 16 **miniature sweet peppers, halved lengthwise**
  Additional fresh cilantro leaves

1. In a dry small skillet, toast cumin seeds over medium heat 1-2 minutes or until aromatic, stirring frequently. Transfer to a food processor. Add chickpeas, cilantro, water, vinegar and salt; pulse until blended.
2. Spoon mixture into pepper halves. Top with additional cilantro. Refrigerate until serving.

★ ★ ★ ★ ★ **READER REVIEW**

"I absolutely loved this recipe, delicious. Such great flavor!"

CINDIHARTLINE TASTEOFHOME.COM

BLUE CHEESE ONION DIP

I decided to tweak the traditional onion soup dip you see at every gathering by adding crumbled blue cheese and walnuts for a little crunch. Everyone loved the result.

—VICKI DESY TUCSON, AZ

PREP: 10 MIN. + CHILLING
MAKES: 12 SERVINGS (¼ CUP EACH)

- 2 **cups (16 ounces) sour cream**
- 1 **cup (4 ounces) crumbled blue cheese**
- ⅔ **cup mayonnaise**
- 2 **tablespoons onion soup mix**
- 1 **garlic clove, minced**
- ⅓ **cup chopped walnuts, toasted**
  Assorted fresh vegetables

Using a small bowl, mix the first five ingredients until they are blended. Refrigerate, covered, at least 2 hours to allow the flavors to blend further. Just before serving, top with walnuts. Serve the dip with vegetables.
NOTE *To toast nuts, bake in a shallow pan in a 350° oven for 5-10 minutes or cook in a skillet over low heat until lightly browned, stirring occasionally.*

SAVORY BLT CHEESECAKE

Served on lettuce, this savory cheesecake is great on its own, but it's also a tasty appetizer alongside crackers. It's a flexible recipe, so use another cheese in place of the Gruyere if you like. Or add olives, crab meat, cooked mushrooms—whatever strikes your fancy.

—JONI HILTON ROCKLIN, CA

PREP: 35 MIN. • **BAKE:** 45 MIN. + CHILLING
MAKES: 24 SERVINGS

- ¾ **cup dry bread crumbs**
- ½ **cup grated Parmesan cheese**
- 3 **tablespoons butter, melted**

FILLING
- 4 **packages (8 ounces each) cream cheese, softened**
- ½ **cup heavy whipping cream**
- 1½ **cups crumbled cooked bacon**
- 1 **cup oil-packed sun-dried tomatoes, patted dry and chopped**
- 1 **cup shredded Gruyere or Swiss cheese**
- 2 **green onions, sliced**
- 1 **teaspoon freshly ground pepper**
- 4 **large eggs, lightly beaten**
  Optional toppings: shredded iceberg lettuce, chopped cherry tomatoes and additional crumbled cooked bacon
  Assorted crackers, optional

1. Preheat oven to 325°. Place a greased 9-in. springform pan on a double thickness of heavy-duty foil (about 18 in. square). Securely wrap foil around pan.
2. In a small bowl, combine the bread crumbs, Parmesan cheese and butter. Press onto the bottom of prepared pan. Place pan on a baking sheet. Bake 12 minutes. Cool on a wire rack.
3. In a large bowl, beat cream cheese and cream until smooth. Beat in the bacon, tomatoes, Gruyere cheese, onions and pepper. Add eggs; beat on low speed just until combined. Pour over crust. Place springform pan in a large baking pan; add 1 in. of boiling water to larger pan.
4. Bake 45-55 minutes or until center is just set and the top appears dull. Remove springform pan from water bath; remove foil. Cool cheesecake on a wire rack 10 minutes; loosen edges from pan with a knife. Cool for 1 hour longer. Refrigerate overnight.
5. Remove rim from pan. Serve cheesecake with toppings and crackers if desired.

BLUE CHEESE ONION DIP

CUCUMBER FRUIT SALSA

We always have way more cucumbers and tomatoes from our garden than we can handle. This recipe is a delightful way to use them up. If making it ahead, stir in the banana and peach right before serving.
—**ANNA DAVIS** SPRINGFIELD, MO

PREP: 25 MIN. + CHILLING
MAKES: 24 SERVINGS (¼ CUP EACH)

- 1 large cucumber, finely chopped
- 2 medium green peppers, finely chopped
- 2 medium tomatoes, finely chopped
- 1 small red onion, finely chopped
- 1 small navel orange, segmented and chopped
- 2 tablespoons lemon juice
- 1 tablespoon minced fresh cilantro
- 1 tablespoon minced fresh parsley
- 1 garlic clove, minced
- ¼ teaspoon salt
- ¼ teaspoon hot pepper sauce
- ⅛ teaspoon pepper
- 1 medium peach, peeled and finely chopped
- 1 small banana, finely chopped

In a large bowl, combine the first 12 ingredients. Refrigerate at least 30 minutes to allow flavors to blend. Just before serving, stir in the peach and banana.

★ ★ ★ ★ ★ **5 STAR TIP**
To easily remove seeds from a cucumber, cut it in half lengthwise, then run a melon baller down the length of both halves to scoop out the seeds. This is much faster than using a knife and wastes little of the cucumber. Finish by chopping the cucumber into small pieces or use as your recipe directs.

DILLY VEGGIE PIZZA

DILLY VEGGIE PIZZA

Here's a fun way to use up leftover chopped veggies. It's a cinch to prepare and you can change the mixture to suit your kids' tastes. It's always popular at special events and tastes just as good the next day.
—**HEATHER AHRENS** COLUMBUS, OH

PREP: 20 MIN. • **BAKE:** 10 MIN. + COOLING
MAKES: 15 SERVINGS

- 1 tube (8 ounces) refrigerated crescent rolls
- 1½ cups vegetable dill dip
- 2 medium carrots, chopped
- 1 cup finely chopped fresh broccoli
- 1 cup chopped seeded tomatoes
- 4 green onions, sliced
- 1 can (2¼ ounces) sliced ripe olives, drained

1. Unroll the crescent dough into one long rectangle. Press onto the bottom of a greased 13x9-in. baking pan; seal seams. Bake at 375° for 10-12 minutes or until the dough is golden brown. Cool completely on a wire rack.
2. Spread dip over crust; sprinkle with the carrots, broccoli, tomatoes, onions and olives. Cut into squares. Refrigerate leftovers.

CRANBERRY
LIMEADE

(5) INGREDIENTS

CRANBERRY LIMEADE

When cranberry and lime juice get together, the result is thirst-quenching. Add ice and you've got a party in a glass.

—**MICHAEL PASSOW** POUGHKEEPSIE, NY

PREP: 15 MIN. + CHILLING
MAKES: 7 SERVINGS

- 2½ to 3½ **cups water, divided**
- 1¼ **cups sugar**
- 2 to 3 **cups cranberry juice**
- 1½ **cups lime juice (10 to 12 medium limes)**
- 1 **tablespoon grated lime peel (2 medium limes)**
  Ice cubes
  Lime slices, optional

Bring 1½ cups water and sugar to a boil. Remove from heat; stir in juices, lime peel and remaining water. Cover; refrigerate at least 1 hour. Serve over ice and, if desired, with lime slices.

★ ★ ★ ★ ★ **READER REVIEW**

"This Cranberry Limeade is wonderfully refreshing and easy to put together. The grated lime peel gives the limeade an extra kick of flavor!"

GLD2BMOM TASTEOFHOME.COM

MINIATURE SHEPHERD'S PIES

These mini pies are ideal for holiday parties. To change up the flavor, replace the ground beef with ground lamb and add a teaspoon of dried rosemary.

—**SUZANNE BANFIELD** BASKING RIDGE, NJ

PREP: 40 MIN. • **BAKE:** 15 MIN.
MAKES: 4 DOZEN

- ½ pound ground beef
- ⅓ cup finely chopped onion
- ¼ cup finely chopped celery
- 3 tablespoons finely chopped carrot
- 1½ teaspoons all-purpose flour
- 1 teaspoon dried thyme
- ¼ teaspoon salt
- ⅛ teaspoon ground nutmeg
- ⅛ teaspoon pepper
- ⅔ cup beef broth
- ⅓ cup frozen petite peas
- 2 packages (17.3 ounces each) frozen puff pastry, thawed
- 3 cups mashed potatoes

1. Preheat oven to 400°. In a large skillet, cook beef, onion, celery and carrot over medium heat until beef is no longer pink; drain. Stir in flour, thyme, salt, nutmeg and pepper until blended; gradually add broth. Bring to a boil; cook and stir 2 minutes or until sauce is thickened. Stir in peas; heat through. Set aside.

2. Unfold puff pastry. Using a floured 2¼-in. round cutter, cut 12 circles from each sheet (save scraps for another use). Press circles onto the bottoms and up the sides of ungreased miniature muffin cups.

3. Fill each with 1½ teaspoons beef mixture; top or pipe with 1 tablespoon mashed potatoes. Bake 13-16 minutes or until heated through and potatoes are lightly browned. Serve warm.

NUTTY STUFFED MUSHROOMS

FAST FIX
NUTTY STUFFED MUSHROOMS

Basil, Parmesan cheese and mushroom blend together well, while buttery pecans give these hot nibblers a surprising crunch. Our kids, grandkids and great-grandkids request them at every family gathering.

—**MILDRED ELDRED** UNION CITY, MI

START TO FINISH: 30 MIN.
MAKES: 18-20 SERVINGS

- 18 to 20 large fresh mushrooms
- 1 small onion, chopped
- 3 tablespoons butter
- ¼ cup dry bread crumbs
- ¼ cup finely chopped pecans
- 3 tablespoons grated Parmesan cheese
- ¼ teaspoon salt
- ¼ teaspoon dried basil
  Dash cayenne pepper

1. Remove stems from mushrooms; set the caps aside. Finely chop stems. In a large skillet, saute the chopped mushrooms and onion in butter for 5 minutes or until the liquid has evaporated. Remove from the heat and set aside.

2. In a small bowl, combine the bread crumbs, pecans, Parmesan cheese, salt, basil and cayenne; add the mushroom mixture. Stuff firmly into mushroom caps.

3. Place in a greased 15x10x1-in. baking pan. Bake, uncovered, at 400° for 15-18 minutes or until tender. Serve warm.

BUFFALO WING BITES

BUFFALO WING BITES

The Buffalo wing fans in my family were happy to taste test when I invented these snacks. We love them anytime.

—JASEY MCBURNETT ROCK SPRINGS, WY

PREP: 25 MIN. • **BAKE:** 15 MIN.
MAKES: 2 DOZEN (2 CUPS DRESSING)

- 2 **tablespoons grated Parmesan cheese**
- 1 **envelope ranch salad dressing mix, divided**
- 1 **cup mayonnaise**
- 1 **cup 2% milk**
- ¼ **cup crumbled blue cheese, optional**
- 1¼ **cups finely chopped cooked chicken breast**
- 1¼ **cups shredded cheddar-Monterey Jack cheese**
- ¼ **cup Buffalo wing sauce**
- 1 **tube (13.8 ounces) refrigerated pizza crust**
- 2 **tablespoons butter, melted**

1. Preheat the oven to 400°. In a small bowl, combine the Parmesan cheese and 1 teaspoon of dressing mix. In another bowl, mix the mayonnaise, milk and remaining dressing mix. If desired, stir in the blue cheese. Refrigerate until serving.
2. In a large bowl, mix the chicken, cheddar-Monterey Jack cheese and wing sauce. Using a lightly floured surface, unroll the pizza crust dough and pat into a 14x12-in. rectangle. Cut into 24 squares.
3. Place 1 rounded tablespoon of the chicken mixture on the center of each square. Pull the corners together to enclose the filling; pinch to seal. Place 1 in. apart on greased baking sheets, seam side down. Brush the tops with butter; sprinkle with the Parmesan cheese mixture.
4. Bake 15-17 minutes or until golden brown. Serve with dressing.

CHEESY PIZZA FONDUE

I love cooking and used to sit for hours reading cookbooks from cover to cover. This dip is so easy to make and transport. You won't have to keep it warm long because it will be gone in a flash.

—JULIE BARWICK MANSFIELD, OH

START TO FINISH: 30 MIN.
MAKES: ABOUT 5 CUPS

- ½ **pound ground beef**
- 1 **medium onion, chopped**
- 2 **cans (15 ounces each) pizza sauce**
- 1½ **teaspoons dried basil or dried oregano**
- ¼ **teaspoon garlic powder**
- 2½ **cups shredded sharp cheddar cheese**
- 1 **cup shredded part-skim mozzarella cheese**
  Breadsticks, garlic toast and green peppers

1. In a large saucepan, cook beef and onion over medium heat until meat is no longer pink; drain. Stir in the pizza sauce, basil and garlic powder. Reduce the heat to low. Add the cheeses; stir until melted.
2. Transfer to a small fondue pot or 1½-qt. slow cooker; keep warm. Serve with breadsticks, garlic toast and green peppers.
NOTE *In addition to breadsticks, serve Cheesy Pizza Fondue with cubes of French or Italian bread.*

CHEESY
PIZZA
FONDUE

TEXAS TACO DIP PLATTER

When I'm entertaining, this colorful dish is my top menu choice. My friends can't resist the hearty appetizer topped with cheese, lettuce, tomatoes and olives.

—KATHY YOUNG WEATHERFORD, TX

PREP: 20 MIN. • **COOK:** 1½ HOURS
MAKES: 20 SERVINGS

- 2 **pounds ground beef**
- 1 **large onion, chopped**
- 1 **can (14½ ounces) diced tomatoes, undrained**
- 1 **can (12 ounces) tomato paste**
- 1 **can (15 ounces) tomato puree**
- 2 **tablespoons chili powder**
- 1 **teaspoon ground cumin**
- ½ **teaspoon garlic powder**
- 2 **teaspoons salt**
- 2 **cans (15 ounces each) Ranch Style beans (pinto beans in seasoned tomato sauce)**
- 1 **package (10½ ounces) corn chips**
- 2 **cups hot cooked rice**

TOPPINGS
- 2 **cups shredded cheddar cheese**
- 1 **medium onion, chopped**
- 1 **medium head iceberg lettuce, shredded**
- 3 **medium tomatoes, chopped**
- 1 **can (2¼ ounces) sliced ripe olives, drained**
- 1 **cup picante sauce, optional**

1. In a large skillet or Dutch oven, cook beef and onion over medium heat until meat is no longer pink; drain. Add next seven ingredients; simmer for 1½ hours.

2. Add beans and heat through. On a platter, layer the corn chips, rice, meat mixture, cheese, onion, lettuce, tomatoes and olives. Serve with picante sauce if desired.

TEXAS TACO DIP PLATTER

MINI MAC & CHEESE BITES

Young relatives were coming for a Christmas party, so I wanted something fun for them to eat. Instead, the adults devoured my mini mac and cheese bites!

—**KATE MAINIERO** ELIZAVILLE, NY

PREP: 35 MIN. • **BAKE:** 10 MIN.
MAKES: 3 DOZEN

- 2 cups uncooked elbow macaroni
- 1 cup seasoned bread crumbs, divided
- 2 tablespoons butter
- 2 tablespoons all-purpose flour
- ½ teaspoon onion powder
- ½ teaspoon garlic powder
- ½ teaspoon seasoned salt
- 1¾ cups 2% milk
- 2 cups shredded sharp cheddar cheese, divided
- 1 cup shredded Swiss cheese
- ¾ cup biscuit/baking mix
- 2 large eggs, lightly beaten

1. Preheat oven to 425°. Cook macaroni according to package directions; drain.
2. Meanwhile, sprinkle ¼ cup bread crumbs into 36 greased mini-muffin cups. In a large saucepan, melt butter over medium heat. Stir in flour and seasonings until smooth; gradually whisk in the milk. Bring to a boil, stirring constantly; cook and stir 1-2 minutes or until thickened. Stir in 1 cup cheddar cheese and Swiss cheese until melted.
3. Remove from heat; stir in biscuit mix, eggs and ½ cup bread crumbs. Add macaroni; toss to coat. Spoon about 2 tablespoons macaroni mixture into prepared mini-muffin cups; sprinkle with remaining cheddar cheese and bread crumbs.
4. Bake 8-10 minutes or until golden brown. Cool in pans for 5 minutes before serving.

CRAWFISH BEIGNETS WITH CAJUN DIPPING SAUCE

Get a taste of the deep South with these slightly spicy beignets. You won't be able to eat just one!

—**DONNA LANCLOS** LAFAYETTE, LA

PREP: 20 MIN. • **COOK:** 5 MIN./BATCH
MAKES: ABOUT 2 DOZEN (¾ CUP SAUCE)

- 1 large egg, beaten
- 1 pound chopped cooked crawfish tail meat or shrimp
- 4 green onions, chopped
- 1½ teaspoons butter, melted
- ½ teaspoon salt
- ½ teaspoon cayenne pepper
- ⅓ cup bread flour
  Oil for deep-fat frying
- ¾ cup mayonnaise
- ½ cup ketchup
- ¼ teaspoon hot pepper sauce
- ¼ teaspoon prepared horseradish, optional

1. In a large bowl, combine the egg, crawfish, onions, butter, salt and cayenne. Stir in flour until blended.
2. In an electric skillet or deep fryer, heat oil to 375°. Drop tablespoonfuls of batter, a few at a time, into hot oil. Fry until golden brown on both sides. Drain on paper towels.
3. Using a small bowl, combine the mayonnaise, ketchup, pepper sauce and, if desired, horseradish. Serve with beignets.

LOADED PULLED PORK CUPS

Potato nests are simple to make and surprisingly handy for pulled pork, cheese, sour cream and other toppings. Make, bake, and then collect the compliments.
—**MELISSA SPERKA** GREENSBORO, NC

PREP: 40 MIN. • **BAKE:** 25 MIN.
MAKES: 1½ DOZEN

- 1 **package (20 ounces) refrigerated shredded hash brown potatoes**
- ¾ **cup shredded Parmesan cheese**
- 2 **large egg whites, beaten**
- 1 **teaspoon garlic salt**
- ½ **teaspoon onion powder**
- ¼ **teaspoon pepper**
- 1 **carton (16 ounces) refrigerated fully cooked barbecued shredded pork**
- 1 **cup shredded Colby-Monterey Jack cheese**
- ½ **cup sour cream**
- 5 **bacon strips, cooked and crumbled**
  Minced chives

1. Preheat oven to 450°. In a large bowl, mix hash browns, Parmesan cheese, egg whites and seasonings until blended. Divide potato mixture among 18 well-greased muffin cups; press onto the bottoms and up the sides to form cups.

2. Bake 22-25 minutes or until edges are dark golden brown. Carefully run a knife around the sides of each cup. Cool 5 minutes before removing from pans to a serving platter. Meanwhile, heat the pulled pork according to the package directions.

3. Sprinkle cheese into cups. Top with pork, sour cream and bacon; sprinkle with chives. Serve warm.

GARDEN VEGGIE SALSA

My family loves this salsa. I make it mostly with fresh vegetables from my garden. It's healthy, and you can easily adjust the ingredients to suit your own tastes.
—**DAWN GILSON** DENMARK, WI

PREP: 20 MIN.
MAKES: 6 CUPS

- 3 **large tomatoes, chopped**
- 1 **cup chopped cucumber**
- 1 **medium sweet yellow or red pepper, chopped**
- ¾ **cup chopped zucchini**
- 1 **small red onion, finely chopped**
- ½ **cup chopped fresh cilantro**
- 1 **jalapeno pepper, seeded and finely chopped**
- 2 **tablespoons olive oil**
- 1 **tablespoon white vinegar**
- ¾ **teaspoon pepper**
- ½ **teaspoon salt**
- ½ **teaspoon ground cumin**
  Tortilla chips

In a large bowl, combine the first 12 ingredients; toss to combine. Refrigerate, covered, until serving. Serve with chips.
NOTE *Wear disposable gloves when cutting hot peppers; the oils can burn skin. Avoid touching your face.*

LOADED PULLED PORK CUPS

PARTY CRAB PUFFS

I received this recipe years ago from my grandmother, who taught me to have fun being creative and experimenting in the kitchen. My friends request these little puffs at every gathering.

—**JEAN BEVILACQUA** RHODODENDRON, OR

PREP: 45 MIN. • **BAKE:** 20 MIN./BATCH
MAKES: 8 DOZEN

- 1 **cup water**
- ½ **cup butter, cubed**
- ¼ **teaspoon salt**
- 1 **cup all-purpose flour**
- 4 **large eggs**

FILLING

- 4 **hard-cooked large eggs, finely chopped**
- 1 **can (6 ounces) lump crabmeat, drained**
- 4 **ounces cream cheese, softened**
- ¼ **cup mayonnaise**
- 2 **tablespoons finely chopped onion**
- 2 **tablespoons prepared horseradish, drained**
  Minced fresh parsley, optional

1. Preheat oven to 400°. In a large saucepan, bring the water, butter and salt to a boil. Add flour all at once and stir until a smooth ball forms. Remove from heat; let stand 5 minutes. Add eggs, one at a time, beating well after each addition. Continue beating until mixture is smooth and shiny.

2. Drop by teaspoonfuls 2 in. apart onto greased baking sheets. Bake for 18-22 minutes or until golden brown. Remove to a wire rack. Immediately split the puffs open; remove the tops and set aside. Discard soft dough from inside. Cool the puffs.

3. In a large bowl, combine filling ingredients. Just before serving, spoon 1 teaspoonful filling into each puff; sprinkle with parsley if desired. Replace tops.

SLOW COOKER SPINACH & ARTICHOKE DIP

SLOW COOKER

SLOW COOKER SPINACH & ARTICHOKE DIP

Thanks to this creamy dip, my daughters will happily eat spinach and artichokes. We serve it with chips, toasted pita bread or fresh veggies on the side.

—**JENNIFER STOWELL** MONTEZUMA, IA

PREP: 10 MIN. • **COOK:** 2 HOURS
MAKES: 32 SERVINGS (¼ CUP EACH)

- 2 **cans (14 ounces each) water-packed artichoke hearts, drained and chopped**
- 2 **packages (10 ounces each) frozen chopped spinach, thawed and squeezed dry**
- 1 **jar (15 ounces) Alfredo sauce**
- 1 **package (8 ounces) cream cheese, cubed**
- 2 **cups shredded Italian cheese blend**
- 1 **cup shredded part-skim mozzarella cheese**
- 1 **cup shredded Parmesan cheese**
- 1 **cup 2% milk**
- 2 **garlic cloves, minced**
  Assorted crackers and/or cucumber slices

In a greased 4-qt. slow cooker, combine the first nine ingredients. Cook, covered, on low 2-3 hours or until heated through. Serve with crackers and/or cucumber slices.

SWEET SRIRACHA WINGS

FAST FIX ▶

GRILLED POTATO SKINS

The creamy topping on these potato skins is so delicious. These make an excellent summertime treat alongside your favorite grilled meat.

—STEPHANIE MOON BOISE, ID

START TO FINISH: 30 MIN.
MAKES: 4 SERVINGS

  2 **medium potatoes**
1½ **teaspoons butter, melted**
  2 **tablespoons picante sauce**
  ¼ **cup shredded cheddar cheese**
  1 **tablespoon real bacon bits**
  ¼ **cup chopped tomato**
  2 **tablespoons chopped green onion**
TOPPING
  3 **tablespoons mayonnaise**
  2 **tablespoons sour cream**
  1 **tablespoon prepared ranch salad dressing**
1½ **teaspoons real bacon bits**
  ¼ **teaspoon garlic powder**

1. Cut each potato lengthwise into four wedges. Cut away the white portion, leaving ¼ in. on the potato skins. Place the skins on a microwave-safe plate.
2. Microwave, uncovered, on high for 8-10 minutes or until tender. Brush butter over shells; top with picante sauce, cheese and bacon bits.
3. Grill potatoes, skin side down, uncovered, over medium heat for 4-6 minutes or until lightly browned. Cover and grill 2-3 minutes longer or until cheese is melted. Sprinkle with tomato and onion. In a small bowl, combine topping ingredients. Serve with potato skins.
NOTE *This recipe was tested in a 1,100-watt microwave.*

SWEET SRIRACHA WINGS

Serve my fiery hot wings on game day or any time friends and family gather. If you don't like a ton of sweetness, add the honey slowly and taste as you go.

—LOGAN HOLSER CLARKSTON, MI

PREP: 20 MIN. + MARINATING
GRILL: 15 MIN. • **MAKES:** 1 DOZEN

 12 **chicken wings (about 3 pounds)**
  1 **tablespoon canola oil**
  2 **teaspoons ground coriander**
  ½ **teaspoon garlic salt**
  ¼ **teaspoon pepper**
SAUCE
  ¼ **cup butter, cubed**
  ½ **cup orange juice**
  ⅓ **cup Sriracha Asian hot chili sauce**
  3 **tablespoons honey**
  2 **tablespoons lime juice**
  ¼ **cup chopped fresh cilantro**

1. Place chicken wings in a large bowl. Mix the oil, coriander, garlic salt and pepper; add to the wings and toss to coat. Refrigerate, covered, for 2 hours or overnight.
2. For sauce, in a small saucepan, melt butter. Stir in orange juice, chili sauce, honey and lime juice until blended.
3. Grill wings, covered, over medium heat 15-18 minutes or until the juices run clear, turning occasionally; brush with some of the sauce during the last 5 minutes of grilling.
4. Transfer chicken to a large bowl; add remaining sauce and toss to coat. Sprinkle with cilantro.

⑤INGREDIENTS

APRICOT LEMONADE ICED TEA

Every special occasion deserves a refreshing beverage. My tea has a tangy flavor from lemonade, apricot nectar and mint.

—**KAY CHON** SHERWOOD, AR

PREP: 10 MIN. • **COOK:** 5 MIN. + COOLING
MAKES: 12 SERVINGS (¾ CUP EACH)

- 4 **cups water**
- 7 **individual tea bags**
- 1 **cup sugar**
- 1 **can (12 ounces) frozen lemonade concentrate, partially thawed**
- 1 **cup chilled apricot nectar**
- 4 **cups cold water**
  Ice cubes
  Mint sprigs

1. In a saucepan, bring 4 cups water to a boil; remove from heat. Add tea bags; steep, covered, 5 minutes.
2. Discard tea bags. Stir in sugar until dissolved; cool slightly. Transfer to a pitcher; cool completely.
3. Add lemonade concentrate and nectar to tea; stir in cold water. Serve over ice with mint.

★ ★ ★ ★ ★ **READER REVIEW**

"I was looking for a new spin on iced tea and this was great! I will definitely be making it again."

ANGEL182009 TASTEOFHOME.COM

CHEESY
PIZZA ROLLS

CHEESY PIZZA ROLLS

The cast-iron skillet browns these rolls to perfection. My family can't get enough. Use whatever pizza toppings you like best.
—**DOROTHY SMITH** EL DORADO, AR

PREP: 15 MIN. • **BAKE:** 25 MIN.
MAKES: 8 APPETIZERS

- 1 loaf (1 pound) frozen pizza dough, thawed
- ½ cup pasta sauce
- 1 cup shredded part-skim mozzarella cheese, divided
- 1 cup coarsely chopped pepperoni (about 64 slices)
- ½ pound bulk Italian sausage, cooked and crumbled
- ¼ cup grated Parmesan cheese
  Minced fresh basil, optional
  Crushed red pepper flakes, optional

1. Preheat oven to 400°. On a lightly floured surface, roll dough into a 16x10-in. rectangle. Brush with pasta sauce to within ½ in. of edges.
2. Sprinkle with ½ cup mozzarella cheese, pepperoni, sausage and parmesan. Roll up jelly-roll style, starting with a long side; pinch seam to seal. Cut into eight slices. Place in a greased 9-in. cast-iron skillet or greased 9-in. round baking pan, cut side down.
3. Bake 20 minutes; sprinkle with remaining mozzarella cheese. Bake until golden brown, about 5-10 more minutes. If desired, sprinkle with minced fresh basil and crushed red pepper flakes.

FISH TACO BITES

I think these appetizers are better than full-size fish tacos I've had as an entree. Enjoy the creamy salsa drizzle not only on these bites, but also on other Mexican dishes.
—**CARMELL CHILDS** FERRON, UT

PREP: 30 MIN. • **BAKE:** 20 MIN.
MAKES: 3 DOZEN

- ½ cup salsa verde
- 4 ounces cream cheese, softened
- 2 tablespoons lime juice, divided
- 2 tablespoons minced fresh cilantro
- 1 teaspoon honey
  Dash salt
- 12 frozen breaded fish sticks
- 1 tablespoon taco seasoning
- 36 tortilla chip scoops
- 1½ cups coleslaw mix
- ¾ cup cubed avocado
- ¾ cup chopped seeded tomato
  Lime wedges and additional minced fresh cilantro

1. In a blender, combine the salsa, cream cheese, 1 tablespoon lime juice, cilantro, honey and salt. Cover and process until smooth; set aside.
2. Place fish sticks on a baking sheet. Bake at 425° for 10 minutes. Sprinkle with half of the taco seasoning. Turn the fish sticks over; sprinkle with remaining taco seasoning. Bake for 7-9 minutes longer or until crisp.
3. Meanwhile, place tortilla chips on a serving platter. In a small bowl, combine the coleslaw mix, avocado, tomato, remaining lime juice and ½ cup salsa mixture. Spoon into chips.
4. Cut each fish stick into three pieces. Place a fish stick piece in each chip; top each with about ½ teaspoon salsa mixture. Garnish with lime wedges and additional cilantro.

STUFFED BREAD APPETIZERS

I recommend doubling the recipe for this tasty stuffed French bread because folks won't be able to stop at just one slice!
—**TRACY WESTROM** LANSDALE, PA

PREP: 20 MIN. + CHILLING
MAKES: ABOUT 2 DOZEN

- 11 ounces cream cheese, softened
- 1 cup chopped celery
- 1 cup shredded cheddar cheese
- ½ cup chopped sweet red pepper
- ½ cup chopped water chestnuts
- 1 teaspoon garlic salt
- 1 loaf (1 pound) French bread, halved lengthwise
- 2 tablespoons mayonnaise
  Dried parsley flakes
- 4 dill pickle spears
- 4 slices deli ham

1. Combine the first six ingredients. Hollow out top and bottom of bread, leaving a ½-in. shell (discard removed bread or save for another use). Spread thin layer of mayonnaise over bread; sprinkle with parsley.
2. Fill each half with cheese mixture. Wrap the pickle spears in ham; place lengthwise over cheese mixture on bottom half of loaf. Replace the top; press to seal. Wrap in foil; refrigerate overnight. Just before serving, cut into 1-in. slices.

BREAKFAST & BRUNCH

Whether you prefer sweet or savory with your morning cup of coffee, turn here to find just what you need to get going. It doesn't matter what side of the bed you woke up on—these delicious dishes will have you smiling and satisfied before you officially start the day!

BLINTZ PANCAKES

Blending sour cream and cottage cheese—ingredients that are traditionally associated with the creamy filling in blintzes—into the batter of these pancakes gives them a classic old-fashioned flavor. Top them with berry syrup to turn an ordinary morning into an extraordinary day.

—**DIANNA DIGOY** SAN DIEGO, CA

START TO FINISH: 30 MIN.
MAKES: 12 PANCAKES

- 1 **cup all-purpose flour**
- 1 **tablespoon sugar**
- ½ **teaspoon salt**
- 1 **cup (8 ounces) sour cream**
- 1 **cup (8 ounces) 4% cottage cheese**
- 4 **large eggs, lightly beaten**
  Strawberry or blueberry syrup
  Sliced fresh strawberries, optional

1. In a large bowl, combine the flour, sugar and salt. Stir in the sour cream, cottage cheese and eggs until blended.
2. Pour batter by ¼ cupfuls onto a greased hot griddle in batches; turn when bubbles form on top. Cook the pancakes until the second side is golden brown. Serve with syrup and, if desired, sliced fresh strawberries.

★ ★ ★ ★ ★ **READER REVIEW**

"I have been using this recipe for many years and just love the flavor and texture. Love the pancakes with fresh blueberry sauce."

ZOOTERCAT TASTEOFHOME.COM

HOW TO TOAST NUTS

Bake in a shallow pan in a 350° oven for 5-10 minutes or cook in a skillet over low heat until lightly browned, stirring occasionally.

BAKED BLUEBERRY-
MASCARPONE
FRENCH TOAST

BAKED BLUEBERRY-MASCARPONE FRENCH TOAST

I turn to this recipe when I want something special to serve guests for a Saturday or Sunday brunch. It is particularly delicious during spring and early summer when fresh blueberries are at their peak.

—PATRICIA QUINN OMAHA, NE

PREP: 15 MIN. + CHILLING
BAKE: 1 HOUR + STANDING
MAKES: 10 SERVINGS

- 8 slices French bread (½ inch thick), cubed (about 4 cups)
- 2 cups fresh or frozen blueberries
- 2 cartons (8 ounces each) mascarpone cheese
- ½ cup confectioners' sugar
- 10 slices French bread (1 inch thick)
- 8 large eggs
- 2 cups half-and-half cream
- 1 cup whole milk
- ⅓ cup granulated sugar
- 1 teaspoon vanilla extract
  Additional confectioners' sugar
- 1 cup sliced almonds, toasted
  Additional fresh blueberries, optional

1. In a greased 13x9-in. baking dish, layer bread cubes and blueberries. In a small bowl, beat mascarpone cheese and confectioners' sugar until smooth; drop by tablespoonfuls over blueberries. Top with bread slices. In a large bowl, whisk eggs, cream, milk, granulated sugar and vanilla; pour over bread. Refrigerate, covered, overnight.

2. Preheat oven to 350°. Remove French toast from refrigerator while oven heats. Bake, covered, 30 minutes. Bake, uncovered, for 30-40 minutes longer or until puffed and golden and a knife inserted in center comes out clean.

3. Let stand 10 minutes before serving. Dust with additional confectioners' sugar; sprinkle with almonds. If desired, serve with additional blueberries.

OVERNIGHT BRUNCH CASSEROLE

I love to cook for company. This breakfast casserole combines scrambled eggs with a rich, creamy cheese sauce.

—CANDY HESCH MOSINEE, WI

PREP: 30 MIN. + CHILLING
BAKE: 40 MIN. + STANDING
MAKES: 12 SERVINGS

- 3 tablespoons butter, divided
- 2 tablespoons all-purpose flour
- ½ teaspoon salt
- ⅛ teaspoon pepper
- 2 cups fat-free milk
- 5 slices reduced-fat process American cheese product, chopped
- 1½ cups sliced fresh mushrooms
- 2 green onions, finely chopped
- 1 cup cubed fully cooked ham
- 2 cups egg substitute
- 4 large eggs

TOPPING

- 3 slices whole wheat bread, cubed
- 4 teaspoons butter, melted
- ⅛ teaspoon paprika

1. In a saucepan, melt 2 tablespoons butter. Stir in flour, salt and pepper until smooth; gradually add milk. Bring to a boil; cook and stir 2 minutes or until slightly thick. Stir in cheese until melted. Remove from heat.

2. In a large nonstick skillet, saute mushrooms and green onions in remaining butter until tender. Add ham; heat through. Whisk the egg substitute and eggs; add to skillet. Cook and stir until almost set. Stir in cheese sauce.

3. Transfer to a 13x9-in. baking dish coated with cooking spray. Toss bread cubes with butter. Arrange over egg mixture; sprinkle with paprika. Cover and refrigerate overnight.

4. Remove from the refrigerator 30 minutes before baking. Preheat oven to 350°. Bake, uncovered, for 40-45 minutes or until a knife inserted near the center comes out clean. Let stand 10 minutes before cutting.

HAM & EGG CASSEROLE

Here's a delicious brunch dish. I prepare this breakfast bake when I have ham leftovers and day-old bread on hand. I love the fact I can prepare it the night before, which allows me to focus on making other dishes for the meal.

—ELIZABETH HESSE SPRINGVILLE, NY

PREP: 15 MIN. + CHILLING • **BAKE:** 45 MIN.
MAKES: 10-12 SERVINGS

- ½ cup chopped green pepper
- ½ cup butter, cubed
- 10 slices white bread, cubed
- 2 cups cubed fully cooked ham
- ½ pound process American cheese, cubed
- 6 large eggs
- 2 cups whole milk
- 1 teaspoon ground mustard

1. In a large skillet, saute the green pepper in butter until tender. Remove the green pepper, reserving drippings. Combine the green pepper, bread and ham; place in an ungreased 13x9-in. baking dish.

2. Add cheese to the drippings; cook and stir over low heat until the cheese melts. Pour it over the bread mixture. Whisk the eggs, milk and mustard; pour over the cheese. Cover the dish and refrigerate overnight.

3. Remove from the refrigerator 30 minutes before baking. Bake it, uncovered, at 350° for 45-55 minutes or until a knife inserted in the center comes out clean. Let casserole stand for 5 minutes before serving.

★ ★ ★ ★ ★ 5 STAR TIP
Day-old bread cubes are made from day-old bread that's been sliced into cubes. Start with a good-quality firm bread that is beginning to dry out— it will better absorb liquid ingredients and seasonings. Using fresh bread can sometimes result in a casserole that is overly moist and compact.

PEAR-STUFFED FRENCH VANILLA TOAST

My trusty handyman, who is originally from Nicaragua, shared this classic breakfast dish his mother used to prepare. He says he makes it frequently for his children and they clean their plates.

—GAIL BORCZYK BOCA RATON, FL

PREP: 20 MIN. + CHILLING
BAKE: 40 MIN.
MAKES: 6 SERVINGS

- 1 cup packed brown sugar
- ½ cup butter, melted
- 1 large pear, peeled and sliced (about 1½ cups)
- ¾ cup raisins
- 4 cups cubed day-old French bread (1½ inch pieces)
- ¾ cup finely chopped pecans
- 4 large eggs
- 2 cups French vanilla ice cream, melted
- 2 teaspoons ground cinnamon
- 2 teaspoons vanilla extract

1. In a small bowl, mix brown sugar and butter. Spread onto bottom of a greased 8-in. square baking dish. Layer with pear, raisins, bread cubes and pecans.

2. In a large bowl, whisk eggs, ice cream, cinnamon and vanilla until blended; pour over top. Refrigerate, covered, several hours or overnight.

3. Preheat oven to 350°. Remove casserole from refrigerator while oven heats. Bake, uncovered, 40-45 minutes or until golden brown and a knife inserted in the center comes out clean. Let stand 5-10 minutes before serving.

PEAR-STUFFED FRENCH VANILLA TOAST

---

(5) INGREDIENTS FAST FIX

SHEEPHERDER'S BREAKFAST

My sister-in-law always made this delicious breakfast dish whenever our families went camping. Served with toast, juice, and milk or coffee, it's a sure hit with everyone. One-dish casseroles like this were a big help while I was raising my nine kids, and now I've passed this recipe on to them.

—PAULETTA BUSHNELL ALBANY, OR

START TO FINISH: 30 MIN.
MAKES: 10 SERVINGS

- ¾ pound bacon strips, finely chopped
- 1 medium onion, chopped
- 1 package (30 ounces) frozen shredded hash brown potatoes, thawed
- 8 large eggs
- ½ teaspoon salt
- ¼ teaspoon pepper
- 1 cup shredded cheddar cheese

1. In a large skillet, cook the bacon and onion over medium heat until bacon is crisp. Drain, reserving ¼ cup drippings in pan.

2. Stir in the hash browns. Cook, uncovered, over medium heat for 10 minutes or until bottom is golden brown; turn potatoes. Using the back of a spoon, make eight evenly spaced wells in the potato mixture. Break one egg into each well, then sprinkle with salt and pepper.

3. Cook, covered, on low 10 minutes or until eggs are set and potatoes are tender. Sprinkle with cheese; let stand until cheese is melted.

CREAMY FROZEN FRUIT CUPS

I prepare these cool, fluffy fruit cups to give a refreshing boost to a variety of meals. They have been well received at family gatherings and summer barbecues. Since you make them in advance, there's no last-minute fuss, either.

—**KAREN HATCHER** ST. AMANT, LA

PREP: 15 MIN. + FREEZING
MAKES: 1½ DOZEN

- 1 **package (8 ounces) cream cheese, softened**
- ½ **cup sugar**
- 1 **jar (10 ounces) maraschino cherries, drained**
- 1 **can (11 ounces) mandarin oranges, drained**
- 1 **can (8 ounces) crushed pineapple, drained**
- ½ **cup chopped pecans**
- 1 **carton (8 ounces) frozen whipped topping, thawed**
  Fresh mint, optional

1. In a large bowl, beat the cream cheese and sugar until fluffy. Halve 9 cherries; chop remaining cherries. Set aside the halved cherries and 18 orange segments for garnish. Add the pineapple, pecans and chopped cherries to cream cheese mixture. Fold in whipped topping and the remaining oranges.
2. Line muffin cups with paper or foil liners. Spoon fruit mixture into cups; garnish with reserved cherries and oranges. Freeze until firm. Remove from the freezer 10 minutes before serving. Top with mint if desired.

BACON ROLL-UPS

BACON ROLL-UPS

This family recipe dates back to the 1930s, when my grandmother started making these hearty breakfast rolls.

—**JANET ABATE** NORTH BRUNSWICK, NJ

PREP: 25 MIN. • **COOK:** 20 MIN.
MAKES: 10 ROLL-UPS

- ⅓ **cup finely chopped onion**
- 1 **tablespoon butter**
- 3 **cups cubed day-old bread**
- ¼ **teaspoon celery salt**
- ¼ **teaspoon garlic powder**
- ⅛ **teaspoon salt**
- ⅛ **teaspoon pepper**
- 1 **large egg, lightly beaten**
- 10 **bacon strips**

1. In a small skillet, saute onion in butter until tender. In a large bowl, combine the bread cubes, celery salt, garlic powder, salt, pepper and onion mixture; toss to mix evenly. Add the egg; toss to coat the bread cubes. Roll into ten 1¼-in. balls. Wrap a bacon strip around each ball. Secure with a toothpick. Repeat with remaining ingredients.
2. In a large skillet, cook the bacon roll-ups on all sides over medium heat for 18 minutes or until bacon is crisp and a thermometer inserted into the stuffing reads at least 160°. Drain on paper towels.

BREAKFAST BISCUIT CUPS

I make these little cups for a variety of events. Folks love how simple and tasty they are.

—**DEBRA CARLSON** COLUMBUS JUNCTION, IA

PREP: 30 MIN. • **BAKE:** 20 MIN.
MAKES: 8 SERVINGS

- ⅓ pound bulk pork sausage
- 1 tablespoon all-purpose flour
- ⅛ teaspoon salt
- ½ teaspoon pepper, divided
- ¾ cup plus 1 tablespoon 2% milk, divided
- ½ cup frozen cubed hash brown potatoes, thawed
- 1 tablespoon butter
- 2 large eggs
- ⅛ teaspoon garlic salt
- 1 can (16.3 ounces) large refrigerated flaky biscuits
- ½ cup shredded Colby-Monterey Jack cheese

1. In a skillet, cook the sausage over medium heat until it is no longer pink; drain. Stir in the flour, salt and ¼ teaspoon pepper until blended; gradually add ¾ cup milk. Bring to a boil; cook and stir for 2 minutes or until thickened. Remove from the heat and set aside.
2. In another skillet over medium heat, cook potatoes in butter until tender. Whisk eggs, garlic salt and remaining milk and pepper; add to skillet. Cook and stir until mixture is almost set.
3. Press each biscuit onto the bottom and up the sides of eight ungreased muffin cups. Spoon the egg mixture, half the cheese, and sausage into cups; sprinkle with remaining cheese.
4. Bake at 375° for 18-22 minutes or until golden brown. Cool 5 minutes before removing from pan.
FREEZE OPTION *Freeze cooled biscuit cups in a freezer container, separating layers with waxed paper. To use, microwave one frozen biscuit cup on high for 50-60 seconds or until heated through.*

ASPARAGUS CREAM CHEESE OMELET

When asparagus is in season, it makes an appearance in almost all of my meals. It tastes fantastic in this omelet.

—**JANE CAIN** JUNCTION CITY, OH

START TO FINISH: 20 MIN.
MAKES: 2 SERVINGS

- 4 fresh asparagus spears, trimmed and cut into 1-inch pieces
- 4 large eggs
- ¼ cup sour cream
- 2 teaspoons dried minced onion
- ¼ teaspoon salt
- ¼ teaspoon crushed red pepper flakes
- 2 teaspoons butter
- 2 ounces cream cheese, cubed and softened

1. Fill a small saucepan three-fourths full with water; bring it to a boil. Add the asparagus; cook, uncovered, 2-4 minutes or until crisp-tender. Remove and immediately drop into ice water. Drain and pat dry.
2. In a small bowl, whisk eggs, sour cream, onion, salt and pepper flakes. In a large nonstick skillet, heat the butter over medium-high heat. Pour in egg mixture. Mixture should set immediately at edge. As eggs set, push cooked portions toward the center, letting the uncooked eggs flow underneath.
3. When eggs are thickened and no liquid egg remains, top one side with cream cheese and asparagus. Fold omelet in half. Reduce heat to low; let stand, covered, 1-2 minutes or until cream cheese is melted. Cut omelet in half before serving.

VEGGIE SAUSAGE STRATA

As a retired home economics teacher, I've made quite a few recipes through the years. This hearty casserole is a favorite.

—**DOROTHY ERICKSON** BLUE EYE, MO

PREP: 15 MIN. + CHILLING
BAKE: 1 HOUR 20 MIN.
MAKES: 10-12 SERVINGS

- 2 pounds bulk Italian sausage
- 2 medium green peppers, coarsely chopped
- 1 medium onion, chopped
- 8 large eggs
- 2 cups whole milk
- 2 teaspoons salt
- 2 teaspoons white pepper
- 2 teaspoons ground mustard
- 12 slices bread, cut into ½-inch pieces
- 1 package (10 ounces) frozen chopped spinach, thawed and squeezed dry
- 2 cups shredded Swiss cheese
- 2 cups shredded cheddar cheese
- 1 medium zucchini, cut into ¼-inch slices

1. In a large skillet, cook the sausage, green peppers and onion on medium heat until the meat is no longer pink; drain. Meanwhile, using a large bowl, whisk the eggs, milk, salt, pepper and mustard. Stir in the sausage mixture, bread, spinach, cheeses and zucchini.
2. Transfer the mixture to a greased 13x9-in. baking dish. Cover it and refrigerate overnight.
3. Remove from the refrigerator 30 minutes before baking. Cover and bake at 350° for 40 minutes. Uncover; bake for 40-45 minutes longer or until a knife inserted in the center comes out clean.

★ ★ ★ ★ ★ 5 STAR TIP

When a recipe calls for frozen spinach, thawed and squeezed dry, I use my salad spinner. It makes it easy to get rid of the excess water without straining my fingers.
—**EDITH L.** LONGWOOD, FL

VEGGIE SAUSAGE
STRATA

GLAZED BACON

GLAZED BACON

Brown sugar, mustard and wine make bacon a little more special. It's so easy to present the morning staple in a new way!

—**JUDITH DOBSON** BURLINGTON, WI

PREP: 10 MIN. • **BAKE:** 30 MIN.
MAKES: 8 SERVINGS

- 1 **pound sliced bacon**
- 1 **cup packed brown sugar**
- ¼ **cup white wine or unsweetened apple juice**
- 2 **tablespoons Dijon mustard**

1. Preheat oven to 350°. Place bacon on a rack in an ungreased 15x10x1-in. baking pan. Bake 10 minutes; drain.
2. Combine brown sugar, wine and mustard; drizzle half over bacon. Bake 10 minutes. Turn bacon and drizzle with remaining glaze. Bake 10 minutes or until golden brown. Place bacon on waxed paper until set. Serve warm.

STRAWBERRY BANANA YOGURT SMOOTHIE

Frozen strawberries combine with banana to keep these frosty smoothies extra thick. The recipe is a delightful way to get a substantial dose of nutrients early in the day.

—**CHRISTY ADKINS** MARTINEZ, GA

START TO FINISH: 5 MIN.
MAKES: 2 SERVINGS

- ½ **cup 2% milk**
- ⅓ **cup strawberry yogurt**
- ⅓ **cup frozen unsweetened strawberries**
- ½ **medium firm banana, chopped**
- 4 **ice cubes**
- 8 **teaspoons sugar**

In a blender, combine all of the ingredients; cover and process for 30-45 seconds or until smooth. Stir if necessary. Pour into chilled glasses; serve immediately.

SAUSAGE & CRESCENT ROLL CASSEROLE

I made this tasty casserole for a baby shower. Preparing it ahead gave me more time to finish other preparations for the party.

—**MELODY CRAFT** CONROE, TX

PREP: 15 MIN. • **BAKE:** 35 MIN.
MAKES: 12 SERVINGS

- 1 **pound bulk pork sausage**
- 1 **tube (8 ounces) refrigerated crescent rolls**
- 2 **cups shredded part-skim mozzarella cheese**
- 8 **large eggs**
- 2 **cups 2% milk**
- ½ **teaspoon salt**
- ¼ **teaspoon pepper**

1. Preheat oven to 375°. In a large skillet, cook sausage over medium heat 6-8 minutes or until no longer pink, breaking into crumbles; drain. Unroll crescent roll dough into a greased 13x9-in. baking dish. Seal seams and perforations. Sprinkle with sausage and cheese.
2. In a large bowl, whisk eggs, milk, salt and pepper. Pour over sausage and cheese.
3. Bake, uncovered, 35-40 minutes or until a knife inserted in the center comes out clean. Let stand for about 5-10 minutes before serving.
TO MAKE-AHEAD *Refrigerate unbaked casserole, covered, several hours or overnight. To use, preheat the oven to 375°. Remove the casserole from the refrigerator while oven heats. Bake as directed, increasing time as necessary until a knife inserted near the center comes out clean. Let stand for 5-10 minutes before serving.*

FARMER'S STRATA

Try my hearty casserole for an inexpensive and easy-to-prepare dish. It includes tasty basic ingredients like bacon, ham, cheese and potatoes. You can assemble it ahead of time and bake just before folks arrive for your brunch.

—**PAT KUETHER** WESTMINSTER, CO

PREP: 25 MIN. + CHILLING
BAKE: 65 MIN. • **MAKES:** 16 SERVINGS

- 1 **pound sliced bacon, cut into ½-inch pieces**
- 2 **cups chopped fully cooked ham**
- 1 **small onion, chopped**
- 10 **slices white bread, cubed**
- 1 **cup cubed cooked potatoes**
- 3 **cups shredded cheddar cheese**
- 8 **large eggs**
- 3 **cups milk**
- 1 **tablespoon Worcestershire sauce**
- 1 **teaspoon ground mustard**
   Dash salt and pepper

1. In a large skillet, cook bacon over medium heat until crisp; add ham and onion. Cook and stir until onion is tender; drain.

2. In a greased 13x9-in. baking dish, layer half the bread cubes, potatoes and cheese. Top with all of the bacon mixture. Repeat layers of bread, potatoes and cheese.

3. In a large bowl, beat the eggs; add the milk, Worcestershire sauce, mustard, salt and pepper. Pour over all. Cover and chill the food overnight.

4. Remove from the refrigerator 30 minutes before baking. Preheat oven to 325°. Bake, uncovered, for about 65-70 minutes or until a knife inserted near the center comes out clean.

FARMER'S STRATA

RAISIN NUT OATMEAL

There's nothing better than waking up to a ready-to-eat breakfast. The oats, fruit and spices in this meal bake together overnight, so the recipe is ideal for busy cooks.
—**VALERIE SAUBER** ADELANTO, CA

PREP: 10 MIN. • **COOK:** 7 HOURS
MAKES: 6 SERVINGS

- 3½ **cups fat-free milk**
- 1 **large apple, peeled and chopped**
- ¾ **cup steel-cut oats**
- ¾ **cup raisins**
- 3 **tablespoons brown sugar**
- 4½ **teaspoons butter, melted**
- ¾ **teaspoon ground cinnamon**
- ½ **teaspoon salt**
- ¼ **cup chopped pecans**

In a 3-qt. slow cooker coated with cooking spray, combine the first eight ingredients. Cover and cook on low for 7-8 hours or until liquid is absorbed. Spoon oatmeal into bowls; sprinkle with pecans.

NOTE *You may substitute 1½ cups quick-cooking oats for the steel-cut oats and increase the fat-free milk to 4½ cups.*

RAISIN NUT OATMEAL

MUSHROOM SAUSAGE STRATA

This delightful casserole is a filling mainstay for our family's Christmas Day brunch. Being able to assemble the recipe ahead of time is an added bonus.
—**JULIE STERCHI** CAMPBELLSVILLE, KY

PREP: 20 MIN. + CHILLING
BAKE: 35 MIN. + STANDING
MAKES: 8-10 SERVINGS

- 1 **pound bulk pork sausage**
- 10 **slices whole wheat bread, cubed**
- 1 **can (4 ounces) mushroom stems and pieces, drained**
- ½ **cup shredded cheddar cheese**
- ½ **cup shredded Swiss cheese**
- 6 **large eggs**
- 1 **cup 2% milk**
- 1 **cup half-and-half cream**
- 1 **teaspoon Worcestershire sauce**
- ½ **teaspoon pepper**

1. In a large skillet, cook sausage over medium heat until no longer pink; drain. Place bread cubes in a greased 13x9-in. baking dish. Sprinkle with the sausage, mushrooms and cheeses.

2. Using a large bowl, whisk the remaining ingredients and pour over the cheese. Cover and refrigerate it overnight.

3. Remove from the refrigerator 30 minutes before baking. Preheat oven to 350°. Bake, uncovered, for 35-45 minutes or until a knife inserted near the center comes out clean.

FREEZE OPTION *After assembling, cover and freeze the strata. To use, partially thaw it in the refrigerator overnight. Remove from refrigerator 30 minutes before baking. Preheat oven to 350°. Bake strata as directed, increasing time as necessary for a knife inserted near the center to come out clean.*

FRESH STRAWBERRY BREAKFAST TACOS

When our son was growing up, this was one of his favorite breakfasts. I've used low-fat ingredients in the past with good results, too.
—**JOAN HALLFORD** NORTH RICHLAND HILLS, TX

START TO FINISH: 30 MIN.
MAKES: 6 SERVINGS

- 2 **tablespoons butter, divided**
- 6 **flour tortillas (6 inches)**
- ⅓ **cup cream cheese, softened**
- 1 **tablespoon honey**
- ½ **teaspoon ground cinnamon**
- ⅓ **cup vanilla yogurt**
- 1¾ **cups quartered fresh strawberries**

1. In a large skillet, heat 1 teaspoon butter over medium-low heat. Add one tortilla; cook each side until light golden, 1-2 minutes. Transfer to wire rack. Repeat with remaining tortillas.
2. Beat together cream cheese, honey and cinnamon; slowly mix in yogurt until blended. Spread tortillas with cream cheese mixture; add berries.

FREEZE STRAWBERRIES FOR LONGER SHELF LIFE

Fresh strawberries don't keep long after picking. To keep your berries past their peak (typically after three days and beyond), wash and place them, whole or cut, on a parchment paper-lined cookie sheet. Freeze until frozen. Then transfer berries to heavy-duty freezer bags that have been labeled and dated for longer storage in the freezer.

FRESH STRAWBERRY BREAKFAST TACOS

BRUNCH PIZZA
SQUARES

BRUNCH PIZZA SQUARES

I love using convenience items, like the crescent rolls in these easy squares. Guests always ask me for the recipe. To hurry along the preparation of this casserole and others like it, I'll brown a few pounds of sausage ahead of time and keep it in the freezer.
—**LACHELLE OLIVET** PACE, FL

START TO FINISH: 30 MIN.
MAKES: 8 SERVINGS

- 1 **pound bulk pork sausage**
- 1 **tube (8 ounces) refrigerated crescent rolls**
- 4 **large eggs**
- 2 **tablespoons milk**
- ⅛ **teaspoon pepper**
- ¾ **cup shredded cheddar cheese**

1. In a large skillet, crumble sausage and cook over medium heat until it is no longer pink; drain. Unroll crescent dough onto the bottom and ½ in. up the sides of a lightly greased 13x9-in. baking pan; seal the seams. Sprinkle with sausage.
2. In a large bowl, beat the eggs, milk and pepper; pour over the sausage. Sprinkle with cheese.
3. Bake, uncovered, at 400° for 15 minutes or until a knife inserted in the center comes out clean.

★ ★ ★ ★ ★ **READER REVIEW**

"We have made this for years and the whole family loves it. For a little different flavor, instead of using pepper, I use cajun seasoning. Gives it a little zip."

OKCOUNTRYGIRL TASTEOFHOME.COM

COFFEE-GLAZED DOUGHNUTS

COFFEE-GLAZED DOUGHNUTS

The coffee-flavored glaze on these tasty doughnuts makes them a perfect way to start the morning. They're also a great way to use up leftover potatoes.
—**PAT SIEBENALER** RANDOM LAKE, WI

PREP: 25 MIN. + RISING
COOK: 5 MIN./BATCH
MAKES: ABOUT 4 DOZEN

- 2 **packages (¼ ounce each) active dry yeast**
- ¼ **cup warm water (110° to 115°)**
- 2 **cups warm 2% milk (110° to 115°)**
- ½ **cup butter, softened**
- 1 **cup hot mashed potatoes (without added milk and butter)**
- 3 **large eggs**
- ½ **teaspoon lemon extract, optional**
- 1 **cup sugar**
- 1½ **teaspoons salt**
- ½ **teaspoon ground cinnamon**
- 9¼ to 9¾ **cups all-purpose flour**

COFFEE GLAZE
- 6 to 8 **tablespoons cold 2% milk**
- 1 **tablespoon instant coffee granules**
- 2 **teaspoons vanilla extract**
- ¾ **cup butter, softened**
- 6 **cups confectioners' sugar**
- ½ **teaspoon ground cinnamon**
  Dash salt
  Oil for deep-fat frying

1. In a large bowl, dissolve yeast in warm water. Add the milk, butter, potatoes, eggs and, if desired, extract. Add the sugar, salt, cinnamon and 3 cups flour. Beat until smooth. Stir in enough remaining flour to form a soft dough. Cover and let rise in a warm place until doubled, about 1 hour.
2. Stir down dough. On a well-floured surface, roll out to ½-in. thickness. Cut with a floured 2½-in. doughnut cutter. Place on greased baking sheets; cover and let rise for 45 minutes.
3. Meanwhile, for glaze, combine 6 tablespoons milk, coffee and vanilla; stir to dissolve coffee. In a large bowl, beat butter, sugar, cinnamon and salt. Gradually add milk mixture; beat until smooth, adding milk to reach a good dipping consistency.
4. In an electric skillet or deep-fat fryer, heat oil to 375°. Fry doughnuts, a few at a time, about 1½ minutes per side or until golden. Drain on paper towels. Dip tops in glaze while warm.

HOMEMADE BISCUITS & MAPLE SAUSAGE GRAVY

I can remember digging into flaky, gravy-smothered biscuits on Christmas morning and other special occasions when I was a child. What a satisfying way to start the day!

—JENN TIDWELL FAIR OAKS, CA

PREP: 30 MIN. • **BAKE:** 15 MIN.
MAKES: 8 SERVINGS

- 2 **cups all-purpose flour**
- 3 **teaspoons baking powder**
- 1 **tablespoon sugar**
- 1 **teaspoon salt**
- ¼ **teaspoon pepper, optional**
- 3 **tablespoons cold butter, cubed**
- 1 **tablespoon shortening**
- ¾ **cup 2% milk**

SAUSAGE GRAVY

- 1 **pound bulk maple pork sausage**
- ¼ **cup all-purpose flour**
- 3 **cups 2% milk**
- 2 **tablespoons maple syrup**
- ½ **teaspoon salt**
- ¼ **teaspoon ground sage**
- ¼ **teaspoon coarsely ground pepper**

1. Preheat oven to 400°. In a large bowl, whisk flour, baking powder, sugar, salt and, if desired, pepper. Cut in butter and shortening until mixture resembles coarse crumbs. Add milk; stir just until moistened. Turn onto a lightly floured surface; knead gently 8-10 times.

2. Pat or roll dough to 1-in. thickness; cut with a floured 2-in. biscuit cutter. Place the pieces 1 in. apart on an ungreased baking sheet. Bake 15-17 minutes or until golden brown.

3. Meanwhile, in a large skillet, cook the sausage over medium heat for 6-8 minutes or until no longer pink, breaking into crumbles. Stir in flour until blended; gradually stir in milk. Bring to a boil, stirring constantly; cook and stir 4-6 minutes or until sauce is thickened. Stir in remaining ingredients. Serve with warm biscuits.

HOMEMADE BISCUITS & MAPLE SAUSAGE GRAVY

ON-THE-GO BREAKFAST MUFFINS

Family members frequently request these savory muffins. I usually prepare them on Sunday night so when we're running late on weekday mornings, the kids can grab these to eat on the bus.

—IRENE WAYMAN GRANTSVILLE, UT

PREP: 30 MIN. **BAKE:** 15 MIN.
MAKES: 1½ DOZEN

- 1 pound bulk Italian sausage
- 7 large eggs, divided use
- 2 cups all-purpose flour
- ⅓ cup sugar
- 3 teaspoons baking powder
- ½ teaspoon salt
- ½ cup 2% milk
- ½ cup canola oil
- 1 cup shredded cheddar cheese, divided

1. Preheat oven to 400°. In a large nonstick skillet, cook the sausage over medium heat 6-8 minutes or until no longer pink, breaking into crumbles. Remove with a slotted spoon; drain on paper towels. Wipe skillet clean.
2. In a bowl, whisk five eggs. Pour into the same skillet; cook and stir over medium heat until thickened and no liquid egg remains. Remove from heat.
3. In a large bowl, whisk flour, sugar, baking powder and salt. In another bowl, whisk the remaining eggs, milk and oil until blended. Add to the flour mixture; stir just until moistened. Fold in ⅔ cup cheese, sausage and scrambled eggs.
4. Fill greased or paper-lined muffin cups three-fourths full. Sprinkle the tops with remaining cheese. Bake 12-15 minutes or until a toothpick inserted in center comes out clean. Cool 5 minutes before removing from pans to wire racks. Serve warm.
FREEZE OPTION *Freeze the cooled muffins in resealable plastic freezer bags. To use, microwave each muffin on high for 45-60 seconds or until heated through.*

RICOTTA-RAISIN COFFEE CAKE

Sharing this beautiful coffee cake with overnight guests is a joy. If you don't have cardamom or don't care for it, substitute nutmeg, cinnamon or allspice.

—CAROL GAUS ELK GROVE VILLAGE, IL

PREP: 15 MIN. + RISING
BAKE: 20 MIN. + COOLING
MAKES: 12 SERVINGS

- 1 loaf (1 pound) frozen bread dough, thawed
- 1 cup part-skim ricotta cheese
- ¼ cup honey
- ¼ teaspoon ground cardamom
- ¼ teaspoon almond extract
- 1 cup golden raisins
- ¼ cup confectioners' sugar
- 2 to 3 teaspoons fat-free milk

1. On a lightly floured surface, roll the dough into a 15x9-in. rectangle. In a small bowl, combine cheese, honey, cardamom and almond extract. Spread the filling to within ½ in. of edges. Sprinkle with raisins. Roll up jelly-roll style, starting with a long side; pinch seam to seal. Pinch ends together to form a ring.
2. Place the ring seam side down in a parchment paper-lined 9-in. round baking pan. Cover and let rise until doubled, about 30 minutes.
3. Preheat oven to 350°. With a sharp knife, make 12 shallow slashes in top of coffee cake. Bake 20-25 minutes or until golden brown. Cool on a wire rack. In a small bowl, combine the confectioners' sugar and milk; drizzle over cake.

RAISIN BREAD & SAUSAGE MORNING CASSEROLE

RAISIN BREAD & SAUSAGE MORNING CASSEROLE

When we used to have Sunday breakfasts with my grandparents, my mom often made this for Grandpa because he enjoyed it so much. Pork sausage and cinnamon bread taste surprisingly good together.
—CAROLYN LEVAN DIXON, IL

PREP: 25 MIN. + CHILLING • **BAKE:** 35 MIN.
MAKES: 12 SERVINGS

- ½ **pound bulk pork sausage**
- 1 **loaf (1 pound) cinnamon-raisin bread, cubed**
- 6 **large eggs**
- 1½ **cups 2% milk**
- 1½ **cups half-and-half cream**
- 1 **teaspoon vanilla extract**
- ¼ **teaspoon ground cinnamon**
- ¼ **teaspoon ground nutmeg**

TOPPING
- 1 **cup chopped pecans**
- 1 **cup packed brown sugar**
- ½ **cup butter, softened**
- 2 **tablespoons maple syrup**

1. In a large skillet, cook sausage over medium heat 4-6 minutes or until no longer pink, breaking into crumbles; drain. In a greased 13x9-in. baking dish, combine bread and sausage.
2. In a large bowl, whisk eggs, milk, cream, vanilla, cinnamon and nutmeg until blended; pour over the bread. Refrigerate, covered, several hours or overnight.
3. Preheat the oven to 350°. Remove casserole from refrigerator while oven heats. In a small bowl, beat topping ingredients until blended. Drop by tablespoonfuls over casserole.
4. Bake, uncovered, 35-45 minutes or until golden brown and a knife inserted in center comes out clean. Let stand 5-10 minutes before serving.

JOLLY JELLY DOUGHNUTS

Plump and filled with jelly, these sugar-coated doughnuts will disappear as fast as you can churn them out.

—**LEE BREMSON** KANSAS CITY, MO

PREP: 25 MIN. + RISING • **COOK:** 30 MIN.
MAKES: ABOUT 2½ DOZEN

- 2 packages (¼ ounce each) active dry yeast
- 2 cups warm milk (110° to 115°)
- 7 cups all-purpose flour
- 4 large egg yolks
- 1 large egg
- ½ cup sugar
- 1 teaspoon salt
- 2 teaspoons grated lemon peel
- ½ teaspoon vanilla extract
- ½ cup butter, melted
  Oil for deep-fat frying
  Red jelly of your choice
  Additional sugar

1. In a large bowl, dissolve yeast in warm milk. Add 2 cups flour; mix well. Let stand in a warm place for 30 minutes. Add the egg yolks, egg, sugar, salt, lemon peel and vanilla; mix well. Beat in the butter and remaining flour. Do not knead. Cover and let rise in a warm place until doubled, about 45 minutes.
2. Punch dough down. On a lightly floured surface, roll out to ½-in. thickness. Cut with a 2½-in. biscuit cutter. Place on lightly greased baking sheets. Cover and let rise until nearly doubled, about 35 minutes.
3. In a deep-fat fryer or an electric skillet, heat oil to 375°. Fry doughnuts, a few at a time, for 1½ to 2 minutes on each side or until browned. Drain on paper towels.
4. Cool for 2-3 minutes; cut a small slit with a sharp knife on one side of each doughnut. Cut a small hole in the corner of a pastry or plastic bag; insert a very small round tip. Fill bag with jelly. Fill each doughnut with about 1 teaspoon jelly. Carefully roll warm doughnuts in sugar. Serve warm.

JOLLY JELLY
DOUGHNUTS

FAST FIX

PINEAPPLE OATMEAL

Oatmeal for breakfast is a standard item, but I like to mix it up a bit. This version gets some natural sweetness from pineapple and pineapple juice. It is definitely worth the extra bit of effort!

—**MARIA REGAKIS** SAUGUS, MA

START TO FINISH: 15 MIN.
MAKES: 3 SERVINGS

- 1¼ cups water
- ½ cup unsweetened pineapple juice
- ¼ teaspoon salt
- 1 cup quick-cooking oats
- ¾ cup unsweetened pineapple tidbits
- ½ cup raisins
- 2 tablespoons brown sugar
- ¼ teaspoon ground cinnamon
- ¼ teaspoon vanilla extract
- ¼ cup chopped walnuts
  Fat-free milk, optional

1. In a large saucepan, bring water, pineapple juice and salt to a boil over medium heat. Stir in oats; cook and stir for 1-2 minutes or until thickened.
2. Remove from heat. Stir in the pineapple, raisins, brown sugar, cinnamon and vanilla. Cover and let stand for 2-3 minutes. Sprinkle with walnuts. Serve with milk if desired.

CHOCOLATE CHIP PANCAKES WITH CINNAMON HONEY SYRUP

Give ordinary pancakes kid-friendly appeal with chocolate chips and cinnamon honey syrup. This is one of those special Saturday morning favorites they're sure to remember.
—**LEEANN HANSEN** KAYSVILLE, UT

START TO FINISH: 25 MIN.
MAKES: 6 SERVINGS

- 2 cups all-purpose flour
- ¼ cup sugar
- 2 tablespoons baking powder
- 1 teaspoon salt
- 2 large eggs
- 1½ cups whole milk
- ¼ cup canola oil
- ½ cup miniature chocolate chips

CINNAMON HONEY SYRUP
- 1 cup honey
- ½ cup butter, cubed
- 1 to 2 teaspoons ground cinnamon

1. In a large bowl, combine the flour, sugar, baking powder and salt. Mix the eggs, milk and oil; add to the dry ingredients just until moistened. Fold in chocolate chips.
2. Pour the batter by ¼ cupfuls onto a lightly greased hot griddle. Turn when bubbles form on top; cook until second side is golden brown. Keep pancakes warm.
3. Combine the syrup ingredients and microwave, uncovered, on high until the butter is melted and syrup is hot, stirring the mix occasionally. Serve with pancakes.

CHOCOLATE CHIP PANCAKES WITH CINNAMON HONEY SYRUP

BRUNCH-STYLE PORTOBELLO MUSHROOMS

I've always loved portobellos for their stuffability. I combined my favorite ingredients for this rich, savory main dish that's wonderful for breakfast, brunch or even dinner.
—**SYLVIA WALDSMITH** ROCKTON, IL

START TO FINISH: 30 MIN.
MAKES: 4 SERVINGS

- 4 large portobello mushrooms, stems removed
- 2 packages (10 ounces each) frozen creamed spinach, thawed
- 4 large eggs
- ¼ cup shredded Gouda cheese
- ½ cup crumbled cooked bacon
  Salt and pepper, optional

1. Place mushrooms, stem side up, in an ungreased 15x10x1-in. baking pan. Spoon the spinach onto mushrooms, building up the sides. Carefully crack an egg into center of each mushroom; sprinkle with cheese and bacon.
2. Bake at 375° for 18-20 minutes or until eggs are set. Sprinkle with salt and pepper if desired.

★ ★ ★ ★ ★ **READER REVIEW**

"These are delicious. Instead of using frozen creamed spinach, I saute fresh spinach with some scallions, salt, pepper and nutmeg."

INVERTEBRATE TASTEOFHOME.COM

SMOKED GOUDA & SWISS CHARD STRATA

I shared this impressive strata with friends at their new home. For your special occasions, change up the veggies and cheese. I've used tomatoes, spinach and cheddar.

—KIMBERLY FORNI LACONIA, NH

PREP: 30 MIN. + CHILLING • **BAKE:** 1 HOUR
MAKES: 10 SERVINGS

- 10 bacon strips, chopped
- 1 pound Swiss chard, leaves chopped and stems julienned
- 1 large sweet onion, thinly sliced
- ½ cup chopped roasted sweet red peppers
- 12 slices white bread, toasted and cubed
- 2 cups smoked Gouda or smoked Gruyere cheese, shredded
- 2 cups Swiss cheese, shredded
- 10 large eggs
- 3½ cups 2% milk
- 2 teaspoons prepared mustard
- 1 teaspoon salt
- ½ teaspoon coarsely ground pepper
- ½ teaspoon cayenne pepper

1. In a large skillet, cook bacon over medium heat until crisp; drain on paper towels, reserving 1 tablespoon drippings. Cook chard stems and onion in reserved drippings over medium heat until tender, about 4 minutes. Add chard leaves and red pepper; cook 2 minutes. Drain.

2. Lightly grease a 13x9-in. baking dish. Layer with half of the bread cubes, half of the vegetable mixture and half of the cheeses. Repeat layers.

3. Mix remaining ingredients until well blended. Pour over layers; press down slightly. Sprinkle bacon over top. Cover and refrigerate several hours or overnight.

4. Preheat oven to 325°. Bake until puffy, lightly browned and set, about 1 hour.

HASH BROWN WAFFLES WITH FRIED EGGS

FAST FIX ▶

HASH BROWN WAFFLES WITH FRIED EGGS

Refrigerated hash brown potatoes help you make quick work of these crunchy waffles. Put out lots of toppings so everyone can design his or her own.

—NANCY JUDD ALPINE, UT

START TO FINISH: 30 MIN.
MAKES: 4 SERVINGS

- 5 large eggs
- ½ teaspoon salt
- ½ teaspoon ground cumin
- ½ teaspoon pepper
- ¼ teaspoon chili powder
- 1¾ cups refrigerated shredded hash brown potatoes
- 1 small onion, finely chopped
- ¼ cup canned chopped green chilies
- 2 tablespoons salsa
- 2 tablespoons canola oil
- ½ cup shredded cheddar-Monterey Jack cheese
  Optional toppings: salsa, guacamole, sour cream and minced fresh cilantro

1. In a large bowl, whisk 1 egg, salt, cumin, pepper and chili powder. Stir in potatoes, onion, green chilies and salsa. Bake in a preheated waffle iron coated with cooking spray until golden brown and potatoes are tender, 8-12 minutes.

2. In a large skillet, heat the oil over medium-high heat. Break the remaining eggs, one at a time, into pan. Reduce heat to low. Cook to desired doneness, turning after whites are set if desired. Remove from heat. Sprinkle with cheese; cover and let stand 3 minutes or until melted.

3. Serve eggs with waffles and toppings of your choice.

HUEVOS RANCHEROS WITH TOMATILLO SAUCE

My husband and I visited Cuernavaca, Mexico, where we had huevos rancheros for the first time. He loved it so much that he wanted to try a homemade version when we returned. This is my take on it, which is suited to our family's preference for sunny-side up eggs. Poached or scrambled eggs would also be delicious.
—**CHERYL WOODSON** LIBERTY, MO

START TO FINISH: 25 MIN.
MAKES: 8 SERVINGS

- 5 tomatillos, husks removed, halved
- 2 tablespoons coarsely chopped onion
- 1 to 2 serrano peppers, halved
- 3 garlic cloves, peeled
- 1 teaspoon chicken bouillon granules
- 1 can (15 ounces) Southwestern black beans, undrained
- 8 large eggs
- 1 cup shredded Manchego cheese
- 8 tostada shells, warmed
- ½ cup sour cream
  Chopped tomato, sliced avocado and minced fresh cilantro, optional

1. Place tomatillos, onion, pepper, garlic and bouillon in food processor. Cover and process until ingredients are finely chopped; set aside. In a small saucepan, mash beans. Cook on low until heated through, stirring occasionally.
2. Meanwhile, break eggs in batches into a large nonstick skillet coated with cooking spray. Cover and cook over low heat for 5-7 minutes or until eggs are set. Sprinkle with cheese.
3. To serve, spread beans over tostada shells; top with eggs, tomatillo sauce and sour cream. Garnish with tomato, avocado and cilantro if desired.
NOTE *Wear disposable gloves when cutting hot peppers; the oils can burn skin. Avoid touching your face.*

CHEESY HASH BROWN EGG CASSEROLE WITH BACON

My husband and sons frequently request this dish, referring to it as "egg pie." The hearty casserole is nice enough for a holiday but is also satisfying enough for a busy weeknight.
—**PATRICIA THROLSON** BECKER, MINNESOTA

PREP: 20 MIN. • **BAKE:** 35 MIN.
MAKES: 8 SERVINGS

- ½ pound sliced bacon, chopped
- ½ cup chopped onion
- ½ cup chopped green pepper
- 12 large eggs, lightly beaten
- 1 cup 2% milk
- 1 teaspoon salt
- ½ teaspoon pepper
- ¼ teaspoon dill weed
- 1 package (16 ounces) frozen shredded hash brown potatoes, thawed
- 1 cup shredded cheddar cheese

1. In a large skillet, cook bacon over medium heat until crisp. Remove with a slotted spoon; drain on paper towels. Discard the drippings, reserving 2 tablespoons. In the same skillet, saute onion and green pepper in drippings until they are tender; remove with a slotted spoon.
2. In a large bowl, whisk eggs, milk and seasonings. Stir in hash browns, cheese, onion mixture and bacon.
3. Transfer to a greased 13x9-in. baking dish. Bake, uncovered, at 350° for 35-45 minutes or until a knife inserted near center comes out clean.

☆ ☆ ☆ ☆ ☆ **READER REVIEW**

"I like this egg bake for its versatility and ease of prep. I add mushrooms and green onions, or chives and some sweet red pepper."

THECREATIVEBAKER TASTEOFHOME.COM

ZUCCHINI EGG SKILLET

My neighbor shared more zucchini from his garden than I knew what to do with. He loved this recipe—it's great for brunch or a special breakfast.
—**DARCY KENNEDY** HENDERSONVILLE, NC

START TO FINISH: 30 MIN.
MAKES: 4 SERVINGS

- 2 tablespoons olive oil
- 2 medium red potatoes (about ½ lb.), cut into ¼-inch cubes
- 1 medium onion, chopped
- 2 small zucchini, shredded (about 3 cups)
- 4 frozen fully cooked breakfast sausage links, thawed and cut into ½-inch slices
- ½ cup chopped roasted sweet red peppers
- 6 cherry tomatoes, quartered
- ¼ teaspoon salt
- ⅛ teaspoon pepper
- ½ cup shredded cheddar cheese
- 4 large eggs

1. In a large skillet, heat the oil over medium-high heat. Add potatoes and onion; cook and stir 4-6 minutes or until potatoes are crisp-tender. Stir in zucchini and sausage; cook another 4-6 minutes or until the vegetables are tender.
2. Gently stir in the red peppers, tomatoes, salt and pepper; sprinkle with cheese. With back of spoon, make four wells in potato mixture; break an egg into each well. Reduce heat to medium. Cook, covered, 4-6 minutes or until egg whites are completely set and yolks begin to thicken but are not hard.

ZUCCHINI
EGG SKILLET

**CHORIZO & EGG
BREAKFAST RING**

CHORIZO & EGG BREAKFAST RING

Friends flip for this loaded crescent ring when I bring it to brunch. It's the result of my love for Mexican food and quick-fix recipes.

—FRANCES BLACKWELDER
GRAND JUNCTION, CO

PREP: 25 MIN. • **BAKE:** 15 MIN.
MAKES: 8 SERVINGS

- 2 tubes (8 ounces each) refrigerated crescent rolls
- ½ pound uncooked chorizo, casings removed, or bulk spicy pork sausage
- 8 large eggs
- ¼ teaspoon salt
- ¼ teaspoon pepper
- 1 tablespoon butter
- 1 cup shredded pepper Jack cheese
- 1 cup salsa

1. Preheat the oven to 375°. Unroll crescent dough and separate into triangles. On an ungreased 12-in. pizza pan, arrange triangles in a ring with points toward the outside and wide ends overlapping. Press overlapping dough to seal.
2. In a large skillet, cook chorizo over medium heat 6-8 minutes or until cooked through, breaking into crumbles. Remove with a slotted spoon; drain on paper towels. Discard drippings, wiping skillet clean.
3. In a small bowl, whisk eggs, salt and pepper until blended. In same skillet, heat butter over medium heat. Pour in egg mixture; cook and stir until eggs are thickened and no liquid egg remains.
4. Spoon egg mixture, chorizo and cheese across wide end of triangles. Fold pointed end of triangles over filling, tucking points under to form a ring (filling will be visible).
5. Bake 15-20 minutes or until golden brown. Serve with salsa.

HOW TO MAKE A BREAKFAST RING

Carefully pull the points of the crescent dough triangles straight over the filling to the inside of the ring. Tuck the points under the base, and bake away.

BREAKFAST BREAD BOWLS

These bread bowls are so elegant, tasty and simple, you'll wonder why you haven't been making them for years. My wife loves it when I make these for her in the morning.

—PATRICK LAVIN JR. BIRDSBORO, PA

PREP: 20 MIN. • **BAKE:** 20 MIN.
MAKES: 4 SERVINGS

- ½ cup chopped pancetta
- 4 crusty hard rolls (4 inches wide)
- ½ cup finely chopped fresh mushrooms
- 4 large eggs
- ⅛ teaspoon salt
- ⅛ teaspoon pepper
- ¼ cup shredded Gruyere or fontina cheese

1. Preheat oven to 350°. In a small skillet, cook pancetta over medium heat until it is browned, stirring occasionally. Remove with a slotted spoon; drain on paper towels.
2. Meanwhile, cut a thin slice off top of each roll. Hollow out bottom of roll, leaving a ½-in.-thick shell (save removed bread for another use); place shells on an ungreased baking sheet.
3. Add mushrooms and pancetta to bread shells. Carefully break an egg into each; sprinkle eggs with salt and pepper. Sprinkle with cheese. Bake 18-22 minutes or until egg whites are completely set and yolks begin to thicken but are not hard.

★ ★ ★ ★ ★ **READER REVIEW**

"These turned out great! I substituted chopped peppers and onion for the pancetta. Add a green salad or fruit and you can have a complete meal anytime!"

PIEHLAR TASTEOFHOME.COM

BREAKFAST
BREAD BOWLS

FAST FIX

BANANA BEIGNET BITES

When I was a little girl, my grandmother took me aside one day and taught me how to make her famous banana beignets. Although we made them during the holidays, they're fantastic any time of the year.

—AMY DOWNING SOUTH RIDING, VA

START TO FINISH: 30 MIN.
MAKES: ABOUT 3 DOZEN

- ¾ cup sugar
- ¼ cup packed brown sugar
- 1½ teaspoons ground cinnamon

BEIGNETS
- 2 cups cake flour
- ¾ cup sugar
- 2½ teaspoons baking powder
- ½ teaspoon ground cinnamon
- 1 teaspoon salt
- 1 large egg
- 1 cup mashed ripe bananas (about 3 medium)
- ½ cup whole milk
- 2 tablespoons canola oil
  Oil for deep-fat frying

1. In a small bowl, mix sugars and cinnamon until blended. In a large bowl, whisk the first five beignet ingredients. In another bowl, whisk egg, bananas, milk and 2 tablespoons oil until blended. Add to the flour mixture; stir just until moistened.
2. In an electric skillet or deep fryer, heat the oil to 375°. Drop tablespoonfuls of batter, a few at a time, into hot oil. Fry about 45-60 seconds on each side or until golden brown. Drain on paper towels. Roll warm beignets in sugar mixture.

FAVORITE LOADED
BREAKFAST POTATOES

FAVORITE LOADED BREAKFAST POTATOES

My four young children love to eat with their hands, and these potatoes make easy finger food. My kids like to call them "brunchskins."

—**MINDY CAMPBELL** RAPID CITY, MI

PREP: 45 MIN. • **BAKE:** 10 MIN.
MAKES: 6 SERVINGS

- 6 **medium baking potatoes (about 3 pounds)**
- 1 **tablespoon butter**
- 1 **each small sweet red, orange and green pepper, finely chopped**
- 1 **cup finely chopped fresh mushrooms**
- ¼ **cup finely chopped red onion**
- ½ **teaspoon salt**
- ¼ **teaspoon pepper**
- 6 **large eggs, beaten**
- 1¼ **cups shredded cheddar cheese, divided**
- ¼ **cup plus 6 tablespoons sour cream, divided**
- 6 **bacon strips, cooked and crumbled or ⅓ cup bacon bits**
- 3 **green onions, chopped**

1. Preheat oven to 375°. Scrub and pierce potatoes with a fork; place on a microwave-safe plate. Microwave, uncovered, on high 15-18 minutes or until tender, turning once.
2. When cool enough to handle, cut a thin slice off the top of each potato; discard slice. Scoop out pulp, leaving ¼-in.-thick shells.
3. In a large skillet, heat butter over medium heat. Add the peppers, mushrooms and red onion; cook and stir 4-6 minutes or until tender. Stir in salt, pepper and 1 cup pulp (save remaining pulp for another use). Add eggs; cook and stir until eggs are thickened and no liquid egg remains. Stir in ½ cup cheese and ¼ cup sour cream.
4. Spoon egg mixture into potato shells. Place on a 15x10x1-in. baking pan. Sprinkle with remaining ¾ cup cheese. Bake 10-12 minutes or until heated through and cheese is melted.

Top with remaining sour cream; sprinkle with bacon and green onions.
NOTE *This recipe was tested in a 1,100-watt microwave.*

MUSHROOM-GOUDA QUICHE

I make a quiche using refrigerated pie pastry for a laid-back Sunday brunch. Load it up with fresh mushrooms, aromatic arugula and creamy Gouda.

—**THOMAS FAGLON** SOMERSET, NJ

PREP: 15 MIN. • **BAKE:** 30 MIN. + STANDING
MAKES: 6 SERVINGS

- 1 **sheet refrigerated pie pastry**
- 4 **large eggs**
- 1 **cup heavy whipping cream**
- ¼ **teaspoon salt**
- ¼ **teaspoon pepper**
- 2 **cups sliced fresh shiitake mushrooms (about 4 ounces)**
- 1 **cup shredded Gouda or Monterey Jack cheese**
- 1 **cup chopped arugula or fresh baby spinach**

1. Preheat oven to 350°. Unroll pastry sheet into a 9-in. pie plate; flute edge. Refrigerate while preparing filling.
2. In a large bowl, whisk eggs, cream, salt and pepper until blended. Stir in the remaining ingredients. Pour into the pie shell.
3. Bake on a lower oven rack for 30-35 minutes or until crust is golden brown and a knife inserted in center comes out clean. Let stand 10 minutes before cutting.
FREEZE OPTION *Cover and freeze unbaked quiche. To use, remove from freezer 30 minutes before baking (do not thaw). Preheat oven to 350°. Place quiche on a baking sheet; cover edge loosely with foil. Bake as directed, increasing time as necessary for a knife inserted near the center to come out clean.*

CRISSCROSS APPLE CROWNS

Wake 'em up on chilly mornings with the tempting aroma of apples and cinnamon wafting through the house. I love these because they're different and easy.

—**TERESA MORRIS** LAUREL, DE

PREP: 30 MIN. • **BAKE:** 20 MIN.
MAKES: 8 SERVINGS

- 1⅓ **cups chopped peeled tart apples**
- ⅓ **cup chopped walnuts**
- ⅓ **cup raisins**
- ½ **cup sugar, divided**
- 2 **tablespoons all-purpose flour**
- 2 **teaspoons ground cinnamon, divided**
  Dash salt
- 1 **package (16.3 ounces) large refrigerated flaky biscuits**
- 2 **teaspoons butter, melted**

1. In a large microwave-safe bowl, combine the apples, walnuts, raisins, 3 tablespoons sugar, flour, ¾ teaspoon cinnamon and salt. Microwave on high for 2-3 minutes or until the mixture is almost tender.
2. Flatten each biscuit into a 5-in. circle. Combine the remaining sugar and cinnamon; sprinkle a rounded teaspoonful of sugar mixture over each. Top each with ¼ cup apple mixture. Bring up edges to enclose mixture; pinch edges to seal.
3. Place seam side down in ungreased muffin cups. Brush tops with butter; sprinkle with the remaining sugar mixture. With a sharp knife, cut an X in the top of each.
4. Bake at 350° for 18-22 minutes or until it is golden brown. Cool about 5 minutes before removing from pan to a wire rack.

ULTIMATE FRUITY GRANOLA

Honey, maple syrup and vanilla coat this wonderfully crunchy treat that's fantastic no matter how you serve it: on its own, with cold milk or in a yogurt parfait.

—**SARAH VASQUES** MILFORD, NH

PREP: 15 MIN. • **BAKE:** 20 MIN. + COOLING
MAKES: 9 CUPS

- 5 cups old-fashioned oats
- 1 cup sliced almonds
- ½ cup sunflower kernels
- ½ cup ground flaxseed
- ½ cup packed brown sugar
- ¼ cup maple syrup
- ¼ cup honey
- 2 tablespoons canola oil
- ½ teaspoon salt
- ½ teaspoon ground cinnamon
- 1 teaspoon vanilla extract
- ½ cup dried cranberries
- ½ cup dried banana chips
- ½ cup dried apricots, halved

1. In a large bowl, combine the oats, almonds, sunflower kernels and flax. In a small saucepan, combine the brown sugar, maple syrup, honey, oil, salt and cinnamon. Cook and stir over medium heat for 2-3 minutes or until brown sugar is dissolved and mixture is heated through. Remove from the heat; stir in vanilla. Pour over oat mixture and toss to coat.

2. Transfer mixture to a 15x10x1-in. baking pan coated with cooking spray. Bake at 350° for 20-25 minutes or until golden brown, stirring every 8 minutes. Cool completely on a wire rack. Stir in dried fruits. Store in an airtight container.

PROSCIUTTO & CHEDDAR BREAKFAST BISCUITS

When my family visits, I love to make my nephew happy by serving breakfast with pork and cheese. I created this as a twist on the traditional breakfast sandwich.

—**KELLY BOE** WHITELAND, IN

PREP: 30 MIN. • **BAKE:** 15 MIN.
MAKES: 6 SERVINGS

- 2⅓ cups biscuit/baking mix
- ½ cup 2% milk
- 3 tablespoons butter, melted
- 1 to 2 tablespoons minced fresh chives

EGGS

- 6 large eggs
- 2 tablespoons 2% milk
- ¼ teaspoon salt
- 2 ounces thinly sliced prosciutto or deli ham, cut into strips
- 2 green onions, chopped
- 1 tablespoon butter
- ½ cup shredded cheddar cheese

1. Preheat oven to 425°. In a bowl, combine biscuit mix, milk, melted butter and chives; mix just until ingredients are moistened.

2. Turn dough onto a lightly floured surface; knead gently 8-10 times. Pat or roll to ¾-in. thickness; cut with a floured 2½-in. biscuit cutter. Place 2 in. apart on an ungreased baking sheet. Bake 12-14 minutes or until golden brown.

3. Meanwhile, in a large bowl, whisk eggs, milk and salt. Place a large skillet over medium heat. Add prosciutto and green onions; cook until the prosciutto begins to brown, stirring occasionally. Stir in the butter until melted. Add egg mixture; cook and stir until eggs are thickened and no liquid egg remains. Stir in cheese; remove from heat.

4. Split warm biscuits in half. Fill with egg mixture.

PROSCIUTTO & CHEDDAR BREAKFAST BISCUITS

PICANTE OMELET PIE

My daughter loves this tasty egg bake. She visits for brunch every week before church, so I serve it often.
—**PHYLLIS CARLSON** GARDNER, KS

START TO FINISH: 30 MIN.
MAKES: 6 SERVINGS

- ½ cup picante sauce
- 1 cup shredded Monterey Jack cheese
- 1 cup shredded cheddar cheese
- 6 large eggs
- 1 cup (8 ounces) sour cream
  Tomato slices and minced fresh cilantro, optional

1. Pour the picante sauce into a lightly greased 9-in. pie plate. Sprinkle with cheeses; set aside. In a blender, combine the eggs and sour cream; cover and process until smooth. Pour over cheese.
2. Bake at 375° for 20-25 minutes or until a knife inserted in the center comes out clean. Let stand 5 minutes before cutting. Garnish with tomato and cilantro if desired.

★ ★ ★ ★ ★ **READER REVIEW**

"This has become my favorite egg dish! I serve it at brunches with other egg dishes and this is the one that receives the compliments and recipe requests."

QUILTINGMONTANA TASTEOFHOME.COM

PICANTE OMELET PIE

CORNMEAL-WHEAT PANCAKES

Drizzled with a touch of honey butter, these tasty hotcakes will brighten the day for everyone at the breakfast table. We sometimes add fruit on the side.
—**ELISABETH LARSEN** PLEASANT GROVE, UT

PREP: 15 MIN. • **COOK:** 5 MIN./BATCH
MAKES: 12 PANCAKES (½ CUP HONEY BUTTER)

- ¾ cup all-purpose flour
- ½ cup whole wheat flour
- ¼ cup cornmeal
- 2 teaspoons sugar
- 1 teaspoon salt
- 1 teaspoon baking powder
- ¾ teaspoon baking soda
- 2 large eggs
- 1½ cups buttermilk
- ¼ cup canola oil

HONEY BUTTER
- ¼ cup butter, softened
- ¼ cup honey
- 1 teaspoon ground cinnamon

1. In a large bowl, combine the first seven ingredients. Combine the eggs, buttermilk and oil; add to the dry ingredients just until moistened.
2. Pour batter by ¼ cupfuls onto a greased hot griddle; turn when bubbles form on top. Cook until the second side is golden brown.
3. Using a small bowl, combine the butter, honey and cinnamon. Serve with pancakes.

APPLE-PEAR PUFF PANCAKE

Whenever I serve this fruity pancake, people think I worked on it for hours. They are surprised that such an attractive, scrumptious dish could be so easy.

—CAROL WILLIAMS ST. JOSEPH, MO

START TO FINISH: 30 MIN.
MAKES: 6 SERVINGS

- 3 **tablespoons butter**
- 4 **large eggs**
- 1 **cup 2% milk**
- 1 **cup all-purpose flour**
- 1 **tablespoon sugar**
- ⅛ **teaspoon ground nutmeg**

TOPPING

- 3 **tablespoons butter**
- 3 **medium apples, sliced**
- 3 **medium pears, sliced**
- 3 **tablespoons sugar**
  Maple syrup, optional

1. Preheat the oven to 425°. Place butter in a 10-in. ovenproof skillet; heat in oven until butter is melted, 2-3 minutes. Tilt pan to coat evenly with butter.

2. Place the eggs, milk, flour, sugar and nutmeg in a blender; cover and process until smooth. Pour into hot skillet. Bake until it is puffed and browned, 17-20 minutes.

3. Meanwhile, for topping, heat butter in a large skillet over medium heat. Add apples, pears and sugar; cook until fruit is tender, stirring occasionally, 12-15 minutes.

4. Remove pancake from oven; fill with the fruit mixture and serve immediately. If desired, serve it with syrup.

**APPLE-PEAR
PUFF PANCAKE**

CREAM CHEESE COFFEE CAKE

This impressive coffee cake drizzled with a vanilla glaze and sprinkled with toasted almonds will shine on your buffet. The recipe yields four loaves.

—MARY ANNE MCWHIRTER PEARLAND, TX

PREP: 35 MIN. + RISING
BAKE: 20 MIN. + COOLING
MAKES: 20-24 SERVINGS

- 1 cup (8 ounces) sour cream
- ½ cup sugar
- ½ cup butter, cubed
- 1 teaspoon salt
- 2 packages (¼ ounce each) active dry yeast
- ½ cup warm water (110° to 115°)
- 2 large eggs, lightly beaten
- 4 cups all-purpose flour

FILLING
- 2 packages (8 ounces each) cream cheese, softened
- ¾ cup sugar
- 1 large egg, lightly beaten
- 2 teaspoons vanilla extract
- ⅛ teaspoon salt

GLAZE
- 2½ cups confectioners' sugar
- ¼ cup milk
- 1 teaspoon vanilla extract
  Toasted sliced almonds, optional

1. In a small saucepan, combine sour cream, sugar, butter and salt. Cook over medium-low heat, stirring it constantly, 5-10 minutes or until well blended. Cool to room temperature.
2. In a large bowl, dissolve yeast in warm water. Add the sour cream mixture and eggs. Beat until smooth. Gradually stir in flour to form a soft dough (dough will be very soft). Cover and refrigerate overnight.
3. Punch the dough down. Turn it onto a floured surface; knead it 5-6 times. Divide into fourths. Roll each piece into a 12x8-in. rectangle. Using a large bowl, combine the filling ingredients until well blended. Spread over each rectangle to within 1 in. of the edges.

4. Roll up jelly-roll style, starting with a long side; pinch seams and ends to seal. Place seam side down on greased baking sheets. Cut six X's on top of each loaf. Cover and let rise until nearly doubled, about 1 hour.
5. Preheat oven to 375°. Bake for 20-25 minutes or until it is golden brown. Remove from pans to wire racks to cool. Using a small bowl, combine confectioners' sugar, milk and vanilla; drizzle over warm loaves. Sprinkle with almonds if desired. Store in the refrigerator.

FAST FIX
OVEN DENVER OMELET

I like omelets but don't always have time to stand by the stove. That's why I favor this oven-baked variety that I can quickly pop into the oven at a moment's notice. My family frequently requests this for Sunday brunch. They always empty the dish.

—ELLEN BOWER TANEYTOWN, MD

START TO FINISH: 30 MIN.
MAKES: 6 SERVINGS

- 8 large eggs
- ½ cup half-and-half cream
- 1 cup shredded cheddar cheese
- 1 cup finely chopped fully cooked ham
- ¼ cup finely chopped green pepper
- ¼ cup finely chopped onion

1. Using a large bowl, whisk eggs and cream. Stir in the cheese, ham, green pepper and onion. Pour into a greased 9-in. square baking dish.
2. Bake at 400° for 25 minutes or until golden brown.

★ ★ ★ ★ ★ 5 STAR TIP
My husband cannot tolerate green peppers, so I use fresh snow peas from my garden in any dish that calls for green pepper. They freeze well, too, so I have a good supply all year long.
GINNY B. CHASE, BC

FRENCH TOAST STICKS

Keep these French toast sticks stockpiled in the freezer so you can pull them out whenever you need an instant, filling breakfast.
—*TASTE OF HOME* TEST KITCHEN

PREP: 20 MIN. + FREEZING
BAKE: 20 MIN.
MAKES: 1½ DOZEN

- 6 **slices day-old Texas toast**
- 4 **large eggs**
- 1 **cup milk**
- 2 **tablespoons sugar**
- 1 **teaspoon vanilla extract**
- ¼ **to ½ teaspoon ground cinnamon**
- 1 **cup crushed cornflakes, optional**
  Confectioners' sugar, optional
  Maple syrup

1. Cut each piece of bread into thirds; place in an ungreased 13x9-in. dish. In a large bowl, whisk the eggs, milk, sugar, vanilla and cinnamon. Pour over the bread; soak for 2 minutes, turning once. If desired, coat bread with cornflake crumbs on all sides.
2. Place in a greased 15x10x1-in. baking pan. Freeze until firm, about 45 minutes. Transfer to an airtight container or resealable freezer bag and store in the freezer.

TO USE FROZEN FRENCH TOAST STICKS *Place desired number on a greased baking sheet. Bake at 425° for 8 minutes. Turn; bake 10-12 minutes longer or until golden brown. Sprinkle with confectioners' sugar if desired. Serve with syrup.*

GRANDMOTHER'S TOAD IN A HOLE

I cherish memories of my grandmother's Yorkshire pudding wrapped around sausages. My kids called this puffy dish "the boat."
—SUSAN KIEBOAM STREETSBORO, OH

PREP: 10 MIN. + STANDING • **BAKE:** 25 MIN.
MAKES: 6 SERVINGS

- 3 **large eggs**
- 1 **cup 2% milk**
- ½ **teaspoon salt**
- 1 **cup all-purpose flour**
- 1 **package (12 ounces) uncooked maple breakfast sausage links**
- 3 **tablespoons olive oil**
  Butter and maple syrup, optional

1. Preheat oven to 400°. In a small bowl, whisk eggs, milk and salt. Whisk flour into egg mixture until blended. Let stand 30 minutes. Meanwhile, cook sausage according to package directions; cut each sausage into three pieces.
2. Place the oil in a 12-in. nonstick ovenproof skillet. Place in oven 3-4 minutes or until hot. Stir batter and pour into prepared skillet; top with sausage. Bake 20-25 minutes or until golden brown and puffed. Remove from the skillet; cut into wedges. If desired, serve with butter and syrup.

★ ★ ★ ★ ★ **READER REVIEW**

"Hole-y Cow, this looks toad-ally delicious! I would like to try this with applesauce."

TASTYWORLD TASTEOFHOME.COM

FRENCH TOAST STICKS

MEXICAN EGG CASSEROLE

Tomatoes and green chilies give color and zip to this extra-cheesy egg bake. It's a favorite for breakfast or brunch, but can be enjoyed for lunch or supper, too.

—MARY STEINER WEST BEND, WI

PREP: 15 MIN. • **BAKE:** 45 MIN.
MAKES: 8 SERVINGS

- ½ cup all-purpose flour
- 1 teaspoon baking powder
- 12 large eggs, lightly beaten
- 4 cups shredded Monterey Jack cheese, divided
- 2 cups (16 ounces) 4% cottage cheese
- 2 plum tomatoes, seeded and diced
- 1 can (4 ounces) chopped green chilies, drained
- 4 green onions, sliced
- ½ teaspoon hot pepper sauce
- 1 teaspoon dried oregano
- 2 tablespoons minced fresh cilantro
- ½ teaspoon salt
- ½ teaspoon pepper
  Salsa, optional

1. In a bowl, combine the flour and baking powder. Add the eggs, 3½ cups Monterey Jack cheese, cottage cheese, tomatoes, chilies, onions, hot pepper sauce, oregano, cilantro, salt and pepper. Pour mixture into a greased 13x9-in. baking dish. Sprinkle with the remaining Monterey Jack cheese.
2. Bake, uncovered, at 400° for 15 minutes. Reduce heat to 350°; bake 30 minutes longer or until a knife inserted near the center comes out clean. Let stand for 5 minutes before cutting. Serve with salsa if desired.

★ ★ ★ ★ ★ 5 STAR TIP

To easily trim cilantro (or flat-leaf parsley) from its stems, hold the bunch, then angle the blade of a chef's knife almost parallel with the stems. With short, downward strokes, shave off the leaves where they meet the stems.

BREAKFAST PIZZA SKILLET

BREAKFAST PIZZA SKILLET

I found the recipe for this hearty stovetop dish several years ago and tweaked it to fit our tastes. When I served it at a Christmas brunch, it was an instant hit.

—MARILYN HASH ENUMCLAW, WA

PREP: 35 MIN. • **COOK:** 10 MIN.
MAKES: 6 SERVINGS

- 1 pound bulk Italian sausage
- 5 cups frozen shredded hash brown potatoes
- ½ cup chopped onion
- ½ cup chopped green pepper
- ¼ to ½ teaspoon salt
  Pepper to taste
- ½ cup sliced mushrooms
- 4 large eggs, lightly beaten
- 1 medium tomato, thinly sliced
- 1 cup shredded cheddar cheese
  Sour cream and salsa, optional

1. In a large skillet, cook sausage over medium heat until no longer pink. Add potatoes, onion, green pepper, salt and pepper. Cook over medium-high heat for 18-20 minutes or until the potatoes are browned.
2. Stir in mushrooms. Pour eggs over the potato mixture. Arrange tomato slices on top. Sprinkle with cheese.
3. Cover and cook over medium-low heat for 10-15 minutes or until eggs are completely set (do not stir). Serve with sour cream and salsa if desired.

CRUSTLESS SPINACH QUICHE

I served this quiche at a church luncheon, and I had to laugh when a gentleman turned to me and said, "This is delicious, and I don't even like broccoli." I replied, "Sir, it isn't broccoli. It's spinach." He quickly answered, "I don't like spinach either, but this is good!"

—MELINDA CALVERLEY JANESVILLE, WI

PREP: 25 MIN. • **BAKE:** 40 MIN.
MAKES: 8 SERVINGS

- 1 cup chopped onion
- 1 cup sliced fresh mushrooms
- 1 tablespoon vegetable oil
- 1 package (10 ounces) frozen chopped spinach, thawed and well drained
- ⅔ cup finely chopped fully cooked ham
- 5 large eggs
- 3 cups shredded Muenster or Monterey Jack cheese
- ⅛ teaspoon pepper

In a large skillet, saute onion and mushrooms in oil until tender. Add spinach and ham; cook and stir until the excess moisture is evaporated. Cool slightly. Beat eggs; add cheese and mix well. Stir in spinach mixture and pepper; blend well. Spread evenly into a greased 9-in. pie plate or quiche dish. Bake at 350° for 40-45 minutes or until a knife inserted in center comes out clean.

★ ★ ★ ★ ★ 5 STAR TIP

To avoid water on the bottom of the pie when making a quiche, use an oven thermometer to check your oven temperature. Then, to avoid overbaking, do the "knife test" when the quiche appears to have set around the edges but still seems a little soft in the very center. The quiche is done if the knife inserted near the center comes out clean.

CRUSTLESS
SPINACH QUICHE

FAST FIX ▶

MINI HAM & CHEESE QUICHES

We bake mini quiches with ham and cheddar in muffin pans. Salad croutons replace the need for a crust.
—**LOIS ENGER** COLORADO SPRINGS, CO

START TO FINISH: 30 MIN.
MAKES: 1 DOZEN

- 1 cup salad croutons
- 1 cup shredded cheddar cheese
- 1 cup chopped fully cooked ham
- 4 large eggs
- 1½ cups 2% milk
- 1½ teaspoons dried parsley flakes
- ½ teaspoon Dijon mustard
- ¼ teaspoon salt
- ⅛ teaspoon onion powder
  Dash pepper

1. Preheat oven to 325°. Divide croutons, cheese and ham among 12 greased muffin cups. In a large bowl, whisk remaining ingredients until blended. Divide egg mixture among prepared muffin cups.
2. Bake 15-20 minutes or until a knife inserted in the center comes out clean. Let stand 5 minutes before removing from pan. Serve warm.

FAST FIX ▶

SAUSAGE BREAKFAST BURRITOS

This is a fun and filling way to enjoy eggs and sausage stuffed inside burritos. The zippy flavor will wake up your taste buds.
—**BRENDA SPANN** GRANGER, IN

START TO FINISH: 20 MIN.
MAKES: 8 SERVINGS

- 1 pound bulk pork sausage
- 1 small onion, chopped
- ½ green pepper, chopped
- 1 can (4 ounces) mushroom stems and pieces, drained
- 1 tablespoon butter
- 6 large eggs, beaten
- 8 flour tortillas (8 inches), warmed
- 1 cup shredded cheddar cheese
  Salsa, optional

1. In a large skillet, brown sausage. Drain, reserving 2 tablespoons drippings. Saute the onion, green pepper and mushrooms in drippings until tender.
2. In another skillet, melt butter over medium-high heat. Add eggs; cook and stir until set.
3. Divide sausage mixture among tortillas; top with eggs and cheese. Fold bottom of tortilla over filling and roll up. Serve with salsa if desired.

FAST FIX ▶

SPICY SCRAMBLED EGG SANDWICHES

When my daughters were young, I'd pile this tasty egg mixture onto toasted English muffins, pour each girl a glass of juice, and let them enjoy their breakfast on the patio.
—**HELEN VAIL** GLENSIDE, PA

START TO FINISH: 30 MIN.
MAKES: 4 SERVINGS

- ⅓ cup chopped green pepper
- ¼ cup chopped onion
- 3 large eggs
- 4 large egg whites
- 1 tablespoon water
- ¼ teaspoon salt
- ¼ teaspoon ground mustard
- ⅛ teaspoon pepper
- ⅛ teaspoon hot pepper sauce
- ⅓ cup fresh or frozen corn, thawed
- ¼ cup real bacon bits
- 4 English muffins, split and toasted

1. In a 10-in. skillet coated with cooking spray, cook green pepper and onion over medium heat until tender, about 8 minutes.
2. In a large bowl, whisk the eggs, egg whites, water, salt, mustard, pepper and hot pepper sauce. Pour into the skillet. Add corn and bacon; cook and stir until the eggs are completely set. Spoon onto English muffin bottoms; replace tops. Serve immediately.

HOW TO SLICE AVOCADOS

Cut into the ripe avocado from stem to stern until you hit the seed. Repeat to cut the avocado into quarters.

Twist to separate.

Pull out the seed.

Pull the skin back like a banana peel. Slice as you like or as recipe directs.

SOUTHWEST HASH WITH ADOBO-LIME CREMA

SOUTHWEST HASH WITH ADOBO-LIME CREMA

If you wake up with a hankering for some south-of-the-border flavor, you'll love this bold and zesty specialty. When I have leftover pulled pork on hand, I'll toss it into the hash for some serious yum!

—**BROOKE KELLER** LEXINGTON, KY

PREP: 20 MIN. • **BAKE:** 25 MIN.
MAKES: 4 SERVINGS

- 3 **medium sweet potatoes (about 1½ pounds), cubed**
- 1 **medium onion, chopped**
- 1 **medium sweet red pepper, chopped**
- 1 **tablespoon canola oil**
- 1 **teaspoon garlic powder**
- 1 **teaspoon smoked paprika**
- ¾ **teaspoon ground chipotle pepper**
- ½ **teaspoon salt**
- ¼ **teaspoon pepper**
- ⅔ **cup canned black beans, rinsed and drained**
- 4 **large eggs**
- ½ **cup reduced-fat sour cream**
- 2 **tablespoons lime juice**
- 2 **teaspoons adobo sauce**
- ½ **medium ripe avocado, peeled and sliced, optional**
- 2 **tablespoons minced fresh cilantro**

1. Preheat oven to 400°. Place the sweet potatoes, onion and red pepper in a 15x10x1-in. baking pan coated with cooking spray. Drizzle with oil; sprinkle with seasonings. Toss to coat. Roast 25-30 minutes or until potatoes are tender, adding beans during the last 10 minutes of cooking time.

2. Place 2-3 in. of water in a large saucepan or skillet with high sides. Bring to a boil; adjust heat to maintain a gentle simmer. Break cold eggs, one at a time, into a small bowl; holding bowl close to surface of water, slip egg into water.

3. Cook, uncovered, 3-5 minutes or until whites are completely set and yolks begin to thicken but are not hard. Using a slotted spoon, lift eggs out of water.

4. In a small bowl, mix sour cream, lime juice and adobo sauce. Serve sweet potato mixture with egg, sour cream mixture and, if desired, avocado. Sprinkle with cilantro.

CHEESY POTATO EGG BAKE

I whip up this cozy egg bake with potato crowns for either breakfast or dinner. If you like, toss in sweet peppers, onions, broccoli or carrots. The possibilities are endless.

—**AMY LENTS** GRAND FORKS, ND

PREP: 20 MIN. • **BAKE:** 45 MIN.
MAKES: 12 SERVINGS

- 1 **pound bulk lean turkey breakfast sausage**
- 1¾ **cups sliced baby portobello mushrooms, chopped**
- 4 **cups fresh spinach, coarsely chopped**
- 6 **large eggs**
- 1 **cup 2% milk**
  Dash seasoned salt
- 2 **cups shredded cheddar cheese**
- 6 **cups frozen potato crowns**

1. Preheat oven to 375°. In a large skillet, cook sausage over medium heat 5-7 minutes or until no longer pink, breaking into crumbles. Add mushrooms and spinach; cook 2-4 minutes longer or until mushrooms are tender and spinach is wilted.

2. Spoon sausage mixture into a greased 13x9-in. baking dish. In a large bowl, whisk eggs, milk and seasoned salt until blended; pour over sausage mixture. Layer with cheese and potato crowns.

3. Bake, uncovered, 45-50 minutes or until set and top is crisp.

BAKED CHEDDAR EGGS & POTATOES

I love having breakfast for dinner, especially this combo of eggs, potatoes and cheese. It starts in a skillet on the stovetop and then I pop it into the oven to bake.

—**NADINE MERHEB** TUCSON, AZ

PREP: 20 MIN. • **BAKE:** 10 MIN.
MAKES: 4 SERVINGS

- 3 **tablespoons butter**
- 1½ **pounds red potatoes, chopped**
- ¼ **cup minced fresh parsley**
- 2 **garlic cloves, minced**
- ¾ **teaspoon kosher salt**
- ⅛ **teaspoon pepper**
- 8 **large eggs**
- ½ **cup shredded extra-sharp cheddar cheese**

1. Preheat oven to 400°. In a 10-in. ovenproof skillet, heat butter over medium-high heat. Add potatoes; cook and stir until golden brown and tender. Stir in parsley, garlic, salt and pepper. With back of a spoon, make four wells in the potato mixture; break two eggs into each well.

2. Bake 9-11 minutes or until egg whites are completely set and yolks begin to thicken but are not hard. Sprinkle with cheese; bake 1 minute or until cheese is melted.

★ ★ ★ ★ ★ **READER REVIEW**

"Loved this! I added onion and peppers to the potatoes. I popped some bacon in the oven while this was cooking and served with toast. So good!"

ROBBIEJACKSON TASTEOFHOME.COM

SPINACH QUICHE WITH POTATO CRUST

Although the recipe calls for refrigerated potatoes and frozen spinach, this breakfast dish is a smart way to use up leftovers. Just sub in 2½ cups mashed potatoes and whatever cooked vegetables you have on hand. And instead of bacon, you can use ½ pound of Italian sausage.
—HEATHER KING FROSTBURG, MD

PREP: 25 MIN. • **BAKE:** 55 MIN. + STANDING
MAKES: 8 SERVINGS

- 1 package (24 ounces) refrigerated mashed potatoes
- 2 tablespoons olive oil, divided
- 8 ounces sliced fresh mushrooms
- 2 garlic cloves, minced
- 5 ounces frozen chopped spinach, thawed and squeezed dry (about ½ cup)
- 6 bacon strips, cooked and crumbled or ⅓ cup bacon bits
- 2 teaspoons minced fresh rosemary or ½ teaspoon dried rosemary, crushed
- 4 large eggs
- 1 cup 2% milk
- ¼ teaspoon pepper
- 1 cup shredded cheddar cheese

1. Preheat oven to 350°. Press mashed potatoes onto bottom and up sides of a greased 9-in. deep-dish pie plate. Brush with 1 tablespoon oil. Bake 30 minutes or until edges are golden brown.
2. Meanwhile, in a large skillet, heat remaining oil over medium-high heat. Add mushrooms; cook and stir 3-4 minutes or until tender. Add garlic; cook 1 minute longer. Remove from heat. Stir in the spinach, bacon and rosemary; spoon over the crust. In a small bowl, whisk the eggs, milk and pepper until blended; stir in cheese. Pour over mushroom mixture.
3. Bake 25-30 minutes longer or until golden brown and a knife inserted near the center comes out clean. Let stand 10 minutes before cutting.

SOUTHERN BRUNCH PASTRY PUFF

My family just about jumps out of bed when the smell of eggs, sausage and buttery pastry hits their noses. It's morning magic!
—MISTY LEDDICK CHESTER, SC

PREP: 30 MIN. • **BAKE:** 30 MIN. + STANDING
MAKES: 8 SERVINGS

- 2 cups plus 1 tablespoon water, divided
- ½ cup quick-cooking grits
- 1 cup shredded cheddar cheese
- ¼ cup butter, cubed
- 2 tablespoons prepared pesto
- ½ teaspoon salt, divided
- ¼ teaspoon coarsely ground pepper, divided
- ½ pound bulk pork sausage
- ¼ cup finely chopped sweet red pepper
- 7 large eggs, divided use
- 1 package (17.3 ounces) frozen puff pastry, thawed

1. Preheat oven to 375°. In a small saucepan, bring 2 cups water to a boil. Slowly stir in grits. Reduce heat to medium-low; cook, covered, about 5 minutes or until thickened, stirring occasionally. Remove from heat. Stir in cheese, butter, pesto, ¼ teaspoon salt and ⅛ teaspoon pepper until blended.
2. Meanwhile, in a large skillet, cook sausage and red pepper over medium heat 4-6 minutes or until sausage is no longer pink and red pepper is tender, breaking up sausage into crumbles; drain.
3. In a small bowl, whisk six eggs and the remaining salt and pepper until blended. Return sausage to skillet. Pour in egg mixture; cook and stir until eggs are thickened and no liquid egg remains.
4. Unfold each puff pastry sheet onto a 12x10-in. sheet of parchment paper. Spread grits to within ½ in. of edges. Spoon sausage mixture over half of grits on each pastry. Fold pastries over sausage mixture to enclose; press

edges with a fork to seal. Transfer to a baking sheet.
5. In a small bowl, whisk remaining egg and water; brush over pastries. If desired, top with additional ground pepper. Bake 30-35 minutes or until golden brown. Let stand 10 minutes. Cut each pastry into four pieces.

SCRAMBLED EGG HASH BROWN CUPS

These cuties manage to pack all of your favorite breakfast foods—eggs, hash browns and bacon—into one single serving-size cup. Grab one and get mingling.
—TALON DIMARE BULLHEAD CITY, AZ

PREP: 10 MIN. • **BAKE:** 25 MIN.
MAKES: 1 DOZEN

- 1 package (20 ounces) refrigerated Southwest-style shredded hash brown potatoes
- 6 large eggs
- ½ cup 2% milk
- ⅛ teaspoon salt
- 1 tablespoon butter
- 10 thick-sliced bacon strips, cooked and crumbled
- 1¼ cups shredded cheddar-Monterey Jack cheese, divided

1. Preheat the oven to 400°. Divide potatoes among 12 greased muffin cups; press onto bottoms and up sides to form cups. Bake 18-20 minutes or until light golden brown.
2. Meanwhile, in a small bowl, whisk eggs, milk and salt. In a large nonstick skillet, heat butter over medium heat. Pour in egg mixture; cook and stir until eggs are thickened and no liquid egg remains. Stir in bacon and ¾ cup cheese. Spoon into cups; sprinkle with remaining ½ cup cheese.
3. Bake 3-5 minutes or until the cheese is melted. Cool 5 minutes before removing from pan.

**SCRAMBLED EGG
HASH BROWN CUPS**

SOUPS & SANDWICHES

Cozy up with terrifically scrumptious soups and sandwiches. Many of these are fast fixes for when you're in a pinch and still want a flavorful meal, and some you can make ahead and freeze to enjoy later. If you're looking for a fresh take on lunch or dinner, this is where it's at. Enjoy!

PORK & BEEF BARBECUE

It's the combination of beef stew meat and tender pork that keeps folks asking about these tangy sandwiches. Add a lettuce leaf and a tomato slice for a crisp contrast.

—**CORBIN DETGEN** BUCHANAN, MI

PREP: 15 MIN. • **COOK:** 6 HOURS
MAKES: 12 SERVINGS

- 1 can (6 ounces) tomato paste
- ½ cup packed brown sugar
- ¼ cup chili powder
- ¼ cup cider vinegar
- 2 teaspoons Worcestershire sauce
- 1 teaspoon salt
- 1½ pounds beef stew meat, cut into ¾-inch cubes
- 1½ pounds pork chop suey meat or pork tenderloin, cut into ¾-inch cubes
- 3 medium green peppers, chopped
- 2 large onions, chopped
- 12 sandwich buns, split
  Lettuce and tomatoes, optional

1. In a 5-qt. slow cooker, combine the first six ingredients. Stir in beef, pork, green peppers and onions. Cover and cook on low for 6-8 hours or until the meat is tender.

2. Shred the meat with two forks. Serve on buns, adding lettuce and tomatoes if desired.

★ ★ ★ ★ ★ **READER REVIEW**

"This was very easy and tasted great. It also made the house smell great while cooking. I used a frozen pepper and onion blend. I served it with slaw, baked beans and a pickle."

CKLEE1403 TASTEOFHOME.COM

CAJUN CORN
SOUP

CAJUN CORN SOUP

I found this recipe years ago and substituted Cajun stewed tomatoes for a bolder taste. I prepare my soup for out-of-state guests who want to try Cajun food. I prefer it spicy, but feel free to adjust the ingredients and seasonings to suit your own taste.
—**SUE FONTENOT** KINDER, LA

PREP: 20 MIN. • **COOK:** 1 HOUR 20 MIN.
MAKES: 12-14 SERVINGS

- 1 **cup chopped onion**
- 1 **cup chopped green pepper**
- 6 **green onions, sliced**
- ½ **cup canola oil**
- ½ **cup all-purpose flour**
- 3 **cups water**
- 2 **packages (16 ounces each) frozen corn**
- 1½ **pounds smoked sausage, cut into ¼-inch pieces**
- 3 **cups cubed fully cooked ham**
- 1 **can (14½ ounces) stewed tomatoes**
- 2 **cups chopped peeled tomatoes**
- 1 **can (6 ounces) tomato paste**
- ⅛ **teaspoon cayenne pepper or to taste**
  Salt to taste
  Hot pepper sauce to taste

1. In a Dutch oven, saute the onion, green pepper and green onions in oil for 5-6 minutes or until tender. Stir in flour and cook until bubbly. Gradually add the water; bring to a boil. Add the corn, sausage, ham, tomatoes, tomato paste, cayenne, salt and pepper sauce.
2. Reduce heat; simmer, uncovered, for 1 hour, stirring occasionally.

★ ★ ★ ★ ★ **5 STAR TIP**
Cayenne pepper is a ground, or powdered, spice that's popular in Cajun cuisine and many others. Also commonly known as ground red pepper, it yields a pungent, hot flavor. Add to soups, stews, chili, sauces, beans, poultry, meat and seafood when you'd like a little heat.

QUICK & EASY TURKEY SLOPPY JOES

FAST FIX ▶
QUICK & EASY TURKEY SLOPPY JOES

When I was first married, I found this simple sloppy joe recipe and adjusted it to taste. The fresh bell pepper and red onion give it a wonderful flavor.
—**KALLEE TWINER** MARYVILLE, TN

START TO FINISH: 30 MIN.
MAKES: 8 SERVINGS

- 1 **pound lean ground turkey**
- 1 **large red onion, chopped**
- 1 **large green pepper, chopped**
- 1 **can (8 ounces) tomato sauce**
- ½ **cup barbecue sauce**
- 1 **teaspoon dried oregano**
- 1 **teaspoon ground cumin**
- 1 **teaspoon chili powder**
- ¼ **teaspoon salt**
- 8 **hamburger buns, split**

1. In a large skillet, cook the turkey, onion and pepper over medium heat 6-8 minutes or until the turkey is no longer pink and vegetables are tender, breaking up turkey into crumbles.
2. Stir in tomato sauce, barbecue sauce and seasonings. Bring to a boil. Reduce heat; simmer, uncovered, 10 minutes to allow flavors to blend, stirring occasionally. Serve on buns.

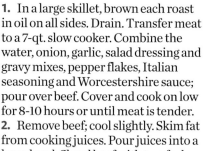

MOM'S ITALIAN BEEF SANDWICHES

My mom made the best Italian beef. I've added to it over the years, but it's still her recipe. She made this for family reunions, and there were never any leftovers.
—**MARY MCVEY** COLFAX, NC

PREP: 20 MIN. • **COOK:** 8 HOURS
MAKES: 16 SERVINGS

- 1 boneless beef rump roast or bottom round roast (2 pounds), halved
- 1 boneless beef chuck roast (2 pounds), halved
- 1 beef sirloin tip roast (1 pound)
- 2 tablespoons canola oil
- 2 cups water
- 1 medium onion, chopped
- 4 garlic cloves, minced
- 2 envelopes Italian salad dressing mix
- 1 envelope zesty Italian salad dressing mix
- 1 envelope (0.87 ounce) brown gravy mix
- 1 to 2 tablespoons crushed red pepper flakes
- 1 tablespoon Italian seasoning
- 2 teaspoons Worcestershire sauce
- 16 hoagie buns, split
   Sliced provolone cheese, optional
   Giardiniera, optional

1. In a large skillet, brown each roast in oil on all sides. Drain. Transfer meat to a 7-qt. slow cooker. Combine the water, onion, garlic, salad dressing and gravy mixes, pepper flakes, Italian seasoning and Worcestershire sauce; pour over beef. Cover and cook on low for 8-10 hours or until meat is tender.
2. Remove beef; cool slightly. Skim fat from cooking juices. Pour juices into a large bowl. Shred beef with two forks; add to bowl. Using a slotted spoon, place ½ cup on each bun. Top with cheese and giardiniera if desired.
FREEZE OPTION *Cool the meat and juices; transfer to freezer containers. Freeze for up to 3 months. To use, thaw in the refrigerator overnight. Place in a Dutch oven; heat through. Using a slotted spoon, place ½ cup on each bun. Top with cheese and giardiniera if desired.*

MOM'S ITALIAN BEEF SANDWICHES

(5) INGREDIENTS FAST FIX

SIMPLE CHICKEN SOUP

I revised a recipe that my family loved so it would be lighter and easier to make. It's a hearty and healthy meal that I serve with a green salad and fresh bread.
—**SUE WEST** ALVORD, TX

START TO FINISH: 20 MIN.
MAKES: 6 SERVINGS

- 2 cans (14½ ounces each) reduced-sodium chicken broth
- 1 tablespoon dried minced onion
- 1 package (16 ounces) frozen mixed vegetables
- 2 cups cubed cooked chicken breast
- 2 cans (10¾ ounces each) reduced-fat reduced-sodium condensed cream of chicken soup, undiluted

In a large saucepan, bring the broth and onion to a boil. Reduce the heat. Add the vegetables; cover and cook 6-8 minutes or until crisp-tender. Stir in chicken and soup; heat through.

AVOCADO QUESADILLAS

Avocado slices give quesadillas a nutritional boost and, fortunately, my son likes them, too. Add chicken or beef for extra protein.

—DEBBIE LIMAS NORTH ANDOVER, MA

START TO FINISH: 20 MIN.
MAKES: 4 SERVINGS (2 QUESADILLAS PER SERVING)

- 1 **tablespoon canola oil**
- 16 **corn tortillas (6 inches)**
- 2 **cups shredded Mexican cheese blend**
- 1 **cup pico de gallo**
- 1 **large ripe avocado, peeled and thinly sliced**
- 3 **tablespoons minced fresh cilantro**
  Additional pico de gallo

1. Grease a griddle with oil; heat over medium heat. Lightly sprinkle the tortillas with water to moisten.
2. Place eight tortillas on griddle; sprinkle with cheese. After cheese has melted slightly, top with 1 cup pico de gallo, avocado and cilantro. Top with remaining tortillas.
3. Cook for 3-4 minutes on each side or until lightly browned and cheese is melted. Serve the dish with additional pico de gallo.

★ ★ ★ ★ ★ **READER REVIEW**

"This recipe is quick and easy to prepare. The quesadillas taste delicious. Even the carnivores in the family didn't seem to notice the lack of meat!"

TOOLBARSCO TASTEOFHOME.COM

AVOCADO
QUESADILLAS

CARAMELIZED HAM & SWISS BUNS

My next-door neighbor shared her version of this recipe with me. You can assemble the sandwiches in advance and bake them right before company arrives. The combination of poppy seeds, ham, cheese, horseradish and brown sugar makes it simply delicious!

—**IRIS WEIHEMULLER** BAXTER, MN

PREP: 25 MIN. + CHILLING • **BAKE:** 30 MIN.
MAKES: 1 DOZEN

- 1 package (12 ounces) Hawaiian sweet rolls, split
- ½ cup horseradish sauce
- 12 slices deli ham
- 6 slices Swiss cheese, halved
- ½ cup butter, cubed
- 2 tablespoons finely chopped onion
- 2 tablespoons brown sugar
- 1 tablespoon spicy brown mustard
- 2 teaspoons poppy seeds
- 1½ teaspoons Worcestershire sauce
- ¼ teaspoon garlic powder

1. Spread the roll bottoms with horseradish sauce. Layer with ham and cheese; replace tops. Arrange in a single layer in a greased 9-in. square baking pan.

2. In a small skillet, heat butter over medium-high heat. Add onion; cook and stir 1-2 minutes or until tender. Stir in remaining ingredients. Pour over the rolls. Refrigerate, covered, several hours or overnight.

3. Preheat the oven to 350°. Bake, covered, 25 minutes. Bake, uncovered, 5-10 minutes longer or until buns are golden brown.

HOW TO SPLIT BUNS

Place one hand over the top of the buns to steady. Using a long serrated knife, gently cut buns horizontally. Carefully remove the top half to separate. Place the bottom half in a baking dish or as recipe directs.

CARAMELIZED HAM & SWISS BUNS

FAST FIX ▶

HEARTY CHICKEN & WILD RICE SOUP

Garlic and herb cream cheese adds subtle notes of flavor to this creamy rice soup. On a chilly day, it's like having a bowlful of comfort.

—**SHELISA TERRY** HENDERSON, NV

START TO FINISH: 25 MIN.
MAKES: 6 SERVINGS (2¼ QUARTS)

- 1 package (6.2 ounces) fast-cooking long grain and wild rice mix
- 2 cans (10¾ ounces each) condensed cream of chicken and mushroom soup, undiluted
- 3 cups 2% milk
- 2 packages (6 ounces each) ready-to-use grilled chicken breast strips
- 2 cups frozen California-blend vegetables, thawed and coarsely chopped
- ¾ cup spreadable garlic and herb cream cheese

Prepare rice mix according to package directions using a Dutch oven. Stir in the remaining ingredients and heat through.

FAST FIX ▶

CRISPY BUFFALO CHICKEN WRAPS

I'm big on wraps, even when I go out to eat. As a busy stay-at-home mom, I rely on these family favorites a lot. They're so good with chips and salsa on the side.

—**CHRISTINA ADDISON** BLANCHESTER, OH

START TO FINISH: 30 MIN.
MAKES: 4 SERVINGS

- 1 package (12 ounces) frozen popcorn chicken
- 1 package (8 ounces) shredded lettuce
- 2 medium tomatoes, finely chopped
- 1 cup shredded cheddar cheese
- ⅓ cup Buffalo wing sauce
- 4 flour tortillas (10 inches), warmed Ranch or chipotle ranch salad dressing, optional

1. Cook chicken according to package directions; coarsely chop the chicken. Using a large bowl, mix the chicken, lettuce, tomatoes and cheese. Drizzle with wing sauce; toss to coat.
2. Spoon 1½ cups of chicken mixture down center of each tortilla. Fold the bottom of tortilla over filling; fold both sides to close. Serve immediately with salad dressing if desired.

FAST FIX ▶

BEST LASAGNA SOUP

All the traditional flavors of lasagna come together in this heartwarming soup. Serve with a crusty loaf of bread.

—**SHERYL OLENICK** DEMAREST, NJ

START TO FINISH: 30 MIN.
MAKES: 8 SERVINGS (2¾ QUARTS)

- 1 pound lean ground beef (90% lean)
- 1 large green pepper, chopped
- 1 medium onion, chopped
- 2 garlic cloves, minced
- 2 cans (14½ ounces each) diced tomatoes, undrained
- 2 cans (14½ ounces each) reduced-sodium beef broth
- 1 can (8 ounces) tomato sauce
- 1 cup frozen corn
- ¼ cup tomato paste
- 2 teaspoons Italian seasoning
- ¼ teaspoon pepper
- 2½ cups uncooked spiral pasta
- ½ cup shredded Parmesan cheese

1. In a large saucepan, cook the beef, green pepper and onion over medium heat 6-8 minutes or until meat is no longer pink, breaking up beef into crumbles. Add garlic; cook 1 minute longer. Drain.
2. Stir in the tomatoes, broth, tomato sauce, corn, tomato paste, Italian seasoning and pepper. Bring to a boil. Stir in pasta. Return to a boil. Reduce heat; simmer, covered, 10-12 minutes or until the pasta is tender. Sprinkle with cheese.

CONTEST-WINNING EASY MINESTRONE

This recipe is special because it's one of the few dinners my entire family loves. And I can feel good about serving it because it is nutritious and low in fat.

—**LAUREN BRENNAN** HOOD RIVER, OR

PREP: 25 MIN. • **COOK:** 40 MIN.
MAKES: 11 SERVINGS (2¾ QUARTS)

- 2 **large carrots, diced**
- 2 **celery ribs, chopped**
- 1 **medium onion, chopped**
- 1 **tablespoon olive oil**
- 1 **tablespoon butter**
- 2 **garlic cloves, minced**
- 2 **cans (14½ ounces each) reduced-sodium chicken broth**
- 2 **cans (8 ounces each) no-salt-added tomato sauce**
- 1 **can (16 ounces) kidney beans, rinsed and drained**
- 1 **can (15 ounces) chickpeas, rinsed and drained**
- 1 **can (14½ ounces) diced tomatoes, undrained**
- 1½ **cups shredded cabbage**
- 1 **tablespoon dried basil**
- 1½ **teaspoons dried parsley flakes**
- 1 **teaspoon dried oregano**
- ½ **teaspoon pepper**
- 1 **cup uncooked whole wheat elbow macaroni**
- 11 **teaspoons grated Parmesan cheese**

1. In a large saucepan, saute the carrots, celery and onion in oil and butter until tender. Add garlic; cook 1 minute longer.
2. Stir in broth, tomato sauce, beans, tomatoes, cabbage, basil, parsley, oregano and pepper. Bring to a boil. Reduce heat; cover and simmer for 15 minutes. Add the macaroni; cook, uncovered, 6-8 minutes or until macaroni and vegetables are tender.
3. Ladle soup into bowls. Sprinkle with cheese.

FREEZE OPTION *Before adding the cheese, freeze cooled soup in freezer containers. To use, partially thaw soup in the refrigerator overnight. Heat through in a saucepan, stirring occasionally and adding a little broth or water if necessary.*

CONTEST-WINNING
EASY MINESTRONE

PIZZA JOES

These Italian-style sloppy joes are an easy twist on the classic. You can prepare the meat early and keep it warm until it's time to eat.

—**JOANNE SCHLABACH** SHREVE, OH

START TO FINISH: 30 MIN.
MAKES: 6 SERVINGS

- 1 **pound lean ground beef (90% lean)**
- 1 **can (15 ounces) pizza sauce**
- 1 **teaspoon dried oregano**
- ½ **medium onion**
- ½ **medium green pepper**
- 1 **ounce sliced pepperoni**
- 6 **hamburger buns, split**
- ½ **cup shredded mozzarella cheese**
- ½ **cup sliced fresh mushrooms**

1. In a large skillet over medium heat, cook beef until no longer pink; drain. Stir in pizza sauce and oregano.
2. In a food processor, combine the onion, pepper and pepperoni; cover and process until chopped. Add to beef mixture. Simmer 20-25 minutes or until vegetables are tender. Spoon mixture onto buns. Top with cheese and mushrooms.

NORTH PACIFIC CHOWDER

Tender veggies and tarragon add fantastic flavor to this chunky fish chowder. It's one of the best I've ever tasted.

—**PAM WOOLGAR** QUALICUM BEACH, BC

PREP: 15 MIN. • **COOK:** 35 MIN.
MAKES: 9 SERVINGS (2¼ QUARTS)

- 8 **bacon strips**
- 1 **small onion, chopped**
- 1 **celery rib, chopped**
- 1 **carton (32 ounces) chicken broth**
- 4 **medium red potatoes, cubed**
- 2 **tablespoons all-purpose flour**
- 1 **pint half-and-half cream**
- 1 **pound halibut fillets, cubed**
- 1 **tablespoon minced fresh tarragon or 1 teaspoon dried tarragon**
- ½ **teaspoon salt**
- ¼ **teaspoon pepper**
    Tarragon sprigs, optional

1. In a large saucepan over medium heat, cook bacon until crisp. Drain, reserving 1 teaspoon of drippings. Crumble bacon and set aside. Saute onion and celery in the drippings. Add broth and potatoes. Bring to a boil. Reduce heat; cover and cook for 15-20 minutes or until potatoes are tender.
2. Combine flour and cream until smooth; gradually stir it into the soup. Bring to a boil; then cook and stir for 2 minutes. Stir in halibut, tarragon, salt, pepper and crumbled bacon. Reduce heat; simmer, uncovered, for 5-10 minutes or until fish flakes easily with a fork. Garnish with tarragon sprigs if desired.

★ ★ ★ ★ ★ 5 STAR TIP

A chowder is a chunky, thick, rich soup frequently made with seafood or vegetables (such as corn), but it can also be made with other meat. Chowders have a milk or cream base and may be thickened with flour. North Pacific Chowder can be very versatile. You can use it as a hearty base when making clam chowder or corn chowder.

BEEF STROGANOFF SANDWICHES

FAST FIX

BEEF STROGANOFF SANDWICHES

For an American take on classic Russian comfort food, we turn beef stroganoff into a sandwich. It comes together fast, and our family devours it.

—**ALISON GARCIA** BEATRICE, NE

START TO FINISH: 25 MIN.
MAKES: 6 SERVINGS

- 1 **pound ground beef**
- 1 **cup sliced fresh mushrooms**
- 1 **small green pepper, finely chopped**
- 1 **small onion, finely chopped**
- 1 **envelope ranch dip mix**
- ¾ **cup sour cream**
- 1 **loaf (about 8 ounces) French bread**
- 2 **cups shredded part-skim mozzarella cheese**

1. Preheat broiler. In a large skillet, cook beef, mushrooms, pepper and onion over medium-high heat 8-10 minutes or until beef is no longer pink, breaking up beef into crumbles; drain. Stir in dip mix and sour cream.
2. Cut French bread horizontally in half; place halves on a baking sheet, cut side up. Broil 3-4 in. from heat 1-2 minutes or until lightly toasted. Remove from broiler.
3. Spoon the beef mixture over the bread. Sprinkle with cheese. Broil 1-2 minutes longer or until cheese is lightly browned. To serve, cut each into three pieces.

FAST FIX ▶
BLT WRAPS

My mom used to make these delicious wraps for all of the kids and grandkids on summer days at the lake. Nowadays, we love to pack them along for picnics and days in the park.
—**SHELLY BURKS** BRIGHTON, MO

START TO FINISH: 15 MIN.
MAKES: 8 SERVINGS

- 16 ready-to-serve fully cooked bacon strips, warmed if desired
- 8 flour tortillas (8 inches), room temperature
- 4 cups chopped lettuce
- 2 cups chopped tomatoes (3 small tomatoes)
- 2 cups shredded cheddar cheese
- ½ cup ranch salad dressing

Place two of the bacon strips across the center of each tortilla. Top with lettuce, tomatoes and cheese; drizzle with salad dressing. Fold the bottom and sides of the tortilla over the filling and roll up.
TO MAKE AHEAD *Assemble wraps without heating bacon; wrap in plastic wrap and store in the refrigerator for up to 2 days.*

FREEZE IT
GRANDMA'S PEA SOUP

Mondays were wash days at our house when I was a child, and because they were busy days, we ate soup. My grandma's pea soup was a family favorite. What makes it different from other pea soups I have tried is the addition of whole peas, homemade spaetzle-like dumplings and sausage.
—**CAROLE TALCOTT** DAHINDA, IL

PREP: 15 MIN. + SOAKING
COOK: 2¾ HOURS
MAKES: 16 SERVINGS (4 QUARTS)

- ½ pound dried whole peas
- ½ pound dried green split peas
- 1 meaty ham bone
- 3 quarts water
- 1 large onion, chopped
- 1 medium carrot, chopped
- 2 celery ribs, chopped
- ½ cup chopped celery leaves
- 1 teaspoon bouquet garni (mixed herbs)
- 1 tablespoon minced fresh parsley
- 1 bay leaf
- 1 teaspoon salt
- ¼ teaspoon pepper
- ½ pound smoked sausage, chopped, optional

SPAETZLE DUMPLINGS
- 1 cup all-purpose flour
- 1 large egg, beaten
- ⅓ cup water

1. Cover peas with water and soak overnight. Drain, rinse and place in a Dutch oven.
2. Add the ham bone, water and remaining soup ingredients except sausage and dumplings. Bring to a boil. Reduce heat; cover and simmer 2 to 2½ hours.
3. Remove ham bone and skim fat. Remove meat from bone; dice. Add ham and, if desired, sausage to pan.
4. For dumplings, place flour in a small bowl. Make a depression in the center of the flour; add egg and water and stir until smooth.
5. Place a colander with 3⁄16-in.-diameter holes over simmering soup; transfer dough to the colander and press through with a wooden spoon. Cook, uncovered, 10-15 minutes. Discard bay leaf.
FREEZE OPTION *Prepare soup without dumplings and freeze in serving-size portions.*

BLT WRAPS

GRANDMA'S
PEA SOUP

QUICK PEPPERONI CALZONES

FAST FIX ▶

QUICK PEPPERONI CALZONES

These toasty pockets come together in no time. Take them to the next level by sprinkling Parmesan and herbs on top.

—**SHANNON ROUM** MILWAUKEE, WI

START TO FINISH: 30 MIN.
MAKES: 4 SERVINGS

- 1 **cup chopped pepperoni**
- ½ **cup pasta sauce with meat**
- ¼ **cup shredded part-skim mozzarella cheese**
- 1 **loaf (1 pound) frozen bread dough, thawed**
- 1 **to 2 tablespoons 2% milk**
- 1 **tablespoon grated Parmesan cheese**
- ½ **teaspoon Italian seasoning**

1. Preheat oven to 350°. In a small bowl, mix pepperoni, pasta sauce and mozzarella cheese.
2. On a lightly floured surface, divide dough into four portions. Roll each into a 6-in. circle; top each with a scant ⅓ cup pepperoni mixture. Fold dough over filling; pinch edges to seal. Place on a greased baking sheet.
3. Brush milk over tops of calzones; sprinkle with Parmesan cheese and Italian seasoning. Bake 20-25 minutes or until golden brown.

★ ★ ★ ★ ★ **READER REVIEW**

"Delicious! I made these for my parents and our family of six. I used my breadmaker to make the calzone dough. Besides the pepperoni filling, we also did pineapple and Canadian bacon. We will be making these a lot!"

POWELLCOU TASTEOFHOME.COM

TURKEY & SWISS BISCUIT SLIDERS

I love to come up with new recipe ideas; I'm always experimenting. One of my favorite things to make is buttermilk biscuits, and I created this sandwich combo to perfectly complement the homemade biscuits.
—**CINDY ESPOSITO** BLOOMFIELD, NJ

PREP: 35 MIN. + RISING • **BAKE:** 10 MIN.
MAKES: 16 SERVINGS

- 1 package (¼ ounce) active dry yeast
- ⅔ cup warm buttermilk (110° to 115°)
- 2 tablespoons warm water (110° to 115°)
- 2 cups bread flour
- 3 tablespoons sugar
- 1½ teaspoons baking powder
- ½ teaspoon salt
- ½ cup shortening
- ¾ pound thinly sliced deli smoked turkey
- ½ pound sliced Swiss cheese
  Dijon mustard, optional

1. In a small bowl, dissolve yeast in warm buttermilk and water. Place flour, sugar, baking powder and salt in a food processor; pulse until blended. Add the shortening; pulse until the shortening is the size of peas. While processing, gradually add the yeast mixture and process just until dough forms a ball.

2. Turn dough onto a lightly floured surface; knead 8-10 times. Pat or roll to ½-in. thickness; cut with a floured 2-in. biscuit cutter. Place 2 in. apart on greased baking sheets. Let rise until almost doubled, about 30 minutes.

3. Preheat oven to 425°. Bake biscuits 7-9 minutes or until golden brown. Remove to wire racks to cool slightly. Preheat broiler.

4. Split biscuits in half; place bottoms on greased baking sheets. Layer with turkey and cheese. Broil 3-4 in. from heat 2-3 minutes or until the cheese is melted. Replace tops. If desired, serve with mustard.

POTATO MINESTRONE

SLOW COOKER
POTATO MINESTRONE

Even the die-hard meat lovers in your family won't be able to get enough of this savory meatless soup. If you prefer a thicker consistency, mash half of the garbanzo beans before adding them to the slow cooker.
—**PAULA ZSIRAY** LOGAN, UT

PREP: 10 MIN. • **COOK:** 8½ HOURS
MAKES: 12 SERVINGS (ABOUT 3 QUARTS)

- 2 cans (14½ ounces each) chicken or vegetable broth
- 1 can (28 ounces) crushed tomatoes
- 1 can (16 ounces) kidney beans, rinsed and drained
- 1 can (15 ounces) garbanzo beans or chickpeas, rinsed and drained
- 1 can (14½ ounces) beef broth
- 2 cups frozen cubed hash brown potatoes, thawed
- 1 tablespoon dried minced onion
- 1 tablespoon dried parsley flakes
- 1 teaspoon salt
- 1 teaspoon dried oregano
- ½ teaspoon garlic powder
- ½ teaspoon dried basil
- ½ teaspoon dried marjoram
- 1 package (10 ounces) frozen chopped spinach, thawed and drained
- 2 cups frozen peas and carrots, thawed

Using a 5-qt. slow cooker, combine the first 13 ingredients. Cover and cook on low for 8 hours. Stir in spinach and the peas and carrots; cook 30 minutes or until heated through.

SOUTHWEST BARLEY & LENTIL SOUP

My family has been making lentil soup every New Year's since I was a child. We have tweaked the recipe over time, and all our family and friends love it.

—KRISTEN HEIGL STATEN ISLAND, NY

PREP: 15 MIN. • **COOK:** 55 MIN.
MAKES: 12 SERVINGS (4½ QUARTS)

- 1 **tablespoon olive oil**
- 1 **package (14 ounces) smoked kielbasa or Polish sausage, halved lengthwise and sliced**
- 4 **medium carrots, chopped**
- 1 **medium onion, chopped**
- 2 **garlic cloves, minced**
- ¾ **teaspoon ground cumin**
- 1 **can (28 ounces) crushed tomatoes**
- 1 **package (16 ounces) dried lentils, rinsed**
- 1 **can (15 ounces) black beans, rinsed and drained**
- ¾ **cup medium pearl barley**
- ½ **cup frozen corn**
- 10 **cups reduced-sodium chicken broth**

1. In a 6-qt. stockpot, heat the oil over medium heat. Add the kielbasa; cook and stir 6-8 minutes or until browned. Remove the meat from the pan with a slotted spoon.

2. Add carrots and onion to same pot; cook and stir 6-8 minutes or until tender. Add garlic and cumin; cook 1 minute longer. Stir in kielbasa and remaining ingredients; bring to a boil. Reduce heat; simmer, covered, 35-45 minutes or until lentils and barley are tender, stirring occasionally.

SOUTHWEST BARLEY & LENTIL SOUP

CHUNKY BEEF & VEGETABLE SOUP

Nothing cures the winter blahs like hot soup, including this beefy one I first cooked up on a snowy day. Serve with artisan bread.
—**BILLY HENSLEY** MOUNT CARMEL, TN

PREP: 25 MIN. • **COOK:** 2¾ HOURS
MAKES: 8 SERVINGS (3 QUARTS)

- 1½ **pounds beef stew meat, cut into ½-inch pieces**
- 1 **teaspoon salt, divided**
- 1 **teaspoon salt-free seasoning blend, divided**
- ¾ **teaspoon pepper, divided**
- 2 **tablespoons olive oil, divided**
- 4 **large carrots, sliced**
- 1 **large onion, chopped**
- 1 **medium sweet red pepper, chopped**
- 1 **medium green pepper, chopped**
- 2 **garlic cloves, minced**
- 1 **cup Burgundy wine or additional reduced-sodium beef broth**
- 4 **cups reduced-sodium beef broth**
- 1 **can (14½ ounces) diced tomatoes, undrained**
- 2 **tablespoons tomato paste**
- 2 **tablespoons Worcestershire sauce**
- 1 **bay leaf**
- 4 **medium potatoes (about 2 pounds), cut into ½-inch cubes**

1. Sprinkle beef with ½ teaspoon each salt, seasoning blend and pepper. In a Dutch oven, heat 1 tablespoon oil over medium heat. Brown beef in batches. Remove from pan.
2. In same pan, heat remaining oil over medium heat. Add carrots, onion and peppers; cook and stir until carrots are crisp-tender. Add garlic; cook 1 minute longer.
3. Add wine; stir to loosen browned bits. Stir in broth, tomatoes, tomato paste, Worcestershire sauce, bay leaf and remaining seasonings. Return beef to pan; bring to a boil. Reduce heat; simmer, covered, 2 hours.
4. Add potatoes; cook 30-40 minutes longer or until beef and potatoes are tender. Skim fat and discard bay leaf.

CUBAN PANINI

A Cuban sandwich is a twist on the traditional ham and cheese, usually with ham, Swiss cheese, pickles and other condiments, and sometimes, as in this tasty version, smoked deli turkey.
—**JANET SANDERS** PINE MOUNTAIN, GA

PREP: 20 MIN. • **COOK:** 5 MIN./BATCH
MAKES: 4 SERVINGS

- 2 **garlic cloves, minced**
- ½ **teaspoon olive oil**
- ½ **cup reduced-fat mayonnaise**
- 8 **slices artisan bread**
- 8 **thick slices deli smoked turkey**
- 4 **slices deli ham**
- 8 **slices Swiss cheese**
- 12 **dill pickle slices**
- 1 **cup fresh baby spinach**

1. In a small skillet, cook and stir garlic in oil over medium-high heat until tender. Cool.
2. Stir garlic into mayonnaise; spread over bread slices. Layer four slices of bread with turkey, ham, cheese, pickles and spinach; close sandwiches.
3. Cook on a panini maker or indoor grill for 2-3 minutes or until browned and cheese is melted.

★ ★ ★ ★ ★ **READER REVIEW**

"Have made this more than once for quite a few people. It's the new favorite. Can't believe how so many different flavors can come together to make this so incredible!"

MISSV TASTEOFHOME.COM

SAUSAGE BREAD SANDWICHES

4. Transfer to greased baking sheets, seam side down. In a small bowl, whisk egg with water; brush over loaves. Bake 20-25 minutes or until golden brown and heated through. Cool 5 minutes before slicing.
FREEZE OPTION *Cool the cooked sandwiches 1 hour on wire racks. Cut each sandwich into thirds; wrap each securely in foil. Freeze until serving. To reheat the sandwiches in the oven, place wrapped frozen sandwiches on a baking sheet. Heat in a preheated 375° oven for 20-25 minutes or until they are heated through.*

PASTA PIZZA SOUP

A steaming bowl of this soup hits the spot on chilly days, which we have in abundance here in Alaska. A bit of oregano adds fast flavor to the pleasant blend of tender vegetables, pasta spirals and ground beef.
—**LINDA FOX** SOLDOTNA, AK

PREP: 10 MIN. • **COOK:** 30 MIN.
MAKES: 8 SERVINGS (ABOUT 2 QUARTS)

- 1 **pound ground beef**
- 1¾ **cups sliced fresh mushrooms**
- 1 **medium onion, chopped**
- 1 **celery rib, thinly sliced**
- 1 **garlic clove, minced**
- 4 **cups water**
- 1 **can (14½ ounces) Italian diced tomatoes, undrained**
- 2 **medium carrots, sliced**
- 4 **teaspoons beef bouillon granules**
- 1 **bay leaf**
- 1½ **teaspoons dried oregano**
- 1½ **cups cooked tricolor spiral pasta**

1. In a large saucepan over medium heat, cook the the beef, mushrooms, onion and celery until the meat is no longer pink. Add garlic; cook 1 minute longer. Drain.
2. Stir in the water, tomatoes, carrots, bouillon, bay leaf and oregano. Bring to a boil. Reduce the heat; cover and simmer for 20-25 minutes or until carrots are tender. Stir in pasta; heat through. Discard bay leaf.

FREEZE IT
SAUSAGE BREAD SANDWICHES

I make these sandwiches in my spare time and freeze them so they're ready when needed. We use them for tailgating when we attend Kansas State games.
—**DONNA ROBERTS** MANHATTAN, KS

PREP: 30 MIN. • **BAKE:** 20 MIN.
MAKES: 4 SANDWICH LOAVES (3 PIECES EACH)

- 1 **package (16 ounces) hot roll mix**
- 2 **pounds reduced-fat bulk pork sausage**
- 2 **tablespoons dried parsley flakes**
- 2 **teaspoons garlic powder**
- 1 **teaspoon onion powder**
- ½ **teaspoon dried oregano**
- 2 **cups shredded part-skim mozzarella cheese**
- ½ **cup grated Parmesan cheese**
- 1 **large egg**
- 1 **tablespoon water**

1. Preheat oven to 350°. Prepare the roll mix dough according to package directions.
2. Meanwhile, in a large skillet, cook the sausage over medium heat for 8-10 minutes or until no longer pink, breaking into crumbles; drain. Stir in the seasonings.
3. Divide dough into four portions. On a lightly floured surface, roll each into a 14x8-in. rectangle. Top each with 1¼ cups sausage mixture to within 1 inch of edges; sprinkle with ½ cup of the mozzarella cheese and 2 tablespoons Parmesan cheese. Roll up jelly-roll style, starting with a long side; pinch seams and ends to seal.

GYRO-STYLE TURKEY PITAS

For a unique twist on gyros, try these tasty pitas stuffed with turkey, sauerkraut and a zesty cream sauce.

—WANDA ALLENDE ORLANDO, FL

START TO FINISH: 30 MIN.
MAKES: 4 SERVINGS

- 1 **pound ground turkey**
- 1 **small onion, chopped**
- ½ **cup sauerkraut, rinsed and well drained**
- 2 **tablespoons brown sugar**
- ½ **teaspoon salt**
- ⅔ **cup sour cream**
- 3 **tablespoons mayonnaise**
- 2 **tablespoons prepared ranch salad dressing**
- 1 **small tomato, chopped**
- ⅓ **cup chopped cucumber**
- 4 **pita breads (6 inches), halved and warmed**
  Shredded lettuce

1. In a large skillet, cook the turkey, onion, sauerkraut, brown sugar and salt over medium heat until meat is no longer pink; drain.

2. Using a small bowl, combine the sour cream, mayonnaise and ranch salad dressing. Stir in the tomato and cucumber. Fill pita halves with turkey mixture, lettuce and sauce.

★ ★ ★ ★ ★ **READER REVIEW**

"Easy, nice blend of flavors. Would definitely make again. Add an apple on the side, a glass of milk and dinner is complete."

LAURIEBIGWOOD TASTEOFHOME.COM

ITALIAN SAUSAGE & ZUCCHINI SOUP

Everyone in my family enjoys this soup. Sometimes I use mini farfalle in this soup because my grandchildren say it looks like tiny butterflies. The recipe also works in a slow cooker.

—NANCY MURPHY MOUNT DORA, FL

START TO FINISH: 30 MIN.
MAKES: 6 SERVINGS

- ½ **pound bulk Italian sausage**
- 1 **medium onion, chopped**
- 1 **medium green pepper, chopped**
- 3 **cups beef broth**
- 1 **can (14½ ounces) diced tomatoes, undrained**
- 1 **tablespoon minced fresh basil or 1 teaspoon dried basil**
- 1 **tablespoon minced fresh parsley or 1 teaspoon dried parsley flakes**
- 1 **medium zucchini, cut into ½-inch pieces**
- ½ **cup uncooked orzo pasta**

1. In a large saucepan, cook sausage, onion and pepper over medium heat 4-6 minutes or until the sausage is no longer pink and vegetables are tender, breaking up sausage into crumbles; drain sausage mixture.

2. Add the broth, tomatoes, basil and parsley; bring the mix to a boil. Stir in the zucchini and orzo; return to a boil. Cook, covered, 10-12 minutes or until zucchini and orzo are tender.

ITALIAN SAUSAGE & ZUCCHINI SOUP

HOW TO MAKE A TOPPER TIN

Use a muffin tin to double as a handy condiment caddy. Fill each compartment with your favorite toppings, and add mini serving spoons so guests can load up their burgers, brats or hot dogs as they like.

BBQ BACON BURGERS

BBQ BACON BURGERS

Every family has a burger of choice, and this is ours. It's stacked tall with bacon and crunchy onion rings.
—**PAULA HOMER** NAMPA, ID

START TO FINISH: 30 MIN.
MAKES: 6 SERVINGS

- 12 **frozen onion rings**
- 2 **pounds ground beef**
- ¼ **teaspoon garlic salt**
- ¼ **teaspoon pepper**
- 6 **slices pepper jack cheese**
- 6 **hamburger buns, split and toasted**
- 1 **cup barbecue sauce**
- 6 **cooked bacon strips**
  Optional toppings: lettuce leaves, sliced tomato and dill pickles

1. Bake onion rings according to the package directions. Meanwhile, in a large bowl, combine the beef, garlic salt and pepper; mix it lightly but thoroughly. Shape mixture into six ¾-in.-thick patties.

2. In a large nonstick skillet, cook the burgers over medium heat for 5-7 minutes on each side or until a thermometer reads 160°, adding cheese during last minute of cooking. Serve on buns with barbecue sauce, bacon and onion rings, and other toppings as desired.

★ ★ ★ ★ ★ **READER REVIEW**

"These were delicious and very easy to put together. Great for family cookouts."
ANGEL182009 TASTEOFHOME.COM

MUSHROOM TORTELLINI SOUP

MUSHROOM TORTELLINI SOUP

This nutritious veggie soup eats like a meal thanks to cheese tortellini. It's a real comfort on a cold or rainy day.
—**JEN LUCAS** BALDWINVILLE, MA

START TO FINISH: 25 MIN.
MAKES: 6 SERVINGS

- 2 **tablespoons olive oil**
- ½ **pound sliced fresh mushrooms**
- 2 **garlic cloves, minced**
- 4 **cups vegetable broth**
- 1 **can (14½ ounces) diced tomatoes with basil, oregano and garlic, undrained**
- 1 **package (19 ounces) frozen cheese tortellini**
- 2 **cups fresh baby spinach, coarsely chopped**
- ⅛ **teaspoon pepper**
  Shredded Parmesan cheese, optional

1. In a Dutch oven, heat the oil over medium-high heat. Add mushrooms; cook and stir for 6-8 minutes or until tender. Add the garlic and cook for 1 minute longer.

2. Add broth and tomatoes; bring to a boil. Add tortellini; cook, uncovered, 3-4 minutes or just until tortellini float (do not boil). Stir in spinach and pepper; cook just until spinach is wilted. If desired, serve with cheese.

ROASTED TOMATO & PEPPER SOUP

You'll want to capture everything the roasted tomatoes, pepper, onion and garlic have to offer in this colorful soup. Add cubed bread pieces to soak up some of the soup.

—**DEBBY HARDEN** LANSING, MI

PREP: 45 MIN. • **COOK:** 45 MIN.
MAKES: 4 SERVINGS

- 2 **pounds plum tomatoes, halved lengthwise**
- 2 **medium sweet red peppers, quartered and seeded**
- 2 **medium onions, finely chopped**
- 2 **tablespoons olive oil**
- 3 **garlic cloves, minced**
- 2 **teaspoons ground cumin**
- 1 **teaspoon ground coriander**
- 1 **carton (32 ounces) reduced-sodium chicken broth**
- 3 **slices day-old French bread (1 inch thick), crusts removed and cubed**
- 1 **tablespoon balsamic vinegar**
- ¼ **teaspoon salt**
- ¼ **teaspoon pepper**
  Shaved Parmesan cheese

1. Place tomatoes and peppers, cut side down, in a 15x10x1-in. baking pan. Bake at 425° for 20 minutes. Turn tomatoes and peppers; bake 10-15 minutes longer or until skins are blistered and blackened.
2. Immediately place peppers and tomatoes in a large bowl; cover and let stand for 10 minutes. Peel off and discard skins; coarsely chop tomatoes and peppers.
3. In a large saucepan, saute onions in oil until tender. Add the garlic, cumin and coriander; saute 1 minute longer. Add the broth, tomatoes and peppers. Bring to a boil. Reduce heat; simmer, uncovered, for 30 minutes.
4. Stir in the bread, vinegar, salt and pepper; heat through. Sprinkle servings with cheese.

ROASTED TOMATO & PEPPER SOUP

CRISPY PITA BLT'S

Pack this sandwich full of fresh produce from your garden or a local farmers market. You'll wow lunch guests with just-picked flavor.

—**MARY MILLER** POPLARVILLE, MS

PREP: 35 MIN. • **BAKE:** 15 MIN.
MAKES: 4 SERVINGS

- ⅓ **cup mayonnaise**
- 1 **garlic clove, minced**
- ¼ **teaspoon grated lemon peel**
- ¼ **cup all-purpose flour**
- ¾ **cup fat-free milk**
- 1 **cup panko (Japanese) bread crumbs**
- 2 **medium yellow summer squash, cut into ¼-inch slices**
- 2 **jalapeno peppers, seeds removed and cut into ¼-inch slices**
  Cooking spray
- 8 **pita pocket halves**
- 8 **romaine leaves**
- 8 **slices tomato**
- 16 **cooked bacon strips, halved**

1. In a small bowl, mix mayonnaise, garlic and lemon peel. Cover and chill until serving.
2. Place flour, milk and bread crumbs in three separate shallow bowls. Coat squash and jalapeno slices with flour, then dip in milk and coat with bread crumbs. Place on baking sheets coated with cooking spray. Spritz vegetables with additional cooking spray.
3. Bake at 475° for 12-14 minutes or until golden brown, turning once.
4. Spread mayonnaise mixture inside pita halves; fill with lettuce, tomatoes, bacon and breaded vegetables. Serve immediately.

ONION BEEF AU JUS

Garlic, sweet onions and soy sauce make a flavorful juice for dipping these savory open-faced sandwiches. Any leftover beef makes delicious cold sandwiches, too.
—**MARILYN BROWN** WEST UNION, IA

PREP: 20 MIN.
BAKE: 2½ HOURS + STANDING
MAKES: 12 SERVINGS

- 1   beef rump roast or bottom round roast (4 pounds)
- 2   tablespoons canola oil
- 2   large sweet onions, cut into ¼-inch slices
- 6   tablespoons butter, softened, divided
- 5   cups water
- ½   cup reduced-sodium soy sauce
- 1   envelope onion soup mix
- 1   garlic clove, minced
- 1   teaspoon browning sauce, optional
- 1   loaf (1 pound) French bread
- 1   cup shredded Swiss cheese

1. In a Dutch oven over medium-high heat, brown roast on all sides in oil; drain. In a large skillet, saute onions in 2 tablespoons of butter until tender. Add the water, soy sauce, soup mix, garlic and, if desired, browning sauce. Pour over roast.

2. Cover and bake at 325° for about 2½ hours or until meat is tender.

3. Let meat stand for 10 minutes, then thinly slice. Return meat to pan juices. Split bread lengthwise; cut into 3-in. sections. Spread with remaining butter. Place on a baking sheet.

4. Broil bread 4-6 in. from the heat for 2-3 minutes or until golden brown. Top with beef and onions; sprinkle with cheese. Broil for 1-2 minutes or until the cheese is melted. Serve with pan juices.

ONION BEEF AU JUS

CHEESY BROCCOLI SOUP IN A BREAD BOWL

Try this creamy, rich, cheesy broccoli soup that tastes just like it's from a restaurant. My family requests it all the time. You can even make your own homemade bread bowls if you like. I have a great recipe on my blog, *Yammie's Noshery.*

—RACHEL PREUS MARSHALL, MI

PREP: 5 MIN. • **COOK:** 30 MIN.
MAKES: 6 SERVINGS

- ¼ **cup butter, cubed**
- ½ **cup chopped onion**
- 2 **garlic cloves, minced**
- 4 **cups fresh broccoli florets (about 8 ounces)**
- 1 **large carrot, finely chopped**
- 3 **cups chicken stock**
- 2 **cups half-and-half cream**
- 2 **bay leaves**
- ½ **teaspoon salt**
- ¼ **teaspoon ground nutmeg**
- ¼ **teaspoon pepper**
- ¼ **cup cornstarch**
- ¼ **cup water or additional chicken stock**
- 2½ **cups shredded cheddar cheese**
- 6 **small round bread loaves (about 8 ounces each)**

1. In a 6-qt. stockpot, heat butter over medium heat; saute onion and garlic until tender, 6-8 minutes. Stir in the broccoli, carrot, stock, cream and seasonings; bring to a boil. Simmer, uncovered, until the vegetables are tender, 10-12 minutes.
2. Mix cornstarch and water until smooth; stir into soup. Bring to a boil, stirring occasionally; cook and stir until thickened, 1-2 minutes. Remove bay leaves. Stir in cheese until melted.
3. Cut a slice off the top of each bread loaf; hollow out the bottoms, leaving ¼-in.-thick shells (save the removed bread for another use). Fill with soup just before serving.

HOW TO MAKE A BREAD BOWL

Cut a thin slice off top of bread loaf.

Hollow out bottom of loaf, leaving a ½-in.-thick shell.

Add soup, stew or chili when ready to serve.

**CHEESY BROCCOLI SOUP
IN A BREAD BOWL**

FAST FIX ▶

CHICKEN SALAD
PARTY SANDWICHES

My famous chicken salad arrives at the party chilled in a plastic container. When it's time to set out the food, I stir in the pecans and assemble the sandwiches. They're great for buffet-style potlucks.

—**TRISHA KRUSE** EAGLE, ID

START TO FINISH: 25 MIN.
MAKES: 15 SERVINGS

- 4 **cups cubed cooked chicken breast**
- 1½ **cups dried cranberries**
- 2 **celery ribs, finely chopped**
- 2 **green onions, thinly sliced**
- ¼ **cup chopped sweet pickles**
- 1 **cup fat-free mayonnaise**
- ½ **teaspoon curry powder**
- ¼ **teaspoon coarsely ground pepper**
- ½ **cup chopped pecans, toasted**
- 15 **whole wheat dinner rolls**
  Torn leaf lettuce

1. In a large bowl, combine the first five ingredients. In a small bowl, combine the mayonnaise, curry and pepper. Add to chicken mixture; toss to coat. Chill until serving.
2. Stir pecans into chicken salad. Serve on rolls lined with lettuce.

FAST FIX ▶

DELI BEEF SANDWICHES
WITH HORSERADISH
MAYONNAISE

Sweet cherry preserves balance the bold horseradish in this hearty beef sandwich. What a delicious noontime treat!

—**GREG FONTENOT** THE WOODLANDS, TX

START TO FINISH: 10 MIN.
MAKES: 4 SERVINGS

- ½ **cup mayonnaise**
- 2 **tablespoons cherry preserves**
- 4 **teaspoons prepared horseradish**
- 8 **slices whole wheat bread**
- ¾ **pound sliced deli roast beef**
- 4 **lettuce leaves**
- 1 **large tomato, thinly sliced**
  Dash each salt and pepper

In a small bowl, combine mayonnaise, preserves and horseradish. Spread 1 tablespoon over each of four bread slices. Layer the slides with roast beef, lettuce and tomato; sprinkle with salt and pepper. Spread the remaining mayonnaise mixture over remaining bread; place over top.

SLOW COOKER 🍲

RICH FRENCH ONION SOUP

When entertaining guests, I bring out this savory soup while we're waiting for the main course. I recommend sauteing the onions early in the day and letting the soup simmer until it's time to eat.

—**LINDA ADOLPH** EDMONTON, AB

PREP: 20 MIN. • **COOK:** 5 HOURS
MAKES: 10 SERVINGS

- 6 **large onions, chopped**
- ½ **cup butter**
- 6 **cans (10½ ounces each) condensed beef broth, undiluted**
- 1½ **teaspoons Worcestershire sauce**
- 3 **bay leaves**
- 10 **slices French bread, toasted**
  Shredded Parmesan and shredded part-skim mozzarella cheese

1. In a large skillet, saute onions in butter until crisp-tender. Transfer to a 5-qt. slow cooker. Add the broth, Worcestershire sauce and bay leaves.
2. Cover the dish and cook on low for 5-7 hours or until onions are tender. Discard bay leaves.
3. Ladle soup into ovenproof bowls. Top each with a slice of toast; sprinkle with the desired amount of cheese. Place the bowls on baking sheet. Broil for 2-3 minutes or until the cheese is lightly golden.

SPICE IT UP SOUP

Turkey Italian sausage and jalapeno peppers add kick to this chunky soup. The original recipe called for a lot of butter and required the use of three cooking pots. I eliminated the butter and tossed the ingredients together in just one pot. My husband really enjoys this meaty soup, so I make plenty and freeze what's left over in individual servings for his lunches.

—GUYLA COOPER ENVILLE, TN

PREP: 10 MIN. • **COOK:** 40 MIN.
MAKES: 8 SERVINGS (2½ QUARTS)

- 1 pound uncooked hot turkey Italian sausage links, sliced
- ½ pound lean ground beef (90% lean)
- 1 large onion, chopped
- 1 medium green pepper, chopped
- 3 garlic cloves, minced
- 2 cans (14½ ounces each) beef broth
- 2 cups water
- 2 cups fresh or frozen corn
- 1 can (14½ ounces) diced tomatoes with green chilies, undrained
- 1 cup diced carrots
- ⅓ cup minced fresh cilantro
- 2 jalapeno peppers, seeded and chopped
- ½ teaspoon salt
- ½ teaspoon ground cumin

1. In a Dutch oven, cook the sausage, beef, onion and green pepper over medium heat until meat is no longer pink. Add the garlic; cook 1 minute longer. Drain.

2. Stir in the remaining ingredients. Bring to a boil. Reduce heat; cover and simmer for 30-40 minutes to allow flavors to blend.

NOTE *Wear disposable gloves when cutting hot peppers; the oils can burn skin. Avoid touching your face.*

SPICE IT UP
SOUP

`FAST FIX`

CHICKEN SALAD CROISSANT SANDWICHES

Parmesan cheese and dill make this the most incredible chicken salad I've ever tasted. For the no-cook version, use canned chicken. These sandwiches are a simple entree to serve at parties, showers or picnics.

—JACLYN BELL LOGAN, UT

START TO FINISH: 25 MIN.
MAKES: 4 SERVINGS

- 2 cups shredded cooked chicken breast
- 1 cup seedless red grapes, halved
- ½ cup chopped cashews
- 1 celery rib, chopped
- ⅓ cup grated Parmesan cheese
- 1 green onion, chopped
- ½ cup mayonnaise
- ⅓ cup buttermilk
- 2 teaspoons lemon juice
- 1 teaspoon dill weed
- 1 teaspoon dried parsley flakes
- ¼ teaspoon salt
- ¼ teaspoon garlic powder
- ¼ teaspoon pepper
- 4 croissants, split

In a small bowl, combine the first six ingredients. In another bowl, whisk mayonnaise, buttermilk, lemon juice and seasonings. Pour over the chicken mixture; mix well. Spoon the chicken salad onto the croissant bottoms. Replace tops.

VEGETABLE CARROT SOUP

This blended soup is so smooth and delicious that you'll forget it packs a powerhouse of nutrition from veggies. Its lovely golden color adds a special touch to the table, too.

—BERTHA MCCLUNG SUMMERSVILLE, WV

PREP: 15 MIN. • **COOK:** 40 MIN.
MAKES: 4 SERVINGS

- 3 cups thinly sliced carrots
- 1 cup chopped onion
- ⅔ cup chopped celery
- 1½ cups diced peeled potatoes
- 1 garlic clove, minced
- ½ teaspoon sugar
- 2 teaspoons canola oil
- 4 cups reduced-sodium chicken broth
  Dash ground nutmeg
  Pepper to taste

1. In a Dutch oven or soup kettle over medium-low heat, saute the carrots, onion, celery, potatoes, garlic and sugar in oil for 5 minutes. Add broth, nutmeg and pepper; bring to a boil. Reduce heat; cover and simmer for 30-40 minutes or until the vegetables are tender.

2. Remove from the heat and cool to room temperature. Puree in batches in a blender or food processor. Return to the kettle and heat through.

FAST FIX ▶
TURKEY GYROS

Greek seasoning, feta cheese and cucumber sauce provide my lightened-up gyros with an authentic taste. Instead of feta cheese, we sometimes use cheddar or Monterey Jack.

—DONNA GARVIN GLENS FALLS, NY

START TO FINISH: 25 MIN.
MAKES: 4 SERVINGS

- 1 medium cucumber, peeled
- ⅔ cup reduced-fat sour cream
- ¼ cup finely chopped onion
- 2 teaspoons dill weed
- 2 teaspoons lemon juice
- 1 teaspoon olive oil
- ½ pound turkey breast tenderloin, cut into ¼-inch slices

TURKEY GYROS

- 1½ teaspoons salt-free Greek seasoning
- 8 thin tomato slices
- 4 whole pita breads, warmed
- 1½ cups shredded lettuce
- 2 tablespoons crumbled feta cheese

1. Finely chop one-third of the cucumber; place it in a small bowl. Toss with sour cream, onion, dill and lemon juice. Thinly slice the remaining cucumber.

2. In a nonstick skillet, heat the oil over medium-high heat. Add the turkey; cook and stir 5-7 minutes or until no longer pink. Sprinkle with Greek seasoning.

3. Serve turkey, tomato and sliced cucumber on pita breads. Top with lettuce, cheese and sauce.

TO MAKE YOUR OWN SALT-FREE GREEK SEASONING *Using a small bowl, combine 1½ tsp. dried oregano, 1 tsp. each dried mint and dried thyme, ½ tsp. each dried basil, dried marjoram and dried minced onion, and ¼ tsp. dried minced garlic. Store airtight in a cool dry place for up to 6 months. Yield: 2 Tbsp.*

CILANTRO-AVOCADO
TUNA SALAD SANDWICHES

FAST FIX ▶
QUICK PORK CHILI

A dear neighbor gave me a pot of this delicious chili, and I asked for the recipe. The pork sausage is a nice change from the ground beef many chili recipes call for.

—**JANICE WESTMORELAND** BROOKSVILLE, FL

START TO FINISH: 30 MIN.
MAKES: 12 SERVINGS (3 QUARTS)

- 1 **pound bulk pork sausage**
- 1 **large onion, chopped**
- 2 **cans (16 ounces each) chili beans, undrained**
- 1 **can (28 ounces) crushed tomatoes**
- 3 **cups water**
- 1 **can (4 ounces) chopped green chilies**
- 1 **envelope chili seasoning mix**
- 2 **tablespoons sugar**

In a Dutch oven, cook the sausage and onion over medium heat 6-8 minutes or until the meat is no longer pink, breaking into crumbles; drain. Add the remaining ingredients; bring to a boil. Reduce heat; simmer, covered, 20 minutes, stirring often.

★ ★ ★ ★ ★ **READER REVIEW**

"Easy and delicious chili. My husband and I love it. I make jalapeno and bacon cornbread with the chili. Five star recipe!"

JELLYBUG TASTEOFHOME.COM

FAST FIX ▶
CILANTRO-AVOCADO TUNA SALAD SANDWICHES

Lime juice and cilantro in tuna salad—who knew? This flavorful recipe came to me as a way to have a protein-packed meal with lots of pizzazz.

—**HEATHER WALDORF** BLACK MOUNTAIN, NC

START TO FINISH: 15 MIN.
MAKES: 4 SERVINGS

- 2 **pouches (5 ounces each) albacore white tuna in water**
- ⅓ **cup mayonnaise**
- 3 **tablespoons minced fresh cilantro**
- 2 **tablespoons lime juice**
- 2 **garlic cloves, minced**
- ¼ **teaspoon salt**
- ⅛ **teaspoon pepper**
- 8 **slices whole wheat bread, toasted if desired**
- 4 **slices Muenster or provolone cheese**
- 1 **medium ripe avocado, peeled and sliced**

In a small bowl, mix the first seven ingredients. Spread the tuna mixture over four slices of bread; top it with cheese, avocado and remaining bread. Serve immediately.

QUICK PORK
CHILI

HONEY-MUSTARD
BRATS

HONEY-MUSTARD BRATS

A honey mustard glaze gives every bite of these brats a sweet and punchy flavor. Everyone agrees they're delicious. Top them with condiments of your choice.
—**LILY JULOW** LAWRENCEVILLE, GA

START TO FINISH: 25 MIN.
MAKES: 4 SERVINGS

- ¼ **cup Dijon mustard**
- ¼ **cup honey**
- 2 **tablespoons mayonnaise**
- 1 **teaspoon steak sauce**
- 4 **uncooked bratwurst links**
- 4 **brat buns, split**

1. In a small bowl, mix mustard, honey, mayonnaise and steak sauce.
2. Grill the bratwurst, covered, over medium heat 15-20 minutes or until a thermometer reads 160°, turning occasionally; brush frequently with mustard mixture during the last 5 minutes. Serve on buns.

ORANGE TURKEY CROISSANTS

Here's an easy sandwich that feels special. Sweet and tangy orange marmalade and crunchy pecans make it one of a kind. And the best part is it's only five ingredients!
—**JENNIFER MOORE** CENTERVILLE, IA

START TO FINISH: 10 MIN.
MAKES: 6 SERVINGS

- 6 **tablespoons spreadable cream cheese**
- 6 **tablespoons orange marmalade**
- 6 **croissants, split**
- ½ **cup chopped pecans**
- 1 **pound thinly sliced deli turkey**

Spread cream cheese and marmalade onto the bottom half of the croissants. Sprinkle with the pecans. Top with turkey; replace tops.

HEARTY LIMA BEAN SOUP

This colorful soup has a golden broth dotted with tender vegetables and lima beans. It makes an excellent lunch or first course.

—**BETTY KORCEK** BRIDGMAN, MI

PREP: 20 MIN. + STANDING
COOK: 2 HOURS 50 MIN.
MAKES: 14 SERVINGS (3½ QUARTS)

- 1 **pound dried lima beans**
- 1 **large meaty ham bone or 2 ham hocks**
- 2½ **quarts water**
- 5 **celery ribs, cut into chunks**
- 5 **medium carrots, cut into chunks**
- 1 **garlic clove, minced**
- 2 **tablespoons butter**
- 2 **tablespoons all-purpose flour**
- 2 **teaspoons salt**
- ½ **teaspoon pepper**
  Pinch paprika
- 1 **cup cold water**
- 1 **can (14½ ounces) stewed tomatoes**

1. Place beans in a Dutch oven; add water to cover by 2 in. Bring to a boil; boil for 2 minutes. Remove from the heat; cover and let stand for 1 hour. Drain and discard liquid; return the beans to pan.
2. Add ham bone and 2½ qt. water; bring to a boil. Reduce heat; cover and simmer for 1½ hours.
3. Debone ham and cut meat into chunks; return to pan. Add celery and carrots. Cover and simmer for 1 hour or until beans are tender.
4. In a small skillet, saute garlic in butter for 1 minute. Stir in the flour, salt, pepper and paprika. Add cold water; bring to a boil. Reduce heat; cook and stir for 2 minutes or until thickened. Add to the soup with tomatoes; simmer for 10 minutes or until heated through.

CHEDDAR POTATO CHOWDER

CHEDDAR POTATO CHOWDER

I would only make this soup on occasion because the original recipe was quite high in fat. I doctored it up a bit, using healthier ingredients, and now we enjoy this flavorful chowder more often.

—**ELLIE RAUSCH** GOODSOIL, SK

PREP: 20 MIN. • **COOK:** 20 MIN.
MAKES: 7 SERVINGS

- 2 **cups water**
- 2 **cups diced unpeeled red potatoes**
- 1 **cup diced carrot**
- ½ **cup diced celery**
- ¼ **cup chopped onion**
- 1 **teaspoon salt**
- ¼ **teaspoon pepper**
- ¼ **cup all-purpose flour**
- 2 **cups 2% milk**
- 2 **cups shredded reduced-fat cheddar cheese**
- 1 **cup cubed fully cooked lean ham**

1. In a Dutch oven, combine the first seven ingredients. Bring to a boil. Reduce heat; cover and simmer for 10-12 minutes or until tender.
2. Meanwhile, place flour in a large saucepan; gradually whisk in milk. Bring to a boil over medium heat; cook and stir for 2 minutes or until thickened. Remove from the heat. Add cheese; stir until melted. Stir the ham and the cheese sauce into undrained vegetables; stir until combined.

ROOT BEER PULLED PORK SANDWICHES

My husband is a huge fan of pulled pork sandwiches, so my sister shared this easy recipe with me. At potlucks and family dinners, nobody can get enough of this root beer-braised version.

—CAROLYN PALM RADCLIFF, KY

PREP: 20 MIN. • **COOK:** 8½ HOURS
MAKES: 12 SERVINGS

- 1 **boneless pork shoulder butt roast (3 to 4 pounds)**
- 1 **can (12 ounces) root beer or cola**
- 1 **bottle (18 ounces) barbecue sauce**
- 12 **kaiser rolls, split**

1. Place roast in a 4- or 5-qt. slow cooker. Add root beer; cook, covered, on low until the meat is tender, about 8-10 hours.
2. Remove the roast; cool it slightly. Discard the cooking juices. Shred the pork with two forks; return to slow cooker. Stir in the barbecue sauce. Cook, covered, until heated through, about 30 minutes. Serve on rolls.

FREEZE OPTION *Freeze cooled meat mixture in freezer containers. To use, partially thaw in the refrigerator overnight. Heat the food through in a saucepan, stirring occasionally and adding a little water if necessary.*

★ ★ ★ ★ ★ **READER REVIEW**

"I typically find that root beer adds little flavor to a recipe. But this one is the exception! What an easy and delicious way to marinade pulled pork. I will be making this again and again!"

REMENEC TASTEOFHOME.COM

ROOT BEER PULLED
PORK SANDWICHES

FAST FIX ▶

FISH PO'BOYS

Whether you're rich or poor, you'll feel like a million bucks after one big bite into this classic sandwich. Use your favorite brand of frozen breaded fish, and adjust the amount of hot pepper sauce to suit your tastes.

—*TASTE OF HOME* TEST KITCHEN

START TO FINISH: 30 MIN.
MAKES: 6 SERVINGS

- 2 **packages (11.4 ounces each) frozen crunchy breaded fish fillets**
- ½ **cup mayonnaise**
- 1 **tablespoon minced fresh parsley**
- 1 **tablespoon ketchup**
- 2 **teaspoons stone-ground mustard**
- 1 **teaspoon horseradish sauce**
- 2 **to 4 drops hot pepper sauce**
- 1½ **cups deli coleslaw**
- 6 **hamburger buns, split**

1. Bake fish according to package directions. Meanwhile, in a small bowl, combine mayonnaise, parsley, ketchup, mustard, horseradish sauce and hot pepper sauce until blended.
2. Spoon ¼ cup coleslaw onto the bottom of each bun; top with two pieces of fish. Spread with sauce; replace bun tops.

PRISCILLA'S VEGETABLE CHOWDER

This is the perfect soup to warm up with on a cold fall or winter day. Serve it in a bread bowl to make it extra special.

—**JENNA JACKSON** SALT LAKE CITY, UT

PREP: 25 MIN. • **COOK:** 30 MIN.
MAKES: 12 SERVINGS (3 QUARTS)

- 3 **cups diced peeled potatoes**
- 2½ **cups broccoli florets**
- 1 **cup chopped onion**
- 1 **cup grated carrots**
- 2 **celery ribs, diced**
- 4 **teaspoons chicken bouillon granules**
- 3 **cups water**
- ¾ **cup butter, cubed**
- ¾ **cup all-purpose flour**
- 4 **cups milk**
- 1 **teaspoon salt**
- ¼ **teaspoon pepper**
- 1 **cup cubed fully cooked ham**
- 1 **cup shredded cheddar cheese**

1. In a Dutch oven, combine the potatoes, broccoli, onion, carrots, celery, bouillon and water; simmer for 20 minutes or until vegetables are tender.
2. In a large saucepan, melt butter; stir in the flour. Cook and stir over medium heat for 2 minutes. Whisk in the milk, salt and pepper. Bring to a boil; cook and stir for 2 minutes or until thickened. Add to vegetable mixture with the ham; simmer 10 minutes until heated through. Stir in cheese just until melted.

FAST FIX ▶

PIZZA WRAPS

This recipe features the flavors of your favorite pie—and there's no cooking or baking required. It's the perfect quick-to-fix lunch for those harried mornings you're rushing to get the kids off to school.

—**ELIZABETH DUMONT** MADISON, MS

START TO FINISH: 15 MIN.
MAKES: 4 WRAPS

- 1 **package (8 ounces) sliced pepperoni**
- 4 **flour tortillas (8 inches), room temperature**
- ½ **cup chopped tomatoes**
- ¼ **cup each chopped sweet onion, chopped fresh mushrooms and chopped ripe olives**
- ¼ **cup chopped green pepper, optional**
- 1 **cup shredded part-skim mozzarella cheese**

Arrange the pepperoni off center on each tortilla. Top with the remaining ingredients. Fold sides and bottom over filling and roll up.

MUSHROOM & ONION GRILLED CHEESE SANDWICHES

GRANDMA'S SEAFOOD CHOWDER

My grandmother makes this recipe every year for Christmas morning—the only time I've ever had it. Why wait when you can enjoy this satisfying chowder anytime?
—**MELISSA OBERNESSER** UTICA, NY

PREP: 15 MIN. • **COOK:** 25 MIN.
MAKES: 10 SERVINGS (3¼ QUARTS)

- 3 **tablespoons plus ¼ cup butter, divided**
- 1 **pound sliced fresh mushrooms**
- ⅓ **cup all-purpose flour**
- 1 **teaspoon salt**
- ⅛ **teaspoon pepper**
- 4 **cups half-and-half cream**
- 1½ **cups 2% milk**
- 1 **pound haddock fillets, skin removed, cut into 1-inch pieces**
- 1 **pound uncooked medium shrimp, peeled and deveined**
- 2 **cups frozen peas (about 10 ounces)**
- ¾ **cup shredded cheddar cheese**
- 1 **cup lump crabmeat (about 5 ounces), drained**
- 1 **jar (4 ounces) diced pimientos, drained**
- 1 **teaspoon paprika**

1. Using a 6-qt. stockpot, heat 3 tablespoons butter over medium-high heat. Add mushrooms; cook and stir for 8-10 minutes or until tender. Remove from pot.
2. In same pot, heat remaining butter over medium heat. Stir in flour, salt and pepper until smooth; gradually whisk in cream and milk. Bring to a boil, stirring constantly; cook and stir 2-3 minutes or until thickened.
3. Stir in the haddock, shrimp, peas and sauteed mushrooms; cook for 5-7 minutes or until fish just begins to flake easily with a fork and shrimp turn pink. Add the cheese, crab and pimientos; stir gently until cheese is melted. Sprinkle individual servings with paprika.

FAST FIX
MUSHROOM & ONION GRILLED CHEESE SANDWICHES

We took grilled cheese up a notch with baby portobello mushrooms, bacon and cheddar. It's good to the very last crumb.
—**BLAIR LONERGAN** ROCHELLE, VA

START TO FINISH: 25 MIN.
MAKES: 4 SERVINGS

- 3 **tablespoons butter, softened, divided**
- 8 **ounces sliced baby portobello mushrooms**
- 1 **small onion, halved and thinly sliced**
- 8 **thin slices cheddar cheese (about 3 ounces)**
- 8 **slices Texas toast**
- 4 **bacon strips, cooked and crumbled**

1. In a large nonstick skillet coated with cooking spray, heat 1 tablespoon butter over medium-high heat. Add mushrooms and onion; cook and stir 4-5 minutes or until tender. Remove from pan. Wipe skillet clean.
2. Place one slice cheese on each of four bread slices. Top with mushroom mixture, bacon and the remaining cheese and bread. Lightly spread the outsides of the sandwiches with the remaining butter.
3. In same skillet, toast sandwiches in batches over medium heat 45-60 seconds on each side or until golden brown and cheese is melted.

TURKEY CHILI WITH PASTA

Some may call it witches' stew, but we think this hearty chili is the ultimate comfort food. It's a perfect warmer on chilly autumn nights.

—**PAT SCHMELING** GERMANTOWN, WI

PREP: 10 MIN. • **COOK:** 30 MIN.
MAKES: 10 SERVINGS (4 QUARTS)

- 1 package (20 ounces) lean ground turkey
- 3 celery ribs with leaves, chopped
- 1 large green pepper, chopped
- 1 large onion, chopped
- 2 garlic cloves, minced
- 1 can (46 ounces) tomato juice
- 1 can (11½ ounces) V8 juice
- 2 cans (8 ounces each) tomato sauce
- 2 tablespoons brown sugar
- 2 tablespoons chili powder
- ½ teaspoon salt
- ½ teaspoon ground cumin
- ¼ teaspoon pepper
- 1 bay leaf
- 1 cup uncooked elbow macaroni
- 2 cans (16 ounces each) kidney beans, rinsed and drained
  Optional toppings: sour cream, shredded cheddar cheese, thinly sliced green onions and ripe olives

1. In a Dutch oven, cook the turkey, celery, green pepper, onion and garlic over medium heat until meat is no longer pink. Add the juices, tomato sauce, brown sugar, seasonings and bay leaf. Bring to a boil. Reduce heat; simmer, uncovered, for 20 minutes.
2. Meanwhile, cook the macaroni according to the package directions; drain. Add the beans and macaroni to turkey mixture; heat through. Discard the bay leaf before serving. Garnish servings with toppings of your choice.

FAST FIX
SOUTHWEST-STYLE WEDDING SOUP

I turned leftover hamburgers into meatballs and added them to this zesty soup.

—**TEENA PETRUS** JOHNSTOWN, PA

START TO FINISH: 30 MIN.
MAKES: 6 SERVINGS

- 1 tablespoon canola oil
- 2 medium carrots, chopped
- 2 medium celery ribs, chopped
- ½ cup frozen corn, thawed
- 2 quarts chicken stock
- 1 cup soft bread crumbs
- 1 envelope reduced-sodium taco seasoning
- 1 large egg
- 1 pound ground chicken
- 1½ cups acini di pepe pasta
- 2 tablespoons minced fresh cilantro
- ¼ teaspoon salt
  Cubed avocado and sour cream

1. In a Dutch oven, heat the oil over medium heat. Add carrots, celery and corn; cook until tender. Stir in stock. Increase heat to high; bring to a boil.
2. Meanwhile, combine the bread crumbs, taco seasoning, egg and chicken; mix lightly. With wet hands, shape into 1½-in. balls. Reduce heat to simmer; gently drop meatballs into stock. Cook, covered, until meatballs are no longer pink, 8-10 minutes. Stir in pasta. Simmer, covered, until pasta is tender, 6-8 minutes. Sprinkle with cilantro and salt.
3. Serve soup with cubed avocado and sour cream.
NOTE *To make soft bread crumbs, tear bread into pieces and place in a food processor or blender. Cover and pulse until crumbs form. One slice of bread yields ½ to ¾ cup crumbs.*

SOUTHWEST-STYLE WEDDING SOUP

CHUNKY TACO
SOUP

CHUNKY TACO SOUP

I get a happy response whenever I bring this easy-to-fix soup to potlucks and church suppers. It features a satisfying Southwestern zip. The flavor is even better in leftovers—if there are any!

—EVELYN BUFORD BELTON, MO

PREP: 20 MIN. • **COOK:** 20 MIN.
MAKES: 12 SERVINGS (ABOUT 3 QUARTS)

- 1½ pounds beef top sirloin or round steak, cut into ¾-inch cubes
- 1 medium onion, chopped
- 1 tablespoon olive oil
- 2 cans (15 ounces each) pinto beans, rinsed and drained
- 2 cans (14½ ounces each) diced tomatoes and green chilies, undrained
- 2 cups water
- 1 can (15 ounces) black beans, rinsed and drained
- 1 can (14¾ ounces) cream-style corn
- 1 envelope ranch salad dressing mix
- 1 envelope taco seasoning
- ¼ cup minced fresh cilantro

In a large stockpot or a Dutch oven, brown beef and onion in oil. Add pinto beans, tomatoes, water, black beans, corn, salad dressing mix and taco seasoning. Bring to a boil. Reduce the heat; cover and simmer for 20-30 minutes or until the meat is tender. Sprinkle with cilantro.

★ ★ ★ ★ ★ 5 STAR TIP
The reason for draining canned beans is to remove the excess salt used in the canning process. If you choose to use the liquid, be sure to adjust the salt level in your recipe.

ASIAN TURKEY BURGERS WITH APPLE SLAW

FREEZE IT | FAST FIX
ASIAN TURKEY BURGERS WITH APPLE SLAW

I wanted to take the flavor of turkey burgers up a notch. On a whim, I added hoisin sauce, gingerroot and garlic. Now we enjoy them about once a week.

—ASHLEY GAYLE ELLICOTT CITY, MD

START TO FINISH: 30 MIN.
MAKES: 4 SERVINGS

- 3 green onions, finely chopped
- 2 tablespoons hoisin sauce
- 1 tablespoon minced fresh gingerroot
- 2 garlic cloves, minced
- ½ teaspoon salt
- ¼ teaspoon pepper
- 1¼ pounds ground turkey
- 1 tablespoon olive oil

SLAW
- 3 tablespoons olive oil
- 1 tablespoon cider vinegar
- 1 teaspoon Dijon mustard
- ¼ teaspoon salt
- ⅛ teaspoon pepper
- 2 medium apples, julienned
- 2 green onions, finely chopped

ASSEMBLY
- 4 hamburger buns, split and toasted
- 2 tablespoons hoisin sauce

1. In a large bowl, mix green onions, hoisin sauce, ginger, garlic, salt and pepper. Add turkey; mix lightly but thoroughly. Shape meat into four ¾-in.-thick patties.

2. In a large nonstick skillet, heat oil over medium heat. Cook the burgers 7-9 minutes on each side or until a thermometer reads 165°.

3. Meanwhile, for slaw, in a large bowl, whisk oil, vinegar, mustard, salt and pepper. Add apples and green onions; toss to coat.

4. To assemble, spread bun bottoms with hoisin sauce. Top with burgers; replace tops. Serve with apple slaw.

FREEZE OPTION *Place patties on a plastic wrap-lined baking sheet; wrap and freeze until firm. Remove from pan and transfer to a resealable plastic freezer bag; return to freezer. To use, cook the frozen patties as directed, increasing time as necessary for a thermometer to read 165°.*

CONTEST-WINNING HAMBURGER SOUP

My crew looks forward to this spirit-warming soup whenever I have them over for family get-togethers. I serve it with a fresh loaf of bread and tall glasses of milk. The soup has a robust flavor and plenty of fresh ingredients.

—BARBARA BROWN JANESVILLE, WI

PREP: 15 MIN. • **COOK:** 30 MIN.
MAKES: 8 SERVINGS (2 QUARTS)

- 1 **pound ground beef**
- 4 **cups water**
- 1 **can (14½ ounces) diced tomatoes, undrained**
- 3 **medium carrots, sliced**
- 2 **medium potatoes, peeled and cubed**
- 1 **medium onion, chopped**
- ½ **cup chopped celery**
- 4 **teaspoons beef bouillon granules**
- 1½ **teaspoons salt**
- ¼ **teaspoon pepper**
- ¼ **teaspoon dried oregano**
- 1 **cup cut fresh or frozen green beans**

1. In a large saucepan, brown beef; drain. Add the next 10 ingredients; bring to a boil.
2. Reduce heat; cover and simmer for 15 minutes or until the potatoes and carrots are tender. Add green beans. Cover and simmer 15 minutes longer or until the beans are tender.

CONTEST-WINNING HAMBURGER SOUP

EMILY'S BEAN SOUP

Served with thick slices of warm homemade bread, my soup makes a wonderful fall or winter meal. The recipe has evolved over the years as I experimented with different ingredients. I often double and freeze what we don't eat—that way I can throw some in a pot for a quick meal or in case unexpected company drops by.

—EMILY CHANEY PENOBSCOT, ME

PREP: 25 MIN. + STANDING
COOK: 3 HOURS
MAKES: 22 SERVINGS (ABOUT 5½ QUARTS)

- ½ **cup each dried great northern beans, kidney beans, navy beans, lima beans, butter beans, split green or yellow peas, pinto beans and lentils**
  Water
- 1 **meaty ham bone**
- 2 **teaspoons chicken bouillon granules**
- 1 **can (28 ounces) tomatoes with liquid, quartered**
- 1 **can (6 ounces) tomato paste**
- 1 **large onion, chopped**
- 3 **celery ribs, chopped**
- 4 **medium carrots, sliced**
- 2 **garlic cloves, minced**
- ¼ **cup minced chives**
- 3 **bay leaves**
- 2 **tablespoons dried parsley flakes**
- 1 **teaspoon dried thyme**
- 1 **teaspoon ground mustard**
- ½ **teaspoon cayenne pepper**

1. Wash all beans thoroughly; drain and place in a large saucepan. Add 5 cups of water. Bring to a rapid boil; boil for 2 minutes. Remove from the heat; cover and let stand for 1 hour.
2. Meanwhile, place ham bone and 3 qts. of water in a stockpot. Simmer until beans have stood for 1 hour.
3. Drain beans and add to the ham stock; add remaining ingredients. Simmer for 2-3 hours or until beans are tender. Cut meat from ham bone; discard bone. Add additional water to soup if desired.

OPEN-FACED GRILLED SALMON SANDWICHES

Our family loves to fish. What better reward from a day of fishing than eating what you just caught? We make salmon several ways, but this one is our favorite.

—STEPHANIE HANISAK PORT MURRAY, NJ

START TO FINISH: 30 MIN.
MAKES: 4 SERVINGS

- 4 **salmon fillets (1 inch thick and 5 ounces each), skin removed**
- ¾ **cup mesquite marinade**
- ¼ **teaspoon pepper**
- 4 **slices sourdough bread (½ inch thick)**
- ¼ **cup tartar sauce**
- 4 **iceberg lettuce leaves**
- 4 **lemon wedges, optional**

1. Place fillets in an 8-in. square dish. Pour marinade over fillets; turn fish to coat. Let stand 15 minutes.
2. Drain the salmon, discarding the marinade. Sprinkle with pepper.
3. Moisten some paper towel with cooking oil; using long-handled tongs, rub on grill rack to coat lightly. Grill salmon, covered, over medium heat or broil 4 in. from heat 4-6 minutes on each side or until fish just begins to flake easily with a fork.
4. Grill bread, covered, over medium heat 1-2 minutes on each side or until lightly toasted. Spread with tartar sauce; top with lettuce and salmon. If desired, serve with lemon wedges.

OPEN-FACED GRILLED SALMON SANDWICHES

SIDE DISHES, SALADS & MORE

It's time to meet your new best picks for picnics and parties. Turn the pages to discover creamy coleslaws, garden fresh salads, flame-kissed veggies and homemade jam, pickles and dressings. Simple yet satisfying, any of these recipes will make you the talk of the potluck.

APPLE SALAD WITH MAPLE-MUSTARD VINAIGRETTE

This seasonal salad will be a hit at any gathering. It's also easy for weeknights; just halve the recipe.

—**BETH DAUENHAUER** PUEBLO, CO

START TO FINISH: 15 MIN.
MAKES: 12 SERVINGS (1 CUP EACH)

- ¼ **cup thawed frozen apple juice concentrate**
- 2 **tablespoons cider vinegar**
- 2 **tablespoons canola oil**
- 2 **tablespoons spicy brown mustard**
- 2 **tablespoons maple syrup**
- ¼ **teaspoon salt**
- ⅛ **teaspoon pepper**

SALAD

- 9 **cups torn mixed salad greens**
- 2 **large tart apples, chopped**
- 1 **small red onion, thinly sliced**
- ⅓ **cup chopped walnuts, toasted**

In a small bowl, whisk the first seven ingredients. In a large bowl, combine the salad greens, apples, onion and walnuts. Drizzle with vinaigrette; toss to coat.

NOTE *To toast nuts, bake in a shallow pan in a 350° oven for 5-10 minutes or cook in a skillet over low heat until lightly browned, stirring occasionally.*

★ ★ ★ ★ ★ **READER REVIEW**

"Wonderful combination of sweet, savory, and crunchy. The vinaigrette was surprisingly simple and so delicious."

KBALLET TASTEOFHOME.COM

MARINATED
THREE-BEAN
SALAD

MARINATED THREE-BEAN SALAD

Fresh herbs and cayenne pepper provide the fantastic flavor in this marinated salad featuring fresh veggies and canned beans.
—**CAROL TUCKER** WOOSTER, OH

PREP: 20 MIN. + CHILLING
MAKES: 8 SERVINGS

- 1 can (15½ ounces) great northern beans, rinsed and drained
- 1 can (15 ounces) chickpeas, rinsed and drained
- 1 can (15 ounces) black beans, rinsed and drained
- 1 medium tomato, chopped
- 1 medium onion, chopped
- 1 celery rib, chopped
- ⅓ cup each chopped green, sweet red and yellow pepper
- ½ cup water
- 3 tablespoons minced fresh basil or 1 tablespoon dried basil
- 2 tablespoons minced fresh parsley
- 2 tablespoons lemon juice
- 2 tablespoons olive oil
- 1½ teaspoons minced fresh oregano or ½ teaspoon dried oregano
- ½ teaspoon salt
- ½ teaspoon pepper
- ¼ teaspoon cayenne pepper

In a large bowl, combine the beans, tomato, onion, celery and peppers. In a small bowl, whisk the remaining ingredients; gently stir into the bean mixture. Cover and refrigerate for 4 hours, stirring occasionally.

LIME-HONEY FRUIT SALAD

Nothing is more refreshing to me than a seasonal fruit salad enhanced with this simple lime-honey dressing.
—**VICTORIA SHEVLIN** CAPE CORAL, FL

PREP: 20 MIN. + CHILLING
MAKES: 12 SERVINGS (¾ CUP EACH)

- 1 teaspoon cornstarch
- ¼ cup lime juice
- ¼ cup honey
- ½ teaspoon poppy seeds
- 3 medium Gala or Red Delicious apples, cubed
- 2 medium pears, cubed
- 2 cups seedless red grapes
- 2 cups green grapes

1. In a small microwave-safe bowl, combine cornstarch and lime juice until smooth. Microwave, uncovered, on high for 20 seconds; stir. Cook for 15 seconds longer; stir. Stir in honey and poppy seeds.
2. In a large bowl, combine apples, pears and grapes. Pour the dressing over the fruit; toss to coat. Cover and refrigerate overnight.
NOTE *This recipe was tested in a 1,100-watt microwave.*

FREEZE IT
CRISPY POTATO PUFFS

Crunchy cornflakes and sesame seeds surround a velvety potato filling in these adorable puffs. They make the perfect side dish.
—**EVA TOMLINSON** BRYAN, OH

PREP: 35 MIN. • **BAKE:** 10 MIN.
MAKES: 12 SERVINGS (2 PUFFS EACH)

- 4 pounds cubed peeled potatoes (about 11 cups)
- ½ cup 2% milk
- ¼ cup butter, cubed
- 1½ teaspoons salt
- ½ cup shredded cheddar cheese
- 1½ cups crushed cornflakes
- 6 tablespoons sesame seeds, toasted

1. Place the potatoes in a large saucepan; add water to cover and bring to a boil. Reduce heat; cook, uncovered, 10-15 minutes or until tender. Drain; return to pan.
2. Mash the potatoes, gradually adding the milk, butter and salt; stir in cheese. Transfer to a large bowl; refrigerate, covered, for 2 hours or until firm enough to shape.
3. Using a shallow dish, combine the cornflakes and sesame seeds. Shape the potato mixture into 1½-in. balls; roll in the cornflake mixture. Place on greased baking sheets. Bake 7-9 minutes or until golden brown.
FREEZE OPTION *Place unbaked puffs on baking sheets; cover and freeze until firm. Transfer them to resealable plastic freezer bags. Freeze up to 3 months. To use them, preheat the oven to 400°. Place the frozen potato puffs on greased baking sheets. Bake 15-20 minutes or until golden brown and heated through.*

FAST FIX
BLT MACARONI SALAD

When a friend served this salad, I just had to get the recipe. My husband loves BLTs, so this has become a favorite of his. It's nice to serve on hot and humid days, which we frequently get during summer here in Virginia!
—**HAMILTON MYERS JR.** CHARLOTTESVILLE, VA

START TO FINISH: 30 MIN.
MAKES: 6 SERVINGS

- ½ cup mayonnaise
- 3 tablespoons chili sauce
- 2 tablespoons lemon juice
- 1 teaspoon sugar
- 3 cups cooked elbow macaroni
- ½ cup chopped seeded tomato
- 2 tablespoons chopped green onions
- 3 cups shredded lettuce
- 4 bacon strips, cooked and crumbled

In a large bowl, combine the first four ingredients. Add the macaroni, tomatoes and onions; toss to coat. Cover and refrigerate. Just before serving, add the lettuce and bacon; toss to coat.

SPICY APPLESAUCE

Every year, we have an apple-picking party and end up with loads of apples. This is one of the recipes I always look forward to making with our harvest.

—**MARIAN PLATT** SEQUIM, WA

PREP: 25 MIN. • **COOK:** 30 MIN.
MAKES: 8 CUPS

- 5 **pounds tart apples (about 16 medium), peeled and sliced**
- 1 **cup apple juice**
- 1 **teaspoon ground cinnamon**
- ½ **teaspoon ground allspice**
- ½ **teaspoon ground cloves**

In a Dutch oven, combine all of the ingredients; bring to a boil. Reduce heat; simmer, covered, 25-35 minutes or until apples are tender, stirring occasionally. Remove from heat; mash apples to desired consistency. Serve warm or cold.

FREEZE OPTION *Freeze the cooled applesauce in freezer containers. To use, thaw in refrigerator overnight. Serve cold or heat it through in a saucepan, stirring occasionally.*

SWEET HONEY ALMOND BUTTER

This homemade butter makes a nice gift along with a fresh-from-the-oven loaf of bread.

—**EVELYN HARRIS** WAYNESBORO, VA

START TO FINISH: 10 MIN.
MAKES: 2 CUPS

- 1 **cup butter, softened**
- ¾ **cup honey**
- ¾ **cup confectioners' sugar**
- ¾ **cup finely ground almonds**
- ¼ **to ½ teaspoon almond extract**

In a bowl, combine all the ingredients; mix well. Refrigerate up to 1 week or freeze up to 3 months.

STRAWBERRY-KIWI JAM

My family always gives jams and jellies as gifts and everyone appreciates it. Strawberries and kiwi make a wonderful combination.

—**KATHY KITTELL** LENEXA, KS

PREP: 20 MIN. • **COOK:** 15 MIN. + STANDING
MAKES: 5¾ CUPS

- 6 **cups fresh strawberries**
- 3 **medium kiwifruit, peeled and finely chopped**
- 1 **tablespoon lemon juice**
- 1 **tablespoon chopped crystallized ginger**
- 1 **package (1¾ ounces) powdered fruit pectin**
- 5 **cups sugar**

1. Rinse six 1-cup plastic containers and lids with boiling water. Dry them thoroughly. In a large bowl, mash the berries; transfer to a Dutch oven. Add kiwi, lemon juice and ginger. Stir in pectin. Bring to a full rolling boil over high heat, stirring constantly.

2. Stir in sugar; return to a full rolling boil. Boil 1 minute, stirring constantly.

3. Remove from heat; skim off foam. Immediately fill all the containers to within ½ in. of tops. Wipe off the top edges of containers and cool to room temperature, about 1 hour. Cover and let stand at room temperature for about 24 hours.

4. The jam is now ready to use. Refrigerate up to 3 weeks or freeze extra containers up to 12 months. Thaw frozen jam in the refrigerator before serving.

SPICY APPLESAUCE

5 INGREDIENTS | FAST FIX ▶

PARMESAN ASPARAGUS

Nothing could be simpler than this side dish!
With just four ingredients, I can assemble it in
no time, then pop it into the oven for about
15 minutes. It turns out perfect every time.

—**MARY ANN MARINO** WEST PITTSBURGH, PA

START TO FINISH: 20 MIN.
MAKES: 10-12 SERVINGS

> 4 **pounds fresh asparagus, trimmed**
> ¼ **pound butter, melted**
> 2 **cups shredded Parmesan cheese**
> ½ **teaspoon pepper**

1. Preheat oven to 350°. In a large
saucepan, bring ½ in. of water to a
boil. Add asparagus; cover and boil for
3 minutes or until crisp-tender. Drain.
2. Arrange asparagus in a greased
13x9-in. baking dish. Drizzle with
butter; sprinkle it with Parmesan
cheese and pepper. Bake the dish,
uncovered, 10-15 minutes or until
the cheese is melted.

5 INGREDIENTS | FAST FIX ▶

HERBED BUTTERNUT SQUASH

This is just one of many ways we prepare
butternut squash—it's a winter staple in
our house.

—**JENN TIDWELL** FAIR OAKS, CA

START TO FINISH: 25 MIN.
MAKES: 6 SERVINGS

> 1 **medium butternut squash**
>   **(about 3 pounds)**
> 1 **tablespoon olive oil**
> 1½ **teaspoons dried oregano**
> 1 **teaspoon dried thyme**
> ½ **teaspoon salt**
> ¼ **teaspoon pepper**

Peel and cut squash crosswise into
½-in.-thick slices; remove and
discard seeds. In a large bowl, toss the
squash with remaining ingredients.
Grill, covered, over medium heat or
broil 4 in. from heat 6-8 minutes on
each side or until tender.

PARMESAN ASPARAGUS

MOM'S SPANISH RICE

My mother is famous for her Spanish rice. When I want a taste of home, I pull out this recipe and prepare it for my own family.
—**JOAN HALLFORD** NORTH RICHLAND HILLS, TX

START TO FINISH: 20 MIN.
MAKES: 4 SERVINGS

- 1 pound lean ground beef (90% lean)
- 1 large onion, chopped
- 1 medium green pepper, chopped
- 1 can (15 ounces) tomato sauce
- 1 can (14½ ounces) no-salt-added diced tomatoes, drained
- 1 teaspoon ground cumin
- 1 teaspoon chili powder
- ½ teaspoon garlic powder
- ¼ teaspoon salt
- 2⅔ cups cooked brown rice

1. In a large skillet, cook beef, onion and pepper over medium heat 6-8 minutes or until the beef is no longer pink and the onion is tender, breaking up beef into crumbles; drain.
2. Stir in tomato sauce, tomatoes and seasonings; bring to a boil. Add rice; heat through, stirring occasionally.

GRILLED GREEK POTATO SALAD

My most requested summer recipe is wonderful warm, cold or at room temperature. The grilled potatoes make this salad sensational.
—**KATHY RUNDLE** FOND DU LAC, WI

PREP: 30 MIN. • **GRILL:** 20 MIN.
MAKES: 16 SERVINGS (¾ CUP EACH)

- 3 pounds small red potatoes, halved
- 2 tablespoons olive oil
- ½ teaspoon salt
- ¼ teaspoon pepper
- 1 large sweet yellow pepper, chopped
- 1 large sweet red pepper, chopped
- 1 medium red onion, halved and sliced
- 1 medium cucumber, chopped
- 1¼ cups grape tomatoes, halved
- ½ pound fresh mozzarella cheese, cubed
- ¾ cup Greek vinaigrette
- ½ cup halved Greek olives
- 1 can (2¼ ounces) sliced ripe olives, drained
- 2 tablespoons minced fresh oregano or 1 teaspoon dried oregano

1. Drizzle the potatoes with oil and sprinkle with salt and pepper; toss to coat. Grill the potatoes, covered, over medium heat or broil 4 in. from the heat for 20-25 minutes or until tender.
2. Place in a large bowl. Add the remaining ingredients; toss to coat. Serve salad warm or cold.

FRESH TOMATO RELISH

My two grown sons actually eat this as a salad, but that's a bit too hot for me! The recipe's from my late husband's mother, and I haven't varied it. I make a batch as soon as the first tomatoes of the season are ready.
—**LELA BASKINS** WINDSOR, MO

PREP: 30 MIN. + CHILLING
MAKES: ABOUT 6 PINTS

- 2 cups white vinegar
- ½ cup sugar
- 8 cups chopped tomatoes (about 11 large)
- ½ cup chopped onion
- 1 medium green pepper, diced
- 1 celery rib, diced
- ¼ cup prepared horseradish
- 2 tablespoons salt
- 1 tablespoon mustard seed
- 1½ teaspoons pepper
- ½ teaspoon ground cinnamon
- ½ teaspoon ground cloves

1. In a large saucepan, bring vinegar and sugar to a boil. Remove from the heat; cool completely.
2. Using a large bowl, combine the remaining ingredients; add vinegar mixture and mix well. Spoon into storage containers, allowing ½-in. headspace. Refrigerate up to 2 weeks or freeze up to 12 months. Serve with a slotted spoon.

⑤INGREDIENTS
BAKED PARMESAN BREADED SQUASH

Yellow summer squash crisps beautifully when baked. You don't have to turn the pieces, but do keep an eye on them.
—**DEBI MITCHELL** FLOWER MOUND, TX

PREP: 20 MIN. • **BAKE:** 20 MIN.
MAKES: 6 SERVINGS

- 4 cups thinly sliced yellow summer squash (3 medium)
- 3 tablespoons olive oil
- ½ teaspoon salt
- ½ teaspoon pepper
- ⅛ teaspoon cayenne pepper
- ¾ cup panko (Japanese) bread crumbs
- ¾ cup grated Parmesan cheese

1. Preheat oven to 450°. Place the squash in a large bowl. Add oil and seasonings; toss to coat.
2. In a shallow bowl, mix bread crumbs and cheese. Dip squash in crumb mixture to coat both sides, patting to help the coating adhere. Place on parchment paper-lined baking sheets. Bake 20-25 minutes or until golden brown, rotating pans halfway through baking.

★ ★ ★ ★ ★ **READER REVIEW**

"I've been looking for something different to do with squash. This was yummy and very easy to prepare."

CINDIAK TASTEOFHOME.COM

**BAKED PARMESAN
BREADED SQUASH**

FRESH HEIRLOOM TOMATO SALAD

This tomato salad is a summertime must. The standout dressing takes these tasty ingredients to a brand-new level.

—*TASTE OF HOME* TEST KITCHEN

START TO FINISH: 20 MIN.
MAKES: 12 SERVINGS

- 1 package (5 ounces) spring mix salad greens
- 3 tablespoons olive oil
- 2 tablespoons balsamic vinegar
- 1 teaspoon Dijon mustard
- 1 garlic clove, minced
- ½ teaspoon sugar
- ¼ teaspoon dried oregano
- 3 large heirloom tomatoes, sliced
- ½ cup fresh basil leaves
- ⅓ cup pine nuts, toasted
- 3 tablespoons chopped red onion
- 2 ounces fresh goat cheese, crumbled

Place salad greens in a large bowl. In a small bowl, whisk oil, vinegar, mustard, garlic, sugar and oregano until blended. Pour over salad greens; toss to coat. Transfer to a large platter. Arrange tomato slices over greens. Top with basil, pine nuts, onion and cheese. Serve immediately.

NOTE *To toast nuts, bake in a shallow pan in a 350° oven for 5-10 minutes or cook them in a skillet over low heat until they are lightly browned, stirring occasionally.*

FRESH HEIRLOOM
TOMATO SALAD

CREAMY CRANBERRY SALAD

One of my piano students taught me the perfect lesson in salad for the holidays. The keys are cranberries, pineapple, marshmallows and nuts.

—ALEXANDRA LYPECKY DEARBORN, MI

PREP: 15 MIN. + CHILLING
MAKES: 16 SERVINGS (½ CUP EACH)

- 3 cups fresh or frozen cranberries (thawed), chopped
- 1 can (20 ounces) unsweetened crushed pineapple, drained
- 2 cups miniature marshmallows
- 1 medium apple, chopped
- ⅔ cup sugar
- ⅛ teaspoon salt
- 2 cups heavy whipping cream
- ¼ cup chopped walnuts

1. In a large bowl, mix the first six ingredients until blended. Refrigerate, covered, overnight.
2. In a large bowl, beat the cream until stiff peaks form. Just before serving, fold cream and walnuts into the cranberry mixture.

BACON-TOMATO SALAD

We love this wonderful salad that tastes like a piled-high BLT without the time, effort or carbs. Plus, you can make it hours ahead and keep it in the fridge till serving time.

—DENISE THURMAN COLUMBIA, MO

START TO FINISH: 15 MIN.
MAKES: 6 SERVINGS

- 1 package (12 ounces) iceberg lettuce blend
- 2 cups grape tomatoes, halved
- ¾ cup coleslaw salad dressing
- ¾ cup shredded cheddar cheese
- 12 bacon strips, cooked and crumbled

In a large bowl, combine lettuce blend and tomatoes. Drizzle with dressing; sprinkle with cheese and bacon.

SLOW COOKER 🍲
SWEET & SOUR BEANS

This recipe is popular on both sides of the border. It came from a friend in Alaska, then traveled with me to old Mexico, where I lived for five years, and is now a potluck favorite in my Arkansas community. It's easy to keep the beans warm and serve from a slow cooker.

—**BARBARA SHORT** MENA, AR

PREP: 20 MIN. • **COOK:** 3 HOURS
MAKES: 20 SERVINGS (½ CUP EACH)

- 8 bacon strips, diced
- 2 medium onions, halved and thinly sliced
- 1 cup packed brown sugar
- ½ cup cider vinegar
- 1 teaspoon salt
- 1 teaspoon ground mustard
- ½ teaspoon garlic powder
- 1 can (28 ounces) baked beans, undrained
- 1 can (16 ounces) kidney beans, rinsed and drained
- 1 can (15 ounces) pinto beans, rinsed and drained
- 1 can (15 ounces) lima beans, rinsed and drained
- 1 can (15½ ounces) black-eyed peas, rinsed and drained

1. In a large skillet, cook bacon over medium heat until crisp. Remove with slotted spoon to paper towels. Drain, reserving 2 tablespoons of the drippings. Saute onions in the drippings until tender. Add brown sugar, vinegar, salt, mustard and garlic powder. Bring to a boil.
2. In a 5-qt. slow cooker, combine beans and peas. Add the onion mixture and bacon; mix well. Cover and cook on high for 3-4 hours or until heated through.

**HOMEMADE
ANTIPASTO SALAD**

HOMEMADE
ANTIPASTO SALAD

This colorful salad is a tasty crowd-pleaser. Guests love the homemade dressing, which is a nice change from bottled Italian.

—**LINDA HARRINGTON** WINDHAM, NH

PREP: 1 HOUR + CHILLING
MAKES: 50 SERVINGS (¾ CUP EACH)

- 2 packages (1 pound each) spiral pasta
- 4 cups chopped green peppers
- 4 cups chopped seeded tomatoes
- 3 cups chopped onions
- 2 cans (15 ounces each) chickpeas, rinsed and drained
- 1 pound thinly sliced Genoa salami, julienned
- 1 pound sliced pepperoni, julienned
- ½ pound provolone cheese, cubed
- 1 cup pitted ripe olives, halved

DRESSING
- 1 cup red wine vinegar
- ½ cup sugar
- 2 tablespoons dried oregano
- 2 teaspoons salt
- 1 teaspoon pepper
- 1½ cups olive oil

1. Cook pasta according to package directions. Drain; rinse with cold water. In several large bowls, combine the pasta, green peppers, tomatoes, onions, chickpeas, salami, pepperoni, cheese and olives.
2. Place vinegar, sugar, oregano, salt and pepper in a blender. While processing, gradually add oil in a steady stream. Pour over the pasta salad; toss to coat. Refrigerate, covered, 4 hours or overnight.

CONTEST-WINNING CAJUN CABBAGE

Looking for a different way to enjoy cabbage? Try this spicy cheese-topped recipe that I adapted from a friend's recipe. Not only do my husband and kids like it, but I also hear rave reviews when I make it for company or church functions.

—**BOBBIE SOILEAU** OPELOUSAS, LA

PREP: 15 MIN. • **BAKE:** 65 MIN.
MAKES: 6-8 SERVINGS

- 1 **pound ground beef**
- 1 **medium green pepper, chopped**
- 1 **medium onion, chopped**
- 2 **garlic cloves, minced**
- 1 **can (10 ounces) diced tomatoes and green chilies**
- 1 **can (8 ounces) tomato sauce**
- ½ **cup uncooked long grain rice**
- 1 **teaspoon salt**
- ½ **teaspoon dried basil**
- ½ **teaspoon dried oregano**
- ¼ **to ½ teaspoon each white, black and cayenne pepper**
- 4 **to 6 drops hot pepper sauce**
- 1 **small head cabbage, chopped**
- 1 **cup shredded Colby cheese**

1. In a skillet, cook the beef, green pepper, onion and garlic over medium heat until the meat is no longer pink; drain. Stir in tomatoes, tomato sauce, rice and seasonings.

2. Spread into ungreased 13x9-in. baking dish. Top with the cabbage and cheese. Cover and bake at 350° for 65-75 minutes or until the rice is tender.

CONTEST-WINNING CAJUN CABBAGE

SPRING GREEN RISOTTO

Once a week, I create a new recipe for my blog, *An Officer and a Vegan*. I first made this risotto when I needed something cheerful and satisfying. It would be fantastic with asparagus, zucchini or summer squash, but use whatever veggies are in season.
—**DEANNA MCDONALD** GRAND RAPIDS, MI

PREP: 15 MIN. • **COOK:** 30 MIN.
MAKES: 8 SERVINGS

- 1 carton (32 ounces) vegetable stock
- 1 to 1½ cups water
- 1 tablespoon olive oil
- 2 cups sliced fresh mushrooms
- 1 medium onion, chopped
- 1½ cups uncooked arborio rice
- 2 garlic cloves, minced
- ½ cup white wine or additional vegetable stock
- 1 teaspoon dried thyme
- 3 cups fresh baby spinach
- 1 cup frozen peas
- 3 tablespoons grated Parmesan cheese
- 1 tablespoon red wine vinegar
- ½ teaspoon salt
- ¼ teaspoon pepper

1. In a large saucepan, bring stock and water to a simmer; keep hot. Using a Dutch oven, heat oil over medium-high heat. Add mushrooms and onion; cook and stir 5-7 minutes or until tender. Add rice and garlic; cook and stir 1-2 minutes or until rice is coated.
2. Stir in wine and thyme. Reduce heat to maintain a simmer; cook and stir until wine is absorbed. Add the hot stock blend, ½ cup at a time, cooking and stirring after each addition until the stock has been absorbed; continue until the rice is tender but firm to the bite and the mixture is creamy. Stir in spinach, peas, cheese, vinegar, salt and pepper; heat through. Serve promptly.

SHARP CHEDDAR SCALLOPED POTATOES

Try as I might, I can never follow a recipe exactly, so here's what I came up with when I made a family friend's scalloped potatoes in my own kitchen. They're so good, you just keep going back for more.
—**SUSAN SIMONS** EATONVILLE, WA

PREP: 30 MIN. • **BAKE:** 70 MIN.
MAKES: 8 SERVINGS

- ¼ cup butter, cubed
- ⅓ cup all-purpose flour
- ¾ teaspoon salt
- ½ teaspoon ground mustard
- ½ teaspoon white pepper
- 2 cups half-and-half cream
- 1½ cups shredded sharp white cheddar cheese
- 1½ cups shredded sharp yellow cheddar cheese
- 6 cups thinly sliced peeled Yukon Gold potatoes (about 2 pounds)
- 2 small onions, finely chopped

1. Preheat oven to 350°. In a large saucepan, heat butter over medium heat. Stir in flour, salt, mustard and pepper until blended; cook and stir 2-3 minutes or until lightly browned. Gradually whisk in cream. Bring to a boil, stirring constantly; cook and stir for 1-2 minutes or until thickened. Remove from heat.
2. Using a small bowl, combine the cheeses. Layer a third of the potatoes, a third of the onions and ¾ cup of the cheese mixture in greased 3-qt. baking dish. Repeat the layers twice. Pour the sauce over the top; sprinkle with the remaining cheese.
3. Bake the dish, covered, 45 minutes. Uncover; bake 25-30 minutes longer or until the potatoes are tender and the top is lightly browned.

[5] INGREDIENTS
EASY LEMON-BLUEBERRY JAM

After one taste of this delightfully sweet and simple jam, people will find it hard to believe that you didn't spend many long hours in a hot kitchen. Of course, you don't have to let them in on your secret!

—**JOYCE ROBBINS** OLD HICKORY, TN

PREP: 5 MIN. • **COOK:** 10 MIN. + CHILLING
MAKES: 4 HALF-PINTS

- 4 cups fresh blueberries
- 2 cups sugar
- 1 package (3 ounces) lemon gelatin

In a large saucepan, slightly crush 2 cups of the blueberries. Add the remaining berries and sugar, mix well. Bring all to a boil, stirring it constantly. Remove from heat; stir in gelatin until dissolved. Pour hot jam into jars or containers. Cover and cool. Refrigerate.

[5] INGREDIENTS | FAST FIX
GRANDMA'S CRANBERRY STUFF

What could taste better than turkey and cranberry on Thanksgiving Day? My grandmother's classic recipe makes the best cranberry dish to share with your family and friends this holiday.

—**CATHERINE CASSIDY** MILWAUKEE, WI

START TO FINISH: 10 MIN.
MAKES: 3 CUPS

- 1 medium navel orange
- 1 package (12 ounces) fresh or frozen cranberries, thawed
- 1 cup sugar
- 1 cup chopped walnuts, toasted

Cut unpeeled orange into wedges, removing any seeds, and place in a food processor. Add cranberries and sugar; pulse until chopped. Add the walnuts; pulse just until combined.
NOTE *To toast nuts, bake in a shallow pan in a 350° oven for 5-10 minutes or cook in a skillet over low heat until lightly browned, stirring occasionally.*

FAST FIX
CHICKEN FIESTA SALAD

My husband gave me the secret of using the broiler to cook chicken faster, and I discovered the accompanying spice blend as I tried out some new ways to use this quick-cooking technique.

—**KATIE RANKIN** COLUMBUS, OH

START TO FINISH: 30 MIN.
MAKES: 2 SERVINGS

- 1½ teaspoons lemon-pepper seasoning
- 1½ teaspoons chili powder
- 1½ teaspoons dried basil
- ¾ pound boneless skinless chicken breasts, cut into 1-inch pieces
- 4 cups torn mixed salad greens
- ⅔ cup canned black beans, rinsed and drained
- ¼ cup thinly sliced red onion
- 1 small tomato, sliced
- ½ cup shredded cheddar cheese Tortilla chips, salsa and ranch salad dressing

1. In a large resealable plastic bag, combine the seasonings. Add the chicken, a few pieces at a time, and shake to coat.
2. Place chicken on a greased broiler pan. Broil 3-4 in. from the heat for 3-4 minutes on each side or until chicken is no longer pink.
3. On two plates, arrange the salad greens, black beans, onion and tomato. Top with the chicken and cheese. Serve with tortilla chips, salsa and ranch dressing.

FAST FIX
CREAMY COLESLAW

Packaged coleslaw mix really cuts down on prep time. My recipe is great for potlucks or to serve your family on a busy weeknight.

—**RENEE ENDRESS** GALVA, IL

START TO FINISH: 10 MIN.
MAKES: 6 SERVINGS

- 1 package (14 ounces) coleslaw mix
- ¾ cup mayonnaise
- ⅓ cup sour cream

- ¼ cup sugar
- ¾ teaspoon seasoned salt
- ½ teaspoon ground mustard
- ¼ teaspoon celery salt

Place coleslaw mix in a large bowl. In a small bowl, combine the remaining ingredients; stir until blended. Pour over the coleslaw mix and toss to coat. Refrigerate until serving.

FAST FIX
BUTTERY HORSERADISH CORN ON THE COB

For a July Fourth barbecue, I whipped up a butter and horseradish topping for the grilled corn. People actually formed a line to get seconds!

—**TRISH LOEWEN** BAKERSFIELD, CA

START TO FINISH: 30 MIN.
MAKES: 12 SERVINGS

- ¾ cup butter, softened
- ¼ cup shredded pepper jack cheese
- ¼ cup prepared horseradish
- 1 tablespoon dried parsley flakes
- 3 teaspoons salt
- 2 teaspoons balsamic vinegar
- ½ teaspoon pepper
- ¼ teaspoon dried thyme
- 12 medium ears sweet corn, husks removed

1. In a small bowl, mix the first eight ingredients until blended; spread over the corn. Wrap each ear of corn with a piece of heavy-duty foil (about 14 in. square), sealing tightly.
2. Grill corn, covered, over medium heat 15-20 minutes or until tender, turning occasionally. Open foil carefully to allow steam to escape.

★ ★ ★ ★ ★ 5 STAR TIP
When buying sweet corn, look for ears with bright green tightly closed husks and golden brown silk; kernels should be plump, milky and in closely spaced rows all the way to the tip. The sugar in corn starts to convert to starch as soon as its picked, so it's best when cooked the day it's picked.

BUTTERY HORSERADISH
CORN ON THE COB

SWEET ONION & RED BELL PEPPER TOPPING

When the Vidalia onions hit the market in spring, this is one of the first recipes I make. I use it on hot dogs, bruschetta, cream cheese and crackers. It is so versatile.

—PAT HOCKETT OCALA, FL

PREP: 20 MIN. • **COOK:** 4 HOURS
MAKES: 4 CUPS

- 4 large sweet onions, thinly sliced (about 8 cups)
- 4 large sweet red peppers, thinly sliced (about 6 cups)
- ½ cup cider vinegar
- ¼ cup packed brown sugar
- 2 tablespoons canola oil
- 2 tablespoons honey
- 2 teaspoons celery seed
- ¾ teaspoon crushed red pepper flakes
- ½ teaspoon salt

In a 5- or 6-qt. slow cooker, combine all ingredients. Cook, covered, on low for 4-5 hours or until vegetables are tender. Serve with a slotted spoon.

SWEET ONION & RED BELL PEPPER TOPPING

VEGGIE-TOPPED POLENTA SLICES

Even though we didn't have too many ingredients in the kitchen at the time, this amazing side came from a stroke of genius I had.

—JENN TIDWELL FAIR OAKS, CA

PREP: 20 MIN. • **COOK:** 20 MIN.
MAKES: 4 SERVINGS

- 1 tube (1 pound) polenta, cut into 12 slices
- 2 tablespoons olive oil, divided
- 1 medium zucchini, chopped
- 2 shallots, minced
- 2 garlic cloves, minced
- 3 tablespoons reduced-sodium chicken broth
- ½ teaspoon pepper
- ⅛ teaspoon salt
- 4 plum tomatoes, seeded and chopped
- 2 tablespoons minced fresh basil or 2 teaspoons dried basil
- 1 tablespoon minced fresh parsley
- ½ cup shredded part-skim mozzarella cheese

1. Using a large nonstick skillet, cook the polenta in 1 tablespoon of oil over medium heat for 9-11 minutes on each side or until golden brown.
2. Meanwhile, in another large skillet, saute zucchini in the remaining oil until tender. Add shallots and garlic; cook 1 minute longer. Add the broth, pepper and salt. Bring to a boil; cook until liquid is almost evaporated.
3. Stir in the tomatoes, basil and parsley; heat through. Serve with polenta; sprinkle with cheese.

★ ★ ★ ★ ★ 5 STAR TIP
Polenta is a popular Italian dish made from cornmeal. Premade polenta (in a tube) does not need to be refrigerated. Depending on your store, tubed polenta may be found with the shredded cheese and refrigerated pasta, with the dried pasta, or in the ethnic food aisle.

LOADED SMASHED POTATOES

If mashed potatoes are a must at your family Thanksgiving, then why not go all out with the works? I love garlic, onions and bacon—this dish has all three!

—**KATHY HARDING** RICHMOND, MO

PREP: 40 MIN. • **BAKE:** 10 MIN.
MAKES: 15 SERVINGS

- 2 whole garlic bulbs
- 1 tablespoon canola oil
- 8 bacon strips
- 3 green onions, chopped
- 4 pounds small red potatoes
- 1 container (16 ounces) sour cream
- 1½ cups shredded cheddar cheese, divided
- ⅓ cup butter, softened
- ¼ cup 2% milk
- ½ teaspoon salt
- ¼ teaspoon pepper
  Minced chives, optional

1. Remove papery outer skin from garlic (do not peel or separate cloves). Cut tops off garlic bulbs. Brush with oil. Wrap each bulb in heavy-duty foil.
2. Bake at 425° for 30-35 minutes or until softened. Cool for 10 minutes.
3. Meanwhile, in a large skillet, cook the bacon over medium heat until crisp. Remove to paper towels; drain, reserving 2 tablespoons drippings. In the same skillet, cook onions in reserved drippings for 2 minutes or until tender; set aside. Crumble bacon.
4. Place potatoes in a large saucepan and cover with water. Bring to a boil. Reduce heat; cover and cook for 10-15 minutes or until tender. Drain and transfer to a large bowl.
5. Mash potatoes. Squeeze softened garlic over top. Stir in the bacon, onions with drippings, sour cream, 1 cup of the cheese, butter, milk, salt and pepper; combine. Spoon mixture into a greased 13x9-in. baking dish; top with the remaining cheese.
6. Bake, uncovered, at 350° for 10-15 minutes or until the cheese is melted. Garnish with chives if desired.

BLUE CHEESE & GRAPE COLESLAW

BLUE CHEESE & GRAPE COLESLAW

Traditional dishes like coleslaw beg for a fresh approach. I update mine with almonds, grapes, blue cheese and bacon for a grand bowl of color and crunch.

—**JEANNINE BUNGE** HARTLEY, IA

PREP: 10 MIN. + CHILLING
MAKES: 8 SERVINGS

- 1 package (14 ounces) coleslaw mix
- ¾ cup sliced almonds, toasted
- ¾ cup quartered green grapes
- ¾ cup quartered seedless red grapes
- ½ cup crumbled blue cheese
- 3 bacon strips, cooked and crumbled
- ¼ teaspoon pepper
- ¾ cup coleslaw salad dressing

Combine the first seven ingredients. Pour dressing over the salad; toss to coat. Refrigerate for 1 hour.
NOTE *To toast nuts, bake in a shallow pan in a 350° oven for 5-10 minutes or cook in a skillet over low heat until lightly browned, stirring occasionally.*

CORN BREAD PUDDING

This makes a comforting side for breakfast or any meal. We often enjoy it with shrimp and other seafood. It's an adaptation of my mom's original recipe. It never fails to please.

—**BOB GEBHARDT** WAUSAU, WI

PREP: 5 MIN. • **BAKE:** 40 MIN.
MAKES: 12 SERVINGS

- 2 **large eggs**
- 1 **cup sour cream**
- 1 **can (15¼ ounces) whole kernel corn, drained**
- 1 **can (14¾ ounces) cream-style corn**
- ½ **cup butter, melted**
- 1 **package (8½ ounces) corn bread/muffin mix**
- ¼ **teaspoon paprika**

1. In a large bowl, combine the first five ingredients. Stir in corn bread mix just until blended. Pour into a greased 3-qt. baking dish. Sprinkle with paprika.

2. Bake it, uncovered, at 350° for about 40-45 minutes or until a knife inserted near the center comes out clean. Serve warm.

PESTO BUTTERMILK DRESSING

My family loves this tangy blend of buttermilk, pesto and Greek yogurt.

—**LIZ BELLVILLE** JACKSONVILLE, NC

PREP: 10 MIN. + CHILLING
MAKES: 1¾ CUPS

- ⅔ **cup buttermilk**
- ½ **cup fat-free plain Greek yogurt**
- ½ **cup prepared pesto**
- ¼ **cup shredded Parmesan cheese**
- 1 **tablespoon white wine vinegar**
- 1 **tablespoon grated lemon peel**
- 1 **garlic clove, minced**
- ½ **teaspoon coarsely ground pepper**
- ⅛ **teaspoon salt**

Place all ingredients in a jar with a tight-fitting lid; shake well. Refrigerate for 1 hour. Just before serving, shake the dressing again.

CORN BREAD PUDDING

FAST FIX ▶

CONTEST-WINNING PICNIC PASTA SALAD

My family's not big on traditional pasta salads made with mayonnaise, so when I served this colorful version that uses Italian dressing, it was a big hit. This crowd-pleaser is loaded with vegetables, beans and tricolor pasta.
—**FELICIA FIOCCHI** VINELAND, NJ

START TO FINISH: 25 MIN.
MAKES: 14-16 SERVINGS

- 1 **package (12 ounces) tricolor spiral pasta**
- 1 **package (10 ounces) refrigerated tricolor tortellini**
- 1 **jar (7½ ounces) marinated artichoke hearts, undrained**
- ½ **pound fresh broccoli florets (about 1¾ cups)**
- 12 **ounces provolone cheese, cubed**
- 12 **ounces hard salami, cubed**
- 1 **medium sweet red pepper, chopped**
- 1 **medium green pepper, chopped**
- 1 **can (15 ounces) chickpeas, rinsed and drained**
- 2 **cans (2¼ ounces each) sliced ripe olives, drained**
- 1 **medium red onion, chopped**
- 4 **garlic cloves, minced**
- 2 **envelopes Italian salad dressing mix**

1. Cook the spiral pasta and tortellini according to package directions. Drain and rinse in cold water. Place in a large bowl; add the artichokes, broccoli, provolone cheese, salami, peppers, chickpeas, olives, onion and garlic.
2. Prepare salad dressing according to package directions; pour over salad and toss to coat. Serve immediately |or cover and refrigerate.

STRAWBERRY-ORANGE SPINACH SALAD WITH TOASTED WALNUTS

Here's a colorful salad packed full of flavor. Toasted walnuts add texture and crunch.
—**MARY BUFORD SHAW** MT. PLEASANT, SC

PREP: 25 MIN. • **COOK:** 10 MIN.
MAKES: 8 SERVINGS

- 3 **bacon strips, chopped**
- 3 **tablespoons rice vinegar**
- 2 **tablespoons honey**
- 5 **teaspoons olive oil**
- 1 **teaspoon Dijon mustard**
- ½ **teaspoon pepper**
- ¼ **teaspoon salt**
- 1 **package (6 ounces) fresh baby spinach**
- 2 **medium navel oranges, peeled and chopped**
- 12 **fresh strawberries, quartered**
- 1 **cup thinly sliced cucumber**
- ½ **cup thinly sliced red onion**
- 1 **medium carrot, shredded**
- ½ **cup chopped walnuts, toasted**

1. In a small skillet, cook bacon over medium heat until crisp. Remove to paper towels with a slotted spoon; drain.
2. Using a small bowl, whisk the vinegar, honey, oil, mustard, pepper and salt. In a large bowl, combine the spinach, oranges, strawberries, cucumber, onion and carrot. Pour dressing over salad; toss to coat. Sprinkle with walnuts and bacon. Serve immediately.

★ ★ ★ ★ ★ **READER REVIEW**

"I took this to a luncheon and the ladies loved it! The dressing is light and refreshing. Definitely a crowd pleaser!"

JVROLLINS TASTEOFHOME.COM

COLORFUL
QUINOA SALAD

COLORFUL QUINOA SALAD

My youngest daughter recently learned she has to avoid gluten, dairy and eggs, which gave me a new challenge in the kitchen. I put this dish together as a side we could all share. We love it for leftovers, too.
—**CATHERINE TURNBULL** BURLINGTON, ON

PREP: 30 MIN. + COOLING
MAKES: 8 SERVINGS

- 2 **cups water**
- 1 **cup quinoa, rinsed**
- 2 **cups fresh baby spinach, thinly sliced**
- 1 **cup grape tomatoes, halved**
- 1 **medium cucumber, seeded and chopped**
- 1 **medium sweet orange pepper, chopped**
- 1 **medium sweet yellow pepper, chopped**
- 2 **green onions, chopped**

DRESSING
- 3 **tablespoons lime juice**
- 2 **tablespoons olive oil**
- 4 **teaspoons honey**
- 1 **tablespoon grated lime peel**
- 2 **teaspoons minced fresh gingerroot**
- ¼ **teaspoon salt**

1. In a large saucepan, bring water to a boil. Add quinoa. Reduce heat; simmer, covered, 12-15 minutes or until liquid is absorbed. Remove from heat; fluff with a fork. Transfer to a large bowl; cool completely.
2. Stir spinach, tomatoes, cucumber, peppers and green onions into the quinoa. In a small bowl, whisk the dressing ingredients until blended. Drizzle over the quinoa mixture; toss to coat. Refrigerate until serving.

EDDIE'S FAVORITE FIESTA CORN

EDDIE'S FAVORITE FIESTA CORN

When sweet corn is available, I love making this splurge of a side dish. Frozen corn works, but taste as you go and add sugar if needed.
—**ANTHONY BOLTON** BELLEVUE, NE

PREP: 15 MIN. • **COOK:** 25 MIN.
MAKES: 8 SERVINGS

- ½ **pound bacon strips, chopped**
- 5 **cups fresh or frozen super sweet corn**
- 1 **medium sweet red pepper, finely chopped**
- 1 **medium sweet yellow pepper, finely chopped**
- 1 **package (8 ounces) reduced-fat cream cheese**
- ½ **cup half-and-half cream**
- 1 **can (4 ounces) chopped green chilies, optional**
- 2 **teaspoons sugar**
- 1 **teaspoon pepper**
- ¼ **teaspoon salt**

1. In a 6-qt. stockpot, cook bacon over medium heat until it is crisp, stirring occasionally. Remove with a slotted spoon; drain on paper towels. Discard the drippings, reserving 1 tablespoon in pan.
2. Add corn, red pepper and yellow pepper to the drippings; cook and stir over medium-high heat 5-6 minutes or until tender. Stir in the remaining ingredients until blended; bring to a boil. Reduce heat; simmer, covered, 8-10 minutes or until thickened.

SMOKED TURKEY & APPLE SALAD

An eye-catching dish, this refreshing salad is a great main course for a summer lunch or light dinner. The dressing's Dijon flavor goes nicely with the turkey, and the apples add crunch.

—**CAROLYN JOHNS** LACEY, WA

START TO FINISH: 20 MIN.
MAKES: 4 SERVINGS

- 5 **tablespoons olive oil**
- 2 **tablespoons cider vinegar**
- 1 **tablespoon Dijon mustard**
- ½ **teaspoon lemon-pepper seasoning**

SALAD

- 6 **to 8 cups watercress or torn romaine**
- 1 **medium carrot, julienned**
- 10 **cherry tomatoes, halved**
- 8 **ounces sliced deli smoked turkey, cut into strips**
- 4 **medium apples, sliced**
- ⅓ **cup chopped walnuts, toasted**

1. Whisk together first four ingredients.
2. Place the watercress on a platter; top with carrot, tomatoes, turkey and apples. Drizzle with dressing; top with walnuts. Serve immediately.

FAST FIX

GERMAN POTATO SALAD

I'd always loved my German grandmother's potato salad. So when I married a potato farmer—and had spuds in abundance— I played with several recipes that sounded similar and came up with this salad that reminds me of hers.

—**SUE HARTMAN** PARMA, ID

START TO FINISH: 25 MIN.
MAKES: 6-8 SERVINGS

- 5 **bacon strips**
- ¾ **cup chopped onion**
- 2 **tablespoons all-purpose flour**
- 1 **teaspoon salt**
- ⅛ **teaspoon pepper**
- 1⅓ **cups water**
- ⅔ **cup cider vinegar**
- ¼ **cup sugar**
- 6 **cups sliced cooked peeled potatoes**

1. In a large skillet, fry bacon until crisp; remove and set aside. Drain all but 2-3 tablespoons of drippings; cook onion until tender. Stir in the flour, salt and pepper until blended. Add water and vinegar; cook and stir for 1 minute or until slightly thickened.
2. Stir in the sugar until dissolved. Crumble bacon; gently stir in bacon and potatoes. Heat through, stirring lightly to coat potatoes. Serve warm.

FAST FIX

WATERMELON & SPINACH SALAD

Now's the perfect time to toss together my melon salad. You'd never expect it, but spinach is awesome in this recipe. You will eat it and keep cool on even the hottest days.

—**MARJORIE AU** HONOLULU, HI

START TO FINISH: 30 MIN.
MAKES: 8 SERVINGS

- ¼ **cup rice vinegar or white wine vinegar**
- 1 **tablespoon grated lime peel**
- 2 **tablespoons lime juice**
- 2 **tablespoons canola oil**
- 4 **teaspoons minced fresh gingerroot**
- 2 **garlic cloves, minced**
- ½ **teaspoon salt**
- ¼ **teaspoon sugar**
- ¼ **teaspoon pepper**

SALAD

- 4 **cups fresh baby spinach or arugula**
- 3 **cups cubed seedless watermelon**
- 2 **cups cubed cantaloupe**
- 2 **cups cubed English cucumber**
- ½ **cup chopped fresh cilantro**
- 2 **green onions, chopped**

In a small bowl, whisk the first nine ingredients. In a large bowl, combine salad ingredients. Drizzle with dressing and toss to coat; serve immediately.

TORTELLINI & CHICKEN CAESAR SALAD

My family loved this pasta salad right from the start, so these days I serve it a lot. When grilling season arrives, grilled chicken is a special treat in this recipe.

—**LEE REESE** ROLLA, MO

START TO FINISH: 25 MIN.
MAKES: 6 SERVINGS

- 1 **package (20 ounces) refrigerated cheese tortellini**
- 1 **pound boneless skinless chicken breasts, cut into 1½-inch pieces**
- ⅓ **cup finely chopped onion**
- 1 **tablespoon olive oil**
- 2 **garlic cloves, minced**
- ¾ **teaspoon salt**
- ¼ **teaspoon pepper**
- 1 **package (10 ounces) hearts of romaine salad mix**
- 1½ **cups grape tomatoes**
- 1 **can (6½ ounces) sliced ripe olives, drained**
- ¾ **cup creamy Caesar salad dressing**
- ¾ **cup shredded Parmesan cheese**
- 6 **bacon strips, cooked and crumbled**

1. Cook the tortellini according to package directions. Drain; rinse with cold water.
2. Meanwhile, in a small bowl, combine chicken, onion, oil, garlic, salt and pepper; toss to coat. Heat a large skillet over medium-high heat. Add the chicken mixture; cook and stir 4-6 minutes or until the chicken is no longer pink. Remove from heat.
3. In a large bowl, combine salad mix, tomatoes, olives, tortellini and the chicken mixture. Drizzle with the dressing; toss to coat. Sprinkle with cheese and bacon. Serve immediately.

TORTELLINI & CHICKEN
CAESAR SALAD

ROASTED CARROTS
WITH THYME

(5) INGREDIENTS FAST FIX ▶

ROASTED CARROTS WITH THYME

Cutting the carrots lengthwise makes this dish look extra pretty.

—**DEIRDRE COX** KANSAS CITY, MO

START TO FINISH: 30 MIN.
MAKES: 4 SERVINGS

- 1 **pound medium carrots, peeled and halved lengthwise**
- 2 **teaspoons minced fresh thyme or ½ teaspoon dried thyme**
- 2 **teaspoons canola oil**
- 1 **teaspoon honey**
- ¼ **teaspoon salt**

Preheat oven to 400°. Place carrots in a greased 15x10x1-in. baking pan. In a small bowl, mix thyme, oil, honey and salt; brush over carrots. Roast for 20-25 minutes or until tender.

(5) INGREDIENTS FAST FIX ▶

TANGY BUTTERMILK SALAD DRESSING

Buttermilk gives a tangy twist to this mild and creamy salad dressing. You'll love drizzling it on your favorite fresh greens and vegetables.

—*TASTE OF HOME* TEST KITCHEN

START TO FINISH: 5 MIN.
MAKES: 2 CUPS

- 1 **cup mayonnaise**
- 1 **cup buttermilk**
- ½ **teaspoon onion salt**
- ¼ **teaspoon paprika**
- ⅛ **teaspoon pepper**
  Mixed salad greens

In a small bowl, whisk the mayonnaise, buttermilk, onion salt, paprika and pepper. Serve the dressing with salad greens. Refrigerate leftovers.

MOM'S SUPER STUPENDOUS POTATO SALAD

In college, my best friend and I debated whose mom made the best potato salad. Turns out their recipes were almost identical! Even though I've since tweaked our recipe, it still takes me home again.

—ELLIE MARTIN CLIFFE MILWAUKEE, WI

PREP: 20 MIN. • **COOK:** 15 MIN. + CHILLING
MAKES: 12 SERVINGS

- 1 garlic clove, peeled
- 3 pounds small red potatoes, quartered
- 2 tablespoons cider vinegar, divided
- 1½ teaspoons salt, divided
- 6 hard-cooked large eggs, divided
- 1 cup mayonnaise
- ½ cup sour cream
- 1 tablespoon Dijon mustard
- ½ teaspoon paprika
- ¼ teaspoon pepper
- 1 medium sweet onion, finely chopped
- 2 celery ribs, finely chopped
- 2 tablespoons minced fresh parsley

1. Skewer garlic with a toothpick (to make it easy to find after cooking). Place potatoes, 1 tablespoon vinegar, 1 teaspoon salt and the skewered garlic in a Dutch oven; add water to cover. Bring to a boil. Reduce heat; simmer until tender, 10-12 minutes. Drain potatoes, reserving garlic; remove skewer and crush garlic.
2. Meanwhile, chop five of the eggs. Whisk together mayonnaise, sour cream, mustard, paprika, pepper, garlic and the remaining vinegar and salt. Stir in potatoes, chopped eggs, onion and celery. Refrigerate 4 hours or until cold.
3. Just before serving, slice the remaining egg. Top the salad with the egg; sprinkle with parsley and, if desired, additional paprika.

PATIO PINTOS

FREEZE IT

PATIO PINTOS

Mom made these pinto beans any time she had the gang over for dinner. Once, she made a batch for my cousin's birthday and he ate the entire thing himself!

—JOAN HALLFORD NORTH RICHLAND HILLS, TX

PREP: 25 MIN. • **BAKE:** 1 HOUR
MAKES: 10 SERVINGS

- ½ pound bacon strips, chopped
- 1 large onion, chopped
- 2 garlic cloves, minced
- 6 cans (15 ounces each) pinto beans, rinsed and drained
- 4 cans (8 ounces each) tomato sauce
- 2 cans (4 ounces each) chopped green chilies
- ⅓ cup packed brown sugar
- 1 teaspoon chili powder
- ¾ teaspoon salt
- ½ teaspoon dried oregano
- ¼ teaspoon pepper

1. Preheat oven to 350°. In a Dutch oven, cook bacon over medium heat until crisp, stirring it occasionally. Remove with a slotted spoon; drain on paper towels. Discard drippings, reserving 2 tablespoons in pan.
2. Add onion to the drippings; cook and stir over medium heat for 6-8 minutes or until tender. Add garlic; cook 1 minute longer. Stir in beans, tomato sauce, green chilies, brown sugar and seasonings. Sprinkle top with bacon. Bake, covered, 60-70 minutes or until heated through.
FREEZE OPTION *Freeze the cooled bean mixture in freezer containers. To use, partially thaw in refrigerator overnight. Heat mixture through in a saucepan, stirring occasionally and adding a little water if necessary.*

MICHIGAN CHERRY SALAD

This recipe reminds me what I love about my home state: picking apples with my children, buying greens at the farmer's market, and tasting fresh cherries on vacations.
—**JENNIFER GILBERT** BRIGHTON, MI

START TO FINISH: 15 MIN.
MAKES: 8 SERVINGS

- 7 **ounces fresh baby spinach (about 9 cups)**
- 3 **ounces spring mix salad greens (about 5 cups)**
- 1 **large apple, chopped**
- ½ **cup coarsely chopped pecans, toasted**
- ½ **cup dried cherries**
- ¼ **cup crumbled Gorgonzola cheese**

DRESSING
- ¼ **cup fresh raspberries**
- ¼ **cup red wine vinegar**
- 3 **tablespoons cider vinegar**
- 3 **tablespoons cherry preserves**
- 1 **tablespoon sugar**
- 2 **tablespoons olive oil**

1. In a large bowl, combine the first six ingredients.
2. Place the raspberries, vinegars, preserves and sugar in a blender. While processing, gradually add oil in a steady stream. Drizzle over the salad; toss to coat.
NOTE *To toast nuts, bake in a shallow pan in a 350° oven for 5-10 minutes or cook in a skillet over low heat until lightly browned, stirring occasionally.*

MICHIGAN CHERRY SALAD

BRUSSELS SPROUTS & KALE SAUTE

This colorful side dish is filled with healthy greens. It pairs well with turkey, potatoes and other holiday staples. The crispy salami—which just happens to be my kid's favorite ingredient—makes it over-the-top delicious.
—**JENNIFER MCNABB** BRENTWOOD, TN

START TO FINISH: 30 MIN.
MAKES: 12 SERVINGS (½ CUP EACH)

- ¼ **pound thinly sliced hard salami, cut into ¼-inch strips**
- 1½ **teaspoons olive oil**
- 2 **tablespoons butter**
- 2 **pounds fresh Brussels sprouts, thinly sliced**
- 2 **cups shredded fresh kale**
- 1 **large onion, finely chopped**
- ½ **teaspoon kosher salt**
- ⅛ **teaspoon cayenne pepper**
- ¼ **teaspoon coarsely ground pepper**
- 1 **garlic clove, minced**
- ½ **cup chicken broth**
- ½ **cup chopped walnuts**
- 1 **tablespoon balsamic vinegar**

1. In a Dutch oven, cook and stir salami in oil over medium-high heat for 3-5 minutes or until crisp. Remove to paper towels with a slotted spoon; reserve the drippings in the pan.
2. Add butter to the drippings; heat over medium-high heat. Add the Brussels sprouts, kale, onion, salt, cayenne and black pepper; cook and stir until vegetables are crisp-tender. Add garlic; cook 1 minute longer.
3. Stir in broth; bring to a boil. Reduce heat; cover and cook for 4-5 minutes or until the Brussels sprouts become tender. Stir in walnuts and vinegar. Serve with the salami strips.

LUSCIOUS BLUEBERRY JAM

Enjoy this jam that boasts a beautiful dark color with a sweetly seasonal flavor. It's amazing spread on fresh bread or biscuits.

—**KAREN HAEN** STURGEON BAY, WI

PREP: 20 MIN. • **COOK:** 20 MIN. + STANDING
MAKES: 8 CUPS

- 8 **cups fresh blueberries**
- 2 **tablespoons lemon juice**
- 1 **package (1¾ ounces) powdered fruit pectin**
- 7 **cups sugar**

1. Mash blueberries; transfer to a Dutch oven. Add lemon juice; stir in pectin. Bring to a full rolling boil over high heat, stirring constantly.
2. Stir in the sugar; return to a full rolling boil. Boil for 1 minute, stirring constantly. Remove from the heat; skim off the foam. Ladle into jars or freezer containers and cool to room temperature, about 1 hour.
3. Cover and let stand overnight or until set, but not longer than 24 hours. Refrigerate for up to 3 weeks or freeze for up to 12 months.

★ ★ ★ ★ ★ **5 STAR TIP**

One day I was in a hurry to make homemade berry jam. Instead of mashing the fruit by hand, I put the berries in the blender and gave it a couple of whirls. I had evenly crushed berries in no time.

GALE S. PEMBROKE, ON

ZESTY COLESLAW

ZESTY COLESLAW

This simple slaw tastes best when it's been refrigerated for at least one hour. The mixture seems to get creamier as it sits.

—**MICHELLE GAUER** SPICER, MN

PREP: 15 MIN. + CHILLING
MAKES: 12 SERVINGS (⅔ CUP EACH)

- 1 **cup mayonnaise**
- ⅓ **cup sugar**
- 3 **tablespoons cider vinegar**
- 1 **teaspoon seasoned salt**
- ¾ **teaspoon pepper**
- ½ **teaspoon celery seed**
- 2 **packages (14 ounces each) coleslaw mix**
- 1 **small sweet red pepper, chopped**
- ½ **cup thinly sliced sweet onion**

Using a large bowl, mix the first six ingredients. Add the coleslaw mix, red pepper and onion; toss them to coat. Refrigerate at least 1 hour before serving.

WATERMELON GRAPE SALAD

This salad is easy to make and it tastes great. Enjoy it on a hot summer day when watermelon is at its best, or serve it with a scoop of lemon sherbet for a refreshing dessert.

—**SUE GRONHOLZ** BEAVER DAM, WI

START TO FINISH: 10 MIN.
MAKES: 2 SERVINGS

- 1 **cup cubed seeded watermelon**
- 1 **cup seedless red grapes**
- 2 **tablespoons white grape juice**
- ½ **teaspoon finely chopped fresh tarragon**
- ½ **teaspoon honey**

In a small bowl, mix watermelon and grapes. In another bowl, whisk the grape juice, tarragon and honey. Pour over the fruit and toss to coat. Serve immediately.

MEDITERRANEAN COBB SALAD

I'm a huge fan of taking classic dishes and adding some flair to them. I also like to change up heavier dishes, like the classic Cobb salad. I've traded out typical chicken for crunchy falafel that's just as satisfying.

—JENN TIDWELL FAIR OAKS, CA

PREP: 1 HOUR • **COOK:** 5 MIN./BATCH
MAKES: 10 SERVINGS

- 1 package (6 ounces) falafel mix
- ½ cup sour cream or plain yogurt
- ¼ cup chopped seeded peeled cucumber
- ¼ cup 2% milk
- 1 teaspoon minced fresh parsley
- ¼ teaspoon salt
- 4 cups torn romaine
- 4 cups fresh baby spinach
- 3 hard-cooked large eggs, chopped
- 2 medium tomatoes, seeded and finely chopped
- 1 medium ripe avocado, peeled and finely chopped
- ¾ cup crumbled feta cheese
- 8 bacon strips, cooked and crumbled
- ½ cup pitted Greek olives, finely chopped

1. Prepare and cook falafel according to package directions. When it is cool enough to handle, crumble or coarsely chop the falafel.

2. In a small bowl, mix sour cream, cucumber, milk, parsley and salt. In a large bowl, combine romaine and spinach; transfer to a platter. Arrange the crumbled falafel and remaining ingredients over the greens. Drizzle with dressing.

MEDITERRANEAN COBB SALAD

SAUSAGE & CORN BREAD DRESSING

At our house, we add sausage and a little steak sauce to our corn bread dressing. It warms us up on even the coldest days.

—**MANDY NALL** MONTGOMERY, AL

PREP: 30 MIN. • **BAKE:** 40 MIN.
MAKES: 12 SERVINGS

- 1 package (19½ ounces) Italian turkey sausage links, casings removed
- 4 medium onions, chopped (about 3 cups)
- ½ cup chopped celery
- 6 cups cubed day-old white or French bread
- 6 cups coarsely crumbled corn bread
- 2 large eggs
- 2 tablespoons steak sauce
- 2 teaspoons onion salt
- 2 teaspoons poultry seasoning
- 2 teaspoons dried parsley flakes
- 1 teaspoon garlic powder
- 1 teaspoon baking powder
- 2½ to 3 cups reduced-sodium chicken broth

1. Preheat oven to 350°. In a 6-qt. stockpot, cook sausage over medium heat 6-8 minutes or until no longer pink, breaking into crumbles. Remove it with a slotted spoon, reserving the drippings in pot.
2. Add the onions and celery to the drippings; cook and stir 6-8 minutes or until tender. Remove from heat; stir in the sausage. Add cubed bread and corn bread; toss to combine.
3. In a small bowl, whisk eggs, steak sauce, seasonings and baking powder until blended; stir into the bread mixture. Stir in enough broth to reach desired moistness.
4. Transfer to a greased 13x9-in. or 3-qt. baking dish. Bake 40-50 minutes or until lightly browned.

ROASTED CABBAGE & ONIONS

I roast veggies to bring out their sweetness, and this works wonders with onions and cabbage. The piquant vinegar-mustard sauce makes this dish similar to a slaw.

—**ANN SHEEHY** LAWRENCE, MA

PREP: 10 MIN. • **COOK:** 30 MIN. + STANDING
MAKES: 6 SERVINGS

- 1 medium head cabbage (about 2 pounds), coarsely chopped
- 2 large onions, chopped
- ¼ cup olive oil
- ¾ teaspoon salt
- ¾ teaspoon pepper
- 3 tablespoons minced fresh chives
- 3 tablespoons minced fresh tarragon

DRESSING
- 2 tablespoons white balsamic vinegar or white wine vinegar
- 2 tablespoons olive oil
- 2 tablespoons Dijon mustard
- 1 tablespoon lemon juice
- ½ teaspoon salt
- ½ teaspoon pepper

1. Preheat the oven to 450°. Place cabbage and onions in a large bowl. Drizzle with oil; sprinkle with salt and pepper and toss to coat. Transfer to a shallow roasting pan, spreading it evenly. Roast 30-35 minutes or until vegetables are tender and lightly browned, stirring halfway.
2. Transfer the cabbage mixture to a large bowl. Add chives and tarragon; toss to combine. Using a small bowl, whisk the dressing ingredients until blended. Drizzle mix over the cabbage mixture; toss to coat. Let it stand 10 minutes to allow flavors to blend. Serve warm or at room temperature.

HOW TO SNIP PARSLEY

Here's a simple trimming tip. Simply place parsley or other herbs in a small glass container and snip sprigs with kitchen shears until minced.

CRISPY SMASHED HERBED POTATOES

CRISPY SMASHED HERBED POTATOES

While scanning a local newspaper, I found a recipe with this intriguing title. Just as advertised, these potatoes are crispy, herbed and smashed.

—ALTHEA DYE HOWARD, OH

PREP: 25 MIN. • **BAKE:** 20 MIN.
MAKES: 4 SERVINGS

- 12 small red potatoes (about 1½ pounds)
- 3 tablespoons olive oil
- ¼ cup butter, melted
- ¾ teaspoon salt
- ¼ teaspoon pepper
- 3 tablespoons minced fresh chives
- 1 tablespoon minced fresh parsley

1. Preheat the oven to 450°. Place the potatoes in a large saucepan; add water to cover. Bring to a boil. Reduce heat; cook, uncovered, 15-20 minutes or until tender. Drain.
2. Drizzle oil over the bottom of a 15x10x1-in. baking pan; arrange the potatoes over oil. Using a potato masher, flatten potatoes to ½-in. thickness. Brush the potatoes with butter; sprinkle with salt and pepper.
3. Roast 20-25 minutes or until golden brown. Sprinkle with chives and parsley.

GREAT GRAIN SALAD

I can't think of a better dish to round out a meal. My grain salad features all my favorite nuts, seeds and fruits. Try adding grilled chicken to make it a meal on its own.

—RACHEL DUEKER GERVAIS, OR

PREP: 15 MIN. • **COOK:** 1 HOUR + CHILLING
MAKES: 12 SERVINGS (¾ CUP EACH)

- 3 cups water
- ½ cup medium pearl barley
- ½ cup uncooked wild rice
- ⅔ cup uncooked basmati rice
- ½ cup slivered almonds
- ½ cup sunflower kernels
- ½ cup salted pumpkin seeds or pepitas
- ½ cup each golden raisins, chopped dried apricots and dried cranberries
- ⅓ cup minced fresh parsley
- 4 teaspoons grated orange peel

VINAIGRETTE
- ⅔ cup walnut oil
- ⅔ cup raspberry vinegar
- 2 teaspoons orange juice
- 2 teaspoons pepper
- 1 teaspoon salt

1. In a large saucepan, bring water to a boil. Add the barley and wild rice. Reduce the heat; cover and simmer for 55-65 minutes or until tender. Meanwhile, cook the basmati rice according to package directions. Cool barley and rices to room temperature.
2. In a large bowl, combine almonds, sunflower kernels, pumpkin seeds, dried fruit, parsley and orange peel; add the barley and rices.
3. In a small bowl, whisk vinaigrette ingredients. Pour over the salad and toss to coat. Cover and refrigerate for at least 2 hours.

GOLDEN MASHED POTATOES

When there's no gravy with the meat, this is great to serve in place of regular mashed potatoes. I make it often for picnics and church socials. My husband even made it for his family reunion one year when I couldn't go!

—CINDY STITH WICKLIFFE, KY

PREP: 40 MIN. • **BAKE:** 30 MIN.
MAKES: 10-12 SERVINGS

- 9 large potatoes (about 4 pounds), peeled and cubed
- 1 pound carrots, cut into ½-inch chunks
- 8 green onions, thinly sliced
- ½ cup butter
- 1 cup (8 ounces) sour cream
- 1½ teaspoons salt
- ⅛ teaspoon pepper
- ¾ cup shredded cheddar cheese

1. In a soup kettle or Dutch oven, cook potatoes and carrots in boiling salted water until tender; drain. Place in a bowl; mash and set aside.
2. In a skillet, saute onions in butter until they are tender. Add them to the potato mixture. Add sour cream, salt and pepper; mix until blended.
3. Transfer to a greased 13x9-in. baking dish. Sprinkle with cheese. Bake, uncovered, at 350° for 30-40 minutes or until heated through.

FREEZE OPTION *Cool unbaked casserole; cover and freeze. To use, partially thaw it in the refrigerator overnight. Remove from refrigerator 30 minutes before baking. Preheat oven to 350°. Bake the casserole as directed, increasing time as necessary to heat through and for a thermometer inserted in center to read 165°.*

SLOW-COOKED GREEN BEANS

I spent hours looking up side dishes for a cooking demo to present to women from my church. These easy green beans became my star attraction.

—ALICE WHITE WILLOW SPRING, NC

PREP: 10 MIN. • **COOK:** 2 HOURS
MAKES: 12 SERVINGS (⅔ CUP EACH)

- 16 cups frozen french-style green beans (about 48 ounces), thawed
- ½ cup butter, melted
- ½ cup packed brown sugar
- 1½ teaspoons garlic salt
- ¾ teaspoon reduced-sodium soy sauce

Place the beans in a 5-qt. slow cooker. Mix remaining ingredients; pour over the beans and toss to coat. Cook it, covered, on low until heated through, 2-3 hours. Serve with a slotted spoon.

WARM SQUASH & QUINOA SALAD

When I see butternut squash available at the supermarket, I buy one. It's amazing tossed with earthy quinoa, Italian spices and crunchy pine nuts. And don't get me started on the browned butter! Yum.

—CARLY TAYLOR LIBERTYVILLE, IL

START TO FINISH: 30 MIN.
MAKES: 6 SERVINGS

- 2 cups quinoa, rinsed
- 3 teaspoons ground cumin
- 3 cups water
- 2 tablespoons butter
- 3½ cups cubed peeled butternut squash (about ½ medium)
- 1 teaspoon sea salt
- ¾ teaspoon Italian seasoning
- ¼ teaspoon coarsely ground pepper
- ½ cup crumbled feta cheese
  Toasted pine nuts, optional

1. Using a large saucepan, combine quinoa, cumin and water; bring to a boil. Reduce heat; simmer, covered, until liquid is absorbed, 10-13 minutes. Remove from heat; keep warm.
2. Meanwhile, in a large skillet, heat butter over medium-low heat until golden brown, 3-5 minutes, stirring constantly. Immediately stir in squash and seasonings; cook, covered, until tender, about 10-12 minutes, stirring occasionally. Stir into the quinoa. Sprinkle with cheese and, if desired, pine nuts.

WARM SQUASH & QUINOA SALAD

LIME & SESAME GRILLED EGGPLANT

When I lived in Greece, I fell in love with eggplant. My recipe's seasonings have an Asian theme, but the dish still makes me think Greek.

—ALLYSON MEYLER GREENSBORO, NC

START TO FINISH: 20 MIN.
MAKES: 6 SERVINGS

- 3 tablespoons lime juice
- 1 tablespoon sesame oil
- 1½ teaspoons reduced-sodium soy sauce
- 1 garlic clove, minced
- ½ teaspoon grated fresh gingerroot or ¼ teaspoon ground ginger
- ½ teaspoon salt
- ⅛ teaspoon pepper
- 1 medium eggplant (1¼ pounds), cut lengthwise into ½-inch slices
- 2 teaspoons honey
- ⅛ teaspoon crushed red pepper flakes
  Thinly sliced green onion and sesame seeds

1. In a small bowl, whisk the first seven ingredients until blended; brush 2 tablespoons juice mixture over both sides of eggplant slices. Grill, covered, over medium heat 4-6 minutes on each side or until tender.
2. Transfer eggplant to a serving plate. Stir honey and pepper flakes into remaining juice mixture; drizzle over eggplant. Sprinkle with green onion and sesame seeds.

★ ★ ★ ★ ★ 5 STAR TIP

Salting eggplant draws out some of the liquid that carries bitter flavors. To salt, place slices, cubes, or strips of eggplant in a colander over a plate; sprinkle with salt and toss. Let stand about 30 minutes. Rinse, drain well and pat dry with paper towels.

HOW TO PEEL AN EGGPLANT

Cut the stem end off the eggplant, and, if desired, a small slice from the bottom so the eggplant can rest flat. Remove the peel with a vegetable peeler. Eggplant peel can be tough and bitter, and is best removed in most recipes. However, some small varieties of eggplant are completely edible, including the peel.

LIME & SESAME GRILLED EGGPLANT

BLT TWICE-BAKED POTATOES

Two favorites go together well in this hearty dish: BLTs and twice-baked potatoes. I often serve these tasty spuds with grilled steaks or barbecued chicken.

—MARY SHENK DEKALB, IL

PREP: 25 MIN. • **BAKE:** 15 MIN.
MAKES: 8 SERVINGS

- 4 medium potatoes (about 8 ounces each)
- ½ cup mayonnaise
- 1 cup shredded cheddar cheese
- 8 bacon strips, cooked and crumbled
- ⅓ cup oil-packed sun-dried tomatoes, patted dry and chopped
- 1 green onion, thinly sliced
- ½ teaspoon salt
- ¼ teaspoon pepper
- 1 cup shredded lettuce

1. Preheat the oven to 400°. Scrub potatoes; pierce several times with a fork. Place on a microwave-safe plate. Microwave, uncovered, on high 12-15 minutes or until tender, turning once.
2. When cool enough to work with, cut each potato lengthwise in half. Scoop out pulp, leaving ¼-in.-thick shells. In a small bowl, mash the pulp with mayonnaise, adding the cheese, bacon, tomatoes, green onion, salt and pepper.
3. Spoon into potato shells. Place on a baking sheet. Bake for 12-15 minutes or until heated through. Sprinkle with lettuce.

★ ★ ★ ★ ★ **5 STAR TIP**
When making twice-baked potatoes, use a melon baller for scooping the cooked potato out of the shells. It will come out quickly and neatly without tearing the skins. I once did 40 potatoes this way in no time!
FAY G. EVERETT, PA

BLT TWICE-BAKED POTATOES

⑤INGREDIENTS
ROSEMARY SWEET POTATO FRIES

A local restaurant got me hooked on sweet potato fries. I started experimenting at home, trying to make them taste like theirs, but healthier and baked, not fried. I'm thrilled with these results!

—**JACKIE GREGSTON** HALLSVILLE, TX

PREP: 15 MIN. • **BAKE:** 30 MIN.
MAKES: 4 SERVINGS

- 3 **tablespoons olive oil**
- 1 **tablespoon minced fresh rosemary**
- 1 **garlic clove, minced**
- 1 **teaspoon cornstarch**
- ¾ **teaspoon salt**
- ⅛ **teaspoon pepper**
- 3 **large sweet potatoes, peeled and cut into ¼-inch julienned strips (about 2¼ pounds)**

1. Preheat oven to 425°. In a large resealable plastic bag, combine the first six ingredients. Add the sweet potatoes; shake to coat.
2. Arrange potatoes in a single layer on two 15x10x1-in. baking pans coated with cooking spray. Bake, uncovered, 30-35 minutes or until tender and lightly browned, turning occasionally.

FAST FIX
DAD'S GREEK SALAD

The heart of a Greek salad is in the olives, feta, cucumbers and tomatoes. Dress it with olive oil and vinegar, then add more olives and cheese.

—**ARGE SALVATORI** WALDWICK, NJ

START TO FINISH: 20 MIN.
MAKES: 8 SERVINGS

- 4 **large tomatoes, seeded and coarsely chopped**
- 2½ **cups (about 6) thinly sliced English cucumbers**
- 1 **small red onion, halved and thinly sliced**
- ¼ **cup olive oil**
- 3 **tablespoons red wine vinegar**
- ¼ **teaspoon salt**
- ⅛ **teaspoon pepper**
- ¼ **teaspoon dried oregano, optional**
- ¾ **cup pitted Greek olives**
- ¾ **cup crumbled feta cheese**

Place the tomatoes, cucumbers and onion in a large bowl. In a small bowl, whisk the oil, vinegar, salt and pepper and, if desired, oregano until they are blended. Drizzle over the salad; toss to coat. Top with olives and cheese.

FAST FIX ▶
CREAMED CORN WITH BACON

My family is addicted to this yummy, crunchy side dish. I like to make it in the summer with farm-fresh corn.

—**TINA MIRILOVICH** JOHNSTOWN, PA

START TO FINISH: 25 MIN.
MAKES: 6 SERVINGS

- 1 **small onion, finely chopped**
- 1 **tablespoon butter**
- 4 **cups fresh or frozen corn, thawed**
- 1 **cup heavy whipping cream**
- ¼ **cup chicken broth**
- 4 **bacon strips, cooked and crumbled**
- ¼ **teaspoon pepper**
- ¼ **cup grated Parmesan cheese**
- 2 **tablespoons minced fresh parsley**

1. In a large skillet, saute onion in butter for 3 minutes. Add corn; saute 1-2 minutes longer or until onion and corn are tender.
2. Stir in cream, broth, bacon and pepper. Cook and stir for 5-7 minutes or until slightly thickened. Stir in cheese and parsley.

CHEESY MASHED POTATOES

CHEESY MASHED POTATOES

Tired of the same old mashed potatoes, I whipped up this new family favorite. Now we can't get enough of it at our house. I'll often prepare the dish ahead and refrigerate it. Then I bake it just before serving.
—**DAWN REUTER** OXFORD, WI

PREP: 20 MIN. • **BAKE:** 30 MIN.
MAKES: 14 SERVINGS

- 5 pounds potatoes, peeled and cubed
- ¾ cup sour cream
- ½ cup milk
- 3 tablespoons butter
  Salt and pepper to taste
- 3 cups shredded cheddar cheese blend, divided
- ½ pound sliced bacon, cooked and crumbled
- 3 green onions, sliced

1. Place the potatoes in a Dutch oven and cover with water. Bring to a boil. Reduce heat; cover and simmer for 10-15 minutes or until tender. Drain and place in a large bowl. Add sour cream, milk, butter, salt and pepper. Beat on medium-low speed until light and fluffy. Stir in 2 cups of the cheese, the bacon and onions.
2. Transfer to a greased 3-qt. baking dish. Top with the remaining cheese. Bake it, uncovered, at 350° for 30 minutes or until heated through and cheese is melted.

★ ★ ★ ★ ★ 5 STAR TIP

My secret to rich, creamy mashed potatoes is to boil the potatoes whole and unpeeled. This method decreases the amount of water they absorb while cooking. Once tender, I drain the water and hold the warm potatoes with an oven mitt while I peel off the skins. It may be easier to peel and cube the potatoes before cooking, but you can sure taste the difference this way!
ROBERTA H. SHERWOOD, OR

REFRIGERATOR JALAPENO DILL PICKLES

I'm passionate about making pickles. My husband is passionate about eating them. He's too impatient to let them cure on the shelf, so I found this quick recipe to make him happy. Add hotter peppers if you like.
—**ANNIE JENSEN** ROSEAU, MN

PREP: 20 MIN. + CHILLING
MAKES: ABOUT 4 DOZEN PICKLE SPEARS

- 3 pounds pickling cucumbers (about 12)
- 1 small onion, halved and sliced
- ¼ cup snipped fresh dill
- 1 to 2 jalapeno peppers, sliced
- 3 garlic cloves, minced
- 2½ cups water
- 2½ cups cider vinegar
- ⅓ cup canning salt
- ⅓ cup sugar

1. Cut each cucumber lengthwise into four spears. In a very large bowl, combine the cucumbers, onion, dill, jalapenos and garlic. Using a large saucepan, combine water, vinegar, salt and sugar. Bring to a boil; cook and stir just until the salt and sugar are dissolved. Pour over the cucumber mixture; cool.
2. Cover tightly and refrigerate at least 24 hours. Store in refrigerator for up to 2 months.
NOTE *Wear disposable gloves when cutting hot peppers; the oils can burn skin. Avoid touching your face.*

FAST FIX
VEGGIE CHOPPED SALAD

My husband's aunt gave me this recipe in 1987, and it's been a staple at our house ever since. I like to make it a day ahead because some time in the fridge makes it even better. Be sure to save yourself some leftovers, too.
—**MADELINE ETZKORN** BURIEN, WA

START TO FINISH: 25 MIN.
MAKES: 12 SERVINGS (¾ CUP EACH)

- 3 cups finely chopped fresh broccoli
- 3 cups finely chopped cauliflower
- 3 cups finely chopped celery
- 2 cups frozen peas (about 8 ounces), thawed
- 6 bacon strips, cooked and crumbled
- 1⅓ cups mayonnaise
- ¼ cup sugar
- 2 tablespoons grated Parmesan cheese
- 1 tablespoon cider vinegar
- ¼ teaspoon salt
- ¾ cup salted peanuts

In a large bowl, combine the first five ingredients. In a small bowl, mix mayonnaise, sugar, cheese, vinegar and salt until blended. Add to salad and toss to coat. Just before serving, stir in peanuts. Refrigerate leftovers.

FAST FIX
ZESTY GARLIC GREEN BEANS

If you've got side-dish duty for your next potluck, change up the usual green bean casserole. These beans travel well, too.
—**CHRISTINE BERGMAN** SUWANEE, GA

START TO FINISH: 25 MIN.
MAKES: 10 SERVINGS

- 2 tablespoons oil from oil-packed sun-dried tomatoes
- 1 cup sliced sweet onion
- ½ cup oil-packed sun-dried tomatoes, chopped
- 3 garlic cloves, minced
- 1½ teaspoons lemon-pepper seasoning
- 2 packages (16 ounces each) frozen french-style green beans

1. In a Dutch oven, heat oil over medium heat. Add onion; cook and stir 3-4 minutes or until tender. Add tomatoes, garlic and lemon pepper; cook and stir 2 minutes longer.
2. Stir in frozen green beans; cook, covered 7-9 minutes or until heated through, stirring them occasionally. Uncover; cook 2-3 minutes longer or until liquid is almost evaporated.

(5)INGREDIENTS
SCORED POTATOES

These well-seasoned baked potatoes make a fun alternative to plain baked potatoes. It's easy to help yourself to just the amount you want, too, since the potato halves are scored into sections. My mother serves the dish alongside any meat.

—BARBARA WHEELER SPARKS GLENCOE, MD

PREP: 10 MIN. • **BAKE:** 50 MIN.
MAKES: 4 SERVINGS

- 4 large baking potatoes
- 2 tablespoons butter, melted, divided
- ⅛ teaspoon paprika
- 1 tablespoon minced fresh parsley
  Salt and pepper to taste

1. With a sharp knife, cut potatoes in half lengthwise. Slice each half widthwise six times, but not all the way through; fan potatoes slightly.
2. Place the potatoes in a shallow baking dish. Brush with 1 tablespoon butter. Sprinkle with paprika, parsley, salt and pepper. Bake, uncovered, at 350° for 50 minutes or until tender. Drizzle with remaining butter.

SCORED POTATOES

(5)INGREDIENTS FAST FIX
FRESH GREEN BEANS & GARLIC

I am a firm believer that fresh is best, so I developed this recipe to take advantage of our garden's bounty. It really shows off the full flavor of the green beans.

—CAROL MAYER SPARTA, IL

START TO FINISH: 25 MIN.
MAKES: 8 SERVINGS

- 2 tablespoons canola oil
- 2 tablespoons butter
- 4 garlic cloves, sliced
- 2 pounds fresh green beans
- 1 cup reduced-sodium chicken broth
- ½ teaspoon salt
- ¼ teaspoon pepper

1. In a Dutch oven, heat oil and butter over medium-high heat. Add garlic; cook and stir 45-60 seconds or until golden. Using a slotted spoon, remove the garlic from pan; reserve. Add green beans to pan; cook and stir for 4-5 minutes or until crisp-tender.
2. Stir in broth, salt and pepper. Bring to a boil. Reduce heat; simmer, uncovered, 8-10 minutes or just until the beans are tender and the broth is almost evaporated, stirring occasionally. Stir in reserved garlic.

★ ★ ★ ★ ★ **READER REVIEW**

"This is such a delicious way to prepare green beans. Even my green bean-hating husband liked them!"

NAN MOCK TASTEOFHOME.COM

ITALIAN SALAD WITH LEMON VINAIGRETTE

For an Italian twist on salad, I mix salad greens with red onion, mushrooms, olives, pepperoncini, lemon juice and seasoning. Add tomatoes and carrots if you like.
—**DEBORAH LOOP** CLINTON TOWNSHIP, MI

START TO FINISH: 20 MIN.
MAKES: 8 SERVINGS (½ CUP VINAIGRETTE)

- 1 **package (5 ounces) spring mix salad greens**
- 1 **small red onion, thinly sliced**
- 1 **cup sliced fresh mushrooms**
- 1 **cup assorted olives, pitted and coarsely chopped**
- 8 **pepperoncini**

  Optional toppings: chopped tomatoes, shredded carrots and grated Parmesan cheese

VINAIGRETTE
- ⅓ **cup extra virgin olive oil**
- 3 **tablespoons lemon juice**
- 1 **teaspoon Italian seasoning**
- ¼ **teaspoon salt**
- ¼ **teaspoon pepper**

1. In a large bowl, combine the first five ingredients; toss lightly. If desired, add toppings.

2. In a small bowl, whisk vinaigrette ingredients until blended. Serve with the salad.

ITALIAN SALAD WITH LEMON VINAIGRETTE

HEARTY MAIN DISHES

Think back to some of the best meals you remember having—there's probably a main dish or two that comes to mind immediately. It's time for a creation of your own to take center stage at your next special meal, and these recipes are all ready for their moment in the spotlight.

MOM'S MEAT LOAF

Mom made the best meat loaf, and now, I do too. When I first met my husband, he wasn't a meat loaf fan, but this recipe won him over.
—**MICHELLE BERAN** CLAFLIN, KS

PREP: 15 MIN. • **BAKE:** 1 HOUR + STANDING
MAKES: 6 SERVINGS

- 2 **large eggs, lightly beaten**
- ¾ **cup 2% milk**
- ⅔ **cup finely crushed saltines**
- ½ **cup chopped onion**
- 1 **teaspoon salt**
- ½ **teaspoon rubbed sage**
  Dash pepper
- 1½ **pounds lean ground beef (90% lean)**
- 1 **cup ketchup**
- ½ **cup packed brown sugar**
- 1 **teaspoon Worcestershire sauce**

1. Preheat the oven to 350°. Using a large bowl, combine the first seven ingredients. Add beef; mix lightly but thoroughly. Shape into an 8x4-in. loaf in ungreased 15x10x1-in. baking pan.
2. Using a small bowl, combine the remaining ingredients, stirring to dissolve the sugar; remove ½ cup for sauce. Spread the remaining mixture over meat loaf.
3. Bake for 60-65 minutes or until a thermometer reads 160°. Let stand for 10 minutes before slicing. Serve with reserved sauce.

★ ★ ★ ★ ★ **READER REVIEW**

"I love this meat loaf. I have been making a similar one for years. Instead of Worcestershire in the topping, I use Tabasco. We love the sweet-hot taste. Yum."

LIMIRSH TASTEOFHOME.COM

TURKEY CLUB
ROULADES

TURKEY CLUB ROULADES

Weeknights quickly turn elegant when these short-prep roulades are on the menu. Not a fan of turkey? Substitute lightly pounded chicken breasts.

—*TASTE OF HOME* TEST KITCHEN

PREP: 20 MIN. • **COOK:** 15 MIN.
MAKES: 8 SERVINGS

- ¾ **pound fresh asparagus, trimmed**
- 8 **turkey breast cutlets (about 1 pound)**
- 1 **tablespoon Dijon-mayonnaise blend**
- 8 **slices deli ham**
- 8 **slices provolone cheese**
- ½ **teaspoon poultry seasoning**
- ½ **teaspoon pepper**
- 8 **bacon strips**

SAUCE
- ⅔ **cup Dijon-mayonnaise blend**
- 4 **teaspoons 2% milk**
- ¼ **teaspoon poultry seasoning**

1. Bring 4 cups water to a boil in a large saucepan. Add the asparagus; cook, uncovered, for 3 minutes or until it is crisp-tender. Drain and immediately place asparagus in ice water. Drain and pat dry. Set aside.

2. Spread the turkey cutlets with Dijon-mayonnaise. Layer with ham, cheese and asparagus. Sprinkle with poultry seasoning and pepper. Roll up tightly and wrap with bacon.

3. Cook roulades in a large skillet over medium-high heat for 12-15 minutes, turning occasionally, or until bacon is crisp and turkey is no longer pink. Combine sauce ingredients; serve with roulades.

★ ★ ★ ★ ★ 5 STAR TIP

To keep asparagus fresh longer, place the cut spears in a container of cold water—similar to flowers in a vase. Store asparagus in the refrigerator, changing the water at least once every three days.

GREEK FISH BAKE

As a military spouse living overseas, I got the chance to try many styles of cooking. Here's a Mediterranean-inspired recipe that we still love today.

—**STACEY BOYD** SPRINGFIELD, VA

START TO FINISH: 30 MIN.
MAKES: 4 SERVINGS

- 4 **cod fillets (6 ounces each)**
- 2 **tablespoons olive oil**
- ¼ **teaspoon salt**
- ⅛ **teaspoon pepper**
- 1 **small green pepper, cut into thin strips**
- ½ **small red onion, thinly sliced**
- ¼ **cup pitted Greek olives, sliced**
- 1 **can (8 ounces) tomato sauce**
- ¼ **cup crumbled feta cheese**

1. Preheat oven to 400°. Place cod in a greased 13x9-in. baking dish. Brush with oil; sprinkle with the salt and pepper. Top with green pepper, onion and olives.

2. Pour tomato sauce over the top; sprinkle with cheese. Bake until fish just begins to flake easily with a fork, 15-20 minutes.

BEEF & SPINACH LO MEIN

If you like good Chinese food, you'll want to try my speedy lo mein. It combines hearty steak strips and colorful veggies with a tangy sauce. It's a cinch to throw together.

—**DENISE PATTERSON** BAINBRIDGE, OH

START TO FINISH: 30 MIN.
MAKES: 5 SERVINGS

- ¼ **cup hoisin sauce**
- 2 **tablespoons soy sauce**
- 1 **tablespoon water**
- 2 **teaspoons sesame oil**
- 2 **garlic cloves, minced**
- ¼ **teaspoon crushed red pepper flakes**
- 1 **pound beef top round steak, thinly sliced**
- 6 **ounces uncooked spaghetti**
- 4 **teaspoons canola oil, divided**

BEEF & SPINACH LO MEIN

- 1 **can (8 ounces) sliced water chestnuts, drained**
- 2 **green onions, sliced**
- 1 **package (10 ounces) fresh spinach, coarsely chopped**
- 1 **red chili pepper, seeded and thinly sliced**

1. In a small bowl, mix the first six ingredients. Remove ¼ cup mixture to a large bowl; add beef and toss to coat. Marinate at room temperature for 10 minutes.

2. Cook spaghetti according to the package directions. Meanwhile, in a large skillet, heat 1½ teaspoons canola oil. Add half of the beef mixture; stir-fry 1-2 minutes or until no longer pink. Remove from the pan. Repeat with another 1½ teaspoons oil and remaining beef mixture.

3. Stir-fry the water chestnuts and green onions in the remaining canola oil for 30 seconds. Stir in the spinach and remaining hoisin mixture; cook until spinach is wilted. Return beef to the pan; heat through.

4. Drain the spaghetti; add to the beef mixture and toss to combine. Sprinkle with chili pepper.

NOTE *Wear disposable gloves when cutting hot peppers; the oils can burn skin. Avoid touching your face.*

EASY CHICKEN ENCHILADAS

These enchiladas get a big thumbs-up from my crew. They're a must for any Mexican meal at our house. Try them as a main dish or include them as part of a buffet.

—CHERYL POMRENKE COFFEYVILLE, KS

PREP: 15 MIN.
BAKE: 25 MIN. + STANDING
MAKES: 10 SERVINGS

- 3 cups shredded cheddar cheese, divided
- 2 cups shredded Monterey Jack cheese
- 2 cups chopped cooked chicken
- 2 cups (16 ounces) sour cream
- 1 can (10¾ ounces) condensed cream of chicken soup, undiluted
- 1 can (4 ounces) chopped green chilies
- 2 tablespoons finely chopped onion
- ¼ teaspoon pepper
- ⅛ teaspoon salt
- 10 flour tortillas (8 inches), warmed
  Pico de gallo, optional

1. Using a large bowl, combine 2 cups cheddar cheese, Monterey Jack cheese, chicken, sour cream, soup, chilies, onion, pepper and salt. Spoon about ½ cup off center on each of the tortillas; roll up. Place seam side down in a greased 13x9-in. baking dish.
2. Cover and bake at 350° for 20 minutes. Uncover; sprinkle with the remaining cheddar cheese. Bake 5 minutes longer or until cheese is melted. Let stand for 10 minutes before serving. If desired, serve with pico de gallo.

★ ★ ★ ★ ★ **5 STAR TIP**

Turn leftover tortillas into a tasty dessert. Cut the leftover tortillas into wedges or strips, then fry them on both sides in a lightly oiled skillet until golden. Then sprinkle them with sugar and a bit of cinnamon for a tasty finale to your Mexican meal.
JUDITH L. LITTLETON, MA

EASY CHICKEN ENCHILADAS

POPCORN & PRETZEL CHICKEN TENDERS

My daughter, Alivia, thought it would be fun to coat chicken tenders with two of our favorite movie-watching snacks—popcorn and pretzels. Crunchy and crispy, they bring a lot of smiles, especially when served with this sweet and creamy mustard sauce.
—SUZANNE CLARK PHOENIX, AZ

PREP: 25 MIN. + MARINATING
BAKE: 20 MIN.
MAKES: 6 SERVINGS (1 CUP SAUCE)

- 1½ **pounds chicken tenderloins**
- 1 **cup buttermilk**
- 2 **teaspoons garlic powder**
- 1 **teaspoon salt**
- 1 **teaspoon onion powder**
- ½ **teaspoon pepper**
- ¾ **cup fat-free plain Greek yogurt**
- ¼ **cup peach preserves**
- 1 **tablespoon prepared mustard**
- 4 **cups miniature pretzels, crushed**
- 2 **cups air-popped popcorn, crushed**
  Cooking spray

1. In a large bowl, combine the first six ingredients; toss to coat chicken. Refrigerate, covered, for at least 30 minutes. In a small bowl, mix yogurt, preserves and mustard; refrigerate until serving.

2. Preheat oven to 400°. In a large shallow dish, combine the crushed pretzels and popcorn. Remove the chicken from marinade, discarding marinade. Dip both sides of chicken in the pretzel mixture, patting to help coating adhere. Place on a parchment paper-lined baking sheet; spritz with cooking spray.

3. Bake 20-25 minutes or until the coating is golden brown and chicken is no longer pink. Serve with sauce.

FAST FIX ▶

SPICY VEGGIE PASTA BAKE

My dad always cooked with cast-iron skillets, so when I do, I remember his amazing culinary skills. I keep the tradition going with my veggie pasta.
—SONYA GOERGEN MOORHEAD, MN

START TO FINISH: 30 MIN.
MAKES: 6 SERVINGS

- 3 **cups uncooked spiral pasta**
- 1 **medium yellow summer squash**
- 1 **small zucchini**
- 1 **medium sweet red pepper**
- 1 **medium green pepper**
- 1 **tablespoon olive oil**
- 1 **small red onion, halved and sliced**
- 1 **cup sliced fresh mushrooms**
- ½ **teaspoon salt**
- ¼ **teaspoon pepper**
- ¼ **teaspoon crushed red pepper flakes**
- 1 **jar (24 ounces) spicy marinara sauce**
- 8 **ounces fresh mozzarella cheese pearls**
  Grated Parmesan cheese and julienned fresh basil, optional

1. Preheat oven to 375°. Cook pasta according to package directions for al dente; drain.

2. Cut the squashes and peppers into ¼-in. julienne strips. Using a 12-in. cast-iron skillet, heat the oil over medium-high heat. Add the onion, mushrooms and julienned vegetables; cook and stir 5-7 minutes or until crisp-tender. Stir in the seasonings. Add marinara sauce and pasta; toss to combine. Top with cheese pearls.

3. Transfer to oven; bake, uncovered, 10-15 minutes or until the cheese is melted. If desired, sprinkle the pasta dish with Parmesan cheese and basil before serving.

SATURN'S
PIZZA RING

BIG JOHN'S CHILI-RUBBED RIBS

When my family thinks of summer grilling, it's ribs all the way. Our recipe is a fun, welcome change from the usual version, with a glaze instead of barbecue sauce.

—GINGER SULLIVAN CUTLER BAY, FL

PREP: 20 MIN. + CHILLING
GRILL: 1½ HOURS
MAKES: 10 SERVINGS

- 3 tablespoons packed brown sugar
- 2 tablespoons paprika
- 2 tablespoons chili powder
- 3 teaspoons ground cumin
- 2 teaspoons garlic powder
- 1 teaspoon salt
- 6 pounds pork baby back ribs

GLAZE

- 1 cup reduced-sodium soy sauce
- 1 cup packed brown sugar
- ⅔ cup ketchup
- ⅓ cup lemon juice
- 1½ teaspoons minced fresh gingerroot

1. Mix the first six ingredients; rub over the ribs. Refrigerate, covered, 30 minutes.
2. Wrap rib racks in large pieces of heavy-duty foil; seal tightly. Grill, covered, over indirect medium heat 1 to 1½ hours or until tender.
3. In a large saucepan, combine glaze ingredients; cook, uncovered, over medium heat 6-8 minutes or until heated through and sugar is dissolved, stirring occasionally.
4. Carefully remove ribs from foil. Place ribs over direct heat; brush with some of the glaze. Grill, covered, over medium heat 25-30 minutes or until browned, turning and brushing ribs occasionally with remaining glaze.

(5) INGREDIENTS FAST FIX

SATURN'S PIZZA RING

My daughter loves pizza. This is a recipe she came up with, and it was a huge success! Other pizza toppings can be added.

—TRICIA RICHARDSON SPRINGDALE, AR

START TO FINISH: 30 MIN.
MAKES: 8 SERVINGS

- 1 pound bulk Italian sausage
- 1 can (15 ounces) pizza sauce, divided
- 1½ cups shredded part-skim mozzarella cheese, divided
- 4 ounces Canadian bacon, chopped
- 2 tubes (8 ounces each) refrigerated crescent rolls

1. Cook sausage in a large skillet over medium heat until it is no longer pink; drain. Stir in ½ cup pizza sauce, 1 cup cheese and Canadian bacon.
2. Unroll the crescent dough and separate into triangles. On ungreased 14-in. pizza pan, arrange triangles in a ring with points toward the outside and wide ends overlapping at center, leaving a 4-in. opening. Press the overlapping dough to seal.
3. Spoon filling onto the wide end of triangles. Fold the pointed end of the triangles over the filling, tucking the points under to form a ring (filling will be visible).
4. Bake at 375° for 12-15 minutes or until golden brown and ingredients are heated through. Sprinkle with remaining cheese. Bake 5 minutes longer or until cheese is melted. Serve with remaining pizza sauce.

BIG JOHN'S
CHILI-RUBBED
RIBS

GERMAN MEATBALLS

This was one of our favorite main dishes when I was growing up. We raised our own pork and beef, so our meat was always freshly ground. For variety, these meatballs can be cooked with a sweet cream gravy or steamed with tomatoes—but we prefer them with our homemade sauerkraut.

—**IONA REDEMER** CALUMET, OK

PREP: 20 MIN. • **COOK:** 25 MIN.
MAKES: 6 SERVINGS

- 1 **pound ground beef**
- ½ **pound ground pork**
- ½ **cup finely chopped onion**
- ¾ **cup fine dry bread crumbs**
- 1 **tablespoon snipped fresh parsley**
- 1½ **teaspoons salt**
- ⅛ **teaspoon pepper**
- 1 **teaspoon Worcestershire sauce**
- 1 **large egg, beaten**
- ½ **cup milk**
- 2 **to 3 tablespoons vegetable oil**
- 1 **can (27 ounces) sauerkraut, undrained**
- ⅓ **to ½ cup water, optional**
  Additional snipped parsley

Using a bowl, combine the first 10 ingredients; shape mixture into 18 meatballs, 2 in. each. Heat the oil in a skillet; brown the meatballs. Remove meatballs and drain fat. Spoon the sauerkraut into the skillet; top with meatballs. Cover and simmer for 15-20 minutes or until the meatballs are cooked through, adding water if necessary. Sprinkle with parsley.

FREEZE OPTION *Freeze the cooled meatball mixture in freezer containers. To use, partially thaw in refrigerator overnight. Microwave, covered, on high in a microwave-safe dish until heated through, stirring gently.*

GERMAN MEATBALLS

CHORIZO PUMPKIN PASTA

I'm a busy student, and this spicy-sweet pasta makes a perfect quick dinner. Even better, it works on a bigger scale to feed a bunch of hungry friends.

—**CHRISTINE YANG** SYRACUSE, NY

START TO FINISH: 30 MIN.
MAKES: 6 SERVINGS

- 3 **cups uncooked gemelli or spiral pasta (about 12 ounces)**
- 1 **package (12 ounces) fully cooked chorizo chicken sausage links or flavor of choice, sliced**
- 1 **cup canned pumpkin**
- 1 **cup half-and-half cream**
- ¾ **teaspoon salt**
- ¼ **teaspoon pepper**
- 1½ **cups shredded manchego or Monterey Jack cheese**
  Minced fresh cilantro, optional

1. Cook pasta according to package directions. Drain, reserving ¾ cup pasta water.
2. Meanwhile, in a large skillet, saute the sausage over medium heat until lightly browned; reduce the heat to medium-low. Add pumpkin, cream, salt and pepper; cook and stir until heated through. Toss with pasta and enough pasta water to moisten; stir in cheese. If desired, sprinkle with minced cilantro.

★ ★ ★ ★ ★ **5 STAR TIP**
Chorizo is a coarsely ground fresh or smoked pork sausage that has Mexican, Spanish and Portuguese origins. It is traditionally flavored with paprika or chili powder, which gives it its reddish color. Add chorizo to egg bakes, soups, casseroles, pasta or your favorite Mexican dish.

ANDOUILLE-STUFFED PEPPERS

I was inspired by the important role of green peppers in Cajun dishes when I created my spiced-up recipe. For a healthy alternative, substitute chicken sausage or cubed cooked chicken breast for the andouille sauasage.

—SARAH LARSON CARLSBAD, CA

PREP: 40 MIN. • **BAKE:** 40 MIN.
MAKES: 4 SERVINGS

- 1 package (8 ounces) jambalaya mix
- 4 small green peppers
- ¾ pound fully cooked andouille sausage links, chopped
- 1 jalapeno pepper, seeded and minced
- 1 can (16 ounces) tomato juice Louisiana-style hot sauce, optional

1. Prepare jambalaya mix according to package directions. Meanwhile, cut peppers lengthwise in half; remove seeds from peppers.
2. In a large skillet, cook and stir the sausage over medium-high heat until it is browned. Add the jalapeno; cook 1 minute longer.
3. Stir sausage mixture into prepared jambalaya. Spoon into pepper halves. Place in a greased 13x9-in. baking dish; pour the tomato juice over and around peppers.
4. Bake, uncovered, at 350° for 40-45 minutes or until peppers are tender. Serve with hot sauce if desired.
NOTE *Wear disposable gloves when cutting hot peppers; the oils can burn skin. Avoid touching your face.*

GRILLED TERIYAKI SALMON

GRILLED TERIYAKI SALMON

For this delectable glaze, I blend maple syrup from our neck of the woods with teriyaki sauce from the other side of the world. It helps the salmon stay moist and tender.

—LENITA SCHAFER ORMOND BEACH, FL

START TO FINISH: 30 MIN.
MAKES: 4 SERVINGS

- ¾ cup reduced-sodium teriyaki sauce
- ½ cup maple syrup
- 4 salmon fillets (6 ounces each) Mixed salad greens, optional

1. In a small bowl, whisk the teriyaki sauce and syrup. Pour 1 cup marinade into a large resealable plastic bag. Add the salmon; seal bag and turn to coat. Refrigerate for 15 minutes. Cover and refrigerate remaining marinade.
2. Drain salmon, discarding marinade in bag. Moisten a paper towel with cooking oil; using long-handled tongs, rub on grill rack to coat lightly.
3. Place salmon on grill rack, skin side down. Grill it, covered, over medium heat or broil 4 in. from the heat 8-12 minutes or until the fish just begins to flake easily with a fork, basting often with reserved marinade. If desired, serve over lettuce salad.

ARTICHOKE & LEMON PASTA

While sailing in the Mediterranean, I tasted a lemony pasta and fell in love with it. When I returned home, I developed my own version that my guests now love. Try it with shrimp and kalamatas, too.

—PETER HALFERTY CORPUS CHRISTI, TX

PREP: 20 MIN. • **COOK:** 20 MIN.
MAKES: 6 SERVINGS

- 2½ teaspoons salt, divided
- ½ pound fresh asparagus, trimmed and cut into 1½-inch pieces
- 4 cups uncooked bow tie pasta (about 12 ounces)
- 3 tablespoons olive oil, divided
- 1 can (14 ounces) water-packed quartered artichoke hearts, well drained
- 2 garlic cloves, minced
- 1 cup crumbled goat cheese
- 2 tablespoons minced fresh parsley
- 1 tablespoon grated lemon peel
- 2 to 3 tablespoons lemon juice
- ⅓ cup grated Parmesan cheese

1. Fill a 6-qt. stockpot three-fourths full with water; add 2 teaspoons salt and bring to a boil. Add asparagus; cook, uncovered, 1-2 minutes or just until crisp-tender. Remove asparagus and immediately drop into ice water. Drain and pat dry.

2. In same pot of water, cook pasta according to package directions for al dente. Drain, reserving 1 cup pasta water. Return pasta to pot.

3. Meanwhile, in a large skillet, heat 1 tablespoon oil over medium-high heat. Add the artichoke hearts; cook and stir 3-4 minutes or until lightly browned. Add garlic; cook 1 minute longer. Add to pasta.

4. Add asparagus, goat cheese, parsley, lemon peel, lemon juice and the remaining salt and oil; toss to combine, adding enough reserved pasta water to coat. Heat through. Serve with Parmesan cheese.

ARTICHOKE & LEMON PASTA

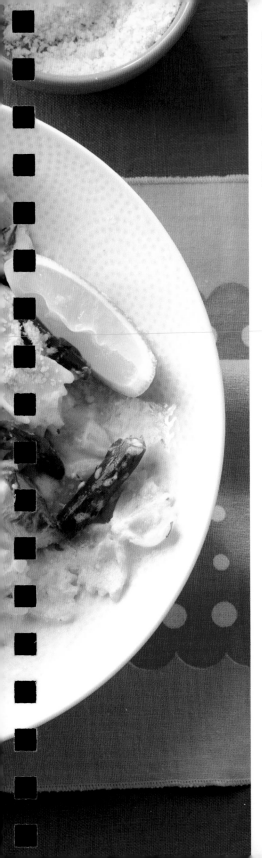

FAST FIX

PINTO BEAN TOSTADAS

Ready-to-go pinto beans and crispy corn tortillas prove how easy it is to make a healthy meal. Sometimes I add some chopped leftover meat to the tostadas, but they're equally satisfying just as they are.

—LILY JULOW LAWRENCEVILLE, GA

START TO FINISH: 30 MIN.
MAKES: 6 SERVINGS

- ¼ cup sour cream
- ¾ teaspoon grated lime peel
- ¼ teaspoon ground cumin
- ½ teaspoon salt, divided
- 2 tablespoons canola oil, divided
- 2 garlic cloves, minced
- 2 cans (15 ounces each) pinto beans, rinsed and drained
- 1 to 2 teaspoons hot pepper sauce
- 1 teaspoon chili powder
- 6 corn tortillas (6 inches)
- 2 cups shredded lettuce
- ½ cup salsa
- ¾ cup crumbled feta cheese or queso fresco
  Lime wedges

1. In a small bowl, mix sour cream, lime peel, cumin and ¼ teaspoon salt. In a large saucepan, heat 1 tablespoon oil over medium heat. Add garlic; cook and stir just until fragrant, about 45 seconds. Stir in beans, pepper sauce, chili powder and remaining salt; heat through, stirring occasionally. Keep bean mixture warm.

2. Brush both sides of tortillas with remaining oil. Place a large skillet over medium-high heat. Add tortillas in two batches; cook 2-3 minutes on each side or until tortillas are lightly browned and crisp.

3. To serve, arrange beans and lettuce over tostada shells; top with the salsa, sour cream mixture and cheese. Serve with lime wedges.

FREEZE IT FAST FIX

SWEET BARBECUED PORK CHOPS

I often prepare a double recipe of these tangy chops, then freeze half to keep on hand for fast dinners. They're so easy and taste so fresh, family and friends never guess my quick entree was frozen!

—SUSAN HOLDERMAN FOSTORIA, OH

START TO FINISH: 25 MIN.
MAKES: 8 SERVINGS

- 2 tablespoons canola oil
- 8 boneless pork loin chops (¾ inch thick and 8 ounces each)
- ½ cup packed brown sugar
- ½ cup chopped sweet onion
- ½ cup each ketchup, barbecue sauce, French salad dressing and honey

1. In a large skillet, heat the oil over medium heat. In batches, brown the pork chops 2-3 minutes on each side. Return all to pan.

2. In a small bowl, mix the remaining ingredients; pour over chops. Bring to a boil. Reduce heat; simmer, covered, 4-5 minutes or until a thermometer reads 145°. Let pork chops stand for 5 minutes before serving.

FREEZE OPTION *Place the pork chops in freezer containers; top with sauce. Cool and freeze. To use, partially thaw in the refrigerator overnight. Heat through in a covered saucepan, gently stirring the sauce and adding a little water if necessary.*

SPICY BEEF & PEPPER STIR-FRY

Think of this stir-fry as your chance to play with heat and spice. I balance the beef with coconut milk and a spritz of lime.

—JOY ZACHARIA CLEARWATER, FL

PREP: 20 MIN. + STANDING • **COOK:** 10 MIN.
MAKES: 4 SERVINGS

- 1 **pound beef top sirloin steak, cut into thin strips**
- 1 **tablespoon minced fresh gingerroot**
- 3 **garlic cloves, minced, divided**
- ¼ **teaspoon pepper**
- ¾ **teaspoon salt, divided**
- 1 **cup light coconut milk**
- 2 **tablespoons sugar**
- 1 **tablespoon Sriracha Asian hot chili sauce**
- ½ **teaspoon grated lime peel**
- 2 **tablespoons lime juice**
- 2 **tablespoons canola oil, divided**
- 1 **large sweet red pepper, cut into thin strips**
- ½ **medium red onion, thinly sliced**
- 1 **jalapeno pepper, seeded and thinly sliced**
- 4 **cups fresh baby spinach**
- 2 **green onions, thinly sliced**
- 2 **tablespoons chopped fresh cilantro**

1. In a large bowl, toss beef with ginger, 2 garlic cloves, pepper and ½ teaspoon salt; let stand 15 minutes. In a small bowl, whisk coconut milk, sugar, chili sauce, lime peel, lime juice and remaining salt until blended.
2. In a large skillet, heat 1 tablespoon oil over medium-high heat. Add beef; stir-fry 2-3 minutes or until no longer pink. Remove from pan.
3. Stir-fry the red pepper, red onion, jalapeno and remaining garlic in remaining oil 2-3 minutes or just until the vegetables are crisp-tender. Stir in coconut milk mixture; heat through. Add the spinach and beef; cook until the spinch is wilted and the beef is heated through, stirring occasionally. Sprinkle with green onions and cilantro.

CRISPY FRIED CHICKEN

Always a picnic favorite, this fried chicken is delicious hot or cold. Serve it alongside potato salad, deviled eggs and watermelon.

—JEANNE SCHNITZLER LIMA, MT

PREP: 10 MIN. • **COOK:** 10 MIN./BATCH
MAKES: 8 SERVINGS

- 4 **cups all-purpose flour, divided**
- 2 **tablespoons garlic salt**
- 1 **tablespoon paprika**
- 3 **teaspoons pepper, divided**
- 2½ **teaspoons poultry seasoning**
- 2 **large eggs**
- 1½ **cups water**
- 1 **teaspoon salt**
- 2 **broiler/fryer chickens (3½ to 4 pounds each), cut up**
  Oil for deep-fat frying

1. In a large resealable plastic bag, combine 2⅔ cups flour, garlic salt, paprika, 2½ teaspoons pepper and poultry seasoning. In a shallow bowl, beat eggs and water; add salt and the remaining flour and pepper. Dip the chicken in egg mixture, then place in the bag, a few pieces at a time. Seal bag and shake to coat.
2. In a deep-fat fryer, heat oil to 375°. Fry chicken, several pieces at a time, for 5-6 minutes on each side or until golden brown and juices run clear. Drain on paper towels.

ULTIMATE GRILLED PORK CHOPS

A little brining and a special dry rub go a long way to making the perfect pork chop. Once you've mastered the techniques, you'll be enjoying them all summer long.

—MATTHEW HASS FRANKLIN, WI

PREP: 20 MIN. + BRINING
GRILL: 10 MIN. • **MAKES:** 4 SERVINGS

- ¼ **cup kosher salt**
- ¼ **cup sugar**
- 2 **cups water**
- 2 **cups ice water**
- 4 **bone-in pork center-cut rib chops (1 inch thick and 8 ounces each)**
- 2 **tablespoons canola oil**

BASIC RUB

- 3 **tablespoons paprika**
- 1 **teaspoon each garlic powder, onion powder, ground cumin and ground mustard**
- 1 **teaspoon coarsely ground pepper**
- ½ **teaspoon ground chipotle pepper**

1. In a large saucepan, combine salt, sugar and 2 cups water; cook and stir over medium heat until salt and sugar are dissolved. Remove from the heat. Add 2 cups of ice water to cool brine to room temperature.
2. Place the pork chops in a large resealable plastic bag; add the cooled brine. Seal the bag, pressing out as much air as possible; turn to coat the chops. Place in a 13x9-in. baking dish. Refrigerate 8-12 hours.
3. Remove chops from brine; rinse and pat dry. Discard brine. Brush both sides of chops with oil. In a small bowl, mix rub ingredients; rub over pork chops. Let stand at room temperature 30 minutes. Grill chops on an oiled rack, covered, over medium heat 4-6 minutes on each side or until a thermometer reads 145°. Let stand 5 minutes before serving.
FOR SMOKY PORK RUB *Prepare rub as directed, using smoked paprika in place of regular paprika.*
FOR SPICY PORK RUB *Add ½ teaspoon cayenne pepper to rub mixture.*
FOR SWEET PORK RUB *Add 3 tablespoons brown sugar to rub mixture.*

★ ★ ★ ★ ★ **READER REVIEW**

"Wow...these are wonderful! Chops were so juicy after being in the brine. My family loved them. Served them with a peach BBQ sauce."

SPINARDO TASTEOFHOME.COM

ULTIMATE GRILLED
PORK CHOPS

HOW TO MAKE CROSSHATCH MARKS

*Mmm...*nothing makes mouths start watering at cookouts like those gorgeous crosshatch grill marks on meat. Want to create them on your pork chops? Place the chops on the grill to sear, then rotate them a quarter turn and cook 2-3 minutes longer before flipping to cook on the other side.

**PINEAPPLE-STUFFED
CORNISH HENS**

PINEAPPLE-STUFFED CORNISH HENS

My mother brought this recipe back with her from Hawaii about 25 years ago. The tender meat, tropical stuffing and sweet-sour sauce made it a favorite with our family and friends. I always keep some copies of the recipe on hand to share.

—VICKI CORNERS ROCK ISLAND, IL

PREP: 20 MIN. • **BAKE:** 1 HOUR 25 MIN.
MAKES: 2 SERVINGS

- ½ **teaspoon salt, divided**
- 2 **Cornish game hens (20 to 24 ounces each)**
- 1 **can (8 ounces) crushed pineapple**
- 3 **cups cubed day-old bread (½-inch cubes), crusts removed**
- 1 **celery rib, chopped**
- ½ **cup flaked coconut**
- ⅔ **cup butter, melted, divided**
- ¼ **teaspoon poultry seasoning**
- 2 **tablespoons steak sauce**
- 2 **tablespoons cornstarch**
- 2 **tablespoons brown sugar**
- 1 **cup cold water**
- 1 **tablespoon lemon juice**

1. Sprinkle ¼ teaspoon salt inside the hens; set aside. Drain the pineapple, reserving the juice. Using a large bowl, combine the pineapple, bread cubes, celery and coconut. Add ⅓ cup butter; toss to coat. Loosely stuff hens with pineapple mixture.
2. Tuck wings under hens; tie legs together. Place on a rack in a greased shallow roasting pan. Place remaining stuffing in a greased 1½-cup baking dish; cover and set aside. Add poultry seasoning and remaining salt to the remaining butter.
3. Spoon some butter mixture over hens. Bake, uncovered, at 350° for 40 minutes, basting twice with the butter mixture.
4. Add steak sauce and reserved pineapple juice to any remaining butter mixture; baste hens. Bake reserved stuffing with hens for 30 minutes, basting hens occasionally with remaining butter mixture.

5. Uncover the stuffing; bake it 15-20 minutes more or until a thermometer reads 185° for the hens and 165° for the stuffing in hens. Remove hens from pan; keep warm.
6. Pour drippings into a saucepan; skim fat. Combine cornstarch, brown sugar, water and lemon juice; add to the drippings. Bring to a boil; cook and stir for 1-2 minutes or until thickened. Serve with hens and stuffing.

FAST FIX

SPINACH & GOUDA-STUFFED PORK CUTLETS

I started this dish in an attempt to copy a restaurant entree I liked. Cheese oozes from the center, and mustard lends a lot of flavor.

—JOAN OAKLAND TROY, MT

START TO FINISH: 30 MIN.
MAKES: 2 SERVINGS

- 3 **tablespoons dry bread crumbs**
- 2 **tablespoons grated Parmesan cheese**
- 2 **pork sirloin cutlets (3 ounces each)**
- ¼ **teaspoon salt**
- ⅛ **teaspoon pepper**
- 2 **slices smoked Gouda cheese (about 2 ounces)**
- 2 **cups fresh baby spinach**
- 2 **tablespoons horseradish mustard**

1. Preheat oven to 400°. In a shallow bowl, mix the bread crumbs and Parmesan cheese.
2. Sprinkle tops of cutlets with salt and pepper. Layer one end of each with Gouda cheese and spinach. Fold cutlets in half, enclosing filling; secure with toothpicks. Brush the mustard over the outsides of pork; dip in bread crumb mixture, patting to help the coating adhere.
3. Place on a greased foil-lined baking sheet. Bake 12-15 minutes or until golden brown and pork is tender. Discard toothpicks before serving.

FAST FIX

EASY CHICKEN PICCATA

My chicken dish is ready to serve in a half hour. It takes just a few minutes in the oven to bake to tender perfection.

—HANNAH WILLIAMS MALIBU, CA

START TO FINISH: 30 MIN.
MAKES: 4 SERVINGS

- 4 **boneless skinless chicken breast halves (6 ounces each)**
- ½ **teaspoon salt**
- ¼ **teaspoon pepper**
- ½ **cup all-purpose flour**
- 3 **tablespoons olive oil**
- 1 **cup chicken stock**
- 3 **to 4 tablespoons capers, drained**
- 2 **to 3 tablespoons lemon juice**
- 3 **tablespoons butter**

1. Preheat oven to 350°. Cut chicken breasts in half crosswise. Pound with a meat mallet to ½-in. thickness; sprinkle with salt and pepper. Place flour in a shallow bowl. Dip chicken halves in flour to coat both sides; shake off excess.
2. In a large skillet, heat 1 tablespoon oil over medium-high heat. Brown chicken in batches, adding additional oil as needed. Transfer chicken to an ungreased 13x9-in. baking dish.
3. Add chicken stock, capers and lemon juice to pan, stirring to loosen browned bits from pan. Whisk in the butter, 1 tablespoon at a time, until creamy. Pour sauce over chicken. Bake 5-10 minutes or until no longer pink.

★ ★ ★ ★ ★ 5 STAR TIP
Buying boneless skinless chicken breasts can cut up to 15 minutes off your cooking time. Save money by buying larger size packages, then rewrap individually or in family-size portions and freeze.

MY BEST-EVER JAMBALAYA

I tried to mimic jambalaya from my favorite restaurant, and it turned out so well that my daughter and husband now prefer my recipe. They won't order the jambalaya when we go out to eat!

—**ALEXIS VAN VULPEN** ST. ALBERT, ALBERTA

PREP: 20 MIN. • **COOK:** 40 MIN.
MAKES: 10 SERVINGS

- 2 **tablespoons canola oil**
- ½ **pound fully cooked Spanish chorizo links, sliced**
- 2 **cups cubed fully cooked ham**
- ¾ **pound boneless skinless chicken breasts, cubed**
- 1 **can (28 ounces) diced tomatoes, undrained**
- 3 **cups chicken broth**
- 2 **large green peppers, chopped**
- 1 **large onion, chopped**
- 1 **tablespoon Cajun seasoning**
- 2 **teaspoons hot pepper sauce**
- 3 **cups instant brown rice**
- ½ **pound uncooked medium shrimp, peeled and deveined**

1. In a Dutch oven, heat the oil over medium-high heat. Add chorizo and ham; cook and stir 3-4 minutes or until browned.

2. Add chicken to pan; cook 5-7 minutes or until no longer pink. Stir in tomatoes, broth, peppers, onion, Cajun seasoning and pepper sauce. Bring to a boil. Reduce heat; simmer, uncovered, 8-10 minutes or until peppers are crisp-tender.

3. Return to a boil; stir in the rice and shrimp. Reduce the heat; simmer, covered, 7-9 minutes or until shrimp turn pink. Remove from heat; let stand, covered, 5 minutes or until rice is tender.

FAST FIX ▶
EASY MEATBALL STROGANOFF

This recipe has fed not only my own family, but many neighborhood kids. They come running when I make this supper. It's one of those things you throw together after work on a busy day because you know it works.

—**JULIE MAY** HATTIESBURG, MS

START TO FINISH: 30 MIN.
MAKES: 4 SERVINGS

- 3 **cups uncooked egg noodles**
- 1 **tablespoon olive oil**
- 1 **package (12 ounces) frozen fully cooked Italian meatballs, thawed**
- 1½ **cups beef broth**
- 1 **teaspoon dried parsley flakes**
- ¾ **teaspoon dried basil**
- ½ **teaspoon salt**
- ½ **teaspoon dried oregano**
- ¼ **teaspoon pepper**
- 1 **cup heavy whipping cream**
- ¾ **cup sour cream**

1. Cook egg noodles according to package directions for al dente; drain.

2. Meanwhile, in a large skillet, heat oil over medium-high heat. Brown meatballs; remove from pan. Add broth, stirring to loosen browned bits from pan. Add seasonings. Bring to a boil; cook 5-7 minutes or until liquid is reduced to ½ cup.

3. Add the meatballs, noodles and cream. Bring to a boil. Reduce the heat; simmer, covered, 3-5 minutes or until slightly thickened. Stir in the sour cream; heat through.

MY BEST-EVER JAMBALAYA

ZUCCHINI BOATS

After working hard all our lives and raising a family, we're now enjoying a simpler life. Getting back to the basics means enjoying old-fashioned comfort foods like this. It's fresh and filling without being heavy.

—MRS. C. THON ATLIN, BC

PREP: 35 MIN. • **BAKE:** 25 MIN.
MAKES: 4 SERVINGS

- 2 **medium zucchini (about 8 inches)**
- ¾ **pound ground beef**
- 1 **small onion, chopped**
- ½ **cup chopped fresh mushrooms**
- ½ **cup chopped sweet red pepper**
- ½ **cup chopped green pepper**
- 1 **cup shredded cheddar cheese, divided**
- 2 **tablespoons ketchup**
  Salt and pepper to taste

1. Trim the ends off zucchini. Cut zucchini in half lengthwise; scoop out pulp, leaving ½-in. shells. Finely chop pulp.

2. In a skillet, cook beef, zucchini pulp, onion, mushrooms and peppers over medium heat until meat is no longer pink; drain. Remove from the heat. Add ½ cup cheese, ketchup, salt and pepper; mix well. Spoon into the zucchini shells. Place in a greased 13x9-in. baking dish. Sprinkle with remaining cheese.

3. Bake, uncovered, at 350° for 25-30 minutes or until zucchini is tender.

NOTE *A teaspoon is just the right size for scooping out the pulp. Use your food processor or blender to finely chop the pulp quickly.*

★ ★ ★ ★ ★ **READER REVIEW**

"I love this recipe. And it's great with fresh zucchini from the garden."

805NESS TASTEOFHOME.COM

ZUCCHINI
BOATS

JUST PEACHY
PORK TENDERLOIN

JUST PEACHY PORK TENDERLOIN

I had a pork tenderloin and ripe peaches and decided to put them together. The results couldn't have been more irresistible! It's a fresh entree that tastes like summer.
—**JULIA GOSLIGA** ADDISON, VT

START TO FINISH: 20 MIN.
MAKES: 4 SERVINGS

- 1 **pound pork tenderloin, cut into 12 slices**
- ½ **teaspoon salt**
- ¼ **teaspoon pepper**
- 2 **teaspoons olive oil**
- 4 **medium peaches, peeled and sliced**
- 1 **tablespoon lemon juice**
- ¼ **cup peach preserves**

1. Flatten each tenderloin slice to ¼-in. thickness. Sprinkle with salt and pepper. In a large nonstick skillet over medium heat, cook pork in oil until tender. Remove and keep warm.
2. Add peaches and lemon juice, stirring to loosen browned bits from pan. Cook and stir for 3-4 minutes or until peaches are tender. Stir in the pork and preserves; heat through.

BARBECUED STRAWBERRY CHICKEN

When it's time to impress family and friends, we serve barbecue chicken garnished with strawberries. It's easier than anyone would ever guess.
—**BONNIE HAWKINS** ELKHORN, WI

PREP: 25 MIN. • **BAKE:** 15 MIN.
MAKES: 4 SERVINGS

- 2 **tablespoons canola oil**
- 4 **boneless skinless chicken breast halves (6 ounces each)**
- 2 **tablespoons butter**
- ¼ **cup finely chopped red onion**
- 1 **cup barbecue sauce**
- 2 **tablespoons brown sugar**
- 2 **tablespoons balsamic vinegar**
- 2 **tablespoons honey**
- 1 **cup sliced fresh strawberries**

1. Preheat oven to 350°. In a large ovenproof skillet, heat the oil over medium-high heat. Brown chicken on both sides. Remove from pan. In same pan, heat butter over medium-high heat. Add onion; cook and stir for 1 minute or until tender.
2. Stir in barbecue sauce, brown sugar, vinegar and honey. Bring to a boil. Reduce heat; simmer, uncovered, for 4-6 minutes or until thickened. Return the chicken to pan. Bake 12-15 minutes or until a thermometer reads 165°. Stir in strawberries.

MONTEREY CHICKEN WITH ROASTED VEGGIES

My clan often requests this tantalizing baked chicken topped with veggies and cheese. Roasting the red peppers and asparagus brings out their sweetness. They're delicious paired with pasta, rice or mashed potatoes.
—**GLORIA BRADLEY** NAPERVILLE, IL

PREP: 15 MIN. • **BAKE:** 25 MIN.
MAKES: 6 SERVINGS

- 1 **pound fresh asparagus, trimmed and cut into 2-inch pieces**
- 2 **large sweet red peppers, cut into strips**
- 1 **tablespoon olive oil**
- 1½ **teaspoons salt, divided**
- ¾ **teaspoon coarsely ground pepper, divided**
- 6 **boneless skinless chicken breast halves (6 ounces each)**
- 5 **tablespoons butter, divided**
- ¼ **cup all-purpose flour**
- 1 **cup chicken broth**
- 1 **cup heavy whipping cream**
- ¼ **cup white wine or additional chicken broth**
- 1½ **cups shredded Monterey Jack cheese, divided**

1. Preheat the oven to 400°. Place the asparagus and red peppers in a greased 13x9-in. baking dish; toss with oil, ½ teaspoon salt and ¼ teaspoon pepper. Roast 5-8 minutes or just until crisp-tender. Remove vegetables from baking dish.
2. Season chicken with the remaining salt and pepper. Using a large skillet, heat 1 tablespoon butter over medium heat; brown 3 chicken breasts on both sides. Transfer chicken to the same baking dish. Repeat with an additional 1 tablespoon of butter and remaining chicken. Top the chicken with the roasted vegetables.
3. In same skillet, melt the remaining butter over medium heat. Stir in flour until smooth; gradually whisk in the broth, cream and wine. Bring to a boil over medium heat, stirring constantly; cook and stir 2-3 minutes or until thickened. Stir in 1 cup cheese until melted. Pour over chicken.
4. Bake, uncovered, 25-30 minutes or until a thermometer inserted in the chicken reads 165°. Sprinkle with remaining cheese.

BIG KAHUNA PIZZA

A prebaked pizza crust and refrigerated barbecued pork make this pizza super fast and super easy. You'll agree it's super delish! This can double as a great last-minute appetizer when cut into bite-sized pieces.
—**JONI HILTON** ROCKLIN, CA

START TO FINISH: 30 MIN.
MAKES: 6 SERVINGS

- 1 **prebaked 12-inch pizza crust**
- 1 **carton (16 ounces) refrigerated fully cooked barbecued shredded pork**
- 1 **can (20 ounces) pineapple chunks, drained**
- ⅓ **cup chopped red onion**
- 2 **cups shredded part-skim mozzarella cheese**

1. Place pizza crust on an ungreased 12-in. pizza pan. Spread shredded pork over crust; top with pineapple and onion. Sprinkle with cheese.
2. Bake at 350° for 20-25 minutes or until cheese is melted.

THAI CHICKEN PEANUT NOODLES

SEARED SALMON WITH STRAWBERRY BASIL RELISH

Take a sweet new approach to salmon by topping it with a relish of strawberries, basil, honey and pepper.
—**STACY MULLENS** GRESHAM, OR

START TO FINISH: 20 MIN.
MAKES: 6 SERVINGS

- 6 **salmon fillets (4 ounces each)**
- 1 **tablespoon butter, melted**
- ¼ **teaspoon salt**
- ⅛ **teaspoon freshly ground pepper**

RELISH

- 1¼ **cups finely chopped fresh strawberries**
- 1 **tablespoon minced fresh basil**
- 1 **tablespoon honey**
  Dash freshly ground pepper

1. Brush fillets with melted butter; sprinkle with salt and pepper. Heat a large skillet over medium-high heat. Add the fillets, skin side up, in batches if necessary; cook 2-3 minutes on each side or until fish just begins to flake easily with a fork.
2. In a small bowl, toss strawberries with basil, honey and pepper. Serve salmon with relish.

★ ★ ★ ★ ★ **READER REVIEW**

"I was intrigued with the strawberries. Tried the recipe and it is delicious! Love it and will be making again...soon!"

IPPERWASH67 TASTEOFHOME.COM

THAI CHICKEN PEANUT NOODLES

My husband loves the spicy Thai flavors in this speedy dish. We break out the chopsticks for a more authentic experience.
—**JENNIFER FISHER** AUSTIN, TX

START TO FINISH: 30 MIN.
MAKES: 6 SERVINGS

- ¼ **cup creamy peanut butter**
- ½ **cup reduced-sodium chicken broth**
- ¼ **cup lemon juice**
- ¼ **cup reduced-sodium soy sauce**
- 4 **teaspoons Sriracha Asian hot chili sauce**
- ¼ **teaspoon crushed red pepper flakes**
- 12 **ounces uncooked multigrain spaghetti**
- 1 **pound lean ground chicken**
- 1½ **cups julienned carrots**
- 1 **medium sweet red pepper, chopped**
- 1 **garlic clove, minced**
- ½ **cup finely chopped unsalted peanuts**
- 4 **green onions, chopped**

1. In a small bowl, whisk the first six ingredients until blended. Cook the spaghetti according to package directions; drain.
2. Meanwhile, using a large skillet, cook the chicken, carrots, pepper and garlic over medium heat for 5-6 minutes or until the chicken is no longer pink, breaking up chicken into crumbles; drain.
3. Stir in peanut butter mixture; bring to a boil. Reduce the heat; simmer, uncovered, 3-5 minutes or until sauce is slightly thickened. Serve with the spaghetti. Top dish with peanuts and green onions.

SEARED SALMON WITH
STRAWBERRY BASIL RELISH

SPICY ROASTED SAUSAGE, POTATOES & PEPPERS

I enjoy sharing my cooking, and this hearty meal-in-one has gotten a tasty reputation. People have actually approached me in public to ask for the recipe!

—**LAURIE SLEDGE** BRANDON, MS

PREP: 20 MIN. • **BAKE:** 30 MIN.
MAKES: 4 SERVINGS

- 1 **pound potatoes (about 2 medium), peeled and cut into ½-inch cubes**
- 1 **package (12 ounces) fully cooked andouille chicken sausage links or flavor of your choice, cut into 1-inch pieces**
- 1 **medium red onion, cut into wedges**
- 1 **medium sweet red pepper, cut into 1-inch pieces**
- 1 **medium green pepper, cut into 1-inch pieces**
- ½ **cup pickled pepper rings**
- 1 **tablespoon olive oil**
- ½ **to 1 teaspoon Creole seasoning**
- ¼ **teaspoon pepper**

1. Preheat oven to 400°. In a large bowl, combine the potatoes, sausage, onion, red pepper, green pepper and pepper rings. Mix the oil, Creole seasoning and pepper; drizzle over potato mixture and toss to coat.

2. Transfer to a 15x10x1-in. baking pan coated with cooking spray. Roast 30-35 minutes or until vegetables are tender, stirring occasionally.

HOW TO PREP A PEPPER

Cut top and bottom off pepper and discard. Cut each side from pepper by slicing close to the center and then down. Scrape out seeds and discard.

Cut away any ribs.

Place skin side down and flatten slightly with your hand. Cut lengthwise into strips or as recipe directs.

SPICY ROASTED SAUSAGE, POTATOES & PEPPERS

TERIYAKI STEAK SKEWERS

When these flavorful skewered steaks are sizzling on the grill, the aroma makes everyone around stop what they're doing and come to see what's cooking. The tasty marinade is easy to make, and these little steaks are quick to cook and fun to eat.

—**JERI DOBROWSKI** BEACH, ND

PREP: 15 MIN. + MARINATING
GRILL: 10 MIN. • **MAKES:** 6 SERVINGS

- ½ cup reduced-sodium soy sauce
- ¼ cup cider vinegar
- 2 tablespoons brown sugar
- 2 tablespoons finely chopped onion
- 1 tablespoon canola oil
- 1 garlic clove, minced
- ½ teaspoon ground ginger
- ⅛ teaspoon pepper
- 2 pounds beef top sirloin steak

1. In a large resealable plastic bag, combine the first eight ingredients. Trim fat from steak and slice across the grain into ½-in. strips. Add the beef to bag; seal bag and turn to coat. Refrigerate for 2-3 hours.
2. Drain and discard marinade. Loosely thread beef onto six metal or soaked wooden skewers. Grill, uncovered, over medium-hot heat for 7-10 minutes or until meat reaches desired doneness, turning often.

RICH CHICKEN ALFREDO PIZZA

Try this tasty twist on pizza night. Spinach and tender chunks of chicken combine with a smooth and buttery Alfredo sauce for a pie that definitely lives up to its name.

—**TAMMY HANKS** GAINESVILLE, FL

PREP: 30 MIN. • **BAKE:** 15 MIN.
MAKES: 1 PIZZA (8 MAIN DISH OR 12 APPETIZER SLICES)

- 2½ teaspoons butter
- 1 garlic clove, minced
- 1½ cups heavy whipping cream
- 3 tablespoons grated Parmesan cheese
- ½ teaspoon salt
- ¼ teaspoon pepper
- 1 tablespoon minced fresh parsley
- 1 prebaked 12-inch thin pizza crust
- 1 cup cubed cooked chicken breast
- 1 cup thinly sliced baby portobello mushrooms
- 1 cup fresh baby spinach
- 2 cups shredded part-skim mozzarella cheese

1. In a small saucepan over medium heat, melt butter. Add garlic; cook and stir for 1 minute. Add cream; cook until liquid is reduced by half, about 15-20 minutes. Add the Parmesan cheese, salt and pepper; cook and stir until thickened. Remove from the heat; stir in parsley. Cool slightly.
2. Place crust on an ungreased baking sheet; spread with cream mixture. Top with chicken, mushrooms, spinach and mozzarella cheese. Bake at 450° for 15-20 minutes or until cheese is melted and crust is golden brown.

⑤ INGREDIENTS **FAST FIX ▶**
ZESTY CHICKEN SOFT TACOS

We've made these tacos with corn and flour tortillas, but flatbread is our favorite wrap. Set out toppings and let your hungry eaters assemble their own tacos.

—**JESSIE GREARSON-SAPAT** FALMOUTH, ME

START TO FINISH: 25 MIN.
MAKES: 6 SERVINGS

- 1 cup (8 ounces) reduced-fat sour cream
- 2 tablespoons Sriracha Asian hot chili sauce
- 2 tablespoons lime juice
- 1½ teaspoons grated lime peel
- ½ teaspoon salt
- ⅛ teaspoon pepper
- 6 naan flatbreads, warmed
- 1 rotisserie chicken, skin removed, shredded
  Minced fresh cilantro, optional

Using a small bowl, mix the first six ingredients. Spread the mix over the flatbreads; top with the chicken and, if desired, cilantro.

QUINOA-STUFFED SQUASH BOATS

MIXED PAELLA

Packed with chicken, shrimp, rice, veggies and olives, this meal is quick and satisfying. It will take the chill off any cool evening.
—**ELIZABETH GODECKE** CHICAGO, IL

PREP: 15 MIN. • **COOK:** 25 MIN.
MAKES: 6 SERVINGS

- 1¼ **pounds boneless skinless chicken breasts, thinly sliced**
- 2 **tablespoons olive oil**
- 1 **medium onion, chopped**
- 2 **garlic cloves, minced**
- 2¼ **cups chicken broth**
- 1 **cup uncooked long grain rice**
- 1 **teaspoon dried oregano**
- ½ **teaspoon ground turmeric**
- ½ **teaspoon paprika**
- ¼ **teaspoon salt**
- ¼ to ½ **teaspoon pepper**
- 1 **pound cooked medium shrimp, peeled and deveined**
- 1 **can (14½ ounces) diced tomatoes, undrained**
- ¾ **cup frozen peas, thawed**
- ½ **cup sliced pimiento-stuffed olives**

1. In a large skillet, saute chicken in oil until no longer pink. Remove and keep warm. In the same skillet, saute onion until tender. Add the garlic; cook 1 minute longer. Stir in the broth, rice and seasonings. Bring to a boil. Reduce heat; cover and simmer for 15-18 minutes or until rice is tender.
2. Stir in the shrimp, tomatoes, peas, olives and chicken; cover and cook for 3-4 minutes or until heated through.

★ ★ ★ ★ ★ **5 STAR TIP**
To cook raw shrimp in water, add 1 pound shrimp (with or without shells) and 1 teaspoon salt to 3 quarts boiling water. Reduce the heat and simmer, uncovered, for 1-3 minutes or until the shrimp turns pink and curls. Watch closely to avoid overcooking—the meat of uncooked shrimp will turn from translucent when raw to pink and opaque when cooked. Drain immediately.

FAST FIX ▶
QUINOA-STUFFED SQUASH BOATS

My colorful boats—with quinoa, chickpeas and pumpkin seeds—use delicata squash, a winter squash that's cream-colored with green stripes. In a pinch, acorn squash will do.
—**LAUREN KNOELKE** MILWAUKEE, WI

START TO FINISH: 30 MIN.
MAKES: 8 SERVINGS

- 4 **delicata squash (about 12 ounces each)**
- 3 **teaspoons olive oil, divided**
- ⅛ **teaspoon pepper**
- 1 **teaspoon salt, divided**
- 1½ **cups vegetable broth**
- 1 **cup quinoa, rinsed**
- 1 **can (15 ounces) chickpeas, rinsed and drained**
- ¼ **cup dried cranberries**
- 1 **green onion, thinly sliced**
- 1 **teaspoon minced fresh sage**
- ½ **teaspoon grated lemon peel**
- 1 **teaspoon lemon juice**
- ½ **cup crumbled goat cheese**
- ¼ **cup salted pumpkin seeds or pepitas, toasted**

1. Preheat oven to 450°. Cut each squash lengthwise in half; remove and discard seeds. Lightly brush cut sides with 1 teaspoon oil; sprinkle with pepper and ½ teaspoon salt. Place on a baking sheet, cut side down. Bake 15-20 minutes or until tender.
2. Meanwhile, in a large saucepan, combine the broth and quinoa; bring to a boil. Reduce the heat; simmer, covered, 12-15 minutes or until the liquid is absorbed.
3. Stir in chickpeas, cranberries, green onion, sage, lemon peel, lemon juice and the remaining oil and salt; spoon into squash. Sprinkle with cheese and pumpkin seeds.

FAMILY-FAVORITE CHEESEBURGER PASTA

I created this recipe to satisfy a cheeseburger craving. The result was a home-style pasta that tastes just like a classic cheeseburger, but makes use of better-for-you ingredients.

—**RAQUEL HAGGARD** EDMOND, OK

START TO FINISH: 30 MIN.
MAKES: 4 SERVINGS

- 1½ cups uncooked whole wheat penne pasta
- ¾ pound lean ground beef (90% lean)
- 2 tablespoons finely chopped onion
- 1 can (14½ ounces) no-salt-added diced tomatoes
- 2 tablespoons dill pickle relish
- 2 tablespoons prepared mustard
- 2 tablespoons ketchup
- 1 teaspoon steak seasoning
- ¼ teaspoon seasoned salt
- ¾ cup shredded reduced-fat cheddar cheese
  Chopped green onions, optional

1. Cook pasta according to package directions. Meanwhile, in a large skillet, cook beef and onion over medium heat until meat is no longer pink; drain. Drain pasta; add to the meat mixture.

2. Stir in the tomatoes, relish, mustard, ketchup, steak seasoning and seasoned salt. Bring to a boil. Reduce heat; simmer, uncovered, for 5 minutes.

3. Sprinkle with cheese. Remove from the heat; cover and let stand until cheese is melted. Garnish with green onions if desired.

NOTE *This recipe was tested with McCormick's Montreal Steak Seasoning. Look for it in the spice aisle at your local grocer.*

SLOPPY JOE BISCUIT CUPS

I'm a busy teacher and mom, so weekday meals with shortcuts like this are definitely a huge help to me. I always have to share the recipe when I take these to school.

—**JULIE AHERN** WAUKEGAN, IL

START TO FINISH: 30 MIN.
MAKES: 5 SERVINGS

- 1 pound lean ground beef (90% lean)
- ¼ cup each finely chopped celery, onion and green pepper
- ½ cup barbecue sauce
- 1 tube (12 ounces) refrigerated flaky biscuits (10 count)
- ½ cup shredded cheddar cheese

1. Heat oven to 400°. In a large skillet, cook the beef and vegetables over medium heat 5-7 minutes or until beef is no longer pink, breaking up the beef into crumbles; drain. Stir in barbecue sauce; bring to a boil. Reduce the heat; simmer, uncovered, for 2 minutes, stirring occasionally.

2. Separate the dough into 10 biscuits; flatten to 5-in. circles. Press onto the bottom and up sides of greased muffin cups. Fill with beef mixture.

3. Bake for 9-11 minutes or until the biscuits are golden brown. Sprinkle with cheese; bake 1-2 minutes longer or until cheese is melted.

SLOPPY JOE BISCUIT CUPS

SWEET POTATO & BEAN QUESADILLAS

SWEET POTATO & BEAN QUESADILLAS

Sweet potatoes and black beans pair up for a quesadilla that's easy, fast and delicious.
—**BRITTANY HUBBARD** ST. PAUL, MN

START TO FINISH: 30 MIN.
MAKES: 4 SERVINGS

- 2 **medium sweet potatoes**
- 4 **whole wheat tortillas (8 inches)**
- ¾ **cup canned black beans, rinsed and drained**
- ½ **cup shredded pepper jack cheese**
- ¾ **cup salsa**

1. Scrub the sweet potatoes; pierce several times with a fork. Place on a microwave-safe plate. Microwave, uncovered, on high 7-9 minutes or until very tender, turning once.
2. When cool enough to handle, cut each potato lengthwise in half. Scoop out pulp. Spread onto one half of each tortilla; top with beans and cheese. Fold other half of tortilla over filling.
3. Heat a griddle or skillet over medium heat. Cook quesadillas 2-3 minutes on each side or until golden brown and cheese is melted. Serve with salsa.

★ ★ ★ ★ ★ **READER REVIEW**

"I am always looking for a vegetarian recipe that is filling and tastes good to this carnivore. These quesadillas do the trick. A definite addition to my recipe book!"

CPILK715 TASTEOFHOME.COM

HONEY CHIPOTLE RIBS

HONEY CHIPOTLE RIBS

Nothing's better than having a finger-lickin' good sauce to smother your baby back ribs. This one calls for Guinness and honey so it's sure to be a winner. You can make the sauce up to a week in advance.
—**CAITLIN HAWES** WESTWOOD, MA

PREP: 5 MIN. • **COOK:** 1½ HOURS
MAKES: 12 SERVINGS

- 6 **pounds pork baby back ribs**
- BARBECUE SAUCE
- 3 **cups ketchup**
- 2 **bottles (11.2 ounces each) Guinness beer**
- 2 **cups barbecue sauce**
- ⅔ **cup honey**
- 1 **small onion, chopped**
- ¼ **cup Worcestershire sauce**
- 2 **tablespoons Dijon mustard**
- 2 **tablespoons chopped chipotle peppers in adobo sauce**
- 4 **teaspoons ground chipotle pepper**
- 1 **teaspoon salt**
- 1 **teaspoon garlic powder**
- ½ **teaspoon pepper**

1. Wrap the ribs in large pieces of heavy-duty foil; seal edges of foil. Grill, covered, over indirect medium heat for 1 to 1½ hours or until tender.
2. Using a large saucepan, combine the sauce ingredients; bring to a boil. Reduce the heat; simmer, uncovered, about 45 minutes or until thickened, stirring occasionally.
3. Carefully remove ribs from foil. Place over direct heat; baste with some of the sauce. Grill, covered, over medium heat about 30 minutes or until browned, turning them once and basting occasionally with additional sauce. Serve with remaining sauce.

GRILLED SIRLOIN WITH CHILI-BEER BARBECUE SAUCE

We came up with this recipe as a tasty way to cook with beer, but the combination of seasonings in the sauce is what makes this recipe a standout.

—TASTE OF HOME TEST KITCHEN

PREP: 40 MIN. • **GRILL:** 20 MIN.
MAKES: 8 SERVINGS

- 1½ cups beer or nonalcoholic beer
- 1 small onion, chopped
- ¾ cup chili sauce
- 2 tablespoons soy sauce
- 1 tablespoon brown sugar
- 2 teaspoons chili powder
- 2 garlic cloves, minced
- ¼ teaspoon cayenne pepper
- ¼ teaspoon ground mustard
- ⅛ teaspoon ground cumin
- 2 beef top sirloin steaks (1½ pounds each)
- ½ teaspoon salt
- ½ teaspoon pepper

1. In a small saucepan, combine the first 10 ingredients. Bring to a boil. Reduce heat; simmer, uncovered, for 25-30 minutes or until thickened. Set aside ¾ cup and keep warm.
2. Sprinkle steaks with salt and pepper. Grill steaks, covered, over medium heat or broil 4 in. from the heat for 9-13 minutes on each side or until meat reaches desired doneness (for medium-rare, a thermometer should read 145°; medium 160°; and well-done 170°), basting occasionally with remaining sauce. Slice meat and serve with reserved sauce.

FREEZE IT

CHICKEN SPINACH DIP BREAD BOWLS

My family loves artichoke spinach dip, so I turned the popular appetizer into a tasty chicken entree. The sourdough bread bowl makes a fun presentation. I love that I can make one bread bowl to eat right away and one to wrap and save in the freezer for later.

—MERRY GRAHAM NEWHALL, CA

PREP: 35 MIN. • **BAKE:** 20 MIN. + STANDING
MAKES: 2 LOAVES (4 SERVINGS EACH)

- 1 package (10 ounces) frozen chopped spinach
- 3 tablespoons olive oil
- 2 garlic cloves, minced
- 2 loaves sourdough bread (1 pound each)
- 1 medium sweet red pepper, chopped
- 1 medium onion, chopped
- 1½ pounds boneless skinless chicken breasts, cut into ½-inch pieces
- 1 can (14 ounces) water-packed artichoke hearts, rinsed, drained and chopped
- 1 package (8 ounces) cream cheese, softened
- ½ cup grated Parmesan cheese, divided
- 1½ teaspoons Italian seasoning
- 1 teaspoon salt
- 6 bacon strips, cooked and crumbled, divided

1. Preheat the oven to 400°. Thaw the frozen spinach, reserving 2 tablespoons of the liquid.
2. In a small microwave-safe bowl, combine oil and garlic. Microwave on high for 30-45 seconds or until warmed. Cut a thin slice off the top of each bread loaf. Hollow out the bottoms, leaving ½-in.-thick shells (save removed bread for another use). Brush 2 tablespoons oil mixture over outside and inside of bread bowls. Place bread bowls on a baking sheet.
3. Strain remaining oil mixture into a large skillet; discard garlic. Heat oil over medium-high heat. Add pepper and onion; cook and stir 5-7 minutes or until tender. Remove from pan.
4. Add chicken to pan; cook and stir over medium-high heat 6-8 minutes or until no longer pink. Reduce heat to medium. Add artichoke hearts, cream cheese, ¼ cup Parmesan cheese, Italian seasoning, salt, spinach, pepper mixture and reserved spinach liquid; cook and stir until the cream cheese is melted. Stir in ¼ cup of crumbled bacon. Remove from heat.
5. Divide mixture between bread bowls; top with remaining bacon. Sprinkle remaining Parmesan cheese over filling and bowls.
6. Bake bread bowls, uncovered, for 10 minutes. Cover loosely with foil; bake 8-12 minutes longer or until filling is heated through. Let stand 10 minutes before serving. To serve, cut each bowl into 4 wedges.

FREEZE OPTION *Cool the chicken mixture before filling bread bowls. Securely wrap unbaked bowls in foil; place in resealable plastic freezer bags and freeze. To use, partially thaw in refrigerator overnight. Unwrap bowls and place on a baking sheet. Cover loosely with foil and bake in preheated 350° oven 1 hour. Bake, uncovered, 10-15 minutes longer or until the filling is heated through and a thermometer inserted in the center reads 165°.*

★ ★ ★ ★ ★ **READER REVIEW**

"I love bread bowls and sometimes make up recipes on my own. Why wait for a party? Make some for yourself!"

WEEDBIND TASTEOFHOME.COM

CHICKEN SPINACH DIP
BREAD BOWLS

FIESTA BEEF & CHEESE SKILLET COBBLER

I tweaked my beefy skillet cobbler until it achieved the wow factor. Top it off with lettuce, avocado, cherry tomatoes and a dollop of sour cream.

—**GLORIA BRADLEY** NAPERVILLE, IL

PREP: 40 MIN.
BAKE: 15 MIN. + STANDING
MAKES: 8 SERVINGS

- 1 pound ground beef
- 1 can (15 ounces) black beans, rinsed and drained
- 1 can (14½ ounces) diced tomatoes with mild green chilies
- 1 can (10 ounces) enchilada sauce
- 1 teaspoon ground cumin
- 4 tablespoons chopped fresh cilantro or parsley, divided
- 1½ cups biscuit/baking mix
- 1½ cups shredded Colby-Monterey Jack cheese, divided
- 4 bacon strips, cooked and crumbled
- ⅔ cup 2% milk
- 1 large egg, lightly beaten
  Sour cream, optional

1. Preheat oven to 400°. In a 10-in. ovenproof skillet, cook beef over medium heat 5-7 minutes or until no longer pink, breaking into crumbles; drain. Stir in beans, tomatoes, enchilada sauce and cumin; bring to a boil. Reduce heat; simmer, uncovered, 20 minutes to allow flavors to blend, stirring occasionally. Stir in 2 tablespoons cilantro.

2. In a bowl, combine baking mix, ½ cup cheese, bacon and remaining cilantro. Add milk and beaten egg; stir just until a soft dough is formed. Spoon over beef mixture.

3. Bake, uncovered, 13-15 minutes or until golden brown. Sprinkle with remaining cheese; bake 2-3 minutes longer or until cheese is melted. Let stand 10 minutes before serving. If desired, serve with sour cream.

FIESTA BEEF & CHEESE SKILLET COBBLER

FAST FIX ▶

CHICKEN NOODLE STIR-FRY

I rely on budget-friendly ramen noodles to stretch this appealing stir-fry. I usually toss in whatever vegetables I happen to have on hand, so it's a unique flavor experiment every time I make it.

—**DARLENE BRENDEN** SALEM, OR

START TO FINISH: 25 MIN.
MAKES: 4 SERVINGS

- 1 package (3 ounces) chicken ramen noodles
- 1 pound boneless skinless chicken breasts, cut into strips
- 1 tablespoon canola oil
- 1 cup fresh broccoli florets
- 1 cup fresh cauliflowerets
- 1 cup sliced celery
- 1 cup coarsely chopped cabbage
- 2 medium carrots, thinly sliced
- 1 medium onion, thinly sliced
- ½ cup canned bean sprouts
- ½ cup teriyaki or soy sauce

1. Set aside seasoning packet from noodles. Cook noodles according to package directions. Meanwhile, in a large skillet or wok, stir-fry chicken in oil for 5-6 minutes or until no longer pink. Add vegetables; stir-fry for 3-4 minutes or until crisp-tender.
2. Drain noodles. Stir the noodles, contents of seasoning packet and teriyaki sauce into the chicken mixture until well combined.

⑤INGREDIENTS FAST FIX ▶

HADDOCK WITH LIME-CILANTRO BUTTER

In Louisiana, the good times roll when we broil fish and serve it with lots of lime juice, cilantro and butter.

—**DARLENE MORRIS** FRANKLINTON, LA

START TO FINISH: 15 MIN.
MAKES: 4 SERVINGS

- 4 haddock fillets (6 ounces each)
- ½ teaspoon salt
- ¼ teaspoon pepper
- 3 tablespoons butter, melted
- 2 tablespoons minced fresh cilantro
- 1 tablespoon lime juice
- 1 teaspoon grated lime peel

1. Preheat broiler. Sprinkle the fillets with salt and pepper. Place them on a greased broiler pan. Broil 4-5 in. from heat 5-6 minutes or until fish flakes easily with a fork.
2. In a small bowl, mix remaining ingredients. Serve over fish.

FAST FIX ▶

PECAN-CRUSTED CHICKEN NUGGETS

I loved chicken nuggets as a child. This baked version is healthier than the original, and it's a great meal for kids.

—**HAILI CARROLL** VALENCIA, CA

START TO FINISH: 30 MIN.
MAKES: 6 SERVINGS

- 1½ cups cornflakes
- 1 tablespoon dried parsley flakes
- 1 teaspoon salt
- ½ teaspoon garlic powder
- ½ teaspoon pepper
- ½ cup panko (Japanese) bread crumbs
- ½ cup finely chopped pecans
- 3 tablespoons 2% milk
- 1½ pounds boneless skinless chicken breasts, cut into 1-inch pieces
  Cooking spray

1. Preheat the oven to 400°. Place cornflakes, parsley, salt, garlic powder and pepper in a blender; cover and pulse until finely ground. Transfer to a shallow bowl; stir in bread crumbs and pecans. Place milk in another shallow bowl. Dip chicken in milk, then roll in crumb mixture to coat.
2. Place on a greased baking sheet; spritz chicken with cooking spray. Bake 12-16 minutes or until chicken is no longer pink, turning once halfway through cooking.

PORK LOIN WITH RASPBERRY SAUCE

Raspberries add lovely color and sweetness to this sauce, which enhances the savory pork roast. It's an easy way to transform everyday pork into something special.

—**FLORENCE NURCZYK** TORONTO, OH

PREP: 5 MIN. • **BAKE:** 1½ HOURS + STANDING
MAKES: 8 SERVINGS

- 1 **boneless whole pork loin roast (3 pounds)**
- 1 **teaspoon salt, divided**
- 1 **teaspoon rubbed sage**
- ½ **teaspoon pepper**
- 1 **package (12 ounces) frozen unsweetened raspberries, thawed, divided**
- ¾ **cup sugar**
- 1 **tablespoon cornstarch**
- ¼ **teaspoon each ground ginger, nutmeg and cloves**
- ¼ **cup white vinegar**
- 1 **tablespoon lemon juice**
- 1 **tablespoon butter**

1. Place roast on a greased rack in a shallow roasting pan. Rub with ¾ teaspoon salt, sage and pepper. Bake, uncovered, at 350° for 1½ hours or until a thermometer reads 160°.
2. Meanwhile, drain raspberries, reserving juice. Set aside ⅓ cup berries. In a sieve, mash remaining berries with the back of a spoon; reserve pulp and discard seeds.
3. In a large saucepan, combine the sugar, cornstarch, ginger, nutmeg, cloves and remaining salt. Stir in the vinegar, reserved raspberry juice and reserved pulp until blended. Add remaining raspberries. Bring to a boil; cook and stir for 2 minutes or until thickened. Remove from the heat; add lemon juice and butter. Stir until butter is melted. Let pork stand for 10 minutes before slicing. Serve with the raspberry sauce.

FREEZE OPTION *Prepare raspberry sauce; transfer to a freezer container. Place sliced pork in freezer containers. Cool and freeze. To use, partially thaw the pork and sauce in the refrigerator overnight. Heat sauce in a saucepan over medium heat until the mixture comes to a boil. Remove from the heat. Microwave pork, covered, on high in a microwave-safe dish until heated through. Serve with sauce.*

PORK LOIN WITH RASPBERRY SAUCE

BROWN SUGAR PINEAPPLE HAM

With pineapple, brown sugar, mustard and cloves, this baked beauty is straightforward and simple. It's everything you're looking for in a succulent ham.

—*TASTE OF HOME* TEST KITCHEN

PREP: 10 MIN. • **BAKE:** 2 HOURS
MAKES: 12 SERVINGS

- 1 **fully cooked bone-in ham (7 to 9 pounds)**
- 1 **can (20 ounces) crushed pineapple, undrained**
- 1 **cup packed brown sugar**
- 1 **tablespoon Dijon mustard**
- ¼ **teaspoon ground cloves**

1. Preheat oven to 325°. Place ham on a rack in a shallow roasting pan. Using a sharp knife, score surface of ham with ½-in.-deep cuts in a diamond pattern. Cover and bake 1½ hours.
2. In a small bowl, mix remaining ingredients. Spread over ham, pressing mixture into cuts. Bake ham, uncovered, 30-60 minutes longer or until a thermometer reads 140°.

GRILLED HULI HULI CHICKEN

When I lived in Hawaii, a friend gave me this recipe for chicken marinated in a ginger-soy sauce. *Huli* means "turn" in Hawaiian and refers to turning the meat on the grill.

—SHARON BOLING SAN DIEGO, CA

PREP: 15 MIN. + MARINATING
GRILL: 15 MIN.
MAKES: 12 SERVINGS

- 1 cup packed brown sugar
- ¾ cup ketchup
- ¾ cup reduced-sodium soy sauce
- ⅓ cup sherry or chicken broth
- 2½ teaspoons minced fresh gingerroot
- 1½ teaspoons minced garlic
- 24 boneless skinless chicken thighs (about 5 pounds)

1. In a small bowl, mix the first six ingredients. Reserve 1⅓ cups for basting; cover and refrigerate. Divide remaining marinade between two large resealable plastic bags. Add 12 chicken thighs to each; seal bags and turn to coat. Refrigerate for 8 hours or overnight.
2. Drain and discard marinade from chicken. Moisten a paper towel with cooking oil; using long-handled tongs, lightly coat the grill rack.
3. Grill the chicken, covered, over medium heat for 6-8 minutes on each side or until no longer pink; baste occasionally with reserved marinade during the last 5 minutes.

★ ★ ★ ★ ★ **5 STAR TIP**

Fresh gingerroot is available in your grocer's produce section. It should have a smooth skin. If wrinkled and cracked, the root is dry and past its prime. Unpeeled gingerroot can be frozen for up to 1 year in a heavy-duty resealable plastic bag. When needed, simply peel and grate.

BLT SKILLET

FAST FIX ▸
BLT SKILLET

With chunks of bacon and tomato, this skillet is reminiscent of a classic BLT. The recipe is fast, too, so it makes a great weeknight meal. The whole wheat linguine gives the dish extra flavor and texture.

—EDRIE O'BRIEN DENVER, CO

START TO FINISH: 25 MIN.
MAKES: 2 SERVINGS

- 4 ounces uncooked whole wheat linguine
- 4 bacon strips, cut into 1½-inch pieces
- 1 plum tomato, cut into 1-inch pieces
- 1 garlic clove, minced
- 1½ teaspoons lemon juice
- ¼ teaspoon salt
- ¼ teaspoon pepper
- 2 tablespoons grated Parmesan cheese
- 1 tablespoon minced fresh parsley

1. Cook the linguine according to package directions. Meanwhile, in a large skillet, cook bacon over medium heat until crisp. Remove to paper towels; drain, reserving 1 teaspoon bacon drippings.
2. In the drippings, saute tomato and garlic for 1-2 minutes or until heated through. Stir in the bacon, lemon juice, salt and pepper.
3. Drain linguine; add to the skillet. Sprinkle with cheese and parsley; toss to coat.

TERIYAKI PINEAPPLE DRUMSTICKS

STRING CHEESE MEAT LOAF

My daughter likes the cheese stuffed into this flavorful meat loaf made with a blend of ground beef and Italian sausage. Served with a salad and sourdough bread, the meal is special enough for company.

—**LAURA LAWRENCE** SALINAS, CA

PREP: 15 MIN.
BAKE: 1 HOUR 25 MIN. + STANDING
MAKES: 6 SERVINGS

- 1 cup meatless spaghetti sauce, divided
- 1 large egg, lightly beaten
- 1 cup seasoned bread crumbs
- 2 garlic cloves, minced
- 1½ teaspoons dried rosemary, crushed
- 1 pound lean ground beef
- 8 ounces bulk Italian sausage
- 3 pieces string cheese

1. In a large bowl, combine ½ cup spaghetti sauce, egg, bread crumbs, garlic and rosemary. Crumble meat over mixture and mix well.
2. Press half into a greased 8x4-in. loaf pan. Place two pieces of cheese, side by side, near one end of loaf. Cut the remaining piece of cheese in half; place side by side on opposite end of loaf. Top with the remaining meat mixture; press down firmly to seal.
3. Bake, uncovered, at 350° for 1¼ to 1½ hours or until meat is no longer pink and a thermometer reads 160°; drain. Drizzle with the remaining spaghetti sauce; bake 10 minutes longer. Let stand for 10 minutes before slicing.
NOTE *Three ounces of mozzarella cheese, cut into four ½-inch sticks, may be substituted for string cheese.*

TERIYAKI PINEAPPLE DRUMSTICKS

We love to throw big backyard parties, so I look for ways to free my hubby from having to be on grill duty all day long. Oven-roasted drumsticks make everyone happy.

—**ERICA ALLEN** TUCKERTON, NJ

PREP: 35 MIN. • **BAKE:** 1½ HOURS
MAKES: 12 SERVINGS

- 1 tablespoon garlic salt
- 1 tablespoon minced chives
- 1½ teaspoons paprika
- 1½ teaspoons pepper
- ½ teaspoon salt
- 24 chicken drumsticks
- ½ cup canola oil
- 1 can (8 ounces) crushed pineapple
- ½ cup water
- ¼ cup packed brown sugar
- ¼ cup Worcestershire sauce
- ¼ cup yellow mustard
- 4 teaspoons cornstarch
- 2 tablespoons cold water

1. Preheat oven to 350°. Mix the first five ingredients; sprinkle over the chicken. In a large skillet, heat oil over medium-high heat. Brown drumsticks in batches. Transfer to a roasting pan.
2. Meanwhile, combine the crushed pineapple, ½ cup water, brown sugar, Worcestershire sauce and mustard; pour mixture over chicken. Cover; bake until the chicken is tender, about 1½ to 2 hours, uncovering during the last 20-30 minutes of baking to let the skin crisp.
3. Remove drumsticks to a platter; keep warm. Transfer cooking juices to a small saucepan; skim fat. Bring cooking juices to a boil. In a small bowl, mix the cornstarch and cold water until smooth; stir into cooking juices. Return to a boil; cook and stir 1-2 minutes or until thickened. Serve with drumsticks.

STRING CHEESE
MEAT LOAF

FONTINA ROLLED CHICKEN

Good food has a way of transporting you to faraway places. My chicken dish with fontina and cream cheese is like a blissful trip to Italy.

—TAMMY REX NEW TRIPOLI, PA

PREP: 30 MIN. • **BAKE:** 30 MIN.
MAKES: 4 SERVINGS

- 4 **ounces cream cheese, softened**
- 1 **cup shredded fontina cheese**
- 5 **bacon strips, cooked and crumbled**
- 4 **green onions, chopped**
- ¼ **cup chopped fresh Italian parsley**
- ¼ **cup julienned oil-packed sun-dried tomatoes, drained, chopped and patted dry**
- ½ **teaspoon salt, divided**
- ¾ **teaspoon pepper, divided**
- 1 **large egg**
- 1½ **cups panko (Japanese) bread crumbs**
- 1 **teaspoon paprika**
- 4 **boneless skinless chicken breast halves (6 ounces each)**
- 1 **tablespoon olive oil**

1. Preheat oven to 375°. In a bowl, mix the first six ingredients; stir in ¼ teaspoon each salt and pepper. In a shallow bowl, whisk egg and the remaining salt and pepper. In another shallow bowl, toss the bread crumbs with paprika.

2. Carefully pound chicken breasts with a meat mallet to ¼-in. thickness. Spread cheese mixture over chicken. Roll up chicken from a short side; secure with toothpicks.

3. Dip chicken in egg, then coat with crumbs. Place in foil-lined 15x10x1-in. baking pan, seam side down. Drizzle tops with oil.

4. Bake, uncovered, 30-35 minutes or until golden brown and chicken is no longer pink. Let stand 5 minutes; discard toothpicks before serving.

FONTINA ROLLED CHICKEN

GARLIC ROSEMARY TURKEY

Garlic, herbs and lemon may seem like simple flavor accents, but they are all you really need to make this turkey shine. Our house smells incredible while the bird is roasting, and my family can hardly wait to eat.

—**CATHY DOBBINS** RIO RANCHO, NM

PREP: 10 MIN. • **BAKE:** 3 HOURS + STANDING
MAKES: 10 SERVINGS

- 1 turkey (10 to 12 pounds)
- 6 to 8 garlic cloves, peeled
- 2 large lemons, halved
- 2 tablespoons olive oil
- 2 teaspoons dried rosemary, crushed
- 1 teaspoon rubbed sage

1. Preheat the oven to 325°. Cut six to eight small slits in the turkey skin; insert garlic under the skin. Squeeze two lemon halves inside the turkey; squeeze the remaining halves over the outside of turkey. Place lemons inside the cavity.
2. Tuck wings under turkey; tie drumsticks together. Place on a rack in a shallow roasting pan, breast side up. Brush with oil; sprinkle with rosemary and sage. Roast 1 hour.
3. Cover turkey with foil; roast for 2 to 2½ hours longer or until a thermometer inserted in thickest part of thigh reads 170°-175°. Baste occasionally with pan drippings.
4. Remove turkey from oven. Let stand 20 minutes before carving. If desired, skim fat and thicken pan drippings for gravy. Serve with turkey.

PAN-FRIED VENISON STEAK

This recipe was a favorite when we had deer meat while I was growing up. I loved it, and now my children do, too!

—**GAYLEEN GROTE** BATTLEVIEW, ND

START TO FINISH: 25 MIN.
MAKES: 4 SERVINGS

- 1 pound venison or beef tenderloin, cut into ½-inch slices
- 2 cups crushed saltines
- 2 large eggs
- ¾ cup milk
- 1 teaspoon salt
- ½ teaspoon pepper
- 5 tablespoons canola oil

1. Flatten venison to ¼-in. thickness. Place the saltines in a shallow bowl. In another shallow bowl, whisk the eggs, milk, salt and pepper. Coat the venison with saltines, then dip in the egg mixture and coat a second time with saltines.
2. In a large skillet over medium heat, cook venison in oil in batches for 2-3 minutes on each side or until meat reaches desired doneness (for medium-rare, a thermometer should read 145°; medium, 160°; well-done, 170°).

★ ★ ★ ★ ★ **READER REVIEW**

"I made this using our venison tenderloin strips, which I soaked in salt water all day. I was out of saltines so I used Keebler Club Crackers, which have a buttery flavor, and I substituted veggie oil for the canola oil. Wow! It turned out delicious."

CHEESECAKEMAVEN
TASTEOFHOME.COM

CASSEROLE ENTREES

Comfort in one convenient pan—
yes, we're talking casseroles! Whether
you want to spice up the usual dinner
rotation or you're looking for a new
awe-inspiring potluck offering, these
family favorites are ready to impress at
breakfast, lunch or dinner.

BURRITO BAKE

Years ago when I was still in college, my roommate would frequently make this economical casserole. It's so easy to put together, and one slice will fill you right up!
—**CINDEE NESS** HORACE, ND

PREP: 25 MIN. • **BAKE:** 30 MIN.
MAKES: 6 SERVINGS

- 1 **pound ground beef**
- 1 **can (16 ounces) refried beans**
- ¼ **cup chopped onion**
- 1 **envelope taco seasoning**
- 1 **tube (8 ounces) refrigerated crescent rolls**
- 1 **to 2 cups shredded cheddar cheese**
- 1 **to 2 cups shredded part-skim mozzarella cheese**
  Optional toppings: chopped green pepper, shredded lettuce, chopped tomatoes and sliced ripe olives

1. Preheat oven to 350°. In a large skillet, cook and crumble the beef over medium heat until no longer pink; drain. Add beans, onion and taco seasoning.
2. Unroll crescent roll dough. Press onto bottom and up the sides of a greased 13x9-in. baking dish; seal seams and perforations.
3. Spread beef mixture over crust; sprinkle with the cheeses. Bake, uncovered, until golden brown, 30 minutes. If desired, add toppings.

★ ★ ★ ★ ★ **READER REVIEW**

"Good, hearty meal. The crescent rolls make it very easy to put together. Add salsa and/or some diced chilies to the mixture for extra spice."

NH-RESCUE TASTEOFHOME.COM

PIZZA NOODLE BAKE

You can throw this yummy, family-pleasing casserole together in a snap. It's perfect for a weeknight meal. Double the recipe and freeze one for later.

—**BERNICE KNUTSON** SOLDIER, IA

PREP: 25 MIN. • **BAKE:** 15 MIN.
MAKES: 6 SERVINGS

- 10 **ounces uncooked egg noodles**
- 1½ **pounds ground beef**
- ½ **cup finely chopped onion**
- ¼ **cup chopped green pepper**
- 1 **jar (14 ounces) pizza sauce**
- 1 **can (4 ounces) mushroom stems and pieces, drained**
- 1 **cup shredded cheddar cheese**
- 1 **cup shredded part-skim mozzarella cheese**
- 1 **package (3½ ounces) sliced pepperoni**

1. Cook noodles according to package directions. Meanwhile, using a large skillet, cook the beef, onion and green pepper over medium heat until meat is no longer pink; drain. Add pizza sauce and mushrooms; heat through.

2. Drain noodles. In a greased 13x9-in. baking dish, layer half of the noodles, beef mixture, cheeses and pepperoni. Repeat layers. Cover and bake at 350° for 15-20 minutes or until heated through.

FREEZE OPTION *Cover and freeze unbaked casserole for up to 3 months. Remove from freezer 30 minutes before baking (do not thaw). Cover and bake at 350° for 45-50 minutes. Uncover; bake 15-20 minutes longer or until heated through.*

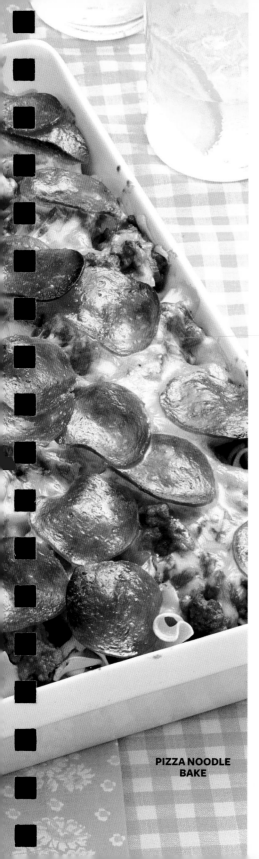

PIZZA NOODLE BAKE

BROCCOLI SCALLOPED POTATOES

The combination of ham and Swiss creates a wonderfully rich, smoky flavor. I also love that I can cook an entire meal—veggie and all—in one standout dish.

—DENELL SYSLO FULLERTON, NE

PREP: 25 MIN. • **BAKE:** 1 HOUR
MAKES: 8 SERVINGS

- ¼ cup butter, cubed
- 2 tablespoons chopped onion
- 4 garlic cloves, minced
- 5 tablespoons all-purpose flour
- ¼ teaspoon white pepper
- ⅛ teaspoon salt
- 2½ cups whole milk
- 2 cups shredded Swiss cheese, divided
- 2 pounds potatoes, peeled and thinly sliced (about 4 cups)
- 2 cups julienned fully cooked ham
- 2 cups frozen broccoli florets, thawed and patted dry

1. Preheat oven to 350°. In a Dutch oven, heat butter over medium-high heat. Add onion and garlic; cook and stir 2-3 minutes or until tender. Stir in flour, white pepper and salt until blended; gradually whisk in milk. Bring to a boil, stirring constantly; cook and stir 2 minutes or until thickened.
2. Stir in 1 cup cheese. Reduce heat; cook 1-2 minutes or until cheese is melted (sauce will be thick). Remove from heat.
3. Add potatoes, ham and broccoli to sauce; stir gently to coat. Transfer to eight greased 8-oz. ramekins.
4. Bake it, covered, for 40 minutes. Sprinkle with remaining cheese. Bake, uncovered, 20-25 minutes longer or until the potatoes are tender and the cheese is melted.

ROAST BEEF WITH CHIVE ROASTED POTATOES

It's hard to believe that last night's beef roast could get any better, but it shines in this heartwarming dish.

—TASTE OF HOME TEST KITCHEN

PREP: 20 MIN. • **BAKE:** 25 MIN.
MAKES: 6 SERVINGS

- 2 pounds red potatoes, cut into 1-inch cubes
- 2 tablespoons olive oil
- 2 teaspoons minced chives
- ¾ teaspoon salt, divided
- 2 medium onions, halved and thinly sliced
- 1 pound sliced fresh mushrooms
- ¼ cup butter, cubed
- 1 garlic clove, minced
- 1 teaspoon dried rosemary, crushed
- ¼ teaspoon pepper
- ⅓ cup dry red wine or beef broth
- 2 cups cubed cooked roast beef
- 1 cup beef gravy

1. Place the potatoes in a greased 15x10x1-in. baking pan. Drizzle with the oil and sprinkle with chives and ¼ teaspoon salt; toss to coat. Bake, uncovered, at 425° for 25-30 minutes or until tender, stirring occasionally.
2. Meanwhile, in a large skillet, saute the onions and mushrooms in butter until tender. Add the garlic, rosemary, pepper and remaining salt; cook for 1 minute longer. Stir in wine. Add the beef and gravy; heat through. Serve with potatoes.

CHURCH SUPPER SPAGHETTI

Because this recipe feeds so many, I often take it to church dinners and potlucks. It also comes in handy when we have lots of hungry folks helping out on our farm.

—VERLYN WILSON WILKINSON, IN

PREP: 50 MIN. • **BAKE:** 20 MIN.
MAKES: 12 SERVINGS

- 1 pound ground beef
- 1 large onion, chopped
- 1 medium green pepper, chopped
- 1 can (14½ ounces) diced tomatoes, undrained
- 1 cup water
- 2 tablespoons chili powder
- 1 package (10 ounces) frozen corn, thawed
- 1 package (10 ounces) frozen peas, thawed
- 1 can (4 ounces) mushroom stems and pieces, drained
  Salt and pepper to taste
- 12 ounces spaghetti, cooked and drained
- 2 cups shredded cheddar cheese, divided

1. In a large skillet, cook beef, onion and green pepper over medium heat until meat is no longer pink. Add tomatoes, water and chili powder. Cover and simmer for 30 minutes. Add the corn, peas, mushrooms, salt and pepper. Stir in spaghetti.
2. Layer half of the mixture in a greased 4-qt. baking dish. Sprinkle with 1 cup cheese; repeat layers.
3. Bake, uncovered, at 350° for 20 minutes or until heated through.
NOTE *To give the Church Supper Spaghetti a new flavor twist, use Italian, Mexican or Cajun diced tomatoes in place of the plain diced tomatoes.*

CHURCH SUPPER SPAGHETTI

DELUXE BAKED MACARONI & CHEESE

By adding diced ham, tomatoes and a crumb topping, I transformed mac and cheese into something extraordinary. It makes a great meal-in-one.

—KATHY YAROSH APOPKA, FL

PREP: 30 MIN. • **BAKE:** 25 MIN.
MAKES: 12 SERVINGS

- 1 package (16 ounces) elbow macaroni
- ¼ cup all-purpose flour
- 2 cups 2% milk
- ½ cup heavy whipping cream
- 1 package (8 ounces) process cheese (Velveeta), cubed
- 1 cup shredded cheddar cheese
- ⅔ cup whipped cream cheese
- ¼ cup grated Parmesan cheese
- 1 can (14½ ounces) diced tomatoes, drained
- 1½ cups cubed fully cooked ham
- 1 cup (8 ounces) sour cream
- 1 teaspoon Dijon mustard
  TOPPING
- 1½ cups soft bread crumbs
- ¼ cup grated Parmesan cheese
- 2 tablespoons butter, melted

1. Preheat oven to 350°. Cook the macaroni according to the package directions. In a Dutch oven, whisk flour, milk and cream until smooth. Bring to a boil; cook and stir 2 minutes or until thickened.
2. Stir in cheeses until melted. Add the tomatoes, ham, sour cream and mustard. Drain the macaroni; add to the cheese mixture and toss to coat.
3. Transfer to a greased 13x9-in. baking dish. In a small bowl, mix the topping ingredients; sprinkle over top. Bake, uncovered, 25-30 minutes or until bubbly and bread crumbs are lightly browned.
NOTE *To make soft bread crumbs, tear bread into pieces and place in a food processor or blender. Cover and pulse until crumbs form. One slice of bread yields ½ to ¾ cup crumbs.*

REUBEN BREAD PUDDING

My Aunt Renee always brought this casserole to our family picnics in Chicago. It became so popular that she started bringing two or three! I have also used dark rye bread or marbled rye, and ham instead of corned beef.
—**JOHNNA JOHNSON** SCOTTSDALE, AZ

PREP: 20 MIN. • **BAKE:** 35 MIN.
MAKES: 6 SERVINGS

- 4 **cups cubed rye bread (about 6 slices)**
- 2 **tablespoons butter, melted**
- 2 **cups cubed or shredded cooked corned beef (about ½ pound)**
- 1 **can (14 ounces) sauerkraut, rinsed and well drained**
- 1 **cup shredded Swiss cheese, divided**
- 3 **large eggs**
- 1 **cup 2% milk**
- ⅓ **cup prepared Thousand Island salad dressing**
- 1½ **teaspoons prepared mustard**
- ¼ **teaspoon pepper**

1. Preheat oven to 350°. In a large bowl, toss bread cubes with butter. Stir in corned beef, sauerkraut and ½ cup cheese; transfer to a greased 11x7-in. baking dish.

2. In same bowl, whisk eggs, milk, salad dressing, mustard and pepper; pour over top. Bake, uncovered, 30 minutes. Sprinkle with remaining cheese. Bake 5-7 minutes longer or until golden and a knife inserted in the center comes out clean.

★ ★ ★ ★ ★ 5 STAR TIP

Don't have a casserole carrier? Here's an easy way to transport a casserole to a party or potluck. Set the dish inside a clear plastic oven bag and close with a twist tie. The bag will trap any spills, it won't melt, and the potluck organizers can see what's inside. Then wrap the dish in a thick beach towel to keep the food warm if traveling a short distance. For long distances, place the cooled casserole dish on ice.

REUBEN BREAD PUDDING

CRAB-SPINACH EGG CASSEROLE

My love of cooking has evolved over the years. I came up with this casserole as a special breakfast for our daughter when she was home for a visit.
—**STEVE HEATON** DELTONA, FL

PREP: 10 MIN. • **BAKE:** 30 MIN. + STANDING
MAKES: 12-16 SERVINGS

- 8 **large eggs**
- 2 **cups half-and-half cream**
- 2 **cans (6 ounces each) crabmeat, drained**
- 1 **package (10 ounces) frozen chopped spinach, thawed and squeezed dry**
- 1 **cup dry bread crumbs**
- 1 **cup shredded Swiss cheese**
- ½ **teaspoon salt**
- ¼ **teaspoon pepper**
- ¼ **teaspoon ground nutmeg**
- 2 **celery ribs, chopped**
- ½ **cup chopped onion**
- ½ **cup chopped sweet red pepper**
- 3 **medium fresh mushrooms, chopped**
- 2 **tablespoons butter**

1. In a large bowl, beat eggs and cream. Stir in the crab, spinach, bread crumbs, cheese, salt, pepper and nutmeg; set aside. In a skillet, saute the celery, onion, red pepper and mushrooms in butter until tender. Add to the spinach mixture.
2. Transfer to a greased shallow 2½-qt. baking dish. Bake, uncovered, at 375° for 30-35 minutes or until a thermometer reads 160°. Let stand for 10 minutes before serving.

CRAB-SPINACH EGG CASSEROLE

FREEZE IT
LASAGNA CASSEROLE

When I was growing up, this was the meal I always wanted on my birthday. If you want more spice, substitute Italian sausage for the ground beef.
—**DEB MORRISON** SKIATOOK, OK

PREP: 15 MIN. • **BAKE:** 1 HOUR + STANDING
MAKES: 6-8 SERVINGS

- 1 **pound ground beef**
- ¼ **cup chopped onion**
- ½ **teaspoon salt**
- ½ **teaspoon pepper, divided**
- 1 **pound medium pasta shells, cooked and drained**
- 4 **cups shredded part-skim mozzarella cheese, divided**
- 3 **cups 4% cottage cheese**
- 2 **large eggs, lightly beaten**
- ⅓ **cup grated Parmesan cheese**
- 2 **tablespoons dried parsley flakes**
- 1 **jar (24 ounces) pasta sauce**

1. In a large skillet, cook beef and onion over medium heat until meat is no longer pink; drain. Sprinkle with salt and ¼ teaspoon pepper; set aside.
2. In a large bowl, combine the pasta, 3 cups mozzarella cheese, cottage cheese, eggs, Parmesan cheese, parsley and remaining pepper. Transfer to a greased shallow 3-qt. baking dish. Top with beef mixture and pasta sauce (dish will be full).
3. Cover and bake at 350° for 45 minutes. Sprinkle with remaining mozzarella cheese. Bake, uncovered, 15 minutes longer or until bubbly and cheese is melted. Let stand for 10 minutes before serving.
FREEZE OPTION *Sprinkle casserole with remaining mozzarella cheese. Cover and freeze unbaked casserole. To use, partially thaw in refrigerator overnight. Remove from refrigerator 30 minutes before baking. Preheat oven to 350°. Bake the casserole as directed, increasing time as necessary to heat through and for a thermometer inserted in center to read 165°.*

LASAGNA
CASSEROLE

CABBAGE ROLL CASSEROLE

I layer cabbage with tomato sauce and beef to create a hearty casserole that tastes like old-fashioned cabbage rolls but without all the work.

—DOREEN MARTIN KITIMAT, BC

PREP: 20 MIN. • **BAKE:** 55 MIN. + STANDING
MAKES: 12 SERVINGS

- 2 pounds ground beef
- 1 large onion, chopped
- 3 garlic cloves, minced
- 2 cans (15 ounces each) tomato sauce, divided
- 1 teaspoon dried thyme
- ½ teaspoon dill weed
- ½ teaspoon rubbed sage
- ¼ teaspoon salt
- ¼ teaspoon pepper
- ¼ teaspoon cayenne pepper
- 2 cups cooked rice
- 4 bacon strips, cooked and crumbled
- 1 medium head cabbage (2 pounds), shredded
- 1 cup shredded part-skim mozzarella cheese
  Coarsely ground pepper, optional

1. Preheat oven to 375°. In a large skillet, cook beef and onion over medium heat, crumbling beef, until meat is no longer pink. Add garlic; cook 1 minute longer. Drain. Stir in one can of tomato sauce and next six ingredients. Bring to a boil. Reduce heat; simmer, covered, 5 minutes. Stir in rice and bacon; remove from heat.

2. Layer a third of the cabbage in a greased 13x9-in. baking dish. Top with half of the meat mixture. Repeat layers; top with remaining cabbage. Pour the remaining tomato sauce over the top.

3. Cover and bake for 45 minutes. Uncover; sprinkle with cheese. Bake until the cheese is melted, about 10 minutes. Let stand 5 minutes before serving. If desired, sprinkle with coarsely ground pepper.

LOADED TATER TOT BAKE

I keep Tater Tots frozen to build quick meals. This one can make a super brunch or side.

—NANCY HEISHMAN LAS VEGAS, NV

PREP: 15 MIN. • **BAKE:** 35 MIN.
MAKES: 6 SERVINGS

- 1 tablespoon canola oil
- 1 medium onion, finely chopped
- 6 ounces Canadian bacon, cut into ½-inch strips
- 4 cups frozen Tater Tots, thawed
- 6 large eggs, lightly beaten
- ½ cup reduced-fat sour cream
- ½ cup half-and-half cream
- 1 tablespoon dried parsley flakes
- ¾ teaspoon garlic powder
- ½ teaspoon pepper
- 1½ cups shredded cheddar cheese

1. Preheat oven to 350°. In a large skillet, heat oil over medium heat. Add onion; cook and stir 2-3 minutes or until tender. Add Canadian bacon; cook for 1-2 minutes or until lightly browned, stirring occasionally. Remove from heat.

2. Line bottom of a greased 11x7-in. baking dish with Tater Tots; top with Canadian bacon mixture. In a large bowl, whisk eggs, sour cream, cream and seasonings until blended. Stir in the cheese; pour over the top. Bake, uncovered, 35-40 minutes or until golden brown.

CABBAGE ROLL CASSEROLE

EASY ZITI BAKE

I enjoy making this dish for family and friends. It's easy to prepare, and I like to get creative with the sauce. For example, sometimes I might add my home-canned tomatoes, mushrooms or vegetables.

—ELAINE ANDERSON NEW GALILEE, PA

PREP: 20 MIN. • **BAKE:** 45 MIN. + STANDING
MAKES: 6-8 SERVINGS

- 12 **ounces uncooked ziti or small tube pasta**
- 2 **pounds ground beef**
- 1 **jar (24 ounces) spaghetti sauce**
- 2 **large eggs, beaten**
- 1 **carton (15 ounces) ricotta cheese**
- 2½ **cups shredded mozzarella cheese, divided**
- ½ **cup grated Parmesan cheese**

1. Cook pasta according to package directions.

2. Meanwhile, preheat oven to 350°. In a large skillet, cook the beef over medium heat until no longer pink; drain. Stir in spaghetti sauce.

3. In a large bowl, combine the eggs, ricotta cheese, 1½ cups mozzarella cheese and the Parmesan cheese. Drain pasta; add to cheese mixture and stir until blended.

4. Spoon a third of the meat sauce into a greased 13x9-in. baking dish; top with half of the pasta mixture. Repeat the layers. Top with the remaining meat sauce.

5. Cover and bake 40 minutes or until a thermometer reads 160°. Uncover; sprinkle with remaining mozzarella cheese. Bake 5-10 minutes longer or until cheese is melted. Let stand 15 minutes before serving.

CORDON BLEU CASSEROLE

CORDON BLEU CASSEROLE

I sometimes roast a turkey just so I have leftovers to bake inside this creamy cordon bleu casserole.

—JOYCE PAUL QU'APPELLE, SK

PREP: 25 MIN. • **BAKE:** 25 MIN.
MAKES: 6 SERVINGS

- 2 **cups cubed fully cooked ham**
- 4 **cups cubed cooked turkey**
- 1 **cup shredded Swiss cheese**
- 1 **large onion, chopped**
- ⅓ **cup butter, cubed**
- ⅓ **cup all-purpose flour**
- ⅛ **teaspoon ground mustard**
- ⅛ **teaspoon ground nutmeg**
- 1¾ **cups whole milk**

TOPPING
- 1½ **cups soft bread crumbs**
- ½ **cup shredded Swiss cheese**
- ¼ **cup butter, melted**

1. In a large nonstick skillet, cook ham 4-5 minutes or until browned; drain and pat dry. In a greased 2-qt. baking dish, layer turkey, cheese and ham; set aside.

2. In a large saucepan, saute onion in butter until tender. Stir in the flour, mustard and nutmeg until blended. Gradually stir in milk. Bring to a boil; cook and stir for 2 minutes or until thickened. Pour over ham.

3. Combine the topping ingredients; sprinkle over top. Bake, uncovered, at 350° for 25-30 minutes or until golden brown and bubbly.

PENNE & SMOKED SAUSAGE

My sausage and pasta dish is a must-try. It just tastes so good when it's hot and bubbly from the oven. The cheddar french-fried onions lend a cheesy, crunchy touch.

—**MARGARET WILSON** SAN BERNARDINO, CA

PREP: 15 MIN. • **BAKE:** 30 MIN.
MAKES: 6 SERVINGS

- 2 **cups uncooked penne pasta**
- 1 **pound smoked sausage, cut into ¼-inch slices**
- 1½ **cups 2% milk**
- 1 **can (10¾ ounces) condensed cream of celery soup, undiluted**
- 1½ **cups cheddar french-fried onions, divided**
- 1 **cup shredded part-skim mozzarella cheese, divided**
- 1 **cup frozen peas**

1. Preheat oven to 375°. Cook pasta according to package directions.
2. Meanwhile, in a large skillet, brown sausage over medium heat 5 minutes; drain. In a large bowl, combine milk and soup. Stir in ½ cup onions, ½ cup cheese, peas and sausage. Drain pasta; stir into sausage mixture.
3. Transfer to a greased 13x9-in. baking dish. Cover and bake 25-30 minutes or until bubbly. Sprinkle with remaining onions and cheese. Bake, uncovered, 3-5 minutes longer or until cheese is melted.

FREEZE OPTION *Sprinkle remaining onions and cheese over the unbaked casserole. Cover and freeze. To use, partially thaw in the refrigerator overnight. Remove from refrigerator 30 minutes before baking. Preheat the oven to 375°. Bake casserole as recipe directs, increasing time as necessary to heat through and for a thermometer inserted in center to read 165°.*

PENNE & SMOKED SAUSAGE

BROCCOLI-HAM HOT DISH

One of my friends gave me this recipe. My family loves it since it includes broccoli, one of our favorite vegetables. I love that it's a colorful addition to the table and a delicious way to use up leftover ham.

—MARGARET ALLEN ABINGDON, VA

PREP: 20 MIN. • **BAKE:** 30 MIN.
MAKES: 8 SERVINGS

- 2 packages (10 ounces each) frozen cut broccoli
- 2 cups cooked rice
- 6 tablespoons butter, cubed
- 2 cups fresh bread crumbs (about 2½ slices)
- 1 medium onion, chopped
- 3 tablespoons all-purpose flour
- 1 teaspoon salt
- ¼ teaspoon pepper
- 3 cups milk
- 1½ pounds fully cooked ham, cubed
  Shredded cheddar or Swiss cheese

1. Preheat oven to 350°. Cook the broccoli according to the package directions; drain. Spoon rice into a 13x9-in. baking pan. Place broccoli over the rice.
2. Melt butter in a large skillet. Sprinkle 2 tablespoons of melted butter over the bread crumbs and set aside. In remaining butter, saute onion until soft. Add flour, salt and pepper, stirring constantly until blended; stir in milk. Bring to a boil; cook and stir 2 minutes or until thickened. Add ham.
3. Pour over rice and broccoli. Sprinkle with crumbs. Bake 30 minutes or until heated through. Sprinkle with cheese; let stand 5 minutes before serving.

FAST FIX
COMPANY MAC & CHEESE

I'm not usually a fan of homemade macaroni and cheese, but when a friend served this, I had to have the recipe. This is by far the creamiest, tastiest and utterly best macaroni and cheese I have ever tried. Since it's simple to make and well received, it's a terrific potluck dish.

—CATHERINE OGDEN MIDDLEGROVE, NY

START TO FINISH: 30 MIN.
MAKES: 6-8 SERVINGS

- 1 package (7 ounces) elbow macaroni
- 6 tablespoons butter, divided
- 3 tablespoons all-purpose flour
- 2 cups milk
- 1 package (8 ounces) cream cheese, cubed
- 2 cups shredded cheddar cheese
- 2 teaspoons spicy brown mustard
- ½ teaspoon salt
- ¼ teaspoon pepper
- ¾ cup dry bread crumbs
- 2 tablespoons minced fresh parsley

1. Preheat oven to 400°. Cook the macaroni according to the package directions. Meanwhile, use a large saucepan to melt 4 tablespoons butter. Stir in the flour until smooth. Gradually add milk. Bring to a boil; cook and stir for 2 minutes.
2. Reduce heat; add cheeses, mustard, salt and pepper. Stir until cheese is melted and sauce is smooth. Drain macaroni; add to cheese sauce and stir to coat.
3. Transfer to a greased shallow 3-qt. baking dish. Melt remaining butter; toss with bread crumbs and parsley. Sprinkle over macaroni. Bake it, uncovered, 15-20 minutes or until golden brown.

BEST-EVER BEANS & SAUSAGE

BEST-EVER BEANS & SAUSAGE

My wife devised this dish, which became extremely popular with our friends and family. It's our go-to whenever we need a dish to pass. We also bring copies of the recipe.
—**ROBERT SAULNIER** CLARKSBURG, MA

PREP: 15 MIN. • **BAKE:** 1 HOUR 20 MIN.
MAKES: 12-16 SERVINGS

- 1½ pounds bulk spicy pork sausage
- 1 medium green pepper, chopped
- 1 medium onion, chopped
- 1 can (31 ounces) pork and beans
- 1 can (16 ounces) kidney beans, rinsed and drained
- 1 can (15½ ounces) great northern beans, rinsed and drained
- 1 can (15½ ounces) black-eyed peas, rinsed and drained
- 1 can (15 ounces) pinto beans, rinsed and drained
- 1 can (15 ounces) chickpeas, rinsed and drained
- 1½ cups ketchup
- ¾ cup packed brown sugar
- 2 teaspoons ground mustard

1. In a large skillet, cook sausage over medium heat until no longer pink; drain. Add green pepper and onion; saute until tender. Drain. Add the remaining ingredients.
2. Pour into a greased 13x9-in. baking dish. Cover casserole and bake at 325° for 1 hour. Uncover; bake for 20-30 minutes longer or until bubbly.

★ ★ ★ ★ ★ **READER REVIEW**

"I have six picky kids and they all love this. It is a regular in my home. Best of all, it makes enough that I can reheat some for lunch the next day!"

TATEVECO TASTEOFHOME.COM

CURRIED CHICKEN & GRITS CASSEROLE

I moved to the South several years ago from Ohio. I've been creating recipes with grits recently and feel like I'm finally getting the Southern vibe! This recipe turns out beautifully every time. I love the mix of veggies, golden sauce and cheese-crusted grits on top.

—LF SHAMSZADEH POINT CLEAR, AL

PREP: 25 MIN. • **BAKE:** 50 MIN.
MAKES: 8 SERVINGS

- 1 **cup water**
- 1½ **cups chicken broth, divided**
- ¼ **teaspoon salt**
- ½ **cup quick-cooking grits**
- 2 **large eggs, beaten**
- 2 **cups shredded cheddar cheese, divided**
- 3 **tablespoons butter, cubed**
- 1 **can (10¾ ounces) condensed cream of chicken and mushroom soup, undiluted**
- 1½ **cups mayonnaise**
- 2 **teaspoons curry powder**
- 1 **package (16 ounces) frozen broccoli-cauliflower blend**
- 2 **cups cubed cooked chicken**
- 2 **cups refrigerated diced potatoes with onion**

1. Bring water, 1 cup broth and salt to a boil in a large saucepan. Slowly stir in the grits. Reduce the heat; cook and stir 5-6 minutes or until thickened. Remove from the heat; stir a small amount of grits into eggs. Return all to pan, stirring constantly. Add 1½ cups cheese and butter; stir until melted.
2. Preheat the oven to 350°. Combine the soup, mayonnaise, curry powder and remaining broth in a large bowl. Add the vegetable blend, chicken and potatoes; toss to coat. Transfer to a greased 13x9-in. baking dish. Top with grits; sprinkle with remaining cheese.
3. Bake, uncovered, 50-55 minutes or until heated through.

HAM & CHEESE POTATO CASSEROLE

FREEZE IT **⑤ INGREDIENTS**

HAM & CHEESE POTATO CASSEROLE

This hammed-up spin on cheesy hash browns makes two hearty casseroles you can use as a main or side dish. Serve one today and save the other for a busy weeknight.

—KARI ADAMS FORT COLLINS, CO

PREP: 15 MIN. • **BAKE:** 50 MIN. + STANDING
MAKES: 2 CASSEROLES (5 SERVINGS EACH)

- 2 **cans (10¾ ounces each) condensed cream of celery soup, undiluted**
- 2 **cups sour cream**
- ½ **cup water**
- ½ **teaspoon pepper**
- 2 **packages (28 ounces each) frozen O'Brien potatoes**
- 1 **package (16 ounces) process cheese (Velveeta), cubed**
- 2½ **cups cubed fully cooked ham**

1. Preheat the oven to 375°. In a large bowl, mix soup, sour cream, water and pepper until blended. Stir in potatoes, cheese and ham.
2. Transfer the blend to two greased 2-qt. baking dishes. Bake, covered, 40 minutes. Uncover; bake 10-15 minutes longer or until bubbly. Let stand 10 minutes before serving.
FREEZE OPTION *Cover and freeze unbaked casseroles. To use, partially thaw in the refrigerator overnight. Remove from refrigerator 30 minutes before baking. Preheat oven to 375°. Bake casseroles as directed, increasing time as necessary to heat through and for a thermometer inserted in center to read 165°.*

CHICKEN POTPIE CASSEROLE

CHICKEN POTPIE CASSEROLE

I always have leftover chicken broth on hand and use it for many things, including this comforting family favorite. You can bake your own biscuits, like I do, or buy them at the store. I often make extra biscuits to eat with butter and jam.

—**LILIANE JAHNKE** CYPRESS, TX

PREP: 40 MIN. • **BAKE:** 15 MIN.
MAKES: 8 SERVINGS

- ⅓ cup butter, cubed
- 1½ cups sliced fresh mushrooms
- 2 medium carrots, sliced
- ½ medium onion, chopped
- ¼ cup all-purpose flour
- 1 cup chicken broth
- 1 cup 2% milk
- 4 cups cubed cooked chicken
- 1 cup frozen peas
- 1 jar (2 ounces) diced pimientos, drained
- ½ teaspoon salt

BISCUIT TOPPING

- 2 cups all-purpose flour
- 4 teaspoons baking powder
- 2 teaspoons sugar
- ½ teaspoon salt
- ½ teaspoon cream of tartar
- ½ cup cold butter, cubed
- ⅔ cup 2% milk

1. Preheat oven to 400°. In a large saucepan, heat butter over medium heat. Add mushrooms, carrots and onion; cook and stir until tender.
2. Stir in the flour until blended; gradually stir in broth and milk. Bring to a boil, stirring constantly; cook and stir 2 minutes or until thickened. Stir in chicken, peas, pimientos and salt; heat through. Transfer to a greased 11x7-in. baking dish.
3. For topping, in a large bowl, whisk flour, baking powder, sugar, salt and cream of tartar. Cut in butter until mixture resembles coarse crumbs. Add milk; stir just until moistened.
4. Turn onto a lightly floured surface; knead gently 8-10 times. Pat or roll dough to ½-in. thickness; cut with a floured 2½-in. biscuit cutter. Place over the chicken mixture. Bake it, uncovered, 15-20 minutes or until biscuits are golden brown.

TUNA & PEA CASSEROLE

Turn to this recipe when you want a tuna casserole with a twist. In this case, the extra flavor comes from horseradish. This dish is an old favorite in our family, and it never fails to win folks over.

—**JACKIE SMULSKI** LYONS, IL

PREP: 20 MIN. • **BAKE:** 40 MIN.
MAKES: 6 SERVINGS

- 8 ounces uncooked egg noodles
- 2 cans (10¾ ounces each) condensed cream of mushroom soup, undiluted
- ½ cup mayonnaise
- ½ cup 2% milk
- 2 to 3 teaspoons prepared horseradish
- ½ teaspoon dill weed
- ⅛ teaspoon pepper
- 1 cup frozen peas, thawed
- 1 can (4 ounces) mushroom stems and pieces, drained
- 1 small onion, chopped
- 1 jar (2 ounces) diced pimientos, drained
- 2 cans (6 ounces each) tuna, drained and flaked
- ¼ cup dry bread crumbs
- 1 tablespoon butter, melted

1. Cook noodles according to package directions. Meanwhile, in a large bowl, combine the soup, mayonnaise, milk, horseradish, dill and pepper. Stir in peas, mushrooms, onion, pimientos and tuna.
2. Drain noodles; stir into the soup mixture. Transfer to a greased 2-qt. baking dish. Toss bread crumbs and butter; sprinkle over the top.
3. Bake, uncovered, at 375° for 40-45 minutes or until bubbly.

ITALIAN CASSEROLE

I come from a huge family, and it seems there is always an occasion for a potluck. I turn to this reliable recipe often.

—**RITA GOSHAW** SOUTH MILWAUKEE, WI

PREP: 40 MIN. • **BAKE:** 25 MIN.
MAKES: 16-20 SERVINGS

- 1½ **pounds bulk Italian sausage**
- 1½ **pounds ground beef**
- 1 **cup chopped onion**
- 1 **cup chopped green pepper**
- 2 **cans (15 ounces each) tomato sauce**
- 2 **cans (6 ounces each) tomato paste**
- ½ **cup water**
- 1 **teaspoon dried basil**
- 1 **teaspoon dried oregano**
- 1 **teaspoon salt**
- 1 **teaspoon pepper**
- ⅛ **teaspoon garlic powder**
- 2 **cans (8¾ ounces each) whole kernel corn, drained**
- 2 **cans (2¼ ounces each) sliced ripe olives, drained**
- 1 **package (16 ounces) wide noodles, cooked and drained**
- 8 **ounces cheddar cheese, cut into strips**

1. In a Dutch oven over medium heat, cook sausage, beef, onion and green pepper until meat is no longer pink; drain. Add the tomato sauce, tomato paste, water and seasonings; bring to a boil. Reduce heat; cover and simmer for 15 minutes. Add corn and olives. Cover and simmer for 5 minutes. Stir in noodles.
2. Pour into two greased 13x9-in. baking dishes. Top with cheese. Cover and bake at 350° for 25-30 minutes or until heated through.

BISCUIT PIZZA BAKE

You'll get all of the flavor of traditional pizza in this easy casserole. It's got everything you could want: ground beef, pepperoni, veggies and two kinds of cheese!

—**EMMA HAGEMAN** WAUCOMA, IA

PREP: 15 MIN. • **BAKE:** 30 MIN.
MAKES: 6-8 SERVINGS

- 1 **pound ground beef**
- 2 **tubes (12 ounces each) refrigerated buttermilk biscuits**
- 1 **package (3½ ounces) sliced pepperoni**
- 1 **can (4 ounces) mushroom stems and pieces, drained**
- 1 **can (15 ounces) pizza sauce**
- 1 **cup chopped green pepper**
- ½ **cup chopped onion**
- 1 **cup shredded cheddar cheese**
- 1 **cup shredded part-skim mozzarella cheese**

1. Preheat oven to 350°. In a large skillet, cook beef over medium heat 6-8 minutes or until no longer pink, breaking into crumbles. Meanwhile, cut biscuits into quarters; place in a greased 13x9-in. baking dish. Drain beef; sprinkle over biscuits.
2. Layer with pepperoni, mushrooms, pizza sauce, green pepper and onion. Bake, uncovered, 15 minutes. Sprinkle with cheeses. Bake 15-20 minutes longer or until cheese is melted. Let stand 5-10 minutes before serving.

BISCUIT PIZZA BAKE

BEST LASAGNA

BEST LASAGNA

For a casual meal, you can't go wrong with this rich and meaty lasagna. My grown kids and their spouses still request it for their birthday dinners.

—PAM THOMPSON GIRARD, IL

PREP: 1 HOUR • **BAKE:** 50 MIN. + STANDING
MAKES: 12 SERVINGS

- 9 lasagna noodles
- 1¼ pounds bulk Italian sausage
- ¾ pound ground beef
- 1 medium onion, diced
- 3 garlic cloves, minced
- 2 cans (one 28 ounces, one 15 ounces) crushed tomatoes
- 2 cans (6 ounces each) tomato paste
- ⅔ cup water
- 2 to 3 tablespoons sugar
- 3 tablespoons plus ¼ cup minced fresh parsley, divided
- 2 teaspoons dried basil
- ¾ teaspoon fennel seed
- ¾ teaspoon salt, divided
- ¼ teaspoon coarsely ground pepper
- 1 large egg, lightly beaten
- 1 carton (15 ounces) ricotta cheese
- 4 cups shredded part-skim mozzarella cheese
- ¾ cup grated Parmesan cheese

1. Cook noodles according to package directions; drain. Meanwhile, using a Dutch oven, cook the sausage, beef and onion over medium heat 8-10 minutes or until meat is no longer pink, breaking up meat into crumbles. Add garlic; cook 1 minute. Drain.
2. Stir in tomatoes, tomato paste, water, sugar, 3 tablespoons parsley, basil, fennel, ½ teaspoon salt and pepper; bring to a boil. Reduce heat; simmer, uncovered, for 30 minutes, stirring occasionally.
3. Using a small bowl, mix the egg, ricotta cheese and the remaining parsley and salt.
4. Preheat the oven to 375°. Spread 2 cups meat sauce into an ungreased 13x9-in. baking dish. Layer with three noodles and a third of the ricotta mixture. Sprinkle this with 1 cup of mozzarella cheese and 2 tablespoons Parmesan cheese. Repeat layers twice. Top with remaining meat sauce and cheeses (dish will be full).
5. Bake, covered, 25 minutes. Bake, uncovered, 25 minutes longer or until bubbly. Let lasagna stand 15 minutes before serving.

CHICKEN TAMALE BAKE

CHICKEN TAMALE BAKE

When I serve this Mexican-style casserole, everyone scrapes their plates clean. Offer fresh toppings like green onions, tomatoes and avocado.

—JENNIFER STOWELL MONTEZUMA, IA

PREP: 10 MIN. • **BAKE:** 25 MIN. + STANDING
MAKES: 8 SERVINGS

- 1 large egg, lightly beaten
- 1 can (14¾ ounces) cream-style corn
- 1 package (8½ ounces) corn bread/muffin mix
- 1 can (4 ounces) chopped green chilies
- ⅓ cup 2% milk
- ¼ cup shredded Mexican cheese blend

TOPPING
- 2 cups coarsely shredded cooked chicken
- 1 can (10 ounces) enchilada sauce
- 1 teaspoon ground cumin
- ½ teaspoon onion powder
- 1¾ cups shredded Mexican cheese blend
  Chopped green onions, tomatoes and avocado, optional

1. Preheat the oven to 400°. Using a large bowl, combine the first six ingredients; stir the mix just until dry ingredients are moistened. Transfer to a greased 13x9-in. baking dish. Bake 15-18 minutes or until light golden brown and a toothpick inserted in center comes out clean.
2. In a large skillet, combine chicken, enchilada sauce, cumin and onion powder; bring to a boil, stirring mix occasionally. Reduce heat; simmer, uncovered, 5 minutes. Spread over corn bread layer; sprinkle with cheese.
3. Bake 10-12 minutes longer or until cheese is melted. Let stand 10 minutes before serving. If desired, top with green onions, tomatoes and avocado.

SOUTHWEST VEGETARIAN BAKE

This veggie-packed casserole hits the spot on chilly nights, and it's great any time I have a taste for Mexican food with all the fixings.
—**TRISH GALE** MONTICELLO, IL

PREP: 40 MIN. • **BAKE:** 35 MIN. + STANDING
MAKES: 8 SERVINGS

- ¾ **cup uncooked brown rice**
- 1½ **cups water**
- 1 **can (15 ounces) black beans, rinsed and drained**
- 1 **can (11 ounces) Mexicorn, drained**
- 1 **can (10 ounces) diced tomatoes and green chilies**
- 1 **cup salsa**
- 1 **cup reduced-fat sour cream**
- 1 **cup shredded reduced-fat cheddar cheese**
- ¼ **teaspoon pepper**
- ½ **cup chopped red onion**
- 1 **can (2¼ ounces) sliced ripe olives, drained**
- 1 **cup shredded reduced-fat Mexican cheese blend**

1. In a large saucepan, bring rice and water to a boil. Reduce the heat; cover and simmer 35-40 minutes or until tender. Preheat the oven to 350°. In a large bowl, combine beans, Mexicorn, tomatoes, salsa, sour cream, cheddar cheese, pepper and rice. Transfer to a shallow 2½-qt. baking dish coated with cooking spray. Sprinkle with onion and olives.

2. Bake, uncovered, 30 minutes. Sprinkle with Mexican cheese. Bake 5-10 minutes or until heated through and cheese is melted. Let stand 10 minutes before serving.

SOUTHWEST VEGETARIAN BAKE

BEEF NOODLE CASSEROLE

I love that I can prepare this dish ahead of time. The flavors blend together to create a delicious combination.

—GRACE LEMA WINTON, CA

PREP: 20 MIN. • **BAKE:** 45 MIN.
MAKES: 8-10 SERVINGS

- 1 package (8 ounces) egg noodles
- 2 pounds ground beef
- 1 large onion, chopped
- 1 medium green pepper, chopped
- 1 can (14¾ ounces) cream-style corn
- 1 can (10¾ ounces) condensed tomato soup, undiluted
- 1 can (8 ounces) tomato sauce
- 1 jar (2 ounces) sliced pimientos, drained
- 2 tablespoons chopped jalapeno pepper
- 1½ teaspoons salt
- ½ teaspoon chili powder
- ¼ teaspoon ground mustard
- ¼ teaspoon pepper
- 1 jar (4½ ounces) sliced mushrooms, drained
- 1½ cups shredded cheddar cheese

1. Cook egg noodles according to the package directions.

2. Meanwhile, in a skillet, cook beef, onion and green pepper over medium heat until meat is no longer pink and vegetables are tender; drain. Add next 10 ingredients. Drain noodles; stir into the mixture.

3. Transfer to a greased 13x9-in. baking dish. Sprinkle with cheese. Bake, uncovered, at 350° for 45 minutes or until heated through.

FREEZE OPTION *Cool unbaked casserole; cover and freeze. To use, partially thaw in the refrigerator overnight. Remove 30 minutes before baking. Bake as directed. Increase bake time as needed to heat through and for a thermometer to read 165°.*

NOTE *Wear disposable gloves when cutting hot peppers; the oils can burn skin. Avoid touching your face.*

CREAMY HAM & CHEESE CASSEROLE

Leftover ham, convenient cooking creme and a garlic-herb seasoning make this pasta toss so simple and delicious.

—BETSY HOWARD KIRKWOOD, MO

PREP: 15 MIN. • **BAKE:** 20 MIN.
MAKES: 6 SERVINGS

- 8 ounces uncooked wide egg noodles
- 3 cups cubed fully cooked ham
- 1 can (10¾ ounces) condensed cream of chicken soup, undiluted
- 1 carton (10 ounces) Philadelphia original cooking creme
- 1 cup 2% milk
- ½ teaspoon garlic-herb seasoning blend
- ¼ teaspoon pepper
- 2 cups shredded Monterey Jack cheese

1. Cook noodles according to package directions. Meanwhile, combine the ham, soup, cooking creme, milk and seasonings in a large bowl.

2. Drain noodles and add to ham mixture; mix well. Transfer to a 13x9-in. baking dish coated with cooking spray; sprinkle with cheese.

3. Bake, uncovered, at 350° for 20-25 minutes or until heated through.

★ ★ ★ ★ ★ **READER REVIEW**

"Great recipe to use up leftover ham. I added broccoli, a small can of mushrooms and red pepper flakes for extra flavor. Will definitely make again!"

MJENSON09 TASTEOFHOME.COM

THREE-CHEESE MEATBALL MOSTACCIOLI

When my husband travels for work, I make a special dinner for my kids to keep their minds off missing Daddy. This tasty mostaccioli is meatball magic.
—JENNIFER GILBERT BRIGHTON, MI

PREP: 15 MIN. • **BAKE:** 35 MIN.
MAKES: 10 SERVINGS

- 1 package (16 ounces) mostaccioli
- 2 large eggs, lightly beaten
- 1 carton (15 ounces) part-skim ricotta cheese
- 1 pound ground beef
- 1 medium onion, chopped
- 1 tablespoon brown sugar
- 1 tablespoon Italian seasoning
- 1 teaspoon garlic powder
- ¼ teaspoon pepper
- 2 jars (24 ounces each) pasta sauce with meat
- ½ cup grated Romano cheese
- 1 package (12 ounces) frozen fully cooked Italian meatballs, thawed
- ¾ cup shaved Parmesan cheese
  Minced fresh parsley or fresh baby arugula, optional

1. Preheat the oven to 350°. Cook the mostaccioli according to package directions for al dente texture; drain. Meanwhile, in a small bowl, mix eggs and ricotta cheese.
2. In a 6-qt. stockpot, cook beef and onion 6-8 minutes or until beef is no longer pink, breaking up beef into crumbles; drain. Stir in brown sugar and seasonings. Add pasta sauce and mostaccioli; toss to combine.
3. Transfer half of the pasta mixture to a greased 13x9-in. baking dish. Layer with ricotta mixture and remaining pasta mixture; sprinkle with Romano cheese. Top with meatballs and Parmesan cheese.
4. Bake, uncovered, 35-40 minutes or until heated through. If desired, top with parsley.

THREE-CHEESE
MEATBALL
MOSTACCIOLI

WINTER DAY DINNER

I rely on this recipe to warm us up during the cold-weather months. When it comes to casseroles, my husband doesn't care for noodles. So I look for creative recipes that call for potatoes.
—LINDA HAGEDORN ROCKVILLE, MD

PREP: 25 MIN. • **BAKE:** 1½ HOURS
MAKES: 8 SERVINGS

- 1½ pounds ground beef
- 1 medium onion, chopped
- 2 tablespoons Worcestershire sauce
- 1 teaspoon salt
- ½ teaspoon pepper
- 8 medium potatoes, sliced
- 1 package (16 ounces) frozen peas, thawed

CHEESE SAUCE
- ¼ cup butter, cubed
- ⅓ cup all-purpose flour
- ½ teaspoon salt
- ¼ teaspoon pepper
- 2 cups milk
- 4 ounces process cheese (Velveeta), cubed

1. In a large skillet, cook the beef and onion over medium heat until meat is no longer pink; drain. Stir in the Worcestershire sauce, salt and pepper.
2. Place half of the potatoes in a greased 13x9-in. baking dish; layer with the meat mixture, peas and remaining potatoes. Set aside.
3. In a large saucepan, melt butter over medium heat. Stir in flour, salt and pepper until smooth. Gradually stir in the milk. Bring to boil; cook and stir for 2 minutes or until thickened. Stir in the cheese until melted. Pour over the potatoes.
4. Cover and bake at 350° for 1½ hours or until potatoes are tender.

CHICKEN CORDON BLEU BAKE

Many years ago, a friend gave me the recipe for this treasured dish. I freeze several in disposable pans so that I can share them with neighbors on a whim.

—REA NEWELL DECATUR, IL

PREP: 20 MIN. • **BAKE:** 40 MIN.
MAKES: 2 CASSEROLES (6 SERVINGS EACH)

- 2 **packages (6 ounces each) reduced-sodium stuffing mix**
- 1 **can (10¾ ounces) condensed cream of chicken soup, undiluted**
- 1 **cup 2% milk**
- 8 **cups cubed cooked chicken**
- ½ **teaspoon pepper**
- ¾ **pound sliced deli ham, cut into 1-inch strips**
- 1 **cup shredded Swiss cheese**
- 3 **cups shredded cheddar cheese**

1. Preheat oven to 350°. Prepare the stuffing mixes according to package directions. Meantime, whisk together the soup and milk.

2. Toss chicken with pepper; divide between two greased 13x9-in. baking dishes. Layer with ham, Swiss cheese, 1 cup cheddar cheese, soup mixture and stuffing. Sprinkle with remaining cheddar cheese.

3. Bake, covered, for 30 minutes. Uncover; bake until cheese is melted, 10-15 minutes.

FREEZE OPTION *Cover and freeze unbaked casseroles. To use, partially thaw in the refrigerator overnight. Remove from refrigerator 30 minutes before baking. Preheat oven to 350°. Bake, covered, until heated through and a thermometer inserted in the center reads 165°, about 45 minutes. Uncover; bake until cheese is melted, 10-15 minutes.*

CHICKEN CORDON
BLEU BAKE

RAVIOLI LASAGNA

2 cups shredded Monterey Jack cheese
2 jalapeno peppers, seeded and chopped

1. Cook the macaroni according to package directions. Meanwhile, in a large saucepan, cook beef and onion over medium heat, crumbling beef, until meat is no longer pink. Add garlic; cook 1 minute longer. Drain. Stir in next eight ingredients. Bring to a boil. Reduce the heat; simmer, uncovered, for 10 minutes. Drain macaroni; stir into beef mixture.
2. Preheat oven to 375°. Transfer macaroni mixture to two greased 2-qt. baking dishes. Top with cheese and jalapenos. Cover and bake at 375° for 30 minutes. Uncover; bake until bubbly and heated through, about 10 minutes longer. Serve one casserole. Cool the second; cover and freeze up to 3 months.

TO USE FROZEN CASSEROLE *Thaw in refrigerator 8 hours. Preheat oven to 375°. Remove from the refrigerator 30 minutes before baking. Cover and bake, increasing time as necessary to heat through and for a thermometer inserted in the center to read 165°, 20-25 minutes.*

NOTE *Wear disposable gloves when cutting hot peppers; the oils can burn skin. Avoid touching your face.*

★ ★ ★ ★ ★ **READER REVIEW**

"This was delicious! I loved how simple it was to make and the jalapenos really added that extra kick of flavor."

ANGEL182009 TASTEOFHOME.COM

---

⑤ INGREDIENTS

RAVIOLI LASAGNA

When people sample this, they think it's a from-scratch recipe. But the lasagna actually starts with frozen ravioli and requires just three other ingredients.

—PATRICIA SMITH ASHEBORO, NC

PREP: 25 MIN. • **BAKE:** 40 MIN.
MAKES: 6-8 SERVINGS

- 1 pound ground beef
- 1 jar (28 ounces) spaghetti sauce
- 1 package (25 ounces) frozen sausage or cheese ravioli
- 1½ cups shredded part-skim mozzarella cheese

1. In a large skillet, cook beef over medium heat until no longer pink; drain. In a greased 2½-qt. baking dish, layer a third of the spaghetti sauce, half of the ravioli and beef, and ½ cup cheese; repeat layers. Top with remaining sauce and cheese.
2. Cover and bake at 400° for 40-45 minutes or until heated through.

FREEZE IT

SOUTHWESTERN CASSEROLE

I've made this family-pleasing casserole for years. It's bold, budget-friendly and, best of all, you get a second casserole to freeze.

—JOAN HALLFORD NORTH RICHLAND HILLS, TX

PREP: 15 MIN. • **BAKE:** 40 MIN.
MAKES: 2 CASSEROLES (6 SERVINGS EACH)

- 2 cups (8 ounces) uncooked elbow macaroni
- 2 pounds ground beef
- 1 large onion, chopped
- 2 garlic cloves, minced
- 2 cans (14½ ounces each) diced tomatoes, undrained
- 1 can (16 ounces) kidney beans, rinsed and drained
- 1 can (6 ounces) tomato paste
- 1 can (4 ounces) chopped green chilies, drained
- 1½ teaspoons salt
- 1 teaspoon chili powder
- ½ teaspoon ground cumin
- ½ teaspoon pepper

HOW TO SEED A JALAPENO

Up to 80 percent of the capsaicin (the compound that gives peppers their heat) is in the seeds and membranes. To reduce the heat, cut the peppers in half, then use a spoon to scrape out the seeds and membranes. If you like very spicy foods, add a few of the seeds to the dish you're making instead of discarding them.

SOUTHWESTERN CASSEROLE

GRILLED CHEESE & TOMATO SOUP BAKE

My superstar of a casserole unites two classic comfort foods: grilled cheese sandwiches and tomato soup. There's no need for hands to get messy dipping into a bowl of hot soup. Best of all, my picky-eater husband devours every bite.

—MEGAN KUNS PERRYSBURG, OH

PREP: 25 MIN. • **BAKE:** 25 MIN. + STANDING
MAKES: 6 SERVINGS

- 3 ounces reduced-fat cream cheese
- 1½ teaspoons dried basil, divided
- 12 slices Italian, sourdough or rye bread (½ inch thick)
- 6 slices part-skim mozzarella cheese
- 6 tablespoons butter, softened
- ½ cup tomato paste
- 1 garlic clove, minced
- ¼ teaspoon salt
- ¼ teaspoon pepper
- 1¾ cups 2% milk
- 2 large eggs
- 1 cup shredded Italian cheese blend or part-skim mozzarella cheese

1. Preheat oven to 350°. In a bowl, mix the cream cheese and 1 teaspoon basil until blended; spread onto six bread slices. Top with mozzarella cheese and remaining bread. Spread outsides of sandwiches with butter. Arrange the sandwiches in a greased 13x9-in. baking dish.

2. Using a small saucepan, combine the tomato paste, garlic, salt, pepper and remaining basil; cook and stir over medium heat for 1 minute. Gradually whisk in milk, bringing it to a boil. Reduce the heat; simmer, uncovered, 4-5 minutes or until thickened, stirring it frequently. Remove from heat.

3. Whisk the eggs in a large bowl; gradually whisk in a third of the milk mixture. Stir in the remaining milk mixture; pour over the sandwiches. Sprinkle with Italian cheese blend.

4. Bake, uncovered, 25-30 minutes or until golden brown and the cheese is melted. Let casserole stand for 10 minutes before serving.

FAST FIX ▶

UNSTUFFED PEPPERS

If you like stuffed peppers, you will love a speedy version that's ready in just half an hour. Instead of cooking the instant rice, you can use 2 cups of leftover cooked rice if you have it on hand.

—BETH DEWYER DU BOIS, PA

START TO FINISH: 30 MIN.
MAKES: 6 SERVINGS

- 1 cup uncooked instant rice
- 1 pound ground beef
- 2 medium green peppers, cut into 1-inch pieces
- ½ cup chopped onion
- 1 jar (26 ounces) marinara sauce
- 1½ teaspoons salt-free seasoning blend
- ½ cup shredded Italian cheese blend
- ½ cup seasoned bread crumbs
- 1 tablespoon olive oil

1. Preheat oven to 350°. Cook rice according to package directions.

2. Meanwhile, in a large skillet, cook beef, green peppers and onion over medium-high heat until meat is no longer pink; drain. Stir in the rice, marinara sauce and seasoning blend. Stir in cheese.

3. Transfer to a greased 2-qt. baking dish. Toss the bread crumbs and oil; sprinkle over the top. Bake for 8-10 minutes or until heated through and topping is golden brown.

GRILLED CHEESE & TOMATO SOUP BAKE

STACKED ENCHILADA

Here's my easy stacked version of a classic Tex-Mex dish. Loaded with chicken, black beans and green pepper, this tortilla pie is both delicious and simple to prepare.
—REBECCA PEPSIN LONGMONT, CO

PREP: 20 MIN. • **BAKE:** 20 MIN.
MAKES: 4 SERVINGS

- ⅔ **cup chopped green pepper**
- 2 **teaspoons canola oil**
- 1 **garlic clove, minced**
- 1 **cup shredded cooked chicken**
- 1 **cup canned black beans, rinsed and drained**
- ⅓ **cup thinly sliced green onions**
- ½ **cup enchilada sauce**
- ½ **cup picante sauce**
- 4 **corn tortillas (6 inches)**
- 1 **cup shredded cheddar cheese**
  Sour cream and shredded lettuce, optional

1. In a large skillet, saute pepper in oil for 3 minutes. Add garlic and cook 2 minutes longer or until pepper is crisp-tender. Stir in the chicken, beans and onions; heat through. Transfer to a bowl and keep warm.
2. In the same skillet, combine enchilada and picante sauces. Coat both sides of one tortilla with sauce mixture; place in a greased 9-in. pie plate. Top with a third of the chicken mixture and ¼ cup cheese. Repeat layers twice. Top with remaining tortilla, sauce and cheese.
3. Cover and bake at 350° for 18-22 minutes or until heated through. Remove to a serving plate and cut into wedges. Serve with sour cream and lettuce if desired.

TURKEY SPAGHETTI CASSEROLE

TURKEY SPAGHETTI CASSEROLE

My mom made this creamy spaghetti when I was growing up. Whenever I have any leftover chicken or turkey, I look forward to preparing this simple, tasty dinner.
—CASANDRA HETRICK LINDSEY, OH

PREP: 30 MIN. • **BAKE:** 1¼ HOURS
MAKES: 6 SERVINGS

- 1 **medium onion, chopped**
- 1 **medium carrot, chopped**
- 1 **celery rib, chopped**
- ⅓ **cup sliced fresh mushrooms**
- 1 **tablespoon butter**
- 2½ **cups reduced-sodium chicken broth**
- 1 **can (10¾ ounces) reduced-fat reduced-sodium condensed cream of mushroom soup, undiluted**
- ¼ **teaspoon salt**
- ¼ **teaspoon pepper**
- 2½ **cups cubed cooked turkey breast**
- 6 **ounces uncooked spaghetti, broken into 2-inch pieces**
- ½ **cup shredded reduced-fat Colby-Monterey Jack cheese**
- ½ **teaspoon paprika**

1. Using a small skillet, saute the vegetables in butter until tender. In a large bowl, combine the broth, soup, salt and pepper.
2. Using a 2½-qt. baking dish coated with cooking spray, layer the turkey, spaghetti and vegetable mixture. Pour broth mixture over the top.
3. Cover casserole and bake at 350° for 70-80 minutes or until spaghetti is tender, stirring it once. Uncover; sprinkle with cheese and paprika. Bake for 5-10 minutes longer or until the cheese is melted.

CHICKEN & SWISS STUFFING BAKE

I love to cook but usually don't have much time to spend in the kitchen. This casserole is both delicious and fast, which makes it my favorite kind of recipe. I serve it with a salad.

—JENA COFFEY SUNSET HILLS, MO

PREP: 20 MIN. • **BAKE:** 25 MIN.
MAKES: 8 SERVINGS

- 1 can (10¾ ounces) condensed cream of mushroom soup, undiluted
- 1 cup whole milk
- 1 package (6 ounces) stuffing mix
- 2 cups cubed cooked chicken breast
- 2 cups fresh broccoli florets, cooked
- 2 celery ribs, finely chopped
- 1½ cups shredded Swiss cheese, divided

1. In a large bowl, combine soup and milk until blended. Add the stuffing mix with the contents of seasoning packet, chicken, broccoli, celery and 1 cup cheese. Transfer to a greased 13x9-in. baking dish.

2. Bake, uncovered, at 375° for 20 minutes or until heated through. Sprinkle with the remaining cheese; bake 5 minutes longer or until the cheese is melted.

FREEZE OPTION *Sprinkle remaining cheese over unbaked casserole. Cover and freeze. To use, partially thaw in refrigerator overnight. Remove from refrigerator 30 minutes before baking. Preheat oven to 375°. Bake casserole as directed, increasing the time as necessary to heat through and for a thermometer inserted in the center to read 165°.*

CHICKEN & SWISS
STUFFING BAKE

SWEET POTATO CHILI BAKE

I'm a vegetarian and wanted to develop dishes that are a little heartier than traditional vegetarian fare. This one's great!

—**JILLIAN TOURNOUX** MASSILLON, OH

PREP: 30 MIN. • **BAKE:** 20 MIN.
MAKES: 7 SERVINGS

- 2 **cups cubed peeled sweet potato**
- 1 **medium sweet red pepper, chopped**
- 1 **tablespoon olive oil**
- 1 **garlic clove, minced**
- 1 **can (28 ounces) diced tomatoes, undrained**
- 2 **cups vegetable broth**
- 1 **can (15 ounces) black beans, rinsed and drained**
- 4½ **teaspoons brown sugar**
- 3 **teaspoons chili powder**
- 1 **teaspoon salt**
- ½ **teaspoon pepper**
- 1 **package (6½ ounces) corn bread/ muffin mix**
- ½ **cup shredded cheddar cheese Optional toppings: sour cream, shredded cheddar cheese and chopped seeded jalapeno pepper**

1. In a Dutch oven, saute the sweet potato and red pepper in oil until crisp-tender. Add the garlic; cook 1 minute longer. Add tomatoes, broth, beans, brown sugar, chili powder, salt and pepper. Bring to a boil. Reduce heat; simmer, uncovered, 15-20 minutes or until potatoes are tender.
2. Meanwhile, preheat oven to 400°. Prepare corn bread batter according to package directions; stir in cheese. Drop by tablespoonfuls over chili.
3. Cover and bake 18-20 minutes or until a toothpick inserted in center comes out clean. Serve with toppings of your choice.
NOTE *Wear disposable gloves when cutting hot peppers; the oils can burn skin. Avoid touching your face.*

BAKED ORANGE ROUGHY & RICE

Believe us when we say that this delectable fish and rice dinner will leave you with just one dish in the sink to wash. Your brood will be lining up to dig in once they see (and smell) the results!

—*TASTE OF HOME* TEST KITCHEN

PREP: 10 MIN. • **BAKE:** 30 MIN.
MAKES: 4 SERVINGS

- 2 **cups uncooked instant rice**
- 1 **package (16 ounces) frozen broccoli-cauliflower blend, thawed**
- 4 **orange roughy fillets (6 ounces each)**
- 1 **can (14½ ounces) chicken broth**
- 1 **can (14½ ounces) fire-roasted diced tomatoes, undrained**
- 1 **teaspoon garlic powder**
- 1 **teaspoon lemon-pepper seasoning**
- ¼ **to ½ teaspoon cayenne pepper**
- ½ **cup shredded cheddar cheese**

1. Place the rice in a greased 13x9-in. baking dish. Layer with the vegetables and fish. Pour the broth and tomatoes over the top; sprinkle with seasonings.
2. Cover and bake at 375° for 25-30 minutes or until fish flakes easily with a fork and rice is tender. Sprinkle with cheese; bake 5 minutes longer or until cheese is melted.

★ ★ ★ ★ ★ 5 STAR TIP
Be careful not to overcook fish, as it loses its flavor and becomes tough. As a general rule, cook fish for 10 minutes for every inch of thickness. For fish fillets, check for doneness by inserting a fork at an angle into the thickest portion of the fish and gently parting the meat. When it is opaque and flakes into sections, it is cooked completely. Whole fish or steaks are done when the flesh is opaque and is easily removed from the bones. The juices in cooked fish are milky white.

CHICKEN NOODLE CASSEROLE

CHICKEN NOODLE CASSEROLE

Everyone who tastes my cheesy chicken casserole asks for the recipe. It's so simple to make that sometimes I feel like I'm cheating!
—**KAY PEDERSON** YELLVILLE, AR

PREP: 15 MIN. • **BAKE:** 40 MIN.
MAKES: 6 SERVINGS

- 1 **can (10¾ ounces) condensed cream of chicken soup, undiluted**
- ½ **cup mayonnaise**
- 2 **tablespoons lemon juice**
- 2 **cups cubed cooked chicken**
- 1 **small onion, chopped**
- ¼ **cup chopped green pepper**
- ¼ **cup chopped sweet red pepper**
- 1 **cup shredded Monterey Jack cheese, divided**
- 1 **cup shredded sharp cheddar cheese, divided**
- 12 **ounces egg noodles, cooked and drained**

1. In a large bowl, combine the soup, mayonnaise and lemon juice. Stir in the chicken, onion, peppers, ½ cup Monterey Jack cheese and ½ cup cheddar cheese. Add the noodles and toss to coat.

2. Transfer to a greased 2-qt. baking dish. Bake, uncovered, at 350° for 30-35 minutes. Sprinkle with the remaining cheeses. Bake 10 minutes longer or until cheese is melted.

FREEZE OPTION *Sprinkle remaining cheeses over unbaked casserole. Cover and freeze. To use, partially thaw in refrigerator overnight. Remove from refrigerator 30 minutes before baking. Preheat oven to 350°. Bake casserole as directed, increasing the time as necessary to heat through and for a thermometer inserted in the center to read 165°.*

OVEN STEW & BISCUITS

Here's a stick-to-the-ribs stew that's sure to warm up any cold day. The recipe came from my brother, who was a wonderful cook.
—**BERTHA BROOKMEIER** EL CAJON, CA

PREP: 20 MIN. • **BAKE:** 45 MIN.
MAKES: 6-8 SERVINGS

- ⅓ cup all-purpose flour
- 1 teaspoon salt
- ½ teaspoon pepper
- 2 pounds beef top sirloin, cut into 1-inch cubes
- ¼ cup canola oil
- 1 can (14½ ounces) stewed tomatoes
- 1 jar (4½ ounces) sliced mushrooms, drained
- 1 large onion, thinly sliced
- 3 tablespoons soy sauce
- 3 tablespoons molasses
- 1 medium green pepper, cut into 1-inch pieces
- 1 tube (12 ounces) refrigerated buttermilk biscuits
- 1 teaspoon butter, melted Sesame seeds

1. In a large resealable plastic bag, combine the flour, salt and pepper. Add beef in batches; shake to coat. In a large skillet, brown beef in batches in oil over medium heat. Return all to the pan; stir in tomatoes, mushrooms, onion, soy sauce and molasses.

2. Transfer to a greased 13x9-in. baking dish. Cover and bake at 375° for 20 minutes. Stir in the green pepper. Cover and bake another 10 minutes.

3. Uncover; top with biscuits. Brush the biscuits with butter and sprinkle with sesame seeds. Bake for 15-18 minutes more or until the biscuits are golden brown.

TURKEY CORDON BLEU CASSEROLE

FREEZE IT
TURKEY CORDON BLEU CASSEROLE

We love everything about traditional cordon bleu, and this turkey variation is a nice change of pace. It's easy to make, too.
—**KRISTINE BLAUERT** WABASHA, MN

PREP: 20 MIN. • **BAKE:** 25 MIN.
MAKES: 8 SERVINGS

- 2 cups uncooked elbow macaroni
- 2 cans (10¾ ounces each) condensed cream of chicken soup, undiluted
- ¾ cup 2% milk
- ¼ cup grated Parmesan cheese
- 1 teaspoon prepared mustard
- 1 teaspoon paprika
- ½ teaspoon dried rosemary, crushed
- ¼ teaspoon garlic powder
- ⅛ teaspoon rubbed sage
- 2 cups cubed cooked turkey
- 2 cups cubed fully cooked ham
- 2 cups shredded part-skim mozzarella cheese
- ¼ cup crushed Ritz crackers

1. Preheat the oven to 350°. Cook the macaroni according to package directions.

2. Meanwhile, whisk together soup, milk, Parmesan cheese, mustard and seasonings. Stir in turkey, ham and mozzarella cheese.

3. Drain the macaroni; add to the soup mixture and toss to combine. Transfer to a greased 13x9-in. baking dish or eight greased 8-oz. ramekins. Sprinkle with the crushed crackers. Bake, uncovered, until bubbly, about 25-30 minutes.

FREEZE OPTION *Cover and freeze unbaked dish or ramekins. To use, partially thaw in the refrigerator overnight. Remove from refrigerator 30 minutes before baking. Preheat the oven to 350°. Bake as directed, increasing the time as necessary to heat through and for a thermometer inserted in the center to read 165°.*

CHICKEN RANCH MAC & CHEESE

CHICKEN RANCH MAC & CHEESE

Prep once, feed the whole gang twice when you double this mac recipe and freeze half. I created it for the people I love most, using the ingredients they love best.

—**ANGELA SPENGLER** TAMPA, FL

PREP: 15 MIN. • **BAKE:** 30 MIN.
MAKES: 8 SERVINGS

- 3 **cups uncooked elbow macaroni**
- 3 **tablespoons butter**
- 2 **tablespoons all-purpose flour**
- ½ **teaspoon salt**
- ¼ **teaspoon pepper**
- 1 **cup 2% milk**
- 1½ **cups shredded cheddar cheese**
- ½ **cup grated Parmesan cheese**
- ½ **cup shredded Swiss cheese**
- ¾ **cup ranch salad dressing**
- 1 **cup coarsely chopped cooked chicken**

TOPPING
- ⅓ **cup seasoned bread crumbs**
- 2 **tablespoons butter, melted**
- 10 **bacon strips, cooked and crumbled**
- 1 **tablespoon minced fresh parsley**

1. Preheat oven to 350°. In a 6-qt. stockpot, cook macaroni according to package directions for al dente; drain and return to pot.
2. Meanwhile, in a medium saucepan, melt butter over medium heat. Stir in flour, salt and pepper until smooth; gradually whisk in milk. Bring to a boil, stirring constantly; cook and stir 1-2 minutes or until thickened. Stir in cheeses until blended. Stir in dressing.
3. Add the chicken and sauce to the cooked macaroni, tossing to combine. Transfer pasta to a greased 13x9-in. baking dish.
4. Toss bread crumbs with melted butter; sprinkle over macaroni. Top with bacon. Bake, uncovered, 30-35 minutes or until topping is golden brown. Sprinkle with parsley.
FREEZE OPTION *Prepare recipe as directed, increasing milk to 1⅓ cups. Cool unbaked casserole; cover and freeze. To use, partially thaw in the refrigerator overnight. Remove from refrigerator 30 minutes before baking. Preheat oven to 350°. Cover casserole with foil; bake 30 minutes. Uncover; continue baking as directed or until heated through and a thermometer inserted in the center reads 165°.*

(5)INGREDIENTS

MASHED POTATO HOT DISH

My cousin gave me this simple savory recipe. Whenever I'm making homemade mashed potatoes, I throw in a few extra spuds so I can make this dish for supper the next night.
—**TANYA ABERNATHY** YACOLT, WA

PREP: 15 MIN. • **BAKE:** 20 MIN.
MAKES: 4 SERVINGS

- 1 **pound ground beef**
- 1 **can (10¾ ounces) condensed cream of chicken soup, undiluted**
- 2 **cups frozen French-style green beans**
- 2 **cups hot mashed potatoes (prepared with milk and butter)**
- ½ **cup shredded cheddar cheese**

1. In a large skillet, cook beef over medium heat until no longer pink; drain. Stir in soup and beans.
2. Transfer mixture to a greased 2-qt. baking dish. Top with the mashed potatoes; sprinkle with cheese. Bake, uncovered, at 350° for 20-25 minutes or until bubbly and cheese is melted.

CHILI TORTILLA BAKE

A home-style Tex-Mex casserole is all it takes to gather my whole family around the dinner table. With its popular flavors and bubbly cheese topping, there's never a need to worry about leftovers.

—**CELINE WELDY** CAVE CREEK, AZ

PREP: 20 MIN. • **BAKE:** 25 MIN.
MAKES: 6 SERVINGS

- 1 **pound extra-lean ground beef (95% lean)**
- 2 **cans (8 ounces each) no-salt-added tomato sauce**
- 1 **can (15 ounces) black beans, rinsed and drained**
- 1 **cup frozen corn**
- 1 **can (4 ounces) chopped green chilies**
- 2 **tablespoons dried minced onion**
- 2 **tablespoons chili powder**
- 1 **teaspoon ground cumin**
- ½ **teaspoon garlic powder**
- ½ **teaspoon dried oregano**
- 6 **whole wheat tortillas (8 inches)**
- 1 **cup shredded reduced-fat cheddar cheese**

1. In a large skillet, cook beef over medium heat until no longer pink. Stir in the tomato sauce, beans, corn, green chilies, onion, chili powder, cumin, garlic powder and oregano; heat through.
2. In an 11x7-in. baking dish coated with cooking spray, layer half of the tortillas, beef mixture and cheese. Repeat the layers. Bake, uncovered, at 350° for about 25-30 minutes or until bubbly.
FREEZE OPTION *Cool unbaked casserole; cover and freeze. To use, partially thaw in the refrigerator overnight. Remove from refrigerator 30 minutes before baking. Preheat oven to 350°. Bake the casserole as directed, increasing time as necessary to heat through and for a thermometer inserted in center to read 165°.*

HAMBURGER CASSEROLE

This "oldie but goodie" is such a hit it's traveled all over the country! My mother originated the recipe in Pennsylvania, I brought it to Texas when I married, I'm still making it in California, and my daughter treats her friends to it in Colorado.

—**HELEN CARMICHALL** SANTEE, CA

PREP: 20 MIN. • **COOK:** 45 MIN.
MAKES: 10 SERVINGS

- 2 **pounds lean ground beef (90% lean)**
- 4 **pounds potatoes, peeled and sliced ¼ inch thick**
- 1 **large onion, sliced**
- 1 **teaspoon salt**
- ½ **teaspoon pepper**
- 1 **teaspoon beef bouillon granules**
- 1 **cup boiling water**
- 1 **can (28 ounces) diced tomatoes, undrained**
  Minced fresh parsley, optional

In a Dutch oven, layer half of the meat, potatoes and onion. Sprinkle with half of the salt and pepper. Repeat layers. Dissolve bouillon in water; pour over all. Top with tomatoes. Cover and cook over medium heat for 45-50 minutes or until potatoes are tender. Garnish with parsley if desired.

HAMBURGER CASSEROLE

**SPINACH
BEEF PIE**

HOW TO SEED A TOMATO

To easily seed a tomato, cut in it half horizontally and remove the stem. Holding one tomato half over a bowl, scrape out the pulp and seeds with a small spoon or squeeze the tomato to force them out. Do the same with the other half. Then slice or dice as your recipe directs.

SPINACH BEEF PIE

I stumbled upon this recipe many years ago, and it's still one I turn to today. If you like meat pies, it's a nice variation from traditional chicken or turkey.

—**MEG STANKIEWICZ** GARFIELD HEIGHTS, OH

PREP: 25 MIN. • **BAKE:** 30 MIN.
MAKES: 6-8 SERVINGS

- 1   **cup all-purpose flour**
- ⅓   **cup old-fashioned oats**
- 7   **tablespoons cold butter**
- 2   **to 3 tablespoons cold water**
- 1   **pound ground beef**
- 1   **medium onion, chopped**
- 1   **medium green pepper, chopped**
- 1   **garlic clove, minced**
- ¼   **cup ketchup**
- 1   **teaspoon salt**
- 1   **teaspoon dried oregano**
- ½   **teaspoon dried basil**
- ½   **teaspoon dried marjoram**
- ¼   **teaspoon pepper**
- 1   **package (10 ounces) frozen chopped spinach, thawed and squeezed dry**
- 3   **large eggs, lightly beaten**
- 2   **cups shredded cheddar cheese, divided**
- 1   **large tomato, seeded and diced**

1. In a large bowl, combine flour and oats; cut in the butter until crumbly. Gradually add water, tossing with a fork until dough forms a ball. Roll out dough to fit a 9-in. pie plate. Transfer to plate; trim and flute edges.
2. In a large skillet, cook the beef, onion, green pepper and garlic over medium heat until meat is no longer pink; drain. Stir in the ketchup and seasonings. Fold in the spinach; cool slightly. Stir in the eggs and 1 cup cheese until combined; spoon into the crust.
3. Bake at 400° for 25-30 minutes or until the center is set. Sprinkle tomato and remaining cheese around edge of pie. Bake 5-10 minutes longer or until cheese is melted. Let stand for 5-10 minutes before cutting.

TACO SALAD CASSEROLE

TACO SALAD CASSEROLE

My family always devours this casserole, which tastes like a taco salad. I like that it's a breeze to prepare.

—**RHONDA MCKEE** GREENSBURG, KS

PREP: 25 MIN. • **BAKE:** 15 MIN.
MAKES: 4 SERVINGS

- 1   **pound ground beef**
- ¼   **cup chopped onion**
- ¼   **cup chopped green pepper**
- 1   **envelope taco seasoning**
- ½   **cup water**
- 1   **cup crushed tortilla chips**
- 1   **can (16 ounces) refried beans**
- 1   **cup shredded cheddar cheese**
     Toppings: chopped lettuce and tomatoes, sliced ripe olives, sour cream and picante sauce

1. In a large skillet, cook beef, onion and green pepper over medium heat until meat is no longer pink; drain. Stir in taco seasoning and water. Cook and stir meat mixture until thickened, about 3 minutes; set aside.
2. Place chips in a greased 8-in. square baking dish. In a small bowl, stir refried beans; spread over chips. Top with beef mixture and cheese.
3. Bake, uncovered, at 375° for 15-20 minutes or until heated through. Top with chopped lettuce, tomatoes and olives. Serve with sour cream and picante sauce.

SAUSAGE HASH BROWN BAKE

Pork sausage sandwiched between layers of crispy hash browns and flavored with cream of chicken soup and French onion dip makes for an all-in-one casserole you soon won't forget. Try it for breakfast or dinner.

—ESTHER WRINKLES VANZANT, MO

PREP: 15 MIN. • **BAKE:** 55 MIN.
MAKES: 10-12 SERVINGS

- 2 **pounds bulk pork sausage**
- 2 **cups shredded cheddar cheese, divided**
- 1 **can (10¾ ounces) condensed cream of chicken soup, undiluted**
- 1 **cup sour cream**
- 1 **carton (8 ounces) French onion dip**
- 1 **cup chopped onion**
- ¼ **cup chopped green pepper**
- ¼ **cup chopped sweet red pepper**
- ⅛ **teaspoon pepper**
- 1 **package (30 ounces) frozen shredded hash brown potatoes, thawed**

1. In a large skillet, cook sausage over medium heat until no longer pink; drain on paper towels. In a large bowl, combine 1¾ cups cheese and the next seven ingredients; fold in potatoes.
2. Spread half into a greased shallow 3-qt. baking dish. Top with sausage and the remaining potato mixture. Sprinkle with the remaining cheese. Cover and bake it at 350° for 45 minutes. Uncover; bake 10 minutes longer or until heated through.

SAUSAGE HASH BROWN BAKE

FIVE-CHEESE JUMBO SHELLS

Using five cheeses in one dish does not typically translate to something light, but this meatless meal is proof that it can be done with great success (and flavor!). The shells freeze beautifully, so the leftovers are a cinch to save for another quick dinner.
—**LISA RENSHAW** KANSAS CITY, MO

PREP: 45 MIN. • **BAKE:** 50 MIN. + STANDING
MAKES: 8 SERVINGS

- 24 **uncooked jumbo pasta shells**
- 1 **tablespoon olive oil**
- 1 **medium zucchini, shredded and squeezed dry**
- ½ **pound baby portobello mushrooms, chopped**
- 1 **medium onion, finely chopped**
- 2 **cups reduced-fat ricotta cheese**
- ½ **cup shredded part-skim mozzarella cheese**
- ½ **cup shredded provolone cheese**
- ½ **cup grated Romano cheese**
- 1 **large egg, lightly beaten**
- 1 **teaspoon Italian seasoning**
- ½ **teaspoon crushed red pepper flakes**
- 1 **jar (24 ounces) meatless spaghetti sauce**
- ¼ **cup grated Parmesan cheese**

1. Preheat oven to 350°. Cook shells according to package directions for al dente; drain and rinse in cold water.
2. In a large skillet, heat oil over medium-high heat. Add vegetables; cook and stir until tender. Remove from heat. In a bowl, combine ricotta, mozzarella, provolone and Romano cheeses; stir in the egg, seasonings and vegetables.
3. Spread 1 cup sauce into a 13x9-in. baking dish coated with cooking spray. Fill pasta shells with cheese mixture; place them in the baking dish. Top with remaining sauce. Sprinkle with Parmesan cheese.

4. Bake, covered, 40 minutes. Bake, uncovered, 10 minutes longer or until cheese is melted. Let stand 10 minutes before serving.
FREEZE OPTION *Cool the unbaked casserole; cover and freeze. To use, partially thaw it in the refrigerator overnight. Remove from refrigerator 30 minutes before baking. Preheat the oven to 350°. Cover casserole with foil; bake 50 minutes. Uncover; bake 15-20 minutes longer or until heated through and a thermometer inserted in center reads 165°.*

EASY TACO CASSEROLE

Your family is sure to enjoy this mildly spicy one-dish meal with Southwestern flair. It's quick and easy to make and fun to serve.
—**FLO BURTNETT** GAGE, OK

PREP: 15 MIN. • **BAKE:** 20 MIN.
MAKES: 6 SERVINGS

- 1 **pound ground beef**
- 1 **cup salsa**
- ½ **cup mayonnaise**
- 2 **teaspoons chili powder**
- 2 **cups crushed tortilla chips**
- 1 **cup shredded Colby cheese**
- 1 **cup shredded Monterey Jack cheese**
- 1 **medium tomato, chopped**
- 2 **cups shredded lettuce**

1. In a large saucepan, cook beef over medium heat until no longer pink; drain. Add the salsa, mayonnaise and chili powder.
2. In an ungreased 2-qt. baking dish, layer half of the meat mixture, chips and cheeses. Repeat layers. Bake, uncovered, at 350° for 20-25 minutes or until heated through. Just before serving, top with tomato and lettuce.

MOZZARELLA BAKED SPAGHETTI

4. Bake, uncovered, for 20 minutes. Sprinkle with the cheese. Bake for 10 minutes longer or until the cheese is melted. Let casserole stand for 10 minutes before cutting.

FREEZE OPTION *Cool spaghetti completely before tossing with egg mixture. Transfer to baking dish; cover and refrigerate. Meanwhile, prepare the meat sauce and cool completely before spooning over the spaghetti mixture. Cover and freeze unbaked casserole. To use, partially thaw in the refrigerator overnight. Remove from refrigerator 30 minutes before baking. Preheat oven to 350°. Bake as directed, increasing time as necessary to heat through and for a thermometer inserted in center of casserole to read 165°.*

SAUERKRAUT CASSEROLE

Mom fermented her own sauerkraut using cabbage we grew in our big farm garden. Blending the kraut with spicy sausage and apples was her favorite way to fix it. I still love this homestyle country dish.

—**ROSEMARY PRYOR** PASADENA, MD

PREP: 20 MIN. • **BAKE:** 1 HOUR
MAKES: 8 SERVINGS

- 1 **pound mild Italian sausage links, cut into 1-inch slices**
- 1 **large onion, chopped**
- 2 **medium apples, peeled and quartered**
- 1 **can (27 ounces) sauerkraut, rinsed and well drained**
- 1 **cup water**
- ½ **cup packed brown sugar**
- 2 **teaspoons caraway seeds**

1. In a large skillet, cook the sausage and onion over medium heat until sausage is no longer pink and onion is tender; drain. Stir in the apples, sauerkraut, water, brown sugar and caraway seeds.
2. Transfer to a 2½-qt. baking dish. Cover and bake at 350° for 1 hour.

FREEZE IT

MOZZARELLA BAKED SPAGHETTI

This cheesy pasta bake is a standby for family gatherings and potlucks. Add a tossed green salad and garlic breadsticks to round out a memorable meal.

—**BETTY RABE** MAHTOMEDI, MN

PREP: 20 MIN. • **BAKE:** 30 MIN. + STANDING
MAKES: 8 SERVINGS

- 8 **ounces uncooked spaghetti, broken into thirds**
- 1 **large egg**
- ½ **cup whole milk**
- ½ **teaspoon salt**
- ½ **pound ground beef**
- ½ **pound bulk Italian sausage**
- 1 **small onion, chopped**
- ¼ **cup chopped green pepper**

- 1 **jar (14 ounces) meatless spaghetti sauce**
- 1 **can (8 ounces) tomato sauce**
- 1 **to 2 cups shredded part-skim mozzarella cheese**

1. Preheat the oven to 350°. Cook the spaghetti according to the package directions.
2. Meanwhile, in a large bowl, beat the egg, milk and salt. Drain spaghetti; add to egg mixture and toss to coat. Transfer pasta to a greased 13x9-in. baking dish.
3. In a large skillet, cook the beef, sausage, onion and green pepper over medium heat until the meat is no longer pink; drain. Stir in spaghetti sauce and tomato sauce. Spoon over the spaghetti mixture.

CHICKEN AMANDINE

With colorful green beans and pimientos, this attractive casserole is terrific for the holidays or family dinners. This is true comfort food at its finest.

—**KAT WOOLBRIGHT** WICHITA FALLS, TX

PREP: 35 MIN. • **BAKE:** 30 MIN.
MAKES: 8 SERVINGS

- ¼ cup chopped onion
- 1 tablespoon butter
- 1 package (6 ounces) long grain and wild rice
- 2¼ cups chicken broth
- 3 cups cubed cooked chicken
- 2 cups frozen french-style green beans, thawed
- 1 can (10¾ ounces) condensed cream of chicken soup, undiluted
- ¾ cup sliced almonds, divided
- 1 jar (4 ounces) diced pimientos, drained
- 1 teaspoon pepper
- ½ teaspoon garlic powder
- 1 bacon strip, cooked and crumbled

1. In a large saucepan, saute onion in butter until tender. Add rice with contents of seasoning packet and broth. Bring to a boil. Reduce heat; cover and simmer for 25 minutes or until liquid is absorbed. Uncover; set aside to cool.

2. Using a large bowl, combine the chicken, green beans, soup, ½ cup of almonds, pimientos, pepper and garlic powder. Stir in rice.

3. Transfer to greased 2½-qt. baking dish. Sprinkle with the bacon and remaining almonds. Cover and bake at 350° for 30-35 minutes or until heated through.

CHICKEN AMANDINE

SLOW COOKER DINNERS

What's on the menu tonight? Maximum deliciousness with minimal effort! Choose any of one of these main entrees, soups, stews or sandwiches to feed your gang— all with the ease of flipping a switch in the morning and coming home to a ready-made meal at night.

SLOW COOKER PIZZA CASSEROLE

A comforting casserole with mass appeal is just what you need when cooking for a crowd. For added convenience, it stays warm in a slow cooker.

—VIRGINIA KRITES CRIDERSVILLE, OH

PREP: 20 MIN. • **COOK:** 2 HOURS
MAKES: 12-14 SERVINGS

- 1 package (16 ounces) rigatoni or large tube pasta
- 1½ pounds ground beef
- 1 small onion, chopped
- 4 cups shredded part-skim mozzarella cheese
- 2 cans (15 ounces each) pizza sauce
- 1 can (10¾ ounces) condensed cream of mushroom soup, undiluted
- 1 package (8 ounces) sliced pepperoni
  Chopped arugula, optional

1. Cook the pasta according to the package directions. Meanwhile, in a skillet, cook the beef and onion over medium heat until the meat is no longer pink; drain.
2. Drain the pasta and place it in a 5-qt. slow cooker. Stir in the beef mixture, cheese, pizza sauce, soup and pepperoni. Cover and cook it on low for 2-3 hours or until heated through. If desired, sprinkle arugula on individual servings.

★ ★ ★ ★ ★ **READER REVIEW**

"I can always tell when a meal is good because the leftovers are gone before noon the next day. This casserole was one such meal."

ALYSSAJEANE TASTEOFHOME.COM

CAROLINA SHRIMP & CHEDDAR GRITS

CARKOLINA SHRIMP & CHEDDAR GRITS

Shrimp and grits are a house favorite...now if only we could agree on a recipe! To find a winner, I stirred things up with cheddar and Cajun seasoning.
—**CHARLOTTE PRICE** RALEIGH, NC

PREP: 15 MIN. • **COOK:** 2¾ HOURS
MAKES: 6 SERVINGS

- 1 **cup uncooked stone-ground grits**
- 1 **large garlic clove, minced**
- ½ **teaspoon salt**
- ¼ **teaspoon pepper**
- 4 **cups water**
- 2 **cups shredded cheddar cheese**
- ¼ **cup butter, cubed**
- 1 **pound peeled and deveined cooked shrimp (31-40 per pound)**
- 2 **medium tomatoes, seeded and finely chopped**
- 4 **green onions, finely chopped**
- 2 **tablespoons chopped fresh parsley**
- 4 **teaspoons lemon juice**
- 2 **to 3 teaspoons Cajun seasoning**

1. Place the first five ingredients in a 3-qt. slow cooker; stir to combine. Cook, covered, on high 2½ to 3 hours or until the water is absorbed and grits are tender, stirring every 45 minutes.
2. Stir in the cheese and butter until they are melted. Stir in the remaining ingredients; cook, covered, on high for about 15-30 minutes or until heated through.

BEEF & BEAN TORTA

This zesty dish is a favorite of mine because it has a wonderful Southwestern taste and is so easy to prepare. I serve it on the nights when we have only a few minutes to eat before running off to meetings or sports events.
—**JOAN HALLFORD** NORTH RICHLAND HILLS, TX

PREP: 30 MIN. • **COOK:** 4 HOURS
MAKES: 4 SERVINGS

- 1 **pound ground beef**
- 1 **small onion, chopped**
- 1 **can (15 ounces) pinto or black beans, rinsed and drained**
- 1 **can (10 ounces) diced tomatoes and green chilies, undrained**
- 1 **can (2¼ ounces) sliced ripe olives, drained**
- 1½ **teaspoons chili powder**
- ½ **teaspoon salt**
- ⅛ **teaspoon pepper**
- 3 **drops hot pepper sauce**
- 4 **flour tortillas (8 inches)**
- 1 **cup shredded cheddar cheese**
  Minced fresh cilantro
  Salsa, sour cream, shredded lettuce and chopped tomatoes, optional

1. Cut four 20x3-in. strips of heavy-duty foil; crisscross so they resemble spokes of a wheel. Place the strips on the bottom and up the sides of a 5-qt. slow cooker. Coat the strips with cooking spray.
2. In a large skillet, cook beef and onion over medium heat until the meat is no longer pink; drain. Stir in beans, tomatoes, olives, chili powder, salt, pepper and hot pepper sauce. Spoon about 1⅔ cups of the beef mixture into prepared slow cooker; top with one tortilla and ¼ cup cheese. Repeat layers three times.
3. Cover and cook on low for 4-5 hours or until heated through. Using the foil strips as handles, remove the tortilla stack to a platter. Sprinkle with cilantro. Serve with salsa, sour cream, lettuce and tomatoes if desired.

BEEF & BEAN
TORTA

CHIPOTLE SHREDDED BEEF

My slow cooker beef is delish when rolled up in a tortilla, burrito style. We also like it over mashed potatoes or in buns. Leftovers make awesome quesadillas.
—**DARCY WILLIAMS** OMAHA, NE

PREP: 25 MIN. • **COOK:** 8 HOURS
MAKES: 10 SERVINGS

- 1 teaspoon canola oil
- 1 small onion, chopped
- 1 can (28 ounces) diced tomatoes, undrained
- ¼ cup cider vinegar
- ¼ cup chopped chipotle peppers in adobo sauce plus 2 teaspoons sauce
- 6 garlic cloves, minced
- 2 tablespoons brown sugar
- 2 bay leaves
- ½ teaspoon ground cumin
- ½ teaspoon paprika
- ½ teaspoon pepper
- ¼ teaspoon ground cinnamon
- 1 boneless beef chuck roast (2½ pounds)
- 5 cups cooked brown rice
  Shredded reduced-fat cheddar cheese and reduced-fat sour cream, optional

1. Using a large skillet coated with cooking spray, heat oil over medium-high heat. Add onion; cook and stir 2-3 minutes or until tender. Stir in the tomatoes, vinegar, peppers with sauce, garlic, brown sugar, bay leaves and spices. Bring to a boil. Reduce the heat; simmer, uncovered, 4-6 minutes or until thickened.
2. Place roast in a 5-qt. slow cooker; add the tomato mixture. Cook it, covered, on low for 8-10 hours or until meat is tender.

3. Discard the bay leaves. Remove the roast; cool slightly. Skim fat from the cooking juices. Shred the beef with two forks. Return the beef and cooking juices to slow cooker; heat through. Serve with rice. If desired, top with cheese and sour cream.
FREEZE OPTION *Freeze the cooled meat mixture and juices in freezer containers. To use, partially thaw in refrigerator overnight. Heat through in a saucepan, stirring occasionally and adding a little water if necessary.*

ITALIAN SAUSAGES WITH PROVOLONE

These sausages with their pepper and onion topping go quickly, so I recommend making a second batch for backup.
—**SHELLY BEVINGTON** HERMISTON, OR

PREP: 15 MIN. • **COOK:** 4 HOURS
MAKES: 10 SERVINGS

- 10 Italian sausage links (4 ounces each)
- 1 tablespoon canola oil
- 1 each small sweet red, yellow and orange peppers, cut into strips
- 2 medium onions, halved and sliced
- 2 cups Italian salad dressing
- 10 slices provolone cheese
- 10 brat buns, split

1. In a large skillet, brown sausages in batches in oil. Drain. Transfer to a 5-qt. slow cooker. Add the peppers, onions and salad dressing. Cover and cook on low for 4-5 hours or until a thermometer reads 160° and the vegetables are tender.
2. Place the sausages and cheese in buns; using a slotted spoon, top with the pepper mixture.

CHIPOTLE SHREDDED BEEF

GREEN CHILI SHREDDED PORK

Slow cooker pork with green chilies always makes my hungry clan happy. And getting creative with the leftovers is always part of the fun.

—MARY SHIVERS ADA, OK

PREP: 10 MIN. • **COOK:** 6 HOURS
MAKES: 8 SERVINGS

- 1 boneless pork loin roast (3 to 4 pounds)
- 1½ cups apple cider or juice
- 1 can (4 ounces) chopped green chilies, drained
- 3 garlic cloves, minced
- 1½ teaspoons salt
- 1½ teaspoons hot pepper sauce
- 1 teaspoon chili powder
- 1 teaspoon pepper
- ½ teaspoon ground cumin
- ½ teaspoon dried oregano
- 16 flour tortillas (8 inches)
  Optional toppings: chopped peeled mango, shredded lettuce, chopped fresh cilantro and lime wedges

1. Place the pork in a 5- or 6-qt. slow cooker. Using a small bowl, mix the cider, green chilies, garlic, salt, pepper sauce, chili powder, pepper, cumin and oregano; pour mix over the pork. Cook, covered, on low 6-8 hours or until the meat is tender.
2. Remove the roast; cool it slightly. Shred pork with two forks. Return the meat to the slow cooker; heat through. Using tongs, serve the pork in tortillas with toppings as desired.

FREEZE OPTION *Place the shredded pork in freezer containers; top with cooking juices. Cool and freeze. To use, partially thaw in refrigerator overnight. Heat it through in a saucepan, stirring occasionally.*

CHICKEN & MUSHROOM ALFREDO

CHICKEN & MUSHROOM ALFREDO

Everyone in my family loves it when I make this dinner, even my kids! You can add any vegetables you like to make it even heartier, such as corn, peas, or diced red bell pepper.

—MONICA WERNER ONTARIO, CA

PREP: 20 MIN. • **COOK:** 4 HOURS
MAKES: 4 SERVINGS

- 4 bone-in chicken breast halves (12 to 14 ounces each), skin removed
- 2 tablespoons canola oil
- 1 can (10¾ ounces) condensed cream of chicken soup, undiluted
- 1 can (10¾ ounces) condensed cream of mushroom soup, undiluted
- 1 cup chicken broth
- 1 small onion, chopped
- 1 jar (6 ounces) sliced mushrooms, drained
- ¼ teaspoon garlic salt
- ¼ teaspoon pepper
- 8 ounces fettuccine
- 1 package (8 ounces) cream cheese, softened and cubed
  Shredded Parmesan cheese, optional

1. In a large skillet, brown chicken in oil in batches. Transfer to a 4- or 5-qt. slow cooker. In a large bowl, combine the soups, broth, onion, mushrooms, garlic salt and pepper; pour over the meat. Cover and cook on low for 4-5 hours or until the chicken is tender.
2. Cook the fettuccine according to package directions; drain. Remove the chicken from slow cooker and keep warm. Turn slow cooker off and stir in cream cheese until melted. Serve the chicken and sauce with the fettuccine. Top with Parmesan cheese if desired.

BROCCOLI-CAULIFLOWER CHICKEN CASSEROLE

A chicken, broccoli and rice casserole is great comfort food. I make my easy variation in the slow cooker, then serve it with rice cooked separately. You can easily swap in whatever cheese you prefer. The dish is also delicious sprinkled with a simple bread crumb topping.

—COURTNEY STULTZ WEIR, KS

PREP: 20 MIN. • **COOK:** 4 HOURS
MAKES: 8 SERVINGS

- 2 **pounds boneless skinless chicken breasts, cut into 1-inch pieces**
- 1 **small head cauliflower, chopped (about 4 cups)**
- 1 **bunch broccoli, chopped (about 4 cups)**
- ½ **pound medium fresh mushrooms, chopped**
- 1 **large onion, chopped**
- 2 **medium carrots, finely chopped**
- 1 **cup reduced-sodium chicken broth**
- 4 **ounces cream cheese, softened**
- 2 **tablespoons olive oil**
- 2 **teaspoons dried sage leaves**
- 1 **teaspoon salt**
- ½ **teaspoon pepper**
- 1 **cup shredded cheddar cheese**
  Hot cooked brown rice

In a 6-qt. slow cooker, combine the first six ingredients. In a small bowl, whisk broth, cream cheese, oil, sage, salt and pepper; pour over the chicken mixture. Sprinkle with cheese. Cook, covered, on low 4-5 hours or until the chicken and vegetables are tender. Serve with rice.

BROCCOLI-CAULIFLOWER CHICKEN CASSEROLE

SLOW-COOKED PORK ROAST

Here's a tasty meal that's wonderful for summer, as the oven never needs heating. It's so flavorful, it's sure to become a favorite.
—**MARION LOWERY** MEDFORD, OR

PREP: 20 MIN. • **COOK:** 6 HOURS + STANDING
MAKES: 12 SERVINGS

- 2 cans (8 ounces each) unsweetened crushed pineapple, undrained
- 1 cup barbecue sauce
- 2 tablespoons unsweetened apple juice
- 1 tablespoon minced fresh rosemary or 1 teaspoon dried rosemary, crushed
- 1 teaspoon minced garlic
- 2 teaspoons grated lemon peel
- 1 teaspoon liquid smoke, optional
- ½ teaspoon salt
- ¼ teaspoon pepper
- 1 boneless pork loin roast (3 to 4 pounds)

1. In a large saucepan, combine the first nine ingredients. Bring to a boil. Reduce heat; simmer, uncovered, for 3 minutes.
2. Meanwhile, cut roast in half. In a nonstick skillet coated with cooking spray, brown pork roast on all sides.
3. Place roast in a 5-qt. slow cooker. Pour sauce over roast and turn to coat. Cover and cook on low for 6-7 hours or until meat is tender. Let stand for 10 minutes before slicing.

SPICED LAMB STEW WITH APRICOTS

My family loves lamb, especially my son. During his first year of college, he claimed to be a vegetarian. When he came home, I had a pot of my lamb stew simmering in the kitchen. When my husband and I wanted to eat dinner, there were only a few shreds of meat left floating in the gravy—and my son confessed that he was the culprit!
—**ARLENE ERLBACH** MORTON GROVE, IL

PREP: 30 MIN. • **COOK:** 5 HOURS
MAKES: 5 SERVINGS

- 2 pounds lamb stew meat, cut into ¾-inch cubes
- 3 tablespoons butter
- 1½ cups chopped sweet onion
- ¾ cup dried apricots
- ½ cup orange juice
- ½ cup chicken broth
- 2 teaspoons paprika
- 2 teaspoons ground allspice
- 2 teaspoons ground cinnamon
- 1½ teaspoons salt
- 1 teaspoon ground cardamom
  Hot cooked couscous
  Chopped dried apricots, optional

1. In a large skillet, brown the lamb in butter in batches. With a slotted spoon, transfer to a 3-qt. slow cooker. In the same skillet, saute the onion in the drippings until tender. Stir in the apricots, orange juice, broth and seasonings; pour over lamb.
2. Cover and cook on high for 5-6 hours or until meat is tender. Serve with couscous. Sprinkle with chopped apricots if desired.

HOW TO TRIM KALE

If your kale is thin and tender, just snip off the bottom of the stems with kitchen shears. If the stems are thicker, you'll need to remove them from the leaves completely. Place each leaf on a cutting board, fold the leaf in in half lengthwise, and use a knife to carefully slice away the stem.

ITALIAN
SAUSAGE &
KALE SOUP

SLOW COOKER

ITALIAN SAUSAGE & KALE SOUP

The first time I made this colorful soup, our home smelled wonderful. We knew it was a keeper to see us through cold winter days.
—**SARAH STOMBAUGH** CHICAGO, IL

PREP: 20 MIN. • **COOK:** 8 HOURS
MAKES: 8 SERVINGS (3½ QUARTS)

- 1 **pound bulk hot Italian sausage**
- 6 **cups chopped fresh kale**
- 2 **cans (15½ ounces each) great northern beans, rinsed and drained**
- 1 **can (28 ounces) crushed tomatoes**
- 4 **large carrots, finely chopped (about 3 cups)**
- 1 **medium onion, chopped**
- 3 **garlic cloves, minced**
- 1 **teaspoon dried oregano**
- ¼ **teaspoon salt**
- ⅛ **teaspoon pepper**
- 5 **cups chicken stock**
  Grated Parmesan cheese

1. In a large skillet, cook sausage over medium heat 6-8 minutes or until no longer pink, breaking into crumbles; drain. Transfer to a 5-qt. slow cooker.
2. Add kale, beans, tomatoes, carrots, onion, garlic, seasonings and stock to slow cooker. Cook, covered, on low for 8-10 hours or until the vegetables are tender. Top each serving with cheese.

SLOW COOKER BUFFALO CHICKEN LASAGNA

When I make this tasty chicken lasagna at home, I use a whole bottle of Buffalo wing sauce because my family likes it nice and spicy. Increase the pasta sauce and use less wing sauce if you prefer.

—HEIDI PEPIN SYKESVILLE, MD

PREP: 25 MIN. • **COOK:** 4 HOURS + STANDING
MAKES: 8 SERVINGS

- 1½ **pounds ground chicken**
- 1 **tablespoon olive oil**
- 1 **bottle (12 ounces) Buffalo wing sauce**
- 1½ **cups meatless spaghetti sauce**
- 1 **carton (15 ounces) ricotta cheese**
- 2 **cups shredded part-skim mozzarella cheese**
- 9 **no-cook lasagna noodles**
- 2 **medium sweet red peppers, chopped**
- ½ **cup crumbled blue cheese or feta cheese**
  Chopped celery and additional crumbled blue cheese, optional

1. In a Dutch oven, cook chicken in oil over medium heat until no longer pink; drain. Stir in wing sauce and spaghetti sauce. In a small bowl, mix ricotta and mozzarella cheeses.
2. Spread 1 cup of the sauce onto the bottom of an oval 6-qt. slow cooker. Layer with three noodles (breaking noodles to fit), 1 cup of the sauce, a third of the peppers and a third of the cheese mixture. Repeat the layers twice. Top with the remaining sauce; sprinkle with blue cheese.
3. Cover and cook on low for 4-5 hours or until the noodles are tender. Let stand 15 minutes before serving. Top with celery and additional blue cheese if desired.

EASY SLOW COOKER MAC & CHEESE

EASY SLOW COOKER MAC & CHEESE

My sons always cheer, "You're the best mom in the world!" whenever I make this creamy mac and cheese perfection. You can't beat a response like that!

—HEIDI FLEEK HAMBURG, PA

PREP: 25 MIN. • **COOK:** 1 HOUR
MAKES: 8 SERVINGS

- 2 **cups uncooked elbow macaroni**
- 1 **can (10¾ ounces) condensed cheddar cheese soup, undiluted**
- 1 **cup 2% milk**
- ½ **cup sour cream**
- ¼ **cup butter, cubed**
- ½ **teaspoon onion powder**
- ¼ **teaspoon white pepper**
- ⅛ **teaspoon salt**
- 1 **cup shredded cheddar cheese**
- 1 **cup shredded fontina cheese**
- 1 **cup shredded provolone cheese**

1. Cook the macaroni according to the package directions for al dente. Meanwhile, using a large saucepan, combine the soup, milk, sour cream, butter and seasonings; cook and stir over medium-low heat until blended. Stir in cheeses until melted.
2. Drain the macaroni; transfer to a greased 3-qt. slow cooker. Stir in the cheese mixture. Cook, covered, on low for 1-2 hours or until heated through.

SLOW COOKER
POT ROAST

SLOW COOKER

SLOW COOKER POT ROAST

I work full time but I still really enjoy making home-cooked meals for my husband and son. It's a comfort to walk in and smell this simmering roast that I know will be fall-apart tender and delicious.

—GINA JACKSON OGDENSBURG, NY

PREP: 15 MIN. • **COOK:** 6 HOURS
MAKES: 6 SERVINGS

- 1 cup warm water
- 1 tablespoon beef base
- ½ pound sliced fresh mushrooms
- 1 large onion, coarsely chopped
- 3 garlic cloves, minced
- 1 boneless beef chuck roast (3 pounds)
- ½ teaspoon pepper
- 1 tablespoon Worcestershire sauce
- ¼ cup butter, cubed
- ⅓ cup all-purpose flour
- ¼ teaspoon salt

1. In a 5- or 6-qt. slow cooker, whisk water and beef base; add mushrooms, onion and garlic. Sprinkle roast with pepper; transfer to the slow cooker. Drizzle with Worcestershire sauce. Cook, covered, on low for 6-8 hours or until the meat is tender.
2. Remove the roast to a serving platter; tent with foil. Strain cooking juices, reserving the vegetables. Skim fat from the cooking juices. In a large saucepan, melt butter over medium heat. Stir in the flour and salt until smooth; then gradually whisk in the cooking juices. Bring to boil, stirring constantly; cook and stir 1-2 minutes or until thickened. Stir in the cooked vegetables. Serve with the roast.
NOTE *At the grocery store, look for beef base near the broth and bouillon.*

SLOW COOKER
FESTIVE SLOW-COOKED BEEF TIPS

We once owned an organic greenhouse and produce business. Weekends were hectic, so I made no-fuss meals like yummy beef tips to fortify us at day's end.

—SUE GRONHOLZ BEAVER DAM, WI

PREP: 45 MIN. • **COOK:** 6 HOURS
MAKES: 8 SERVINGS

- 1 boneless beef chuck roast (about 2 pounds), cut into 2-inch pieces
- 1 teaspoon salt
- ¼ teaspoon pepper
- 2 tablespoons canola oil
- 1 medium onion, coarsely chopped
- 1 celery rib, coarsely chopped
- 6 garlic cloves, halved
- 2 cups beef broth
- 1½ cups dry red wine
- 1 fresh rosemary sprig
- 1 bay leaf
- 2 cans (4 ounces each) sliced mushrooms
- 2 tablespoons cornstarch
- ½ cup water
- 1 tablespoon balsamic vinegar
   Hot cooked egg noodles

1. Sprinkle beef with salt and pepper. In a large skillet, heat the oil over medium-high heat. Brown the beef in batches. Remove with a slotted spoon to a 3- or 4-qt. slow cooker.
2. In same pan, add onion and celery; cook and stir 6-8 minutes or until tender. Add garlic; cook 1 minute longer. Add broth, wine, rosemary and bay leaf. Bring to a boil; cook for 8-10 minutes or until the liquid is reduced to about 2 cups.
3. Pour over beef in the slow cooker; stir in the mushrooms. Cook, covered, on low for 6-8 hours or until the meat is tender. Remove the rosemary and bay leaf.
4. In a small bowl, mix cornstarch, water and vinegar until smooth; gradually stir into the beef mixture. Serve with noodles.

VEGETARIAN CHILI OLE!

I combine ingredients for this hearty chili the night before, start my trusty slow cooker in the morning, and come home to a rich, spicy meal at night!

—**MARJORIE AU** HONOLULU, HI

PREP: 35 MIN. • **COOK:** 6 HOURS
MAKES: 7 SERVINGS

- 1 can (16 ounces) kidney beans, rinsed and drained
- 1 can (15 ounces) black beans, rinsed and drained
- 1 can (14½ ounces) diced tomatoes, undrained
- 1½ cups frozen corn
- 1 large onion, chopped
- 1 medium zucchini, chopped
- 1 medium sweet red pepper, chopped
- 1 can (4 ounces) chopped green chilies
- 1 ounce Mexican chocolate, chopped
- 1 cup water
- 1 can (6 ounces) tomato paste
- 1 tablespoon cornmeal
- 1 tablespoon chili powder
- ½ teaspoon salt
- ½ teaspoon dried oregano
- ½ teaspoon ground cumin
- ¼ teaspoon hot pepper sauce, optional
  Optional toppings: diced tomatoes, chopped green onions and crumbled queso fresco

1. In a 4-qt. slow cooker, combine the first nine ingredients. In a separate bowl, combine water, tomato paste, cornmeal, chili powder, salt, oregano, cumin and, if desired, pepper sauce until smooth; stir into slow cooker. Cover and cook on low for 6-8 hours or until the vegetables are tender.
2. Serve with toppings of your choice.

ISLAND PORK ROAST

ISLAND PORK ROAST

This fork-tender roast is a nice mixture of sweet and tangy. It is especially good when served over rice, and the leftovers make wonderful sandwiches.

—**HEATHER CAMPBELL** LAWRENCE, KS

PREP: 25 MIN. • **COOK:** 5 HOURS
MAKES: 10 SERVINGS

- 1 boneless pork loin roast (about 4 pounds)
- 1 large onion, sliced
- 2 cans (8 ounces each) unsweetened pineapple chunks, undrained
- ½ cup sugar
- ½ cup lime juice
- ½ cup soy sauce
- ¼ cup packed brown sugar
- 2 tablespoons teriyaki sauce
- 2 garlic cloves, minced
- 1 teaspoon ground ginger
- 1 teaspoon curry powder
- ¼ teaspoon salt
- ¼ teaspoon pepper
- 1 bay leaf
- ¼ cup cornstarch
- ½ cup cold water

1. Cut roast in half. Place onion in a 4- or 5-qt. slow cooker. Add the pork. Drain pineapple, reserving juice; set the pineapple aside. In a small bowl, combine sugar, lime juice, soy sauce, brown sugar, teriyaki sauce, garlic, ginger, curry, salt, pepper, bay leaf and the reserved pineapple juice. Pour over the roast.
2. Cover and cook on low for 5-6 hours or until a thermometer reads 160°. Add the pineapple during the last hour of cooking.
3. Remove the meat, onion and pineapple to a serving platter; keep warm. Discard the bay leaf. Skim fat from the cooking juices; transfer the juices to a small saucepan and bring to a boil. Combine cornstarch and water until smooth; gradually stir into the pan with the cooking juices. Bring to a boil; cook and stir for 2 minutes or until thickened. Serve with pork.

STUFFED
FLANK STEAK

STUFFED FLANK STEAK

Flank steak cuts easily into appetizing spirals for serving, and extra stuffing cooks conveniently in a foil packet on top of the steak.

—DIANE HIXON NICEVILLE, FL

PREP: 25 MIN. • **COOK:** 6 HOURS
MAKES: 6 SERVINGS

- 1 **package (8 ounces) crushed corn bread stuffing**
- 1 **cup chopped onion**
- 1 **cup chopped celery**
- ¼ **cup minced fresh parsley**
- ½ **cup egg substitute**
- 1¼ **cups beef broth**
- ⅓ **cup butter, melted**
- ½ **teaspoon seasoned salt**
- ½ **teaspoon pepper**
- 1 **beef flank steak (1½ pounds)**

1. In a large bowl, combine stuffing, onion, celery and parsley. In a small bowl, beat the egg substitute; stir in broth and butter. Pour over the stuffing mixture. Sprinkle with seasoned salt and pepper; stir well.
2. Pound steak to ½-in. thickness. Spread 1½ cups of the stuffing mixture over the steak. Roll up, starting with a short side; tie with string. Place in a 5-qt. slow cooker. The remaining stuffing can be wrapped tightly in foil and placed over the rolled steak.
3. Cover and cook on low for 6-8 hours or until a meat thermometer inserted in the stuffing reads 160° and the meat is tender. Remove the string before slicing.
NOTE *Do not add liquid to the slow cooker. The moisture comes from the meat.*

UPSIDE-DOWN FRITO PIE

UPSIDE-DOWN FRITO PIE

Using ground turkey is a smart way to lighten up this hearty family-pleaser!

—MARY BERG LAKE ELMO, MN

PREP: 15 MIN. • **COOK:** 2 HOURS
MAKES: 6 SERVINGS

- 2 **pounds ground turkey or beef**
- 1 **medium onion, chopped**
- 2 **envelopes chili seasoning mix**
- 1 **can (10 ounces) diced tomatoes and green chilies, undrained**
- 1 **can (8 ounces) tomato sauce**
- 1 **can (15 ounces) pinto beans, rinsed and drained**
- 1 **cup shredded cheddar cheese**
- 3 **cups corn chips**
  Sour cream, minced fresh cilantro and additional chopped onion, optional

1. Using a large skillet, cook turkey and onion over medium heat for 8-10 minutes or until the turkey no longer is pink, breaking into crumbles; stir in the chili seasoning. Transfer to a 3- or 4-qt. slow cooker. Pour tomatoes and tomato sauce over the turkey.
2. Cook, covered, on low for 2-3 hours or until heated through. Stir turkey mixture to combine. Top with beans. Sprinkle with cheese. Cook, covered, 5-10 minutes or until the cheese is melted. Top with corn chips. Serve, if desired, with sour cream, minced cilantro and additional onion.

COUNTRY RIBS DINNER

This is my favorite recipe for the classic ribs dinner. It's always a treat for my family when we have this for dinner.
—**ROSE INGALL** MANISTEE, MI

PREP: 10 MIN. • **COOK:** 6¼ HOURS
MAKES: 4 SERVINGS

- 2 **pounds boneless country-style pork ribs**
- ½ **teaspoon salt**
- ¼ **teaspoon pepper**
- 8 **small red potatoes (about 1 pound), halved**
- 4 **medium carrots, cut into 1-inch pieces**
- 3 **celery ribs, cut into ½-inch pieces**
- 1 **medium onion, coarsely chopped**
- ¾ **cup water**
- 1 **garlic clove, crushed**
- 1 **can (10¾ ounces) condensed cream of mushroom soup, undiluted**
  Chopped fresh parsley, optional

1. Sprinkle ribs with salt and pepper; transfer to a 4-qt. slow cooker. Add potatoes, carrots, celery, onion, water and garlic. Cook, covered, on low for 6-8 hours or until the meat and vegetables are tender.
2. Remove the meat and vegetables; skim fat from the cooking juices. Whisk soup into the cooking juices; return the meat and vegetables to slow cooker. Cook, covered, 15-30 minutes longer or until heated through. If desired, sprinkle with some parsley.

COUNTRY RIBS DINNER

SLOW COOKER BEEF AU JUS

It's easy to fix this roast, which has lots of onion flavor. Sometimes I also add cubed potatoes and baby carrots to the slow cooker to make a terrific meal with plenty of leftovers.

—**CAROL HILLE** GRAND JUNCTION, CO

PREP: 20 MIN.
COOK: 6 HOURS + STANDING
MAKES: 10 SERVINGS

- 1 beef rump roast or bottom round roast (3 pounds)
- 1 large onion, sliced
- ¾ cup reduced-sodium beef broth
- 1 envelope (1 ounce) au jus gravy mix
- 2 garlic cloves, halved
- ¼ teaspoon pepper

1. Cut the roast in half. Using a large nonstick skillet coated with cooking spray, brown the meat on all sides over medium-high heat.
2. Place onion in a 5-qt. slow cooker. Top with the meat. Combine broth, gravy mix, garlic and pepper; pour over the meat. Cover and cook on low for 6-7 hours or until meat is tender.
3. Remove meat to a cutting board. Let stand for 10 minutes. Thinly slice meat and return to the slow cooker; serve with cooking juices and onion.

SLOW COOKER LIME CHICKEN CHILI

Lime juice gives this chili a zesty twist, while canned tomatoes and beans make preparation a breeze. It's fun to serve with toasted tortilla strips.

—**DIANE RANDAZZO** SINKING SPRING, PA

PREP: 25 MIN. • **COOK:** 4 HOURS
MAKES: 6 SERVINGS (2 QUARTS)

- 1 medium onion, chopped
- 1 each medium sweet yellow, red and green peppers, chopped
- 2 tablespoons olive oil
- 3 garlic cloves, minced
- 1 pound ground chicken
- 2 cans (14½ ounces each) diced tomatoes, undrained
- 1 can (15 ounces) cannellini beans, rinsed and drained
- ¼ cup lime juice
- 1 tablespoon all-purpose flour
- 1 tablespoon baking cocoa
- 1 tablespoon ground cumin
- 1 tablespoon chili powder
- 2 teaspoons ground coriander
- 1 teaspoon grated lime peel
- ½ teaspoon salt
- ½ teaspoon garlic pepper blend
- ¼ teaspoon pepper
- 2 flour tortillas (8 inches), cut into ¼-inch strips
- 6 tablespoons reduced-fat sour cream

1. Using a large skillet, saute onion and peppers in oil for 7-8 minutes or until crisp-tender. Add garlic; cook 1 minute longer. Add chicken; cook and stir on medium heat 8-9 minutes or until meat is no longer pink.
2. Transfer to a 3-qt. slow cooker. Stir in tomatoes, beans, lime juice, flour, cocoa, cumin, chili powder, coriander, lime peel, salt, garlic pepper and pepper.
3. Cover and cook on low for 4-5 hours or until heated through.
4. Place the tortilla strips on a baking sheet coated with cooking spray. Bake at 400° for 8-10 minutes or until crisp. Serve the chili with sour cream and tortilla strips.

★ ★ ★ ★ ★ **READER REVIEW**

"Fantastic flavor! I will definitely be making this chili again, probably doubling it!"

PSCHUBE TASTEOFHOME.COM

SLOW-COOKED SHEPHERD'S PIE

Shepherd's pie is to the British what meat loaf is to Americans. When I was a young child in the U.K., shepherd's pie was a weekly staple. This is my go-to recipe when I'm longing for the sights and smells of my mother's kitchen.

—MARI SITKIEWICZ DOWNERS GROVE, IL

PREP: 35 MIN. • **COOK:** 5¼ HOURS
MAKES: 5 SERVINGS

- 2 pounds medium Yukon Gold potatoes, peeled and quartered
- 2 tablespoons butter
- ¼ to ⅓ cup 2% milk
- ¾ teaspoon salt, divided
- ½ teaspoon pepper, divided
- 1 pound ground beef
- 1 large onion, chopped
- 2 garlic cloves, minced
- 3 tablespoons tomato paste
- 1¾ cups sliced fresh mushrooms
- 2 medium carrots, chopped
- 1 cup beef broth
- ¼ cup dry white wine
- 2 teaspoons Worcestershire sauce
- ½ teaspoon dried thyme
- ⅓ cup frozen peas
- ½ cup shredded Monterey Jack cheese
- 1 tablespoon minced fresh parsley

1. Put the potatoes in large saucepan and cover with water. Bring to a boil. Reduce heat; cover and cook for 10-15 minutes or until tender. Drain, then shake the potatoes over low heat for 1 minute to dry. Mash the potatoes, gradually adding butter and enough milk to reach the desired consistency. Stir in ½ teaspoon of the salt and ¼ teaspoon pepper.

2. Meanwhile, using a large skillet, cook the beef, onion, and garlic over medium heat until the meat is no longer pink; drain.

3. Add the tomato paste; cook it for 2 minutes. Add mushrooms, carrots, broth, wine, Worcestershire sauce and thyme. Bring to a boil. Reduce the heat; simmer, uncovered, until most of the liquid is evaporated. Stir in the peas. Season with the remaining salt and pepper.

4. Transfer the beef mixture to a greased 4-qt. slow cooker. Spread the mashed potatoes over top. Cover and cook on low for 5-6 hours or until it is bubbly. Sprinkle with cheese. Cover and cook 10 minutes longer or until the cheese is melted. Just before serving, sprinkle with parsley.

BAKE OPTION *Transfer the cooked beef mixture to a greased 8-in. square baking dish. Spread mashed potatoes over top. Sprinkle with cheese. Bake, uncovered, at 350° for 30-40 minutes or until it is bubbly and the topping is lightly browned. Sprinkle with parsley.*

POLYNESIAN HAM SANDWICHES

The sweetness of the brown sugar and pineapple combined with the tanginess of the Dijon mustard are a perfect match in the tasty sandwich filling.

—JACKIE SMULSKI LYONS, IL

PREP: 20 MIN. • **COOK:** 3 HOURS
MAKES: 12 SERVINGS

- 2 pounds fully cooked ham, finely chopped
- 1 can (20 ounces) crushed pineapple, undrained
- ¾ cup packed brown sugar
- ⅓ cup chopped green pepper
- ¼ cup Dijon mustard
- 1 green onion, chopped
- 1 tablespoon dried minced onion
- 12 hamburger buns or kaiser rolls, split

In a 3-qt. slow cooker, combine the first seven ingredients. Cover and cook on low for 3-4 hours or until heated through. Using a slotted spoon, place ½ cup on each bun.

SLOW-COOKED SHEPHERD'S PIE

SLOW COOKER

SLOW-COOKED PORK STEW

This comforting stew is easy to put together, but it tastes like you've been working hard in the kitchen all day! It's even better when you serve it over polenta, egg noodles or creamy mashed potatoes.

—NANCY ELLIOTT HOUSTON, TX

PREP: 15 MIN. • **COOK:** 5 HOURS
MAKES: 8 SERVINGS

- 2 **pork tenderloins (1 pound each), cut into 2-inch pieces**
- 1 **teaspoon salt**
- ½ **teaspoon pepper**
- 2 **large carrots, cut into ½-inch slices**
- 2 **celery ribs, coarsely chopped**
- 1 **medium onion, coarsely chopped**
- 3 **cups beef broth**
- 2 **tablespoons tomato paste**
- ⅓ **cup pitted dried plums, chopped**
- 4 **garlic cloves, minced**
- 2 **bay leaves**
- 1 **fresh rosemary sprig**
- 1 **fresh thyme sprig**
- ⅓ **cup Greek olives, optional**
  Chopped fresh parsley, optional
  Hot cooked mashed potatoes, optional

1. Sprinkle pork with salt and pepper; transfer to a 4-qt. slow cooker. Add carrots, celery and onion. In a small bowl, whisk broth and tomato paste; pour over the vegetables. Add plums, garlic, bay leaves, rosemary, thyme and, if desired, olives. Cook, covered, on low for 5-6 hours or until the meat and vegetables are tender.

2. Discard the bay leaves, rosemary and thyme. If desired, sprinkle stew with parsley and serve with potatoes.

SLOW-COOKED
PORK STEW

SLOW COOKER
PORK POZOLE

SLOW COOKER

CRAZY DELICIOUS BABY BACK RIBS

My husband craves baby back ribs, so we cook them multiple ways. This low and slow method with a tangy sauce is the best we've found so far.

—**JAN WHITWORTH** ROEBUCK, SC

PREP: 15 MIN. • **COOK:** 5¼ HOURS
MAKES: 8 SERVINGS

- 2 **tablespoons smoked paprika**
- 2 **teaspoons chili powder**
- 2 **teaspoons garlic salt**
- 1 **teaspoon onion powder**
- 1 **teaspoon pepper**
- ½ **teaspoon cayenne pepper**
- 4 **pounds pork baby back ribs**

SAUCE
- ½ **cup Worcestershire sauce**
- ½ **cup mayonnaise**
- ½ **cup yellow mustard**
- ¼ **cup reduced-sodium soy sauce**
- 3 **tablespoons hot pepper sauce**

1. In a small bowl, combine the first six ingredients. Cut ribs into serving-size pieces; rub them with seasoning mixture. Place ribs in a 6-qt. slow cooker. Cook, covered, on low 5-6 hours or until meat is tender.
2. Preheat oven to 375°. In a small bowl, whisk the sauce ingredients. Transfer the ribs to a foil-lined 15x10x1-in. baking pan; brush with some of the sauce. Bake 15-20 minutes or until browned, turning once and brushing occasionally with sauce. Serve with remaining sauce.

★ ★ ★ ★ ★ **5 STAR TIP**
Baby back ribs are ribs that come from the blade and center section of the pork loin. They are called baby back because they are smaller than spareribs. If you are transporting hot cooked ribs to a party and don't want to haul the slow cooker, place them in a container inside heavy-duty foil and then in a brown paper bag. The ribs can stand this way for up to 1 hour.

SLOW COOKER

SLOW COOKER PORK POZOLE

When the snow begins to fall, I prepare this heartwarming stew featuring pork ribs and hominy. It's a fill-you-up recipe of lightly spiced comfort.

—**GENIE GUNN** ASHEVILLE, NC

PREP: 10 MIN. • **COOK:** 3 HOURS
MAKES: 6 SERVINGS

- 1 **can (15½ ounces) hominy, rinsed and drained**
- 1 **can (14½ ounces) diced tomatoes, undrained**
- 1 **can (14½ ounces) diced tomatoes with mild green chilies, undrained**
- 1 **can (10 ounces) green enchilada sauce**
- 2 **medium carrots, finely chopped**
- 1 **medium onion, finely chopped**
- 3 **garlic cloves, minced**
- 2 **teaspoons ground cumin**
- ¼ **teaspoon salt**
- 1 **pound boneless country-style pork ribs**
  Lime wedges and minced fresh cilantro
  Corn tortillas, optional

1. Using a 3- or 4-qt. slow cooker, combine the first nine ingredients; add pork. Cook, covered, on low 3-4 hours or until pork is tender.
2. Remove pork from slow cooker. Cut the pork into bite-size pieces; return to slow cooker. Serve with lime wedges and cilantro and, if desired, corn tortillas.

CRAZY DELICIOUS
BABY BACK RIBS

SLOW COOKER BOEUF BOURGUIGNON

I've wanted to make boeuf bourguignon ever since I got one of Julia Child's cookbook, but I wanted to find a way to fix it in a slow cooker. My version of the popular beef stew is still rich and delicious, but there's no need to watch it on the stovetop or in the oven.

—CRYSTAL JO BRUNS ILIFF, CO

PREP: 30 MIN. + MARINATING
COOK: 8 HOURS
MAKES: 12 SERVINGS (⅔ CUP EACH)

- 3 pounds beef stew meat
- 1¾ cups dry red wine
- 3 tablespoons olive oil
- 3 tablespoons dried minced onion
- 2 tablespoons dried parsley flakes
- 1 bay leaf
- 1 teaspoon dried thyme
- ¼ teaspoon pepper
- 8 bacon strips, chopped
- 1 pound whole fresh mushrooms, quartered
- 24 pearl onions, peeled (about 2 cups)
- 2 garlic cloves, minced
- ⅓ cup all-purpose flour
- 1 teaspoon salt
  Hot cooked whole wheat egg noodles, optional

1. Place beef in a large resealable plastic bag; add the wine, oil and seasonings. Seal bag and turn to coat. Refrigerate overnight.
2. In a large skillet, cook bacon over medium heat until crisp, stirring it occasionally. Remove with a slotted spoon; drain on paper towels. Discard the drippings, reserving 1 tablespoon in the pan.
3. Add the mushrooms and onions to drippings; cook and stir over medium-high heat until tender. Add the garlic; cook 1 minute longer.
4. Drain beef, reserving marinade; transfer the beef to a 4- or 5-qt. slow cooker. Sprinkle beef with flour and salt; toss to coat. Top with the bacon and mushroom mixture. Add the reserved marinade.
5. Cook, covered, on low 8-10 hours or until beef is tender. Remove bay leaf. If desired, serve stew with noodles.

SLOW COOKER BOEUF BOURGUIGNON

SLOW-COOKED CURRY CHICKEN

Our three children all love the spicy flavors found in this dish. Add more or less curry depending on your taste preferences.

—HELEN TOULANTIS WANTAGH, NY

PREP: 25 MIN. • **COOK:** 4½ HOURS
MAKES: 6 SERVINGS

- 6 boneless skinless chicken breast halves (6 ounces each)
- 1¼ teaspoons salt
- 1 can (13.66 ounces) light coconut milk
- 1 teaspoon curry powder
- ½ teaspoon ground turmeric
- ½ teaspoon cayenne pepper
- 3 green onions, sliced, divided
- 2 tablespoons cornstarch
- 2 tablespoons cold water
- 1 to 2 tablespoons lime juice
- 3 cups hot cooked rice

1. Sprinkle chicken with salt. In a large nonstick skillet coated with cooking spray, brown the chicken on both sides. Place in a 5-qt. slow cooker.
2. Combine the coconut milk, curry, turmeric and cayenne; pour over chicken. Sprinkle with half of the onions. Cover and cook on low for 4-5 hours or until chicken is tender.
3. Combine cornstarch and water until smooth; stir into slow cooker. Cover and cook on high 30 minutes or until sauce is thickened. Stir in the lime juice. Serve chicken with the rice and sauce; sprinkle the dish with remaining onions.

LOUISIANA ROUND STEAK

The men in our family really enjoy this beefy main dish. After simmering for hours, the steak takes on a robust taste, and the filling portions are just wonderful.

—MEGAN ROHLCK VERMILLION, SD

PREP: 20 MIN. • **COOK:** 7 HOURS
MAKES: 6 SERVINGS

- 2 **pounds sweet potatoes, peeled and cut into 1-inch pieces**
- 1 **large onion, chopped**
- 1 **medium green pepper, sliced**
- 2 **beef top round steaks (¾ inch thick and 1 pound each)**
- 1 **teaspoon salt, divided**
- 2 **tablespoons olive oil**
- 1 **garlic clove, minced**
- 3 **tablespoons all-purpose flour**
- 1 **can (28 ounces) diced tomatoes, undrained**
- ½ **cup beef broth**
- 1 **teaspoon sugar**
- ½ **teaspoon dried thyme**
- ½ **teaspoon pepper**
- ¼ **teaspoon hot pepper sauce**

1. Place the sweet potatoes, onion and green pepper in a 6-qt. slow cooker. Cut each steak into three serving-size pieces; sprinkle with ½ teaspoon salt. In a large skillet over medium heat, brown steaks in oil in batches on both sides. Place steaks over vegetables, reserving the meat drippings in pan.
2. Add the garlic to drippings; cook and stir for 1 minute. Stir in the flour until blended. Stir in the remaining ingredients and remaining salt. Bring to a boil, stirring constantly. Cook and stir for 4-5 minutes or until thickened. Pour over meat. Cover and cook on low 7-9 hours or until beef is tender.

**BARBECUE PORK TACOS
WITH APPLE SLAW**

BARBECUE PORK TACOS WITH APPLE SLAW

At my house we like to celebrate taco Tuesdays, so I keep things interesting by switching up the varieties. These pork tacos are super simple to make.

—JENN TIDWELL FAIR OAKS, CA

PREP: 15 MIN. • **COOK:** 2¼ HOURS
MAKES: 8 SERVINGS

- 2 **pork tenderloins (1 pound each)**
- 1 **can (12 ounces) root beer**
SLAW
- 6 **cups shredded red cabbage (about 12 ounces)**
- 2 **medium Granny Smith apples, julienned**
- ⅓ **cup cider vinegar**
- ¼ **cup minced fresh cilantro**
- ¼ **cup lime juice**
- 2 **tablespoons sugar**
- ½ **teaspoon salt**
- ½ **teaspoon pepper**
ASSEMBLY
- 1 **bottle (18 ounces) barbecue sauce**
- 16 **taco shells**

1. Place pork in a 3-qt. slow cooker. Pour the root beer over the top. Cook, covered, on low 2 to 2½ hours or just until tender (a thermometer inserted in pork should read at least 145°).
2. Meanwhile, in a large bowl, toss the slaw ingredients. Refrigerate, covered, until serving.
3. Remove tenderloins to a cutting board; let stand, covered, 5 minutes. Discard cooking juices.
4. Coarsely chop pork; return to slow cooker. Stir in barbecue sauce; heat through. Serve in taco shells; top with some of the slaw. Serve the remaining slaw on the side.

SASSY POT ROAST

We lost this recipe for several years, so it's even more special to us now that we found it again. I love walking into my home after a long day at the office and smelling this lovely pot roast.

—SUSAN BURKETT MONROEVILLE, PA

PREP: 15 MIN. • **COOK:** 8 HOURS
MAKES: 8 SERVINGS

- 1 **boneless beef chuck roast (2 pounds)**
- ½ **teaspoon salt**
- ½ **teaspoon pepper**
- 2 **teaspoons olive oil**
- 1 **large onion, chopped**
- 1 **can (8 ounces) tomato sauce**
- ¼ **cup water**
- ¼ **cup lemon juice**
- ¼ **cup cider vinegar**
- ¼ **cup ketchup**
- 2 **tablespoons brown sugar**
- 1 **tablespoon Worcestershire sauce**
- ½ **teaspoon ground mustard**
- ½ **teaspoon paprika**

1. Sprinkle beef with salt and pepper. In a large skillet, brown beef in oil on all sides; drain.

2. Transfer to a 4-qt. slow cooker. Sprinkle with onion. Combine the remaining ingredients; pour over the meat. Cover and cook on low for 8-10 hours or until meat is tender. Skim fat. If desired, thicken cooking liquid.

SASSY
POT
ROAST

PICANTE BEEF ROAST

I created Picante Beef Roast because I love the flavor of taco seasoning and think it shouldn't be reserved just for tacos! My recipe couldn't be easier, and it works great with a pork roast, too.
—**MARGARET THIEL** LEVITTOWN, PA

PREP: 15 MIN. • **COOK:** 8 HOURS
MAKES: 8 SERVINGS

- 1 beef rump roast or bottom round roast (3 pounds), trimmed
- 1 jar (16 ounces) picante sauce
- 1 can (15 ounces) tomato sauce
- 1 envelope taco seasoning
- 3 tablespoons cornstarch
- ¼ cup cold water

1. Cut roast in half; place in a 5-qt. slow cooker. In a large bowl, combine the picante sauce, tomato sauce and taco seasoning; pour over roast. Cover and cook on low for 8-9 hours or until meat is tender.
2. Remove meat to a serving platter; keep warm. Skim the fat from the cooking juices; transfer 3 cups to a small saucepan. Bring liquid to a boil. Combine cornstarch and water until smooth. Gradually stir into the pan. Bring to a boil; cook and stir about 2 minutes or until thickened. Serve with roast.

SLOW-COOKED CHICKEN ENCHILADA SOUP

This soup delivers a big bowl of summery comfort. Toppings like avocado, sour cream and tortilla strips are a must.
—**HEATHER SEWELL** HARRISONVILLE, MO

PREP: 25 MIN. • **COOK:** 6 HOURS
MAKES: 8 SERVINGS (3¼ QUARTS)

- 1 tablespoon canola oil
- 2 Anaheim or poblano peppers, finely chopped
- 1 medium onion, chopped
- 3 garlic cloves, minced
- 1 pound boneless skinless chicken breasts
- 1 carton (48 ounces) chicken broth
- 1 can (14½ ounces) Mexican diced tomatoes, undrained
- 1 can (10 ounces) enchilada sauce
- 2 tablespoons tomato paste
- 1 tablespoon chili powder
- 2 teaspoons ground cumin
- ½ teaspoon pepper
- ½ to 1 teaspoon chipotle hot pepper sauce, optional
- ⅓ cup minced fresh cilantro
  Optional toppings: shredded cheddar cheese, cubed avocado, sour cream and crispy tortilla strips

1. In a large skillet, heat the oil over medium heat. Add peppers and onion; cook and stir 6-8 minutes or until tender. Add garlic; cook 1 minute longer. Transfer pepper mixture and chicken to a 5- or 6-qt. slow cooker. Stir in broth, tomatoes, enchilada sauce, tomato paste, seasonings and, if desired, the pepper sauce. Cook, covered, on low 6-8 hours or until chicken is tender (a thermometer should read at least 165°).
2. Remove chicken from slow cooker. Shred with two forks; return to slow cooker. Stir in cilantro. Serve with toppings as desired.
FREEZE OPTION *Freeze the cooled soup in freezer containers. To use, partially thaw in the refrigerator overnight. Heat it through in a saucepan, stirring occasionally and adding a little water if necessary.*

☆ ☆ ☆ ☆ ☆ **READER REVIEW**

"This soup is so tasty and easy to make, it will become a part of my permanent soup collection."

PAGERD TASTEOFHOME.COM

SLOW-COOKED STUFFED PEPPERS

SLOW COOKER

SLOW-COOKED STUFFED PEPPERS

My favorite kitchen appliance is my slow cooker, and I use mine more than anyone else I know. It does a great job with this good-for-you dish.

—**MICHELLE GURNSEY** LINCOLN, NE

PREP: 15 MIN. • **COOK:** 3 HOURS
MAKES: 4 SERVINGS

- 4 **medium sweet red peppers**
- 1 **can (15 ounces) black beans, rinsed and drained**
- 1 **cup shredded pepper jack cheese**
- ¾ **cup salsa**
- 1 **small onion, chopped**
- ½ **cup frozen corn**
- ⅓ **cup uncooked converted long grain rice**
- 1¼ **teaspoons chili powder**
- ½ **teaspoon ground cumin**
  Reduced-fat sour cream, optional

1. Cut and discard tops from peppers; remove seeds. In a large bowl, mix beans, cheese, salsa, onion, corn, rice, chili powder and cumin; spoon into peppers. Place in a 5-qt. slow cooker coated with cooking spray.
2. Cook, covered, on low 3-4 hours or until peppers are tender and filling is heated through. If desired, serve with sour cream.

★ ★ ★ ★ ★ **5 STAR TIP**
Stuffed peppers are my specialty for potlucks. So, in the summer, when peppers are abundant, I freeze them. To prepare peppers for freezing, wash well; remove seeds and stem. Blanch for 3 minutes; drain well and freeze on a waxed paper-lined cookie sheet. Once they are frozen, place them in plastic freezer bags and enjoy them all fall and winter long.
RUTH J. ALBUQUERQUE, NM

HARVEST TIME CHICKEN WITH COUSCOUS

HAWAIIAN KIELBASA SANDWICHES

If you are looking for a different way to use kielbasa, the sweet and mildly spicy flavor of these sandwiches is a nice change of pace.

—**JUDY DAMES** BRIDGEVILLE, PA

PREP: 15 MIN. • **COOK:** 3 HOURS
MAKES: 12 SERVINGS

- 3 pounds smoked kielbasa or Polish sausage, cut into 3-inch pieces
- 2 bottles (12 ounces each) chili sauce
- 1 can (20 ounces) pineapple tidbits, undrained
- ¼ cup packed brown sugar
- 12 hoagie buns, split

Place kielbasa in a 3-qt. slow cooker. Combine the chili sauce, pineapple and brown sugar; pour over kielbasa. Cover and cook on low for 3-4 hours or until heated through. Serve meat mixture on buns.

HARVEST TIME CHICKEN WITH COUSCOUS

Even on busy days, I can start this chicken in a slow cooker and still get to work on time. When I come home, I add a spinach salad and warm crescent rolls.

—**HEIDI RUDOLPH** OREGON, IL

PREP: 30 MIN. • **COOK:** 3 HOURS
MAKES: 6 SERVINGS

- 2 medium sweet potatoes (about 1¼ pounds), peeled and cut into ½-inch pieces
- 1 medium sweet red pepper, coarsely chopped
- 1½ pounds boneless skinless chicken breasts
- 1 can (14½ ounces) stewed tomatoes, undrained
- ½ cup peach or mango salsa
- ¼ cup golden raisins
- ½ teaspoon salt
- ¼ teaspoon ground cumin
- ¼ teaspoon ground cinnamon
- ¼ teaspoon pepper

COUSCOUS
- 1 cup water
- ½ teaspoon salt
- 1 cup uncooked whole wheat couscous

1. In a 4-qt. slow cooker, layer sweet potatoes, red pepper and chicken breasts. In a small bowl, mix tomatoes, salsa, raisins and seasonings; pour over chicken. Cook, covered, on low 3-4 hours or until sweet potatoes and chicken are tender.

2. About 10 minutes before serving, prepare the couscous. Using a small saucepan, bring the water and salt to a boil. Stir in the couscous. Remove from the heat; let stand, covered, 5 minutes or until water is absorbed. Fluff with a fork.

3. Remove chicken from slow cooker; coarsely shred with two forks. Return chicken to slow cooker, stirring gently to combine. Serve with couscous.

FREEZE OPTION *Place the cooled chicken mixture in freezer containers. To eat it, partially thaw the food in the refrigerator overnight. Microwave, covered, on high in a microwave-safe dish until heated through, stirring gently and adding a little broth or water if necessary.*

CHIPOTLE PULLED CHICKEN

SLOW COOKER 🍲
SLOW-COOKED BEEF

I serve this popular German entree with potato pancakes and vegetables. Crushed gingersnaps, lemon and vinegar give the marinated slow-cooked beef and gravy their appetizing sweet-sour flavor.

—SUSAN GAROUTTE GEORGETOWN, TX

PREP: 10 MIN. + MARINATING
COOK: 6 HOURS 10 MIN.
MAKES: 12 SERVINGS

- 1½ cups water, divided
- 1¼ cups cider vinegar, divided
- 2 large onions, sliced, divided
- 1 medium lemon, sliced
- 15 whole cloves, divided
- 6 bay leaves, divided
- 6 whole peppercorns
- 2 tablespoons sugar
- 2 teaspoons salt
- 1 beef sirloin tip roast (3 pounds), cut in half
- ¼ teaspoon pepper
- 12 gingersnap cookies, crumbled

1. In a large resealable plastic bag, combine 1 cup water, 1 cup vinegar, half of the onions, lemon, 10 cloves, 4 bay leaves, peppercorns, sugar and salt; mix well. Add roast. Seal bag and turn to coat; refrigerate overnight, turning occasionally.
2. Drain and discard marinade. Place the roast in a 5-qt. slow cooker; add pepper and remaining water, vinegar, onions, cloves and bay leaves. Cover and cook on low until meat is tender, about 6-8 hours.
3. Remove the roast and keep warm. Discard the bay leaves. Stir in the gingersnaps. Cover and cook on high for 10-15 minutes or until the gravy has thickened. Slice the roast; serve it with gravy.

FREEZE IT **SLOW COOKER** 🍲
CHIPOTLE PULLED CHICKEN

I love chicken that has a chipotle kick to it. This is a go-to meal when I'm looking for something extra tasty.

—TAMRA PARKER MANLIUS, NY

PREP: 15 MIN. • **COOK:** 3 HOURS
MAKES: 12 SERVINGS

- 2 cups ketchup
- 1 small onion, finely chopped
- ¼ cup Worcestershire sauce
- 3 tablespoons reduced-sodium soy sauce
- 2 tablespoons brown sugar
- 2 tablespoons cider vinegar
- 3 garlic cloves, minced
- 1 tablespoon molasses
- 2 teaspoons dried oregano
- 2 teaspoons minced chipotle pepper in adobo sauce plus 1 teaspoon sauce
- 1 teaspoon ground cumin
- 1 teaspoon smoked paprika
- ¼ teaspoon salt
- ¼ teaspoon crushed red pepper flakes
- 2½ pounds boneless skinless chicken breasts
- 12 sesame seed hamburger buns, split and toasted

1. In a 3-qt. slow cooker, combine the first 14 ingredients; add chicken. Cook, covered, on low 3-4 hours or until the chicken is tender and a thermometer reads at least 165°.
2. Remove chicken from slow cooker. Shred with two forks; return to slow cooker. Using tongs, place the chicken mixture on bun bottoms. Replace the bun tops.
FREEZE OPTION *Freeze the cooled meat mixture and sauce in the freezer containers. To use, partially thaw in refrigerator overnight. Heat through in a saucepan, stirring occasionally.*

LIME-CHIPOTLE CARNITAS TOSTADAS

Here's a great recipe for your next party! Set out various toppings and garnishes so guests can custom-make their own tostadas with the lime-kissed shredded pork.
—**JAN VALDEZ** CHICAGO, IL

PREP: 20 MIN. • **COOK:** 8 HOURS
MAKES: 16 SERVINGS

- ½ cup chicken broth
- 4 teaspoons ground chipotle pepper
- 4 teaspoons ground cumin
- 1 teaspoon salt
- 1 boneless pork shoulder roast (4 to 5 pounds), halved
- 1 large onion, peeled and halved
- 8 garlic cloves, peeled
- 1 to 2 limes, halved
- 16 tostada shells
    Optional toppings: warmed refried beans, salsa, sour cream, shredded lettuce, chopped avocado, crumbled queso fresco and minced fresh cilantro
    Lime wedges

1. Add broth to a 5-qt. slow cooker. Mix seasonings; rub over all sides of pork. Place in slow cooker. Add onion and garlic cloves. Cook, covered, on low 8-10 hours or until meat is tender.
2. Remove pork; cool slightly. Strain cooking juices, reserving garlic cloves; discard onion. Skim fat from cooking juices. Mash garlic with a fork. Shred pork with two forks.
3. Return cooking juices, garlic and pork to slow cooker. Squeeze the lime juice over pork; heat through, stirring to combine. Layer tostada shells with pork mixture and toppings as desired. Serve with lime wedges.

SLOW COOKER SPLIT PEA SOUP

When I have leftover ham in the fridge, I always like to make this soup. Just throw the ingredients in the slow cooker, turn it on and dinner is done.
—**PAMELA CHAMBERS** WEST COLUMBIA, SC

PREP: 15 MIN. • **COOK:** 8 HOURS
MAKES: 8 SERVINGS

- 1 package (16 ounces) dried green split peas, rinsed
- 2 cups cubed fully cooked ham
- 1 large onion, chopped
- 1 cup julienned or chopped carrots
- 3 garlic cloves, minced
- ½ teaspoon dried rosemary, crushed
- ½ teaspoon dried thyme
- 1 carton (32 ounces) reduced-sodium chicken broth
- 2 cups water

In a 4- or 5-qt. slow cooker, combine all ingredients. Cover and cook on low for 8-10 hours or until peas are tender.
FREEZE OPTION *Freeze cooled soup in freezer containers. To use, thaw overnight in the refrigerator. Heat through in a saucepan over medium heat, stirring occasionally.*

SLOW COOKER SPLIT PEA SOUP

**CHEESY HAM &
CORN CHOWDER**

CHEESY HAM & CORN CHOWDER

When the day calls for a warm bowl of chunky soup, I haul out the slow cooker and whip up a big batch of this satisfying favorite.
—**ANDREA LAIDLAW** SHADY SIDE, MD

PREP: 25 MIN. • **COOK:** 8½ HOURS
MAKES: 12 SERVINGS (3¾ QUARTS)

- 1½ **pounds potatoes (about 3 medium), peeled and cut into ½-inch cubes**
- 4 **cups fresh or frozen corn, thawed (about 20 ounces)**
- 4 **cups cubed deli ham**
- 2 **small onions, chopped**
- 4 **celery ribs, chopped**
- 4 **garlic cloves, minced**
- ¼ **teaspoon pepper**
- 3 **cups chicken broth**
- 2 **tablespoons cornstarch**
- 2 **cups whole milk**
- 2 **cups shredded sharp cheddar cheese**
- 1 **cup sour cream**
- 3 **tablespoons minced fresh parsley**

1. Place the first eight ingredients in a 6-qt. slow cooker. Cook, covered, on low 8-10 hours or until the potatoes are tender.
2. In a small bowl, mix cornstarch and milk until smooth; stir into soup. Cook, covered, on high for 20-30 minutes or until thickened, stirring occasionally. Stir in the cheese, sour cream and parsley until the cheese is melted.

★ ★ ★ ★ ★ **5 STAR TIP**
Fresh corn is at its peak May through September. Look for ears of corn with bright green tightly closed husks and golden brown silk. The kernels should be plump, milky and in closely spaced rows all the way to the tip. As soon as the corn is picked, the sugar gradually begins to convert to starch, reducing its natural sweetness. So corn is best cooked and served the same day it's picked and purchased.

MELT-IN-YOUR-MOUTH CHUCK ROAST

MELT-IN-YOUR-MOUTH CHUCK ROAST

My husband and I like well-seasoned foods, so this recipe is terrific. You'll also love how flavorful this roast turns out.
—**BETTE MCCUMBER** SCHENECTADY, NY

PREP: 20 MIN. • **COOK:** 5 HOURS
MAKES: 6 SERVINGS

- 1 **can (14½ ounces) Italian stewed tomatoes, undrained**
- ½ **cup beef broth**
- ½ **cup ketchup**
- 3 **tablespoons brown sugar**
- 2 **tablespoons Worcestershire sauce**
- 4 **teaspoons prepared mustard**
- 3 **garlic cloves, minced**
- 1 **tablespoon soy sauce**
- 2 **teaspoons pepper**
- ¼ **teaspoon crushed red pepper flakes**
- 1 **large onion, halved and sliced**
- 1 **medium green pepper, halved and sliced**
- 1 **celery rib, chopped**
- 1 **boneless beef chuck roast (2 to 3 pounds)**
- 3 **tablespoons cornstarch**
- ¼ **cup cold water**

1. Mix first 10 ingredients. Place the onion, green pepper and celery in a 5-qt. slow cooker; place roast over top. Pour tomato mixture over the roast. Cook, covered, on low until meat is tender, 5-6 hours.
2. Remove the roast. Strain cooking juices, reserving vegetables. Transfer juices to a small saucepan; skim the fat. Mix the cornstarch and water until smooth; stir into cooking juices. Bring to a boil; cook and stir until thickened, about 1-2 minutes. Serve the roast and vegetables with gravy.
FREEZE OPTION *Place the sliced beef and vegetables in freezer containers; top with gravy. Cool and freeze. To use, partially thaw in the refrigerator overnight. Heat through slowly in a covered saucepan, stirring gently and adding a little broth or water if needed.*

SLOW-COOKED SWISS STEAK

This is a favorite of mine to make, because I can flour and season the steaks and then refrigerate them overnight. In the morning, I just put all the ingredients in the slow cooker, and I have a delicious dinner waiting for us when I arrive home from work.

—SARAH BURKS WATHENA, KS

PREP: 10 MIN. • **COOK:** 6 HOURS
MAKES: 6 SERVINGS

- 2 **tablespoons all-purpose flour**
- ½ **teaspoon salt**
- ¼ **teaspoon pepper**
- 1½ **pounds beef round steak, cut into six pieces**
- 1 **medium onion, cut into ¼-inch slices**
- 1 **celery rib, cut into ½-inch slices**
- 2 **cans (8 ounces each) tomato sauce**

1. In a large resealable plastic bag, combine the flour, salt and pepper. Add the steak; seal the bag and shake to coat.

2. Place the sliced onion in a greased 3-qt. slow cooker. Top with the steak, celery and tomato sauce. Cover and cook on low for 6-8 hours or until the meat is tender.

★ ★ ★ ★ ★ **READER REVIEW**

"This is in the slow cooker for the second time this week. So good."

WOKKER TASTEOFHOME.COM

SLOW-COOKED
SWISS STEAK

BEAN & BEEF SLOW-COOKED CHILI

This chili may be chock-full, but we love to build it up even more with toppings like pico de gallo, red onion, cilantro and cheese.

—**MALLORY LYNCH** MADISON, WI

PREP: 20 MIN. • **COOK:** 6 HOURS
MAKES: 6 SERVINGS (2¼ QUARTS)

- 1 pound lean ground beef (90% lean)
- 1 large sweet onion, chopped
- 3 garlic cloves, minced
- 2 cans (14½ ounces each) diced tomatoes with mild green chilies
- 2 cans (15 ounces each) pinto beans, rinsed and drained
- 2 cans (15 ounces each) black beans, rinsed and drained
- 2 to 3 tablespoons chili powder
- 2 teaspoons ground cumin
- ½ teaspoon salt
  Optional toppings: sour cream, chopped red onion and minced fresh cilantro

1. In a large skillet, cook the beef, onion and garlic over medium heat 6-8 minutes or until the beef is no longer pink, breaking up beef into crumbles; drain.

2. Transfer the beef mixture to a 5-qt.slow cooker. Drain one can of tomatoes, discarding liquid; add to slow cooker. Stir in the beans, chili powder, cumin, salt and remaining tomatoes. Cook, covered, on low for 6-8 hours to allow flavors to blend.

3. Mash beans to desired consistency. Serve with toppings as desired.

FREEZE OPTION *Freeze cooled chili in freezer containers. To use, partially thaw it in the refrigerator overnight. Heat through in a saucepan, stirring occasionally and adding a little water if necessary.*

SLOW-COOKED BARBECUED PORK SANDWICHES

These saucy sandwiches are great for hungry crowds and easy to prepare. Just keep the meat warm in the slow cooker until it's time to serve.

—**KIMBERLY WALLACE** DENNISON, OH

PREP: 20 MIN. • **COOK:** 7 HOURS
MAKES: 10 SERVINGS

- 1 medium onion, chopped
- 1 tablespoon butter
- 1 can (15 ounces) tomato puree
- ½ cup packed brown sugar
- ¼ cup steak sauce
- 2 tablespoons lemon juice
- ½ teaspoon salt
- 1 boneless pork shoulder butt roast (3 pounds)
- 10 hard rolls, split
  Coleslaw, optional

1. In a large skillet, saute the onion in butter until it is tender. Stir in the tomato puree, brown sugar, steak sauce, lemon juice and salt. Cook over medium heat until sugar is dissolved and heated through.

2. Place roast in a 5-qt. slow cooker; pour sauce over the top. Cover and cook on low for 7-9 hours or until meat is tender. Remove roast; cool slightly. Skim fat from cooking juices. Shred the meat with two forks and return it to the slow cooker; heat it through. Serve on rolls. Top it with coleslaw if desired.

TOP-RATED
ITALIAN
POT ROAST

Remove roast from slow cooker; keep warm. Discard the spice bag; skim fat from sauce. Serve roast and sauce with noodles and parsley if desired.

FREEZE OPTION *Place the sliced pot roast in freezer containers; top it with sauce. Cool and freeze. To use, partially thaw in the refrigerator overnight. Then heat it through in a covered saucepan, stirring it gently and adding a little broth if necessary.*

SLOW COOKER

EASY CITRUS HAM

I created this recipe many years ago with items I already had on hand. The succulent ham has a mild citrus flavor. It was so popular at a church social that I knew I had a winner!

—**SHEILA CHRISTENSEN** SAN MARCOS, CA

PREP: 15 MIN. • **COOK:** 4 HOURS + STANDING
MAKES: 10-12 SERVINGS

- 1 **boneless fully cooked ham (3 to 4 pounds)**
- ½ **cup packed dark brown sugar**
- 1 **can (12 ounces) lemon-lime soda, divided**
- 1 **medium navel orange, thinly sliced**
- 1 **medium lemon, thinly sliced**
- 1 **medium lime, thinly sliced**
- 1 **tablespoon chopped crystallized ginger**

1. Cut ham in half; place in a 5-qt. slow cooker. In a small bowl, combine brown sugar and ¼ cup soda; rub over ham. Top with orange, lemon and lime slices. Add the candied ginger and remaining soda to the slow cooker.
2. Cover and cook on low for 4-5 hours or until a meat thermometer reads 140°, basting occasionally with cooking juices. Let it stand about 10 minutes before slicing.

FREEZE IT SLOW COOKER

TOP-RATED ITALIAN POT ROAST

I am always saving recipes from newspapers and magazines, and this one just sounded too good not to try! You will love the the blend of wholesome ingredients and aromatic spices.

—**KAREN BURDELL** LAFAYETTE, CO

PREP: 30 MIN. • **COOK:** 6 HOURS
MAKES: 8 SERVINGS

- 1 **cinnamon stick (3 inches)**
- 6 **whole peppercorns**
- 4 **whole cloves**
- 3 **whole allspice berries**
- 2 **teaspoons olive oil**
- 1 **boneless beef chuck roast (2 pounds)**
- 2 **celery ribs, sliced**
- 2 **medium carrots, sliced**
- 1 **large onion, chopped**
- 4 **garlic cloves, minced**
- 1 **cup dry sherry or reduced-sodium beef broth**

- 1 **can (28 ounces) crushed tomatoes**
- ¼ **teaspoon salt**
  Hot cooked egg noodles and minced parsley, optional

1. Place the cinnamon stick, peppercorns, cloves and allspice on a double thickness of cheesecloth. Gather corners of cloth to enclose spices; tie securely with string.
2. In a large skillet, heat the oil over medium-high heat. Brown roast on all sides; transfer to a 4-qt. slow cooker. Add celery, carrots and spice bag.
3. Add onion to same skillet; cook and stir until tender. Add the garlic; cook 1 minute longer. Add sherry, stirring to loosen browned bits from the pan. Bring to a boil, then cook and stir until liquid is reduced to ⅔ cup. Stir in the tomatoes and salt; pour mixture over roast and vegetables.
4. Cook, covered, on low 6-7 hours or until meat and vegetables are tender.

CHICKEN SLIDERS WITH SESAME SLAW

These tangy, spicy chicken sliders have an Asian style that tingles the taste buds. At our potlucks, they quickly vanish.

—PRISCILLA YEE CONCORD, CA

PREP: 25 MIN. • **COOK:** 6 HOURS
MAKES: 20 SERVINGS

- 1 medium onion, coarsely chopped
- 3 pounds boneless skinless chicken thighs
- ½ cup ketchup
- ¼ cup reduced-sodium teriyaki sauce
- 2 tablespoons dry sherry or reduced-sodium chicken broth
- 2 tablespoons minced fresh gingerroot
- ½ teaspoon salt

SESAME SLAW
- ¼ cup mayonnaise
- 1 tablespoon rice wine vinegar
- 1 tablespoon sesame oil
- 1 teaspoon Sriracha Asian hot chili sauce
- 3 cups coleslaw mix
- ⅓ cup dried cherries or cranberries
- 2 tablespoons minced fresh cilantro
- 20 slider buns or dinner rolls, split

1. Place onion and chicken in a 4-qt. slow cooker. In a small bowl, mix the ketchup, teriyaki sauce, sherry, ginger and salt. Pour over the chicken. Cook, covered, on low 6-7 hours or until a thermometer reads 170°.
2. Remove chicken; cool it slightly. Skim fat from cooking juices. Shred the chicken with two forks. Return chicken to slow cooker. Meanwhile, in a small bowl, whisk mayonnaise, vinegar, sesame oil and Sriracha sauce until blended. Stir in coleslaw mix, cherries and cilantro. Using a slotted spoon, place ¼ cup chicken mixture on each bun bottom; top with about 2 tablespoons slaw. Replace tops.

CHICKEN SLIDERS WITH SESAME SLAW

RED PEPPER CHICKEN

Chicken breasts are treated to black beans, red peppers and juicy tomatoes in this Southwestern supper. We love it served with rice cooked in chicken broth.

—PIPER SPIWAK VIENNA, VA

PREP: 15 MIN. • **COOK:** 6 HOURS
MAKES: 4 SERVINGS

- **4 boneless skinless chicken breast halves (4 ounces each)**
- **1 can (15 ounces) black beans, rinsed and drained**
- **1 can (14½ ounces) Mexican stewed tomatoes, undrained**
- **1 jar (12 ounces) roasted sweet red peppers, drained and cut into strips**
- **1 large onion, chopped**
- **½ teaspoon salt**
   Pepper to taste
   Hot cooked rice

Place the chicken in a 3-qt. slow cooker. In a bowl, combine the beans, tomatoes, red peppers, onion, salt and pepper. Pour over the chicken. Cover and cook on low for 6 hours or until chicken is tender. Serve with rice.

SLOW COOKER SHORT RIBS

These ribs are an easy alternative to traditionally braised short ribs—you don't need to pay any attention to them once you get them started.

—REBEKAH BEYER SABETHA, KS

PREP: 30 MIN. • **COOK:** 6¼ HOURS
MAKES: 6 SERVINGS

- **3 pounds bone-in beef short ribs**
- **½ teaspoon salt**
- **½ teaspoon pepper**
- **1 tablespoon canola oil**
- **4 medium carrots, cut into 1-inch pieces**
- **1 cup beef broth**
- **4 fresh thyme sprigs**
- **1 bay leaf**
- **2 large onions, cut into ½-inch wedges**
- **6 garlic cloves, minced**
- **1 tablespoon tomato paste**
- **2 cups dry red wine or beef broth**
- **4 teaspoons cornstarch**
- **3 tablespoons cold water**
   Salt and pepper to taste

1. Sprinkle ribs with ½ teaspoon each salt and pepper. In a large skillet, heat oil over medium heat. In batches, brown ribs on all sides; transfer to a 4- or 5-qt. slow cooker. Add carrots, broth, thyme and bay leaf to ribs.
2. Add onions to the same skillet; cook and stir over medium heat 8-9 minutes or until tender. Add garlic and tomato paste; cook and stir 1 minute longer. Stir in wine. Bring to a boil; cook 8-10 minutes or until liquid is reduced by half. Add to slow cooker. Cook, covered, on low 6-8 hours or until meat is tender.
3. Remove the ribs and vegetables; keep them warm. Transfer cooking juices to a small saucepan; skim fat. Discard the thyme and bay leaf. Bring the juices to a boil. In a small bowl, mix the cornstarch and water until smooth; stir into the cooking juices. Return to a boil; cook and stir about 1-2 minutes or until it is thickened. Season with salt and pepper to taste. Serve with ribs and vegetables.

★ ★ ★ ★ ★ 5 STAR TIP
Bay leaves are aromatic leaves used in cooking for their distinctive savory and spicy flavor. They are available as whole, fresh or dried, dull green leaves. Add them to soups, stews, casseroles and meat dishes during the cooking process. Bay leaves should always be removed from the cooked food before eating.

RED PEPPER CHICKEN

SLOW COOKER
SHORT RIBS

SLOW COOKER TWO-MEAT MANICOTTI

SLOW COOKER TWO-MEAT MANICOTTI

I wanted to create my ideal version of a stuffed manicotti, which requires a fantastic filling and a meat sauce to die for. This recipe is the final result, and I don't mind saying it's a huge success!

—**SHALIMAR WIECH** GLASSPORT, PA

PREP: 45 MIN. • **COOK:** 4 HOURS
MAKES: 7 SERVINGS

- ½ **pound medium fresh mushrooms, chopped**
- 2 **small green peppers, chopped**
- 1 **medium onion, chopped**
- 1½ **teaspoons canola oil**
- 4 **garlic cloves, minced**
- ¾ **pound ground sirloin**
- ¾ **pound bulk Italian sausage**
- 2 **jars (23½ ounces each) Italian sausage and garlic spaghetti sauce**
- 1 **carton (15 ounces) ricotta cheese**
- 1 **cup minced fresh parsley**
- ½ **cup shredded part-skim mozzarella cheese, divided**
- ½ **cup grated Parmesan cheese, divided**
- 2 **large eggs, lightly beaten**
- ½ **teaspoon salt**
- ¼ **teaspoon pepper**
- ⅛ **teaspoon ground nutmeg**
- 1 **package (8 ounces) manicotti shells**

1. In a large skillet over medium-high heat, saute the mushrooms, peppers and onion in oil until tender. Add the garlic; cook 1 minute longer. Remove from pan.
2. In the same skillet, cook beef and sausage over medium heat until no longer pink; drain. Stir in mushroom mixture and spaghetti sauce; set aside.
3. In a small bowl, combine ricotta cheese, parsley, ¼ cup mozzarella cheese, ¼ cup Parmesan cheese, eggs and seasonings. Stuff into uncooked manicotti shells.
4. Spread 2¼ cups sauce onto the bottom of a 6-qt. slow cooker. Arrange five stuffed manicotti shells over the sauce; repeat this two times, using four shells on the top layer. Top with the remaining sauce. Sprinkle with the remaining cheeses. Cover and cook on low for 4-5 hours or until the pasta is tender.
BAKE OPTION *Spread half of the sauce mixture into a greased 13x9-in. baking dish. Arrange the stuffed manicotti shells in a single layer over sauce. Top with remaining sauce. Cover and bake at 375° for 45-55 minutes or until pasta is tender. Uncover; sprinkle with remaining cheeses. Bake 10-15 minutes longer or until cheese is melted. Let stand 5 minutes before serving.*

GREAT NORTHERN BEAN CHILI

My easy version of Southwestern chicken chili uses just a few ingredients. I like to serve it with tortilla chips, sour cream and a dash of hot sauce on top. It's a great alternative to traditional chili.

—**MAMESMOM** TASTE OF HOME.COM

PREP: 20 MIN. • **COOK:** 4 HOURS
MAKES: 8 SERVINGS

- 2 **pounds boneless skinless chicken breasts, cut into 1-inch cubes**
- 1 **tablespoon canola oil**
- 1 **jar (48 ounces) great northern beans, rinsed and drained**
- 1 **jar (16 ounces) salsa**
- 1 **can (14½ ounces) chicken broth**
- 1 **teaspoon ground cumin, optional**
- 2 **cups shredded Monterey Jack cheese**

In a large skillet, brown the chicken in the oil. Using a 4- or 5-qt. slow cooker, combine the beans, salsa, broth, cumin if desired and chicken. Cover and cook on low for 4-6 hours or until chicken is tender. Serve with cheese.

MANGO-PINEAPPLE CHICKEN TACOS

I lived in the Caribbean as a child and the fresh tropical fruits in this delectable chicken entree bring me back to my childhood.
—**LISSA NELSON** PROVO, UT

PREP: 25 MIN. • **COOK:** 5 HOURS
MAKES: 16 SERVINGS

- 2 **medium mangoes, peeled and chopped**
- 1½ **cups cubed fresh pineapple or canned pineapple chunks, drained**
- 2 **medium tomatoes, chopped**
- 1 **medium red onion, finely chopped**
- 2 **small Anaheim peppers, seeded and chopped**
- 2 **green onions, finely chopped**
- 1 **tablespoon lime juice**
- 1 **teaspoon sugar**
- 4 **pounds bone-in chicken breast halves, skin removed**
- 3 **teaspoons salt**
- ¼ **cup packed brown sugar**
- 32 **taco shells, warmed**
- ¼ **cup minced fresh cilantro**

1. In a large bowl, combine the first eight ingredients. Place chicken in a 6-qt. slow cooker; sprinkle with salt and brown sugar. Top with mango mixture. Cover and cook on low for 5-6 hours or until chicken is tender.
2. Remove chicken; cool slightly. Strain the cooking juices, reserving the mango mixture and ½ cup juices. Discard remaining juices. When cool enough to handle, remove chicken from bones; discard bones.
3. Shred the chicken with two forks. Return chicken and reserved mango mixture and cooking juices to slow cooker; heat through. Serve in taco shells; sprinkle with cilantro.
FREEZE OPTION *Freeze cooled meat mixture in freezer containers. To use, partially thaw it in the refrigerator overnight. Heat it through in a saucepan, stirring occasionally and adding a little broth if necessary.*

SLOW-COOKED STROGANOFF

I've been preparing Stroganoff in the slow cooker for more than 30 years. Once you've done it this way, you'll never cook it on the stovetop again. It's great for family gatherings or when you're hosting company.
—**KAREN HERBERT** PLACERVILLE, CA

PREP: 20 MIN. • **COOK:** 5 HOURS
MAKES: 8-10 SERVINGS

- 3 **pounds beef top round steaks**
- ½ **cup all-purpose flour**
- 1½ **teaspoons salt**
- ½ **teaspoon ground mustard**
- ⅛ **teaspoon pepper**
- 1 **medium onion, sliced and separated into rings**
- 1 **can (8 ounces) mushroom stems and pieces, drained**
- 1 **can (10½ ounces) condensed beef broth, undiluted**
- 1½ **cups (12 ounces) sour cream**
  Hot cooked noodles

1. Cut beef into thin strips. Using a shallow bowl, mix flour, salt, mustard and pepper. Add the beef in batches; toss to coat.
2. In a 5-qt. slow cooker, layer onion, mushrooms and beef. Pour broth over top. Cook, covered, on low 5-7 hours or until the meat is tender. Just before serving, stir in the sour cream. Serve with noodles.

SLOW-COOKED STROGANOFF

BREADS & ROLLS

"Please pass the bread...and pass the recipe, too!" That's what folks will say when they try any of the golden specialties found here. Shared by home bakers, these loaves, biscuits, muffins and scones are sure to turn out right.

SKILLET HERB BREAD

My grandmother, aunts and mom were all good bakers, and each had her own specialty when it came to making bread. Mom's was my favorite—she started baking this skillet bread over 40 years ago. The flavors call to mind the taste of corn bread stuffing.

—**SHIRLEY SMITH** YORBA LINDA, CA

PREP: 10 MIN. • **BAKE:** 35 MIN.
MAKES: 10 SERVINGS

- 1½ cups all-purpose flour
- 2 tablespoons sugar
- 4 teaspoons baking powder
- 1½ teaspoons salt
- 1 teaspoon rubbed sage
- 1 teaspoon dried thyme
- 1½ cups yellow cornmeal
- 1½ cups chopped celery
- 1 cup chopped onion
- 1 jar (2 ounces) chopped pimientos, drained
- 3 large eggs, beaten
- 1½ cups fat-free milk
- ⅓ cup vegetable oil

In a large bowl, combine the flour, sugar, baking powder, salt, sage and thyme. Combine cornmeal, celery, onion and pimientos; add to the dry ingredients and mix well. Add eggs, milk and oil; stir just until moistened. Pour this into a greased 10- or 11-in. ovenproof skillet. Bake at 400° for 35-45 minutes or until bread tests done. Serve warm.

★ ★ ★ ★ ★ **READER REVIEW**

"The submitter is right! This bread does taste like stuffing. I already have requests to make it again."

ISOLDA TASTEOFHOME.COM

EVELYN'S SOUR CREAM TWISTS

FREEZE IT
APPLE-RHUBARB BREAD

Rhubarb is such a jewel that I freeze it to have all year. Here's how my mother used rhubarb—in an apple bread spiced with cinnamon. I hope you like it, too!

—**LINDA TOM** SIOUX FALLS, SD

PREP: 15 MIN. • **BAKE:** 50 MIN. + COOLING
MAKES: 2 LOAVES (12 SLICES EACH)

- 4 **large eggs**
- 1½ **cups sugar**
- ½ **cup canola oil**
- 1 **teaspoon vanilla extract**
- 3 **cups all-purpose flour**
- 4½ **teaspoons baking powder**
- 1 **teaspoon salt**
- 1 **teaspoon ground cinnamon**
- 1½ **cups chopped peeled apple**
- 1½ **cups finely chopped fresh or frozen rhubarb, thawed**
- 1 **cup chopped walnuts**

1. Preheat oven to 350°. In a large bowl, whisk eggs, sugar, oil and vanilla until blended. In another bowl, whisk the flour, baking powder, salt and cinnamon. Add to egg mixture; stir just until moistened. Fold in apples, rhubarb and walnuts.
2. Transfer to two greased 8x4-in. loaf pans. Bake 50-60 minutes or until a toothpick inserted in center comes out clean. Cool in pans 10 minutes before removing to wire racks to cool.
FREEZE OPTION *Securely wrap and freeze cooled loaves in plastic wrap and foil. To use, thaw the loaves at room temperature.*
NOTE *If using frozen rhubarb, measure rhubarb while still frozen, then thaw completely. Drain in a colander, but do not press liquid out.*

EVELYN'S SOUR CREAM TWISTS

Keep some of these flaky twists stored in your freezer to serve in a pinch at breakfast, lunch or dinner. They're delectable.

—**LINDA WELCH** NORTH PLATTE, NE

PREP: 40 MIN. + CHILLING • **BAKE:** 15 MIN.
MAKES: 4 DOZEN

- 1 **package (¼ ounce) active dry yeast**
- ¼ **cup warm water (110° to 115°)**
- 3 **cups all-purpose flour**
- 1½ **teaspoons salt**
- ½ **cup cold butter**
- ½ **cup shortening**
- 2 **large eggs**
- ½ **cup sour cream**
- 3 **teaspoons vanilla extract, divided**
- 1½ **cups sugar**

1. Using a small bowl, dissolve the yeast in water. In a bowl, combine the flour and salt. Cut in the butter and shortening until the mixture resembles coarse crumbs. Stir in eggs, sour cream, 1 teaspoon vanilla and the yeast mixture; mix thoroughly. Cover and refrigerate overnight.
2. Combine the sugar and remaining vanilla; lightly sprinkle ½ cup over a pastry cloth or countertop surface. On the sugared surface, roll half of the dough into a 12x8-in. rectangle; refrigerate remaining dough. Sprinkle rolled dough with about 1 tablespoon of the sugar mixture. Fold rectangle into thirds.
3. Give the dough a quarter turn and repeat rolling, sugaring and folding two more times. Roll into a 12x8-in. rectangle. Cut into 4x1-in. strips; twist each strip two or three times. Place on chilled ungreased baking sheets. Repeat with remaining sugar mixture and dough.
4. Bake at 375° for 12-14 minutes or until lightly browned. Immediately remove the twists from the pan and cool on wire racks.

APPLE-
RHUBARB
BREAD

PUMPKIN SWIRL BREAD

PUMPKIN SWIRL BREAD

This combination of pumpkin, nuts and dates creates a flavorful bread with a beautiful golden look. The surprise inside is almost like a luscious layer of cheesecake in each slice.
—CINDY MAY TROY, MI

PREP: 15 MIN. • **BAKE:** 65 MIN. + COOLING
MAKES: 3 LOAVES (16 SLICES EACH)

FILLING
- 2 packages (8 ounces each) cream cheese, softened
- ¼ cup sugar
- 1 large egg
- 1 tablespoon milk

BREAD
- 3 cups sugar
- 1 can (15 ounces) solid-pack pumpkin
- 4 large eggs
- 1 cup canola oil
- 1 cup water
- 4 cups all-purpose flour
- 4 teaspoons pumpkin pie spice
- 2 teaspoons baking soda
- 1½ teaspoons ground cinnamon
- 1 teaspoon salt
- 1 teaspoon baking powder
- 1 teaspoon ground nutmeg
- ½ teaspoon ground cloves
- 1 cup chopped walnuts
- 1 cup raisins
- ½ cup chopped dates

OPTIONAL TOPPINGS
- 1 cup confectioners' sugar
- ¼ teaspoon vanilla extract
- 2 to 3 tablespoons 2% milk
  Additional chopped walnuts

1. Preheat the oven to 350°. Grease and flour three 8x4-in. loaf pans. In a small bowl, beat the filling ingredients until smooth.

2. Using a large bowl, beat the sugar, pumpkin, eggs, oil and water until well blended. In another bowl, whisk flour, pie spice, soda, cinnamon, salt, baking powder, nutmeg and cloves; gradually beat into pumpkin mixture. Stir in the walnuts, raisins and dates.

3. Pour half of the batter into the prepared pans, dividing evenly. Spoon filling over the batter. Cover filling completely with remaining batter.

4. Bake 65-70 minutes or until a toothpick inserted in bread portion comes out clean. Cool 10 minutes before removing from pans to wire racks to cool completely. Wrap in foil; refrigerate until serving.

5. Just before serving, if desired, in a small bowl, mix confectioners' sugar, vanilla and enough milk to reach a drizzling consistency. Drizzle over bread; sprinkle with walnuts.

FAST FIX ▸

HERB-HAPPY GARLIC BREAD

You'll love the fresh garlic and herbs in this recipe. The mild goat cheese that's sprinkled on top makes this bread extra rich.
—*TASTE OF HOME* TEST KITCHEN

START TO FINISH: 15 MIN.
MAKES: 12 SERVINGS

- ½ cup butter, softened
- ¼ cup grated Romano cheese
- 2 tablespoons minced fresh basil or 2 teaspoons dried basil
- 1 tablespoon minced fresh parsley
- 3 garlic cloves, minced
- 1 French bread baguette
- 4 ounces crumbled goat cheese

1. In a small bowl, mix the first five ingredients until blended. Cut the baguette crosswise in half; cut each piece lengthwise in half. Spread cut sides with butter mixture. Place on an ungreased baking sheet.

2. Bake, uncovered, at 425° for 7-9 minutes or until lightly toasted. Sprinkle with goat cheese; bake 1-2 minutes longer or until goat cheese is softened. Cut into slices.

FLAKY WHOLE WHEAT BISCUITS

Whole wheat flour gives these biscuits a nutty flavor. Ever since I started making them, white flour biscuits just don't taste as good! Pair them with soup or stew, or dollop on whipped cream and sweetened berries for an easy dessert.

—TRISHA KRUSE EAGLE, ID

START TO FINISH: 25 MIN.
MAKES: 10 BISCUITS

- 1 cup all-purpose flour
- 1 cup whole wheat flour
- 3 teaspoons baking powder
- 1 tablespoon brown sugar
- 1 teaspoon baking soda
- ½ teaspoon salt
- ¼ cup cold butter
- 1 cup 2% milk

1. In a large bowl, combine the first six ingredients. Cut in butter until mixture resembles coarse crumbs. Stir in milk just until moistened. Turn onto a lightly floured surface; knead 8-10 times.

2. Pat or roll out to ½-in. thickness; cut with a floured 2½-in. biscuit cutter. Place 2 in. apart on ungreased baking sheet. Bake at 425° for 8-10 minutes or until golden brown.

BUTTERMILK SUBSTITUTES

Milk and Lemon
For each cup of buttermilk, you can use 1 tablespoon lemon juice plus enough milk to measure 1 cup. Stir and let stand 5 minutes.

Powdered Buttermilk
For each cup of buttermilk, you can use ¼ cup buttermilk powder plus 1 cup water.

SOFT BUTTERMILK DINNER ROLLS

Warm, buttery dinner rolls are absolutely irresistible. I save time and use a stand mixer to make my dough.

—JENNIFER PATTERSON SHOSHONE, ID

PREP: 40 MIN. + RISING
BAKE: 20 MIN. + COOLING
MAKES: 20 SERVINGS

- 1 package (¼ ounce) active dry yeast
- ¼ cup warm water (110° to 115°)
- 1 cup plus 2 tablespoons warm buttermilk (110° to 115°), divided
- ½ cup plus 1 teaspoon softened butter, divided
- 1 large egg
- ⅓ cup sugar
- 1 teaspoon salt
- 4 cups bread flour

1. Dissolve the yeast in warm water until foamy. In a large bowl, combine 1 cup buttermilk, ½ cup butter, egg, sugar, salt and yeast mixture, then add 3 cups of flour; beat on medium speed until smooth, about 1 minute. Add the remaining flour, ¼ cup at a time, to form a soft dough.

2. Turn dough onto a lightly floured surface; knead until it is smooth and elastic, 6-8 minutes. Place in a greased bowl, turning once to grease the top. Cover it with plastic wrap and let it rise in a warm place until doubled, about 1 hour.

3. Punch down dough. Turn onto a lightly floured surface; divide and shape into 20 balls. Place in a greased 13x9-in. pan. Cover with a kitchen towel; let rise in a warm place until almost doubled, about 45 minutes.

4. Preheat oven to 350°. Brush rolls lightly with remaining buttermilk and butter. Bake until golden brown, 20-25 minutes. Cool in the pan for 20 minutes. Remove to a wire rack; serve warm.

SOFT BUTTERMILK DINNER ROLLS

OAT DINNER ROLLS

These delicious homemade rolls provide a delightful addition to any holiday or special occasion. They're simple and only call for a few ingredients.

—PATRICIA RUTHERFORD WINCHESTER, IL

PREP: 30 MIN. + RISING • **BAKE:** 20 MIN.
MAKES: 2 DOZEN

- 2⅓ cups water, divided
- 1 cup quick-cooking oats
- ⅔ cup packed brown sugar
- 3 tablespoons butter
- 1½ teaspoons salt
- 2 packages (¼ ounce each) active dry yeast
- 5 to 5¾ cups all-purpose flour

1. In a large saucepan, bring 2 cups water to a boil. Stir in the oats; reduce the heat. Simmer, uncovered, for 1 minute. Stir in brown sugar, butter, salt and remaining water.

2. Transfer to a large bowl; let stand until mixture reaches 110°-115°. Stir in the yeast. Add 3 cups flour; beat well. Add enough remaining flour to form a soft dough.

3. Turn onto a floured surface; knead until smooth and elastic, about 6-8 minutes. Place in a greased bowl; turn once to grease the top. Cover and let rise in a warm place until doubled, about 1 hour.

4. Punch dough down; shape into 24 rolls. Place on greased baking sheets. Cover and let rise until doubled, about 30 minutes.

5. Bake at 350° for 20-25 minutes or until golden brown. Remove from pan and cool on wire racks.

CRUSTY
HOMEMADE
BREAD

CRUSTY HOMEMADE BREAD

Crackling homemade bread like this makes an average day extraordinary. Enjoy this beautiful loaf as is, or stir in a few favorites like cheese, garlic, herbs and dried fruits.

—MEGUMI GARCIA MILWAUKEE, WI

PREP: 20 MIN. + RISING
BAKE: 50 MIN. + COOLING
MAKES: 1 LOAF (16 SLICES)

- 1½ teaspoons active dry yeast
- 1¾ cups water (70° to 75°)
- 3½ cups plus 1 tablespoon all-purpose flour, divided
- 2 teaspoons salt
- 1 tablespoon cornmeal or additional flour

1. In a small bowl, dissolve yeast in water. In a large bowl, mix 3½ cups flour and salt. Using a rubber spatula, stir in yeast mixture to form a soft, sticky dough. Do not knead. Cover with plastic wrap; let rise at room temperature 1 hour.

2. Punch down dough. Turn onto a lightly floured surface; pat into a 9-in. square. Fold the square into thirds, forming a 9x3-in. rectangle. Fold rectangle into thirds, forming a 3-in. square. Turn dough over; place in a greased bowl. Cover with plastic wrap; let rise at room temperature until almost doubled, about 1 hour.

3. Punch down dough and repeat folding process. Return dough to bowl; refrigerate, covered, overnight.

4. Dust bottom of a disposable foil roasting pan with cornmeal. Turn dough onto a floured surface. Knead gently 6-8 times; shape into a 6-in. round loaf. Place in prepared pan; dust top with remaining 1 tablespoon flour. Cover the pan with plastic wrap; let rise at room temperature until the dough expands to a 7½-in. loaf, about 1¼ hours.

5. Preheat the oven to 500°. Using a sharp knife, make a slash (¼ in. deep) across top of loaf. Cover pan tightly with foil. Bake on lowest oven rack 25 minutes.

6. Reduce the oven setting to 450°. Remove the foil; bake bread 25-30 minutes longer or until deep golden brown. Remove the loaf to a wire rack to cool.

FOR CHEDDAR CHEESE BREAD
Prepare the dough as directed. After refrigerating dough overnight, knead in 4 ounces diced sharp cheddar cheese before shaping.

FOR RUSTIC CRANBERRY & ORANGE BREAD *Prepare dough as directed. After refrigerating dough overnight, knead in 1 cup of dried cranberries and 4 teaspoons grated orange peel before shaping.*

FOR GARLIC & OREGANO BREAD
Prepare the dough as directed. After refrigerating the dough overnight, microwave ½ cup of peeled and quartered garlic cloves with ¼ cup 2% milk on high for 45 seconds. Drain garlic, discarding milk; knead garlic and 2 tablespoons of minced fresh oregano into dough before shaping.

★ ★ ★ ★ ★ **READER REVIEW**

"Foolproof! And easy, too. This homemade bread recipe is the perfect one to start with if you've never made bread before. It's also perfect if you are an experienced baker."

LINDAS_WI TASTEOFHOME.COM

ARIZONA CORN BREAD

Unlike other corn breads, this one uses yeast. The oil and sour cream make the loaf tender, and it has a bit of bite from the two jalapenos.

—MARGARET PACHE MESA, AZ

PREP: 20 MIN. + RISING • **BAKE:** 30 MIN.
MAKES: 2 LOAVES (16 SLICES EACH)

- 1 **cup cornmeal**
- 2 **tablespoons sugar**
- 2 **packages (¼ ounce each) active dry yeast**
- 1 **teaspoon salt**
- ½ **teaspoon baking soda**
- ¼ **teaspoon pepper**
- 1 **cup sour cream**
- ½ **cup canola oil**
- ½ **cup chopped green onions**
- 2 **large eggs**
- 1¼ **cups shredded pepper jack cheese**
- 1 **cup cream-style corn**
- 2 **jalapeno peppers, seeded and chopped**
- 5 **to 6 cups all-purpose flour**
  Additional cornmeal
  Melted butter

1. In a large bowl, combine the first six ingredients; set aside. Using a saucepan, heat the sour cream, oil and onions to 120°-130°. Add to cornmeal mixture; beat until blended. Beat in eggs, cheese, corn and jalapenos. Stir in enough flour to form a stiff dough.
2. Turn onto a floured surface; knead until smooth and elastic, 6-8 minutes. Place in a greased bowl, turning once to grease the top. Cover and let rise in a warm place until doubled, for about 1 hour.

3. Punch dough down. Turn onto a lightly floured surface; divide in half. Shape into two loaves. Grease two 9x5-in. loaf pans; dust with additional cornmeal. Place loaves seam side down in prepared pans. Cover and let rise until doubled, about 30 minutes.
4. Brush butter over loaves. Bake at 375° for 30-35 minutes or until golden brown; cover loosely with foil if top browns too quickly. Remove from pans to wire racks to cool.
NOTE *Wear disposable gloves when cutting hot peppers; the oils can burn skin. Avoid touching your face.*

EMPIRE STATE MUFFINS

These muffins are loaded with fruit and nuts. They're perfect to share when the autumn apple harvest is abundant.

—BEVERLY COLLINS NORTH SYRACUSE, NY

PREP: 15 MIN. • **BAKE:** 20 MIN.
MAKES: 18 MUFFINS

- 2 **cups shredded tart apples**
- 1⅓ **cups sugar**
- 1 **cup chopped fresh or frozen cranberries**
- 1 **cup shredded carrots**
- 1 **cup chopped walnuts or pecans**
- 2½ **cups all-purpose flour**
- 1 **tablespoon baking powder**
- 2 **teaspoons baking soda**
- ½ **teaspoon salt**
- 2 **teaspoons ground cinnamon**
- 2 **large eggs, lightly beaten**
- ½ **cup canola oil**

1. In a large bowl, combine apples and sugar. Gently fold in cranberries, carrots and nuts. Combine the dry ingredients; add to bowl. Mix well to moisten dry ingredients. Combine eggs and oil; stir into apple mixture.
2. Fill 18 greased muffin cups two-thirds full. Bake at 375° for 20-25 minutes. Cool for 5 minutes before removing muffins from tins.

ARIZONA CORN BREAD

DELICIOUS ALMOND BRAIDS

Similar to an almond crescent, this coffee cake is light and flaky, with a rich almond center. It's so versatile that you can serve it for dessert, breakfast or brunch. It will taste as if it was made from scratch at a bakery, yet the packaged puff pastry makes the recipe quick and easy.
—**GINA IDONE** STATEN ISLAND, NY

PREP: 25 MIN. • **BAKE:** 30 MIN. + COOLING
MAKES: 2 BRAIDS (6 SLICES EACH)

- 1 **package (7 ounces) almond paste**
- ½ **cup butter**
- ½ **cup sugar**
- 1 **large egg**
- 2 **tablespoons all-purpose flour**
- 1 **package (17.3 ounces) frozen puff pastry, thawed**

GLAZE
- ¾ **cup plus 1 tablespoon confectioners' sugar**
- 2 **tablespoons 2% milk**
- ½ **teaspoon almond extract**
- ¼ **cup sliced almonds, toasted**

1. Place the almond paste, butter and sugar in a food processor; cover and pulse until chopped. Add the egg and flour; process until smooth.
2. Unfold puff pastry sheets onto a greased baking sheet. Spread half of the filling mixture down the center third of one pastry sheet. On each side, cut eight strips about 3½ in. into the center. Then, starting at one end, fold alternating strips at an angle across filling. Pinch ends to seal. Repeat with remaining pastry and filling. Bake at 375° for 30-35 minutes or until golden brown. Remove to a wire rack.
3. For glaze, combine confectioners' sugar, milk and almond extract. Drizzle over braids; sprinkle with almonds. Cut into slices.

CHOCOLATE CHIP-
CRANBERRY SCONES

FREEZE IT | FAST FIX
CHOCOLATE CHIP-CRANBERRY SCONES

My daughter started making these as a healthier alternative to cookies, since we enjoy cookies of any kind. For a more citrusy flavor, use cranberries flavored with orange.
—**NICHOLE JONES** IDAHO FALLS, ID

START TO FINISH: 30 MIN.
MAKES: 1 DOZEN

- 2 **cups all-purpose flour**
- 3 **tablespoons brown sugar**
- 2 **teaspoons baking powder**
- 1 **teaspoon grated orange peel**
- ½ **teaspoon salt**
- ½ **teaspoon baking soda**
- ¼ **cup cold butter**
- 1 **cup plain yogurt**
- 1 **large egg yolk**
- ½ **cup dried cranberries**
- ½ **cup semisweet chocolate chips**

1. Preheat oven to 400°. In a large bowl, whisk the first six ingredients. Cut in the butter until the mixture resembles coarse crumbs. In another bowl, whisk the yogurt and egg yolk; stir into the crumb mixture just until moistened. Stir in the cranberries and chocolate chips.
2. Turn onto a floured surface; knead gently 10 times. Pat the dough into an 8-in. circle. Cut into 12 wedges. Place wedges on a baking sheet coated with cooking spray. Bake 10-12 minutes or until golden brown. Serve warm.
FREEZE OPTION *Freeze the cooled scones in resealable plastic freezer bags. To use, thaw the scones at room temperature or, if desired, microwave each scone on high for 20-30 seconds or until heated through.*

HONEY WHOLE WHEAT ROLLS

HONEY WHOLE WHEAT ROLLS

There's nothing quite like a warm yeast roll fresh from the oven. I bake these rolls often, especially when I'm making soup or stew.
—**CELECIA STOUP** HOBART, OK

PREP: 20 MIN. + RISING • **BAKE:** 20 MIN.
MAKES: 15 ROLLS

- 2 packages (¼ ounce each) active dry yeast
- 1 cup warm water (110° to 115°)
- ¼ cup butter, melted
- ¼ cup honey
- 1 large egg
- ¾ cup whole wheat flour
- ½ cup old-fashioned oats
- 1 teaspoon salt
- 2½ to 3 cups all-purpose flour
  Additional melted butter, optional

1. In a small bowl, dissolve yeast in warm water. In a large bowl, combine butter, honey, egg, whole wheat flour, oats, salt, yeast mixture and 1 cup all-purpose flour; beat on medium speed until smooth. Stir in enough remaining flour to form a soft dough.
2. Turn dough onto a floured surface; knead until smooth and elastic, about 6-8 minutes. Place in a greased bowl, turning once to grease the top. Cover with plastic wrap and let rise in warm place until doubled, about 1 hour.
3. Punch down dough; shape into 15 balls. Place in a greased 13x9-in. pan. Cover with a kitchen towel; let rise in warm place until doubled, about 45 minutes. Preheat oven to 375°.
4. Bake until golden brown, about 20 minutes. If desired, brush with additional butter. Serve warm.

CINNAMON-SUGAR SCONES

I turn to these lighter-than-air scones whenever I need to bake something for an event. They're always a hit!

—KATHY MONAHAN JACKSONVILLE, FL

PREP: 20 MIN. • **BAKE:** 20 MIN.
MAKES: 8 SCONES

- 3 cups biscuit baking mix
- ¼ cup sugar
- ½ cup vanilla yogurt
- ⅓ cup 2% milk
- 1 tablespoon vanilla extract
- 1 cup cinnamon baking chips or semisweet chocolate chips
  Cinnamon sugar or coarse sugar

1. Preheat oven to 375°. In a large bowl, mix baking mix and sugar. In another bowl, whisk yogurt, milk and vanilla; stir into dry ingredients just until moistened. Stir in chips. Turn onto a lightly floured surface; knead gently 10 times.
2. Pat into a 9-in. circle. Sprinkle with cinnamon sugar. Cut into eight wedges. Place wedges on an ungreased baking sheet. Bake 20-25 minutes or until golden brown. Serve warm.

★ ★ ★ ★ ★ 5 STAR TIP

You can buy bottles of prepared cinnamon-sugar in the spice aisle of your grocery store. Or make your own by combining ½ cup sugar and 1 tablespoon ground cinnamon. Store in an airtight container to use in a variety of recipes or to sprinkle over buttered toast at breakfast.

WALNUT ZUCCHINI MUFFINS

FREEZE IT
WALNUT ZUCCHINI MUFFINS

Shredded zucchini adds moisture to these tender muffins which are dotted with raisins and chopped walnuts. If you have a surplus of zucchini in summer, this is a tasty way to put it to good use.

—HARRIET STICHTER MILFORD, IN

PREP: 20 MIN. • **BAKE:** 20 MIN.
MAKES: 1 DOZEN

- 1 cup all-purpose flour
- ¾ cup whole wheat flour
- ⅔ cup packed brown sugar
- 2 teaspoons baking powder
- ¾ teaspoon ground cinnamon
- ½ teaspoon salt
- 2 large eggs
- ¾ cup 2% milk
- ½ cup butter, melted
- 1 cup shredded zucchini
- 1 cup chopped walnuts
- ½ cup raisins

1. Preheat oven to 375°. In a large bowl, whisk the first six ingredients. In another bowl, whisk eggs, milk and melted butter until blended. Add to the flour mixture; stir just until moistened. Fold in zucchini, walnuts and raisins.
2. Fill greased muffin cups three-fourths full. Bake 18-20 minutes or until a toothpick inserted in center comes out clean. Cool 5 minutes before removing from pan to a wire rack. Serve warm.

FREEZE OPTION *Freeze cooled muffins in resealable plastic freezer bags. To use, thaw the muffins at room temperature or, if desired, microwave each muffin on high for 20-30 seconds or until heated through.*

HOW TO CUT BISCUITS

Turn dough onto a lightly floured surface and knead gently for as many times as the recipe directs. Be careful not to overknead, as it will keep the dough from rising.

Roll dough evenly to ¾-in. thickness.

Cut dough with a floured biscuit cutter, using a straight downward motion. Do not twist the cutter; twisting will make the layers stick together and the biscuits will not rise as high.

Place biscuits on a greased baking sheet. Place 2 in. apart to create biscuits with crusty sides, or almost touching for softer-sided biscuits.

HAM & GREEN ONION BISCUITS

HAM & GREEN ONION BISCUITS

I added a bit of personality to my grandma's biscuit recipe. When I make them with my kids, it feels like she's with us.
—**AMY CHASE** VANDERHOOF, BC

PREP: 20 MIN. • **BAKE:** 10 MIN.
MAKES: ABOUT 1 DOZEN

- 2 **cups all-purpose flour**
- 3 **teaspoons baking powder**
- 1 **teaspoon sugar**
- ¼ **teaspoon garlic salt**
  Dash pepper
- 6 **tablespoons cold butter, cubed**
- 1 **cup finely chopped fully cooked ham**
- 2 **green onions, chopped**
- ¾ **cup 2% milk**

1. Preheat oven to 450°. In a large bowl, whisk the first five ingredients. Cut in butter until mixture resembles coarse crumbs. Stir in the ham and green onions. Add the milk; stir just until moistened.
2. Turn dough onto a lightly floured surface; knead gently 8-10 times. Pat or roll dough to ½-in. thickness; cut with a floured 2½-in. biscuit cutter. Place 2 in. apart on an ungreased baking sheet. Bake 10-12 minutes or until golden brown. Serve warm.

★ ★ ★ ★ ★ **5 STAR TIP**
For biscuits to bake properly, arrange your oven rack so that the baking sheet is in the center of the oven. Be sure to use a hot oven (425°-450°) and a baking time of 10-12 minutes for standard-size biscuits. Insulated baking sheets will not allow the bottom of biscuits to brown like regular baking sheets do.

LOUISIANA PECAN BACON BREAD

LOUISIANA PECAN BACON BREAD

One Christmas, our babysitter brought gifts for my daughter and a basket of goodies, including pecan bread. When I make this bread, I remember her kind soul.
—**MARINA CASTLE KELLEY**
CANYON COUNTRY, CA

PREP: 20 MIN. • **BAKE:** 50 MIN. + COOLING
MAKES: 1 LOAF (16 SLICES)

- 6 **bacon strips, chopped**
- 6 **ounces cream cheese, softened**
- ⅓ **cup sugar**
- 1 **large egg**
- 2 **cups all-purpose flour**
- 2½ **teaspoons baking powder**
- ½ **teaspoon salt**
- ¾ **cup 2% milk**
- 1 **cup chopped pecans**
- ¼ **cup finely chopped onion**
- ¼ **cup chopped green pepper**

1. Preheat oven to 350°. In a large skillet, cook bacon over medium-low heat until crisp, stirring occasionally. Remove with a slotted spoon; drain on paper towels. Reserve drippings (about 2 tablespoons); cool slightly.
2. In a large bowl, beat cream cheese, sugar and reserved drippings until smooth. Beat in egg. In another bowl, whisk flour, baking powder and salt; add to the cream cheese mixture alternately with milk, beating well after each addition. Fold in pecans, onion, pepper and bacon. Transfer to a greased 9x5-in. loaf pan.
3. Bake 50-60 minutes or until a toothpick inserted in center comes out clean. Cool in pan 10 minutes before removing to a wire rack to cool.
FREEZE OPTION *Securely wrap cooled loaves in plastic wrap and foil, then freeze. To use, thaw the loaves in the refrigerator.*

VEGETABLE & CHEESE FOCACCIA

My family eats up this flavorful bread as fast as I can make it. Sometimes I add different herbs, red onion or crumbled bacon.

—MARY CASS BALTIMORE, MD

PREP: 20 MIN. + RISING • **BAKE:** 30 MIN.
MAKES: 15 SERVINGS

- 1 **cup water (70° to 80°)**
- 4½ **teaspoons olive oil**
- 4½ **teaspoons sugar**
- 2 **teaspoons dried oregano**
- 1¼ **teaspoons salt**
- 3¾ **cups bread flour**
- 1½ **teaspoons active dry yeast**

TOPPING

- 1 **tablespoon olive oil**
- 1 **tablespoon dried basil**
- 2 **medium tomatoes, thinly sliced**
- 1 **medium onion, thinly sliced**
- 1 **cup frozen chopped broccoli, thawed**
- ¼ **teaspoon salt**
- ¼ **teaspoon pepper**
- ¾ **cup grated Parmesan cheese**
- 1 **cup shredded part-skim mozzarella cheese**

1. In bread machine pan, place the first seven ingredients in the order suggested by manufacturer. Select dough setting (check dough after 5 minutes of mixing; if needed, add 1-2 tablespoons of water or flour).

2. When cycle is completed, turn dough onto a lightly floured surface. Punch the dough down. Roll into a 13x9-in. rectangle; transfer it to a 13x9-in. baking dish coated with cooking spray.

3. For topping, brush dough with olive oil; sprinkle with basil. Layer with the tomatoes, onion and broccoli; sprinkle with the salt, pepper and Parmesan cheese. Cover and let rise in a warm place until doubled, about 30 minutes.

4. Bake at 350° for 20 minutes. Then sprinkle with mozzarella cheese; bake 10-15 minutes longer or until golden brown and cheese is melted.

VEGETABLE & CHEESE FOCACCIA

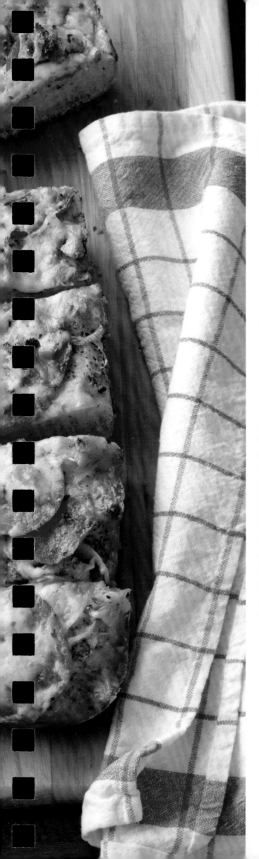

BLUEBERRY BRUNCH LOAF

I make special breakfasts on the weekend for my husband and children. This recipe's glaze makes the already delicious blueberry bread even tastier with a hint of orange.

—**JEAN NIETERT** CLAREMONT, SD

PREP: 15 MIN. • **BAKE:** 50 MIN. + COOLING
MAKES: 1 LOAF

- ¼ **cup butter, softened**
- ¾ **cup packed brown sugar**
- 1 **large egg**
- 1 **tablespoon grated orange peel**
- 2¼ **cups all-purpose flour**
- 1 **tablespoon baking powder**
- ½ **teaspoon salt**
- ½ **cup whole milk**
- ¼ **cup orange juice**
- 1 **cup fresh or frozen blueberries**

GLAZE

- ½ **cup confectioners' sugar**
- 2 **teaspoons butter, softened**
- ½ **teaspoon grated orange peel**
- 1 **to 1½ tablespoons whole milk**

1. In a bowl, cream butter and brown sugar. Stir in the egg and orange peel. Combine the flour, baking powder and salt; add to the creamed mixture alternately with the milk and juice, mixing well after each addition. Fold in blueberries. Pour into a greased 9x5-in. loaf pan.

2. Bake at 350° for 50-55 minutes or until the bread tests done. Cool in the pan for 10 minutes before removing to a wire rack.

3. For glaze, combine sugar, butter and orange peel. Gradually add milk until glaze is of spreading consistency; drizzle over warm bread.

FREEZE IT

CINNAMON RAISIN QUICK BREAD

Cinnamon and raisins bring heartwarming flavor to these mildly sweet loaves. Slices are ideal for on-the-go breakfasts, quick snacks or anytime treats.

—**FLO BURTNETT** GAGE, OK

PREP: 15 MIN. • **BAKE:** 55 MIN. + COOLING
MAKES: 2 LOAVES (12 SLICES EACH)

- 4 **cups all-purpose flour**
- 2 **cups sugar, divided**
- 2 **teaspoons baking soda**
- 1 **teaspoon salt**
- 2 **large eggs**
- 2 **cups buttermilk**
- ½ **cup canola oil**
- ½ **cup raisins**
- 3 **teaspoons ground cinnamon**

1. Preheat oven to 350°. In a large bowl, combine flour, 1½ cups sugar, soda and salt. In a small bowl, whisk eggs, buttermilk and oil. Stir into dry ingredients just until moistened. Fold in raisins. Combine cinnamon and remaining sugar; set aside.

2. Spoon half the batter into two greased 8x4-in. loaf pans. Sprinkle with half of the reserved cinnamon sugar; repeat layers. Cut through batter with a knife to swirl.

3. Bake 55-60 minutes or until a toothpick inserted in center comes out clean. Cool 10 minutes before removing from pans to wire racks.

FREEZE OPTION *Wrap cooled bread in foil and freeze for up to 3 months. To use, thaw at room temperature.*

MOIST & SWEET CORN BREAD

MINI SWISS CHEESE LOAVES

I usually make these tender little loaves in the morning, so they're ready to eat at lunchtime. There's nothing better than a sandwich prepared with homemade bread.

—HELEN WANAMAKER VAIL GLENSIDE, PA

PREP: 25 MIN. + RISING
BAKE: 25 MIN. + COOLING
MAKES: 4 MINI LOAVES

- 1 package (¼ ounce) active dry yeast
- ½ cup warm water (110° to 115°)
- 1 cup (8 ounces) sour cream
- 2 tablespoons sugar
- 1 teaspoon salt
- ¼ teaspoon baking soda
- 1 large egg
- 2⅓ cups all-purpose flour
- 1 cup shredded Swiss cheese
- 2 teaspoons sesame seeds

1. In a large bowl, dissolve yeast in warm water. Add the sour cream, sugar, salt, baking soda, egg and 1⅓ cups flour. Beat on medium for 3 minutes. Stir in Swiss cheese and remaining flour. Do not knead.
2. Spread batter into four greased 5¾x3x2-in. loaf pans. Sprinkle with the sesame seeds. Cover and let rise in a warm place until doubled, about 45 minutes.
3. Bake at 350° for 25-30 minutes or until golden brown. Remove from pans to wire racks to cool.

★ ★ ★ ★ ★ **5 STAR TIP**
Cool unsliced yeast bread completely before placing in an airtight container or resealable plastic bag. Yeast bread will stay fresh at room temperature for 2 to 3 days. Bread with cream cheese or other perishable ingredients should be stored in the refrigerator. For longer storage, freeze the bread in an airtight container or resealable plastic bag for up to 3 months.

MOIST & SWEET CORN BREAD

We prefer good old Southern corn bread with our beans, but sometimes we want it sweeter. Here's a sweet version to hold up the butter.

—STACEY FEATHER JAY, OK

PREP: 10 MIN. • **BAKE:** 25 MIN.
MAKES: 15 SERVINGS

- 2½ cups all-purpose flour
- 1½ cups cornmeal
- 1 cup sugar
- 4 teaspoons baking powder
- 1½ teaspoons salt
- ¾ cup shortening
- 2 large eggs
- 2½ cups whole milk

1. Preheat oven to 400°. In a large bowl, combine first five ingredients. Cut in the shortening until mixture resembles coarse crumbs. In another bowl, whisk eggs and milk; stir into crumb mixture just until moistened.
2. Pour into a greased 13x9-in. baking pan. Bake 25-30 minutes or until a toothpick inserted in center comes out clean. Serve warm.

NO-KNEAD KNOT ROLLS

My mom, Velma Perkins, served these light, golden rolls when I was growing up on our Iowa farm. They pair well with any entree and they're quick to prep since they require no kneading. The dough rises in the refrigerator overnight, so there's no last-minute fuss before popping them in the oven.

—**TONI HILSCHER** OMAHA, NE

PREP: 25 MIN. + RISING • **BAKE:** 10 MIN.
MAKES: 4 DOZEN

- 2 **packages (¼ ounce each) active dry yeast**
- 2 **cups warm water (110° to 115°)**
- ½ **cup sugar**
- 2 **teaspoons salt**
- 6 **to 6½ cups all-purpose flour**
- 1 **large egg**
- ½ **cup shortening**
- ½ **cup butter, softened**

1. In a large bowl, dissolve the yeast in warm water. Add the sugar, salt and 2 cups flour. Beat on medium speed for 2 minutes. Beat in the egg and shortening. Stir in enough of the remaining flour to form a soft dough (do not knead it). Then cover and refrigerate overnight.

2. Punch the dough down and divide into four portions; roll each portion into a 14x12-in. rectangle. Spread 2 tablespoons butter over the dough. Fold in half lengthwise; cut into 12 strips. Tie each strip into a knot; tuck and pinch ends under. Place 2 in. apart on greased baking sheets. Repeat with remaining dough.

3. Cover and let rise until doubled, about 1 hour. Bake at 400° for 10-12 minutes or until golden brown. Remove to a wire rack to cool.

NO-KNEAD
KNOT ROLLS

TENDER CRESCENT ROLLS

My family's holiday meal consists of different soups and breads. These crescents are a favorite during that special dinner.

—BONNIE MYERS CALLAWAY, NE

PREP: 45 MIN. + RISING
BAKE: 10 MIN./BATCH
MAKES: 4 DOZEN

- 2 envelopes (¼ ounce each) active dry yeast
- 1 cup warm water (110° to 115°)
- 1 cup warm 2% milk (110° to 115°)
- 3 large eggs
- ½ cup sugar
- 6 tablespoons shortening
- 1 teaspoon salt
- 6½ to 7 cups all-purpose flour

1. In a small bowl, dissolve yeast in warm water. In a large bowl, combine the milk, eggs, sugar, shortening, salt, yeast mixture and 3 cups flour; beat on medium speed for 3 minutes until smooth. Stir in enough of remaining flour to form a soft dough (the dough will be sticky).

2. Turn dough onto a floured surface; knead until smooth and elastic, about 6-8 minutes. Place in a greased bowl, turning once to grease the top. Cover the bowl with plastic wrap and let the dough rise in a warm place until it has doubled, about 1 hour.

3. Punch down the dough. Turn it onto a lightly floured surface; divide into four portions. Roll each portion into a 12-in. circle; cut each into 12 wedges. Roll up wedges from the wide ends. Place 2 in. apart on greased baking sheets, point side down; curve to form crescents.

4. Cover with kitchen towels; let rise in a warm place until doubled, about 30 minutes. Preheat the oven to 350°.

5. Bake 8-10 minutes or until golden brown. Remove from pans to wire racks; serve warm.

CARAWAY SEED RYE BREAD

It was probably 45 years ago when my mother first served this bread. Today, every time I bake it, I get nostalgic for those days and all of that delicious food!

—MILLIE FEATHER BARODA, MI

PREP: 20 MIN. + RISING • **BAKE:** 25 MIN.
MAKES: 2 LOAVES

- 2 packages (¼ ounce each) active dry yeast
- 2 cups warm water (110° to 115°), divided
- ¼ cup packed brown sugar
- 1 tablespoon caraway seeds
- 1 tablespoon canola oil
- 2 teaspoons salt
- 2½ cups rye flour
- 2¾ to 3¼ cups all-purpose flour, divided

1. In a large bowl, dissolve the yeast in ½ cup warm water. Add brown sugar, caraway, oil, salt and remaining water; mix well. Stir in rye flour and 1 cup all-purpose flour; beat until smooth. Add enough remaining all-purpose flour to form a soft dough.

2. Turn onto a floured surface; knead until smooth and elastic, 6-8 minutes. Place in a greased bowl, turning once to grease top. Cover bowl and let the dough rise in a warm place until it has doubled, about 1 hour.

3. Punch dough down; divide in half. Shape each half into a ball; place in two greased 8-in. round baking pans or ovenproof skillets. Flatten balls to a 6-in. diameter. Cover and let rise until nearly doubled, about 30 minutes. Bake at 375° for 25-30 minutes or until golden brown.

TENDER CRESCENT ROLLS

CARAWAY SEED RYE BREAD

BUTTONS & BOWS

FREEZE IT FAST FIX

BUTTONS & BOWS

A biscuit mix hurries along these nutmeg-spiced buttons and bows. This recipe remains a Saturday morning favorite at our house. Serve the sugar-coated treats with hot coffee for dunking.

—MARCIE HOLLADAY IRVING, TX

START TO FINISH: 30 MIN.
MAKES: 1 DOZEN BUTTONS AND BOWS

- 2 **cups biscuit/baking mix**
- 2 **tablespoons plus ¼ cup sugar, divided**
- 1 **teaspoon ground nutmeg**
- ⅛ **teaspoon ground cinnamon**
- 1 **large egg, beaten**
- ⅓ **cup 2% milk**
- ¼ **cup butter, melted**

1. In a large bowl, combine the biscuit mix, 2 tablespoons sugar, nutmeg and cinnamon. Combine the egg and milk; stir into the dry ingredients just until the mixture is moistened.

2. Turn it onto a heavily floured surface; knead 5-6 times. Roll out to ¼-in. thickness. Cut with a floured 2½-in. doughnut cutter; set centers aside for buttons.

3. For bows, twist each circle to form a figure eight; place them on a greased baking sheet. Bake at 400° for 8-10 minutes or until golden brown. Place buttons on another greased baking sheet. Bake for 6-7 minutes.

4. Brush tops of buttons and bows with butter; sprinkle with remaining sugar. Remove from pans to wire racks. Serve warm.

FREEZE OPTION *Freeze cooled biscuits in resealable plastic freezer bags, putting the bows in one bag and buttons in another. To use, place the bows on one baking sheet and the buttons on another. Heat in preheated 350° oven about 6-8 minutes for bows and 2-4 minutes for buttons or until heated through.*

⑤ INGREDIENTS

VIRGINIA BOX BREAD

When I lived in the South, someone was kind enough to share the recipe for this melt-in-your-mouth bread. Cutting the dough in the baking pan lets you easily separate the rolls for serving. My family devours these tender treats as soon as they come out of the oven!

—THELMA RICHARDSON LA CROSSE, WI

PREP: 20 MIN. + RISING • **BAKE:** 20 MIN.
MAKES: 16 SERVINGS

- 1 package (¼ ounce) active dry yeast
- ⅔ cup warm water (110° to 115°)
- 2 large eggs, lightly beaten
- 5 tablespoons butter, melted and cooled
- 2 tablespoons sugar
- 1 teaspoon salt
- 3¼ to 3¾ cups all-purpose flour

1. In a large bowl, dissolve yeast in warm water. Add the eggs, butter, sugar, salt and 2 cups flour; beat until smooth. Add enough remaining flour to form a soft dough.

2. Turn onto a floured surface; knead until smooth and elastic, about 6-8 minutes. Place in a greased bowl, turning once to grease top. Cover and let rise in a warm place until doubled, about 1½ hours.

3. Punch dough down. On a lightly floured surface, roll the dough into a 13x9-in. rectangle. Transfer it to a greased 13x9-in. baking pan. Using a sharp knife, cut dough into 16 pieces. Cover and let rise until doubled, about 30 minutes. Preheat oven to 375°.

4. Bake 20 minutes or until golden brown. To serve, separate into rolls.

CHEESE-FILLED GARLIC ROLLS

To change up plain old dinner rolls, I added mozzarella. Now my family wants them at every gathering.

—ROSALIE FITTERY PHILADELPHIA, PA

PREP: 20 MIN. + RISING • **BAKE:** 15 MIN.
MAKES: 2 DOZEN

- 1 loaf (1 pound) frozen bread dough, thawed
- 24 cubes part-skim mozzarella cheese (¾ inch each), about 10 ounces
- 3 tablespoons butter, melted
- 2 teaspoons minced fresh parsley
- 1 garlic clove, minced
- ½ teaspoon Italian seasoning
- ½ teaspoon crushed red pepper flakes
- 2 tablespoons grated Parmigiano-Reggiano cheese

1. Divide the dough into 24 portions. Shape each portion around a cheese cube to cover completely; pinch to seal. Put each roll in a greased muffin cup, seam side down. Cover cups with kitchen towels; let rise in a warm place until doubled, about 30 minutes. Preheat oven to 350°.

2. In a small bowl, mix butter, parsley, garlic, Italian seasoning and pepper flakes. Brush over rolls; sprinkle with cheese. Bake 15-18 minutes or until golden brown.

3. Cool 5 minutes before removing from pans. Serve warm.

RHUBARB SCONES

RHUBARB SCONES

My grandfather grows rhubarb and gives us a generous supply of his harvest. With tartness similar to that of a cranberry, rhubarb is perfect for tossing into a scone.
—**DANIELLE ULAM** HOOKSTOWN, PA

PREP: 30 MIN. • **BAKE:** 20 MIN.
MAKES: 16 SCONES

- 1¼ cups whole wheat pastry flour
- 1¼ cups all-purpose flour
- ½ cup sugar
- 1 tablespoon baking powder
- 1 teaspoon ground cardamom
- ½ teaspoon salt
- ½ cup cold unsalted butter, cubed
- 1½ cups finely chopped fresh or frozen rhubarb, thawed (3-4 stalks)
- ½ cup heavy whipping cream
- ¼ cup fat-free milk
- 1 teaspoon vanilla extract
  Coarse sugar

1. Preheat oven to 400°. In a large bowl, whisk the first six ingredients. Cut in butter until mixture resembles coarse crumbs. Add the rhubarb; toss to coat.
2. In another bowl, whisk cream, milk and vanilla; stir into crumb mixture just until moistened.
3. Turn onto a floured surface; knead gently 4-5 times. Divide dough in half; pat into two 6-in. circles. Cut each into eight wedges. Place the wedges on parchment paper-lined baking sheets; sprinkle with coarse sugar. Bake 18-22 minutes or until golden brown. Serve them warm.
NOTE *If using frozen rhubarb, measure rhubarb while still frozen, then thaw completely. Drain in a colander, but do not press liquid out.*

ALMOND & CRANBERRY COCONUT BREAD

This is an all-around fantastic bread for any season, but the red bursts of cranberry lend a lovely look for Thanksgiving or Christmas.

—ROSEMARY JOHNSON IRONDALE, AL

PREP: 20 MIN. • **BAKE:** 1 HOUR + COOLING
MAKES: 2 LOAVES (16 SLICES EACH)

- 2 cups flaked coconut
- 1 cup slivered almonds
- 1 cup butter, softened
- 1 cup sugar
- 4 large eggs
- 1 cup (8 ounces) vanilla yogurt
- 1 teaspoon almond extract
- 4½ cups all-purpose flour
- 3 teaspoons baking powder
- ½ teaspoon salt
- ½ teaspoon baking soda
- 1 can (15 ounces) cream of coconut
- 1 cup dried cranberries

1. Place coconut and almonds in an ungreased 15x10x1-in. pan. Bake at 350° for 10-15 minutes or until lightly toasted, stirring occasionally. Cool.
2. In a large bowl, cream butter and sugar until light and fluffy. Add eggs, one at a time, beating well after each addition. Beat in yogurt and extract until blended. Combine the flour, baking powder, salt and baking soda. Add to creamed mixture alternately with cream of coconut, beating well after each addition. Then fold in the cranberries, coconut and almonds.
3. Transfer to two greased, floured 9x5-in. loaf pans. Bake at 350° for 60-70 minutes or until a toothpick inserted near the center comes out clean. Cool for 10 minutes before removing from pans to wire racks to cool completely.

BASIC BANANA MUFFINS

FAST FIX
BASIC BANANA MUFFINS

These muffins go over well with kids and adults alike. Not only are they loaded with big banana flavor, they're ready in just half an hour. Toss in walnuts for a little crunch.

—LORNA GREENE HARRINGTON, ME

START TO FINISH: 30 MIN.
MAKES: 1 DOZEN

- 1½ cups all-purpose flour
- 1 cup sugar
- 1 teaspoon baking soda
- ½ teaspoon salt
- 3 medium ripe bananas
- 1 large egg
- ⅓ cup vegetable oil
- 1 teaspoon vanilla extract

1. In a large bowl, combine the dry ingredients. In another bowl, mash the bananas. Add egg, oil and vanilla; mix well. Stir into the dry ingredients just until moistened. Fill greased or paper-lined muffin cups half full.
2. Bake at 375° for 18-22 minutes or until a toothpick inserted near the center comes out clean. Cool for 10 minutes; remove from pan to a wire rack to cool completely.

CRANBERRY SWEET
POTATO MUFFINS

CRANBERRY SWEET POTATO MUFFINS

Sweet potatoes, cranberries and cinnamon give seasonal appeal to these cheery muffins. I recommend them for a change-of-pace treat with a meal, packed into a lunch box or enjoyed as a snack.
—**DIANE MUSIL** LYONS, IL

PREP: 20 MIN. • **BAKE:** 20 MIN. + COOLING
MAKES: 1 DOZEN

- 1½ cups all-purpose flour
- ½ cup sugar
- 2 teaspoons baking powder
- ¾ teaspoon salt
- ½ teaspoon ground cinnamon
- ½ teaspoon ground nutmeg
- 1 large egg
- ½ cup milk
- ½ cup cold mashed sweet potatoes (without added butter or milk)
- ¼ cup butter, melted
- 1 cup chopped fresh or frozen cranberries
  Cinnamon-sugar

1. In a large bowl, combine the flour, sugar, baking powder, salt, cinnamon and nutmeg. In a small bowl, combine the egg, milk, sweet potatoes and butter; stir into dry ingredients just until moistened. Fold in cranberries.
2. Fill 12 greased or paper-lined muffin cups half full. Sprinkle with cinnamon-sugar. Bake at 375° for 18-22 minutes or until a toothpick inserted in muffins comes out clean. Cool 10 minutes before removing from pan to a wire rack. Serve warm.

★ ★ ★ ★ ★ **READER REVIEW**

"A great change-of-pace, seasonal muffin. All sorts of good flavors going on, with holiday spice, tart cranberry and a sweet sugar topping."

GRAMMYDEBBIE TASTEOFHOME.COM

A BIT NUTTY BOSTON BROWN BREAD

A BIT NUTTY BOSTON BROWN BREAD

Hearty and dense, my homemade Boston brown bread features hazelnuts that provide a delightfully nutty taste. Thick slices pair well with just about anything, from soups and stews to roasts and casseroles.
—**LORRAINE CALAND** SHUNIAH, ON

PREP: 30 MIN. • **BAKE:** 45 MIN. + COOLING
MAKES: 2 LOAVES (12 SLICES EACH)

- 3 cups whole wheat flour
- 1 cup all-purpose flour
- 2½ teaspoons baking soda
- 1 teaspoon salt
- 2½ cups buttermilk
- 1 cup molasses
- 1 cup golden raisins
- ¾ cup chopped hazelnuts

1. In a large bowl, combine the flours, baking soda and salt. In a small bowl, whisk the buttermilk and molasses. Stir into the dry ingredients just until moistened. Fold in the raisins and nuts. Transfer to two greased 8x4-in. loaf pans.
2. Bake at 350° for 45-50 minutes or until a toothpick inserted in the center comes out clean. Cool for 10 minutes before removing from pans to wire racks.
NOTE *To toast nuts, bake in a shallow pan in a 350° oven for 5-10 minutes or cook in a skillet over low heat until lightly browned, stirring occasionally.*

APPLE & CHEDDAR MINI SCONES

Cheese and sage go well with apples, so why not put them all in scones? These mini bites make a brunch, tailgate or other party that much more fun.

—**SUE GRONHOLZ** BEAVER DAM, WI

PREP: 25 MIN. • **BAKE:** 10 MIN.
MAKES: 32 SCONES

- 3 **cups all-purpose flour**
- 3 **teaspoons baking powder**
- ½ **teaspoon salt**
- ½ **teaspoon baking soda**
- 1 **cup cold butter, cubed**
- 1 **large egg**
- ¾ **cup (6 ounces) vanilla yogurt**
- 3 **tablespoons 2% milk, divided**
- ⅓ **cup shredded peeled apple**
- ⅓ **cup shredded sharp cheddar cheese**
- 1 **tablespoon minced fresh sage**
- 1 **tablespoon sugar**

1. Preheat oven to 425°. In a large bowl, whisk flour, baking powder, salt and baking soda. Cut in butter until mixture resembles coarse crumbs. In another bowl, whisk egg, yogurt and 2 tablespoons milk; stir into crumb mixture just until moistened. Stir in apple, cheese and sage.

2. Turn onto a lightly floured surface; knead gently 10 times. Divide dough in half; pat each portion into a 6-in. circle. Cut each circle into eight wedges; cut each wedge in half.

3. Transfer to parchment paper-lined baking sheets. Brush the tops with remaining milk; sprinkle with sugar. Bake 10-12 minutes or until golden brown. Serve warm.

FOR REGULAR-SIZE SCONES *Do not cut the wedges in half. Bake as directed, increasing baking time to 12-14 minutes. Yield: 16 regular scones*

APPLE & CHEDDAR MINI SCONES

HONEY-SQUASH DINNER ROLLS

These puffy dinner rolls take on rich color when you add squash to the dough. Any squash variety works. I've even used cooked carrots with great results.

—**MARCIA WHITNEY** GAINESVILLE, FL

PREP: 40 MIN. + RISING • **BAKE:** 20 MIN.
MAKES: 2 DOZEN

- 2 **packages (¼ ounce each) active dry yeast**
- 2 **teaspoons salt**
- ¼ **teaspoon ground nutmeg**
- 6 **to 6½ cups all-purpose flour**
- 1¼ **cups 2% milk**
- ½ **cup butter, cubed**
- ½ **cup honey**
- 1 **package (12 ounces) frozen mashed winter squash, thawed (about 1⅓ cups)**
- 1 **large egg, lightly beaten**
  Poppy seeds, salted pumpkin seeds or pepitas, or sesame seeds

1. In a large bowl, mix yeast, salt, nutmeg and 3 cups flour. In a small saucepan, heat milk, butter and honey to 120°-130°. Add to dry ingredients; beat on medium speed 2 minutes. Add squash; beat on high 2 minutes. Stir in enough remaining flour to form a soft dough (dough will be sticky).
2. Turn dough onto a floured surface; knead until smooth and elastic, about 6-8 minutes. Place in a greased bowl, turning once to grease the top. Cover the bowl with plastic wrap and let the dough rise in a warm place until it has doubled, about 1 hour.
3. Punch down dough. Turn onto a lightly floured surface; divide and shape into 24 balls. Divide between two greased 9-in. round baking pans. Cover with kitchen towels; let rise in a warm place until doubled, about 45 minutes.

4. Preheat oven to 375°. Brush tops with beaten egg; sprinkle with seeds. Bake 20-25 minutes or until dark golden brown. Cover loosely with foil during the last 5-7 minutes if needed to prevent overbrowning. Remove from pans to wire racks; serve warm.

CHOCOLATE ZUCCHINI BREAD

My family loves this chocolaty treat. I shred and freeze zucchini from my garden each summer so that I can make this bread all winter long.

—**SHARI MCKINNEY** BIRNEY, MT

PREP: 15 MIN. • **BAKE:** 50 MIN. + COOLING
MAKES: 2 LOAVES (12 SLICES EACH)

- 2 **cups sugar**
- 1 **cup canola oil**
- 3 **large eggs**
- 3 **teaspoons vanilla extract**
- 2½ **cups all-purpose flour**
- ½ **cup baking cocoa**
- 1 **teaspoon salt**
- 1 **teaspoon baking soda**
- 1 **teaspoon ground cinnamon**
- ¼ **teaspoon baking powder**
- 2 **cups shredded peeled zucchini**

1. In a large bowl, beat the sugar, oil, eggs and vanilla until well blended. Combine the flour, cocoa, salt, baking soda, cinnamon and baking powder; gradually beat into sugar mixture until blended. Stir in the zucchini. Transfer to two 8x4-in. loaf pans coated with cooking spray.
2. Bake at 350° for 50-55 minutes or until a toothpick inserted near the center comes out clean. Cool for 10 minutes before removing from pans to wire racks to cool completely.

BERRY CREAM MUFFINS

PUMPKIN CHOCOLATE LOAF

This no-fuss recipe bakes into three moist chocolate loaves. Featuring a tasty hint of pumpkin and spice, they've been a favorite for years. The loaves can be sliced to serve as a snack or dessert.

—KATHY GARDNER ROCKVILLE, MD

PREP: 15 MIN. • **BAKE:** 55 MIN. + COOLING
MAKES: 3 LOAVES

- 3¾ cups all-purpose flour
- 3½ cups sugar
- 1½ teaspoons salt
- 1½ teaspoons baking powder
- 1¼ teaspoons baking soda
- 1¼ teaspoons ground cinnamon
- 1 to 1¼ teaspoons ground cloves
- ½ teaspoon ground nutmeg
- 3 large eggs
- 1 can (29 ounces) solid-pack pumpkin
- 1¼ cups canola oil
- 3 ounces unsweetened chocolate, melted and cooled
- 1½ teaspoons vanilla extract
- 2 cups (12 ounces) semisweet chocolate chips

1. In a large bowl, combine the flour, sugar, salt, baking powder, baking soda, cinnamon, cloves and nutmeg. In another large bowl, whisk the eggs, pumpkin, oil, chocolate and vanilla. Stir into dry ingredients just until moistened. Fold in chips.
2. Transfer to three greased 9x5-in. loaf pans. Bake at 350° about 55-65 minutes or until a toothpick inserted in the center comes out clean. Cool for 10 minutes before removing from pans to wire racks. Wrap and freeze for up to 6 months.

BERRY CREAM MUFFINS

If you can't decide which berries to use in these muffins, try using half raspberries and half blueberries. They're fantastic!

—LINDA GILMORE HAMPSTEAD, MD

PREP: 15 MIN. • **BAKE:** 20 MIN.
MAKES: ABOUT 2 DOZEN

- 4 cups all-purpose flour
- 2 cups sugar
- 1¼ teaspoons baking powder
- 1 teaspoon baking soda
- 1 teaspoon salt
- 3 cups fresh or frozen raspberries or blueberries
- 4 large eggs, lightly beaten
- 2 cups (16 ounces) sour cream
- 1 cup canola oil
- 1 teaspoon vanilla extract

1. In a large bowl, combine the flour, sugar, baking powder, baking soda and salt; add the berries and toss gently. Combine the eggs, sour cream, oil and vanilla; mix well. Stir into the dry ingredients just until moistened.
2. Fill greased muffin cups two-thirds full. Bake at 400° for 20-25 minutes or until a toothpick inserted near the center comes out clean. Cool for about 5 minutes before removing from pans to a wire rack. Serve warm.

AUSTRIAN APPLE TWISTS

The addition of apples makes these sweet butterhorns stand out. The recipe is easy to prepare because you don't have to wait for the dough to rise.

—**KATHY BLESS** FAYETTEVILLE, PA

PREP: 30 MIN. + CHILLING • **BAKE:** 20 MIN.
MAKES: 64 TWISTS

- 1 package (¼ ounce) active dry yeast
- 3 cups all-purpose flour
- 1 cup butter, softened
- 3 large egg yolks, beaten
- 1 cup (8 ounces) sour cream
- ½ cup sugar
- ½ cup finely chopped pecans
- ¾ teaspoon ground cinnamon
- 1 medium tart apple, peeled and finely chopped

ICING

- 1 cup confectioners' sugar
- 4 teaspoons whole milk
- ¼ teaspoon vanilla extract
  Finely chopped pecans

1. In a large bowl, combine the yeast and flour; add butter and mix well. Add egg yolks and sour cream; mix well. Shape into four balls. Place in separate resealable plastic bags or wrap in plastic; refrigerate overnight.

2. Combine the sugar, pecans and cinnamon; set aside. On a floured surface, roll each ball of dough into a 9-in. circle. Sprinkle with the sugar mixture and apple. Cut each circle into 16 wedges; roll up from wide edge and pinch to seal. Place with point side down on greased baking sheets.

3. Bake at 350° for 16-20 minutes or until lightly browned. Immediately remove to wire racks to cool. For icing, combine sugar, milk and vanilla until smooth; drizzle over the twists. Sprinkle with pecans.

NOTE *The yeast does not need to be dissolved in liquid, and no rising time is necessary before baking.*

AUSTRIAN APPLE TWISTS

CINNAMON-WALNUT STICKY BUNS

The sweet honey-walnut topping and tender texture make these sticky rolls a surefire crowd-pleaser.

—DEBBIE BROEKER ROCKY MOUNT, MO

PREP: 1 HOUR + RISING • **BAKE:** 30 MIN.
MAKES: 2 DOZEN

- 2 packages (¼ ounce each) active dry yeast
- 1½ cups warm water (110° to 115°)
- 1 cup mashed potatoes (without added milk and butter)
- ½ cup sugar
- ½ cup butter, softened
- 2 large eggs
- 2 teaspoons salt
- 6 to 6½ cups all-purpose flour

TOPPING
- ¼ cup butter
- 1 cup packed brown sugar
- 1 cup honey
- 1 teaspoon ground cinnamon
- 1 cup chopped walnuts

FILLING
- ½ cup sugar
- 2 teaspoons ground cinnamon
- 2 tablespoons butter, melted

1. In a small bowl, dissolve yeast in warm water. In a large bowl, combine mashed potatoes, sugar, butter, eggs, salt, yeast mixture and 2 cups flour; beat on medium speed until smooth. Stir in enough remaining flour to form a soft dough.

2. Turn dough onto a floured surface; knead until smooth and elastic, about 6-8 minutes. Place in a greased bowl, turning once to grease the top. Cover the dough with plastic wrap and let it rise in a warm place until doubled, about 1 hour.

3. For topping, in a small saucepan, melt the butter. Stir in the brown sugar, honey and cinnamon. Divide the mixture among three greased 9-in. round baking pans, spreading evenly. Sprinkle with walnuts.

4. For filling, in a small bowl, mix the sugar and cinnamon. Punch down the dough. Turn onto a lightly floured surface; divide in half. Then roll one portion into an 18x12-in. rectangle. Brush with 1 tablespoon melted butter to within ½ in. of edges; sprinkle with ¼ cup sugar mixture.

5. Roll up jelly-roll style, starting with a long side; pinch the seam to seal. Cut into 12 slices. Repeat with remaining dough, butter and sugar mixture. Put eight slices in each pan, with cut side down. Cover with kitchen towels; let rise until doubled, about 30 minutes. Preheat oven to 350°.

6. Bake about 30-35 minutes or until golden brown. Immediately invert onto serving plates. Serve warm.

★ ★ ★ ★ ★ 5 STAR TIP
To keep homemade sticky buns or cinnamon rolls from separating or unrolling when serving, dust off any excess flour from your dough after rolling it out. Then be careful not to spread or sprinkle too much filling over the dough—abundant filling does not allow the roll to seal as it rises. Tightly roll up the dough and allow the rolls to rise until doubled before baking.

CINNAMON-WALNUT STICKY BUNS

(5) INGREDIENTS
PULL-APART GARLIC BREAD

People go wild over this golden, garlicky loaf whenever I serve it. There's intense flavor in every bite.

—**CAROL SHIELDS** SUMMERVILLE, PA

PREP: 10 MIN. + RISING • **BAKE:** 30 MIN.
MAKES: 1 LOAF

- ¼ **cup butter, melted**
- 1 **tablespoon dried parsley flakes**
- 1 **teaspoon garlic powder**
- ¼ **teaspoon garlic salt**
- 1 **loaf (1 pound) frozen white bread dough, thawed**

1. In a small bowl, combine butter, parsley, garlic powder and garlic salt. Cut dough into 1-in. pieces; dip into butter mixture. Layer in a greased 9x5-in. loaf pan. Cover and let rise until doubled, about 1 hour.
2. Bake at 350° for 30 minutes or until golden brown.

(5) INGREDIENTS | FAST FIX
CHOCOLATE BISCUIT PUFFS

I know my favorite snack is fun for kids to make and eat because I dreamed it up at age 9! The puffs are shaped to hide the chocolate inside for a tasty surprise.

—**JOY CLARK** SEABECK, WA

START TO FINISH: 20 MIN.
MAKES: 10 SERVINGS

- 1 **tube (12 ounces) refrigerated buttermilk biscuits**
- 1 **milk chocolate candy bar (1.55 ounces)**
- 2 **teaspoons cinnamon sugar**

1. Preheat the oven to 450°. Flatten each biscuit into a 3-in. circle. Break candy bar into 10 pieces; place a piece on each biscuit. Bring up the edges to enclose candy and pinch to seal.
2. Place biscuits seam side down on an ungreased baking sheet. Sprinkle with cinnamon sugar. Bake 8-10 minutes or until golden brown.

PULL-APART GARLIC BREAD

SOUR CREAM CHIP MUFFINS

(5) INGREDIENTS
BASIC HOMEMADE BREAD

I enjoy the aroma of fresh homemade bread in my kitchen. Here's a simple yeast version that bakes up golden brown.
—**SANDRA ANDERSON** NEW YORK, NY

PREP: 20 MIN. + RISING
BAKE: 30 MIN. + COOLING
MAKES: 2 LOAVES (16 SLICES EACH)

    1 **package (¼ ounce) active dry yeast**
   2¼ **cups warm water (110° to 115°)**
    3 **tablespoons sugar**
    1 **tablespoon salt**
    2 **tablespoons canola oil**
  6¼ to 6¾ **cups all-purpose flour**

1. In a large bowl, dissolve yeast in warm water. Add the sugar, salt, oil and 3 cups flour. Beat until smooth. Stir in enough remaining flour, ½ cup at a time, to form a soft dough.
2. Turn onto a floured surface; knead the dough until smooth and elastic, about 8-10 minutes. Place in a greased bowl, turning once to grease the top. Cover and let rise in a warm place until doubled, about 1½ hours.
3. Punch the dough down. Turn onto a lightly floured surface; divide the dough in half. Shape each half into a loaf. Place in two greased 9x5-in. loaf pans. Cover and let rise until doubled, about 30-45 minutes.
4. Bake at 375° for 30-35 minutes or until golden brown and bread sounds hollow when tapped. Remove from pans to wire racks to cool.

★ ★ ★ ★ ★ **5 STAR TIP**
To make sure active dry yeast (not quick-rise yeast) is alive and active, you first want to proof it. Simply dissolve one package of yeast and 1 teaspoon sugar in ¼ cup warm water (110° to 115°). Let stand for 5 to 10 minutes. If the mixture foams, the yeast is active and the mixture can be used. If it doesn't foam, the yeast should be discarded.

FAST FIX ▸
SOUR CREAM CHIP MUFFINS

Take one bite and you'll see why I think these rich, tender muffins are the best I've ever tasted. Mint chocolate chips make them a big hit with my family and friends.
—**STEPHANIE MOON** BOISE, ID

START TO FINISH: 30 MIN.
MAKES: 1 DOZEN

  1½ **cups all-purpose flour**
   ⅔ **cup sugar**
   ¾ **teaspoon baking powder**
   ¾ **teaspoon baking soda**
   ¼ **teaspoon salt**
    1 **large egg**
    1 **cup (8 ounces) sour cream**
    5 **tablespoons butter, melted**
    1 **teaspoon vanilla extract**
   ¾ **cup mint or semisweet chocolate chips**

1. In a large bowl, combine the flour, sugar, baking powder, baking soda and salt. Combine the egg, sour cream, butter and vanilla. Stir into the dry ingredients just until moistened. Fold in the chocolate chips.
2. Fill greased or paper-lined muffin cups three-fourths full. Bake at 350° for 18-20 minutes or until a toothpick inserted near the center comes out clean. Cool for 5 minutes before removing from pan to a wire rack.

HOW TO MAKE YEAST DOUGH

Fold top of dough toward you. With your palms, push dough with a rolling motion away from you. Turn dough a quarter turn; repeat folding, kneading and turning until dough is smooth and elastic. Add flour to surface as needed to prevent sticking during rising.

Press two fingers ½ in. into the dough. If the dents remain, the dough has doubled in size.

Place in greased pans. Cover with a towel and let rise in a warm (80° to 85°), draft-free area until dough has doubled.

BASIC HOMEMADE BREAD

AUNT BETTY'S BLUEBERRY MUFFINS

My Aunt Betty bakes many items each Christmas, but I look forward to these mouthwatering muffins the most.
—SHEILA RALEIGH KECHI, KS

PREP: 15 MIN. • **BAKE:** 20 MIN.
MAKES: ABOUT 1 DOZEN

- ½ cup old-fashioned oats
- ½ cup orange juice
- 1 large egg
- ½ cup canola oil
- ½ cup sugar
- 1½ cups all-purpose flour
- 1¼ teaspoons baking powder
- ½ teaspoon salt
- ¼ teaspoon baking soda
- 1 cup fresh or frozen blueberries

TOPPING
- 2 tablespoons sugar
- ½ teaspoon ground cinnamon

1. In a bowl, combine oats and orange juice; let stand for 5 minutes. Beat in the egg, oil and sugar until blended. Combine flour, baking powder, salt and baking soda; stir into oat mixture just until moistened. Fold in berries.
2. Fill greased or paper-lined muffin cups two-thirds full. Combine topping ingredients; sprinkle over batter. Bake at 400° for 20-25 minutes or until a toothpick inserted near the center comes out clean. Cool for 5 minutes before removing from pan to a wire rack. Serve warm.
NOTE *If using frozen blueberries, use without thawing to avoid discoloring the batter.*

★ ★ ★ ★ ★ **5 STAR TIP**
If the berries settle to the bottoms of the muffins during baking, try lightly coating them with flour first, before you add them to the batter. Reserve 1 or 2 tablespoons of the flour in the recipe and gently toss the berries in it. Also, if you're using frozen fruit, pat the blueberries dry (do not thaw) before tossing with flour. Carefully fold in the berries and bake as usual.

**AUNT BETTY'S
BLUEBERRY MUFFINS**

ORANGE CRANBERRY BREAD

The beauty of this quick bread is that it makes a delicious post-meal snack. I also like to toast leftover slices and spread them with cream cheese or butter for breakfast.

—**RON GARDNER** GRAND HAVEN, MI

PREP: 20 MIN. • **BAKE:** 50 MIN. + COOLING
MAKES: 2 LOAVES (16 SLICES EACH)

- 2¾ cups all-purpose flour
- ⅔ cup sugar
- ⅔ cup packed brown sugar
- 3½ teaspoons baking powder
- 1 teaspoon salt
- ½ teaspoon ground cinnamon
- ¼ teaspoon ground nutmeg
- 1 large egg
- 1 cup 2% milk
- ½ cup orange juice
- 3 tablespoons canola oil
- 2 to 3 teaspoons grated orange peel
- 2 cups coarsely chopped fresh or frozen cranberries
- 1 large apple, peeled and chopped

1. In a large bowl, combine the flour, sugars, baking powder, salt, cinnamon and nutmeg. Then whisk the egg, milk, orange juice, oil and orange peel; stir these into the dry ingredients just until blended. Fold in the cranberries and apple.

2. Pour into two greased 8x4-in. loaf pans. Bake at 350° for 50-55 minutes or until a toothpick inserted in the center comes out clean. Cool for 10 minutes before removing from pans to wire racks.

FREEZE OPTION *Securely wrap and freeze cooled loaves in plastic wrap and foil. To use, thaw the loaves at room temperature.*

HAWAIIAN DINNER ROLLS

Crushed pineapple and flaked coconut give a subtle sweetness to these golden rolls, and leftovers are perfect for sandwiches.

—**KATHY KURTZ** GLENDORA, CA

PREP: 35 MIN. + RISING • **BAKE:** 15 MIN.
MAKES: 15 ROLLS

- 1 can (8 ounces) crushed pineapple, undrained
- ¼ cup warm pineapple juice (70° to 80°)
- ¼ cup water (70° to 80°)
- 1 large egg
- ¼ cup butter, cubed
- ¼ cup nonfat dry milk powder
- 1 tablespoon sugar
- 1½ teaspoons salt
- 3¼ cups bread flour
- 2¼ teaspoons active dry yeast
- ¾ cup flaked coconut

1. In bread machine pan, place the first 10 ingredients in order suggested by manufacturer. Select dough setting (check the dough after 5 minutes of mixing; add 1 to 2 tablespoons of water or flour if needed). Just before final kneading (your machine may audibly signal this), add coconut.

2. When the cycle is complete, turn dough onto a lightly floured surface. Cover with plastic wrap; let rest for 10 minutes. Divide into 15 portions; roll each into a ball. Place in a greased 13x9-in. baking pan.

3. Cover and let rise in a warm place for 45 minutes or until doubled. Bake at 375° for 15-20 minutes or until the rolls are golden brown.

NOTE *We recommend that you do not use a bread machine's time-delay feature for this recipe.*

HAWAIIAN DINNER ROLLS

APPLE PULL-APART BREAD

Drizzled with icing, each finger-licking piece of this bread has a yummy filling of apples and pecans. I think you'll agree the recipe is well worth the bit of extra effort.

—**CAROLYN GREGORY** HENDERSONVILLE, TN

PREP: 40 MIN. + RISING
BAKE: 35 MIN. + COOLING
MAKES: 1 LOAF

- 1 package (¼ ounce) active dry yeast
- 1 cup warm milk
- ½ cup butter, melted, divided
- 1 large egg
- ⅔ cup plus 2 tablespoons sugar, divided
- 1 teaspoon salt
- 3 to 3½ cups all-purpose flour
- 1 medium tart apple, peeled and chopped
- ½ cup finely chopped pecans
- ½ teaspoon ground cinnamon

ICING

- 1 cup confectioners' sugar
- 3 to 4½ teaspoons hot water
- ½ teaspoon vanilla extract

1. In a large bowl, dissolve yeast in milk. Add 2 tablespoons butter, egg, 2 tablespoons sugar, salt and 3 cups flour; beat until smooth. Add enough remaining flour to form a stiff dough. Turn dough onto a floured surface; knead until smooth and elastic, about 6-8 minutes. Place in a greased bowl, turning once to grease the top. Cover and let rise in a warm place until doubled, about 1 hour.

2. Combine apple, pecans, cinnamon and remaining sugar; set aside. Punch dough down; divide in half. Cut each half into 16 pieces. On a lightly floured surface, pat or roll out each piece into a 2½-in. circle. Place 1 teaspoon apple mixture in center of circle; pinch the edges together and seal, forming a ball. Dip in remaining butter.

3. In a greased 10-in. tube pan, place 16 balls, seam side down; sprinkle the balls with ¼ cup apple mixture. Layer the remaining balls; then sprinkle with the remaining apple mixture. Cover them and let rise until nearly doubled, about 45 minutes.

4. Bake at 350° for 35-40 minutes or until golden brown. Cool about 10 minutes; remove from pan to a wire rack. Combine icing ingredients; drizzle over warm bread.

LEMON BREAD

I often bake this sunshiny-sweet bread when company is coming. It has a texture similar to pound cake and it tastes just as rich, with a slight hint of lemon.

—**KATHY SCOTT** LINGLE, WY

PREP: 10 MIN. • **BAKE:** 45 MIN. + COOLING
MAKES: 1 LOAF (12 SLICES)

- ½ cup butter, softened
- 1 cup sugar
- 2 large eggs
- 2 tablespoons lemon juice
- 1 tablespoon grated lemon peel
- 1½ cups all-purpose flour
- 1 teaspoon baking powder
- ⅛ teaspoon salt
- ½ cup 2% milk

GLAZE

- ½ cup confectioners' sugar
- 2 tablespoons lemon juice

1. In a large bowl, cream butter and sugar until light and fluffy. Beat in the eggs, lemon juice and peel. Combine the flour, baking powder and salt; gradually stir into creamed mixture alternately with milk, beating well after each addition.

2. Pour into a greased 8x4-in. loaf pan. Bake at 350° for 45 minutes or until a toothpick inserted near the center comes out clean.

3. Combine the glaze ingredients. Remove bread from pan; immediately drizzle with glaze. Cool on a wire rack. Serve warm.

APPLE PULL-APART BREAD

BANANA MOCHA-CHIP MUFFINS

These moist muffins combine my two favorite things—chocolate and coffee. The banana is just an added bonus.

—**MELISSA WILLIAMS** TAYLORVILLE, IL

PREP: 20 MIN. • **BAKE:** 20 MIN.
MAKES: 2 DOZEN

- 5 teaspoons instant coffee granules
- 5 teaspoons hot water
- ¾ cup butter, softened
- 1¼ cups sugar
- 1 large egg
- 1⅓ cups mashed ripe bananas
- 1 teaspoon vanilla extract
- 2¼ cups all-purpose flour
- 1½ teaspoons baking powder
- ½ teaspoon baking soda
- ½ teaspoon salt
- 1½ cups semisweet chocolate chips

1. Preheat oven to 350°. In a small bowl, dissolve coffee granules in hot water. In a large bowl, cream butter and sugar until light and fluffy. Add egg; beat well. Beat in bananas, vanilla and coffee mixture. Combine flour, baking powder, baking soda and salt; add to creamed mixture just until moistened. Fold in chocolate chips.

2. Fill paper-lined muffin cups two-thirds full. Bake 18-20 minutes or until a toothpick inserted in muffin comes out clean. Cool 5 minutes before removing from pans to wire racks. Serve warm.

★ ★ ★ ★ ★ **READER REVIEW**

"Boy, were these good! The only thing I did different was I used mini chocolate chips. They are moist and addicting!"

TWINS1111 TASTEOFHOME.COM

DILLY ROLLS

DILLY ROLLS

These versatile rolls are great served warm alongside any dinner entree. I always make a big batch since my family enjoys the rolls after they're cool, too, stuffed with sandwich fillings like egg salad or ham salad.

—**MARY BICKEL** TERRE HAUTE, IN

PREP: 25 MIN. + RISING • **BAKE:** 20 MIN.
MAKES: 2 DOZEN

- 2 cups 4% cottage cheese
- 2 tablespoons butter
- 2 packages (¼ ounce each) active dry yeast
- ½ cup warm water (110° to 115°)
- 2 large eggs
- ¼ cup sugar
- 2 tablespoons dried minced onion
- 1 to 2 tablespoons dill weed
- 1 tablespoon salt
- ½ teaspoon baking soda
- 4½ to 5 cups all-purpose flour

1. In a large saucepan over medium heat, cook cottage cheese and butter until butter is melted. Cool to 110° to 115°. In a large bowl, dissolve the yeast in water. Add eggs, sugar, onion, dill, salt, baking soda and cottage cheese mixture. Add 3 cups of flour; beat until smooth. Add enough remaining flour to form a soft dough.

2. Turn onto a floured surface; knead until smooth and elastic, 6-8 minutes. Place in a greased bowl, turning once to grease top. Cover and let rise in a warm place until dough has doubled, about 1 hour.

3. Punch the dough down. Form into 24 balls; place in a 13x9-in. baking pan that has been sprayed with cooking spray. Cover and let rise until doubled, about 45 minutes.

4. Bake at 350° for 20-25 minutes.

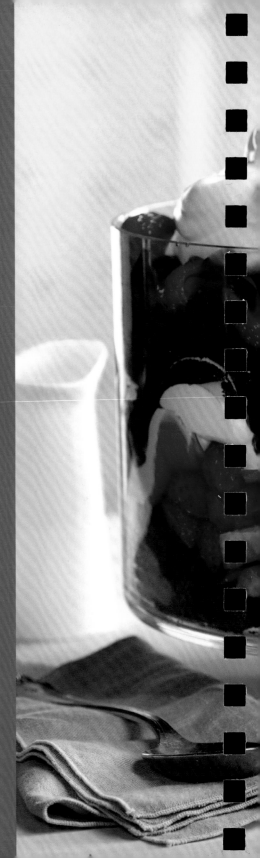

CAKES, PIES & DESSERTS

Dinner is done and the table is cleared. Time for dessert! It doesn't get any better than homemade pies and cakes. But the delicious goodness doesn't end there! Flip through this chapter for frozen treats, cheesecake, brownies, tarts, trifles and so much more.

[5] INGREDIENTS

CHOCOLATE STRAWBERRY PUNCH BOWL TRIFLE

I created this dessert together when I needed something quick to take to my in-laws' house. Because the dish is so beautiful, everyone thought I fussed, but it's very easy. And since it makes so much, it's perfect for potlucks, reunions and large get-togethers.

—**KRISTI JUDKINS** MORRISON, TN

PREP: 20 MIN. • **BAKE:** 20 MIN.
MAKES: 24-28 SERVINGS

- 1 **package chocolate cake mix (regular size)**
- 1 **quart fresh whole strawberries, sliced**
- 1 **carton (13½ ounces) strawberry glaze**
- 2 **cartons (12 ounces each) frozen whipped topping, thawed, divided**
- 1 **cup chocolate frosting**
  Shaved chocolate, optional

1. Prepare and bake cake according to package directions, using a 13x9-in. baking pan. Cool the cake completely on a wire rack.

2. Cut the cake into 1-in. cubes. Place half of the cake cubes in a 6-qt. glass punch bowl. Top cubes with half of the sliced strawberries; drizzle with half of the strawberry glaze. Spread with 3½ cups whipped topping.

3. In a microwave-safe bowl, heat the frosting on high for 20-30 seconds or until pourable, stirring it often; cool slightly. Drizzle half over the whipped topping. Repeat layers of cake, berries, glaze and whipped topping. If desired, drizzle with remaining frosting and sprinkle with shaved chocolate.

★ ★ ★ ★ ★ **READER REVIEW**

"This is fabulous. I made the cake the night before and threw everything together the next day."

SJHEMP TASTEOFHOME.COM

HOW TO FILL A CAKE

Insert toothpicks an inch from the top of the cake on all sides as a guide for your knife. Slice the top off the cake with a serrated knife.

Cut the outline of the tunnel with a small paring knife, leaving a 1-in. shell on each side. Use your fingers to gently pull out the cake.

Fill the hollow with lemon or other flavored filling. Replace the top of the cake, then finish with your favorite glaze or topping.

LEMON CURD-FILLED ANGEL FOOD CAKE

LEMON CURD-FILLED ANGEL FOOD CAKE

For a sunny angel food cake, I make an easy filling of mascarpone, whipping cream and lemon curd, and then drizzle the cake with a lemony sweet glaze.

—LEAH REKAU MILWAUKEE, WI

PREP: 55 MIN. + CHILLING
BAKE: 45 MIN. + COOLING
MAKES: 16 SERVINGS

- 12 large egg whites (about 1⅔ cups)
- 1 cup cake flour
- 1½ cups sugar, divided
- 1 vanilla bean (see Note) or 1 teaspoon vanilla extract
- ½ teaspoon cream of tartar
- ¼ teaspoon salt

FILLING
- ½ cup heavy whipping cream
- ½ cup mascarpone cheese
- 2 tablespoons confectioners' sugar
- 1 jar (10 ounces) lemon curd, divided
- 1 cup sliced fresh strawberries, patted dry

GLAZE
- 2 cups confectioners' sugar
- 1 teaspoon grated lemon peel
- 3 to 4 tablespoons lemon juice

1. Place egg whites in a large bowl; let stand at room temperature for 30 minutes.
2. Preheat oven to 325°. In a small bowl, mix the flour and ¾ cup sugar until blended.
3. Add seeds from vanilla bean (or extract if using), cream of tartar and salt to egg whites. Beat on medium speed until soft peaks form. Gradually add the remaining ¾ cup of sugar, 1 tablespoon at a time, beating on high after each addition until the sugar is dissolved. Continue beating until soft glossy peaks form. Gradually fold in flour mixture, about ½ cup at a time.
4. Gently transfer batter to ungreased 10-in. tube pan. Cut through the batter with a knife to remove air pockets. Bake on lowest oven rack 45-55 minutes or until top springs back when it is lightly touched. Immediately invert the pan; cool completely in pan, about 1½ hours.
5. Run a knife around the sides and center tube of pan. Remove cake to a serving plate. Using a serrated knife, cut a 1-in. slice off top of cake. Hollow out remaining cake, leaving a 1-in.-thick shell (save removed cake for another use).
6. For filling, in a small bowl, beat the cream until it begins to thicken. Add the mascarpone and confectioners' sugar; beat until soft peaks form. Fold in ¼ cup of the lemon curd.
7. Line the bottom of the tunnel with strawberries. Spoon the mascarpone mixture over the berries; top with remaining lemon curd. Replace cake top; refrigerate, covered, at least 4 hours or overnight.
8. For glaze, in a small bowl, mix the confectioners' sugar, lemon peel and enough juice to reach the desired consistency. Unwrap cake; spread glaze over top, allowing some to drip down sides. Refrigerate until serving.

NOTE *To remove the seeds from a vanilla bean, cut the bean lengthwise in half with a sharp knife; scrape out the dark, pulpy seeds.*

CHERRY CHOCOLATE COCONUT CUPCAKES

These cupcakes are a bit time-consuming but worth it! Chocolate-covered coconut candy is tucked inside each morsel. The fluffy white ganache frosting is complemented by coarse sugar and chocolate-covered cherries.

—SANDY PLOY WHITEFISH BAY, WI

PREP: 35 MIN. + CHILLING
BAKE: 20 MIN. + COOLING
MAKES: 2 DOZEN

- 1 package (10 to 12 ounces) vanilla or white chips
- ½ cup butter, cubed
- 1 cup heavy whipping cream
- 1 teaspoon coconut extract
- 1 can (21 ounces) cherry pie filling
- 1 cup buttermilk
- 2 large eggs
- 2 cups all-purpose flour
- 2 cups sugar
- ¾ cup baking cocoa
- 2 teaspoons baking soda
- 1 teaspoon baking powder
- ½ teaspoon salt
- 6 packages (1.9 ounces each) chocolate-covered coconut candy bars
- ½ cup semisweet chocolate chips
- 1 teaspoon shortening
- 24 maraschino cherries, well drained
- 3¾ cups confectioners' sugar
- 2 tablespoons coarse sugar

1. For ganache, place vanilla chips and butter in a large bowl. In a small saucepan, bring cream just to a boil. Pour over chip mixture; whisk until smooth. Stir in the extract. Cover and refrigerate for at least 4 hours, stirring occasionally.
2. In a large bowl, beat the pie filling, buttermilk and eggs until they are well blended. Combine the flour, sugar, cocoa, baking soda, baking powder and salt; gradually beat into pie filling mixture until blended.
3. Fill 24 paper-lined muffin cups one-third full. Cut candy bars in half; place half of a candy bar in the center of each cupcake. Cover each with 2 tablespoonfuls batter.
4. Bake at 375° for 16-20 minutes or until a toothpick inserted near the center comes out clean. Cool for 10 minutes before removing from pans to wire racks to cool completely.
5. Meanwhile, in a microwave, melt chocolate chips and shortening; stir until smooth. Dip the cherries in the chocolate mixture; allow excess to drip off. Place on a waxed paper-lined baking sheet. Refrigerate until set.
6. Remove ganache from refrigerator; gradually beat in the confectioners' sugar until frosting is light and fluffy. Pipe over the cupcakes; sprinkle with coarse sugar. Garnish with chocolate-dipped cherries.

WHITE CHOCOLATE-STRAWBERRY TIRAMISU

BLUEBERRY-BLACKBERRY RUSTIC TART

My dad would always stop the car on the side of the road in Maine and say, "I smell blueberries!" He had a pail ready to go. Once home, Mom would bake the wild berries in a cornmeal crust.

—PRISCILLA GILBERT
INDIAN HARBOUR BEACH, FL

PREP: 20 MIN. + CHILLING • **BAKE:** 55 MIN.
MAKES: 8 SERVINGS

- 2 **cups all-purpose flour**
- ⅓ **cup sugar**
- ¼ **cup yellow cornmeal**
- ⅔ **cup cold butter, cubed**
- ½ **cup buttermilk**
FILLING
- 4 **cups fresh blueberries**
- 2 **cups fresh blackberries**
- ⅔ **cup sugar**
- ⅓ **cup all-purpose flour**
- 2 **tablespoons lemon juice**
- 1 **large egg, beaten**
- 2 **tablespoons turbinado (washed raw) sugar or coarse sugar**
  Whipped cream, optional

1. In a large bowl, mix flour, sugar and cornmeal; cut in butter until crumbly. Gradually add the buttermilk, tossing with a fork until dough holds together when pressed. Shape into a disk; wrap in plastic wrap. Refrigerate it for 30 minutes or overnight.
2. Preheat oven to 375°. On a lightly floured surface, roll the dough into a 14-in. circle. Transfer to a parchment paper-lined baking sheet.
3. In a large bowl, combine berries, sugar, flour and lemon juice; spoon over pastry to within 2 in. of edges. Fold the pastry edge over the filling, leaving the center uncovered. Brush the folded pastry with beaten egg; sprinkle with turbinado sugar.
4. Bake 55-60 minutes or until crust is golden brown and filling is bubbly. Using parchment paper, slide tart onto a wire rack to cool. If desired, serve with whipped cream.

FAST FIX ▶

WHITE CHOCOLATE-STRAWBERRY TIRAMISU

Here's a fast twist on a classic dessert that highlights one of our favorite flavor combos: strawberries and white chocolate. Lighten it up if you'd like—I've had good luck with light whipped topping and reduced-fat cream cheese, for example.

—ANNA GINSBERG CHICAGO, IL

START TO FINISH: 30 MIN.
MAKES: 15 SERVINGS

- 2 **cups heavy whipping cream**
- 1 **package (8 ounces) cream cheese, softened**
- ½ **cup (4 ounces) mascarpone cheese**
- 9 **ounces white baking chocolate, melted and cooled**
- 1 **cup confectioners' sugar, divided**
- 1 **teaspoon vanilla extract**
- 2 **packages (3 ounces each) ladyfingers, split**
- ⅔ **cup orange juice**
- 4 **cups sliced fresh strawberries**
  Chocolate syrup, optional

1. In a large bowl, beat cream until soft peaks form. In another bowl, beat the cheeses until they are light and fluffy. Beat in cooled chocolate, ½ cup confectioners' sugar and vanilla. Fold in 2 cups of the whipped cream.
2. Brush half of the ladyfingers with half of the orange juice; arrange in a 13x9-in. dish. Spread with 2 cups of cream cheese mixture; top with half of the strawberries. Brush remaining ladyfingers with remaining orange juice; arrange over berries.
3. Now gently stir the remaining confectioners' sugar into remaining cream cheese mixture; fold in the remaining whipped cream. Spread over the ladyfingers. Top with the remaining strawberries. Refrigerate until serving. If desired, drizzle with chocolate syrup before serving.

MINIATURE PEANUT BUTTER CHEESECAKES

The recipe for these yummy treats, with a peanut butter cup inside, was handed down to me from my mother. They're perfect for holidays or any special occasion.

—MARY ANN DELL PHOENIXVILLE, PA

PREP: 20 MIN. • **BAKE:** 15 MIN. + CHILLING
MAKES: 6 SERVINGS

- ⅓ cup graham cracker crumbs
- 1 tablespoon sugar
- 5 teaspoons butter, melted

FILLING
- 4 ounces cream cheese, softened
- ¼ cup sugar
- 2 teaspoons all-purpose flour
- 2 tablespoons beaten egg
- ¼ teaspoon vanilla extract
- 6 miniature peanut butter cups

1. In a small bowl, combine the cracker crumbs, sugar and butter. Press onto the bottoms of six paper-lined muffin cups; set aside.
2. In a small bowl, beat the cream cheese, sugar and flour until smooth. Add egg and vanilla; beat on low speed just until combined. Place a peanut butter cup in the center of each muffin cup; fill with cream cheese mixture.
3. Bake at 350° for 15-18 minutes or until center is set. Cool on a wire rack for 10 minutes before removing from pan to a wire rack to cool completely. Refrigerate for at least 2 hours.

★ ★ ★ ★ ★ 5 STAR TIP
Switch things up by cutting the peanut butter cups into halves or quarters first, then set the pieces into the center of the muffin cups before adding the cream cheese mixture. You can also substitute small chocolate-covered caramels for the peanut cups if you'd like.

CREAM CHEESE-PINEAPPLE PIE

I've made this light and refreshing pie many times for friends, relatives, guests and church suppers, and I'm always getting requests for the recipe. It has become one of our favorite ways to complete a meal. I've lived on farms all my life, and I love the old-fashioned appeal of down-home desserts like this one.

—ELIZABETH BROWN CLAYTON, DE

PREP: 20 MIN. • **BAKE:** 1 HOUR + COOLING
MAKES: 8 SERVINGS

PINEAPPLE LAYER
- ⅓ cup sugar
- 1 tablespoon cornstarch
- 1 can (8 ounces) crushed pineapple with juice

CREAM CHEESE LAYER
- 1 package (8 ounces) cream cheese, softened to room temperature
- ½ cup sugar
- 1 teaspoon salt
- 2 large eggs
- ½ cup milk
- ½ teaspoon vanilla extract
- 1 9-inch unbaked pie shell
- ¼ cup chopped pecans

1. Combine the sugar, cornstarch and pineapple with juice in a small saucepan. Cook over medium heat, stirring constantly until mixture is thick and clear. Cool; set aside.
2. Blend cream cheese, sugar and salt in mixer bowl. Add eggs, one at a time, beating after each addition. Blend in the milk and vanilla. (The mixture may look curdled.)
3. Spread cooled pineapple mixture over bottom of pie shell. Pour cream cheese mixture over pineapple layer; sprinkle with pecans.
4. Bake at 400° for 10 minutes; then reduce heat to 325° and bake for 50 minutes. Cool.

CREAM CHEESE-PINEAPPLE PIE

RHUBARB DREAM BARS

Dreaming of a different way to use rhubarb? Try these sweet bars! A tender shortbread-like crust is the perfect addition to rhubarb, walnuts and coconut.

—**MARION TOMLINSON** MADISON, WI

PREP: 15 MIN. • **BAKE:** 45 MIN. + COOLING
MAKES: 2 DOZEN

- 1¼ cups all-purpose flour, divided
- ⅓ cup confectioners' sugar
- ½ cup cold butter, cubed
- 1¼ to 1½ cups sugar
- 2 large eggs
- 2 cups diced fresh or frozen rhubarb
- ½ cup chopped walnuts
- ½ cup flaked coconut

1. In a large bowl, combine 1 cup flour and the confectioners' sugar. Cut in butter until crumbly. Pat into a lightly greased 13x9-in. baking dish. Bake at 350° for 13-15 minutes or until edges are lightly browned.

2. In a large bowl, combine sugar and remaining flour. Add eggs. Stir in the rhubarb, walnuts and coconut; pour over crust. Bake 30-35 minutes longer or until set. Cool on a wire rack. Cut into bars.

NOTE *If you are using frozen rhubarb, measure the rhubarb while still frozen, then thaw it completely. Drain in a colander, but do not press liquid out.*

★ ★ ★ ★ ★ **READER REVIEW**

"I made these for a birthday party and everyone went crazy over them. I don't even like rhubarb, and I couldn't keep my hands off them."

HAG2NUT2000 TASTEOFHOME.COM

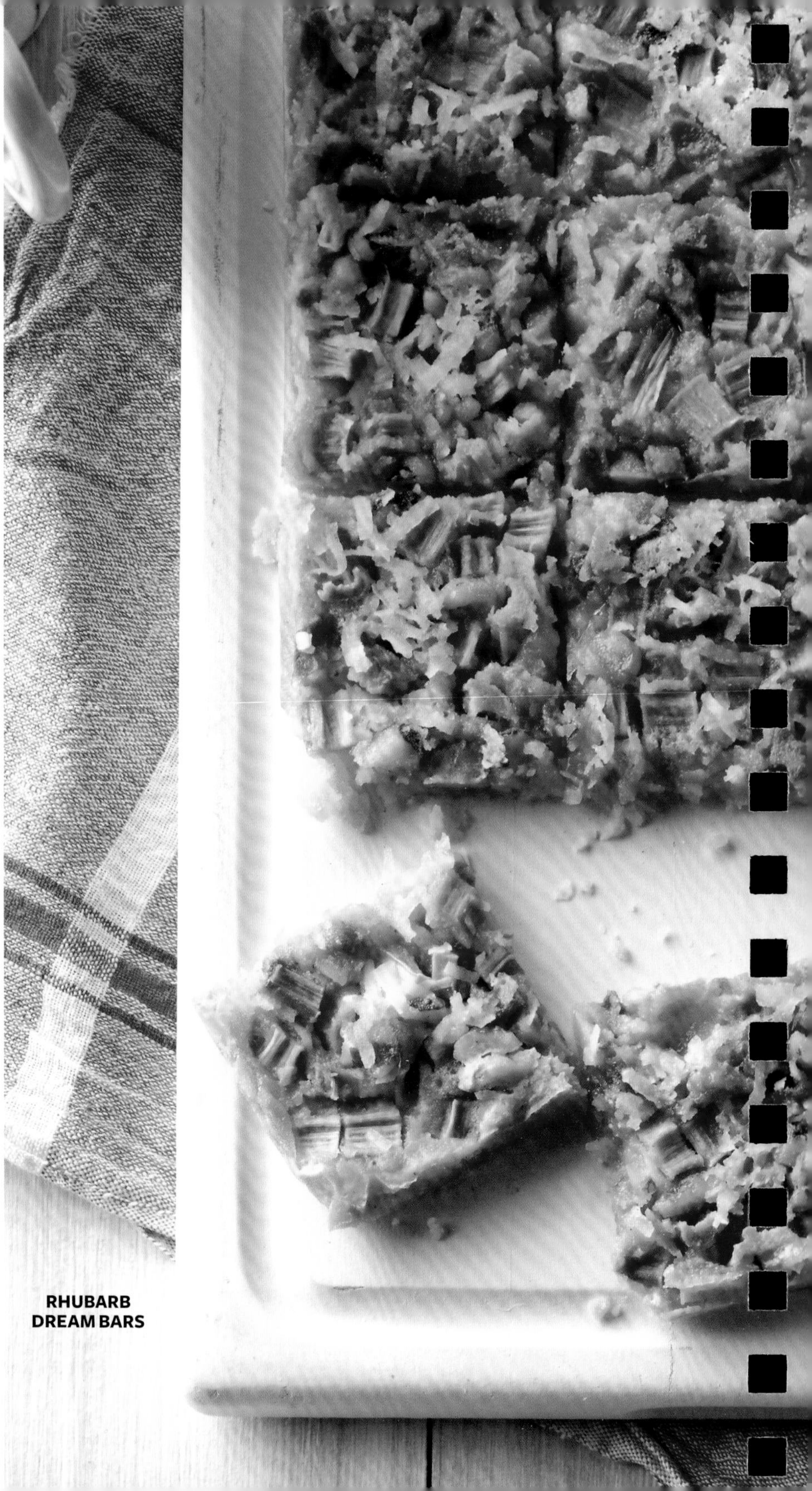

RHUBARB DREAM BARS

(5) INGREDIENTS

BIRTHDAY CAKE FREEZER POPS

During my quest to find birthday cake ice cream—my favorite flavor—I came up with these easy ice pops. Now, instead of going to the store whenever a craving hits, I just head to my freezer.

—DAWN LOPEZ WESTERLY, RI

PREP: 20 MIN. + FREEZING
MAKES: 1½ DOZEN

- ⅔ cup sprinkles, divided
- 18 paper or plastic cups (3 ounces each) and wooden pop sticks
- 2 cups cold 2% milk
- 1 package (3.4 ounces) instant vanilla pudding mix
- 1 carton (8 ounces) frozen whipped topping, thawed
- 2 cups crushed vanilla wafers (about 60 wafers)

1. Spoon 1 teaspoon of sprinkles into each cup. In a large bowl, whisk milk and pudding mix 2 minutes. Let stand 2 minutes or until soft-set. Stir in the whipped topping, crushed wafers and remaining sprinkles.

2. Cut a 1-in. hole in the tip of a pastry bag or in a corner of a food-safe plastic bag. Transfer the mixture to bag. Pipe into prepared cups. Top with foil and insert sticks through foil. Freeze until firm, about 4 hours. Let stand at room temperature 5 minutes before gently removing pops.

KEY LIME PIE CUPCAKES

I bake over 200 of these cupcakes for our church suppers, and we always run out. If you can't find Key lime juice, use lime juice. Just add a tad more sugar.

—JULIE HERRERA-LEMLER ROCHESTER, MN

PREP: 45 MIN. • **BAKE:** 20 MIN. + COOLING
MAKES: 32 CUPCAKES

- 2 packages (14.1 ounces each) refrigerated pie pastry
- 1 cup butter, softened
- 2½ cups sugar
- 4 large eggs
- ½ cup Key lime juice
- 2 cups all-purpose flour
- 1½ cups self-rising flour
- 1½ cups buttermilk

FROSTING

- 12 ounces cream cheese, softened
- 1½ cups butter, softened
- 1½ teaspoons vanilla extract
- 2¾ to 3 cups confectioners' sugar
- 6 tablespoons Key lime juice
  Fresh raspberries

1. Preheat the oven to 350°. Line 32 muffin cups with foil liners. On a lightly floured work surface, unroll the pastry sheets. Cut 32 circles with a floured 2¼-in. round cookie cutter (discard the remaining pastry or save for another use). Press one pastry circle into each liner. Bake for 10-12 minutes or until lightly browned. Cool in wire racks.

2. In a large bowl, beat butter and sugar until crumbly. Add eggs, one at a time, beating them well after each addition. Beat in lime juice. In another bowl, whisk flours; add to butter mixture alternately with buttermilk, beating well after each addition.

3. Pour batter into prepared cups. Bake for 20-22 minutes or until a toothpick inserted in center comes out clean. Cool in pans 10 minutes before removing to wire racks to cool completely.

4. In a large bowl, beat cream cheese, butter and vanilla until blended. Beat in enough of the confectioners' sugar, alternately with lime juice, to reach the desired consistency. Frost the cupcakes; top them with raspberries. Refrigerate the leftovers.

NOTE *As a substitute for 1½ cups self-rising flour, place 2¼ teaspoons baking powder and ¾ teaspoon salt in a measuring cup. Add all-purpose flour to measure 1 cup. Combine with an additional ½ cup all-purpose flour.*

BANANA PUDDING

I didn't see my son for more than two years after he enlisted in the Marines after high school. When he finally arrived back home, I just grabbed hold of him at the airport and burst out crying. And when we got to our house, the first thing he ate was two bowls of my banana pudding.

—**STEPHANIE HARRIS** MONTPELIER, VA

PREP: 35 MIN. + CHILLING
MAKES: 9 SERVINGS

- ¾ **cup sugar**
- ¼ **cup all-purpose flour**
- ¼ **teaspoon salt**
- 3 **cups 2% milk**
- 3 **large eggs**
- 1½ **teaspoons vanilla extract**
- 8 **ounces vanilla wafers (about 60 cookies), divided**
- 4 **large ripe bananas, cut into ¼-inch slices**

1. In a large saucepan, mix the sugar, flour and salt. Whisk in milk. Cook and stir over medium heat until mix is thickened and bubbly. Reduce heat to low; cook and stir 2 minutes longer. Remove from heat.
2. In a small bowl, whisk eggs. Whisk small amount of the hot mixture into eggs; return all to the pan, whisking it constantly. Bring to a gentle boil; cook and stir 2 minutes. Remove from heat. Stir in the vanilla. Cool for 15 minutes, stirring occasionally.
3. In ungreased 8-in. square baking dish, layer 25 vanilla wafers, half of the banana slices and half of the pudding. Repeat the layers.
4. Press plastic wrap onto surface of pudding. Refrigerate for 4 hours or overnight. Just before serving, crush remaining wafers and sprinkle over the top.

BANANA PUDDING

CARAMEL BROWNIES

My family can't possibly eat all of the sweets I whip up, so my co-workers are more than happy to sample them. They're especially fond of these rich, chewy brownies that are full of gooey caramel, chocolate chips and crunchy walnuts.

—**CLARA BAKKE** COON RAPIDS, MN

PREP: 20 MIN. • **BAKE:** 35 MIN. + COOLING
MAKES: 2 DOZEN

- 2 **cups sugar**
- ¾ **cup baking cocoa**
- 1 **cup canola oil**
- 4 **large eggs**
- ¼ **cup 2% milk**
- 1½ **cups all-purpose flour**
- 1 **teaspoon salt**
- 1 **teaspoon baking powder**
- 1 **cup (6 ounces) semisweet chocolate chips**
- 1 **cup chopped walnuts, divided**
- 1 **package (14 ounces) caramels**
- 1 **can (14 ounces) sweetened condensed milk**

1. Using a large bowl, beat the sugar, cocoa, oil, eggs and milk. Combine the flour, salt and baking powder; then gradually add to egg mixture until well blended. Fold in chocolate chips and ½ cup walnuts.
2. Spoon two-thirds of the batter into a greased 13x9-in. baking pan. Bake 350° for 12 minutes.
3. Meanwhile, in large saucepan, heat the caramels and condensed milk over low heat until caramels are melted. Pour over the baked brownie layer. Sprinkle with remaining walnuts.
4. Drop the remaining batter by teaspoonfuls over the caramel layer; carefully swirl the brownie batter with a knife.
5. Bake for 35-40 minutes or until a toothpick inserted near the center comes out with moist crumbs (do not overbake). Cool on a wire rack.

WHOLE WHEAT STRAWBERRY SHORTCAKES

Nothing says spring better than a fresh strawberry shortcake. Heaven! My mother and I usually make this recipe with the strawberries we picked ourselves.

—SARAH HATTER BRODHEAD, WI

PREP: 45 MIN. + CHILLING
BAKE: 15 MIN. + COOLING
MAKES: 6 SERVINGS

WHOLE WHEAT STRAWBERRY SHORTCAKES

- 2½ cups fresh strawberries, hulled, divided
- 1 to 2 tablespoons maple syrup

SHORTCAKES
- 2 cups whole wheat flour
- 2½ teaspoons baking powder
- ½ teaspoon salt
- ¼ teaspoon baking soda
- ½ cup cold butter, cubed
- 1 large egg
- ½ cup 2% milk
- ¼ cup honey
  Whipped cream

1. In a bowl, thoroughly mash ¾ cup strawberries; stir in the syrup. Cut the remaining strawberries into ¼-in. slices; add to the crushed strawberries and toss to coat. Refrigerate, covered, for 1 hour.

2. Meanwhile, preheat oven to 400°. In a large bowl, whisk flour, baking powder, salt and baking soda. Cut in butter until mixture resembles coarse crumbs. In a small bowl, whisk egg, milk and honey until blended; stir into flour mixture just until moistened.

3. Turn onto a lightly floured surface; knead gently 8-10 times. Pat or roll dough to ¾-in. thickness; cut with a floured 2½-in. biscuit cutter. Place 2 in. apart on parchment paper-lined baking sheets. Bake 12-15 minutes or until light brown. Remove to wire racks to cool slightly.

4. To serve, split shortcakes in half. Fill with strawberry mixture and whipped cream. Top with additional whipped cream.

PECAN
BUTTER
TARTS

CHERRY ALMOND MOUSSE PIE

Anytime is the right time to treat your family and friends to a luscious pie with chocolate, cherries and nuts in a creamy vanilla mousse. It's a sweet yet light dessert.

—DOROTHY PRITCHETT WILLS POINT, TX

PREP: 25 MIN. + CHILLING
MAKES: 10 SERVINGS

- 1 **can (14 ounces) sweetened condensed milk, divided**
- 1 **ounce unsweetened chocolate**
- ½ **teaspoon almond extract, divided**
- 1 **frozen pie shell (9 inches), baked**
- 1 **jar (10 ounces) maraschino cherries, drained**
- 1 **package (8 ounces) cream cheese, softened**
- 1 **cup cold water**
- 1 **package (3.4 ounces) instant vanilla pudding mix**
- 1 **cup heavy whipping cream, whipped**
- ½ **cup chopped toasted almonds Chopped chocolate, optional**

1. In a small saucepan over low heat, cook and stir ½ cup milk and the chocolate until chocolate is melted and mixture is thickened, about 4 minutes. Stir in ¼ teaspoon extract. Pour into pie shell; set aside.
2. Set aside eight whole cherries for garnish. Chop the remaining cherries; set aside. In a large bowl, beat cream cheese until fluffy. Gradually beat in water and remaining milk. Beat in pudding mix and remaining extract. Fold in the whipped cream. Stir in chopped cherries and almonds.
3. Pour over pie. Chill 4 hours or until set. Garnish with whole cherries and, if desired, chopped chocolate.

PECAN BUTTER TARTS

I searched for the perfect butter tart for ages. After many attempts, I finally discovered this favorite that simply begs for a scoop of ice cream on top.

—SUSAN KIEBOAM STREETSBORO, OH

PREP: 30 MIN. • **BAKE:** 10 MIN + COOLING
MAKES: 1 DOZEN

- 1 **package (14.1 ounces) refrigerated pie pastry**

FILLING
- ½ **cup raisins**
- 1 **cup water**
- 1 **large egg, lightly beaten**
- ½ **cup packed dark brown sugar**
- ½ **cup packed light brown sugar**
- ⅓ **cup butter, melted**
- 1½ **teaspoons vanilla extract**
- ¼ **teaspoon salt**
- ⅓ **cup coarsely chopped pecans Vanilla ice cream, optional**

1. Preheat oven to 425°. Line 12 muffin cups with foil liners. (Do not use paper-lined foil liners.)
2. On a work surface, unroll pastry sheets. Cut 12 circles with a floured 4-in. round cookie cutter (save remaining pastry for another use). Gently press pastry circles onto bottom and up sides of foil liners. Refrigerate while preparing filling.
3. In a microwave-safe bowl, combine raisins and water; microwave on high 2 minutes. Drain; cool slightly.
4. In a small bowl, mix egg, brown sugars, melted butter, vanilla and salt until blended; stir in the pecans and raisins. Spoon into pastry cups, dividing evenly.
5. Bake on a lower oven rack 7-9 minutes or until the filling just begins to bubble up and the crusts are light golden brown (do not overbake). Cool completely in pan on a wire rack. If desired, serve with ice cream.

CHERRY ALMOND MOUSSE PIE

GIANT PEANUT BUTTER ICE CREAM SANDWICH

I created this treat for my husband, adding light and low-fat products to the cookie dough. It was so fantastic that I fixed it with conventional ingredients for guests. Since it can be made ahead of time and frozen, it cuts stress for busy hostesses and really, who doesn't love peanut butter?

—JOANN BELACK BRADENTON, FL

PREP: 30 MIN. • **BAKE:** 20 MIN. + FREEZING
MAKES: 12 SERVINGS

- 2 **packages (16 ounces each) ready-to-bake refrigerated chocolate peanut butter cookie dough**
- 6 **whole chocolate graham crackers, crushed**
- 1 **cup cold milk**
- 1 **cup heavy whipping cream**
- 1 **package (3.4 ounces) instant vanilla pudding mix**
- 1 **package (8 ounces) cream cheese, softened**
- 1⅓ **cups creamy peanut butter**
- 3 **cups vanilla ice cream, softened**
- ¼ **cup Nutella**

1. Preheat oven to 350°. Let dough stand at room temperature for 5-10 minutes to soften. Press into two ungreased 9-in. springform pans; sprinkle with graham cracker crumbs. Bake for 20-25 minutes or until set. Cool completely.

2. In a large bowl, whisk milk, cream and pudding mix 2 minutes. Let stand 2 minutes or until soft-set. In another large bowl, beat the cream cheese and peanut butter until they are smooth. Add the pudding and ice cream; beat until smooth.

3. Spread over one cookie crust. Remove sides of second pan; place crust, crumb side down, over filling.

Wrap in plastic wrap; freeze on a baking sheet 4 hours or until firm.

4. Remove from freezer 15 minutes before serving. Place the Nutella in a small microwave-safe bowl; cover and microwave at 50% power 1-2 minutes or until it is smooth, stirring it twice. Remove sides of pan; cut dessert into slices. Drizzle with Nutella.

FAST FIX ▶
BLUEBERRY CRUMBLE TARTS

Pop one in a lunch box, share a batch at work or wait until after dinner—these are sweet anytime, anywhere. Sometimes, I refrigerate prepared tarts overnight and bake them while making dinner the next day. Foolproof.

—CAROLE FRASER NORTH YORK, ON

START TO FINISH: 30 MIN.
MAKES: 6 SERVINGS

- 2 **cups fresh blueberries**
- ¼ **cup sugar**
- 1 **tablespoon cornstarch**
- 1 **package (6 count) individual graham cracker tart shells**
- ¼ **cup all-purpose flour**
- ¼ **cup quick-cooking oats**
- ¼ **cup packed brown sugar**
- 2 **tablespoons cold butter**
  Ice cream or whipped cream, optional

1. Preheat oven to 375°. In a bowl, toss the blueberries with sugar and cornstarch; spoon into tart shells. In a small bowl, mix the flour, oats and brown sugar; cut in the butter until crumbly. Sprinkle over blueberries.

2. Place tarts on a baking sheet. Bake 20-25 minutes or until topping is golden brown and filling is bubbly. Serve warm or at room temperature. If desired, top with ice cream.

GIANT PEANUT BUTTER ICE CREAM SANDWICH

CREAMY CARAMEL FLAN

It's easy to prepare flan with this recipe! Try it and see. One warning, though—this yummy dessert is filling. A small slice goes a long way!
—PAT FORETE MIAMI, FL

PREP: 25 MIN. + STANDING
BAKE: 50 MIN. + CHILLING
MAKES: 8-10 SERVINGS

- ¾ cup sugar
- 1 package (8 ounces) cream cheese, softened
- 5 large eggs
- 1 can (14 ounces) sweetened condensed milk
- 1 can (12 ounces) evaporated milk
- 1 teaspoon vanilla extract

1. In a heavy saucepan, cook and stir the sugar over medium-low heat until melted and golden, about 15 minutes. Quickly pour it into an ungreased 2-qt. round baking or souffle dish, tilting to coat the bottom; let it stand for 10 minutes.
2. In a bowl, beat the cream cheese until smooth. Beat in eggs, one at a time, until thoroughly combined. Add remaining ingredients; mix well. Pour over the caramelized sugar.
3. Place the dish in a larger baking pan. Pour boiling water into larger pan to a depth of 1 in. Bake at 350° for 50-60 minutes or until center is just set (mixture will jiggle).
4. Remove the dish from a larger pan to a wire rack; cool it about 1 hour. Refrigerate overnight.
5. To unmold, run a knife around edges and invert onto a large rimmed serving platter. Cut into wedges or spoon onto dessert plates; spoon sauce over each serving.

STRAWBERRY
PRETZEL DESSERT

STRAWBERRY PRETZEL DESSERT

Here, a salty pretzel crust nicely contrasts cream cheese and gelatin layers.
—ALDENE BELCH FLINT, MI

PREP: 20 MIN. • **BAKE:** 10 MIN. + CHILLING
MAKES: 12-16 SERVINGS

- 2 cups crushed pretzels (about 8 ounces)
- ¾ cup butter, melted
- 3 tablespoons sugar

FILLING
- 2 cups whipped topping
- 1 package (8 ounces) cream cheese, softened
- 1 cup sugar

TOPPING
- 2 packages (3 ounces each) strawberry gelatin
- 2 cups boiling water
- 2 packages (16 ounces each) frozen sweetened sliced strawberries, thawed
  Additional whipped topping, optional

1. In a bowl, combine the pretzels, butter and sugar. Press the mix into an ungreased 13x9-in. baking dish. Bake at 350° for 10 minutes. Cool on a wire rack.
2. For filling, in a small bowl, beat whipped topping, cream cheese and sugar until smooth. Spread it over pretzel crust. Refrigerate until chilled.
3. For topping, dissolve gelatin in boiling water in a large bowl. Stir in strawberries with syrup; chill until partially set. Carefully spoon over filling. Chill for 4-6 hours or until firm. Cut into squares; serve with whipped topping if desired.

CHOCOLATE-STRAWBERRY CREAM CHEESE TART

Sure to impress, this dessert features velvety cream cheese, red strawberries and a drizzle of fudge, all piled on a crunchy chocolate-almond crust. It's too gorgeous to resist.
—PRISCILLA YEE CONCORD, CA

PREP: 20 MIN. • **BAKE:** 15 MIN. + CHILLING
MAKES: 12 SERVINGS

- ¾ cup all-purpose flour
- ½ cup finely chopped almonds, toasted
- 6 tablespoons butter, melted
- ⅓ cup baking cocoa
- ¼ cup packed brown sugar

FILLING
- 16 ounces cream cheese, softened
- 1 cup confectioners' sugar
- 1 teaspoon vanilla extract
- 3 cups halved fresh strawberries
- 3 tablespoons hot fudge ice cream topping

1. Preheat the oven to 375°. Using a small bowl, combine the first five ingredients; press onto the bottom and up the sides of an ungreased 9-in. fluted tart pan with a removable bottom. Bake 12-15 minutes or until crust is set. Cool on a wire rack.

2. In another small bowl, beat cream cheese, confectioners' sugar and vanilla until smooth. Spread over bottom of prepared crust. Arrange the strawberry halves, cut side down, over the filling. Cover and refrigerate for at least 1 hour.

3. Just before serving, drizzle the fudge topping over tart. Refrigerate any leftovers.

BLUEBERRY ZUCCHINI SQUARES

BLUEBERRY ZUCCHINI SQUARES

I saw a bar recipe using apple and lemon peel on a muffin mix box. I tried it from scratch with shredded zucchini and fresh blueberries instead. It's a nifty combo.
—**SHELLY BEVINGTON** HERMISTON, OR

PREP: 30 MIN. • **BAKE:** 30 MIN. + COOLING
MAKES: 2 DOZEN

- 2 cups shredded zucchini (do not pack)
- ½ cup buttermilk
- 1 tablespoon grated lemon peel
- 3 tablespoons lemon juice
- 1 cup butter, softened
- 2½ cups sugar
- 2 large eggs
- 3¼ cups plus 2 tablespoons all-purpose flour, divided
- 1 teaspoon baking soda
- ½ teaspoon salt
- 2 cups fresh or frozen blueberries

GLAZE
- 2 cups confectioners' sugar
- ¼ cup buttermilk
- 1 tablespoon grated lemon peel
- 2 teaspoons lemon juice
- ⅛ teaspoon salt

1. Preheat oven to 350°. Grease a 15x10x1-in. baking pan.
2. In a small bowl, combine zucchini, buttermilk, lemon peel and lemon juice; toss to combine. In a large bowl, cream butter and sugar until light and fluffy. Beat in eggs, one at a time. In another bowl, whisk 3¼ cups flour, baking soda and salt; gradually add to creamed mixture alternately with zucchini mixture, mixing well after each addition. Toss blueberries with remaining flour; fold into batter.
3. Transfer batter to prepared pan, spreading evenly (pan will be full). Bake for 30-35 minutes or until light golden brown and a toothpick pushed in center comes out clean. Cool it completely in pan on a wire rack.
4. Using a small bowl, mix the glaze ingredients until smooth; spread over top. Let stand until set.

NOTE *If using frozen blueberries, use without thawing to avoid discoloring the batter.*

NUTELLA HAND PIES

These pint-size Nutella hand pies made with puff pastry are too good to keep to yourself!
—*TASTE OF HOME* **TEST KITCHEN**

PREP: 10 MIN. • **BAKE:** 20 MIN.
MAKES: 9 SERVINGS

- 1 large egg
- 1 tablespoon water
- 1 sheet frozen puff pastry, thawed
- 3 tablespoons Nutella
- 1 to 2 teaspoons grated orange peel

ICING
- ⅓ cup confectioners' sugar
- ½ teaspoon orange juice
- ⅛ teaspoon grated orange peel
  Additional Nutella, optional

1. Preheat oven to 400°. In a small bowl, whisk egg with water.
2. Unfold puff pastry; cut into nine squares. Place 1 teaspoon Nutella in center of each; sprinkle with orange peel. Brush edges of pastry with the egg mixture. Fold one corner over the filling to form a triangle; press the edges to seal. Transfer to ungreased baking sheet.
3. Bake 17-20 minutes or until golden brown. Cool slightly.
4. In a small bowl, mix confectioners' sugar, orange juice and orange peel; drizzle over pies. If desired, warm additional Nutella in a microwave and drizzle over tops.

★ ★ ★ ★ ★ **READER REVIEW**

"My family loves hand pies, and these are so simple and easy to make. They taste amazing and look so much harder than they actually are."

RANDCBRUKNS TASTEOFHOME.COM

**TOFFEE-PEAR CRISP
BREAD PUDDING**

TOFFEE-PEAR CRISP BREAD PUDDING

My son loves pear crisp, but one night I was making bread pudding. He asked if I could make both. I compromised by combining two desserts into this one dish. We love it! It's absolutely fantastic!

—KURT WAIT REDWOOD CITY, CA

PREP: 20 MIN. + STANDING
BAKE: 40 MIN. + COOLING
MAKES: 12 SERVINGS

- 1¾ **cups 2% milk**
- 1 **cup butterscotch-caramel ice cream topping**
- ¼ **cup butter, cubed**
- 1 **teaspoon ground cinnamon**
- ½ **teaspoon ground ginger**
- 2 **large eggs**
- 4 **cups cubed day-old French bread**
- 2 **cups sliced peeled fresh pears (about 2 medium)**

TOPPING
- ½ **cup all-purpose flour**
- ½ **cup packed brown sugar**
- ⅓ **cup cold butter**
- ⅓ **cup English toffee bits**

1. Preheat oven to 350°. In a small saucepan, combine milk, caramel topping, butter, cinnamon and ginger. Cook and stir over medium-low heat until the butter is melted. Remove from heat.

2. Whisk the eggs in a large bowl; gradually whisk in a third of the milk mixture. Stir in the remaining milk mixture. Add bread; stir to coat. Let stand 10 minutes. Gently stir in pears; transfer to a greased 11x7-in. baking dish. Bake, uncovered, 20 minutes.

3. Meanwhile, for topping, in a small bowl, combine flour and brown sugar; cut in butter until crumbly. Stir in the toffee bits; sprinkle over the bread pudding. Bake, uncovered, for 20-25 minutes longer or until puffed, golden and a knife inserted near the center comes out clean. Let it stand for 10 minutes before serving. Serve warm. Refrigerate leftovers.

BLUE-RIBBON BUTTER CAKE

I found this recipe in an old cookbook I bought at a garage sale and couldn't wait to try it. I knew it had been someone's favorite because of the well-worn page.
—**JOAN GERTZ** PALMETTO, FL

PREP: 20 MIN. • **BAKE:** 65 MIN. + COOLING
MAKES: 16 SERVINGS

- 1 **cup butter, softened**
- 2 **cups sugar**
- 4 **large eggs**
- 2 **teaspoons vanilla extract**
- 3 **cups all-purpose flour**
- 1 **teaspoon baking powder**
- ½ **teaspoon baking soda**
- ½ **teaspoon salt**
- 1 **cup buttermilk**
BUTTER SAUCE
- 1 **cup sugar**
- ½ **cup butter, cubed**
- ¼ **cup water**
- 1½ **teaspoons almond extract**
- 1½ **teaspoons vanilla extract**

1. In a large bowl, cream butter and sugar until light and fluffy. Add eggs, one at a time, beating well after each addition. Beat in vanilla. Combine the flour, baking powder, baking soda and salt; add to the creamed mixture alternately with buttermilk, beating well after each addition.
2. Pour into a greased and floured 10-in. tube pan. Bake at 350° for 65-70 minutes or until a toothpick inserted in center comes out clean. Cool 10 minutes. Run a knife around edges and center tube of pan. Invert cake onto a wire rack over waxed paper.
3. For sauce, combine the sugar, butter and water in a small saucepan. Cook over medium heat just until butter is melted and sugar is dissolved. Remove from the heat; stir in extracts.
4. Poke holes in the top of the warm cake; spoon ¼ cup sauce over cake. Let stand until sauce is absorbed. Repeat twice. Poke holes into sides of cake; brush remaining sauce over sides. Cool completely.

SIMPLE TURTLE CHEESECAKE

FAST FIX
SIMPLE TURTLE CHEESECAKE

For an almost instant dessert, I spread some homemade ganache and caramel sauce over pre-made cheesecake. It makes entertaining feel slightly less hectic.
—**LAURA MCDOWELL** LAKE VILLA, IL

START TO FINISH: 25 MIN.
MAKES: 8 SERVINGS

- 1 **frozen New York-style cheesecake (30 ounces), thawed**
- ½ **cup semisweet chocolate chips**
- ½ **cup heavy whipping cream, divided**
- 3 **tablespoons chopped pecans, toasted**
- ¼ **cup butter, cubed**
- ½ **cup plus 2 tablespoons packed brown sugar**
- 1 **tablespoon light corn syrup**

1. Place cheesecake on a serving plate. Place chocolate chips in a small bowl. Using a small saucepan, bring ¼ cup cream just to a boil. Pour over the chocolate; stir with a whisk until smooth. Cool slightly, stirring the mix occasionally. Pour over cheesecake; sprinkle with pecans. Refrigerate until set.
2. In a small saucepan, melt butter; stir in brown sugar and corn syrup. Bring to a boil. Reduce heat; cook and stir until sugar is dissolved. Stir in the remaining cream and return to a boil. Remove from the heat. Serve warm with cheesecake or, if desired, cool it completely and drizzle it over the cheesecake.
NOTE *To toast nuts, bake in a shallow pan in a 350° oven for 5-10 minutes or cook in a skillet over low heat until lightly browned, stirring occasionally.*

TOFFEE BROWNIE
TRIFLE

TOFFEE BROWNIE TRIFLE

This decadent combination of pantry items is a terrific way to dress up a brownie mix. Try it with other flavors of pudding or substitute your favorite candy bar. It tastes great with low-fat and sugar-free products, too.

—WENDY BENNETT SIOUX FALLS, SD

PREP: 20 MIN. • **BAKE:** 25 MIN. + COOLING
MAKES: 16 SERVINGS

- 1 package fudge brownie mix (13x9-inch pan size)
- 2½ cups cold milk
- 1 package (3.4 ounces) instant cheesecake or vanilla pudding mix
- 1 package (3.3 ounces) instant white chocolate pudding mix
- 1 carton (8 ounces) frozen whipped topping, thawed
- 2 to 3 Heath candy bars (1.4 ounces each), chopped

1. Prepare and bake the brownies according to package directions for cake-like brownies, using a greased 13x9-in. baking pan. Cool completely on a wire rack.
2. Using a large bowl, beat the milk and pudding mixes on low speed for 2 minutes. Let them stand 2 minutes or until they are soft-set. Fold in the whipped topping.
3. Cut the brownies into 1-in. cubes; place half in a 3-qt. glass trifle bowl or serving dish. Cover with half of the pudding. Repeat the layers. Sprinkle with chopped candy bars. Refrigerate the leftovers.

★ ★ ★ ★ ★ **READER REVIEW**

"This has been a family favorite for years. My 24-year-old son requests this for his birthday every year. It's always a hit!"

BKYOUNGFAMILY TASTEOFHOME.COM

BANANA CREAM PIE

BANANA CREAM PIE

Made from our farm-fresh dairy products, this pie was a sensational creamy treat anytime that Mom served it. Her recipe is a real treasure, and I've never found one that tastes better!

—BERNICE MORRIS MARSHFIELD, MO

PREP: 20 MIN. + COOLING
MAKES: 6-8 SERVINGS

- ¾ cup sugar
- ⅓ cup all-purpose flour
- ¼ teaspoon salt
- 2 cups milk
- 3 egg yolks, lightly beaten
- 2 tablespoons butter
- 1 teaspoon vanilla extract
- 3 medium firm bananas
- 1 pastry shell (9 inches), baked
  Whipped cream and additional sliced bananas

1. In a saucepan, combine sugar, flour and salt; stir in the milk and mix well. Cook over medium-high heat until mixture is thickened and bubbly. Cook and stir for 2 minutes longer. Remove from the heat. Stir a small amount into egg yolks; return all to saucepan. Bring to a gentle boil. Cook for and stir 2 minutes; remove from the heat. Add the butter and vanilla; cool slightly.
2. Slice the bananas into pastry shell; pour filling over top. Cool on wire rack for 1 hour. Store in the refrigerator. Before serving, garnish with whipped cream and bananas.

CHERRY GELATIN SUPREME

TROPICAL CARROT CAKE

I look forward to August because that's when we enjoy our annual family reunion. Everyone loves this classic cake with the special flair it gets from pineapple. My great-aunt gave me her recipe, and I've made it a tradition to bring it every year.
—**VICTORIA CASEY** ENTERPRISE, OR

PREP: 15 MIN. • **BAKE:** 45 MIN. + COOLING
MAKES: 12-16 SERVINGS

- 3 **large eggs**
- ¾ **cup canola oil**
- ¾ **cup buttermilk**
- 2 **cups all-purpose flour**
- 2 **cups sugar**
- 2 **teaspoons baking soda**
- 2 **teaspoons ground cinnamon**
- ½ **teaspoon salt**
- 2 **teaspoons vanilla extract**
- 2 **cups finely shredded carrots**
- 1 **cup raisins**
- 1 **can (8 ounces) crushed pineapple, undrained**
- 1 **cup chopped walnuts**
- 1 **cup flaked coconut**

FROSTING
- 1 **package (8 ounces) cream cheese, softened**
- 4 **to 4½ cups confectioners' sugar**
- 1 **to 2 tablespoons heavy whipping cream**
- 1 **teaspoon vanilla extract**

1. In a large bowl, beat eggs, oil and buttermilk. Combine flour, sugar, baking soda, cinnamon and salt; add to egg mixture and mix well. Stir in vanilla, carrots, raisins, pineapple, walnuts and coconut; mix well. Pour into a greased 13x9-in. baking pan. Bake at 350° for 45-50 minutes or until cake tests done. Cool.
2. For frosting, beat all ingredients in a bowl until smooth. Frost cake.

CHERRY GELATIN SUPREME

When I was growing up, this easy-to-make, yummy dessert was always on the menu at holiday get-togethers. Years ago, my aunt gave me the recipe, and now when I make it for my family I think of her.
—**JANICE RATHGEB** BRIGHTON, IL

PREP: 20 MIN. + CHILLING
MAKES: 12 SERVINGS

- 2 **cups water, divided**
- 1 **package (3 ounces) cherry gelatin**
- 1 **can (21 ounces) cherry pie filling**
- 1 **package (3 ounces) lemon gelatin**
- 3 **ounces cream cheese, softened**
- ⅓ **cup mayonnaise**
- 1 **can (8 ounces) crushed pineapple, undrained**
- 1 **cup miniature marshmallows**
- ½ **cup heavy whipping cream, whipped**
- 2 **tablespoons chopped pecans**

1. In a large saucepan, bring 1 cup water to a boil. Stir in cherry gelatin until dissolved. Stir in the pie filling. Pour into an 11x7-in. dish. Cover and refrigerate for 2 hours or until set.
2. In a small saucepan, bring the remaining water to a boil. Stir in lemon gelatin until dissolved. In a small bowl, beat the cream cheese and mayonnaise until smooth. Beat in lemon gelatin and pineapple. Cover and refrigerate for 45 minutes.
3. Fold in the marshmallows and whipped cream. Spoon over cherry layer; sprinkle with pecans. Cover and refrigerate for 2 hours or until set.

FRUIT PIZZA

This pretty dessert has been a hit every time I've served it, and it makes a great change of pace from chocolate treats.

—JANET O'NEAL POPLAR BLUFF, MO

PREP: 30 MIN. + CHILLING
BAKE: 15 MIN. + COOLING
MAKES: 16-20 SERVINGS

- 1 tube (16½ ounces) refrigerated sugar cookie dough
- 1 package (8 ounces) cream cheese, softened
- ¼ cup confectioners' sugar
- 1 carton (8 ounces) frozen whipped topping, thawed
- 2 to 3 kiwifruit, peeled and thinly sliced
- 1 to 2 firm bananas, sliced
- 1 can (11 ounces) mandarin oranges, drained
- ½ cup red grape halves
- ¼ cup sugar
- ¼ cup orange juice
- 2 tablespoons water
- 1 tablespoon lemon juice
- 1½ teaspoons cornstarch
  Pinch salt

1. Pat the cookie dough into an ungreased 14-in. pizza pan. Bake at 350° for 15-18 minutes or until deep golden brown; cool.

2. In a bowl, beat the cream cheese and confectioners' sugar until the blend is smooth. Fold in whipped topping. Spread over crust. Arrange fruit on the top.

3. In a saucepan, bring the sugar, orange juice, water, lemon juice, cornstarch and salt to a boil, stirring constantly for 2 minutes or until thickened. Cool; brush over fruit. Chill. Store in refrigerator.

BUTTERMILK POUND CAKE

A true Southern classic, this cake is the one I make most often. Once people taste it, they say they won't go back to their other pound cake recipes.

—GRACIE HANCHEY DERIDDER, LA

PREP: 10 MIN. • **BAKE:** 70 MIN. + COOLING
MAKES: 16-20 SERVINGS

- 1 cup butter, softened
- 2½ cups sugar
- 4 large eggs
- 1 teaspoon vanilla extract
- 3 cups all-purpose flour
- ¼ teaspoon baking soda
- 1 cup buttermilk
  Confectioners' sugar, optional

1. In a large bowl, cream butter and sugar until light and fluffy. Add eggs, one at a time, beating well after each addition. Beat in vanilla. Combine flour and baking soda; add alternately with buttermilk and beat well.

2. Pour into a greased and floured 10-in. fluted tube pan. Bake at 325° for 70 minutes or until a toothpick inserted near the center comes out clean. Cool in the pan for 15 minutes before removing to a wire rack to cool completely. Dust with confectioners' sugar if desired.

BUTTERMILK POUND CAKE

CHOCOLATE S'MORES TART

I created this tart for my kids, who love having s'mores on the fire pit. It's truly indulgent. We simply can't get enough of the billowy marshmallow topping.

—**DINA CROWELL** FREDERICKSBURG, VA

PREP: 55 MIN. + CHILLING
MAKES: 16 SERVINGS

- 1½ **cups graham cracker crumbs**
- ¼ **cup sugar**
- ⅓ **cup butter, melted**

FILLING

- 10 **ounces bittersweet chocolate, chopped**
- ¼ **cup butter, cubed**
- 1½ **cups heavy whipping cream**

TOPPING

- 5 **large egg whites**
- 1 **cup sugar**
- ¼ **teaspoon cream of tartar**

1. Using a small bowl, mix the cracker crumbs and sugar; stir in butter. Press onto bottom and ½ in. up sides of an ungreased 9-in. fluted tart pan with removable bottom. Refrigerate about 30 minutes.

2. Place chocolate and butter in a large bowl. In a small saucepan, bring the cream just to a boil. Pour over the chocolate and butter; let it stand for 5 minutes. Stir with a whisk until smooth. Pour into prepared tart shell. Refrigerate 1 hour or until set. Place egg whites in a large bowl; let stand at room temperature 30 minutes.

3. In top of a double boiler or a metal bowl over simmering water, combine egg whites, sugar and cream of tartar. Beat on low speed 1 minute. Continue beating on low until a thermometer reads 160°, about 5 minutes. Transfer to a large bowl; beat on high until stiff glossy peaks form and mixture is slightly cooled, about 5 minutes.

4. Spread the meringue over tart. If desired, heat meringue with a kitchen torch or broil 2 in. from heat 30-45 seconds or until meringue is lightly browned. Refrigerate leftovers.

CHOCOLATE S'MORES TART

FREEZE IT ⑤ INGREDIENTS
BLUEBERRY CREAM POPS
Blueberries and cream combine for a fun after-school snack. Make these pops in the morning so they're ready to go when the kids come in the door.
—CINDY REAMS PHILIPSBURG, PA

PREP: 15 MIN. + FREEZING
MAKES: 8 POPS

- ⅔ **cup sugar**
- ⅔ **cup water**
- 2 **cups fresh or frozen blueberries, thawed**
- ¼ **cup heavy whipping cream**
- 8 **freezer pop molds or 8 paper cups (3 ounces each) and wooden pop sticks**

1. For sugar syrup, using a small saucepan, combine sugar and water; bring to a boil, stirring to dissolve sugar. Cool completely.
2. Meanwhile, in a bowl, coarsely mash blueberries; stir in cream and sugar syrup. Spoon into molds or paper cups. Top molds with holders. If using cups, top with foil and insert sticks through foil. Freeze until firm. To serve, let the pops stand at room temperature for 10 minutes before unmolding.

FREEZE IT ⑤ INGREDIENTS
EASY GRASSHOPPER ICE CREAM PIE
This quick pie is such an ego booster! My family compliments me the entire time they're eating it. A big hit at work potlucks, too, it's good to the last crumb.
—KIM MURPHY ALBIA, IA

PREP: 15 MIN. + FREEZING
MAKES: 8 SERVINGS

- 4 **cups mint chocolate chip ice cream, softened**
- 1 **chocolate crumb crust (8 inches)**
- 5 **Oreo cookies, chopped**
- ⅓ **cup chocolate-covered peppermint candies**
  Chocolate hard-shell ice cream topping

Spread ice cream into crust. Sprinkle with cookies and candies; drizzle with ice cream topping. Freeze until firm. Remove from the freezer 15 minutes before serving.
NOTE *This recipe was tested with Junior Mints chocolate-covered peppermint candies.*

PEACH MELBA TRIFLE
This dream of a dessert tastes extra good on a busy day because you can make it ahead of time. If you don't have fresh peaches handy, use the canned variety.
—CHRISTINA MOORE CASAR, NC

PREP: 20 MIN. + CHILLING
MAKES: 12 SERVINGS

- 2 **packages (12 ounces each) frozen unsweetened raspberries, thawed**
- 1 **tablespoon cornstarch**
- 1½ **cups (12 ounces) fat-free peach yogurt**
- ⅛ **teaspoon almond extract**
- 1 **carton (8 ounces) frozen reduced-fat whipped topping, thawed**
- 2 **prepared angel food cakes (8 to 10 ounces each), cut into 1-inch cubes (about 8 cups)**
- 4 **small peaches, peeled and sliced (about 2 cups)**

1. Using a large saucepan, mix the raspberries and cornstarch until they are blended. Bring to a boil; cook and stir 1-2 minutes or until thickened. Strain seeds; cover and refrigerate.
2. In a large bowl, mix the yogurt and extract; fold in whipped topping. In a 4-qt. bowl, layer half of the cake cubes, yogurt mixture and peaches. Repeat layers. Refrigerate, covered, for at least 3 hours before serving. Serve with raspberry sauce.

STRAWBERRY BANANA TRIFLE

GRITS PIE

Simple, southern and scrumptious, this pie will be a definite hit—even with people who dislike grits! It has the perfect custardy texture if you ask me.

—VICTORIA HUDSON PICKENS, SC

PREP: 15 MIN. • **BAKE:** 30 MIN.
MAKES: 10 SERVINGS

- ¾ **cup water**
- ⅛ **teaspoon salt**
- ¼ **cup quick-cooking grits**
- ½ **cup butter, cubed**
- ¾ **cup sugar**
- 2 **tablespoons all-purpose flour**
- 3 **large eggs**
- ¼ **cup buttermilk**
- 1 **teaspoon vanilla extract**
  Pastry for single-crust pie (9 inches)
  Whipped cream, orange slices or sliced fresh strawberries, optional

1. In a small saucepan, bring water and salt to a boil. Slowly stir in grits. Reduce heat; cook and stir for 4-5 minutes or until thickened. Add butter; stir until melted. Remove from the heat; cool to room temperature.
2. In a small bowl, whisk the sugar, flour, eggs, buttermilk and vanilla. Slowly stir into grits. Roll out pastry to fit a 9-in. pie plate. Transfer pastry to pie plate. Trim pastry to ½ in. beyond edge of plate; flute edges. Add filling.
3. Bake at 325° for 30-35 minutes or just until set. Serve warm or cool to room temperature. Garnish with whipped cream and orange slices or strawberries if desired.

STRAWBERRY BANANA TRIFLE

No matter where I take this dessert, the bowl is emptied in minutes. It's especially fun to make because everyone oohs and aahs over how pretty it is.

—KIM WATERHOUSE RANDOLPH, ME

PREP: 20 MIN. + COOLING
MAKES: 14 SERVINGS

- 1 **cup sugar**
- ¼ **cup cornstarch**
- 3 **tablespoons strawberry gelatin powder**
- 1 **cup cold water**
- 1 **pint fresh strawberries, sliced**
- 1¾ **cups cold milk**
- 1 **package (3.4 ounces) instant vanilla pudding mix**
- 3 **medium firm bananas, sliced**
- 1 **tablespoon lemon juice**
- 6 **cups cubed angel food cake**
- 2 **cups heavy whipping cream, whipped**
  Additional strawberries or banana slices, optional

1. In a saucepan, combine the sugar, cornstarch and gelatin; stir in water until smooth. Bring to a boil; cook and stir for 2 minutes or until thickened. Remove from the heat. Stir in the strawberries; set aside.
2. In a large bowl, combine milk and pudding mix. Beat on low speed for 2 minutes; set aside. Toss bananas with lemon juice; drain and set aside.
3. Place half of the cake cubes in a trifle bowl or 3-qt. serving bowl. Layer with half of the pudding, bananas, strawberry sauce and whipped cream. Repeat layers. Cover and refrigerate for at least 2 hours. Garnish with additional fruit if desired.

APPLE PIE A LA MODE

I was planning a dinner party, and wanted a dessert that truly wowed. My ice cream pie certainly does the trick. Loaded with caramel, it's a family favorite.

—TRISHA KRUSE EAGLE, ID

PREP: 15 MIN. + FREEZING
MAKES: 8 SERVINGS

- 1 can (21 ounces) apple pie filling
- 1 graham cracker crust (9 inches)
- 2 cups butter pecan ice cream, softened if necessary
- 1 jar (12 ounces) hot caramel ice cream topping
- ¼ cup chopped pecans, toasted

1. Spread half of the pie filling over crust. Top with half of the ice cream; freeze 30 minutes. Drizzle with half of the caramel topping; layer with the remaining pie filling. Freeze for 30 minutes. Scoop remaining ice cream over top. Freeze, covered, until firm.

2. Remove from freezer 30 minutes before serving. In a microwave, warm remaining caramel topping. Serve pie with warm caramel topping; sprinkle with pecans.

NOTE *To toast nuts, bake in a shallow pan in a 350° oven for 5-10 minutes or cook in a skillet over low heat until lightly browned, stirring occasionally.*

★ ★ ★ ★ ★ **5 STAR TIP**

If a recipe calls for a 9-in. graham cracker crust, you can make one from scratch in a pretty pie plate. Begin by crushing 24 graham cracker squares to yield 1½ cups crumbs. In a mixing bowl, combine the crumbs with ¼ cup sugar. Melt ⅓ cup butter; add to crumb mixture and blend well. Press the mixture onto the bottom and up the sides of an ungreased 9-in. pie plate. Refrigerate crust for 30 minutes before filling.

APPLE PIE A LA MODE

SHORTCUT TRES LECHES CAKE

My mom's favorite cake is tres leches, a butter cake soaked with three kinds of milk. I developed this no-fuss version that's oh-so rich and tender.

—MARINA CASTLE KELLEY
CANYON COUNTRY, CA

PREP: 20 MIN. + CHILLING
BAKE: 30 MIN. + COOLING
MAKES: 20 SERVINGS

- 1 package butter recipe golden cake or yellow cake mix (regular size)
- 3 large eggs
- ⅔ cup 2% milk
- ½ cup butter, softened
- 1 teaspoon vanilla extract

TOPPING
- 1 can (14 ounces) sweetened condensed milk
- 1 can (12 ounces) evaporated milk
- 1 cup heavy whipping cream

WHIPPED CREAM
- 1 cup heavy whipping cream
- 3 tablespoons confectioners' sugar
- 1 teaspoon vanilla extract

1. Preheat the oven to 350°. Grease a 13x9-in. baking pan.

2. In a large bowl, combine cake mix, eggs, milk, softened butter and vanilla; beat on low speed 30 seconds. Beat on medium for 2 minutes. Transfer to prepared pan. Bake 30-35 minutes or until a toothpick inserted in center comes out clean.

3. Cool in pan on a wire rack for 20 minutes. In a 4-cup measuring cup, whisk the topping ingredients until blended. Using a skewer, generously poke holes in top of warm cake. Pour milk mixture slowly over cake, filling the holes. Cool 30 minutes longer. Refrigerate, covered, at least 4 hours or overnight.

4. In a bowl, beat cream until it begins to thicken. Add confectioners' sugar and vanilla; beat until soft peaks form. Spread over cake.

SHORTCUT TRES LECHES CAKE

PEANUT BUTTER SHEET CAKE

I received the recipe for Peanut Butter Sheet Cake from a minister's wife, and my family just loves it.

—BRENDA JACKSON GARDEN CITY, KS

PREP: 15 MIN. • **BAKE:** 20 MIN. + COOLING
MAKES: 24 SERVINGS

- 2 cups all-purpose flour
- 2 cups sugar
- 1 teaspoon baking soda
- ½ teaspoon salt
- 1 cup water
- ¾ cup butter, cubed
- ½ cup chunky peanut butter
- ¼ cup canola oil
- 2 large eggs
- ½ cup buttermilk
- 1 teaspoon vanilla extract

GLAZE
- ⅔ cup sugar
- ⅓ cup evaporated milk
- 1 tablespoon butter
- ⅓ cup chunky peanut butter
- ⅓ cup miniature marshmallows
- ½ teaspoon vanilla extract

1. Preheat oven to 350°. Grease a 15x10x1-in. baking pan.

2. In a large bowl, whisk flour, sugar, baking soda and salt. Using a small saucepan, combine water and butter; bring just to a boil. Stir in the peanut butter and oil until blended. Stir into flour mixture. In a small bowl, whisk the eggs, buttermilk and vanilla until blended; add to the flour mixture, whisking constantly.

3. Transfer to prepared pan. Bake 20-25 minutes or until a toothpick inserted in center comes out clean.

4. Meanwhile, for glaze, combine sugar, milk and butter in a saucepan. Bring to a boil, stirring constantly; cook and stir for 2 minutes. Remove from the heat; stir in the peanut butter, marshmallows and vanilla until blended. Spoon over warm cake, spreading evenly. Cool on a wire rack.

PEANUT
BUTTER
SHEET CAKE

LEMON BARS

This dessert is a delightful recipe from my mother's file. I've been serving it for many years. The bars have a wonderful tangy flavor, and they're always a hit. Their color and shape make them a nice addition to a platter of cookies.

—ETTA SOUCY MESA, AZ

PREP: 10 MIN. • **BAKE:** 45 MIN. + COOLING
MAKES: 9 SERVINGS

- **1 cup all-purpose flour**
- **½ cup butter, softened**
- **¼ cup confectioners' sugar**

FILLING

- **2 large eggs**
- **1 cup sugar**
- **2 tablespoons all-purpose flour**
- **½ teaspoon baking powder**
- **2 tablespoons lemon juice**
- **1 teaspoon grated lemon peel**
  Additional confectioners' sugar

1. In a bowl, combine the flour, butter and confectioners' sugar. Pat into an ungreased 8-in. square baking pan. Bake at 350° for 20 minutes.
2. For filling, in a small bowl, beat eggs. Add the sugar, flour, baking powder, lemon juice and peel; beat until frothy. Pour over the crust. Bake 25 minutes longer or until light golden brown. Cool on a wire rack. Dust with confectioners' sugar. Cut into bars.

LEMON BARS

PEANUT BUTTER CUPCAKES

Peanut butter lovers can conveniently double their pleasure with these tender treats. I use the popular ingredient in the cupcakes as well as in the creamy homemade frosting.

—RUTH HUTSON WESTFIELD, IN

PREP: 20 MIN. • **BAKE:** 20 MIN. + COOLING
MAKES: ABOUT 1½ DOZEN

- **⅓ cup butter, softened**
- **½ cup peanut butter**
- **1¼ cups packed brown sugar**
- **1 large egg**
- **1 teaspoon vanilla extract**
- **2 cups all-purpose flour**
- **½ teaspoon salt**
- **½ teaspoon baking powder**
- **½ teaspoon baking soda**
- **¼ teaspoon ground cinnamon**
- **¾ cup 2% milk**

FROSTING

- **⅓ cup peanut butter**
- **2 cups confectioners' sugar**
- **2 teaspoons honey**
- **1 teaspoon vanilla extract**
- **3 to 4 tablespoons 2% milk**

1. In a large bowl, cream the butter, peanut butter and brown sugar until light and fluffy. Beat in egg and vanilla. Combine the dry ingredients; add to creamed mixture alternately with milk, beating well after each addition.
2. Fill the paper-lined muffin cups two-thirds full. Bake at 350° for 18-22 minutes or until a toothpick inserted near the center comes out clean. Cool for 10 minutes before removing from pans to wire racks to cool completely.
3. For the frosting, in a small bowl, cream the peanut butter and sugar until light and fluffy. Beat in the honey and vanilla. Beat in enough milk to achieve a spreading consistency. Frost the cupcakes.
NOTE *Reduced-fat peanut butter is not recommended for this recipe.*

BANANA CREAM CHEESECAKE

Here is a lovely no-bake dessert. Add a dash of cinnamon to the graham cracker crust if you prefer.
—**MARGIE SNODGRASS** WILMORE, KY

PREP: 25 MIN. + CHILLING
MAKES: 10 SERVINGS

- 1¾ cups graham cracker crumbs
- ¼ cup sugar
- ½ cup butter, melted

FILLING

- 1 package (8 ounces) cream cheese, softened
- ½ cup sugar
- 1 carton (8 ounces) frozen whipped topping, thawed, divided
- 3 to 4 medium firm bananas, sliced
- 1¾ cups cold milk
- 1 package (3.4 ounces) instant banana cream pudding mix

1. In a small bowl, combine cracker crumbs and sugar; stir in butter. Set aside ½ cup for topping. Press the remaining crumb mixture onto the bottom and up the sides of a greased 9-in. springform pan or 9-in. square baking pan. Bake at 350° for 5-7 minutes. Cool on wire rack.

2. In a large bowl, beat cream cheese and sugar until smooth. Fold in 2 cups whipped topping. Arrange half of the banana slices in crust; top with half of the cream cheese mixture. Repeat the layers.

3. In a small bowl, whisk milk and pudding mix for 2 minutes. Let stand for 2 minutes or until soft-set; fold in remaining whipped topping. Pour over the cream cheese layer. Sprinkle with the reserved crumb mixture. Refrigerate for 1-2 hours or until set.

EASY FRESH STRAWBERRY PIE

⑤ INGREDIENTS

EASY FRESH STRAWBERRY PIE

I often use whole fresh strawberries and arrange them pointed side up in the pastry shell for a different presentation. It also is a time-saver because I don't have to slice all of the berries.
—**SUE JURACK** MEQUON, WI

PREP: 20 MIN. + COOLING
BAKE: 15 MIN. + CHILLING
MAKES: 6-8 SERVINGS

- 1 unbaked pastry shell (9 inches)
- ¾ cup sugar
- 2 tablespoons cornstarch
- 1 cup water
- 1 package (3 ounces) strawberry gelatin
- 4 cups sliced fresh strawberries
  Fresh mint, optional

1. Line unpricked pastry shell with a double thickness of heavy-duty foil. Bake at 450° for 8 minutes. Remove foil; bake 5 minutes longer. Cool on a wire rack.

2. Using a small saucepan, combine the sugar, cornstarch and water until smooth. Bring to a boil; cook and stir for 2 minutes or until the mixture is thickened. Remove from heat; stir in gelatin until dissolved. Refrigerate for 15-20 minutes or until slightly cooled.

3. Meanwhile, arrange strawberries in the crust. Pour gelatin mixture over berries. Refrigerate until set. Garnish with mint if desired.

BUTTERY COCONUT BARS

My coconut bars are an American version of a Filipino coconut cake called bibingka. These are a crispier, sweeter take on the Christmas tradition I grew up with.

—DENISE NYLAND PANAMA CITY, FL

PREP: 20 MIN. + COOLING
BAKE: 40 MIN. + COOLING
MAKES: 3 DOZEN

- 2 **cups all-purpose flour**
- 1 **cup packed brown sugar**
- ½ **teaspoon salt**
- 1 **cup butter, melted**

FILLING

- 3 **large eggs**
- 1 **can (14 ounces) sweetened condensed milk**
- ½ **cup all-purpose flour**
- ¼ **cup packed brown sugar**
- ¼ **cup butter, melted**
- 3 **teaspoons vanilla extract**
- ½ **teaspoon salt**
- 4 **cups flaked coconut, divided**

1. Preheat the oven to 350°. Line a 13x9-in. baking pan with parchment paper, letting ends extend up sides.
2. In a large bowl, mix flour, brown sugar and salt; stir in 1 cup melted butter. Press onto bottom of prepared pan. Bake 12-15 minutes or until light brown. Cool 10 minutes on a wire rack. Reduce oven setting to 325°.
3. In a large bowl, whisk the first seven filling ingredients until blended; stir in 3 cups coconut. Pour over crust; sprinkle with remaining coconut. Bake 25-30 minutes or until light golden brown. Cool in pan on a wire rack. Lifting with parchment paper, remove from pan. Cut into bars.

CHOCOLATE CHIFFON CAKE

HOW TO MAKE A CHIFFON CAKE

Gently fold in the ingredients: Using a rubber spatula, slowly cut down through the ingredients/batter, pull across the bottom of the bowl and bring up part of the mixture.

To avoid large air pockets in the baked cake, cut through the batter with a knife to break air bubbles.

Chiffon cakes are done when the top springs back when touched, and the cracks at the top of the cake look and feel dry.

Cool chiffon cake upside down in the pan. Otherwise, it will collapse and flatten. If your tube pan has legs, invert it onto its legs until the cake is completely cool. If your tube plan does not have legs, place the pan over a funnel or the neck of a narrow bottle until cake is completely cool.

CHOCOLATE CHIFFON CAKE

If you want to offer family and friends a dessert that really stands out from the rest, this is the cake to make. Beautiful high layers of rich sponge cake are drizzled with a succulent chocolate glaze.

—**ERMA FOX** MEMPHIS, MO

PREP: 25 MIN. + COOLING
BAKE: 1 HOUR + COOLING
MAKES: 20 SERVINGS

- 7 **large eggs, separated**
- ½ **cup baking cocoa**
- ¾ **cup boiling water**
- 1¾ **cups cake flour**
- 1¾ **cups sugar**
- 1½ **teaspoons baking soda**
- 1 **teaspoon salt**
- ½ **cup canola oil**
- 2 **teaspoons vanilla extract**
- ¼ **teaspoon cream of tartar**

ICING
- ⅓ **cup butter**
- 2 **cups confectioners' sugar**
- 2 **ounces unsweetened chocolate, melted and cooled**
- 1½ **teaspoons vanilla extract**
- 3 **to 4 tablespoons hot water**
  Chopped nuts, optional

1. Let eggs stand at room temperature for 30 minutes. In a bowl, combine the cocoa and water until smooth; cool for 20 minutes. In a large bowl, combine flour, sugar, baking soda and salt. In a bowl, whisk egg yolks, oil and vanilla; add to dry ingredients along with the cocoa mixture. Beat until this is well blended. In another large bowl and with clean beaters, beat egg whites and cream of tartar on high speed until stiff peaks form. Gradually fold into egg yolk mixture.

2. Gently spoon the batter into an ungreased 10-in. tube pan and cut through the batter with a knife to remove the air pockets. Bake on the lowest rack at 325° for 60-65 minutes or until top springs back when lightly touched. Immediately invert pan; cool completely. Run a knife around sides and center tube of pan. Invert cake onto a serving plate.

3. For the icing, melt the butter in a saucepan. Remove from the heat; stir in the confectioners' sugar, chocolate, vanilla and water. Drizzle over cake. Sprinkle with nuts if desired.

**CINNAMON-APPLE
BROWN BETTY**

SLOW COOKER
CINNAMON-APPLE BROWN BETTY

For this sweet dish, spiced apples are slow-cooked between layers of cinnamon-raisin bread cubes for a wonderful twist on the traditional oven-baked classic.

—HEATHER DEMERITTE SCOTTSDALE, AZ

PREP: 15 MIN. • **COOK:** 2 HOURS
MAKES: 6 SERVINGS

- 5 **medium tart apples, cubed**
- 2 **tablespoons lemon juice**
- 1 **cup packed brown sugar**
- 1 **teaspoon ground cinnamon**
- ¼ **teaspoon ground nutmeg**
- 6 **tablespoons butter, melted**
- 6 **cups cubed day-old cinnamon-raisin bread (about 10 slices)**
  Sweetened whipped cream, optional

1. In a large bowl, toss apples with lemon juice. In a small bowl, mix brown sugar, cinnamon and nutmeg; add to apple mixture and toss to coat. In a large bowl, drizzle butter over bread cubes; toss to coat.
2. Place 2 cups of bread cubes in a greased 3- or 4-qt. slow cooker. Layer with half of the apple mixture and 2 cups bread cubes. Repeat layers. Cook, covered, on low 2-3 hours or until apples are tender. Stir before serving. If desired, top with whipped cream.

★ ★ ★ ★ ★ **READER REVIEW**

"My husband enjoys almost any dessert with apples. This is one of his favorites. It smells wonderful as it bakes, especially when you lift the lid off the slow cooker."

NANZIM TASTEOFHOME.COM

FUDGE-TOPPED BROWNIES

These exquisite brownies are the ultimate chocolate dessert.

—JUDY OLSON WHITECOURT, AB

PREP: 25 MIN. • **BAKE:** 25 MIN. + FREEZING
MAKES: ABOUT 10 DOZEN

- 1 cup butter
- 4 ounces unsweetened chocolate, chopped
- 2 cups sugar
- 2 teaspoons vanilla extract
- 4 large eggs
- 1½ cups all-purpose flour
- 1 teaspoon baking powder
- ½ teaspoon salt
- 1 cup chopped walnuts

TOPPING

- 4½ cups sugar
- 1 can (12 ounces) evaporated milk
- ½ cup butter, cubed
- 1 package (12 ounces) semisweet chocolate chips
- 1 package (11½ ounces) milk chocolate chips
- 1 jar (7 ounces) marshmallow creme
- 2 teaspoons vanilla extract
- 2 cups chopped walnuts

1. Using a heavy saucepan, melt the butter and chocolate; stir until they're smooth. Remove from heat; blend in sugar and vanilla. Add eggs; mix well. Combine the flour, baking powder and salt; add to chocolate mixture. Stir in walnuts. Pour into a greased 13x9-in. baking pan. Bake at 350° for 25-30 minutes or until top springs back when lightly touched. Cool on a wire rack while preparing the topping.

2. Combine the sugar, milk and butter in a large heavy saucepan; bring to a boil over medium heat. Reduce heat; simmer, uncovered, for 5 minutes, stirring constantly. Remove from the heat. Stir in the chocolate chips, marshmallow creme and vanilla until smooth. Add walnuts. Spread over warm brownies. Freeze for 3 hours or until firm. Cut into 1-in. squares. Store in the refrigerator.

PEANUT BUTTER CREAM PIE

PEANUT BUTTER CREAM PIE

During the warm months, it's nice to have a fluffy, no-bake dessert that's a snap to make. Packed with peanut flavor, this pie gets quickly gobbled up even after a big meal!

—JESSE & ANNE FOUST BLUEFIELD, WV

PREP: 10 MIN. + CHILLING
MAKES: 6-8 SERVINGS

- 1 package (8 ounces) cream cheese, softened
- ¾ cup confectioners' sugar
- ½ cup peanut butter
- 6 tablespoons milk
- 1 carton (8 ounces) frozen whipped topping, thawed
- 1 graham cracker crust (9 inches)
- ¼ cup chopped peanuts

In a large bowl, beat cream cheese until fluffy. Beat in sugar and peanut butter. Gradually add the milk. Fold in whipped topping; spoon into the crust. Sprinkle with the peanuts. Chill overnight.

WHITE
CHOCOLATE
FRUIT TART

WHITE CHOCOLATE FRUIT TART

This tart is absolutely marvelous, especially in summer when fresh fruit is in abundance.

—**CLAIRE DAILEY** NEW CASTLE, DE

PREP: 30 MIN. • **BAKE:** 25 MIN. + CHILLING
MAKES: 16 SERVINGS

- ¾ **cup butter, softened**
- ½ **cup confectioners' sugar**
- 1½ **cups all-purpose flour**

FILLING
- 1 **package (10 to 12 ounces) white baking chips, melted and cooled**
- ¼ **cup heavy whipping cream**
- 1 **package (8 ounces) cream cheese, softened**
- 1 **can (20 ounces) pineapple chunks**
- 1 **pint fresh strawberries, sliced**
- 1 **can (11 ounces) mandarin oranges, drained**
- 2 **kiwifruit, peeled and sliced**

GLAZE
- 3 **tablespoons sugar**
- 2 **teaspoons cornstarch**
- ½ **teaspoon lemon juice**

1. In a bowl, cream butter and confectioners' sugar until fluffy. Gradually add flour and mix well.
2. Press into an ungreased 11-in. fluted tart pan with removable bottom or 12-in. pizza pan with sides. Bake at 300° for 25-30 minutes or until lightly browned. Cool on a wire rack.
3. For filling, in a small bowl, beat melted chips and cream. Add cream cheese; beat until smooth. Spread over crust. Refrigerate for 30 minutes.
4. Drain pineapple, reserving ½ cup of the juice. Arrange the pineapple, strawberries, oranges and kiwi over the filling.
5. For glaze, using a small saucepan, combine sugar and cornstarch. Stir in lemon juice and reserved pineapple juice until smooth. Bring to a boil over medium heat; cook and stir 2 minutes or until thickened. Cool.
6. Brush glaze over fruit. Refrigerate for 1 hour before serving. Refrigerate the leftovers.

CHOCOLATE
BAVARIAN TORTE

CHOCOLATE BAVARIAN TORTE

Whenever I take this torte to a potluck, I get so many requests for the recipe.

—**EDITH HOLMSTROM** MADISON, WI

PREP: 15 MIN. + CHILLING
BAKE: 30 MIN. + COOLING
MAKES: 12 SERVINGS

- 1 **package devil's food cake mix (regular size)**
- 1 **package (8 ounces) cream cheese, softened**
- ⅓ **cup packed brown sugar**
- 1 **teaspoon vanilla extract**
- ⅛ **teaspoon salt**
- 2 **cups heavy whipping cream, whipped**
- 2 **tablespoons grated semisweet chocolate**

1. Prepare and bake cake according to package directions, using two 9-in. round baking pans. Cool in pans for 10 minutes before removing to wire racks to cool completely.
2. In a large bowl, beat the cream cheese, sugar, vanilla and salt until smooth. Fold in cream.
3. Cut each cake horizontally into two layers. Place bottom layer on a serving plate; top with a fourth of the cream mixture. Sprinkle with a fourth of the chocolate. Repeat the layers three times. Cover and refrigerate 8 hours or overnight.

BUTTER PECAN
LAYER CAKE

APPLE DUMPLINGS WITH SAUCE

Covered in a luscious caramel sauce, these dumplings are amazing served alone or with a big scoop of vanilla ice cream.
—ROBIN LENDON CINCINNATI, OH

PREP: 1 HOUR + CHILLING • **BAKE:** 50 MIN.
MAKES: 8 SERVINGS

- 3 cups all-purpose flour
- 1 teaspoon salt
- 1 cup shortening
- ⅓ cup cold water
- 8 medium tart apples, peeled and cored
- 8 teaspoons butter
- 9 teaspoons cinnamon-sugar, divided

SAUCE
- 1½ cups packed brown sugar
- 1 cup water
- ½ cup butter, cubed

1. In a large bowl, combine flour and salt; cut in shortening until crumbly. Gradually add the water, tossing with a fork until the dough forms a ball. Divide into eight portions. Cover and refrigerate at least 30 minutes or until easy to handle.
2. Preheat the oven to 350°. Roll each portion of dough between two lightly floured sheets of waxed paper into a 7-in. square. Place an apple on each square. Place 1 teaspoon butter and 1 teaspoon cinnamon-sugar in the center of each apple.
3. Gently bring up the corners of the pastry to each center; pinch edges to seal. If desired, cut out apple leaves and stems from dough scraps; attach to dumplings with water. Place in a greased 13x9-in. baking dish. Sprinkle with the remaining cinnamon-sugar.
4. In a large saucepan, combine sauce ingredients. Bring them just to a boil, stirring until blended. Pour the mix over the apples.
5. Bake 50-55 minutes or until the apples are tender and pastry is golden brown, basting occasionally with sauce. Serve warm.

BUTTER PECAN LAYER CAKE

Pecans and butter give this cake the same irresistible flavor as the popular ice cream.
—BECKY MILLER TALLAHASSEE, FL

PREP: 40 MIN. • **BAKE:** 25 MIN. + COOLING
MAKES: 12-16 SERVINGS

- 2⅔ cups chopped pecans, divided
- 1¼ cups butter, softened, divided
- 2 cups sugar
- 4 large eggs
- 2 teaspoons vanilla extract
- 3 cups all-purpose flour
- 2 teaspoons baking powder
- ½ teaspoon salt
- 1 cup milk

FROSTING
- 1 cup butter, softened
- 8 to 8½ cups confectioners' sugar
- 1 can (5 ounces) evaporated milk
- 2 teaspoons vanilla extract

1. Place pecans and ¼ cup butter in a baking pan. Bake at 350° for 10-15 minutes or until toasted, stirring frequently; set aside.
2. In a large bowl, cream sugar and remaining butter until light and fluffy. Add eggs, one at a time, beating well after each addition. Stir in vanilla. Combine the flour, baking powder and salt; add to the creamed mixture alternately with milk, beating well after each addition. Stir in 1⅓ cups of toasted pecans.
3. Pour into three greased and floured 9-in. round baking pans. Bake at 350° for 25-30 minutes or until a toothpick inserted in the center comes out clean. Cool for 10 minutes before removing from pans to wire racks to cool completely.
4. For frosting, cream butter and confectioners' sugar in a large bowl. Add milk and vanilla; beat until smooth. Stir in remaining toasted pecans. Spread frosting between layers and over top and sides of cake.

VERY BERRY CRISP

I love this recipe because it's easy, low-fat, versatile and delicious! The crispy topping is flavored with graham cracker crumbs, cinnamon and almonds and doesn't taste light at all. It's great with frozen yogurt or whipped topping.

—SCARLETT ELROD NEWNAN, GA

PREP: 20 MIN. • **BAKE:** 25 MIN.
MAKES: 8 SERVINGS

- 2 **cups fresh raspberries**
- 2 **cups sliced fresh strawberries**
- 2 **cups fresh blueberries**
- ⅓ **cup sugar**
- 2 **tablespoons plus ¼ cup all-purpose flour, divided**
- ⅓ **cup graham cracker crumbs**
- ⅓ **cup quick-cooking oats**
- ¼ **cup packed brown sugar**
- 2 **tablespoons sliced almonds**
- ½ **teaspoon ground cinnamon**
- 1 **tablespoon canola oil**
- 1 **tablespoon butter, melted**
- 1 **tablespoon water**

1. Using a large bowl, combine the berries, sugar and 2 tablespoons flour; transfer to an 11x7-in. baking dish coated with cooking spray.

2. Using a small bowl, combine the cracker crumbs, oats, brown sugar, almonds, cinnamon and remaining flour. Stir in the oil, butter and water until moistened. Sprinkle the blend over the berries.

3. Bake at 375° for 25-30 minutes or until filling is bubbly and topping is golden brown.

★ ★ ★ ★ ★ **5 STAR TIP**

Purchase strawberries that are shiny, firm and fragrant. A strawberry should be almost completely red, though some whiteness near the cap is acceptable. Look for fresh blueberries that are firm, dry, plump and smooth-skinned. Raspberries should be brightly colored without the hulls attached.

FREEZE IT

BUTTERMILK PEACH ICE CREAM

My mother's family owned peach orchards in Missouri. I live in Tennessee, a top consumer of buttermilk. This summery ice cream combines both my past and present!

—KIM HIGGINBOTHAM KNOXVILLE, TN

PREP: 15 MIN. + CHILLING
PROCESS: 30 MIN./BATCH + FREEZING
MAKES: 2 QUARTS

- 2 **pounds ripe peaches (about 7 medium), peeled and quartered**
- ½ **cup sugar**
- ½ **cup packed brown sugar**
- 1 **tablespoon lemon juice**
- 1 **teaspoon vanilla extract**
  Pinch salt
- 2 **cups buttermilk**
- 1 **cup heavy whipping cream**

1. Place peaches in a food processor; process until smooth. Add sugars, lemon juice, vanilla and salt; process until blended.

2. In a large bowl, mix the buttermilk and the cream. Stir in peach mixture. Refrigerate, covered, for 1 hour or until cold.

3. Fill cylinder of ice cream maker no more than two-thirds full. Freeze according to the manufacturer's directions, refrigerating any of the remaining mixture to process later.

4. Transfer the ice cream to freezer containers, allowing headspace for expansion. Freeze for 2-4 hours or until firm. Let the ice cream stand at room temperature for 10 minutes before serving.

BUTTERMILK PEACH ICE CREAM

COOKIES & CANDIES

Just about everybody has a sweet tooth. Here you'll find a treasure trove of recipes to satisfy that craving. Whether it's a classic cookie or a mouthwatering candy, these sweet sensations are sure to get people talking.

PEANUT BUTTER CHIPPERS

My cookie-loving family always comes running to the kitchen when they smell peanut butter and chocolate baking. This recipe is so quick and easy, I often stir up a batch while making dinner.
—**PAT DOERFLINGER** CENTERVIEW, MO

PREP: 10 MIN. • **BAKE:** 15 MIN./BATCH
MAKES: 3½ DOZEN

- 6 **tablespoons butter, softened**
- ¼ **cup peanut butter**
- ½ **cup sugar**
- ½ **cup packed brown sugar**
- 1 **large egg**
- 1 **teaspoon vanilla extract**
- 1¼ **cups all-purpose flour**
- ½ **teaspoon baking soda**
- ¼ **teaspoon salt**
- 1 **cup milk chocolate chips**

1. In a small bowl, cream the butter, peanut butter and sugars until light and fluffy. Beat in egg and vanilla. Combine the flour, baking soda and salt; gradually add to creamed mixture and mix well. Stir in chocolate chips.
2. Drop by tablespoonfuls 2 in. apart onto ungreased baking sheets. Bake at 350° for 11-14 minutes or until golden brown. Remove to wire racks.
NOTE *Reduced-fat peanut butter is not recommended for this recipe.*

★ ★ ★ ★ ★ **READER REVIEW**

"I replaced the PB with Nutella and it was great. Chocolaty, hazelnutty, delicious!"

REGAL_S TASTEOFHOME.COM

EASY OATMEAL CREAM PIES

EASY OATMEAL CREAM PIES

These easy cookies use only five ingredients and bake up tender and moist.

—**CRYSTAL SCHLUETER** NORTHGLENN, CO

PREP: 20 MIN. + CHILLING
BAKE: 10 MIN./BATCH + COOLING
MAKES: 1½ DOZEN

- ¾ **cup butter, softened**
- 2 **large eggs**
- 1 **package spice cake mix (regular size)**
- 1 **cup quick-cooking oats**
- 1 **can (16 ounces) vanilla frosting**

1. Beat butter and eggs until blended. Beat in cake mix and oats. Refrigerate, covered, 2 hours or until firm enough to roll, though dough will remain fairly soft.

2. Preheat oven to 350°. On a well-floured surface, roll half of dough to ¼-in. thickness. Cut with a floured 2½-in. round cookie cutter. Place 1 in. apart on parchment paper-lined baking sheets. Bake 8-10 minutes or until set. Remove from pans to wire racks to cool completely. Repeat with remaining dough.

3. Spread frosting on the bottoms of half of the cookies; cover with the remaining cookies.

FREEZE OPTION *Freeze the cookies in freezer containers, separating the layers with waxed paper. To use, thaw before serving.*

★ ★ ★ ★ ★ **5 STAR TIP**

Quick-cooking oats and old-fashioned oats are interchangeable in recipes, as long as you consider the differences between the two. Both types have been flattened with large rollers, but quick-cooking oats are cut into smaller pieces first. As a result, quick-cooking oats cook faster, and offer a more delicate texture in baked goods. If you prefer a heartier texture, use old-fashioned oats.

BUTTERY GANACHE COOKIE CUPS

BUTTERY GANACHE COOKIE CUPS

Our family wanted to share our love of ganache-filled cupcakes, so we made them into cookies—and because we bake the cookies into muffin cups, we get the best of both worlds.

—**ADELA SRINIVASAN** PARKER, CO

PREP: 30 MIN. + CHILLING
BAKE: 10 MIN./BATCH + COOLING
MAKES: ABOUT 4 DOZEN

- 1 **cup butter, softened**
- 1 **cup sugar**
- 2 **large eggs**
- 2 **tablespoons orange juice**
- 1 **teaspoon orange extract**
- 3 **cups all-purpose flour**
- 1 **teaspoon baking powder**
- ¼ **teaspoon salt**
- 1 **tablespoon confectioners' sugar**
- 6 **ounces bittersweet chocolate, chopped**
- 1 **cup heavy whipping cream**

1. In a large bowl, cream butter and sugar until light and fluffy. Add eggs, one at a time, beating well after each addition. Beat in orange juice and extract. In another bowl, whisk flour, baking powder and salt; gradually beat into creamed mixture. Refrigerate, covered, 1 hour or until firm.

2. Preheat the oven to 350°. Shape level tablespoons of dough into balls; press evenly onto the bottom and up the sides of greased or foil-lined mini-muffin cups. Bake 7-9 minutes or until the edges are light brown. Cool in pans for 2 minutes. Remove to wire racks to cool completely. Dust with confectioners' sugar.

3. Meanwhile, place chocolate in a small bowl. Using a small saucepan, bring cream just to a boil. Pour over the chocolate; stir with a whisk until smooth. Cool slightly. Refrigerate, covered, about 1 hour or until the ganache thickens to a spreading consistency, stirring occasionally. Pipe onto cookie cups. Refrigerate in airtight containers.

FREEZE OPTION *Freeze shaped balls of dough on waxed paper-lined baking sheets until they are firm. Transfer to resealable plastic freezer bags; return to freezer. To use, thaw the dough in the refrigerator overnight. Bake and decorate cookies as directed.*

GINGER & MAPLE MACADAMIA NUT COOKIES

GINGER & MAPLE MACADAMIA NUT COOKIES

This spiced cookie has a real kick of ginger, similar to traditional German lebkuchen. If you don't have crystallized ginger on hand, use colored sprinkles.
—**THOMAS FAGLON** SOMERSET, NJ

PREP: 45 MIN. + CHILLING
BAKE: 10 MIN./BATCH + COOLING
MAKES: ABOUT 7 DOZEN

1½ **cups butter, softened**
½ **cup sugar**
¾ **cup maple syrup**
4 **cups all-purpose flour**
3 **teaspoons ground ginger**
3 **teaspoons ground cinnamon**
1 **teaspoon ground allspice**
½ **teaspoon ground cloves**
1½ **teaspoons salt**
1½ **teaspoons baking soda**
1½ **cups finely chopped macadamia nuts**
24 **ounces dark chocolate candy coating, melted**
⅓ **cup finely chopped crystallized ginger**

1. In a large bowl, cream butter and sugar until light and fluffy. Gradually beat in syrup. In another bowl, whisk the flour, spices, salt and baking soda; gradually beat into creamed mixture. Stir in nuts.
2. Divide dough in half; shape each into a 12-in.-long roll. Wrap in plastic wrap; refrigerate 2 hours or until firm.
3. Preheat oven to 350°. Unwrap and cut dough crosswise into ¼-in. slices. Place 1 in. apart on ungreased baking sheets. Bake 8-10 minutes or until set. Cool on pans 2 minutes. Remove to wire racks to cool completely.
4. Dip each cookie halfway into the melted candy coating; allow excess to drip off. Place the cookies on waxed paper-lined baking sheets; sprinkle with crystallized ginger. Refrigerate until set.

⑤INGREDIENTS

CARAMEL TRUFFLES

My caramel-filled candies disappear just as fast as I can make them. The five-ingredient microwave recipe is fun to make.
—**CHARLOTTE MIDTHUN** GRANITE FALLS, MN

PREP: 1 HOUR + CHILLING
MAKES: 2½ DOZEN

26 **caramels**
1 **cup milk chocolate chips**
¼ **cup heavy whipping cream**
1⅓ **cups semisweet chocolate chips**
1 **tablespoon shortening**

1. Line an 8-in. square dish with plastic wrap; set it aside. Using a microwave-safe bowl, combine the caramels, milk chocolate chips and cream. Microwave, uncovered, on high for 1 minute; stir. Microwave for 1 minute longer, stirring every 15 seconds or until the caramels are melted and the mixture is smooth. Spread into prepared dish; refrigerate for 1 hour or until firm.
2. Using plastic wrap, lift candy out of pan. Cut into 30 pieces; roll each piece into a 1-in. ball. Cover and refrigerate for 1 hour or until firm.
3. In a microwave-safe bowl, melt semisweet chips and shortening; stir until smooth. Dip the caramels in chocolate; allow excess to drip off. Place on waxed paper; let stand until set. Refrigerate until firm.
NOTE *This recipe was tested in a 1,100-watt microwave.*

ALMOND CRUNCH

Once you start eating this taste-tempting treat, you may not be able to stop! Matzo crackers are topped with buttery caramel, chocolate and slivered almonds...and then baked to perfection.

—**SHARALYN ZANDER** JACKSONVILLE, AL

PREP: 20 MIN. • **BAKE:** 15 MIN. + CHILLING
MAKES: 1 POUND

- 4 to 6 **unsalted matzo crackers**
- 1 **cup butter, cubed**
- 1 **cup packed brown sugar**
- ¾ **cup semisweet chocolate chips**
- 1 **teaspoon shortening**
- 1 **cup slivered almonds, toasted**

1. Line a 15x10x1-in. baking pan with foil; line the foil with parchment paper. Arrange the crackers in the pan; set aside.

2. In a large, heavy saucepan over medium heat, melt the butter. Stir in the brown sugar. Bring to a boil; cook and stir for 3-4 minutes or until the sugar is dissolved. Spread evenly over the crackers.

3. Bake at 350° for 15-17 minutes (cover loosely with foil if top browns too quickly). Cool on a wire rack for 5 minutes. Meanwhile, melt chocolate chips and shortening; stir until they are smooth. Stir in almonds; spread over top. Cool for 1 hour.

4. Break it into pieces. Cover and refrigerate for at least 2 hours or until set. Store in an airtight container.

★ ★ ★ ★ ★ **READER REVIEW**

"This recipe is so easy and so delicious! I use lightly salted matzo crackers to get that salty/sweet combo. Yum!"

ASH5563 TASTEOFHOME.COM

ALMOND CRUNCH

LEMON MELTAWAYS

Both the cookie and the frosting are spiked with lemon juice in these divine goodies. You'll be happy you baked them.

—MARY HOUCHIN LEBANON, IL

PREP: 15 MIN. + CHILLING
BAKE: 10 MIN./BATCH + COOLING
MAKES: ABOUT 5 DOZEN

- ¾ **cup butter, softened**
- ⅓ **cup confectioners' sugar**
- 1 **teaspoon lemon juice**
- 1¼ **cups all-purpose flour**
- ½ **cup cornstarch**

FROSTING
- ¼ **cup butter, softened**
- ¾ **cup confectioners' sugar**
- 1 **teaspoon grated lemon peel**
- 1 **teaspoon lemon juice**
- 1 **to 3 drops yellow food coloring, optional**

1. In a bowl, beat the butter and confectioners' sugar until blended. Beat in lemon juice. In a small bowl, whisk flour and cornstarch; gradually beat into butter mixture. Divide dough in half; shape each into an 8-in.-long roll. Wrap in plastic wrap; refrigerate 2 hours or until firm.

2. Preheat the oven to 350°. Unwrap and cut the dough crosswise into ¼-in. slices. Place them 2 in. apart on ungreased baking sheets.

3. Bake 8-12 minutes or until firm. Remove from pans to wire racks to cool completely.

4. For frosting, in a small bowl, beat butter and confectioners' sugar until smooth. Beat in lemon peel, lemon juice and, if desired, food coloring. Spread over cookies.

LEMON MELTAWAYS

CREAM-FILLED CHOCOLATE COOKIES

I have been making these cookies for years. My children and grandchildren always gobble them up.

—**MAXINE FINN** EMMETSBURG, IA

PREP: 15 MIN. + CHILLING
BAKE: 10 MIN./BATCH + COOLING
MAKES: ABOUT 4½ DOZEN

- 1 **cup butter, softened**
- 2 **cups sugar**
- 2 **large eggs**
- 1 **teaspoon vanilla extract**
- 3 **cups all-purpose flour**
- ⅔ **cup baking cocoa**
- 1 **teaspoon baking soda**
- 1 **teaspoon salt**
- ½ **cup whole milk**

FILLING

- ½ **cup butter, softened**
- 1½ **cups confectioners' sugar**
- 1 **cup marshmallow creme**
- 1 **teaspoon vanilla extract**

1. In a large bowl, cream butter and sugar until light and fluffy. Add eggs, one at a time, beating well after each addition. Beat in vanilla. Combine the flour, cocoa, baking soda and salt; gradually add to creamed mixture alternately with milk, beating well after each addition. Refrigerate for at least 2 hours.

2. Drop by rounded teaspoonfuls 2 in. apart onto greased baking sheets. Bake at 375° for 10-12 minutes or until the edges are set. Remove to wire racks to cool.

3. In a small bowl, combine filling ingredients; beat until smooth. Spread on the bottoms of half of the cookies; top with remaining cookies. Store in the refrigerator.

AUNT MYRTLE'S COCONUT OAT COOKIES

These cookies are the stuff of happy memories. Coconut and oatmeal give them rich flavor and texture. Store them in your best cookie jar.

—**CATHERINE CASSIDY** MILWAUKEE, WI

PREP: 30 MIN. • **BAKE:** 10 MIN./BATCH
MAKES: ABOUT 5 DOZEN

- 1 **cup butter, softened**
- 1 **cup packed brown sugar**
- 2 **large eggs**
- 2 **teaspoons vanilla extract**
- 2⅓ **cups all-purpose flour**
- 1 **teaspoon salt**
- 1 **teaspoon baking soda**
- ¾ **teaspoon baking powder**
- 2 **cups flaked coconut**
- 1 **cup old-fashioned or quick-cooking oats**
- ¾ **cup chopped walnuts, toasted**

1. Preheat oven to 375°. In a large bowl, cream butter and brown sugar until light and fluffy. Beat in eggs and vanilla. In another bowl, whisk flour, salt, baking soda and baking powder; gradually beat into creamed mixture. Stir in coconut, oats and walnuts.

2. Drop dough by tablespoonfuls 2 in. apart onto ungreased baking sheets. Bake for 8-10 minutes or until light brown. Remove from pans to wire racks to cool.

NOTE *To toast nuts, bake in a shallow pan in a 350° oven for 5-10 minutes or cook in a skillet over low heat until lightly browned, stirring occasionally.*

TOFFEE ALMOND SANDIES

These yummy classics are just loaded with crunchy chopped toffee and almonds, so there's no doubt as to why they're my husband's all-time favorite cookie. I used to bake them in large batches when our four sons still lived at home. Now I whip them up for our grandchildren.

—**ALICE KAHNK** KENNARD, NE

PREP: 35 MIN. • **BAKE:** 15 MIN./BATCH
MAKES: ABOUT 12 DOZEN

- 1 **cup butter, softened**
- 1 **cup sugar**
- 1 **cup confectioners' sugar**
- 1 **cup canola oil**
- 2 **large eggs**
- 1 **teaspoon almond extract**
- 3½ **cups all-purpose flour**
- 1 **cup whole wheat flour**
- 1 **teaspoon baking soda**
- 1 **teaspoon cream of tartar**
- 1 **teaspoon salt**
- 2 **cups chopped almonds**
- 1 **package (8 ounces) milk chocolate English toffee bits**
  Additional sugar

1. In a large bowl, cream butter and sugars until light and fluffy. Beat in the oil, eggs and extract. Combine the flours, baking soda, cream of tartar and salt; gradually add to creamed mixture and mix well. Stir in almonds and toffee bits.

2. Shape into 1-in. balls; roll in sugar. Place on ungreased baking sheets and flatten with a fork. Bake the cookies at 350° for 12-14 minutes or until they are lightly browned.

TOFFEE ALMOND SANDIES

BLACK WALNUT COOKIES

These crispy cookies are studded with black walnuts, yielding a more distinctive flavor than cookies that call for traditional English walnuts. They always get raves!

—**DOUG BLACK** CONOVER, NC

PREP: 20 MIN. + CHILLING
BAKE: 15 MIN./BATCH
MAKES: 10 DOZEN

- 1 **cup butter, softened**
- 2 **cups packed brown sugar**
- 2 **large eggs**
- 1 **teaspoon vanilla extract**
- 3½ **cups all-purpose flour**
- 1 **teaspoon baking soda**
- ¼ **teaspoon salt**
- 2 **cups chopped black walnuts or walnuts, divided**

1. In a large bowl, cream the butter and brown sugar until light and fluffy. Beat in eggs and vanilla. Combine the flour, baking soda and salt; gradually add to the creamed mixture. Stir in 1¼ cups walnuts. Finely chop the remaining nuts.

2. Shape dough into two 15-in. rolls. Roll in chopped nuts, pressing gently. Wrap each in plastic wrap. Refrigerate for 2 hours or until firm.

3. Unwrap dough; cut into ¼-in. slices. Place 2 in. apart on greased baking sheets. Bake at 300° for 12 minutes or until lightly browned. Remove to wire racks.

★ ★ ★ ★ ★ **5 STAR TIP**
The walnuts you most commonly find in grocery stores are mild-tasting English walnuts. This type has a semi-firm light brown shell. Native American black walnuts have a very hard thick black shell. The flavor is richer and more intense than the English walnut. Because the black walnuts are difficult to shell, they are not as widely available commercially as English walnuts.

OATMEAL SANDWICH CREMES

These hearty cookies appeal to everyone whenever I take them to a family get-together or church bake sale. They're worth the little extra effort.

—LESLEY MANSFIELD MONROE, NC

PREP: 20 MIN.
BAKE: 15 MIN./BATCH + COOLING
MAKES: 3 DOZEN

- ¾ cup shortening
- 1 cup sugar
- 1 cup packed brown sugar
- 1 large egg
- ¼ cup water
- 1 teaspoon vanilla extract
- 1½ cups self-rising flour
- 1 teaspoon baking soda
- 1 teaspoon ground cinnamon
- 3 cups quick-cooking oats
- ¾ cup raisins

FILLING
- ½ cup butter, softened
- ½ cup shortening
- 3¾ cups confectioners' sugar
- 2 tablespoons 2% milk
- 1 teaspoon vanilla extract
  Dash salt

1. In a large bowl, cream shortening and sugars until light and fluffy. Beat in the egg, water and vanilla. Combine the flour, baking soda and cinnamon; gradually add to creamed mixture and mix well. Stir in oats and raisins.

2. Drop by tablespoonfuls 3 in. apart onto ungreased baking sheets. Flatten with a glass. Bake at 325° for 13-14 minutes or until lightly browned. Remove to wire racks to cool.

3. In a large bowl, combine the filling ingredients; beat until smooth. Spread on the bottoms of half of the cookies; top with remaining cookies.

NOTE *As a substitute for each cup of self-rising flour, place 1½ teaspoons baking powder and ½ teaspoon salt in a measuring cup. Add all-purpose flour to measure 1 cup.*

CHOCOLATE PECAN CARAMELS

CHOCOLATE PECAN CARAMELS

I haven't missed a year making this candy for the holidays since a friend gave me the recipe in 1964! It's a tradition I cherish.

—JUNE HUMPHREY STRONGSVILLE, OH

PREP: 20 MIN. • **COOK:** 15 MIN. + COOLING
MAKES: ABOUT 2½ POUNDS (ABOUT 6¾ DOZEN)

- 1 tablespoon plus 1 cup butter, softened, divided
- 1½ cups coarsely chopped pecans, toasted
- 1 cup (6 ounces) semisweet chocolate chips
- 2 cups packed brown sugar
- 1 cup light corn syrup
- ¼ cup water
- 1 can (14 ounces) sweetened condensed milk
- 2 teaspoons vanilla extract

1. Line a 13x9-in. pan with foil; butter the foil with 1 tablespoon of butter. Sprinkle with pecans and chocolate chips; set aside.

2. Using a heavy saucepan, melt the remaining butter over medium heat. Add the brown sugar, corn syrup and water. Cook and stir until the mixture comes to a boil. Stir in the milk. Cook, stirring the mixture constantly, until a candy thermometer reads 248° (firm-ball stage).

3. Remove from the heat and add the vanilla. Pour into prepared pan (do not scrape the saucepan). Cool completely before cutting.

CHOCOLATE MEXICAN WEDDING CAKES

WALNUT SANDWICH COOKIES

I've made this recipe many times over the years, and the cookies are always a hit with my family and friends.
—**SHIRLEY BARKER** NORMAL, IL

PREP: 15 MIN.
BAKE: 15 MIN./BATCH + COOLING
MAKES: 2 DOZEN

- ¾ cup butter, softened
- 1 cup sugar
- 1 tablespoon water
- 1½ cups all-purpose flour
- ½ teaspoon salt
- ¾ cup ground walnuts

FILLING
- 3 ounces cream cheese, softened
- 1 tablespoon butter, softened
- 1½ cups confectioners' sugar
- ½ teaspoon grated orange peel

1. In a large bowl, cream butter and sugar until light and fluffy. Beat in water. Combine the flour and salt; gradually add to creamed mixture and mix well. Stir in walnuts. Roll into 1-in. balls.
2. Place balls 1 in. apart on ungreased baking sheets. Coat bottom of a glass with cooking spray, then dip in sugar. Flatten cookies with prepared glass, redipping in sugar as needed.
3. Bake at 350° for 12-15 minutes or until edges are lightly browned. Cool for 2 minutes. Remove to wire racks; cool completely.
4. For filling, in a small bowl, beat cream cheese and butter until fluffy. Gradually add confectioners' sugar and orange peel; beat until smooth. Spread over the bottoms of half of the cookies; top with remaining cookies. Store in the refrigerator.

CHOCOLATE MEXICAN WEDDING CAKES

Cinnamon adds warmth to this twist on a traditional Mexican treat. Sometimes I add mini chocolate chips to the dough and, after baking, dip the cooled cookies in melted almond bark.
—**JOANNE VALKEMA** FREEPORT, IL

PREP: 20 MIN. • **BAKE:** 15 MIN./BATCH
MAKES: ABOUT 3½ DOZEN

- 1 cup butter, softened
- 1¾ cups confectioners' sugar, divided
- 1 teaspoon vanilla extract
- 1½ cups all-purpose flour
- ¼ cup cornstarch
- ¼ cup baking cocoa
- ½ teaspoon salt
- 1¼ cups finely chopped pecans or almonds
- ½ teaspoon ground cinnamon

1. Preheat oven to 325°. In a large bowl, cream the butter and 1 cup confectioners' sugar until light and fluffy. Beat in vanilla. Combine flour, cornstarch, cocoa and salt; gradually add to creamed mixture and mix well. Stir in nuts.
2. Shape tablespoonfuls of dough into 1-in. balls. Place balls 2 in. apart on ungreased baking sheets. Bake 12-14 minutes or until set.
3. In a bowl, combine the cinnamon and remaining confectioners' sugar. Roll the warm cookies in the sugar mixture; cool on wire racks. Store in an airtight container.

MAKE THE MOST OF CITRUS PEELS

The peel from citrus fruit adds a burst of flavor to recipes and color to garnishes. Citrus peel, also called zest, can be grated into fine shreds with a Microplane grater. For slightly thicker and longer shreds, use the zester; for long, continuous strips, use a stripper. Remove only the colored portion of the peel, not the bitter white pith.

WALNUT SANDWICH COOKIES

CHOCOLATE MINT WAFERS

CHOCOLATE MINT WAFERS

These chocolaty treats with a cool mint filling won't last long around your house. They're so pretty stacked on a glass plate.

—**ANNETTE ESAU** DURHAM, ON

PREP: 30 MIN. + CHILLING
BAKE: 5 MIN./BATCH + COOLING
MAKES: ABOUT 7½ DOZEN

⅔ **cup butter, softened**
½ **cup sugar**
½ **cup packed brown sugar**
¼ **cup whole milk**
1 **large egg**
2 **cups all-purpose flour**
¾ **cup baking cocoa**
1 **teaspoon baking powder**
½ **teaspoon baking soda**
¼ **teaspoon salt**
FILLING
2¾ **cups confectioners' sugar**
¼ **cup half-and-half cream**
¼ **teaspoon peppermint extract**
¼ **teaspoon salt**
 Green food coloring

1. In a large bowl, cream butter and sugars until light and fluffy. Beat in milk and egg. Combine the flour, cocoa, baking powder, baking soda and salt; gradually add to creamed mixture and mix well. Cover and refrigerate for 2 hours or until firm.
2. On a lightly floured surface, roll out dough to ⅛-in. thickness. Cut with a 1½-in. cookie cutter and place 1 in. apart on greased baking sheets. Bake at 375° for 5-6 minutes or until edges are lightly browned. Remove to wire racks to cool completely.
3. Combine filling ingredients; spread on bottoms of half of the cookies and top with remaining cookies.

GIANT LEMON SUGAR COOKIES

My chewy cookies have a light lemon flavor from the juice and zest. The sanding of sugar on top adds sparkle and crunch.

—**MICHAEL VYSKOCIL** GLEN ROCK, PA

PREP: 25 MIN. • **BAKE:** 15 MIN./BATCH
MAKES: 14 COOKIES

- 1 **cup unsalted butter, softened**
- 1½ **cups sugar**
- ½ **cup packed brown sugar**
- 2 **large eggs**
- 1½ **teaspoons grated lemon peel**
- 2 **tablespoons lemon juice**
- 3 **cups all-purpose flour**
- 1 **teaspoon baking soda**
- ¼ **teaspoon salt**
- ¼ **teaspoon cream of tartar**
- 4 **teaspoons coarse sugar**

1. Preheat oven to 350°. In a large bowl, cream butter and sugars until light and fluffy. Beat in eggs. Beat in lemon peel and juice. In another bowl, whisk flour, baking soda, salt and cream of tartar; gradually beat into creamed mixture.

2. Shape ¼ cupfuls of dough into balls. Place 6 in. apart on greased baking sheets. Flatten to ¾-in. thickness with bottom of a measuring cup. Lightly brush tops with water; sprinkle with coarse sugar.

3. Bake 12-15 minutes or until light brown. Remove from pans to wire racks to cool completely. Store in airtight containers.

★ ★ ★ ★ ★ **5 STAR TIP**

When a recipe calls for lemon juice, you can use either fresh, frozen or bottled lemon juice in equal amounts. When lemons are in season or you have excess lemons on hand, juice them and freeze the juice in ice cube trays. Measure 1 or 2 tablespoons of juice into each compartment in your ice cube tray. When frozen, remove the lemon cubes and place them in resealable freezer bags.

OATMEAL CRISPIES

OATMEAL CRISPIES

My husband, who normally isn't fond of oatmeal, thinks these old-fashioned cookies are great. With a hint of nutmeg, their aroma is wonderful as they bake...and they taste even better!

—**KAREN HENSON** ST. LOUIS, MO

PREP: 15 MIN. • **BAKE:** 10 MIN./BATCH
MAKES: 5½ DOZEN

- 1 **cup shortening**
- 1 **cup sugar**
- 1 **cup packed brown sugar**
- 2 **large eggs**
- 1 **teaspoon vanilla extract**
- 3 **cups quick-cooking oats**
- 1½ **cups all-purpose flour**
- 1 **teaspoon baking soda**
- 1 **teaspoon salt**
- ¼ **teaspoon ground nutmeg**
- ¼ **teaspoon ground cinnamon**

1. In a large bowl, cream shortening and sugars until light and fluffy. Add the eggs, one at a time, beating well after each addition. Beat in the vanilla.

2. Combine the oats, flour, baking soda, salt, nutmeg and cinnamon and mix it well; gradually add to the creamed mixture.

3. Drop by tablespoonfuls 2 in. apart onto ungreased baking sheets. Flatten with a fork. Bake at 350° for 10-12 minutes or until lightly browned. Remove to wire racks to cool.

AUNT ROSE'S FANTASTIC BUTTER TOFFEE

I don't live in the country, but I do love everything about it—especially the good old-fashioned home cooking! Every year, you'll find me at our County Fair, entering a different recipe contest. This toffee is a family favorite!

—KATHY DORMAN SNOVER, MI

PREP: 25 MIN. • **COOK:** 15 MIN.
MAKES: ABOUT 2 POUNDS

- 2 **cups unblanched whole almonds**
- 11 **ounces milk chocolate, chopped**
- 1 **cup butter, cubed**
- 1 **cup sugar**
- 3 **tablespoons cold water**

1. Preheat oven to 350°. In a shallow baking pan, toast the almonds until golden brown, 5-10 minutes, stirring occasionally. Cool. Pulse chocolate in a food processor until finely ground (do not overprocess); transfer to a bowl. Pulse almonds in food processor or until coarsely chopped. Sprinkle 1 cup almonds over bottom of a greased 15x10-in. pan. Sprinkle with 1 cup chocolate.

2. In a heavy saucepan, combine the butter, sugar and water. Cook the mix over medium heat until a candy thermometer reads 290° (soft-crack stage), stirring occasionally.

3. Immediately pour the mixture over almonds and chocolate in pan. Sprinkle with remaining chocolate and almonds. Refrigerate until set; break into pieces.

AUNT ROSE'S FANTASTIC BUTTER TOFFEE

HOW TO USE A CANDY THERMOMETER

Always use a thermometer designed for candy making. It must have a movable clip that's used to secure it to the side of the pan and to keep the end of the thermometer off the bottom of the pan. Be sure to read the thermometer at eye level.

Check your candy thermometer for accuracy each time you make candy. Place the thermometer in a saucepan of boiling water for several minutes before reading. If the thermometer reads 212° in boiling water, it is accurate. If it rises above or does not reach 212°, add or subtract the difference to the temperature called for in the recipe.

A candy mixture will cook very slowly when boiling until it reaches 220°, then it will cook quickly. It's important to closely watch the thermometer at this point.

To avoid breakage, allow the candy thermometer to cool completely before washing it.

FREEZE IT

MINI PEANUT BUTTER SANDWICH COOKIES

Peanut butter lovers go nuts for these rich little sandwich cookies. To cool down on a hot day, sandwich ice cream between the cookies instead of frosting.
—**KERI WOLFE** NAPPANEE, IN

PREP: 25 MIN.
BAKE: 15 MIN./BATCH + COOLING
MAKES: ABOUT 3½ DOZEN

- 1 **cup shortening**
- 1 **cup creamy peanut butter**
- 1 **cup sugar**
- 1 **cup packed brown sugar**
- 3 **large eggs**
- 1 **teaspoon vanilla extract**
- 3½ **cups all-purpose flour**
- 2 **teaspoons baking soda**
- ½ **teaspoon salt**

FILLING
- ¾ **cup creamy peanut butter**
- ½ **cup 2% milk**
- 1½ **teaspoons vanilla extract**
- 4 **cups confectioners' sugar**

1. Preheat oven to 350°. In a large bowl, cream shortening, peanut butter and sugars until blended. Beat in eggs and vanilla. In another bowl, whisk flour, baking soda and salt; gradually beat into creamed mixture.
2. Shape into 1-in. balls; place 2 in. apart on ungreased baking sheets. Bake 11-13 minutes or until set. Remove from pans to wire racks to cool completely.
3. In a small bowl, beat the peanut butter, milk and vanilla until blended. Beat in the confectioners' sugar until smooth. Spread filling on bottoms of half of the cookies; cover with the remaining cookies.
FREEZE OPTION *Freeze unfilled cookies in freezer containers. To use, thaw cookies and fill as directed.*
NOTE *Reduced-fat peanut butter is not recommended for this recipe.*

FAVORITE MACAROON KISSES

These cookies are a holiday favorite around our house. You can top them off with cherries or chocolate—or some of each!
—**ALICE MCTARNAGHAN** CASTLETON, NY

PREP: 20 MIN. • **BAKE:** 10 MIN./BATCH
MAKES: ABOUT 4 DOZEN

- ⅓ **cup butter, softened**
- 3 **ounces cream cheese, softened**
- ¾ **cup sugar**
- 1 **large egg yolk**
- 1½ **teaspoons almond extract**
- 2 **teaspoons orange juice**
- 1¼ **cups all-purpose flour**
- 2 **teaspoons baking powder**
- ¼ **teaspoon salt**
- 5 **cups coconut, divided**
  Candied cherries and/or chocolate kisses

1. In a large bowl, cream the butter, cream cheese and sugar until light and fluffy. Beat in the egg yolk, extract and juice. Combine flour, baking powder and salt; gradually add to the creamed mixture and mix well. Stir in 3 cups of the coconut. Cover and chill for at least 1 hour.
2. Shape into 1-in. balls; roll in the remaining coconut. Place 2 in. apart on ungreased baking sheets. Bake at 350° for 10-12 minutes or until lightly browned. Immediately place a cherry or a chocolate kiss on top of each cookie. Cool 5 minutes; remove to a wire rack to cool completely.

**CARAMEL
PRETZEL BITES**

CARAMEL PRETZEL BITES

I created this recipe to put my own twist on a pretzel log dipped in caramel, chocolate and nuts—similar to a version from a popular candy store. These homemade treats are a delight any time of year.

—**MICHILENE KLAVER** GRAND RAPIDS, MI

PREP: 45 MIN. + COOLING
MAKES: 6 DOZEN

- 2 **teaspoons butter, softened**
- 4 **cups pretzel sticks**
- 2½ **cups pecan halves, toasted**
- 2¼ **cups packed brown sugar**
- 1 **cup butter, cubed**
- 1 **cup corn syrup**
- 1 **can (14 ounces) sweetened condensed milk**
- ⅛ **teaspoon salt**
- 1 **teaspoon vanilla extract**
- 1 **package (11½ ounces) milk chocolate chips**
- 1 **tablespoon plus 1 teaspoon shortening, divided**
- ⅓ **cup white baking chips**

1. Line a 13x9-in. pan with foil; grease foil with softened butter. Spread pretzels and pecans on bottom of prepared pan.
2. In a large heavy saucepan, combine the brown sugar, cubed butter, corn syrup, milk and salt; cook and stir mixture over medium heat until a candy thermometer reads 240°(soft-ball stage). Remove from heat. Stir in vanilla. Pour over pretzel mixture.
3. In a microwave, melt chocolate chips and 1 tablespoon shortening; stir until smooth. Spread over caramel layer. In microwave, melt baking chips and remaining shortening; stir until smooth. Drizzle over top. Let stand until set.

4. Using foil, lift candy out of pan; remove foil. Using a buttered knife, cut candy into bite-size pieces.

FROSTED MAPLE COOKIES

Living in New England, I have learned to appreciate the unique qualities of our area. Many people here enjoy the flavor of maple in their recipes, and I love this adaptation of an old favorite.

—**CONNIE BORDEN** MARBLEHEAD, MA

PREP: 20 MIN. + CHILLING
BAKE: 10 MIN./BATCH + COOLING
MAKES: 4 DOZEN (2½-INCH COOKIES)

- ½ **cup shortening**
- 1½ **cups packed brown sugar**
- 2 **large eggs**
- 1 **cup (8 ounces) sour cream**
- 1 **tablespoon maple flavoring**
- 2¾ **cups all-purpose flour**
- 1 **teaspoon salt**
- ½ **teaspoon baking soda**
- 1 **cup chopped nuts**

FROSTING
- ½ **cup butter**
- 2 **cups confectioners' sugar**
- 2 **teaspoons maple flavoring**
- 2 **to 3 tablespoons hot water**

1. In a large bowl, cream shortening and brown sugar until light and fluffy. Add eggs, one at a time, beating well after each addition. Stir in sour cream and maple flavoring. Combine the flour, salt and baking soda; add to creamed mixture and mix well. Stir in nuts. Cover and refrigerate for 1 hour.
2. Drop the dough by rounded tablespoonfuls 2 in. apart onto some greased baking sheets. Bake at 375° for 8-10 minutes or until edges are lightly browned. Cool completely on wire racks.
3. For frosting, in a small saucepan, heat butter over low heat until golden brown. Remove from the heat; blend in the confectioners' sugar, maple flavoring and enough water to achieve spreading consistency. Frost cookies.

SALTINE TOFFEE BARK

(5) INGREDIENTS

These salty-sweet treasures make great gifts, and their flavor is simply irresistible. The bark is like brittle, but better and with only a few ingredients. Get ready for a new favorite!

—LAURA COX SOUTH DENNIS, MA

PREP: 25 MIN. + CHILLING
MAKES: 2 POUNDS

40 saltines
1 cup butter, cubed
¾ cup sugar
2 cups (12 ounces) semisweet chocolate chips
1 package (8 ounces) milk chocolate English toffee bits

1. Line a 15x10x1-in. baking pan with heavy-duty foil. Arrange saltines in a single layer on foil; set aside.
2. In a large heavy saucepan over medium heat, melt butter. Stir in sugar. Bring to a boil; cook and stir for 1-2 minutes or until sugar is dissolved. Pour evenly over crackers.
3. Bake at 350° for 8-10 minutes or until bubbly. Immediately sprinkle with chocolate chips. Allow the chips to soften a few minutes, then spread over the top. Sprinkle with the toffee bits. Cool.
4. Cover and refrigerate for 1 hour or until set. Break into pieces. Store in an airtight container.

★ ★ ★ ★ ★ **READER REVIEW**

"Try the bark with a layer of pretzels instead of saltines. Just be sure the pretzels are all flat and packed tightly together. Yum!"

JKHUGGYBEAR TASTEOFHOME.COM

CHEWY OATMEAL COOKIES

I pack chocolate chips, raisins, nuts and cinnamon into my oatmeal cookies. Our kids love them!

—JANIS PLAGEMAN LYNDEN, WA

PREP: 15 MIN.
BAKE: 10 MIN./BATCH + COOLING
MAKES: ABOUT 5 DOZEN

1 cup butter, softened
1 cup sugar
1 cup packed brown sugar
2 large eggs
1 tablespoon molasses
2 teaspoons vanilla extract
2 cups all-purpose flour
2 cups quick-cooking oats
1½ teaspoons baking soda
1 teaspoon ground cinnamon
½ teaspoon salt
1 cup each raisins and chopped pecans
1 cup (6 ounces) semisweet chocolate chips

1. In a large bowl, cream butter and sugars until light and fluffy. Add the eggs, molasses and vanilla; beat well.
2. Combine the flour, oats, baking soda, cinnamon and salt; gradually add to creamed mixture and mix well. Stir in raisins, pecans and chocolate chips. Drop dough by tablespoonfuls 2 in. apart onto greased baking sheets.
3. Bake at 350° for 9-10 minutes or until lightly browned. Cool on pans for 2 minutes before removing the cookies to wire racks.

CHEWY OATMEAL COOKIES

APRICOT-FILLED
TRIANGLES

APRICOT-FILLED TRIANGLES

It's a good thing this recipe makes a big batch because no one can stop eating just one! These crisp, buttery cookies truly do melt in your mouth.

—**MILDRED LORENCE** CARLISLE, PA

PREP: 1¼ HOURS + CHILLING
BAKE: 10 MIN./BATCH + COOLING
MAKES: 6 DOZEN

- 1 **pound dried apricots (2½ cups)**
- 1½ **cups water**
- ½ **cup sugar**

DOUGH
- ⅔ **cup shortening**
- 3 **tablespoons 2% milk**
- 1⅓ **cups sugar**
- 2 **large eggs**
- 1 **teaspoon lemon extract**
- 4 **cups cake flour**
- 2 **teaspoons baking powder**
- 1 **teaspoon salt**

1. In a small saucepan, cook apricots and water over low heat for 45 minutes or until the water is absorbed and apricots are soft. Cool slightly; transfer to a blender. Cover and process until smooth. Add sugar; cover and process until blended. Set aside.
2. In a large saucepan over low heat, melt shortening and milk. Remove from the heat; stir in sugar. Add eggs, one at a time, whisking well after each addition. Stir in the extract. Combine the flour, baking powder and salt; gradually add to the saucepan and mix well. Cover and refrigerate for 4 hours or until easy to handle.
3. On a lightly floured surface, roll out to ⅛-in. thickness. Cut with a floured 3-in. round cookie cutter. Place 1 teaspoon apricot filling in the center of each. Bring three edges together over filling, overlapping slightly (a small portion of filling will show in the center); pinch the edges gently. Place 1 in. apart on ungreased baking sheets.
4. Bake at 400° for 8-10 minutes or until golden brown. Remove to wire racks to cool.

CONFETTI CAKE BATTER COOKIES

CONFETTI CAKE BATTER COOKIES

Mom and I took up cake decorating. Funfetti was our favorite cake, so we used the mix to make cutout cookies. Plain or decorated, they're a favorite at parties.

—**DANIELLE DEMARCO** BASKING RIDGE, NJ

PREP: 15 MIN. + CHILLING
BAKE: 10 MIN./BATCH + COOLING
MAKES: ABOUT 2 DOZEN

- ½ **cup butter, softened**
- 2 **large eggs**
- 1 **teaspoon vanilla extract**
- 1 **package Funfetti cake mix**

1. In a large bowl, beat butter, eggs and vanilla until combined. Beat in cake mix. Refrigerate, covered, for 2 hours or until firm enough to roll.
2. Preheat oven to 350°. On a well-floured surface, roll dough to ¼-in. thickness. Cut with a floured 2½-in. cookie cutter. Place 1 in. apart on ungreased baking sheets. Bake 8-10 minutes or until set. Remove from pans to wire racks to cool completely. Decorate as desired.
FREEZE OPTION *Transfer the dough to a resealable plastic freezer bag; freeze. To use, thaw the dough in the refrigerator until soft enough to roll. Prepare and bake cookies as directed; decorate as desired.*

CHOCOLATE LINZER COOKIES

Living where I do, it's no surprise that I enjoy holiday baking. My mom and I used to make these cookies together. Now that I'm married and living in Alaska, I love to make them for my own family. They remind me of home.
—**HEATHER PETERS** NORTH POLE, AK

PREP: 30 MIN. + CHILLING
BAKE: 10 MIN./BATCH + COOLING
MAKES: 2 DOZEN

- ¾ cup butter, softened
- 1 cup sugar
- 2 large eggs
- ½ teaspoon almond extract
- 2⅓ cups all-purpose flour
- 1 teaspoon baking powder
- ½ teaspoon salt
- ½ teaspoon ground cinnamon
- 1 cup (6 ounces) semisweet chocolate chips, melted
  Confectioners' sugar
- 6 tablespoons seedless raspberry jam

1. In a small bowl, cream butter and sugar until light and fluffy. Add eggs, one at a time, beating well after each addition. Beat in extract. Combine the flour, baking powder, salt and cinnamon; gradually add to creamed mixture and mix well. Refrigerate for 1 hour or until easy to handle.

2. Divide dough in half. On a lightly floured surface, roll out one portion to ⅛-in. thickness; cut with a floured 2½-in. round cookie cutter. Roll out remaining dough; cut with a 2½-in. floured doughnut cutter so the center is cut out of each cookie.

3. Place 1 in. apart on ungreased baking sheets. Bake cookies at 350° for 8-10 minutes or until the edges are lightly browned. Remove to wire racks to cool.

4. Spread melted chocolate over the bottoms of solid cookies. Place cookies with cutout centers over the chocolate. Sprinkle the cookies with confectioners' sugar. Then spoon ½ teaspoon jam in each cookie center.

MAPLE WHOOPIE PIES

In New York, we have a huge maple syrup industry. I took a basic whoopie pie and gave it a twist using our beloved maple flavor.
—**HOLLY BALZER** MALONE, NY

PREP: 40 MIN.
BAKE: 10 MIN./BATCH + COOLING
MAKES: ABOUT 2 DOZEN

- ⅓ cup butter, softened
- ¾ cup sugar
- 1 large egg
- 1 teaspoon vanilla extract
- 1 teaspoon maple flavoring
- 2¼ cups all-purpose flour
- 1¼ teaspoons baking powder
- 1 teaspoon salt
- ½ cup heavy whipping cream
- ½ cup maple syrup
- ½ cup chopped pecans

FILLING
- ½ cup butter, softened
- ½ cup shortening
- 1 teaspoon maple flavoring
- 4 cups confectioners' sugar
- ¼ cup heavy whipping cream
- 2 tablespoons maple syrup

1. Preheat oven to 375°. In a large bowl, cream butter and sugar until light and fluffy. Beat in egg, vanilla and flavoring. In another bowl, whisk flour, baking powder and salt; add to creamed mixture alternately with cream and syrup, beating well after each addition. Stir in pecans.

2. Drop the dough by rounded tablespoonfuls 2 in. apart onto greased baking sheets. Bake 8-10 minutes or until edges are light brown and tops spring back when lightly touched. Remove from pans to wire racks to cool completely.

3. For filling, in a large bowl, beat butter, shortening and flavoring until creamy. Beat in confectioners' sugar alternately with cream and syrup until smooth. Spread the filling on the bottoms of half of the cookies; cover with the remaining cookies. Store in airtight containers.

CHOCOLATE LINZER COOKIES

CASHEW CLUSTERS

I make this recipe for many bake sales at the local community college where I work. They are always the first to sell out.

—BETSY GRANTIER CHARLOTTESVILLE, VA

PREP: 20 MIN. + STANDING • **COOK:** 5 MIN.
MAKES: ABOUT 6 DOZEN

- 1 **pound white candy coating, coarsely chopped**
- 1 **cup (6 ounces) semisweet chocolate chips**
- 4 **ounces German sweet chocolate, chopped**
- ⅓ **cup milk chocolate chips**
- 2 **cups salted whole cashews (about 9 ounces)**
- 2 **cups salted cashew halves and pieces (about 9 ounces)**

1. Put first four ingredients in a large microwave-safe bowl; microwave, covered, at 50% power until melted, 5-6 minutes, stirring about every 30 seconds. Stir in cashews.

2. Drop mixture by tablespoonfuls onto waxed paper-lined pans; let it stand until it is set. Then store in an airtight container.

NOTE *This recipe was tested in a 1,100-watt microwave.*

★ ★ ★ ★ ★ **5 STAR TIP**

Before melting chocolate, be certain that bowl and utensils are completely dry. Any moisture may cause the chocolate to seize (to become stiff, thick and lumpy). Chocolate that has seized can sometimes be saved by immediately adding 1 tablespoon vegetable oil for each 6 ounces of chocolate. Slowly heat the mixture and stir until smooth.

CASHEW CLUSTERS

WALNUT-FILLED PILLOWS

These tender cookie pillows filled with a delicious walnut mixture are my husband's favorite. He says it wouldn't be Christmas without them.

—NANCY KOSTREJ CANONSBURG, PA

PREP: 30 MIN. + CHILLING
BAKE: 10 MIN./BATCH
MAKES: 28 COOKIES

- ½ **cup cold butter, cubed**
- 1 **package (3 ounces) cold cream cheese**
- 1¼ **cups all-purpose flour**
- ¾ **cup ground walnuts**
- ¼ **cup sugar**
- 2 **tablespoons whole milk**
- ½ **teaspoon vanilla or almond extract**
- 1 **large egg, lightly beaten**
  Confectioners' sugar

1. In a large bowl, cut butter and cream cheese into flour until mixture resembles coarse crumbs. Blend mixture together until smooth dough forms, about 3 minutes. Pat into a rectangle; wrap in plastic wrap. Refrigerate for 1 hour or until firm. For filling, combine the walnuts, sugar, milk and vanilla.

2. Unwrap dough and place on a lightly floured surface. Roll into a 17½x10-in. rectangle; cut into 2½-in. squares. Place a level teaspoonful of filling in the center of each square. Moisten edges with water; fold in half and seal with a fork. Place 1 in. apart on ungreased baking sheets. Brush with egg.

3. Bake at 375° for 10-12 minutes or until edges are golden brown. Remove to wire racks to cool. Dust the cookies with confectioners' sugar.

WALNUT-FILLED PILLOWS

TIPS FOR ROLLING COOKIE DOUGH

For tender cookies that bake perfectly every time, follow these handy hints.

For easier handling, refrigerate the dough before rolling.

Use a light touch when handling the dough; overhandling will cause the cookies to be tough.

Lightly flour the rolling pin and work surface. Too much flour added to the dough can cause cookies to be tough.

Work with one portion of dough at a time. Keep the remaining dough in the refrigerator to prevent it from getting too warm.

CHOCOLATE-COVERED CHIPS

These are great conversation starters. I think the salty-sweet combination makes them simply irresistible.
—**MARCILLE MEYER** BATTLE CREEK, NE

START TO FINISH: 25 MIN.
MAKES: ABOUT 4 POUNDS

- 1½ **pounds white candy coating, coarsely chopped**
- 1 **package (14 ounces) ridged potato chips**
- 1½ **pounds milk chocolate or dark chocolate candy coating, coarsely chopped**

1. In a microwave, melt white coating, stir until it is smooth. Dip the chips halfway in coating; allow excess to drip off. Place on waxed paper-lined baking sheets to set.
2. Melt milk or dark chocolate. Dip other half of chips, allow excess to drip off. Place on waxed paper to set. Store in an airtight container.

SALTED TOFFEE CASHEW COOKIES

I might be addicted to the sweet and salty flavor combo of these cookies. Lucky for me, these nutty cookies are also quick to make.
—**CRYSTAL SCHLUETER** NORTHGLENN, CO

PREP: 25 MIN. • **BAKE:** 10 MIN./BATCH
MAKES: ABOUT 5 DOZEN

- 1 **cup butter, softened**
- 1½ **cups packed brown sugar**
- 2 **large eggs**
- 1 **teaspoon vanilla extract**
- 2⅔ **cups all-purpose flour**
- 1 **teaspoon salt**
- 1 **teaspoon baking soda**
- 1½ **cups chopped salted cashews**
- 1 **cup brickle toffee bits**
- 1 **cup butterscotch chips**
  Salted whole cashews

1. Preheat oven to 375°. In a large bowl, cream butter and brown sugar until light and fluffy. Beat in the eggs and vanilla. In another bowl, whisk flour, salt and baking soda; gradually beat into creamed mixture. Stir in chopped cashews, toffee bits and butterscotch chips.
2. Drop cookie dough by rounded tablespoonfuls 2 in. apart onto ungreased baking sheets. Press one whole cashew into each cookie. Bake 7-9 minutes or until golden brown. Cool on pans 2 minutes. Remove to wire racks to cool.
FREEZE OPTION *Freeze the cookies in freezer containers. To use, thaw before serving.*

MARSHMALLOW PUFFS

Since they blend peanut butter, chocolate and marshmallows, these treats were popular with our three kids as they were growing up. Now I make them for our grandchildren. The puffs are quick to make, too, so they're perfect for the holidays or anytime you're short on time.
—**DODY CAGENELLO** SIMSBURY, CT

PREP: 10 MIN. + CHILLING
MAKES: 3 DOZEN

- 36 **large marshmallows**
- 1½ **cups semisweet chocolate chips**
- ½ **cup chunky peanut butter**
- 2 **tablespoons butter**

Line a 9-in. square pan with foil; butter the foil. Arrange marshmallows in pan. In a microwave, melt the chocolate chips, peanut butter and butter; stir until smooth. Pour and spread over the marshmallows. Chill completely. Cut into 1½-in. squares.
NOTE *This recipe was tested in a 1,100-watt microwave.*

CREAMY ORANGE CARAMELS

Each Christmas I teach myself a new candy recipe. Last year I started with my caramel recipe and added a splash of orange extract for fun. This year I just might try buttered rum extract.

—SHELLY BEVINGTON HERMISTON, OR

PREP: 10 MIN. • **COOK:** 30 MIN. + STANDING
MAKES: ABOUT 2½ POUNDS (80 PIECES)

- 1 teaspoon plus 1 cup butter, divided
- 2 cups sugar
- 1 cup light corn syrup
- 1 can (14 ounces) sweetened condensed milk
- 1 teaspoon orange extract
- 1 teaspoon vanilla extract

1. Line an 11x7-in. dish with foil; grease foil with 1 teaspoon butter.
2. In a large heavy saucepan, combine the sugar, corn syrup and remaining butter. Bring to a boil over medium heat, stirring constantly. Reduce heat to medium-low; boil gently, without stirring, for 4 minutes.
3. Remove from the heat; gradually stir in milk. Cook and stir until a candy thermometer reads 244° (firm-ball stage). Remove from the heat; stir in extracts. Immediately pour into prepared dish (do not scrape saucepan). Let stand until firm.
4. Using foil, lift out candy; remove foil. Using a buttered knife, cut the caramel into 1x¾-in. pieces. Wrap individually in waxed paper; twist the ends.

CREAMY ORANGE CARAMELS

WHITE CHOCOLATE MACADAMIA COOKIES

White baking chips and macadamia nuts are a fantastic duo in these buttery cookies. They are a nice change from the classic chocolate chip ones.

—CATHY LENNON NEWPORT, TN

PREP: 15 MIN. • **BAKE:** 10 MIN./BATCH
MAKES: 4½ DOZEN

- ½ cup butter, softened
- ⅔ cup sugar
- 1 large egg
- 1 teaspoon vanilla extract
- 1 cup plus 2 tablespoons all-purpose flour
- ½ teaspoon baking soda
- 1 cup macadamia nuts, chopped
- 1 cup white baking chips

1. Preheat oven to 350°. In a large bowl, cream butter and sugar until light and fluffy. Beat in egg and vanilla. In another bowl, whisk flour and baking soda; gradually beat into creamed mixture. Stir in nuts and baking chips.
2. Drop by heaping teaspoonfuls 2 in. apart onto ungreased baking sheets. Bake 10-12 minutes or until they are golden brown. Cool on pans 1 minute. Remove to wire racks to cool the cookies completely.

FREEZE OPTION *Freeze cookies, layered between waxed paper, in freezer containers. To use, thaw before serving or, if desired, reheat them on a baking sheet in a preheated 350° oven 3-4 minutes.*

CARAMEL-DARK CHOCOLATE COOKIES

FREEZE IT

These taste like my favorite coffeehouse beverage. In cookie form, they're crispy outside but nice and soft in the middle.
—**ANGELA SPENGLER** TAMPA, FL

PREP: 20 MIN. • **BAKE:** 10 MIN./BATCH
MAKES: ABOUT 3 DOZEN

- 6 tablespoons butter, softened
- ⅓ cup shortening
- ½ cup packed brown sugar
- ⅓ cup sugar
- 1 large egg
- 2 tablespoons hot caramel ice cream topping
- 1 teaspoon vanilla extract
- 1½ cups all-purpose flour
- 4 teaspoons dark roast instant coffee granules
- ½ teaspoon baking soda
- ½ teaspoon salt
- 1½ cups (9 ounces) dark chocolate chips

Preheat oven to 350°. In a large bowl, cream butter, shortening and sugars until light and fluffy. Beat in the egg, ice cream topping and vanilla. Using another bowl, whisk the flour, coffee granules, baking soda and salt; gradually beat into creamed mixture. Fold in chocolate chips.

3. Drop the dough by rounded tablespoonfuls 2 in. apart onto ungreased baking sheets. Bake the cookies 8-10 minutes or until set. Cool on pans 2 minutes. Remove to wire racks to cool.

FREEZE OPTION *Drop dough by rounded tablespoonfuls onto waxed paper-lined baking sheets; freeze until firm. Transfer to resealable plastic freezer bags; return to freezer. To use, bake frozen cookies as directed, increasing time by 1-2 minutes.*

TRUFFLE CHERRIES

TRUFFLE CHERRIES

My family and I are a bunch of chocolate lovers, especially during the holidays. Double chocolate gems like these don't stand a chance of lasting long at our house.
—**ANNE DROUIN** DUNNVILLE, ON

PREP: 20 MIN. + CHILLING
MAKES: ABOUT 2 DOZEN

- ⅓ cup heavy whipping cream
- 2 tablespoons butter
- 2 tablespoons sugar
- 4 ounces semisweet chocolate, chopped
- 1 jar (8 ounces) maraschino cherries with stems, well drained

COATING
- 6 ounces semisweet chocolate, chopped
- 2 tablespoons shortening

1. In a small saucepan, bring the cream, butter and sugar to a boil, stirring constantly. Remove from the heat; stir in chocolate until melted. Cover and refrigerate for at least 4 hours or until easy to handle.

2. Pat cherries with paper towels until very dry. Shape a teaspoonful of chocolate mixture around each cherry, forming a ball. Cover and refrigerate for 2-3 hours or until firm.

3. In a microwave, melt chocolate and shortening; stir until smooth. Dip cherries until coated; allow excess to drip off. Place on waxed paper to set.

SALTED PECAN SHORTBREAD SQUARES

SALTED PECAN SHORTBREAD SQUARES

My shortbread squares are the ultimate go-to for cookie trays and gift-giving. The buttery caramel and toasted nuts make it tough to eat just one.

—**DIANA ASHCRAFT** MONMOUTH, OR

PREP: 25 MIN. • **BAKE:** 25 MIN. + COOLING
MAKES: 4 DOZEN

- 1½ **cups all-purpose flour**
- 1 **cup confectioners' sugar**
- ½ **cup cornstarch**
- 1 **teaspoon sea salt**
- 1 **cup cold unsalted butter, cubed**

FILLING
- ¾ **cup unsalted butter, cubed**
- 1½ **cups packed brown sugar**
- ½ **cup dark corn syrup**
- ½ **teaspoon sea salt**
- ½ **cup milk chocolate chips**
- ¼ **cup heavy whipping cream**
- 1 **teaspoon vanilla extract**
- 4 **cups coarsely chopped pecans, toasted**

1. Preheat oven to 350°. Line two 13x9-in. baking pans with foil, letting ends extend up sides of pan.
2. Place the flour, confectioners' sugar, cornstarch and salt in a food processor; pulse until blended. Add butter; pulse until butter is the size of peas. Divide the mixture between prepared pans; press onto bottom of pans. Bake 10-12 minutes or until light brown. Cool on a wire rack.
3. For filling, melt butter in a large saucepan. Stir in brown sugar, corn syrup and salt; bring to a boil. Reduce heat to medium; cook and stir until sugar is completely dissolved, about 3 minutes. Remove from heat; stir in chocolate chips, cream and vanilla until smooth. Stir in pecans. Spread over the crusts.
4. Bake 12-15 minutes or until the filling is bubbly. Cool completely in pans on wire racks. Using foil, lift the shortbread out of the pans. Gently peel off foil; cut into bars. Store in an airtight container.

NOTE To toast nuts, bake in a shallow pan in a 350° oven for 5-10 minutes or cook in a skillet over low heat until lightly browned, stirring occasionally.

⑤INGREDIENTS SLOW COOKER

CRUNCHY CANDY CLUSTERS

Before I retired, I'd take these yummy peanut butter bites to work for special occasions. I still make them for holidays—my family looks forward to the coated cereal and marshmallow clusters.

—**FAYE O'BRYAN** OWENSBORO, KY

PREP: 15 MIN. • **COOK:** 1 HOUR
MAKES: 6½ DOZEN

- 2 **pounds white candy coating, coarsely chopped**
- 1½ **cups peanut butter**
- ½ **teaspoon almond extract, optional**
- 4 **cups Cap'n Crunch cereal**
- 4 **cups crisp rice cereal**
- 4 **cups miniature marshmallows**

1. Place candy coating in a 5-qt. slow cooker. Cover and cook on high for 1 hour. Add peanut butter. Stir in extract if desired.
2. Using a large bowl, combine the cereals and marshmallows. Stir in the peanut butter mixture until well coated. Drop by tablespoonfuls onto waxed paper. Let stand until set. Store at room temperature.

★ ★ ★ ★ ★ **READER REVIEW**

"I am asked to make this every year for my family reunion. I put it in a foil-lined 13x9-in. pan and cut it into squares."

DIRVAN57 TASTEOFHOME.COM

CRUNCHY CANDY CLUSTERS

LAYERED MINT CANDIES

LAYERED MINT CANDIES

These incredible melt-in-your-mouth candies have the perfect amount of mint nestled between layers of mild chocolate. Even when I make a double batch at Christmas, the supply doesn't last long.

—RHONDA VAUBLE SAC CITY, IA

PREP: 15 MIN. + CHILLING
MAKES: ABOUT 2 POUNDS (ABOUT 9½ DOZEN)

- 1 **tablespoon butter**
- 1½ **pounds white candy coating, coarsely chopped, divided**
- 1 **cup (6 ounces) semisweet chocolate chips**
- 1 **teaspoon peppermint extract**
- 4 **drops green food coloring, optional**
- 3 **tablespoons heavy whipping cream**

1. Line a 13x9-in. pan with foil. Grease foil with butter.

2. Microwave 1 pound candy coating and chocolate chips until smooth, stirring every 30 seconds. Spread half into prepared pan, reserving half. Microwave remaining candy coating until melted; stir in extract and, if desired, food coloring. Stir in cream until smooth (mixture will be stiff). Spread over first layer; refrigerate until firm, about 10 minutes. Warm the reserved chocolate mixture if necessary; spread over mint layer. Refrigerate until firm, about 1 hour.

3. Using foil, lift the candy out of the pan, then remove the foil. Cut the candy into 1-in. squares. Refrigerate in airtight container.

CHERRY DIVINITY

It's not a Valentine's Day party without these light and airy confections on my dessert platter. You can replace the cherry gelatin with any flavor to suit your tastes.

—CRYSTAL RALPH-HAUGHN

BARTLESVILLE, OK

PREP: 35 MIN. • **COOK:** 25 MIN. + STANDING
MAKES: 5 DOZEN

2 large egg whites
3 cups sugar
¾ cup water
¾ cup light corn syrup
1 package (3 ounces) cherry gelatin
1 cup chopped walnuts

1. Place the egg whites in the bowl of a large stand mixer; let them stand at room temperature for 30 minutes. Meanwhile, line three 15x10x1-in. baking pans with waxed paper.
2. In a heavy saucepan, combine the sugar, water and corn syrup; cook and stir until sugar is dissolved and the mixture comes to a boil. Cook over medium heat, without stirring, until a candy thermometer reads 250° (hard-ball stage).
3. Just before the temperature is reached, beat egg whites until foamy. Gradually beat in gelatin. Beat until stiff peaks form. With mixer running on high speed, carefully pour the hot syrup in a slow, steady stream into the bowl. Beat just until the candy loses its gloss and holds its shape, about 5 minutes. Promptly stir in walnuts.
4. Quickly drop by tablespoonfuls onto prepared pans. Let stand at room temperature overnight or until dry to the touch. Store in airtight container at room temperature.

ROLL-OUT COOKIES

ROLL-OUT COOKIES

I collect cookie cutters (I have over 5,000!), so a good cutout recipe is a must. These sweet delights are crisp and buttery-tasting with just a hint of lemon, and the dough handles nicely.

—BONNIE PRICE YELM, WA

PREP: 25 MIN. • **BAKE:** 10 MIN./BATCH
MAKES: ABOUT 6 DOZEN (2¼ INCH COOKIES)

1 cup butter, softened
1 cup sugar
1 large egg
1 teaspoon vanilla extract
½ teaspoon lemon extract
3 cups all-purpose flour
2 teaspoons baking powder
GLAZE
1 cup confectioners' sugar
2 tablespoons water
1 tablespoon light corn syrup
Food coloring, optional

1. In a bowl, cream butter and sugar. Add egg and extracts. Combine flour and baking powder; gradually add to the creamed mixture and mix well. (Dough will be very stiff. If necessary, stir in the last cup of flour mixture by hand. Do not chill.)
2. On a lightly floured surface, roll dough to ⅛-in. thickness. Cut out the cookies into desired shapes. Place 2 in. apart on ungreased baking sheets. Bake at 400° for 6-7 minutes or until the edges are lightly browned. Cool for 2 minutes before removing to wire racks; cool completely.
3. For the glaze, combine the sugar, water and corn syrup until smooth. Tint with food coloring if desired. Using a small brush and stirring glaze often, brush on cookies, decorating as desired.

(5)INGREDIENTS

MINI S'MORES

I created my s'mores at a time when I couldn't afford store-bought gifts. They're awesome for parties and bake sales—and kids love to help put them together.

—STEPHANIE TEWELL ELIZABETH, IL

PREP: 50 MIN. + STANDING • **COOK:** 5 MIN.
MAKES: ABOUT 4 DOZEN

- 2 **cups milk chocolate chips**
- ½ **cup heavy whipping cream**
- 1 **package (14.4 ounces) graham crackers, quartered**
- 1 **cup marshmallow creme**
- 2 **cartons (7 ounces each) milk chocolate for dipping**
- 4 **ounces white candy coating, melted, optional**

1. Place chocolate chips in a small bowl. Using a small saucepan, bring the cream just to a boil. Pour over the chocolate; stir with a whisk until smooth. Cool to room temperature or until mixture reaches a spreading consistency, about 10 minutes.

2. Spread chocolate mixture over half of the graham crackers. Spread marshmallow creme over remaining graham crackers; then place over the chocolate-covered crackers, pressing to adhere.

3. Melt dipping chocolate according to package directions. Dip each s'more halfway into dipping chocolate; allow excess to drip off. Place on waxed paper-lined baking sheets; let stand until dipping chocolate is set.

4. If desired, drizzle tops with melted white candy coating; let stand until set. Store in an airtight container in the refrigerator.

MINI S'MORES

SUGAR COOKIES

This is truly an oldie, dating back to a Swedish woman born in 1877. Her daughter, Esther Davis, came up with the exact measurements (the original cookies were mixed by feel and taste) and shared the recipe with me. These are my favorite cookies, and I hope they'll become yours as well.

—**HELEN WALLIS** VANCOUVER, WA

PREP: 30 MIN. • **BAKE:** 10 MIN./BATCH
MAKES: 5 DOZEN

- ½ **cup butter, softened**
- ½ **cup shortening**
- 1 **cup sugar**
- 1 **large egg**
- 1 **teaspoon vanilla extract**
- 2¼ **cups all-purpose flour**
- ½ **teaspoon baking powder**
- ½ **teaspoon baking soda**
  Additional sugar

1. Preheat oven to 350°. Cream butter, shortening and sugar until light and fluffy. Beat in egg and vanilla. In another bowl, whisk flour, baking powder and baking soda; gradually beat into creamed mixture.
2. Shape into 1-in. balls. Roll in additional sugar. Place on greased baking sheets; flatten with a glass. Bake until set, 10-12 minutes. Remove to wire racks to cool.
IF COOKING FOR TWO *Freeze the baked cookies in airtight containers or freezer bags to enjoy anytime!*

COOKIE JAR GINGERSNAPS

My grandma kept two cookie jars in her pantry. One of the jars, which I now have, always contained these crisp and chewy gingersnaps. My daughter entered this recipe in a 4-H competition and won a blue ribbon.

—**DEB HANDY** POMONA, KS

PREP: 20 MIN. • **BAKE:** 15 MIN./BATCH
MAKES: 3 DOZEN

- ¾ **cup shortening**
- 1 **cup plus 2 tablespoons sugar, divided**
- 1 **large egg**
- ¼ **cup molasses**
- 2 **cups all-purpose flour**
- 2 **teaspoons baking soda**
- 1½ **teaspoons ground ginger**
- 1 **teaspoon ground cinnamon**
- ½ **teaspoon salt**

1. Preheat oven to 350°. Cream the shortening and 1 cup sugar until light and fluffy. Beat in egg and molasses. In another bowl, combine next five ingredients; gradually add to creamed mixture and mix well.
2. Shape level tablespoonfuls of dough into balls. Dip one side into remaining sugar; place 2 in. apart, sugary side up, on greased baking sheets. Bake until lightly browned and crinkly, 12-15 minutes. Remove to wire racks to cool.

BABY RUTH COOKIES

I love Baby Ruth candy bars and usually have a few on hand, so I decided to put them to good use in my favorite cookie recipe.

—**ELINOR NIELD** SOQUEL, CA

PREP: 15 MIN. • **BAKE:** 10 MIN./BATCH
MAKES: 4 DOZEN

- ½ **cup butter, softened**
- ¾ **cup sugar**
- 1 **large egg**
- ½ **teaspoon vanilla extract**
- 1⅓ **cups all-purpose flour**
- ½ **teaspoon baking soda**
- ½ **teaspoon salt**
- 2 **Baby Ruth candy bars (2.1 ounces each), chopped**

1. In a large bowl, cream butter and sugar until light and fluffy. Beat in egg and vanilla. Combine flour, baking soda and salt; gradually add to the creamed mixture. Stir in candy bars.
2. Drop by rounded teaspoonfuls 2 in. apart onto greased baking sheets. Bake at 350° for 10 minutes or until edges of cookies are lightly browned. Immediately remove cookies to wire racks to cool.

RASPBERRY COCONUT COOKIES

4. In a small bowl, beat the butter, confectioners' sugar, milk and vanilla until smooth. Place ½ teaspoon preserves and a scant teaspoon of filling on the bottoms of half of the cookies; top with remaining cookies. Store in an airtight container in the refrigerator.

MAPLE WALNUT TRUFFLES

You'll be surprised and delighted when you bite into one of these little goodies. The velvety maple and white chocolate coating surrounds a sweet nutty center.
—**ROXANNE CHAN** ALBANY, CA

PREP: 45 MIN. + CHILLING
MAKES: 2 DOZEN

- ⅔ **cup ground walnuts**
- 2 **teaspoons maple syrup**
- 1 **teaspoon brown sugar**
- 1 **package (10 to 12 ounces) white baking chips**
- 4 **ounces cream cheese, softened**
- ⅔ **cup butter, softened**
- ¾ **teaspoon maple flavoring**
- 1½ **cups finely chopped walnuts, toasted**

1. Place the ground walnuts, syrup and brown sugar in a small bowl; mix well. Scoop teaspoonfuls and form into 24 balls; transfer to a waxed paper-lined baking sheet. Chill.
2. Meanwhile, in a microwave, melt chips; stir until smooth. Set aside. In a large bowl, beat cream cheese and butter until smooth. Beat in melted chips and maple flavoring; mix well. Refrigerate for 1 hour or until set.
3. Shape tablespoonfuls of cream cheese mixture around each walnut ball. Roll in the chopped walnuts. Refrigerate for 2 hours or until firm. Store in an airtight container in the refrigerator.

RASPBERRY COCONUT COOKIES

My mother gave me the recipe for these rich, buttery cookies. Raspberry preserves and a cream filling make them doubly delicious.
—**JUNE BROWN** VENETA, OR

PREP: 20 MIN.
BAKE: 15 MIN./BATCH + COOLING
MAKES: 2½ DOZEN

- ¾ **cup butter, softened**
- ½ **cup sugar**
- 1 **large egg**
- 1 **teaspoon vanilla extract**
- 2 **cups all-purpose flour**
- ½ **cup flaked coconut**
- 1½ **teaspoons baking powder**
- ¼ **teaspoon salt**

FILLING
- ¼ **cup butter, softened**
- ¾ **cup confectioners' sugar**
- 2 **teaspoons 2% milk**
- ½ **teaspoon vanilla extract**
- ½ **cup raspberry preserves**

1. In a large bowl, cream butter and sugar until light and fluffy. Beat in the egg and vanilla. Combine the flour, coconut, baking powder and salt; gradually add to the creamed mixture and mix well.
2. Shape into 1-in. balls. Place 1½ in. apart on ungreased baking sheets; flatten with a glass dipped in flour.
3. Bake at 350° for 12-14 minutes or until edges begin to brown. Cool on wire racks.

ICED ORANGE COOKIES

I often make these bite-size cookies at Christmastime, when oranges in Florida are plentiful. Every time I experience their wonderful aroma, I remember my grandmother, who shared the recipe.

—LORI DIPIETRO NEW PORT RICHEY, FL

PREP: 15 MIN.
BAKE: 10 MIN./BATCH + COOLING
MAKES: ABOUT 5½ DOZEN

- ½ cup shortening
- 1 cup sugar
- 2 large eggs
- ½ cup orange juice
- 1 tablespoon grated orange peel
- 2½ cups all-purpose flour
- 1½ teaspoons baking powder
- ½ teaspoon salt

ICING

- 2 cups confectioners' sugar
- ¼ cup orange juice
- 2 tablespoons butter, melted
  Orange paste food coloring, optional

1. In a large bowl, cream shortening and sugar until light and fluffy. Add eggs, one at a time, beating well after each addition. Beat in orange juice and peel. Combine the flour, baking powder and salt; gradually add to the creamed mixture.

2. Drop by heaping teaspoonfuls 2 in. apart onto ungreased baking sheets. Bake at 350° for 10-12 minutes or until edges begin to brown. Remove to wire racks to cool. In a small bowl, combine icing ingredients until smooth; drizzle over cooled cookies.

★ ★ ★ ★ ★ READER REVIEW

"I own a pastry company and am always trying new recipes. This is one of my customer favorites."

SLUMMY41 TASTEOFHOME.COM

---

⑤ INGREDIENTS
DARK CHOCOLATE RASPBERRY FUDGE

Something about the combination of dark chocolate and raspberry is so appealing. This fudge makes a heartfelt homemade gift, or a treat that's worth sharing in the candy dish.

—BARBARA LENTO HOUSTON, PA

PREP: 15 MIN. + FREEZING
COOK: 5 MIN. + CHILLING
MAKES: 3 POUNDS (81 PIECES)

- 1 package (10 to 12 ounces) white baking chips
- 1 teaspoon butter, softened
- 3 cups dark chocolate chips
- 1 can (14 ounces) sweetened condensed milk
- ¼ cup raspberry liqueur
- ⅛ teaspoon salt

1. Place baking chips in a single layer on a small baking sheet. Freeze 30 minutes. Line a 9-in. square pan with foil; grease foil with butter.

2. In a large microwave-safe bowl, combine the dark chocolate chips and milk. Microwave, uncovered, on high for 2 minutes; stir. Microwave in additional 30-second intervals, stirring until smooth. Stir in liqueur and salt. Add white baking chips; stir just until partially melted. Spread into prepared pan. Refrigerate 1 hour or until firm.

3. Using foil, lift the fudge out of pan. Remove the foil; cut the fudge into 1-in. squares. Store in an airtight container in the refrigerator.

NOTE *This recipe was tested in a 1,100-watt microwave.*

DARK CHOCOLATE RASPBERRY FUDGE

MERINGUE MAGIC

Since humidity is the most critical factor in making a successful meringue, choose a dry day. Meringues can absorb moisture on a humid day and become limp or sticky.

Separate the eggs while they are still cold from the refrigerator, then allow the egg whites to stand at room temperature for 30 minutes before beating.

For the greatest volume, place egg whites in a small clean metal or glass bowl. Even a drop of fat from the egg yolk or a film sometimes found on plastic bowls will prevent egg whites from foaming. For this reason, be sure to use a clean whisk or clean beaters.

After stiff peaks form, check that the sugar is dissolved. It should feel silky smooth when rubbed between your thumb and index finger.

Continue as recipe directs.

MERINGUE KISSES

MERINGUE KISSES

There's a chocolate surprise inside these frothy kisses. They're my husband's top choice at Christmas.

—TAMI HENKE LOCKPORT, IL

PREP: 15 MIN.
BAKE: 30 MIN./BATCH + COOLING
MAKES: 44 COOKIES

- 3 **large egg whites**
- ¼ **teaspoon cream of tartar**
  Pinch salt
- 1 **cup sugar**
- 1 **teaspoon vanilla extract**
  Red and green food coloring, optional
- 44 **milk chocolate kisses**
  Baking cocoa, optional

1. Place egg whites in a small bowl; let stand at room temperature for 30 minutes. Beat egg whites until foamy. Sprinkle with cream of tartar and salt; beat until soft peaks form. Gradually add sugar and vanilla, beating until stiff peaks form, about 5-8 minutes. If desired, divide batter in half and fold in red and green food coloring.
2. Drop by rounded tablespoonfuls 1½-in. apart onto lightly greased baking sheets. Press a chocolate kiss into the center of each cookie and cover it with meringue, using a knife.
3. Bake at 275° for 30-35 minutes or until firm to the touch. Immediately remove to a wire rack to let it cool. If desired, sprinkle with cocoa. Store in an airtight container.

★ ★ ★ ★ ★ **5 STAR TIP**

Meringue is a sweetened egg white foam that can be shaped into cups to hold fruit or mousse, made into cookies, or spread onto pie filling to create a golden crown. Depending on the amount of sugar beaten into the egg whites, meringue is classified as a soft meringue (as used for Baked Alaska or meringue-topped pies) or hard meringue (as used for meringue shells or cookies).

ANISE ICEBOX COOKIES

ANISE ICEBOX COOKIES

These old-fashioned crisp cookies have just the right accent of anise.

—SHARON NICHOLS BROOKINGS, SD

PREP: 25 MIN. + CHILLING
BAKE: 10 MIN./BATCH
MAKES: ABOUT 5½ DOZEN

- 1 **cup butter, softened**
- 1 **cup sugar**
- 1 **cup packed brown sugar**
- 1 **large egg**
- 2½ **cups all-purpose flour**
- 1 **teaspoon baking soda**
- ½ **teaspoon salt**
- ½ **teaspoon ground cinnamon**
- ½ **teaspoon ground cloves**
- ½ **cup finely chopped pecans**
- 1 **tablespoon aniseed**

1. In a large bowl, cream butter and sugars until light and fluffy. Beat in egg. Combine the flour, baking soda, salt, cinnamon and cloves; gradually add to creamed mixture and mix well. Stir in pecans and aniseed.
2. Shape into two 10-in. rolls; wrap each in plastic wrap. Refrigerate for 4 hours.
3. Unwrap; cut ¼ in. off the ends of each roll. Cut dough into ¼-in. slices. Place 2 in. apart on ungreased baking sheets. Bake at 375° for 8-10 minutes or until golden brown. Remove to wire racks to cool.

VIENNESE COOKIES

I love to cook and bake. When I worked at a medical clinic, I became known as the "cookie lady." A Swedish friend gave me the recipe for these delights. I often triple or quadruple it so I have plenty to share and send.

—BEVERLY STIRRAT MISSION, BC

PREP: 35 MIN. + CHILLING
BAKE: 10 MIN./BATCH + COOLING
MAKES: ABOUT 3 DOZEN

- 1¼ cups butter, softened
- ⅔ cup sugar
- 2¼ cups all-purpose flour
- 1⅔ cups ground almonds
- 1 cup apricot preserves
- 2 cups (12 ounces) semisweet chocolate chips
- 2 tablespoons shortening

1. In a large bowl, cream butter and sugar until light and fluffy. Combine flour and ground almonds; gradually add to creamed mixture and mix well. Cover and refrigerate 1 hour.

2. Preheat oven to 350°. On a lightly floured surface, roll dough to ¼-in. thickness. Cut with a floured 2¼-in. round cookie cutter. Place 2 in. apart on ungreased baking sheets. Bake 7-9 minutes or until edges are lightly browned. Remove to wire racks to cool completely.

3. Spread jam on the bottoms of half of the cookies; top with remaining cookies. In a microwave, melt the chocolate chips and shortening; stir until they are smooth. Dip half of each sandwich cookie into the chocolate mixture; allow excess to drip off. Place on waxed paper until set. Store in an airtight container.

VIENNESE COOKIES

FAST FIX

GERMAN SPICE COOKIES

These chewy spice cookies are great with coffee and taste even better the next day. The recipe has been in my family for more than 40 years.

—JOAN TYSON BOWLING GREEN, OH

START TO FINISH: 20 MIN.
MAKES: 3½ DOZEN

- 3 large eggs
- 2 cups packed brown sugar
- 1 teaspoon ground cloves
- 1 teaspoon ground cinnamon
- ½ teaspoon pepper
- 2 cups all-purpose flour
- ½ teaspoon baking soda
- ½ teaspoon salt
- 1 cup raisins
- 1 cup chopped walnuts

1. In a large bowl, beat eggs. Add the brown sugar, cloves, cinnamon and pepper. Combine the flour, baking soda and salt; gradually add to the egg mixture. Stir in raisins and walnuts.

2. Drop by tablespoonfuls 2 in. apart onto lightly greased baking sheets. Bake at 400° for 8-10 minutes or until the surface cracks. Remove to wire racks to cool.

NOTE *This recipe contains no butter or shortening.*

PISTACHIO THUMBPRINTS

My mild pistachio-flavored cookies disappear in a flash. For more pistachio flavor, roll the cookies in finely chopped pistachios instead of pecans.

—ELIZABETH PROBELSKI

PORT WASHINGTON, WI

PREP: 45 MIN. • **BAKE:** 10 MIN./BATCH
MAKES: ABOUT 4 DOZEN

- 1 **cup butter, softened**
- ⅓ **cup confectioners' sugar**
- 1 **large egg**
- 1 **teaspoon vanilla extract**
- ¾ **teaspoon almond extract**
- 2 **cups all-purpose flour**
- 1 **package (3.4 ounces) instant pistachio pudding mix**
- ½ **cup miniature chocolate chips**
- 2 **cups finely chopped pecans**

FILLING

- 2 **tablespoons butter, softened**
- 2 **cups confectioners' sugar**
- 1 **teaspoon vanilla extract**
- 2 **to 3 tablespoons 2% milk**

GLAZE

- ½ **cup semisweet chocolate chips**
- 2 **teaspoons shortening**

1. In a large bowl, cream butter and sugar until smooth and fluffy. Beat in egg and extracts. Combine flour and dry pudding mix; gradually add to creamed mixture and mix well. Stir in chocolate chips.

2. Shape into 1-in. balls; roll in nuts. Place 2 in. apart on greased baking sheets; make a thumbprint in the center of each cookie. Bake at 350° for 10-12 minutes. Remove to a wire rack to cool.

3. For the filling, beat the butter, confectioners' sugar, vanilla and enough milk to achieve the desired consistency. Spoon into the center of cooled cookies.

4. For glaze, if desired, melt chocolate chips and shortening; drizzle over cookies. Let stand until set.

PISTACHIO
THUMBPRINTS

SEASONAL SPECIALTIES

Winter, spring, summer or fall—the recipes here will cover them all! Holidays and the changing of the seasons offer opportunities to experiment with new ingredients and flavors for festive celebrations year-round.

PEANUT BUTTER CUTOUT COOKIES

I used peanut butter in place of the butter in this take on a traditional cutout cookie. My kids love to decorate them with frosting and sprinkles for Valentine's Day.

—**CINDI BAUER** MARSHFIELD, WI

PREP: 30 MIN. + CHILLING
BAKE: 10 MIN./BATCH + COOLING
MAKES: ABOUT 4½ DOZEN

- 1 **cup creamy peanut butter**
- ¾ **cup sugar**
- ¾ **cup packed brown sugar**
- 2 **large eggs**
- ⅓ **cup 2% milk**
- 1 **teaspoon vanilla extract**
- 2½ **cups all-purpose flour**
- ½ **teaspoon baking powder**
- ½ **teaspoon baking soda**
  Vanilla frosting
  Red food coloring
  Assorted colored sprinkles

1. In a large bowl, cream the peanut butter and sugars until light and fluffy, about 4 minutes. Beat in the eggs, milk and vanilla. Combine the flour, baking powder and baking soda; add to the creamed mixture and mix well. Cover and refrigerate for 2 hours or until easy to handle.

2. On a lightly floured surface, roll out dough to ¼-in. thickness. Cut with 2-in. to 4-in. cookie cutters. Place 2 in. apart on ungreased baking sheets.

3. Bake at 375° for 7-9 minutes or until edges are browned. Cool for 1 minute before removing from pans to wire racks to cool completely. Frost cookies and decorate as desired.

★ ★ ★ ★ ★ **READER REVIEW**

"These are great! I placed jelly between two cookies and they tasted just like a PB&J sandwich."

JULIEANDKAVIN TASTEOFHOME.COM

CHOCOLATE CHIP RED VELVET WHOOPIE PIES

Baking a yummy treat is a must when my grandkids come to visit. These heart-shaped sandwich cookies spread the love.

—LINDA SCHEND KENOSHA, WI

PREP: 45 MIN.
BAKE: 10 MIN./BATCH + COOLING
MAKES: ABOUT 2 DOZEN

- 1 package red velvet cake mix (regular size)
- 3 large eggs
- ½ cup canola oil
- 2 teaspoons vanilla extract

FILLING
- 8 ounces cream cheese, softened
- ½ cup butter, softened
- 2 cups confectioners' sugar
- 1 cup (6 ounces) miniature semisweet chocolate chips

1. Preheat oven to 350°. In a large bowl, combine cake mix, eggs, oil and extract; beat on low speed 30 seconds. Beat on medium 2 minutes.
2. Cut a ½-in. hole in the tip of a pastry bag or the corner of a food-safe plastic bag. Transfer dough to bag. Pipe 1½x1-in. hearts onto parchment paper-lined baking sheets, spacing hearts 1 in. apart.
3. Bake 6-8 minutes or until edges are set. Cool on pans 2 minutes. Remove to wire racks to cool completely.
4. For the filling, in a large bowl, beat the cream cheese and butter until blended. Gradually beat in the confectioners' sugar until smooth. Stir in chocolate chips. Spread filling on bottoms of half of the cookies. Top with remaining cookies. Refrigerate any leftovers.

CHOCOLATE CHIP RED VELVET WHOOPIE PIES

ULTIMATE FUDGY BROWNIES

Coffee granules bump up the chocolate flavor in these ultra-fudgy brownies. Add chocolate chips to the batter to make them even more irresistible.

—SARAH THOMPSON GREENFIELD, WI

PREP: 20 MIN. • **BAKE:** 40 MIN. + COOLING
MAKES: 16 SERVINGS

- 1 cup sugar
- ½ cup packed brown sugar
- ⅔ cup butter, cubed
- ¼ cup water
- 2 teaspoons instant coffee granules, optional
- 2¾ cups bittersweet chocolate chips, divided
- 4 large eggs
- 2 teaspoons vanilla extract
- 1½ cups all-purpose flour
- ½ teaspoon baking soda
- ½ teaspoon salt

1. Preheat oven to 325°. Line a 9-in. square baking pan with parchment paper, letting ends extend up sides. In a large heavy saucepan, combine sugars, butter, water and, if desired, coffee granules; bring to a boil, stirring constantly. Remove from heat; add 1¾ cups chocolate chips and stir until melted. Cool slightly.
2. In a large bowl, whisk eggs until foamy, about 3 minutes. Add vanilla; gradually whisk in chocolate mixture. In another bowl, whisk flour, baking soda and salt; stir into the chocolate mixture. Fold in the remaining chocolate chips.
3. Pour into prepared pan. Bake on a lower oven rack 40-50 minutes or until a toothpick inserted in center comes out with moist crumbs (do not overbake). Cool completely in pan on a wire rack.
4. Lifting with parchment paper, remove the brownies from pan. Cut into squares.

SLOW COOKER 🍲

MOLTEN MOCHA CAKE

When I first made this slow cooker chocolate cake, my husband and daughter loved it—it's one of my daughter's favorite desserts. I also shared the cake with my son, who liked it so much that he ate the whole thing without telling anyone!

—AIMEE FORTNEY FAIRVIEW, TN

PREP: 10 MIN. • **COOK:** 2½ HOURS
MAKES: 4 SERVINGS

- 4 **large eggs**
- 1½ **cups sugar**
- ½ **cup butter, melted**
- 3 **teaspoons vanilla extract**
- 1 **cup all-purpose flour**
- ½ **cup baking cocoa**
- 1 **tablespoon instant coffee granules**
- ¼ **teaspoon salt**
   Fresh raspberries or sliced fresh strawberries and vanilla ice cream, optional

1. In a large bowl, beat eggs, sugar, butter and vanilla until blended. In another bowl, whisk flour, cocoa, coffee granules and salt; gradually beat into egg mixture.

2. Transfer to a greased 1½-qt. slow cooker. Cook, covered, on low 2½-3 hours or until a toothpick comes out with moist crumbs. If desired, serve warm cake with berries and ice cream.

★ ★ ★ ★ ★ **5 STAR TIP**

Always choose the correct size slow cooker for your recipe. A slow cooker should be from half to two-thirds full. The lid on your slow cooker seals in steam that cooks the food. So unless the recipe instructs you to stir in or add ingredients, do not lift the lid while the slow cooker is cooking. Every time you sneak a peek, it adds cooking time to the food you're making. Most slow cookers on the market have clear plastic or glass lids to satisfy curious cooks.

MOLTEN MOCHA CAKE

ST. PADDY'S IRISH
BEEF DINNER

ST. PADDY'S IRISH BEEF DINNER

A variation on shepherd's pie, this hearty dish brings saucy beef together with mashed potatoes, parsnips and other vegetables. It's always the star of our March 17th meal.

—**LORRAINE CALAND** SHUNIAH, ON

PREP: 25 MIN. • **COOK:** 35 MIN.
MAKES: 4 SERVINGS

- 2 **medium Yukon Gold potatoes**
- 2 **small parsnips**
- ¾ **pound lean ground beef (90% lean)**
- 1 **medium onion, chopped**
- 2 **cups finely shredded cabbage**
- 2 **medium carrots, halved and sliced**
- 1 **teaspoon dried thyme**
- 1 **teaspoon Worcestershire sauce**
- 1 **tablespoon all-purpose flour**
- ¼ **cup tomato paste**
- 1 **can (14½ ounces) reduced-sodium chicken or beef broth**
- ½ **cup frozen peas**
- ¾ **teaspoon salt, divided**
- ½ **teaspoon pepper, divided**
- ¼ **cup 2% milk**
- 1 **tablespoon butter**

1. Peel potatoes and parsnips and cut into large pieces; place in a large saucepan and cover with water. Bring to a boil. Reduce heat; cover and cook for 10-15 minutes or until vegetables are tender. Drain.
2. Meanwhile, in a large skillet, cook beef and onion over medium heat until meat is no longer pink; drain. Stir in cabbage, carrots, thyme and Worcestershire sauce.
3. In a small bowl, combine the flour, tomato paste and broth until smooth. Gradually stir into the meat mixture. Bring to a boil. Reduce the heat; cover and simmer for 15-20 minutes or until the vegetables are tender. Stir into the mixture the peas, ¼ teaspoon salt and ¼ teaspoon pepper.
4. Drain potatoes and parsnips; mash with milk, butter and the remaining salt and pepper. Serve potatoes with meat mixture.

IRISH CREAM CUPCAKES

IRISH CREAM CUPCAKES

If you're looking for a grown-up cupcake this St. Patrick's Day, give these beauties a try!

—**JENNY LEIGHTY** WEST SALEM, OH

PREP: 25 MIN. • **BAKE:** 20 MIN. + COOLING
MAKES: 2 DOZEN

- ½ **cup butter, softened**
- 1½ **cups sugar**
- 2 **large eggs**
- ¾ **cup unsweetened applesauce**
- 2 **teaspoons vanilla extract**
- 2½ **cups all-purpose flour**
- 3 **teaspoons baking powder**
- ½ **teaspoon salt**
- ½ **cup Irish cream liqueur**

FROSTING

- ⅓ **cup butter, softened**
- 4 **ounces reduced-fat cream cheese**
- 6 **tablespoons Irish cream liqueur**
- 4 **cups confectioners' sugar**

1. In a large bowl, beat butter and sugar until crumbly, about 2 minutes. Add eggs, one at a time, beating well after each addition. Beat in applesauce and vanilla (the mixture may appear curdled). Combine the flour, baking powder and salt; add to the creamed mixture alternately with the liqueur, beating well after each addition.
2. Fill paper-lined muffin cups two-thirds full. Bake at 350° for 18-22 minutes or until a toothpick inserted in the center comes out clean. Cool for 10 minutes before removing from pans to wire racks to cool completely.
3. For frosting, in a large bowl, beat butter and cream cheese until fluffy. Beat in liqueur. Add the confectioners' sugar; beat until smooth. Pipe frosting over tops of the cupcakes. Refrigerate any leftovers.

GLAZED SPIRAL-SLICED HAM

In my mind, few foods in an Easter spread are as tempting as a big baked ham. I always hope for leftovers so we can have ham sandwiches in the following days.
—**EDIE DESPAIN** LOGAN, UT

PREP: 10 MIN. • **BAKE:** 1 HOUR 35 MIN.
MAKES: 12 SERVINGS

- 1 spiral-sliced fully cooked bone-in ham (7 to 9 pounds)
- ½ cup pineapple preserves
- ½ cup seedless raspberry jam
- ¼ cup packed brown sugar
- ¼ teaspoon ground cloves

1. Preheat oven to 300°. Place ham directly on roasting pan, cut side down. Bake, covered, 1¼ to 1¾ hours.
2. In a small bowl, mix the remaining ingredients. Spread over ham. Bake, uncovered, 20-30 minutes longer or until a thermometer reads 140° (do not overcook).

LEMON-ROASTED ASPARAGUS

When it comes to fixing asparagus, it's hard to go wrong. The springy flavors in this easy recipe burst with every bite.
—**JENN TIDWELL** FAIR OAKS, CA

START TO FINISH: 20 MIN.
MAKES: 8 SERVINGS

- 2 pounds fresh asparagus, trimmed
- ¼ cup olive oil
- 4 teaspoons grated lemon peel
- 2 garlic cloves, minced
- ½ teaspoon salt
- ½ teaspoon pepper

Preheat oven to 425°. Place asparagus in a greased 15x10x1-in. baking pan. Mix remaining ingredients; drizzle over asparagus. Toss to coat. Roast 8-12 minutes or until crisp-tender.

GLAZED
SPIRAL-SLICED
HAM

GRANDMA'S FAVORITE HOT CROSS BUNS

My husband's grandmother used to make these every year for Good Friday, and I carry on the tradition with my own version of her recipe. I make six dozen every year, and they all disappear.

—JILL EVELY WILMORE, KY

PREP: 45 MIN. + RISING
BAKE: 15 MIN./BATCH
MAKES: 6 DOZEN

 4 packages (¼ ounce each) active dry yeast
 3 cups warm 2% milk (110° to 115°)
 2 cups canola oil
 8 large eggs
 4 large eggs, separated
 1⅓ cups sugar
 4 teaspoons ground cinnamon
 3 teaspoons salt
 2 teaspoons ground cardamom
 13 to 15 cups all-purpose flour
 2⅔ cups raisins
 2 teaspoons water
ICING
 3 cups confectioners' sugar
 2 tablespoons butter, melted
 4 to 5 tablespoons 2% milk

1. In a very large bowl, dissolve the yeast in warm milk. Add the oil, eggs, egg yolks, sugar, cinnamon, salt, cardamom, yeast mixture and 10 cups flour. Beat mixture until smooth. Stir in enough remaining flour to form a firm dough. Stir in raisins.
2. Turn dough onto a floured surface; knead until smooth and elastic, about 6-8 minutes. Place in a greased bowl, turning once to grease the top. Cover the dough and let rise in a warm place until doubled, about 1¼ hours.
3. Punch dough down. Turn onto a lightly floured surface. Cover and let rest 10 minutes. Divide into 72 pieces; shape each into a ball. Place 2 in. apart in four greased 15x10x1-in. baking pans. Cover; let rise in a warm place until doubled, about 40 minutes.
4. Preheat oven to 375°. Combine the egg whites and water; brush over tops. Bake 12-15 minutes or until golden brown. Remove from the pans to wire racks to cool. For the icing, combine the confectioners' sugar, butter and enough milk to achieve the desired spreading consistency. Pipe a cross on top of each bun.

FAST FIX ▸
SNAP PEA SALAD

When snap peas are in season, I can't resist making this crunchy salad. I usually serve it cold, but it's also good warm, with the peas straight from the pot.

—JEAN ECOS HARTLAND, WI

START TO FINISH: 20 MIN.
MAKES: 12 SERVINGS (¾ CUP EACH)

 ¼ cup white wine vinegar
 ¼ cup Dijon mustard
 2 tablespoons minced fresh parsley
 2 tablespoons olive oil
 2 tablespoons honey
 1 tablespoon lemon juice
 1 teaspoon salt
 ½ teaspoon pepper
 3 pounds fresh sugar snap peas
 Grated lemon peel, optional

1. For vinaigrette, in a small bowl, whisk the first eight ingredients until blended. In a 6-qt. stockpot, bring 16 cups water to a boil. Add snap peas; cook, uncovered, 2-3 minutes or just until peas turn bright green. Remove peas and immediately drop into ice water. Drain and pat dry; place in a large bowl.
2. Drizzle with vinaigrette and toss to coat. Serve immediately or refrigerate, covered, up to 4 hours before serving. If desired, sprinkle with lemon peel.

FRESH FRUIT BOWL

This fruity salad boasts glorious color. Slightly sweet and well-chilled, it makes a refreshing accompaniment to a spring meal.

—**MARION KIRST** TROY, MI

PREP: 15 MIN. + CHILLING
MAKES: 3-4 QUARTS

- **8 to 10 cups fresh melon cubes**
- **1 to 2 tablespoons white corn syrup**
- **1 pint fresh strawberries, halved**
- **2 cups fresh pineapple chunks**
- **2 oranges, sectioned**
  Fresh mint leaves, optional

In a large bowl, combine melon cubes and corn syrup. Cover and refrigerate overnight. Just before serving, stir in the remaining fruit. If desired, garnish with fresh mint leaves.

LEMON-BLUEBERRY POUND CAKE

Pair a slice of this moist cake with a scoop of vanilla ice cream or sweetened whipped cream. It's a staple at our family gatherings.

—**REBECCA LITTLE** PARK RIDGE, IL

PREP: 25 MIN. • **BAKE:** 55 MIN. + COOLING
MAKES: 12 SERVINGS

- **⅓ cup butter, softened**
- **4 ounces cream cheese, softened**
- **2 cups sugar**
- **3 large eggs**
- **1 large egg white**
- **1 tablespoon grated lemon peel**
- **2 teaspoons vanilla extract**
- **2 cups fresh or frozen unsweetened blueberries**
- **3 cups all-purpose flour, divided**
- **1 teaspoon baking powder**
- **½ teaspoon baking soda**
- **½ teaspoon salt**
- **1 cup (8 ounces) lemon yogurt**

GLAZE
- **1¼ cups confectioners' sugar**
- **2 tablespoons lemon juice**

1. Preheat oven to 350°. Grease and flour a 10-in. fluted tube pan. In a large bowl, cream the butter, cream cheese and sugar until blended. Add eggs and egg white, one at a time, beating well after each addition. Beat in lemon peel and vanilla.
2. Toss berries with 2 tablespoons flour. In another bowl, mix remaining flour with baking powder, baking soda and salt; add to the creamed mixture alternately with yogurt, beating after each addition just until combined. Fold in blueberry mixture.
3. Transfer batter to prepared pan. Bake for 55-60 minutes or until a toothpick inserted in center comes out clean. Cool in pan 10 minutes before removing to wire rack; cool cake completely.
4. In a small bowl, mix confectioners' sugar and lemon juice until smooth. Drizzle over cake.

NOTE *For easier cake removal, use solid shortening when greasing a fluted or plain tube pan.*

★ ★ ★ ★ ★ **READER REVIEW**

"Made this cake for Easter dinner. Excellent! Followed the recipe except that I added 1 teaspoon lemon extract and cut vanilla extract to 1 teaspoon. Also added extra lemon zest to cake and to the icing as well— perfect! Everyone had a second slice."

JESKELLINGTON TASTEOFHOME.COM

FRESH FRUIT BOWL

BOURBON-GLAZED HAM

Smoky and sweet flavors come through in every bite of this Kentucky-style ham. It's now my go-to recipe.

—SUSAN SCHILLER TOMAHAWK, WI

PREP: 15 MIN.
BAKE: 2½ HOURS + STANDING
MAKES: 16 SERVINGS

- 1 fully cooked bone-in ham (8 to 10 pounds)
- ¾ cup bourbon, divided
- 2 cups packed brown sugar
- 1 tablespoon ground mustard
- 1 tablespoon orange marmalade
- ⅛ teaspoon ground coriander

1. Place ham on a rack in a shallow roasting pan. Score the surface of the ham, making diamond shapes ½ in. deep. Brush ham with 2 tablespoons bourbon. Bake, uncovered, at 325° for 2 hours.

2. In a small bowl, combine the brown sugar, mustard, marmalade, coriander and remaining bourbon; spoon over ham. Bake 30 minutes longer or until a thermometer reads 140°. Let ham stand for 15 minutes before slicing.

TRIPLE CITRUS SCONES

I love the bright and buttery flavor of these tender scones. Serve them with jam, or try them as a base for strawberry shortcake.

—ANGELA LEMOINE HOWELL, NJ

PREP: 20 MIN. • **BAKE:** 15 MIN.
MAKES: 8 SCONES

- 2¼ cups all-purpose flour
- ¼ cup plus 1 tablespoon sugar, divided
- 4 teaspoons grated orange peel
- 2 teaspoons grated lemon peel
- 1½ teaspoons grated lime peel
- 3 teaspoons baking powder
- ½ teaspoon salt
- 6 tablespoons cold butter, cubed
- 1 large egg
- ¼ cup orange juice
- ¼ cup buttermilk
- 1 tablespoon butter, melted

TRIPLE CITRUS SCONES

GLAZE
- ¼ cup confectioners' sugar
- 1½ teaspoons grated lime peel
- 1 tablespoon lime juice
- 1 tablespoon orange juice

1. Preheat oven to 400°. Place flour, ¼ cup sugar, citrus peels, baking powder and salt in a food processor; pulse until blended. Add cold butter; pulse until butter is the size of peas. Transfer to a large bowl. In a small bowl, whisk egg, orange juice and buttermilk until blended; stir into crumb mixture just until moistened.

2. Turn onto a lightly floured surface; knead gently 6-8 times. Pat dough into a 6-in. circle. Cut the dough into eight wedges. Place wedges on a parchment paper-lined baking sheet. Brush the scones with melted butter; sprinkle with the remaining sugar.

3. Bake 14-18 minutes or until golden brown. Meanwhile, in a small bowl, mix the glaze ingredients until smooth. Remove scones from oven; immediately brush with glaze. Serve scones warm.

FISH TACOS WITH GUACAMOLE

Hosting a Cinco de Mayo fiesta? Then you'll love my new favorite recipe for tacos. They're lighter than traditional beef tacos smothered in cheese. Add hot sauce, onions, tomatoes or jalapenos on top to suit your spice level.

—**DEB PERRY** TRAVERSE CITY, MI

PREP: 25 MIN. • **COOK:** 10 MIN.
MAKES: 4 SERVINGS

- 2 cups angel hair coleslaw mix
- 1½ teaspoons canola oil
- 1½ teaspoons lime juice

GUACAMOLE

- 1 medium ripe avocado, peeled and quartered
- 2 tablespoons fat-free sour cream
- 1 tablespoon finely chopped onion
- 1 tablespoon minced fresh cilantro
- ⅛ teaspoon salt
  Dash pepper

TACOS

- 1 pound tilapia fillets, cut into 1-inch pieces
- ¼ teaspoon salt
- ⅛ teaspoon pepper
- 2 teaspoons canola oil
- 8 corn tortillas (6 inches), warmed
  Optional toppings: hot pepper sauce and chopped tomatoes, green onions and jalapeno pepper

1. In a small bowl, toss coleslaw mix with oil and lime juice; refrigerate until serving. In another bowl, mash avocado with a fork; stir in sour cream, onion, cilantro, salt and pepper.
2. Sprinkle tilapia with salt and pepper. In a large nonstick skillet coated with cooking spray, heat oil over medium-high heat. Add tilapia; cook 3-4 minutes on each side or until fish just begins to flake easily with a fork. Serve in tortillas with coleslaw, guacamole and toppings as desired.

**FISH TACOS
WITH GUACAMOLE**

TRES LECHES CAKE

(5) INGREDIENTS FAST FIX ▶

REFRESHING BEER MARGARITAS

I'm always surprised when people say they didn't know this drink existed. It's an ideal warm-weather cocktail, and it's easy to double or triple the recipe for a crowd.
—**ARIANNE BARNETT** KANSAS CITY, MO

START TO FINISH: 5 MIN.
MAKES: 6 SERVINGS

	Lime slices and kosher salt, optional
2	**bottles (12 ounces each) beer**
1	**can (12 ounces) frozen limeade concentrate, thawed**
¾	**cup tequila**
¼	**cup sweet and sour mix**
	Ice cubes

GARNISH
    Lime slices

1. If desired, use lime slices to moisten the rims of six margarita or cocktail glasses. Sprinkle salt on a plate; hold each glass upside down and dip rims into salt. Discard the remaining salt on plate.

2. In a pitcher, combine the beer, concentrate, tequila and sweet and sour mix. Serve in prepared glasses over ice. Garnish with lime slices.

TRES LECHES CAKE

A staple dessert in Mexican kitchens for generations, this cake gets its name from the three types of milk—evaporated, sweetened condensed and heavy whipping cream—that create its moist and tender texture.
—*TASTE OF HOME* TEST KITCHEN

PREP: 45 MIN. • **BAKE:** 20 MIN. + CHILLING
MAKES: 10 SERVINGS

4	**large eggs, separated**
⅔	**cup sugar, divided**
⅔	**cup cake flour**
	Dash salt
¾	**cup heavy whipping cream**
¾	**cup evaporated milk**
¾	**cup sweetened condensed milk**
2	**teaspoons vanilla extract**
¼	**teaspoon rum extract**

TOPPING

1¼	**cups heavy whipping cream**
3	**tablespoons sugar**
	Dulce de leche, optional

1. Place egg whites in a large bowl; let stand at room temperature for 30 minutes. Line the bottom of a 9-in. springform pan with parchment paper; grease paper.

2. Meanwhile, preheat oven to 350°. In another large bowl, beat egg yolks until slightly thickened. Gradually add ⅓ cup sugar, beating on high speed until thick and lemon-colored. Fold in flour, a third at a time.

3. Add salt to egg whites; with clean beaters, beat on medium until soft peaks form. Gradually add remaining sugar, 1 tablespoon at a time, beating on high after each addition until sugar is dissolved. Continue beating until soft glossy peaks form. Fold a third of the whites into batter, then fold in remaining whites. Gently spread into prepared pan.

4. Bake until top springs back when lightly touched, 20-25 minutes. Cool 10 minutes before removing from pan to a wire rack to cool completely.

5. Place cake on a rimmed serving plate. Poke holes in top with a skewer. In a small bowl, mix the whipping cream, evaporated milk, sweetened condensed milk and extracts; brush slowly over cake. Refrigerate, covered, for 2 hours.

6. For topping, beat cream until it begins to thicken. Add sugar; beat until peaks form. Spread over top of cake. If desired, top with dulce de leche just before serving.

MARINATED PORK CHOPS

FAST FIX ▶
WATERMELON FETA FLAG SALAD

Our family celebrates the Fourth of July with a watermelon salad that resembles the flag. Here's an all-American centerpiece that's truly red, white and blue.

—**JAN WHITWORTH** ROEBUCK, SC

START TO FINISH: 25 MIN.
MAKES: 12 SERVINGS (¾ CUP EACH)

- ¼ cup red wine vinegar
- 1 tablespoon Dijon mustard
- 1 tablespoon grated lemon peel
- 1 teaspoon sugar
- ¼ teaspoon salt
- ¼ teaspoon pepper
- ⅓ cup olive oil
- ¼ cup finely chopped red onion

SALAD
- 6 cups fresh arugula (about 5 ounces)
- 1½ cups fresh blueberries
- 5 cups cubed seedless watermelon
- 1 package (8 ounces) feta cheese, cut into ½-in. cubes

1. For vinaigrette, in a small bowl, whisk the first six ingredients; gradually whisk in oil until blended. Stir in onion.
2. In a large bowl, lightly toss arugula with ¼ cup vinaigrette. Arrange the greens evenly in a large rectangular serving dish.
3. For stars, place blueberries over arugula at the top left corner. For stripes, arrange watermelon and cheese in alternating rows. Drizzle with remaining vinaigrette. Serve immediately.

FREEZE IT
MARINATED PORK CHOPS

I make these tender chops all summer long, and my family never tires of them. My secret? Marinate the meat overnight.

—**JEAN NEITZEL** BELOIT, WI

PREP: 5 MIN. + MARINATING
GRILL: 20 MIN.
MAKES: 6 SERVINGS

- ¾ cup canola oil
- ⅓ cup reduced-sodium soy sauce
- ¼ cup white vinegar
- 2 tablespoons Worcestershire sauce
- 1 tablespoon lemon juice
- 1 tablespoon prepared mustard
- 1 teaspoon salt
- 1 teaspoon pepper
- 1 teaspoon dried parsley flakes
- 1 garlic clove, minced
- 6 bone-in pork loin chops (1 inch thick and 8 ounces each)

1. In a large resealable plastic bag, combine the first 10 ingredients; add the pork. Seal bag and turn to coat; refrigerate overnight.
2. Drain pork, discarding marinade. Grill, covered, over medium heat, for 4-5 minutes on each side or until a thermometer reads 145°. Let meat stand for 5 minutes before serving.
FREEZE OPTION *Freeze uncooked pork in bag with marinade. To use, completely thaw in refrigerator. Grill as directed.*

WATERMELON
FETA FLAG SALAD

FAST FIX ▶

HOT DOG SLIDERS WITH MANGO-PINEAPPLE SALSA

For parties, we shrink down lots of foods to slider size, including these quick hot dogs. Pile on the easy but irresistible fruit salsa for a burst of fresh flavor.
—**CAROLE RESNICK** CLEVELAND, OH

START TO FINISH: 30 MIN.
MAKES: 2 DOZEN (2 CUPS SALSA)

- **3 tablespoons lime juice**
- **2 tablespoons honey**
- **¼ teaspoon salt**
- **1 cup cubed fresh pineapple (½ inch)**
- **1 cup cubed peeled mango (½ inch)**
- **¼ cup finely chopped red onion**
- **2 tablespoons finely chopped sweet red pepper**
- **12 hot dogs**
- **12 hot dog buns, split**

1. In a small bowl, whisk lime juice, honey and salt until blended. Add pineapple, mango, onion and pepper; toss to coat.
2. Grill the hot dogs, covered, over medium heat or broil 4 in. from heat 7-9 minutes or until heated through, turning occasionally.
3. Place hot dogs in buns; cut each crosswise in half. Serve the sliders with fruit salsa.

HOT DOG SLIDERS WITH MANGO-PINEAPPLE SALSA

FAST FIX ▶

SWISS HAM KABOBS

With warm cheese, juicy pineapple and salty ham, these kabobs are my daughter's birthday dinner request every year. They're a fantastic way to welcome grilling season.
—**HELEN PHILLIPS** HORSEHEADS, NY

START TO FINISH: 20 MIN.
MAKES: 4 SERVINGS

- **1 can (20 ounces) pineapple chunks**
- **½ cup orange marmalade**
- **1 tablespoon prepared mustard**
- **¼ teaspoon ground cloves**
- **1 pound fully cooked ham, cut into 1-inch cubes**
- **½ pound Swiss cheese, cut into 1-inch cubes**
- **1 medium green pepper, cut into 1-inch pieces, optional**

1. Drain the pineapple, reserving 2 tablespoons juice; set pineapple aside. In a small bowl, mix marmalade, mustard, cloves and the reserved pineapple juice. On eight metal or soaked wooden skewers, alternately thread ham, cheese, pineapple and, if desired, green pepper.
2. Place kabobs on greased grill rack. Grill, uncovered, over medium heat or broil 4 in. from heat 5-7 minutes or until heated through, turning and basting frequently with marmalade sauce. Serve with remaining sauce.

★ ★ ★ ★ ★ 5 STAR TIP

Before grilling meats, trim any excess fat to avoid flare-ups. Thick or sweet sauces can be used to add flavor to meat and vegetables. If a sauce is also used as a basting or dipping sauce, reserve a portion before adding the uncooked foods to the grill. Lightly brush on during the last few minutes of cooking. Baste and turn every few minutes to prevent burning.

FAJITA IN A BOWL

Get out the skewers and take a stab at grilling peppers, onions and corn for an awesome steak salad that's pure summer.

—PEGGY WOODWARD SHULLSBURG, WI

START TO FINISH: 30 MIN.
MAKES: 4 SERVINGS

- 1 **tablespoon brown sugar**
- 1 **tablespoon chili powder**
- ½ **teaspoon salt**
- 1 **beef flank steak (1 pound)**
- 12 **miniature sweet peppers, halved and seeded**
- 1 **medium red onion, cut into thin wedges**
- 2 **cups cherry tomatoes**
- 2 **medium ears sweet corn, husks removed**

SALAD
- 12 **cups torn mixed salad greens**
- 1 **cup fresh cilantro leaves**
- ½ **cup reduced-fat lime vinaigrette**
   Optional ingredients: cotija cheese, lime wedges and tortillas

1. In a small bowl, mix brown sugar, chili powder and salt. Rub onto both sides of steak.

2. Place peppers and onion on a grilling grid; place on grill rack over medium heat. Grill, covered, 9-11 minutes or until crisp-tender, stirring occasionally; add tomatoes during the last 2 minutes. Remove from grill.

3. Place steak and corn directly on grill rack; close lid. Grill steak 8-10 minutes on each side or until a thermometer reads 145° for medium rare; grill corn 10-12 minutes or until lightly charred, turning occasionally.

4. Divide greens and cilantro among four bowls. Cut corn from cobs and thinly slice steak across the grain; place in bowls. Top with vegetables; drizzle with vinaigrette. If desired, serve with cheese, lime and tortillas.

NOTE *If you do not have a grilling grid, use a disposable foil pan with holes poked into the bottom with a meat fork.*

PATRIOTIC
FROZEN DELIGHT

PATRIOTIC FROZEN DELIGHT

My husband and I pick lots of fruit at local farms, then freeze our harvest to enjoy all year long. This frozen dessert showcases both blueberries and strawberries and has a refreshing lemon flavor.

—BERNICE RUSS BLADENBORO, NC

PREP: 10 MIN. + FREEZING
MAKES: 12 SERVINGS

- 1 **can (14 ounces) sweetened condensed milk**
- ⅓ **cup lemon juice**
- 2 **teaspoons grated lemon peel**
- 2 **cups (16 ounces) plain yogurt**
- 2 **cups miniature marshmallows**
- ½ **cup chopped pecans**
- 1 **cup sliced fresh strawberries**
- 1 **cup fresh blueberries**

In a bowl, combine milk, lemon juice and peel. Stir in yogurt, marshmallows and pecans. Spread half of the mixture into an ungreased 11x7-in. dish. Sprinkle with half of the strawberries and blueberries. Cover with the remaining yogurt mixture; top with remaining berries. Cover and freeze. Remove dish from the freezer 15-20 minutes before serving.

SWEET POTATO, ORANGE & PINEAPPLE CRUNCH

I combined my two favorite sweet potato casseroles to create a new version for the Thanksgiving Day table.

—LISA VARNER EL PASO, TX

PREP: 35 MIN. • **BAKE:** 40 MIN.
MAKES: 12 SERVINGS (½ CUP EACH)

- 2 pounds sweet potatoes, peeled and cubed (about 6 cups)
- ¾ cup sugar
- 1 can (8 ounces) crushed pineapple, drained
- 2 large eggs, lightly beaten
- ½ cup sour cream or plain yogurt
- ½ teaspoon grated orange peel
- ¼ cup orange juice
- ¼ cup butter, melted
- 1 teaspoon vanilla extract

TOPPING

- 1 cup flaked coconut
- 1 cup chopped pecans
- 1 cup packed brown sugar
- ½ cup all-purpose flour
- ¼ cup butter, melted

1. Preheat oven to 350°. Place sweet potatoes in a large saucepan; add water to cover. Bring to a boil over high heat. Reduce heat to medium; cook, uncovered, 10-15 minutes or until tender. Drain.

2. Place the sweet potatoes in a large bowl; mash potatoes. Stir in sugar, pineapple, eggs, sour cream, orange peel, juice, butter and vanilla; transfer to a greased 13x9-in. baking dish. For topping, in a large bowl, mix coconut, pecans, brown sugar and flour. Add butter; mix until crumbly. Sprinkle over top.

3. Bake, uncovered, 40-45 minutes or until heated through and topping is golden brown.

SWEET POTATO, ORANGE & PINEAPPLE CRUNCH

TURKEY SAUSAGE-STUFFED ACORN SQUASH

Finding healthy recipes the whole family will eat is a challenge. This elegant squash is one dish we love. It works with pork, turkey and chicken sausage.

—MELISSA PELKEY HASS WALESKA, GA

PREP: 30 MIN. • **BAKE:** 50 MIN.
MAKES: 8 SERVINGS

- 4 **medium acorn squash (about 1½ pounds each)**
- 1 **cup cherry tomatoes, halved**
- 1 **pound Italian turkey sausage links, casings removed**
- ½ **pound sliced fresh mushrooms**
- 1 **medium apple, peeled and finely chopped**
- 1 **small onion, finely chopped**
- 2 **teaspoons fennel seed**
- 2 **teaspoons caraway seeds**
- ½ **teaspoon dried sage leaves**
- 3 **cups fresh baby spinach**
- 1 **tablespoon minced fresh thyme**
- ¼ **teaspoon salt**
- ⅛ **teaspoon pepper**
- 8 **ounces fresh mozzarella cheese, chopped**
- 1 **tablespoon red wine vinegar**

1. Preheat oven to 400°. Cut squash lengthwise in half; remove and discard seeds. Using a sharp knife, cut a thin slice from bottom of each half to allow them to lie flat. Place the squash in a shallow roasting pan, hollow the side down; add ¼ in. of hot water and the halved tomatoes. Bake, uncovered, for 45 minutes.
2. Meanwhile, in a large skillet, cook sausage, mushrooms, apple, onion and dried seasonings over medium heat 8-10 minutes or until sausage is no longer pink, breaking up sausage into crumbles; drain. Add spinach, thyme, salt and pepper; cook and stir 2 minutes. Remove from heat.
3. Carefully remove squash from the roasting pan. Drain cooking liquid, reserving tomatoes. Return squash to pan, hollow side up.

4. Stir cheese, vinegar and reserved tomatoes into sausage mixture. Spoon into squash cavities. Bake for 5-10 minutes longer or until heated through and squash is easily pierced with a fork.

FAST FIX ▶
TASTE-OF-FALL SALAD

My parents stayed with me at a friend's beautiful ranch for the holidays, and I made everyone this impressive salad. It became every night's first course!

—KRISTIN KOSSAK BOZEMAN, MT

START TO FINISH: 25 MIN.
MAKES: 6 SERVINGS

- ⅔ **cup pecan halves**
- ¼ **cup balsamic vinegar, divided**
  Dash cayenne pepper
  Dash ground cinnamon
- 3 **tablespoons sugar, divided**
- 1 **package (5 ounces) spring mix salad greens**
- ¼ **cup olive oil**
- 1 **teaspoon Dijon mustard**
- ⅛ **teaspoon salt**
- 1 **medium pear, thinly sliced**
- ¼ **cup shredded Parmesan cheese**

1. In a large heavy skillet, cook the pecans, 2 tablespoons vinegar, cayenne and cinnamon over medium heat until nuts are toasted, about 4 minutes. Sprinkle with 1 tablespoon sugar. Cook and stir for 2-4 minutes or until sugar is melted. Spread pecans on foil to cool.
2. Place salad greens in a large bowl. In a small bowl, whisk oil, mustard, salt and remaining vinegar and sugar; drizzle over greens and toss to coat. Arrange the greens, pear slices and pecans on six salad plates. Sprinkle with cheese.

CREAMY BUTTERNUT SQUASH & SAGE SOUP

I recently started experimenting with new soup recipes and finally created a rich squash version that omits heavy cream altogether, making it a healthier way to indulge my fondness for creamy foods.

—**NITHYA KUMAR** DAVIS, CA

PREP: 20 MIN. • **COOK:** 50 MIN.
MAKES: 4 SERVINGS

- 4 **cups cubed peeled butternut squash**
- 1 **tablespoon olive oil**
- 2 **tablespoons minced fresh sage**
- ¼ **teaspoon salt**
- ¼ **teaspoon pepper**

CREAMY BUTTERNUT SQUASH & SAGE SOUP

SOUP
- 1 **tablespoon olive oil**
- 2 **tablespoons butter, divided**
- 1 **medium onion, chopped**
- 1 **garlic clove, minced**
- ¾ **teaspoon salt**
- ¼ to ½ **teaspoon crushed red pepper flakes**
- ⅛ **teaspoon pepper**
- 4 **cups water**
- 1 **medium sweet potato, chopped**
- 1 **medium carrot, chopped**

1. Preheat oven to 400°. Place squash in a foil-lined 15x10x1-in. baking pan. Drizzle with oil; sprinkle with sage, salt and pepper. Toss to coat. Roast squash for 30-35 minutes or until tender, stirring occasionally.
2. Meanwhile, in a large saucepan, heat oil and 1 tablespoon butter over medium heat. Add onion and garlic; cook and stir 3-4 minutes or until softened. Reduce heat to medium-low; cook 30-40 minutes or until deep golden brown, stirring occasionally. Stir in salt, pepper flakes and pepper.
3. Add water, sweet potato and carrot to saucepan. Bring to a boil. Reduce heat; cook, uncovered, 10-15 minutes or until vegetables are tender. Add squash mixture and remaining butter to soup. Puree the soup using an immersion blender. Or, cool soup slightly and puree in batches in a blender; return the soup to pan and heat through.

⑤INGREDIENTS
ROASTED FRESH PUMPKIN SEEDS

I learned how to roast pumpkin seeds from my mother, who learned it from her mother. They're a wholesome, healthy snack and fun to make after you finish carving Halloween jack-o'-lanterns with the kids!

—**MARGARET DRYE** PLAINFIELD, NH

PREP: 20 MIN. + SOAKING
BAKE: 1½ HOURS + COOLING
MAKES: 1½ CUPS

- 2 **cups fresh pumpkin seeds**
- 1 **teaspoon salt**
- 1 **tablespoon olive oil**
- ¾ **teaspoon kosher or fine sea salt**

1. Place seeds in a 1-qt. bowl; cover with water. Stir in salt; let stand, covered, overnight.
2. Preheat oven to 200°. Drain and rinse seeds; drain again and pat dry. Transfer to a 15x10x1-in. baking pan. Toss with oil and kosher salt; spread in a single layer.
3. Roast 1½ to 1¾ hours or until the seeds are crisp and lightly browned, stirring occasionally. Cool completely. Store in an airtight container.

TRAIL MIX COOKIE CUPS

My granddaughter helped create these cookie cups by using ingredients from my pantry and fridge. We used trail mix to jazz them up.

—PAMELA SHANK PARKERSBURG, WV

PREP: 20 MIN. • **BAKE:** 15 MIN. + COOLING
MAKES: 2 DOZEN

1 **tube (16½ ounces) refrigerated peanut butter cookie dough**
½ **cup creamy peanut butter**
½ **cup Nutella**
1½ **cups trail mix**

1. Preheat oven to 350°. Shape dough into twenty-four balls (about 1¼ in.). Press evenly onto bottom and up sides of greased mini-muffin cups.

2. Bake 12-14 minutes or until golden brown. Using the end of a wooden spoon handle, reshape the cups as necessary. Cool in pans 15 minutes. Remove to wire racks to cool cookie cups completely.

3. Fill each with 1 teaspoon each peanut butter and Nutella. Top with trail mix.

PUMPKIN BREAD

I keep this deliciously spicy, pumpkin-rich quick bread stocked in my freezer along with other home-baked goodies.

—JOYCE JACKSON BRIDGETOWN, NS

PREP: 15 MIN. • **BAKE:** 65 MIN. + COOLING
MAKES: 1 LOAF (16 SLICES)

1⅔ **cups all-purpose flour**
1½ **cups sugar**
1 **teaspoon baking soda**
1 **teaspoon ground cinnamon**
¾ **teaspoon salt**
½ **teaspoon baking powder**
½ **teaspoon ground nutmeg**
¼ **teaspoon ground cloves**
2 **large eggs**
1 **cup canned pumpkin**
½ **cup canola oil**
½ **cup water**
½ **cup chopped walnuts**
½ **cup raisins, optional**

PUMPKIN BREAD

1. Preheat oven to 350°. Combine first eight ingredients. Whisk together eggs, pumpkin, oil and water; stir into dry ingredients just until moistened. Fold in walnuts and, if desired, raisins.

2. Pour into a greased 9x5-in. loaf pan. Bake until a toothpick inserted in the center comes out clean, 65-70 minutes. Cool bread in pan 10 minutes before removing to a wire rack.

★ ★ ★ ★ ★ **5 STAR TIP**
For best results with quick breads, bake in a light aluminum pan rather than a darker nonstick pan. Position the oven rack so the top of the loaf is in the center of the oven. After baking, tightly wrap a cooled quick bread and wait a day to enjoy it— you'll find the flavors have mellowed and the sides have softened.

FUN WITH FONDANT

To prevent fondant from sticking to the surface while rolling, sprinkle with confectioners' sugar.

Fondant dries out quickly, so while working with it, always keep excess tightly wrapped in plastic wrap and stored in a resealable plastic bag.

To save for future use, lightly coat the surface with shortening to prevent it from drying out. Wrap in plastic wrap and store in a resealable plastic bag.

JACK-O'-LANTERN CAKE

I sandwiched two bundt cakes together to make this gap-toothed grinner—it's the best Halloween centerpiece ever!

—JULIANNE JOHNSON GROVE CITY, MN

PREP: 35 MIN. • **BAKE:** 30 MIN. + COOLING
MAKES: 12-16 SERVINGS

- 2 **packages spice cake mix (regular size)**
- 4 **cans (16 ounces each) vanilla frosting**
  Red and yellow food coloring
- 1 **ice cream cake cone (about 3 inches tall)**
- 2 **Oreo cookies**
- 1 **package (24 ounces) ready-to-use rolled black fondant**

1. Prepare and bake cakes according to package directions using two 10-in. fluted tube pans. Invert cakes onto wire racks; cool completely. Meanwhile, tint the frosting orange using red and yellow food coloring.
2. Cut thin slice off bottom of each cake. Spread one cake bottom with frosting; press flat sides together to make a pumpkin shape. Place a foil ball in the center to support the stem; top with an ice cream cake cone. Frost cake with remaining frosting.
3. To decorate face, roll out fondant to 1/8-in. thickness; cut into desired shapes for mouth and nose. Remove the tops from two Oreo cookies; cut half-circles in filling for eyes. Press cookies and fondant into frosting to make the face.

WICKED WITCH STUFFED POTATOES

WICKED WITCH STUFFED POTATOES

These rich, cheesy potatoes are a savory way to work Halloween into your menu. They're sure to cast a smile-producing spell on those fun-loving folks around your table.

—*TASTE OF HOME* TEST KITCHEN

PREP: 5 MIN. • **BAKE:** 70 MIN.
MAKES: 4 SERVINGS

- 2 **large baking potatoes**
- 3 **ounces Jarlsberg or Swiss cheese, shredded, divided**
- 1/4 **cup milk**
- 2 **tablespoons butter**
- 1/2 **teaspoon salt**
- 4 **grape tomatoes, halved**
- 8 **slices ripe olives**
- 4 **small serrano peppers, stems removed**
- 4 **green pepper strips**
- 4 **blue corn chips**

1. Scrub and pierce potatoes. Bake at 375° for 1 hour or until tender.
2. When potatoes are cool enough to handle, cut in half lengthwise. Scoop out pulp, leaving a thin shell. In a small bowl, mash the pulp. Stir in 1/2 cup cheese, milk, butter and salt. Spoon into the potato shells. Sprinkle with remaining cheese.
3. Place on a baking sheet. Bake at 375° for 5-10 minutes or until cheese is melted.
4. Using the tomato halves, olive slices, serrano peppers and pepper strips, create a face on each potato half. Add corn chip hats.

NOTE *Wear disposable gloves when cutting hot peppers; the oils can burn skin. Avoid touching your face.*

SLITHERING HUMMUS BITES

Friends often ask me to make my hummus dip for parties. One year at Halloween, I took it a step further by piping it into mini phyllo shells and topping it with olives and roasted red peppers to make creepy creatures.

—**AMY WHITE** MANCHESTER, CT

START TO FINISH: 20 MIN.
MAKES: 2½ DOZEN

- 1 jar (7½ ounces) roasted sweet red peppers, drained
- 1 can (15 ounces) garbanzo beans or chickpeas, rinsed and drained
- 1 garlic clove, halved
- 3 tablespoons lemon juice
- 2 tablespoons olive oil
- 2 tablespoons tahini
- ½ teaspoon salt
- 2 packages (1.9 ounces each) frozen miniature phyllo tart shells
- 30 pitted ripe olives

1. Cut one roasted pepper into 30 strips; place remaining peppers in a food processor. Add beans and garlic; pulse until chopped. Add lemon juice, oil, tahini and salt; process until the mixture is blended.
2. Pipe into shells. Stuff a strip of red pepper into each olive; press into filled shells.

SPIDERWEB BROWNIES

I drizzle a chocolate spiderweb over white icing to turn these brownies into a fun Halloween treat. They're so delicious and chocolaty that you may end up making them for gatherings throughout the year.

—**SANDY PICHON** SLIDELL, LA

PREP: 20 MIN. • **BAKE:** 30 MIN. + COOLING
MAKES: 2 DOZEN

- ¾ cup butter, cubed
- 4 ounces unsweetened chocolate, chopped
- 2 cups sugar
- 3 large eggs, lightly beaten
- 1 teaspoon vanilla extract
- 1 cup all-purpose flour
- 1 cup chopped pecans or walnuts
- 1 jar (7 ounces) marshmallow creme
- 1 ounce semisweet chocolate

1. In a large microwave-safe bowl, melt the butter and unsweetened chocolate; stir until smooth. Remove from the heat; stir in sugar. Cool for 10 minutes. Whisk in eggs and vanilla. Stir in the flour and nuts. Pour into a greased foil-lined 13x9-in. baking pan.
2. Bake at 350° for 25-30 minutes or until a toothpick inserted in the center comes out clean (do not overbake). Immediately drop the marshmallow cream by spoonfuls over hot brownies; spread evenly. Cool on a wire rack.
3. Lift out of the pan; remove foil. For the web decoration, melt semisweet chocolate in a microwave; stir until smooth. Transfer to a small resealable plastic bag. Cut a small hole in one corner of the bag; drizzle chocolate over top in a spiderweb design. Let set before cutting into bars.

SLITHERING
HUMMUS BITES

CANDY CORN QUESADILLAS

Celebrate the season with a savory touch. These candy corn triangles will be a smash hit. Let kids join in the fun by using a rolling pin to crush a bag filled with nacho tortilla chips while you do the rest.

—MARIE PARKER MILWAUKEE, WI

PREP: 25 MIN. • **COOK:** 10 MIN.
MAKES: 2 DOZEN

- 1 rotisserie chicken, cut up
- 1 jar (16 ounces) salsa
- 1 cup frozen corn, thawed
- ¼ cup barbecue sauce
- ½ teaspoon ground cumin
- ½ cup butter, melted
- 8 flour tortillas (10 inches)
- 1 jar (15½ ounces) salsa con queso dip, warmed
- 4 cups (16 ounces) shredded Mexican cheese blend
- 2⅔ cups crushed nacho-flavored tortilla chips
- ½ cup sour cream

1. In a Dutch oven, combine the first five ingredients; heat through, stirring occasionally. Brush butter over one side of each tortilla.

2. Place one tortilla in a large skillet, buttered side down. Spread with 1 cup chicken mixture; top with another tortilla, buttered side up. Cook over medium heat for 1-2 minutes or until bottom is lightly browned. Turn the quesadilla.

3. Spread ½ cup queso dip over quesadilla; carefully sprinkle cheese along the outer edge. Cook, covered, 1-2 minutes or until the cheese begins to melt.

4. Remove quesadilla to a cutting board. Sprinkle crushed chips over queso dip. Cut quesadilla into six wedges. Place a small dollop of sour cream at the point of each wedge. Repeat with remaining ingredients.

CANDY CORN
QUESADILLA

BUTTERNUT-SWEET POTATO PIE

If you're looking for a memorable autumn dessert, this custard-like pie is one folks soon won't forget. It's super easy to put together, and it slices like a dream.

—MARY ANN DELL PHOENIXVILLE, PA

PREP: 15 MIN. • **BAKE:** 50 MIN. + COOLING
MAKES: 8 SERVINGS

- Pastry for single-crust pie (9 inches)
- 4 large eggs
- 1⅓ cups half-and-half cream
- 1 cup mashed cooked butternut squash
- 1 cup mashed cooked sweet potato (about 1 medium)
- ½ cup honey
- 1 tablespoon all-purpose flour
- ½ teaspoon salt
- 1 teaspoon ground cinnamon
- ½ teaspoon ground ginger
- ¼ teaspoon ground nutmeg
- Dash ground cloves
- Whipped cream, optional

1. Preheat oven to 375°. On a lightly floured surface, roll pastry dough to a ⅛-in.-thick circle; transfer to a 9-in. deep-dish pie plate. Trim pastry to ½ in. beyond rim of plate; flute edge.

2. In a large bowl, whisk eggs, cream, squash, sweet potato, honey, flour, salt and spices. Pour into pastry shell.

3. Bake 50-60 minutes or until a knife inserted near the center comes out clean. Cover edge loosely with foil during the last 15 minutes if needed to prevent overbrowning. Remove foil. Cool on a wire rack; serve within 2 hours or refrigerate and serve cold. If desired, top with whipped cream.

PASTRY FOR SINGLE-CRUST PIE (9 INCHES) *Combine 1¼ cups all-purpose flour and ¼ teaspoon salt; cut in ½ cup cold butter until crumbly. Gradually add 3-5 tablespoons ice water, tossing with a fork until dough holds together when pressed. Wrap in plastic wrap and refrigerate 1 hour.*

CITRUS & HERB ROASTED TURKEY BREAST

⑤ INGREDIENTS

CREAM CHEESE MASHED POTATOES

The bowl is always scraped clean when I serve this easy mash. Before holiday feasts, I make it early and keep it warm in a slow cooker so I can focus on last-minute details.

—JILL THOMAS WASHINGTON, IN

PREP: 20 MIN. • **COOK:** 15 MIN.
MAKES: 20 SERVINGS

- 8 pounds russet potatoes
- 1 package (8 ounces) cream cheese, softened
- ½ cup butter, melted
- 2 teaspoons salt
- ¾ teaspoon pepper
  Additional melted butter, optional
- ¼ cup finely chopped green onions

1. Peel and cube potatoes. Place in a large stockpot; add water to cover. Bring to a boil. Reduce heat; cook, uncovered, until tender, for 12-15 minutes. Drain.
2. With a mixer, beat cream cheese, ½ cup melted butter, salt and pepper until smooth. Add potatoes; beat until light and fluffy. If desired, top with additional melted butter. Sprinkle with green onions.

CITRUS & HERB ROASTED TURKEY BREAST

This recipe will make you love turkey in a whole new way. Brining with lemon, rosemary and orange juice makes it so flavorful. It's the star attraction at our Thanksgiving table.

—FAY MORELAND WICHITA FALLS, TX

PREP: 1 HOUR + CHILLING
BAKE: 2 HOURS + STANDING
MAKES: 10 SERVINGS

- 4 cups water
- ¾ cup kosher salt
- ¾ cup sugar
- 2 medium lemons, quartered
- 6 fresh rosemary sprigs
- 6 fresh thyme sprigs
- 8 garlic cloves, halved
- 1 tablespoon coarsely ground pepper
- 2 cups cold apple juice
- 2 cups cold orange juice
- 2 large oven roasting bags
- 1 bone-in turkey breast (5 to 6 pounds)

HERB BUTTER
- ⅓ cup butter, softened
- 4 teaspoons grated lemon peel
- 1 tablespoon minced fresh rosemary
- 1 tablespoon minced fresh thyme
- 1½ teaspoons coarsely ground pepper

SEASONED SALT BUTTER
- ¼ cup butter, melted
- 1½ teaspoons seasoned salt

1. In a 6-qt. stockpot, combine the first eight ingredients. Bring to a boil. Remove from heat. Add cold juices to brine; cool to room temperature.
2. Place one oven roasting bag inside the other. Place turkey breast inside both bags; pour in cooled brine. Seal bags, pressing out as much air as possible, and turn to coat. Place in a roasting pan. Refrigerate 8 hours or overnight, turning occasionally.
3. In a small bowl, beat herb butter ingredients until blended. Remove turkey from brine; rinse and pat dry. Discard brine. Place turkey on a rack in a 15x10x1-in. baking pan. With fingers, carefully loosen skin from turkey breast; rub herb butter under the skin. Secure skin to underside of breast with toothpicks. Refrigerate, covered, 18-24 hours.
4. Preheat oven to 425°. In a small bowl, mix butter and seasoned salt; brush over outside of turkey. Roast for 15 minutes.
5. Reduce oven setting to 325°. Roast for 1¾-2¼ hours longer or until a thermometer reads 170°. (Cover loosely with foil if turkey browns too quickly.) Remove turkey from oven; tent with foil. Let stand 15 minutes before carving.

GRANDMA'S CORN BREAD DRESSING

One of our favorite Thanksgiving dishes growing up was our grandmother's chicken corn bread dressing. Now we leave out the chicken, but it's still just as good.
—**SUZANNE MOHME** BASTROP, TX

PREP: 40 MIN. + COOLING • **BAKE:** 45 MIN.
MAKES: 12 SERVINGS (⅔ CUP EACH)

- 1 cup all-purpose flour
- 1 cup cornmeal
- 2 teaspoons baking powder
- 1 teaspoon salt
- 2 large eggs
- 1 cup buttermilk
- ¼ cup canola oil

DRESSING
- 1 tablespoon canola oil
- 1 medium onion, chopped
- 2 celery ribs, chopped
- 3 large eggs
- 2 cans (10¾ ounces each) condensed cream of chicken soup, undiluted
- 3 teaspoons poultry seasoning
- 1 teaspoon pepper
- ½ teaspoon salt
- 2 cups chicken broth

1. Preheat oven to 400°. In a large bowl, whisk flour, cornmeal, baking powder and salt. In another bowl, whisk eggs and buttermilk. Pour oil into an 8-in. ovenproof skillet; place skillet in oven for 4 minutes.
2. Meanwhile, add the buttermilk mixture to the flour mixture; stir just until moistened.
3. Carefully tilt and rotate skillet to coat bottom with oil; add batter. Bake 20-25 minutes or until a toothpick inserted in center comes out clean. Cool completely in pan on a wire rack.
4. Reduce oven setting to 350°. For dressing, in a large skillet, heat oil over medium-high heat. Add onion and celery; cook and stir 4-6 minutes or until tender. Remove from heat. Coarsely crumble corn bread into skillet; toss to combine. In a small bowl, whisk eggs, condensed soup and seasonings; stir into bread mixture. Stir in broth.
5. Transfer to a greased 13x9-in. baking dish. Bake 45-55 minutes or until lightly browned.

FAST FIX
HARVARD BEETS

The bright, citrusy flavors of this pretty side dish are a great perk-up for down-to-earth entrees—and for people who usually shy away from beets.
—**JEAN ANN PERKINS** NEWBURYPORT, MD

START TO FINISH: 15 MIN.
MAKES: 4-6 SERVINGS

- 1 can (16 ounces) sliced beets
- ¼ cup sugar
- 1½ teaspoons cornstarch
- 2 tablespoons vinegar
- 2 tablespoons orange juice
- 1 tablespoon grated orange peel

Drain beets, reserving 2 tablespoons juice; set beets and juice aside. In a saucepan, combine the sugar and cornstarch. Add vinegar, orange juice and beet juice; bring to a boil. Reduce heat and simmer for 3-4 minutes or until thickened. Add beets and orange peel; heat through.

GRANDMA'S CORN BREAD DRESSING

BUTTERNUT SQUASH ROLLS

With their cheery yellow color and delicious aroma, these appealing rolls will brighten your buffet table. I've found this recipe is a great way to utilize squash from the garden.

—BERNICE MORRIS MARSHFIELD, MO

PREP: 30 MIN. + RISING • **BAKE:** 20 MIN.
MAKES: 2 DOZEN

- 1 package (¼ ounce) active dry yeast
- 1 cup warm whole milk (110° to 115°)
- ¼ cup warm water (110° to 115°)
- 3 tablespoons butter, softened
- 2 teaspoons salt
- ½ cup sugar
- 1 cup mashed cooked butternut squash
- 5 to 5½ cups all-purpose flour, divided

1. In a large bowl, dissolve yeast in milk and water. Add the butter, salt, sugar, squash and 3 cups flour; beat until smooth. Add enough remaining flour to form a soft dough.

2. Turn onto a floured surface; knead until smooth and elastic, 6-8 minutes. Place in a greased bowl, turning once to grease top. Cover dough and let rise in a warm place until doubled, about 1 hour.

3. Punch dough down. Form into rolls; place in two greased 10-in. cast-iron skillets or 9-in. round baking pans. Cover and let rise until doubled, about 30 minutes.

4. Bake at 375° for 20-25 minutes or until golden brown.

PRETZEL TURKEY TREATS

PRETZEL TURKEY TREATS

Get the kids in the Turkey Day spirit with these festive treats. With a sturdy pretzel base, colorful chewy fruit tail feathers and funny turkey faces made out of thin mints, they are clever edible favors.

—LORRI REINHARDT BIG BEND, WI

PREP: 2 HOURS + STANDING
MAKES: 1 DOZEN

- 6 Fruit by the Foot fruit rolls
- 6 circus peanut candies
- 1 cup butterscotch chips, divided
- 24 candy eyeballs
- 12 chocolate-covered thin mints
- 12 large sourdough pretzels
- 36 milk chocolate kisses, unwrapped
- 12 vanilla wafers

1. Using kitchen scissors, cut feathers and 12 wattles from fruit rolls. Cut 24 turkey feet from circus peanuts.

2. Reserve 12 butterscotch chips for beaks. In a microwave, melt ½ cup of the remaining chips; stir until smooth. Using melted chips, attach two candy eyeballs, a wattle and a beak to each chocolate-covered thin mint to make turkey heads.

3. Place a pretzel on a waxed paper-lined microwave-safe plate. Place a chocolate kiss in each of the three holes. Microwave on high for 15-20 seconds or until melted. While still warm, arrange feathers in a fan shape over pretzel, pressing gently into melted chocolate to adhere. Repeat with remaining pretzels and kisses.

4. Melt remaining butterscotch chips. Using melted chips, attach a vanilla wafer to each pretzel for body; attach heads. Attach circus peanut pieces for feet. Let stand until set.

POTATO PUMPKIN MASH

WALNUT PUMPKIN CAKE ROLL

This is one of my family's favorite dessert recipes, especially for holiday gatherings.
—**MARY GECHA** CENTER RUTLAND, VT

PREP: 20 MIN. + CHILLING
BAKE: 15 MIN. + COOLING
MAKES: 12 SERVINGS

- 3 **large eggs**
- 1 **cup sugar**
- ⅔ **cup canned pumpkin**
- 1 **teaspoon lemon juice**
- ¾ **cup all-purpose flour**
- 2 **teaspoons ground cinnamon**
- 1 **teaspoon baking powder**
- 1 **teaspoon ground ginger**
- ½ **teaspoon salt**
- ½ **teaspoon ground nutmeg**
- 1 **cup finely chopped walnuts**
  Confectioners' sugar

FILLING
- 6 **ounces cream cheese, softened**
- 1 **cup confectioners' sugar**
- ¼ **cup butter, softened**
- ½ **teaspoon vanilla extract**

1. Line a greased 15x10x 1-in. baking pan with waxed paper. Grease the paper; set aside. In a bowl, beat eggs for 3 minutes. Gradually add sugar; beat for 2 minutes or until mixture is thick and lemon-colored. Stir in the pumpkin and lemon juice. Combine dry ingredients; fold into pumpkin mixture. Spread batter evenly in prepared pan. Sprinkle with walnuts.
2. Bake at 375° for 12-14 minutes or until cake springs back when lightly touched in center. Cool for 5 minutes. Turn onto a kitchen towel dusted with confectioners' sugar. Gently peel off waxed paper. Roll up cake in towel jelly-roll style, starting with a short side *(image 1)*. Cool on a wire rack.
3. In a bowl, combine filling the ingredients; beat until smooth. Unroll cake; spread evenly with filling to within ½ in. of edges *(image 2)*. Roll up again *(image 3)*. Cover cake and refrigerate for 1 hour before cutting. Refrigerate leftovers.

POTATO PUMPKIN MASH

No more plain white potatoes for us! I swirl fresh pumpkin into our holiday spuds for an extra kick of flavor and color. You can also substitute butternut squash for pumpkin.
—**MICHELLE MEDLEY** DALLAS, TX

PREP: 20 MIN. • **COOK:** 25 MIN.
MAKES: 8 SERVINGS

- 8 **cups cubed peeled pie pumpkin (about 2 pounds)**
- 8 **medium Yukon Gold potatoes, peeled and cubed (about 2 pounds)**
- ½ **to ¾ cup 2% milk, divided**
- 8 **tablespoons butter, softened, divided**
- 1 **teaspoon salt, divided**
- 1 **tablespoon olive oil**
- ¼ **teaspoon coarsely ground pepper**

1. Place pumpkin in a large saucepan; add water to cover. Bring to a boil. Reduce heat; cook, uncovered, for 20-25 minutes or until tender.
2. Meanwhile, place the potatoes in another saucepan; add water to cover. Bring to a boil. Reduce the heat; cook, uncovered, for 10-15 minutes or until potatoes are tender.
3. Drain potatoes; return to the pan. Mash potatoes, adding ¼ cup milk, 4 tablespoons butter and ½ teaspoon salt. Add additional milk if needed to reach desired consistency. Transfer to a serving bowl; keep warm.
4. Drain pumpkin; return to pan. Mash pumpkin, gradually adding the remaining butter and salt and enough of the remaining milk to reach desired consistency; spoon mixture evenly over potatoes. Cut through mashed vegetables with a spoon or knife to swirl. Drizzle with olive oil; sprinkle with pepper. Serve immediately.

COMMON CAKE CONUNDRUM

To avoid cracking the cake as you roll it up, be sure to not overbake. Most cake rolls bake in 10-15 minutes. Check the cake at 8-9 minutes and watch it closely until it tests done.

WALNUT PUMPKIN CAKE ROLL

LITTLE BUTTER COOKIE
SANDWICHES

LITTLE BUTTER COOKIE SANDWICHES

This spritz recipe originally came from my sister-in-law, but I tweaked it a bit to make doubly delicious sandwich cookies. You can make all different kinds of shapes.

—**PATRICIA KUTCHINS** LAKE ZURICH, IL

PREP: 30 MIN.
BAKE: 10 MIN./BATCH + COOLING
MAKES: 7 DOZEN

- 2 **cups butter, softened**
- 1 **cup sugar**
- 1 **large egg**
- 1 **teaspoon almond extract**
  Food coloring, optional
- 4 **cups all-purpose flour**
  Colored sugar, optional

FILLING
- 2 **cups confectioners' sugar**
- ¼ **cup plus 2 tablespoons apricot preserves**
- ½ **teaspoon almond extract**
- 3 **to 4 teaspoons orange juice**

1. Preheat oven to 350°. In a large bowl, cream butter and sugar until light and fluffy. Beat in egg, extract and, if desired, food coloring. Gradually beat flour into creamed mixture (dough will be sticky).
2. Using a cookie press fitted with disk of your choice, press dough 1 in. apart onto ungreased baking sheets. Decorate as desired with colored sugar. Bake 7-9 minutes or until set. Remove from pans to wire racks to cool completely.
3. Mix the confectioners' sugar, preserves, extract and enough orange juice to reach spreading consistency. Spread about ½ teaspoon filling on the bottoms of half of the cookies; top with remaining cookies.
FREEZE OPTION *Transfer dough to a resealable plastic freezer bag; freeze. To use, thaw dough in refrigerator overnight or until soft enough to press. Prepare and bake cookies as directed.*

HONEY GARLIC GREEN BEANS

Green beans are a great side dish for the holidays, but they can seem ordinary on their own. Add a few extra ingredients to give them sweet and salty attitude.

—**SHANNON DOBOS** CALGARY, AB

START TO FINISH: 20 MIN.
MAKES: 8 SERVINGS

- 4 **tablespoons honey**
- 2 **tablespoons reduced-sodium soy sauce**
- 4 **garlic cloves, minced**
- ¼ **teaspoon salt**
- ¼ **teaspoon crushed red pepper flakes**
- 2 **pounds fresh green beans, trimmed**

1. Whisk together the first five ingredients; set aside. In a 6-qt. stockpot, bring 10 cups water to a boil. Add beans in batches; cook, uncovered, for 2-3 minutes or just until crisp-tender. Remove beans; immediately drop into ice water. Drain and pat dry.
2. Coat stockpot with cooking spray. Add beans; cook, stirring constantly, over high heat until slightly blistered, 2-3 minutes. Add sauce; continue stirring until beans are coated and sauce starts to evaporate slightly, 2-3 minutes. Remove from heat.

★ ★ ★ ★ ★ **5 STAR TIP**

To trim fresh green beans quickly, simply line up the ends of the beans; then, using a chef's knife, slice several at a time.

CROWN ROAST WITH APRICOT DRESSING

CROWN ROAST WITH APRICOT DRESSING

I have been making crown roasts for many years but was only satisfied with the results when I combined a few recipes to come up with this version. It's beautifully roasted with a sweet glaze and a nicely browned dressing.

—**ISABELL COOPER** CAMBRIDGE, NS

PREP: 20 MIN.
BAKE: 2½ HOURS + STANDING
MAKES: 12 SERVINGS

- 1 **pork crown roast (12 ribs and about 8 pounds)**
- ½ **teaspoon seasoned salt**
- ⅓ **cup apricot preserves**

APRICOT DRESSING

- ¼ **cup butter, cubed**
- 1 **cup sliced fresh mushrooms**
- 1 **medium onion, finely chopped**
- 1 **celery rib, finely chopped**
- 1 **cup chopped dried apricots**
- ½ **teaspoon dried savory**
- ½ **teaspoon dried thyme**
- ¼ **teaspoon salt**
- ¼ **teaspoon pepper**
- 3 **cups soft bread crumbs**

1. Preheat oven to 350°. Place roast on a rack in a shallow roasting pan. Sprinkle with seasoned salt. Bake, uncovered, 1 hour.
2. Brush sides of roast with preserves. Bake 1½-2 hours longer or until the meat reaches desired doneness (for medium-rare, a thermometer should read 145°; medium, 160°). Transfer roast to a serving platter. Let stand for 20 minutes before carving.
3. For dressing, in a large skillet, heat butter over medium-high heat. Add mushrooms, onion and celery; cook and stir 6-8 minutes or until tender. Stir in apricots and seasonings. Add bread crumbs; toss to coat. Transfer to a greased 8-in. square baking dish. Bake 15-20 minutes or until lightly browned. Carve roast between ribs; serve with dressing.

WINTER SQUASH, SAUSAGE & FETA BAKE

My special side dish is a feast for the eyes and the taste buds! The butternut and acorn squash bake up tender and golden, and the bright color looks perfect on your holiday table. It's a guaranteed hit at potlucks, too.

—CRAIG SIMPSON SAVANNAH, GA

PREP: 30 MIN. • **BAKE:** 45 MIN.
MAKES: 20 SERVINGS (¾ CUP EACH)

- 1 **pound bulk Italian sausage**
- 2 **large onions, chopped**
- ½ **teaspoon crushed red pepper flakes, divided**
- ¼ **cup olive oil**
- 2 **teaspoons minced fresh rosemary**
- 1½ **teaspoons salt**
- 1 **teaspoon Worcestershire sauce**
- 1 **teaspoon pepper**
- 1 **medium butternut squash (about 4 pounds), peeled and cut into 1-inch cubes**
- 1 **medium acorn squash, peeled and cut into 1-inch cubes**
- 2 **cups (8 ounces) crumbled feta cheese**
- 2 **small sweet red peppers, chopped**

1. Preheat oven to 375°. In a large skillet, cook the sausage, onions and ¼ teaspoon pepper flakes over medium heat 8-10 minutes or until sausage is no longer pink and onions are tender, breaking up sausage into crumbles; drain.

2. In a large bowl, combine the oil, rosemary, salt, Worcestershire sauce, pepper and remaining pepper flakes. Add butternut and acorn squash, cheese, red peppers and sausage mixture; toss to coat.

3. Transfer to an ungreased shallow roasting pan. Cover and bake for 35 minutes. Uncover; bake 10-15 minutes longer or until squash is tender.

CHRISTMAS STAR
TWISTED BREAD

CHRISTMAS STAR TWISTED BREAD

This gorgeous sweet bread swirled with jam may look tricky, but it's not. The best part is opening the oven to find this star-shaped beauty in all its glory.

—DARLENE BRENDEN SALEM, OR

PREP: 45 MIN. + RISING
BAKE: 20 MIN. + COOLING
MAKES: 16 SERVINGS

- 1 package (¼ ounce) active dry yeast
- ¼ cup warm water (110° to 115°)
- ¾ cup warm whole milk (110° to 115°)
- 1 large egg
- ¼ cup butter, softened
- ¼ cup granulated sugar
- 1 teaspoon salt
- 3¼ to 3¾ cups all-purpose flour
- ¾ cup seedless raspberry jam
- 2 tablespoons butter, melted
  Confectioners' sugar

1. Dissolve yeast in warm water until foamy. In another bowl, combine milk, egg, butter, sugar and salt; add yeast mixture and 3 cups flour. Beat on medium speed until smooth, about 1 minute. Stir in enough remaining flour to form a soft dough.

2. Turn onto a floured surface; knead until smooth and elastic, 6-8 minutes. Place in a greased bowl, turning once to grease top. Cover with plastic wrap; let rise in a warm place until doubled, about 1 hour.

3. Punch down dough. Turn onto a lightly floured surface; divide into four portions. Roll one portion into a 12-in. circle. Place on a greased 14-in. pizza pan. Spread with one-third of the jam to within ½ in. from edge *(image 1)*. Repeat twice, layering dough and jam, and ending with final portion of dough.

4. Place a 2½-in. round cutter on top of the dough in center of circle (do not press down). With a sharp knife, make 16 evenly spaced cuts from round cutter to edge of dough *(image 2)*. Remove cutter; grasp two strips and rotate twice outward *(image 3)*. Pinch ends together. Repeat with remaining dough strips.
Cover with plastic wrap; let dough rise until almost doubled, about 30 minutes. Preheat oven to 375°. Bake until golden brown, 18-22 minutes. (Watch during final 5 minutes for any dripping.) Remove from oven; brush with melted butter, avoiding areas where jam is visible. Cool completely on a wire rack. Lightly dust with confectioners' sugar.

FLAVOR TWIST

Raspberry jam is divine and lends a gorgeous ruby-red color to this golden bread. But if you feel like changing it up, use blueberry jam and 1 teaspoon grated lemon peel. Or try blackberry jam and ½ teaspoon cardamom.

RED VELVET CANDY CANE FUDGE

HOLIDAY PORK ROAST WITH GINGER GRAVY

This special dish is perfect for Christmas or New Year's Eve. A mouthwatering ginger gravy and tender vegetables complement the herbed roast.

—**MARY ANN DELL** PHOENIXVILLE, PA

PREP: 30 MIN.
BAKE: 1 HOUR 40 MIN. + STANDING
MAKES: 16 SERVINGS

- 1 **boneless whole pork loin roast (5 pounds)**
- 1 **tablespoon minced fresh gingerroot**
- 2 **garlic cloves, minced**
- 1 **teaspoon rubbed sage**
- ¼ **teaspoon salt**
- ⅓ **cup apple jelly**
- ½ **teaspoon hot pepper sauce**
- 2 **medium carrots, sliced**
- 2 **medium onions, sliced**
- 1½ **cups water, divided**
- 1 **teaspoon browning sauce, optional**

1. Place pork roast on a rack in a shallow roasting pan. Combine the ginger, garlic, sage and salt; rub over meat. Bake, uncovered, at 350° for 1 hour.

2. Combine jelly and pepper sauce; brush over roast. Arrange carrots and onions around roast. Pour ½ cup water into pan. Bake 40-50 minutes longer or until a thermometer reads 145°. Remove the roast to a serving platter; let roast stand for 10 minutes before slicing.

3. Skim fat from the pan drippings. Transfer drippings and vegetables to a food processor; cover and process until smooth. Pour mixture into a small saucepan. Add remaining water and, if desired, browning sauce; heat through. Slice roast; serve with gravy.

RED VELVET CANDY CANE FUDGE

My favorite kind of cake, red velvet, inspired me to create this delectable fudge. If you prefer a different shape, spoon the candy mixture into paper-lined mini muffin cups instead of spreading it in a 13x9 pan.

—**CRYSTAL SCHLUETER** NORTHGLENN, CO

PREP: 25 MIN. + CHILLING
MAKES: 3¾ POUNDS

- 1 **teaspoon butter**
- 2 **packages (12 ounces each) white baking chips, divided**
- ⅔ **cup semisweet chocolate chips**
- 3 **teaspoons shortening, divided**
- 1 **can (14 ounces) sweetened condensed milk**
- 1½ **teaspoons red paste food coloring**
- 4 **cups confectioners' sugar, divided**
- 6 **ounces cream cheese, softened**
- 1 **teaspoon vanilla extract**
- ¼ **teaspoon peppermint extract**
- 3 **tablespoons crushed peppermint candies**

1. Line a 13x9-in. pan with foil; grease foil with butter.

2. In a large microwave-safe bowl, combine 3¼ cups white baking chips, chocolate chips and 2 teaspoons shortening. Microwave, uncovered, on high 1 minute; stir. Microwave at additional 15-second intervals, stirring until smooth. Stir in milk and food coloring; gradually add 1 cup confectioners' sugar. Spread into prepared pan.

3. In another large microwave-safe bowl, melt remaining white baking chips and shortening; stir until smooth. Beat in cream cheese and extracts. Gradually beat in remaining confectioners' sugar until smooth. Spread over red layer; sprinkle with crushed candies. Refrigerate 2 hours or until firm.

4. Using foil, lift fudge out of pan. Remove foil; cut fudge into 1-in. squares. Store between layers of waxed paper in an airtight container.

GARLIC-HERB PARMESAN ROLLS

Fresh-baked yeast rolls are always a hit at holiday dinners. To keep prep easy, start them in a bread machine. For the Yuletide season, I arrange them in a tree shape, but you can also make them in a 13x9-inch pan.
—**LORRI REINHARDT** BIG BEND, WI

PREP: 20 MIN. • **BAKE:** 20 MIN. + COOLING
MAKES: 16 SERVINGS

- 1 cup water (70° to 80°)
- 2 tablespoons butter, softened
- 1 large egg, lightly beaten
- 3 tablespoons sugar
- 2 teaspoons dried minced garlic
- 1 teaspoon Italian seasoning
- 1 teaspoon salt
- 2¼ cups bread flour
- 1 cup whole wheat flour
- 1 package (¼ ounce) active dry yeast

TOPPING
- 1 tablespoon butter, melted
- 1 tablespoon grated Parmesan cheese
- 1 teaspoon Italian seasoning
- ½ teaspoon coarse salt

1. In bread machine pan, place the first 10 ingredients in order suggested by manufacturer. Select dough setting (check the dough after 5 minutes of mixing; add 1 to 2 tablespoons of water or flour if needed).
2. When cycle is completed, turn dough onto a lightly floured surface; divide into 16 balls. Line a baking sheet with foil and grease the foil. Center one roll near the top of the prepared baking sheet. Arrange rolls snugly into four additional rows, adding one more roll for each row, forming a tree.
3. Center remaining ball under tree for trunk. Cover and let rise until doubled, about 1 hour.
4. Brush rolls with butter. Combine cheese and Italian seasoning and sprinkle over rolls. Sprinkle with salt. Bake at 350° for 20-25 minutes or until golden brown. Serve warm.

CRANBERRY-WHITE CHOCOLATE COOKIES

These are among my favorite Christmas cookies. I prepare a few batches early in the season, then freeze them to pull out as needed. The tartness of the berries perfectly balances the sweet white chocolate.
—**SHERRY CONLEY** NOEL HANTS COUNTY, NS

PREP: 25 MIN.
BAKE: 10 MIN./BATCH + COOLING
MAKES: ABOUT 7 DOZEN

- 1 cup butter, softened
- ¾ cup sugar
- ¾ cup packed brown sugar
- 2 large eggs
- ⅓ cup cranberry juice
- 1 teaspoon vanilla extract
- 3 cups all-purpose flour
- 2 teaspoons baking powder
- ½ teaspoon salt
- 2 cups dried cranberries
- 2 cups vanilla or white chips

GLAZE
- 2 cups vanilla or white chips
- 2 tablespoons plus 1½ teaspoons shortening

1. In a large bowl, cream butter and sugars until light and fluffy. Beat in the eggs, cranberry juice and vanilla. Combine the flour, baking powder and salt; gradually add to creamed mixture and mix well. Fold in cranberries and vanilla chips.
2. Drop by rounded teaspoonfuls 2 in. apart onto greased baking sheets. Bake at 350° for 10-12 minutes or until edges begin to brown. Cool cookies for 2 minutes before removing to wire racks to cool completely.
3. For glaze, microwave vanilla chips and shortening at 70% power until melted; stir until smooth. Drizzle the glaze over cookies.

CRANBERRY-WHITE CHOCOLATE COOKIES

CHRISTMAS
GINGERBREAD TRIFLE

CHRISTMAS GINGERBREAD TRIFLE

Trifles make eye-catching centerpieces. To add color, I sometimes garnish mine using candy canes and red and green M&M's. All the possibilities make this a very merry, kid-friendly project.

—**CHERYL TOMPKINS** KINGSVILLE, MO

PREP: 45 MIN. + CHILLING
MAKES: 14 SERVINGS

- 1 package (14½ ounces) gingerbread cake/cookie mix
- 2 cups cold 2% milk
- 2 cups cold eggnog
- 2 packages (3.4 ounces each) instant French vanilla pudding mix
- 1 package (5 ounces) gingerbread man cookies
- 1 carton (16 ounces) frozen whipped topping, thawed

1. Prepare cake mix according to package directions and bake using a 9-in. square baking pan. Cool cake completely on a wire rack. Cut into 1-in. cubes.
2. In a large bowl, whisk milk, eggnog and pudding mix for 2 minutes. Let stand 2 minutes or until soft-set.
3. Arrange nine gingerbread cookies around the sides of a 4-qt. glass bowl, using a third of the cake cubes to stand cookies upright. Top with a third of the pudding and whipped topping. Repeat layers. Top with remaining cake, pudding and whipped topping. Refrigerate trifle, covered, for 4 hours or overnight.
4. Just before serving, top with remaining cookies.
NOTE *This recipe was tested with commercially prepared eggnog.*

FROSTED ANISE COOKIES

I love anise flavoring, and my nana loved sugar cookies, so I put them together in one delicious cookie. They have a soft, from-scratch texture that's hard to resist.

—**RACHELE ANGELONI** NORTH PROVIDENCE, RI

PREP: 30 MIN.
BAKE: 10 MIN./BATCH + COOLING
MAKES: 3½ DOZEN

- 1 cup butter, softened
- 1½ cups sugar
- 1 large egg
- 1 teaspoon anise extract
- 2¾ cups all-purpose flour
- 1 teaspoon baking soda
- ½ teaspoon baking powder
- 1 can (16 ounces) vanilla frosting Holiday sprinkles

1. Cream butter and sugar in a large bowl until light and fluffy. Beat in egg and extract. Combine the flour, baking soda and baking powder; gradually add to creamed mixture and mix well.
2. Drop by tablespoonfuls 2 in. apart onto ungreased baking sheets. Bake at 375° for 9-11 minutes or until golden brown. Remove cookies to wire racks to cool completely.
3. Spread the cookies with vanilla frosting and decorate with sprinkles. Let stand until set. Store in an airtight container.
TO MAKE AHEAD *Package cookies in an airtight container, separating layers with waxed paper, and freeze for up to 1 month.*

CRANBERRY-ORANGE CORDIALS

I like recipes that are elegant but quick. These refreshing cordials are just the right touch after a full meal. The fruit and cream layers make a pretty presentation in clear glasses.

—**SUELLEN CALHOUN** DES MOINES, IA

START TO FINISH: 15 MIN.
MAKES: 6 SERVINGS

- 1 can (14 ounces) whole-berry cranberry sauce
- 1 cinnamon stick (3 inches)
- 1 whole star anise
- ⅓ cup orange liqueur
- ¾ cup plain Greek yogurt
- 2 ounces cream cheese, softened
- 2 tablespoons honey
- 6 small mint sprigs

1. In a small saucepan, combine the cranberry sauce, cinnamon stick and star anise. Bring to a boil. Reduce heat; simmer, uncovered, for 2 minutes, stirring constantly. Stir in liqueur. Set aside to cool; discard cinnamon stick and star anise.
2. In a small bowl, beat the yogurt, cream cheese and honey until blended. Divide among six shot or cordial glasses. Top with the cooled cranberry mixture. Save any remaining sauce for another use. Garnish with mint sprigs.
TO MAKE AHEAD *Cranberry mixture can be made the day before serving. Cover and refrigerate.*

GENERAL RECIPE INDEX

This handy index lists every recipe by food category, major ingredient and/or cooking method.

ALPHABETICAL RECIPE INDEX

This convenient index lists every recipe in alphabetical order, so you can easily find your favorite dishes.

INGREDIENT SUBSTITUTIONS

WHEN YOU NEED:	IN THIS AMOUNT:	SUBSTITUTE:
Baking Powder	1 teaspoon	½ teaspoon cream of tartar plus ¼ teaspoon baking soda
Broth	1 cup	1 cup hot water plus 1 teaspoon bouillon granules *or* 1 bouillon cube
Buttermilk	1 cup	1 tablespoon lemon juice *or* white vinegar plus enough milk to measure 1 cup (let stand 5 minutes), *or* 1 cup plain yogurt
Cajun Seasoning	1 teaspoon	¼ teaspoon cayenne pepper, ½ teaspoon dried thyme, ¼ teaspoon dried basil and 1 minced garlic clove
Chocolate	1 ounce	3 tablespoons baking cocoa plus 1 tablespoon shortening *or* canola oil
Chocolate, Semisweet	1 ounce	1 ounce unsweetened chocolate plus 1 tablespoon sugar, *or* 3 tablespoons semisweet chocolate chips
Corn Syrup, Dark	1 cup	¾ cup light corn syrup plus ¼ cup molasses
Corn Syrup, Light	1 cup	1 cup sugar plus ¼ cup water
Cornstarch	1 tablespoon	2 tablespoons all-purpose flour (for thickening)
Cracker Crumbs	1 cup	1 cup dry bread crumbs
Cream, Half-and-Half	1 cup	1 tablespoon melted butter plus enough whole milk to measure 1 cup
Egg, Large	1 whole	2 large egg whites *or* 2 large egg yolks *or* ¼ cup egg substitute
Flour, Cake	1 cup	1 cup minus 2 tablespoons (⅞ cup) all-purpose flour
Flour, Self-Rising	1 cup	1½ teaspoons baking powder, ½ teaspoon salt and enough all-purpose flour to measure 1 cup
Garlic, Fresh	1 clove	⅛ teaspoon garlic powder
Gingerroot, Fresh	1 teaspoon	¼ teaspoon ground ginger
Honey	1 cup	1¼ cups sugar plus ¼ cup water
Lemon Juice	1 teaspoon	¼ teaspoon cider vinegar
Lemon Peel	1 teaspoon	½ teaspoon lemon extract
Milk, Whole	1 cup	½ cup evaporated milk plus ½ cup water, *or* 1 cup water plus ⅓ cup nonfat dry milk powder
Molasses	1 cup	1 cup honey
Mustard, Prepared	1 tablespoon	½ teaspoon ground mustard plus 2 teaspoons cider *or* white vinegar
Onion	1 small onion (⅓ cup chopped)	1 teaspoon onion powder *or* 1 tablespoon dried minced onion
Poultry Seasoning	1 teaspoon	¾ teaspoon rubbed sage plus ¼ teaspoon dried thyme
Sour Cream	1 cup	1 cup plain yogurt
Sugar	1 cup	1 cup packed brown sugar *or* 2 cups sifted confectioners' sugar
Tomato Juice	1 cup	½ cup tomato sauce plus ½ cup water
Tomato Sauce	2 cups	¾ cup tomato paste plus 1 cup water

GET COOKING WITH A WELL-STOCKED KITCHEN

In a perfect world, you would plan weekly or even monthly menus and have all the ingredients on hand to make each night's dinner. The reality, however, is that you likely haven't thought about dinner until you've walked through the door.

With a reasonably stocked pantry, refrigerator and freezer, you'll still be able to serve a satisfying meal in short order. Consider these tips:

QUICK-COOKING MEATS—such as boneless chicken breasts, chicken thighs, pork tenderloin, pork chops, ground meats, Italian sausage, sirloin and flank steaks, fish fillets and shrimp—should be stocked in the freezer. Wrap them individually (except shrimp), so you can remove only the amount you need. For the quickest defrosting, wrap meats for freezing in small, thin packages.

FROZEN VEGETABLES packaged in plastic bags are a real time-saver. Simply pour out the amount needed. No preparation is required!

PASTAS, RICE, RICE MIXES AND COUSCOUS are great staples to have in the pantry—and they generally have a long shelf life. Remember, thinner pastas, such as angel hair, cook faster than thicker pastas. Fresh (refrigerated) pasta cooks faster than dried.

DAIRY PRODUCTS like milk, sour cream, cheeses (shredded, cubed or crumbled), eggs, yogurt, butter and margarine are perishable, so check the use-by date on packages and replace as needed.

CONDIMENTS such as ketchup, mustard, mayonnaise, salad dressings, salsa, taco sauce, soy sauce, stir-fry sauce, lemon juice, etc., add flavor to many dishes. Personalize the list to suit your family's needs.

FRESH FRUIT AND VEGETABLES can make a satisfying predinner snack. Oranges and apples are not as perishable as bananas. Ready-to-use salad greens are perfect for an instant salad.

DRIED HERBS, SPICES, VINEGARS and seasoning mixes add lots of flavor and keep for months.

PASTA SAUCES, OLIVES, BEANS, broths, canned tomatoes, canned vegetables, and canned or dried soups are ideal to have on hand for a quick meal—and many of these items are common recipe ingredients.

GET YOUR FAMILY INTO THE HABIT of posting a grocery list. When an item is used up or is almost gone, just add it to your list for the next shopping trip. This way you won't run completely out of an item, and you'll also save time when writing your grocery list.

MAKE THE MOST OF YOUR TIME EVERY NIGHT

With recipes in hand and your kitchen stocked, you're well on your way to a relaxing family meal. Here are some pointers to help you get dinner on the table fast:

PREHEAT THE OVEN OR GRILL before starting on the recipe.

PULL OUT ALL THE INGREDIENTS, mixing tools and cooking tools before beginning any prep work.

USE CONVENIENCE ITEMS whenever possible, such as prechopped garlic, onion and peppers, shredded or cubed cheese, seasoning mixes, jarred sauces, etc.

MULTITASK! While the meat is simmering for a main dish, toss a salad, cook a side dish or start on dessert.

ENCOURAGE HELPERS. Have younger children set the table. Older ones can help prepare ingredients or even assemble simple recipes themselves.

TAKE CARE OF TWO MEALS IN ONE NIGHT by planning main dish leftovers or making a double batch of favorite sides.

TRICKS TO TAME HUNGER WHEN IT STRIKES

Are the kids begging for a before-supper snack? Calm their rumbling tummies with some nutritious, not-too-filling noshes.

START WITH A SMALL TOSSED SALAD. Try a ready-to-serve salad mix and add their favorite salad dressing and a little protein, like cubed cheese or julienned slices of deli meat.

CUT UP AN APPLE and smear a little peanut butter on each slice. Or offer other fruits such as seedless grapes, cantaloupe, oranges or bananas. For variety, give kids vanilla yogurt or reduced-fat ranch dressing as a dipper for the fruit, or combine a little reduced-fat sour cream with a sprinkling of brown sugar. Too tired to cut up the fruit? A fruit snack cup will do the trick, too.

DURING THE COLD MONTHS, serve up a small mug of soup with a few oyster crackers to hit the spot.

RAW VEGGIES such as carrots, cucumbers, mushrooms, broccoli and cauliflower are tasty treats, especially when served with a little hummus for dipping. Many of these vegetables can be purchased precut.

GIVE KIDS A SMALL SERVING of cheese and crackers. Look for sliced cheese and cut the slices into smaller squares to fit the crackers. Choose a cracker that's made from whole wheat, such as an all-natural, seven-grain cracker.